THE COLLECTED TRAVELER

ALSO EDITED BY BARRIE KERPER

Istanbul: The Collected Traveler

Tuscany and Umbria: The Collected Traveler

Barrie Kerper

PARIS

Barrie Kerper is an avid traveler and reader who has lived abroad. She has over a thousand books in her home library—and an even greater number of file clippings—and has filled up four passports.

PARIS

THE COLLECTED TRAVELER

Edited by Barrie Kerper

An Inspired Companion Guide

Vintage Departures
Vintage Books
A Division of Random House, Inc.
New York

A VINTAGE DEPARTURES ORIGINAL, JULY 2011

Copyright © 2000, 2011 by Barrie Kerper

All rights reserved. Published in the United States by Vintage Books,
a division of Random House, Inc., New York, and in Canada
by Random House of Canada Limited, Toronto.

Some of the material originally published in the United States as part of
Paris by Three Rivers Press, an imprint of the Crown Publishing Group,
a division of Random House, Inc., New York, in 2000.

Vintage is a registered trademark and Vintage Departures and
colophon are trademarks of Random House, Inc.

Owing to limitations of space, all acknowledgments to reprint
previously published material can be found on pages 719–721.

Library of Congress Cataloging-in-Publication Data
Paris : the collected traveler / edited by Barrie Kerper.
    p.   cm.—(Vintage departures)
"An inspired companion guide."
Includes bibliographical references.
ISBN 978–0–307–47489–6
1. Paris (France)—Description and travel—Sources.   2. Travelers' writings.
3. Paris (France)—Social life and customs—Sources.   4. Paris (France)—Guidebooks.
5. Paris (France)—Biography.   6. Interviews—France—Paris.   I. Kerper, Barrie.
DC707.P2546 2011
914.4'3610484—dc22
2011013200

Book design by Jo Anne Metsch

www.vintagebooks.com

Printed in the United States of America

10 9 8 7 6 5 4 3 2

Once again, to my mother, Phyllis,
who always believed my boxes of files
held something of value,
and, in memorium, to my father, Peter.
The memory of their first visit to Paris in 1979,
when I lived there as a student,
remains one of the fondest of my life.

CONTENTS

Paris is a city that might well be spoken of in the plural, as the Greeks used to speak of Athens, for there are many Parises, and the tourists' Paris is only superficially related to the Paris of the Parisians. The foreigner driving through Paris from one museum to another is quite oblivious to the presence of a world he brushes past without seeing. Until you have wasted time in a city, you cannot pretend to know it well. The soul of a big city is not to be grasped so easily; in order to make contact with it, you have to have been bored, you have to have suffered a bit in those places that contain it. Anyone can get hold of a guide and tick off all the monuments, but within the very confines of Paris there is another city as difficult of access as Timbuktu once was.

—JULIAN GREEN, *Paris*

INTRODUCTION

A breath of Paris preserves the soul.
—Victor Hugo, *Les Misérables*

Those who have experienced Paris have the advantage over those who haven't. We are the ones who have glimpsed a little bit of heaven, down here on earth.
—Deirdre Kelly, *Paris Times Eight*

Paris is truly an ocean. Plumb its depths, knowing you will never touch bottom. Run its length, describe it. Whatever care you take in exploring or detailing, however many and determined the navigators of this sea, there always will be virgin territory, unknown grottoes, flowers, pearls, monsters, something amazing, overlooked by literary divers.
—Honoré de Balzac, *Le Père Goriot*

PARIS HAS LONG been a beacon—of light, beauty, culture, and civilization—to people and nations around the world. The city has been called the undisputed capital of the nineteenth century, though Gertrude Stein, writing in the early half of the 1900s, could also make the claim that "Paris was where the twentieth century was." Though the city unquestionably lost some of its luster in the mid to late twentieth century, there is also no doubt that Paris is reemerging as a city of grace, significance, and prominence in the twenty-first. As anywhere, it is currently faced with some formidable urban challenges, yet as it works toward solutions to its ills, Paris retains its allure, and its image as a beacon will survive. Paris is still remarkably beautiful; it still has cachet and prestige, grandeur and distinction. "Oh, Paris!" writes Joyce Slayton Mitchell. "Even with modern and economic changes, the value of the beautiful is conserved." The city still brings a sparkle to many an eye, and makes grown adults sigh at the mention of its name.

One of those adults is me. Though I will always have a soft spot in my heart for Spain—that's where I took my very first overseas trip, with my tenth-grade Spanish class in 1975—it was Paris that changed my life, made me realize who I wanted to be, made me who I am today. It was in Paris that I lived as a student and learned to think in another language and grasped what was really important in life. Though I have only recently become familiar with the late historian Richard Cobb, a passage from his book *Paris and Elsewhere* perfectly sums up how I felt then: "To live in France is to live double, every moment counts, the light of the sky of the Île-de-France is unique and a source of joy, there is joy too in a small rectangle of sunshine at the top of a tall, greying, leprous building, the colour of Utrillo, and in the smell of chestnuts that brings the promise of autumn, *la rentrée*, and the beloved repetition of the Paris year." I sometimes wonder if I would feel the same way if I'd gone as a student to live in London, or another European country, or somewhere in Asia, Africa, or South America—after all, *every* experience abroad is enriching and worthwhile. But I honestly don't believe I would have. Paris was and remains a city that so very many other places emulate and aspire to.

If it sometimes seems that the world is shrinking (it is) and Paris appears clichéd and too popular and too much like anywhere else (occasionally it is), understand that things *are* different there. And, today, due to the influx of inhabitants from France's former colonies, visitors may feel in certain *quartiers* that they are in a far-flung city nowhere near Paris. While it is true that there are too many of the same retailers and fast-food chains in Paris that we have in North America, thankfully there are enough one-of-a-kind shops, local places to eat, and only-in-Paris experiences to make you feel the journey you've made is worth it.

It's easy in Paris to succumb to Stendhal Syndrome, named for the French novelist Stendhal, who felt physically sick after he visited Santa Croce in Florence; it refers to the sensation of being completely overwhelmed by your surroundings. (My translation: seeing and doing way too much.) Visitors to Paris who arrive with too long a list of must-sees are prime candidates for the syndrome. Author and Italy expert Fred Plotkin counsels against falling into this trap in his foreword to Claudio Gatti's *Florence in Detail* (an excellent guidebook, by the way) by advising, "Like it or not, one must adopt a policy of '*Poco, ma buono*' (loosely translated as 'Do less, but do it really well') to experience what Florence has to offer. A mad dash through a gallery will leave you with only fleeting impressions. Spend ten minutes in front of one painting and you will see remarkable things that a two-minute look could not reveal; spend an hour in front of that same painting and your life will be changed. To really pause and reflect, whether in front of a sculpture or a dish of gelato, is to find the presence of art and genius in all things." For Paris, one may easily substitute the phrase *Peu, mais bien,* an image of the Louvre rather than the Uffizi, and a dish of *glace* instead of gelato. I would add that by creating more reasonable itineraries, you give yourself the opportunity to acquire more than a superficial understanding of a place. I particularly enjoy simply sitting at a café table, looking, listening, and wondering. What is life like in the beautiful apartment building off the *place*, the one the young boy has just entered carrying a purchase from the *pâtisserie*? I am curious about the elderly man in his antiques shop, the mother and daughter walking arm in arm, the fruit vendor at the rue Mouffetard outdoor market who talks nonstop and greets everyone like she's known them all her life. And, enviously, I wonder where the woman walking on the rue Saint-Honoré bought her beautiful handbag.

In addition to a reasonable schedule, I also counsel adjusting to daily life, and one of the fastest ways to do this in France is to abandon whatever schedule you observe at home and eat when the French eat. Mealtimes in France are well established, and if you have not purchased provisions for a picnic or found a place to eat lunch by one o'clock, many restaurants will be full—or sold out of that day's specials—and many shops closed. Likewise, dinner is not typically served at six, an hour that is entirely too early for anyone in France to contemplate his or her next meal. The phrase *cinq à sept* (five to seven) refers to a sort of French happy hour, or *apéro*. (It once more commonly was the time of day when men and their mistresses would rendezvous, but today it usually refers to an accepted time to meet for drinks before dinner.) While cocktails between five and seven are not unfamiliar to North Americans, I continue to be amazed at how many of us still eat dinner at six p.m. (my hypothesis is that North Americans eat dinner earlier than any other people in the world, which I don't consider to be a positive custom). Adjust

your schedule and you'll be on French time, doing things when the French do them, eliminating possible disappointment and frustration and the feeling of being utterly out of step.

ABOUT THIS BOOK

> A traveler without knowledge is a bird without wings.
> —Sa'adi, Persian poet, *Gulistan*

The Collected Traveler editions are meant to be companion volumes to guidebooks that go beyond the practical information that traditional guidebooks supply. Each individual volume is perfect to bring along, but each is also a sort of planning package—the books guide readers to many other sources, and they are sources of inspiration. James Pope-Hennessy, in his wonderful book *Aspects of Provence,* notes that "if one is to get best value out of places visited, some skeletal knowledge of their history is necessary. . . . Sight-seeing is by no means the only object of a journey, but it is as unintelligent as it is lazy not to equip ourselves to understand the sights we see." Immerse yourself in a destination and you'll acquire a deeper understanding and appreciation of the place and the people who live there, and, not surprisingly, you'll have more fun.

This series promotes the strategy of staying longer within a smaller area so as to experience it more fully. Susan Allen Toth refers to this in one of her many wonderful books, *England as You Like It,* in which she subscribes to the "thumbprint theory of travel": spending at least a week in one spot no larger than her thumbprint covers on a large-scale map of England. Excursions are encouraged, as long as they're about an hour's drive away.

I have discovered in my own travels that a week in one place, even a spot no bigger than my thumbprint, is rarely long enough to see and enjoy it all. For this reason, most of the books in *The Collected Traveler* series focus on either cities or regions, as opposed to entire countries. There will not be a book on all of France, for example. I am mindful that France is a member of two communities, European and Mediterranean, and that an understanding of both is essential to understanding Paris, and I have tried to reflect this wider-world sense of community throughout the book. But even though some visitors to Paris may travel on to points farther afield in France, each of its regions deserves to be covered in a separate book and is too far outside this particular thumbprint.

The major portion of this book features a selection of articles and essays from various periodicals and recommended reading relevant to the theme of each section. The articles and books were chosen from my own files and home library, which I've maintained for more than two decades. (I often feel I am the living embodiment of a comment that Samuel Johnson made in 1775, that "a man will turn over half a library to make one book.") The selected writings reflect the culture, politics, history, current social issues, religion, cuisine, and arts of the people you'll be visiting. They represent the observations and opinions of a wide variety of novelists, travel writers, journalists, and others whom I refer to as "observant enthusiasts." These writers are typically authorities on Paris, or France, or both; they either live there (as permanent or part-time residents) or visit there often for business or pleasure. I'm very discriminating in seeking opinions and recommendations, and I am not interested in the remarks of unobservant wanderers. I am not implying that first-time visitors to France have nothing noteworthy or interesting to share—they very often do, and are often keen observers. Conversely, frequent travelers can be jaded and apt to miss the finer details that make Paris the exceptional place it is. Above all, I am interested in the opinions of people who want to *know* France, not just *see* it.

I've included numerous older articles because they were particularly well-written, thought-provoking, or unique in some way, and because the authors' views stand as a valuable record of a certain time in history. Even after the passage of many years you may share the emotions and opinions of the writer, and you may find that *plus ça change, plus c'est la même chose*. I have many, many more articles in my files than I was able to reprint here, and I ask for your forgiveness if it seems a particular neighborhood or monu-

ment gets more attention than others, or if I have highlighted certain topics more than others. The truth is, I embrace it all, the complete picture, if you will. To borrow a lovely phrase from *One Hundred & One Beautiful Small Towns in France,* I claim, "as you will after your own visit, a surfeit of abundance, and a divine temptation to be reckless." Though there are a few pieces whose absence I very much regret, I believe the anthology you're holding is very comprehensive.

Some notes about the cuisine and restaurant sections, "La Cuisine Française" and "À Table!," are in order. Food, and the enjoyment of it, still holds a place of honor in French life, prompting Elizabeth Bard, in *Lunch in Paris,* to write, "So much of what I'd learned about France I'd discovered *autour de la table*—around the table." Likewise, Suzy Gershman, in her book *C'est la Vie,* relates a revealing tale about the first time she made the French dessert *clafoutis.* Even though she'd cooked it for the proper amount of time, it appeared completely liquified. Just then her doorbell rang. It was the telephone repairman, and though he was there to fix a damaged telephone line, she explained her predicament with the *clafoutis*. He complimented her on its appearance and said that she simply had to let it cool and it would congeal, or she could put it in the fridge and it would set more quickly. "Only in France would the telephone repairman know how to rescue a *clafoutis*." And as Edward Behr notes in his excellent journal *The Art of Eating,* "The French still care enormously about food. In a luxury restaurant in Paris not long ago, I felt an extraordinary sense of comfort and of intimate contact with craftsmen working without inhibition to accomplish their best. Even the welcome was a lesson in the craft of the server—not friendliness (there's no skill in that) but a concern for my happiness during my time in the restaurant. I was certain that the warmth reflected pride in the chef, all the cooks, the entire restaurant."

For all of these reasons and more, I hope you will take my book as merely the first step in investigating this crucial area of French culture. I have great respect for restaurant reviewers, and though their work may seem glamorous—it sometimes is—it is also very hard. It's an all-consuming, full-time job, and that is why I urge you to consult the very good recommended cookbooks as well as restaurant guidebooks. Restaurant (and hotel) reviewers are, for the most part, professionals who have dined in hundreds of eating establishments (and spent hundreds of nights in hotels). They are far more capable of assessing the qualities and flaws of a place than I am. I don't always agree with every opinion of a reviewer, but I am far more inclined to defer to their opinion over that of someone who is unfamiliar with French food in general, for example, or someone who doesn't dine out frequently enough to recognize what good restaurants have in common. My files are filled with restaurant reviews, and I could have included many more articles, but that would have been repetitive and ultimately beside the point. I have selected a few articles that give you a feel for eating out in Paris, alert you to some things to look for in selecting a truly worthwhile place versus a mediocre one, and highlight notable dishes and culinary specialties visitors will encounter.

The recommended reading for each section in my book is one of its most important features and represents my favorite aspect of this series. (My annotations are, however, *much* shorter than I would prefer—did I mention that I love encyclopedias?—but they are still nothing less than enormously enthusiastic endorsements and I encourage you to read as many of the books as you can.) One reason I do not include many excerpts from books in my series is that I am not convinced an excerpt will always lead a reader to the book in question, and good books deserve to be read in their entirety. Art critic John Russell wrote an essay, in 1962, entitled "Pleasure in Reading," in which he stated, "Not for us today's selections, readers, digests, and anthologizings: only the Complete Edition will do." Years later, in 1986, he noted that "bibliographies make dull reading, some people say, but I have never found them so. They remind us, they prompt us, and they correct us. They double and treble as history, as biography, and as a freshet of surprises. They reveal the public self, the private self, and the buried self of the person commemorated. How should we not enjoy them, and be grateful to the devoted student who has done the compiling?" The section of a nonfiction book I always turn to first is the bibliography, as it is there that I learn something about the author who has done the compiling as well as about other notable books I know I will want to read.

When I read about travel in the days before transatlantic flights, I always marvel at the number of steamer trunks and baggage people were accustomed to taking. If I were traveling back then, however, my trunks would have been filled with books, not clothes. Although I travel light and seldom check bags, I have been known to fill an entire suitcase with books, secure in the knowledge that I'll have them all with me for the duration of my trip. The advent of lightweight electronic reading devices can make luggage much less heavy, but there are always some titles I absolutely have to have in a paper-and-cover format.

Each recommended reading section features titles I feel are the best available and most worth your time. I realize that "best" is subjective; readers will simply have to trust me that I have been extremely thorough in deciding which books to recommend. I have not hesitated to list out-of-print titles because some of the most excellent books ever written about Paris and France are (sadly) out of print (and deserve to be returned to print!), and are worthy of your best efforts to track them down—most of them can be found at libraries, used-book stores, or online booksellers that deal in out-of-print volumes. (Abebooks.com is my favorite online source.) A wonderful online piece called "Tales of the Un-read," at the nifty Web site The Second Pass, makes the observation that "publishers naturally want to tell you about what's new or what's evergreen. But most readers know the pleasure of somehow discovering and falling in love with a book that has fallen from view." Great books are great books, *whenever* they were published, and what's "old" to one reader is "new" to another. That's the wonderful thing about books! There are undoubtedly titles with which I'm unfamiliar and therefore do not appear here, and I hope you'll let me know if a favorite of yours is missing. Bibliophiles, no matter how many books they have, love nothing better than to discover yet another book or author on a subject about which they're passionate.

I also believe the leisure reading you bring along should be related in some way to where you're going, so these lists include fiction and poetry titles that feature Parisian or French characters or

settings. (I do not always annotate these titles, as my aim is simply to inform you of the numerous choices available.) I'm especially fond of historical fiction, and recently I was pleased to discover that Roger Sutton, editor in chief of *The Horn Book,* a wonderful magazine dedicated to children's and young adult literature, is, too. "Historical fiction," he writes, "is not only one excellent way to explain our parents (or grandparents) to ourselves, it can also explain *ourselves* to ourselves, allowing readers to consider what they might have done, or how they might have been different, in circumstances unlike their own. We don't read historical fiction to find out 'what it was like back then' so much as to get a fresh look at who we are now. And if I want to take another look at who I was then? All I have to do is remember what I was reading." I do not adhere to the belief seemingly so prevalent at many periodicals today that unless a book or online source is utterly *au courant* it isn't worthy of a reader's time. I strongly believe that my books should evoke a sense of history and emphasize context, which has become increasingly important in today's world. Reading a biography, a cookbook, a memoir, *and* a work of history, or reading a novel, a guidebook, *and* a photography or art book provides travelers with context.

Sprinkled throughout this book I have included the brief observations of a number of visitors to Paris and northern France— ranging from friends and colleagues to notable Francophiles such as Judith Jones, Mark Greenside, Mireille Guiliano, Steven Barclay, Barbara Fairchild, and Molly Wizenberg—describing their favorite sites or experiences from their visits. There are also interviews throughout the book, with Ina Garten, Suzy Gershman, Alexander Lobrano, and Patricia Wells, among others.

An "A to Z Miscellany" appears at the end of the book. This is an alphabetical assemblage of information about words, phrases, foods, people, themes, historical notes, and personal favorites of mine that are unique to Paris and France. Will you learn of some nontouristy things to see and do? Yes. Will you also learn more about the better-known aspects of Paris? Yes. The Eiffel Tower, a little neighborhood park in the twentieth, the Canal Saint-Martin, Notre-Dame, a perfect *café crème,* the Musée d'Orsay, Chartres Cathedral, Versailles, Giverny, and the experience of being the only tourist in the local bistro are all equally representative of Paris and its surrounding regions. Seeing and doing them *all* is what makes for a memorable visit, and no one, by the way, should make you feel guilty for wanting to see some famous sites. They have become famous for a reason: they are really something to see, the Eiffel Tower included. Canon number eighty-four in Bruce Northam's *Globetrotter Dogma* is "The good old days are now," in which he wisely reminds us that destinations are not ruined even though they may have been more "real" however many years ago. "'Tis a haughty condescension to insist that because a place has changed or lost its innocence that it's not worth visiting; change requalifies a destination. Your first time is your first time; virgin turf simply is. The moment you commit to a trip, there begins the search for adventure."

Ultimately, this is the compendium of information that I wish I'd had between two covers years ago. I admit it isn't the "perfect" book; for that, I envision a waterproof jacket and pockets inside the front and back covers, pages and pages of accompanying maps, lots of blank pages for notes, a bookmark, mileage and size conversion charts . . . in other words, something so encyclopedic in both weight and size that no one would want to carry it, let alone read it. I envision such a large volume because I believe that to really get to know a place, to truly understand it in a non-superficial way, one must either live there or travel there again and again. Just as Henry Miller noted that "to know Paris is to know a great deal," it seems to me that it can take nothing short of a lifetime of studying and traveling to grasp Paris. I do not pretend to have completely grasped it now, many years later, nor do I pretend to have completely grasped the other destinations that are featured in *The Collected Traveler* series, but I am trying, by continuously reading, collecting, and traveling. And I presume readers like you are, too. That said, I am exceedingly happy with this edition, and I believe it will prove helpful in the anticipation of your upcoming journey, in the enjoyment of your trip while it's happening, and in the remembrance of it when you're back home.

Tous mes vœux pour un bon voyage!

FRANCE

There is, I think, something that sets France apart from many other parts of the world. I know of no other country that is so fascinating yet so frustrating, so aware of the world and its place within it but at the same time utterly insular. A nation touched by nostalgia, with a past so great—so marked by brilliance and achievement—that French people today seem both enriched and burdened by it. France is like a maddening, moody lover who inspires emotional highs and lows. One minute it fills you with a rush of passion, the next you're full of fury itching to smack the mouth of some sneering shopkeeper or smug civil servant. Yes, it's a love-hate relationship. But it's charged with so much mystery, longing and that French specialty—*séduction*—that we can't resist coming back for more.

—Sarah Turnbull,
*Almost French: Love and a New
Life in Paris*

PAVILLON DE LESDIGUIERES

France: The Outsider

IAN JACK

☙❧❧

THIS EDITORIAL WAS the introductory essay in an issue of the fine, thought-provoking literary magazine *Granta*. Though it appeared in the autumn 1997 issue, the references made to society and politics remain very much similar today. (Though the unemployment rate in France, for one thing, has fallen.) The essay as it appears here is an edited version of the original.

IAN JACK was the editor of *Granta* from 1995 to 2008. He edited London's *Independent on Sunday* from 1991 to 1995, and currently he writes a weekly column for the *Guardian*. Jack has also served as a foreign correspondent in South Asia and is the author of *The Country Formerly Known as Great Britain* (Jonathan Cape, 2009).

THE FIRST MAN to fly solo across the Atlantic and the hero of his age, Charles Lindbergh, saw France from the air on May 21, 1927. He had been flying for more than thirty hours and seen nothing but ocean since he left New York, and now the green fields and woods of Normandy were below him. Journey's end! Time for a bite! He took a sandwich from its wrapper and stretched to throw the wrapper from the cockpit. Then he looked down and decided that just wouldn't do. "My first act," Lindbergh said to himself, "will not be to sully such a beautiful garden." His American waste paper remained in the air-craft—scrunched, one assumes, in a ball at his feet.

The French writer Jean-Marie Domenach, who died this summer, tells this story in his last book: *Regarder la France: essai sur le malaise français*. It is for Domenach yet another small stone in a large mountain of anecdotal evidence gathered to demonstrate the singularity of France as a state, a people, a culture and (in this case) a landscape. But, as Domenach's subtitle indicates, all isn't well with this singularity. The fields that Lindbergh flew over are larger now, the roads straighter and wider, the peasants (should Lindbergh have spotted any, bending their backs in this beautiful garden) dramatically fewer. All of these changes have happened to most other western countries as agriculture has adopted new machines and new techniques to plough out hedges and plough in chemical fertilizers, to relegate agricultural labourers to models in museums of folklore. But in none of these other countries (even England, where the countryside supplies a large part of the national idea) would rural transformation be seen as such a blow to the nation's identity. There would be nostalgia, of course, and ecological concern. In France, things go much further. Implied in Domenach's story is the notion that, had Lindbergh been flying over some other, less top-quality country (Portugal, say, or Belgium), he might have nonchalantly tossed the paper into the windstream and had a good spit at the same time. But, as General and President Charles de Gaulle was fond of saying, France is . . . France. Even Lindbergh, high up in his frail aeroplane, and with a hundred other things to worry about, could see the specialness of the place and respect it.

Nobody doubts that France is special; certainly not the French. It is the largest, though not the most populous country, in Europe, and was once the most powerful. Its linguistic unity and its natural boundaries—France can be seen as a hexagonal fortress with sea on three sides and mountains on two—have given it a clearer identity, a less contested nationalism, than most countries which share a continent. Its history is alive with symbols, events, heroes and slogans which have not been shuttered in to the cob-webbed past—which form part of France's grand and still unfold-ing story, as the French tell it to themselves. France sees itself as the birthplace of modern ideas and modern politics. The words of the American constitution are fine, but a snappier political credo than "Liberty, Equality, Fraternity" has still to be invented. The terms "Left" and "Right" as in left-wing and right-wing come from the seating arrangements in the National Assembly of 1789, when the pro-revolutionaries took the benches on the left side of the chamber. When Britain was manufacturing industrial and necessarily temporary objects, France was taking the lead in cre-ating enduring, and now universal, abstractions. These ideals, which have dignified humankind, form part of France's claim to its status as a universal nation. Add them to a cultural preemi-nence which has lasted through most of the last and the present century—think of the French novel and French painting in the nineteenth, French film in the twentieth—and a way of living no-torious for its discriminating pleasure in philosophy, love, food, drink and fashion, and France's claim to be the global model for civilization can seem unanswerable. "Ah, the French," as the maxim goes on the northbound Channel ferry and the jet head-ing west to North America, "they know how to *live!*"

The paradox is that, while France has thought of itself as a tutor to the world, it has never really believed that it can be imitated. France is distinctive. It may believe, as the USA affects to believe (or simply assumes), that it is a country with values which can be franchised anywhere; but unlike perfumes, croissants and fizzy water—unlike, in fact, the Statue of Liberty—some items are not for export. There is the French soul; there is an even mistier item, *la France profonde.* Here normal rules do not apply. Sooner or later, in almost every area of human activity, one comes across the phrase: *l'exception française.* Exceptionally, France has retained sev-eral parts of its empire with little sense of post-imperial shame. Exceptionally, in the 1990s it began again to explode nuclear devices under one of these old outposts (when on British television a French government spokesman was asked why, if these tests were so safe, they were not conducted under French waters rather than in the far-away Pacific, he replied: "But Tahiti *is* France"). Exceptionally, it still regards French as the near-rival to English as the triumphant world language, when nearly four times as many people speak English (and three times as many use Spanish, and twice as many Bengali—or Arabic). Exceptionally, it is the most anti-American country in western (or for that matter eastern) Europe.

Nearly all of these exceptions flow from what is now the greatest exception of all: the power of the French state to regulate, subsidize, satisfy and inspire the lives and ambitions of France's fifty-eight million citizens. The urge to standardize and centralize in France predates the Revolution, but it was the precepts of the Revolution, later codified by Napoleon, which allowed French citizens to feel that they played equal parts in a grand and unifying design. There would be standard courts dispensing standard law, standard schools teaching the same French history, standard forms of local administration sitting in headquarters with *Liberté, Egalité, Fraternité* standardly engraved in their stone. The language would be standard despite its many regional variants, the measurements (metres, litres, kilos) also. All standards would be set by the government in Paris. The state interfered but it also sheltered, and it became one of the glories of France, inseparable from the idea of the French way of life. Today France employs five million civil servants (proportionately five times as many as the USA) and industries run by the state comprise more than a third of the French economy.

The state, then, matters in France as it does in few other countries. It has never been, unlike in Britain or the USA, the bogey of the tax-paying middle classes. For one thing, it keeps a large part of the middle class in work; more than half the families in France depend on income from the state. For another, its regulations and subsidies have sustained the attractive variousnesses of France, which still produces four hundred (or a thousand; the boast varies) different kinds of cheese, and where a town of one thousand seven hundred people can contain (this is a real but typical example, from Beaujolais) three bakeries, a butcher, two grocers, a pharmacy, a jeweller's, two clothes shops, a flower shop, two hardware stores, a newsagent, two garages, several bars, two hotels and two restaurants, one of which is mentioned honourably in the Michelin guide. In Britain and North America, supermarkets and shopping malls would have closed most of them, while politicians spoke airily about the free market's great virtue of consumer choice.

But—reenter *le malaise français*—unemployment runs at 12.5 percent (double the British figure) and the centralized political and bureaucratic elites of Paris have become deeply unpopular and sometimes corrupt. And the nation state is now retreating throughout the world as a custodian of economies and cultures, abandoning its old remits to the capricious pressures of the global market. France has many phrases for this phenomenon—*le capitalisme sauvage, le capitalisme dur* (hard), *le capitalisme Anglo-Saxon*—and most of them could be heard in the elections of June this year, when France ditched its right-wing government and replaced it with an alliance of Socialists and Communists. On the face of it, the Left had capitalized on France's prevailing moods of *sinistrose* (dismalness) and *morosité* (gloom) by promising that the two great forces for change in French life could be resisted: that France needn't bow to Chinese wage rates or cut its public spending so that it could qualify for membership of the European Monetary Union. The Left pledged that it would create seven hundred thousand jobs, half of them funded by the state, and cut the statutory working week from forty to thirty-five hours with no reduction in earnings. In Britain, where Mrs. Thatcher expunged socialism from the politics of her Labour successors, there was mockery and also half a cheer.

France was being exceptional once again, struggling to preserve its cherished ideas of Frenchness. To the rest of the world,
which has accepted globalism as an inevitability, the way things
are and will be, it seemed as though its fourth-largest economy
had recoiled in the face of modernity; that Fortress France was
pulling up the drawbridge.

Where does French writing stand in all this? The awkward truth
here is that, outside France and small pockets of Francophilia,
hardly anyone knows. Name six living French novelists. Name six
contemporary French novels. The French, of course, blame this
neglect on Anglo-Saxon ignorance and hostility, but the truth

(our truth, at least) is that, in literature, France pulled up the drawbridge long ago. Saul Bellow, writing in *Granta* in 1984, remembered how Paris had been the capital of international culture before the Second World War and how, on his first visit in 1948, the city had still seemed "one of the permanent settings, a theatre if you like, where the greatest problems of existence might be represented." Thirty years later that feeling had gone. "Marxism, Euro-communism, Existentialism, Structuralism, Deconstructionism could not restore the potency of French civilization," Bellow wrote. "Sorry about that."

Today in France there are arguments about the purpose of writing and a movement to put the world back into the book; it hasn't escaped the French that the failure of French writing to sell abroad may have, to put it strictly in terms of the market, more to do with the producer than the consumer. Today a younger generation of writers is emerging which is more willing to look outward again. Many of these writers come from present or former French territories outside Europe, or are the children of migrants from those places. What their writing has in common is the desire to dramatize the deed rather than the thought, the story above the idea.

They reflect a France that is richer and more complicated than the beleaguered monolith of newspaper headlines, and which cannot be accommodated by old ideas of Frenchness, no matter what its government may say or do. France, we should never forget, has the largest Muslim community in Europe, between three and five million people, and Europe's largest Jewish community (about seven hundred thousand people) outside Russia. A third of France's population has ancestry from outside its borders.

Beneath the crust of its mythology, France has already changed. Why otherwise would Jean-Marie Le Pen and his anti-immigrant, anti-Europe, anti-American party, the National Front, exist? And why in June would they have won 15 percent of the vote? The real challenge to France is not the Anglo-Saxon world. It is to find a new and more plural identity, freed from the burden of glorious memory.

Dreyfus Is Decorated

ON DECEMBER 22, 1894, in Paris, Jewish army captain Alfred Dreyfus was unjustly accused of treason for passing military secrets to the Germans. The Dreyfus Affair—often simply referred to as *l'affaire*—was "the most celebrated affair of the Belle Époque and the conflict that helped shape the political landscape of modern France," according to Michael Burns, author of *Dreyfus: A Family Affair* (HarperCollins, 1991). *L'affaire* inspired writer Émile Zola to write an open letter addressed to Félix Faure, then president of France, which appeared on the front page of the newspaper *L'Aurore* on January 13, 1898. It was Georges Clemenceau, a member of the National Assembly and later prime minister, who had some influence at the newspaper and who titled Zola's letter "*J'accuse . . . !*" The accusatory letter was scathing and landed Zola a libel lawsuit, but this was what he'd intended all along as he believed a public trial would force the military authorities to reopen the Dreyfus case, in turn revealing the military cover-up. *L'affaire* is also a key underlying theme in Proust's *Remembrance of Things Past*, and through its successive volumes Proust reveals which characters are for or against Dreyfus. Patrick Alexander, in *Marcel Proust's Search for Lost Time: A Reader's Guide to The Remembrance of Things Past* (Vintage, 2009), notes that the Dreyfus Affair "ripped French society down the middle and created enmities and cultural divisions that were to last decades." For journalist Theodor Herzl, a Hungarian Jew who was a Paris correspondent for the Austrian newspaper *Neue Freie Presse, l'affaire* would solidify his belief in a separate homeland for Jews. In 1896 he first explored this idea in a pamphlet entitled *Der Judenstaat,* and Dreyfus's tragedy, according to author Michael Burns, "gave his dreams added urgency. If religious tolerance and racial harmony were impossible in France, the home of the Rights of Man, they were, Herzl was now convinced, impossible everywhere." Herzl, considered the father of modern Zionism, organized the First Zionist Congress in Switzerland in 1897, and fifty years later the state of Israel was established.

An excellent book that I think approaches *l'affaire* in a never-before-examined way is *For the Soul of France: Culture Wars in the Age of Dreyfus* by Frederick Brown (Knopf, 2010). Brown (also the author of acclaimed biographies of Zola and Flaubert) details how the Dreyfus Affair can be understood only by fully grasping what happened in France in the previous decades: the revolution of 1848, France's defeat in the Franco-Prussian War of 1870–71, the ceding of Alsace-Lorraine, civil war, the Paris Commune, and the rise of nationalism. By the late 1800s, two cultural factions emerged in France: moderates, who espoused a secular state, and militants, who were Catholic and royalist. "Science" and "technological advancement" were pitted against "supernatural intervention," and these were reflected in two of Paris's most iconic monuments, the Eiffel Tower and Sacré-Coeur. Brown notes that "these two forces converged as never before during the tumultuous nineties, in the Dreyfus Affair." The uncertain atmosphere made "cosmopolitan," "modern," and "intellectual" dirty words among the very vocal militants. Anti-Semitism and xenophobia reared their ugly heads, and foreign-born Jews in particular were singled out for every kind of vice. (And indeed, the line drawn from this to Vichy, little more than forty years later, is perfectly straight: the Nazis first asked for all foreign-born Jews to be rounded up, and Vichy officials were only too happy to comply.) Brown delves deep into fin de siècle Paris and France, and he brilliantly reveals how the conflicting opinions of the 1800s were not resolved when Dreyfus was acquitted, twelve years after his arrest.

Here is the original article that appeared on the front page of

the *New York Times* on July 22, 1906, detailing the official ceremony that marked his army reinstatement.

Dreyfus Is Decorated Where He Was Degraded
Cross of the Legion of Honor Pinned on His Breast.
Officers Congratulate Him
Ceremony in the Courtyard of the Military School—
An Attack of Heart Weakness Afterward.

Paris, July 21—In the presence of a distinguished military assemblage Major Alfred Dreyfus, wearing the full uniform of his
rank, this afternoon received the Cross of Chevalier of the Legion of Honor. The ceremony, which took place in the courtyard of the military school, was rendered doubly impressive by
being held on the very spot where the buttons and gold lace

52 - PARIS - Les Fêtes de la Victoire - 14 Juillet 1919
Le Maréchal Pétain et les Troupes Françaises sur les Grands Boulevards

were stripped off Dreyfus's uniform and his sword was broken twelve years ago.

The decoration of the Major assumed the aspect of a notable demonstration. His brother officers, who were prominent figures in various stages of the controversy, were among the spectators, and outside the circle of troops stood Mme. Dreyfus and the little son of Dreyfus, Brig. Gen. Picquart, who shared in the court's acquittal of the famous prisoner, Anatole France of the French Academy, and Alfred Capus, and other literary men, who aided in Zola's campaign for a revision of the first trial.

Previous to the ceremony Major Dreyfus was presented to Gen. Gillain, commander of the First Division of Cavalry, Gen. Percin, and other prominent officers, who warmly shook hands with him, testifying their satisfaction at his return to the army. The officers then repaired to the courtyard, where trumpeters sounded four calls announcing the ceremony.

The courtyard, from which the general public were excluded, as the ceremony was purely official, was encircled by two batteries of the thirteenth artillery, commanded by Col. Targe, who made the recent discoveries at the war office leading to the re-hearing of the case against Dreyfus and his acquittal.

Gen. Gillain, accompanied by a number of army officials, entered the circle with trumpets and drums sounding. Major Dreyfus took up a position by the side of Col. Targe, while Gen. Gillain, stepping into the center of the circle, announced the decoration of Targe as a Commander and Dreyfus as a Chevalier of the Legion of Honor. Dreyfus and Targe, with their sabers drawn, then advanced to the center of the troops, taking a position before Gen. Gillain. The latter first bestowed the decoration on Targe, and then, turning to Dreyfus, the General said:

"In the name of the President of the Republic and in virtue of the powers intrusted to me, Major Dreyfus, I hereby name you a Chevalier of the National Order of the Legion of Honor."

After pinning the cross on Dreyfus's breast and felicitating him on his well-earned honor, the General gave the Major the military accolade, the trumpets sounding and the spectators applauding. Dreyfus briefly expressed his acknowledgements.

The troops then defiled before Gen. Gillain, Dreyfus occupying the post of honor on Gen. Gillain's right, Col. Targe and the other generals being stationed on his left.

When the march past was completed, the trumpets again sounded four calls, announcing the close of the ceremony, which had lasted only about five minutes, and Dreyfus and Targe were immediately the center of an eager crowd of officers and friends. One of the first to reach Dreyfus was his little son, who rushed forward and threw his arms around his father's neck, sobbing violently.

The officers who had not taken official part in the ceremony also came forward to greet their comrade. As Dreyfus received the well wishes of his relatives and the officers, his face, usually impassive, twitched with emotion, and it was with difficulty that he preserved his soldierly calm.

Turning to Anatole France, Dreyfus said:

"I thank you more than I can say, you who have always struggled for my cause."

M. France replied:

"We merit no thanks, for what has been done was in the interest of right and justice. We felicitate you all the more since so many others who have struggled for justice have died before it was attained."

Col. Targe terminated his felicitations by conducting Major Dreyfus to the officers' quarters, where Mme. Dreyfus was waiting for him. The meeting between the husband and wife was most affectionate, the spectators withdrawing to permit them to be alone. Shortly after this Dreyfus, accompanied by his wife and son, emerged from the military school and entered a carriage. As the Major appeared the crowd in front of the main entrance gave him a hearty ovation, waving handkerchiefs and shouting "Vive Dreyfus!" "Vive la République!" "Vive l'Armée!"

The carriage was then driven swiftly in the direction of Dreyfus's home. On reaching his residence the Major, who is affected with heart weakness, suffered a violent attack, but thanks to his strong will power the faintness soon passed away and he was able to receive Procurator General Baudouin and Brig. Gen. Picquart, to whom he expressed his sincerest thanks for their exertions on his behalf.

La Poste and I

BARBARA WILDE

𝕊𝕫𝕊𝕫

BEFORE IT WAS fashionably renamed La Poste, the French postal system was called the PTT, which stood for Poste, Télégraphes et Téléphones. Though the average visitor to France will do no more than buy stamps and mail postcards at *la poste,* residents have much more contact there, with varying degrees of success, as the piece below attests. But *la poste* is also, according to Philippe Meyer in his revealing book *A Parisian's Paris,* one of the best places in the city to really observe Parisians. Meyer was actually given permission, while working on his book, to sit behind the counter at a Paris post office, and he gained a new perspective on his fellow Parisians, both behind and in front of the counter. He notes that *la poste* "is the place par excellence for Parisians, irascible by nature, to find somebody to lay into. And not just any old body, but an individual who, when being told off, represents a telling-off of the Government, the Civil Service, and moribund Public Spirit all in one." Dialogue between clerk and customer is "characterized by absurdity cloaked in diplomacy." Diplomacy because one lady (as related in one transaction), "who hoped to be relieved of her anxiety even as she places the blame for the shoddy performance on the postal clerk, does her best to remain impersonal in her criticisms and polite in asking for help. It's a question of making the person behind the window feel duty-bound toward her, and therefore guilty about the firm's poor showing. But this guilt must be sparked and fueled without uttering a single insulting word, which would give the employee room to put an end to the discussion by insisting that the customer hurry up and make a decision on her own (*'I'm sorry, but people be-*

hind you are waiting . . .')." A trip to *la poste,* therefore, can be an adventure.

The two most significant points to remember about *la poste* are that there are very few slow periods in a Paris post office and that Parisians are in a hurry. Therefore, visitors should be mindful of the etiquette code at *la poste,* just as it exists at a busy *pâtisserie.* Clients expect to move through the line quickly, and clerks expect clients to be prepared. Before you join the line—there will almost always be one, no matter what the hour—make sure you have euros handy so you don't earn glares as you dig for coins in your bag. It never pays, even if you feel frustrated, to lose your temper. Be as deferential as you possibly can. If you're mailing a box or a small package, none of the customers will want to be behind you as a package, of any size, is perceived as being time-consuming—don't take offense if the clerks take other customers first and come back to you. If all of this sounds a bit like the Soup Nazi episode on *Seinfeld,* it isn't meant to, though sometimes you might wonder.

When I lived in Paris as a student, I once tried to mail a box of books home, and I was chastised for not tying the string properly around one of the boxes designated for shipping books by boat. The clerk would not accept it until I had retied it to her satisfaction. It seemed, in those days, that each visit to the PTT was an exercise in humility, as the clerks were always the victors. But in fairness, in the years since, I've had nothing but uneventful, even pleasant, exchanges at *la poste.* And by the way, you can still place calls at the *téléphonique* part of some post offices today, which I think is a far better option than using a cell phone or a phone booth on a busy street. You wait your turn for a private (and quiet) *cabine,* and after you're finished an attendant informs you of the sum you owe.

If, like me, you have a yen for stamps and old-fashioned letter writing, you may enjoy the Musée de la Poste, at 34 boulevard de Vaugirard in the fifteenth arrondissement (museedelaposte.fr).

This little-known museum exhibits a wonderful collection of French stamps, letter boxes, postal uniforms, and virtually everything connected to the history of written communication in France.

BARBARA WILDE, a passionate gardener and cook who lives in France, is the founder of a wonderful company called L'Atelier Vert (frenchgardening.com), which is a "green studio" of great French gardening items for both garden and home. The L'Atelier Web site is filled with gardening information, tips, recipes, and some travel insights, as well as authentic garden-related products from all over France. "We started this company," she notes, "with a commitment to offering only French-made products, and we hope to keep it that way. Don't look here for 'French-look' garden urns made in China." Wilde gets three cheers from me for that mission! Also the author of *Growing Roses Organically* (Rodale, 2002), she is currently working on a cookbook featuring recipes she created at her *mas* (farmhouse) in Provence.

Wilde writes a great Paris Postcard feature on her site, in which she shares "the frustrations, humor, and sometimes almost heartbreaking beauty of daily life from the perspective of an American expatriate living in Paris." This one is among the best tales of a postal adventure *anywhere* that I've ever read.

THE MINUTE I see any combination of golden yellow and navy blue, I think of La Poste. Those are the colors of the French post office, where I seem to be spending more and more of my life. Those of you who picture me whiling away a rainy winter afternoon with friends in a cozy Parisian café or discussing Franco-American relations in a smoky brasserie? Uh-uh. Like as not (and like it or not), I'm probably either *at* the post office or getting ready to go to the post office.

If neither of those options applies, I'm probably sticking close to home (-office) during the peak hours of postal delivery, in the hope that I won't miss the drop-off of a package, a registered letter for Denis, or, God forbid, an item sent by Chronoposte, the "express delivery" arm of La Poste. Trying to outguess the French postal service on their delivery times is next to impossible. While the regular mailman delivers registered letters (and he comes twice a day), packages are delivered by a separate department. Packages or documents sent Chronoposte, on the other hand, are delivered by ghosts, which manage to slip unseen into the building to leave an *avis de passage* (notice of passage), even when I am bodily present in my apartment.

It is commonly accepted by the French public that one's physical presence has little to do with whether or not an item requiring one's presence will in fact be delivered. On the yellow *avis de passage* slips, there is not one but several reasons which may be checked to indicate why your package could not be delivered. If none of the choices seems to apply, the agent will feel free to add one of his own, inscrutably encoded in private acronym.

Needless to say, you will then have to hunt your package down yourself. In the simplest scenario for me, this involves going to my postal office branch, bringing along the yellow slip and a piece of

identification. If by chance the item has been addressed to my company, I must also bring along my documents of its organization. Already I'm weighed down and I haven't even picked up the package yet.

When picking up a missed delivery, I usually walk to *la poste* because there is absolutely nowhere to park nearby, except in the bus stop zone, which stretches the entire length of the building (the length of several buses). I take a shopping caddy with me as I have no indication on my yellow slip as to the origin of the item, so I have no way of judging what it might be or how heavy. I yank my empty caddy up the three steps of the post office, avoiding the eyes of the *chômeur* (unemployed person) who is allowed to station himself at the door, opening it for you in the hopes of getting a handout.

A wave of stifling heat blasts my face, and I immediately unwind the scarf from my neck. Three seasons of the year, the post office is heated to broiling temperatures. In summer it is not air conditioned.

I eye *la queue,* or line, gauging its length against the number of *guichets,* or windows, open and functioning, in order to estimate the probable length of my wait. Appropriately, there is a chair available for aged or ill persons who cannot remain standing this long.

One of the main reasons that the line in the post office advances so interminably slowly is that, in France, the post office offers financial services similar to those of a bank. This means that in any given line, over half of the customers are likely there for a financial transaction of some sort. And given the enormous seriousness and discretion required for any financial transaction in France . . . well, you get the picture.

Add to this the fact that any public transaction here requires the exchange of pleasantries, and the attitude of the French that, after they've waited through everyone else's interminable transaction, they're darned well going to take their time for their own turns, and—well, let's just say you never go to the post office if you have a pressing appointment in the near future.

If the wait looks as if it will be lengthy, I take off my coat, so that perspiration won't soak my inner garments while I wait, an eventuality that I know will add to my sense of panic at the amount of time I'm wasting. French people absolutely never remove their coats—not in the boiling-hot post office, not in the ovenlike department stores, not in stuffy, overheated Métro cars. This is one of the things that makes me realize I'll never be French enough to be French.

On such a Monday last month, right before the holidays, I was standing in line, clutching a letter from Chronoposte in my hand. Somehow I had missed the delivery of a Wi-Fi network setup and ADSL modem sent by France Télécom, who had notified me in a very well-organized and efficient manner that the package would be delivered between nine a.m. and one p.m. the previous Friday.

During those hours I had stayed in the house, not even daring to take a shower, play the radio, or talk too loudly on the phone for fear of not hearing the door buzzer. I was especially anxious to receive this delivery because it meant that we could switch from our fiber-optic cable connection, which had been down an inexplicable almost 40 percent of the last two months, to a more reliable and even faster ADSL line. Of course, it didn't arrive, so I was in line at the post office with my Chronoposte letter, feeling just the tiniest bit more anxious than usual as I couldn't figure out why I had received this letterlike object instead of the usual yellow slip. I feared, well, some sort of irregularity which I might find confusing or be somehow unequipped to deal with (e.g. missing the necessary documents).

At last my turn came. I handed over my letter, explaining I was here to collect my Chronoposte delivery which *I* had missed! The postal service employee gravely took my letter and scanned it. Maintaining a carefully noncommittal expression, he typed the reference number of the delivery into his computer. While I watched anxiously, he scrolled and clicked around through several screens. Finally he looked up. "We don't have this item," he informed me. "You must pick it up at the Chronoposte depot." He shoved the letter at me, his eyes already seeking the next customer.

"Wait!" I implored. "Where is this depot?"

"In the rue Cardinet," he replied shortly.

"*Where* in the rue Cardinet?" I asked, relieved that it was in a street which was just a couple of blocks away, but also worried because it is a very long street, stretching through several neighborhoods.

"In the middle," he replied in dismissal. At which I planted myself squarely in front of his *guichet,* getting an inkling but no real idea of the extent of the saga that lay before me.

"Is it west or east of where we are now?" I asked, narrowing his choices. "What is the address?" Which, under the circumstances, seemed like a reasonable request.

"I don't know, madame," he answered, looking at me with the panic of a cornered animal in his eyes. "Here, I'll give you their phone number." And he scribbled some digits on a slip of paper. I looked at the number to make sure I could decipher the French handwriting and went on my way, muttering and cursing under my breath.

I went back home and maneuvered my car out of the interior courtyard into the street, heading toward rue Cardinet. Doing some quick thinking, I headed east, because the part of this street that heads west I go down almost every day and I'd never noticed a Chronoposte building. I drove slowly, eliciting honks and obscene gestures. I was trying to peer at all buildings, because it's amazing how well hidden a building can be in Paris. After having gone some distance with no sign of Chronoposte, I pulled over to the side of the street and phoned information to get the number for said depot on rue Cardinet. "*Ça n'existe pas, madame,*" I was told. Not "No such number is listed," but rather "It doesn't exist," setting the tone for the surreal events to follow.

I called the post office where I had just been and explained my situation to the person answering. After a hold of a few minutes, he returned to the phone. "It's at 147 rue Cardinet, madame," he informed me politely.

Somewhat mollified, I pulled back into traffic. When I got to the 120s, I seized a parking space. The rest of the search I would do on foot, as I was now in a rather bizarre industrial area near the enormous artery of train tracks that runs down into the Gare du Nord. Perhaps due to the fact that I was now in a warehouse area, the numbers on the street progressed incredibly slowly on the odd-numbered north side, while progressing busily into the 160s already on the more inhabited south side. (Beware if you're ever in Paris searching for an address: the numbers on either side of the street may bear little or no relation to each other.)

After walking about a half a mile, I came to 143 rue Cardinet. At last, I thought, and walked a little farther past the entrance to a weird, grungy sort of industrial park, which was numbered 145. The next building with a number was 149. *Where is 147?!* I felt like wailing. I took shelter from the traffic noise in a doorway and redialed the post office. The same guy answered. After a brief hold, he apologized. "It's 145, in fact, madame!"

Okay, at least I wasn't going crazy. Inside the industrial park, I identified the Chronoposte terminal by the scores of yellow and blue delivery vans parked outside its loading dock. Less obvious was how to access the building, which seemed to admit only trucks. I walked around it, finding no entry door. Finally, passing a pollution-smeared office window behind which were living human beings, I gestured wildly. A man opened the window and let me in on the secret entry.

I found myself in the selfsame office, and wearily showed the gentleman who had guided me in my by now rumpled Chronoposte letter. A stern lady sat imperviously at a computer behind him. After scanning my letter, he showed it to her. They exchanged significant looks. "Where do you live?" he asked me.

I gestured at the address clearly visible on my letter and added it was just by Parc Monceau. Now eyebrows were raised and a slight smile played around his lips. Even the stern woman seemed on the point of snickering. Just what was so funny?

After checking a list, on which I was sure I saw my address, he gave me the explanation. On the previous Friday—the day my delivery was due—the driver had simply aborted his run, stealing the delivery truck with all its contents. It had not been recovered. My delivery had fallen victim to a disgruntled postal worker! It was so absurd that I had to laugh. We all shook our heads. They advised me to call France Télécom and report what had happened, and request another shipment.

I was back in my car headed toward home before I wondered why this information could not have been relayed in the original letter, saving everyone involved—especially me—a lot of time and hassle. There must have been some sort of weird face-saving involved. Would that this were the end of my story.

I duly reported to France Télécom. Another delivery was scheduled and not delivered. I think you'll have to agree that at this point we must invoke déjà vu, in all its corny glory. Just rewind the tape back to the beginning and replay it up to where

I'm at the Chronoposte depot, minus, of course, the address confusion. By now I'm feeling like a regular.

In the office, the same man takes my letter. He summons an employee from the non-office side of the place and they head out into the warehouse together. Twenty minutes later they come back, without the package, and begin an explanation of breathtaking complexity. I'm thinking about Occam's razor when I'm brought up short by a glimmer of recognition in the eye of the office man.

"You're the lady with the package on the stolen truck, aren't you? Wait just a minute . . ." And he disappears for another five minutes, this time reappearing with a tattered box which has obviously been retaped shut using bright yellow and blue post office tape. "We found the truck! Most of the packages on it had been emptied, but yours wasn't."

Together we inspected the contents, which seemed to be intact and filled the dimensions of the carton. After a serious discussion on the best route to take, I decided to go with the bird in the hand, in spite of a slight risk of invisible damage. "Just refuse the new shipment when it comes!" my new friend cheerily advised.

Indeed! Refuse to trudge to the post office—or here!—to retrieve it, is more like it, I reflected as I navigated back to my car, clutching my precious if tattered cargo.

That evening, Denis asked me for the latest update on the arrival of the modem. I gestured at the dog-eared box on the floor, bearing its layers of blue and yellow tape like bandages over war wounds. "Let me tell you a story," I began.

"Whenever I travel to Europe I'm astounded by the beauty you can find by simply walking down the street. The basalt blocks in Rome, the cobblestones in Aix-en-Provence . . . the roads themselves are perfectly laid puzzles for all to experience. In Paris, the roads wind and the buildings curve, soar, and expand. Everything feels a bit romantic and magical. The sign for the Métro pulls you in with its twists and turns; its lavish curls seem exotic and exciting. Strolling along the Seine in the evening from Notre-Dame to the Eiffel Tower, different parts of the city slip in and out of view. The Eiffel Tower radiates blue light, in contrast to the white light filling I. M. Pei's Louvre pyramid. When it's cool outside and I'm finished looking at the buildings and streets, my eye wanders to the beautiful people walking around and their wonderful scarves! And then I move on to the food: even something as simple as a *croque-monsieur*—toasted ham and cheese sandwich—seems divine. My favorite way to experience Paris is on foot with my eyes wide open and ready to take it all in! From the big museums and cooking schools to the streetside vendors and markets, there is always something to see and appreciate."

—Lindsey Elias,
children's books marketer and
Paris enthusiast

The French, Rude? *Mais Non!*

JOSEPH VOELKER

꧁꧂

LOTS OF VISITORS to France have amusing language faux pas tales to tell. One common mistake, for example, is to say "*Je suis plein*" for "I'm full" after a meal—since the phrase *Je suis plein* means "I'm pregnant" ("*J'ai assez mangé*" is a better way to say you don't want seconds). No matter how well one might know the language, it's still hard to speak it flawlessly, as the author of this piece attests.

JOSEPH VOELKER is dean of the College of Arts and Sciences at the University of Hartford. Previously he held the position of associate dean at Franklin & Marshall College, where he also served on the English department faculty for many years.

IT IS FUNNY that we Americans, in our current enthusiasm for cultural diversity, have collectively decided to be tolerant of all national and ethnic groups on the planet *except the French*. If a Bororo chieftain starts beating his wife in their hut, the visiting American anthropologist—though feminist to the core—will stand by and say nothing. But she'll tell you a story that vilifies the French waiter who refused to bring her a wine list.

No doubt there are complex historical reasons for this acceptability of French-bashing: their arrogance as inheritors of a two-thousand-year-old culture, their irksomely deserved reputation for elegance and knowing how to live. And the fact that they are rude.

If we speak English, French waiters and hotel receptionists ignore us. If we try to speak French, they respond in English—and not always the best English at that. We are humiliated by this response. Why do they act so superior? Having recently spent a year living just outside Nantes, I venture a couple of amateurish explanations, in the spirit that *tout comprendre est tout pardonner*—to understand everything is to forgive everything.

First, the French language is simply much harder than the English. It certainly seems to have more tenses, moods, and genders, and it's full of subtle and numerous irregularities. For instance, they don't pronounce the *f* in *oeufs* (eggs); for *deux oeufs* you have to say "duhz uhh." French is hard to articulate. The French mouth is far more tense than the English and makes its sounds farther to the front, where seemingly minor errors can create major shifts in significance.

French people, from elementary school onward, learn their language in an atmosphere of intimidation. As corporal punishment was the medium in which our ancestors learned Latin, so humiliation is the medium in which the French learn French. As a result, they associate speaking badly with stupidity. At a dinner party recently, a French friend who is by no means pedantic told me she couldn't drink another glass of wine because it would cause her to make mistakes in the subjunctive.

Two of the best speakers of the French language in public life are François Mitterrand and Jean-Marie Le Pen, who correspond roughly in our political system to George H. W. Bush and Jesse Helms respectively. The two men are politically opposed on every count: Mitterrand is a socialist; Le Pen is a far-right xenophobe. But they share one attribute: they are able to employ the imperfect subjunctive spontaneously, in public speeches. It's a risky business; errors will be reported in the press. But doing it wins them respect and even votes.

In any given year, the French middle schooler will have one course in French orthography, one in French grammar, and one in French literature. All are hard, and all present the risk of humiliation. One reason the French are generally not good at foreign languages and avoid learning them is that they have no desire to suffer the agonies of French class all over again in another tongue. The vast majority—who by the way are not Paris waiters—are shy about speaking English because they fear they will sound funny.

A French academic I know (he's a Spanish professor) told me the story of a confrontation he witnessed in Paris. A retirement-aged American couple approached a Parisian and asked him where

"Noder Daaame" was. The man responded by shrugging his shoulders and making a sound that I'm going to spell "PFFFFFT." Then he walked away.

Now, first of all, "PFFFFFT" is part of the French language. It means "I don't know" or "I don't understand." It is neither rude nor hostile. Children respond to teachers and parents with it. It is utterly unrelated to our "raspberry," which is spelled "PHGF-PGHFPFRRRT." The man made this gesture because he was a prisoner inside the difficult French phonetic system, in which *Noder Daaame* cannot by any stretch of the ear and brain be transformed into *Nuhtr Dom-uh.*

Okay, you answer. He didn't understand and he said, "I don't know." But why did he walk away instead of trying to help?

Well, France has been invaded a lot. Caesar arrived in 52 BC. Then there were a half dozen Germanic and Hungarian migrations, followed by the Vikings, who stayed a century. And let's not forget three modern German invasions within a period of seventy years. Sometimes it is difficult for people whose country has never been invaded and occupied to understand people for whom that is a central fact of their national history. It is not admirable on the part of the French that they are not crazy about foreigners, but it runs very, very deep.

Hence, when the French insist on answering our noble efforts at their language by speaking English, we should be more forgiving. First, these are tired people trying to get through a day's work with dead-end jobs in the tourism industry. Second, they are sparing us from looking ridiculous, and thus embarrassing them in turn.

Early in my own sojourn in France, when I was by no means linguistically up to snuff, I found myself in the express lane of a grocery store. A tall young man challenged me—I didn't catch all the words—for being in the wrong lane. I stammered out an answer, to which he replied, "*Oh, m'sieur, vous ne parlez pas Français*" ("You don't speak French"). Instead of letting it go, I said, "*Mais, essayez-moi*" ("Try me"), unaware that the phrase is a standard homosexual come-on. Only his wife derived any enjoyment from the scene, and her "*Oh, Jean-Pierre, oh la la la la la la!*" will stay with me until I die.

Once I inadvertently told a French family gathered at the dinner table that my mother used to make wonderful jellies and she never put condoms in them (*les préservatifs*). Once I phoned a neighbor to ask directions to a famous château and, wanting to know if she thought it was worth a visit, tried to ask, "*Vous l'avez vu?*" ("Have you seen it?"). But the American phonetic system (and my untrained mouth) couldn't distinguish among the different French *u*'s, and so what I actually said was "*Vous lavez-vous?*" ("Do you bathe yourself?"). She laughed inexplicably. An hour after hanging up, I realized what I'd said.

Just learning the body language to enter and order something in a bakery in France is a small challenge. Somehow we Americans never know where to stand. We end up dead center in the store, with everyone staring at us. I can offer some advice for negotiating small shops.

Begin with "*Bonjour,*" followed always by "*m'sieur*" or "*madame.*" ("*Bonjour*" by itself is rather abrupt—even, well, rude. In fact, I'd bet that that retired American couple approached that Parisian in a manner that seemed awfully brusque by his lights.) When you are handed your bag of croissants, say "*Merci, m'sieur*" or "*Merci, madame.*" And always say "*Au revoir*" or "*Bonne journée*" or something equivalent when you leave. If that's all the French you ever speak, you'll be thought of as an intriguingly polite American.

And if you want to try the language, don't do it in the American Express office in Paris, for heaven's sake. That poor guy may have spent the last six hours in that cage. Get out of Paris, off the beaten track, where the people don't speak English, and where some of them will be delighted to chat with you. Try retired people: they've generally got the time, and therefore the patience, to let you practice.

If you need a subject, ask a question about food—or wine. Here's a sure thing. Ask if the region produces good asparagus—or, if you're near the coast, good oysters. These are questions so subtle, so complex, so rife with possibilities for a Frenchman to display a Cartesian clarity, that you will likely have a full hour in which you won't have to do anything but listen. If you want to say *"Ah, bon?"* ("Oh, really?") once in a while, go ahead. It's thought to be encouraging.

It pleases me to remember that the story I used to tell most often in conversation with new French acquaintances was the one about the grocery store, the *"essayez-moi"* story. I suppose I was shrewd enough to see that it endeared me to them. It was the sort of moment that they, as French people, feared the most. It is hard to explain, but it got me over a bridge. It made me human, rather than another bossy, abrupt American. *"Oh, le pauvre!"* they would say—"Poor thing!"—laughing in genuine sympathy.

"I seem to have accidentally on purpose devised a tradition of celebrating my birthday (in February) in Paris. I've been there consistently over the course of the last ten years or so. *Bon Appétit* magazine is based in Los Angeles, and one of the best birthday trips was definitely along the lines of "You can take the girl out of Hollywood, but . . ." I managed to find out which brasserie was featured in *Something's Gotta Give,* that delightful comedy with Diane Keaton, Jack Nicholson, and Keanu Reeves. Not only did my friend Stephanie Curtis track down the restaurant for us—Le Grand Colbert behind the Opéra—but she managed to reserve for Paul (Nagle, my life partner) and me the same table where Keaton and Reeves

sat; there was a very discreet poster for the movie placed behind the banquette. That night we had all the classics—
superb fresh oysters, perfectly cooked chateaubriand for two,
pommes dauphine, profiteroles, Champagne, a great bottle of
Margaux. I can't think of a better place—or more delicious
way—to mark the passing of another year."

> —Barbara Fairchild, food
> writer, editor, consultant,
> and former editor in chief,
> *Bon Appétit*

RECOMMENDED READING

EUROPE

For European history and a sense of the European community of
which France is a member, all of these are excellent reads:

The Civilization of Europe in the Renaissance, John Hale (Atheneum, 1994).

Europe: A History, Norman Davies (Oxford University Press, 1996).

Fifty Years of Europe: An Album, Jan Morris (Villard, 1997).

*History of the Present: Essays, Sketches, and Dispatches from Europe in
the 1990s,* Timothy Garton Ash (Random House, 2000).

The Penguin Atlas of Ancient History (1967; revised 2002), *The
Penguin Atlas of Medieval History* (1968; revised 1992), *The Penguin Atlas of Modern History: to 1815* (1973; revised 1986), and

The Penguin Atlas of Recent History: Europe Since 1815 (1982, revised 2003), all by Colin McEvedy and published by Penguin. The concept for each of these paperbacks is brilliant: a chronological sequence of maps that illustrate political and military developments, which in turn illustrate history via geography. Each volume is remarkably fascinating, and the four volumes as a whole present an enlightening read. Maps appear on the right-hand pages while one page of explanatory text accompanies them on the left-hand page. Essential for history novices and mavens alike. (*The Penguin Atlas of Diasporas,* published in 1995 by Gérard Chaliand and Jean-Pierre Rageau is equally fascinating.)

Travel Guide to Europe, 1492: Ten Itineraries in the Old World, Lorenzo Camusso (Henry Holt, 1992). This unique book, published to coincide with the five hundredth anniversary of the discovery of the Americas, deserves more than short-lived appreciation. Italian historian Camusso presents ten real (or probable) journeys in chronological order, so that readers may imagine the passing of time and events. The first portion of the book gives an overview of Europe in the fifteenth century and includes descriptions of what travel was like by horse, river, and seaworthy boats, as well as of road conditions, inns, money, royal families, artists and artwork, and food and drink. Of the ten itineraries, Paris and cities nearby are featured in three. It's interesting to note that in a population chart of twenty cities on the itineraries, Paris was then the fifth largest after Istanbul (four hundred thousand) and Florence, Naples, and Venice (each with one hundred thousand).

WORLD WARS

France lost nearly two million men in World War I, equivalent to two out of every nine, and if today's younger generations visiting

Paris feel a bit removed from this war, all they have to do is visit a smaller French city or town; just about every one has its requisite World War I monument. (And if World War II too feels remote, a visit to the Normandy American Cemetery, with its seemingly endless rows of grave markers, should solidify a very real and present link—and this is only one World War II cemetery of more than 120 in France.) Over the years I have found these monuments quite moving, and I've taken numerous photographs of them, probably enough for a book. As renowned military historian John Keegan notes, the list of names on these monuments is "heartrendingly long," and even more heartrending is that you'll often notice several names repeated, testifying to more than one death in the same family.

Keegan writes that "the First World War was a tragic and unnecessary conflict," and "the Second World War, when it came in 1939, was unquestionably the outcome of the First, and in large measure its continuation. . . . In 1914, by contrast, war came, out of a cloudless sky, to populations which knew almost nothing of it and had been raised to doubt that it could ever again trouble their

continent." In any compilation of recommended books on the world wars, Keegan's top the list, and are on my short list, too. Keegan has served as senior lecturer in military history at the Royal Military Academy in England and was named by the *New York Times Book Review* "the best military historian of our day." His *The First World War* (Knopf, 1999) was widely acclaimed, and referred to by the *Washington Post* as "a grand narrative history [and] a pleasure to read." *An Illustrated History of the First World War* (Knopf, 2001) includes some text from his previous World War I book and some that is new, as well as photographs, paintings, cartoons, and posters belonging to archives in both Europe and America.

Other world war reads I highly recommend include:

Bad Faith: A Forgotten History of Family, Fatherland and Vichy France, Carmen Callil (Knopf, 2006). I'm fascinated by the opening sentences of books, and the opening line for this one hooked me right away: "There are many things to make one wretched on this earth." Callil's childhood was the thing to make her wretched, and when she was twenty-one she tried to commit suicide by overdosing on sleeping pills. The London doctor into whose care she was admitted, Anne Darquier, once told Callil that "there are some things and some people you can never forgive." In 1970, Callil arrived at Dr. Darquier's for an appointment, but there was no answer at the door, and later that day she received word that Anne was dead. When she attended Anne's funeral, she thought it was odd that Anne's name appeared with the addition of "de Pellepoix," and it would have remained only an oddity if Callil had not later seen the documentary *Le Chagrin et la pitié* (*The Sorrow and the Pity*) by Marcel Ophüls. The English subtitles contained Anne's full surname, but in reference to a Vichy government official. Callil's curiosity was piqued, and she began to investigate Anne's story and that of her father, who had been a leading French anti-Semite before the war and who had added the fictitious "de Pellepoix" to his original name. He later became commissioner for Jewish affairs, and in July 1942 he was put in charge of the Vél' d'Hiv' (Vélodrome d'Hiver) roundup in Paris, which led to the deportation of nearly thirteen thousand Jews, almost a third of whom were children. According to Callil, Darquier "worked tirelessly to provide more Jews for deportation. He introduced the yellow star and took life-and-death decisions over the fate of the Jews of France." She also informs us that after the German occupation of France ended in 1944, the *épuration* (purge) followed, and it was reported that a man believed to be Darquier was lynched by a mob in either Limoges or Brive. But apparently the mob got the wrong man. Callil's book is a much bigger story than Anne's and is a monumental work.

The Collapse of the Third Republic: An Inquiry into the Fall of France in 1940, William Shirer (Simon & Schuster, 1969). As you might expect, Shirer (*The Rise and Fall of the Third Reich*) has written another work that is thoroughly researched and revealing, and he carefully illustrates, point by point, how the fall of France was an absolute debacle. Until reading this, I hadn't realized the extent of the utter chaos—the complete lack of communication among government officials as well as with the general public—that followed the news that the Germans were en route to Paris. In the words of the French historian Marc Bloch, "It was the most terrible collapse in all the long story of our national life."

D-Day June 6, 1944: The Climactic Battle of World War II, Stephen Ambrose (Simon & Schuster, 1994). There is a plethora of books available about the D-Day battles, but none of them is as definitive as this. Ambrose, who passed away in 2002, was a World War II historian and the author of more than a dozen books, including a biography of Dwight D. Eisenhower; he also founded the National World War II Museum in New Orleans. He was devoted to D-Day scholarship and has been referred to as the premier American narrative and military historian. For this work he drew upon fourteen hundred oral histories from the men who lived through it. This is the story of the enlisted men and junior officers who freed the Normandy coastline, and it is not exaggeration when Operation Overlord is called "the most important day of the twentieth century."

Decisive Battles of the Western World and Their Influence upon History, J. F. C. Fuller (Eyre and Spottiswoode, London): volume 1, *From the Earliest Times to the Battle of Lepanto* (1954); volume 2, *From the Defeat of the Spanish Armada to the Battle of Waterloo* (1955); and volume 3, *From the American Civil War to the End of the Second World War* (1956). Though only the third volume in this trio deals with the two world wars, all three books are worth your most determined efforts to obtain. Fuller wisely notes that it may be disputed whether war is necessary to mankind, "but a fact which cannot be questioned is that, from the earliest records of man to the present age, war has been his dominant preoccupation. There has never been a period in human history altogether free from war, and seldom one of more than a generation which has not witnessed a major conflict: great wars flow and ebb almost as regularly as the tides."

Europe's Last Summer: Who Started the Great War in 1914?, David Fromkin (Knopf, 2004). I was predisposed to like this as I'm a huge fan of Fromkin's *A Peace to End All Peace*, and I wasn't disappointed. Fromkin maintains that "the sky out of which Europe fell was not empty; on the contrary, it was alive with processes and powers. The forces that were to devastate it—nationalism, socialism, imperialism, and the like—had been in motion for a long time." Interestingly, he asked students in one of his classes to pinpoint the first steps toward the war before

1908. Their responses, which included events dating back to the fourth century AD, illustrate "how many roads can be imagined to have led to Sarajevo."

France Under the Germans: Collaboration and Compromise, Philippe Burrin (New Press, 1996). None other than Robert Paxton— an internationally recognized expert on Vichy France who served as an expert witness at the trial of Maurice Papon in 1997—referred to this work as "unsurpassed." It's thorough and exhaustively researched. Burrin, a Swiss historian, focuses on three sections of French society that accommodated the Germans: French government, civil society, and a small but significant circle of journalists, politicians, and "ordinary" French people who voiced collaborationist opinions. Burrin seeks to dissect the meaning of the word "collaboration" itself, as it was first used by Marshal Pétain in October 1940 and then passed into German as *Kollaboration.* No photos but a good map showing where the free and occupied zones began and ended.

The Great War: Perspectives on the First World War, edited by Robert Cowley (Random House, 2003). In his introduction, Cowley writes that a good argument may be made that the Great War was the true turning point of the century just past: "It brought down dynasties and empires—including the Ottoman, one of the roots of our present difficulties. It changed the United States from a provincial nation into a world power. It made World War II inevitable and the Cold War as well. It created the modern world—and that greatest of growth industries, violent death." Cowley is founding editor of *MHQ: The Quarterly Journal of Military History,* and the thirty essays, articles, and letters featured in this volume originally appeared in *MHQ.* In addition to writing eight other books, Cowley has traveled the entire length of the western front, from the North Sea to the Swiss border.

The Greatest Generation, Tom Brokaw (Random House, 1998). Brokaw opens his acknowledgements by saying, "When I first came to fully understand what effect members of the World War II generation had on my life and the world we occupy today, I quickly resolved to tell their stories as a small gesture of personal appreciation." If, amidst all the hype and publicity this book received, you missed reading it, I encourage you to pick it up—it's truly wonderful, as are Brokaw's other books, *An Album of Memories: Personal Histories from the Greatest Generation* and *The Greatest Generation Speaks: Letters and Reflections,* all published by Random House in hardcover and paperback editions.

The Guns of August, Barbara Tuchman (Macmillan, 1962; Ballantine, 1994). William Shirer, mentioned above, described this as "one of the finest books of our time," and I completely concur. I *love* this book, and the paperback Ballantine edition includes a foreword by Robert K. Massie, who explains in his final paragraph that Tuchman's opening paragraph took her eight hours to complete and was the most famous passage in the book. Massie's own concludes with "By turning the page, the fortunate person who has not yet encountered this book can begin to read." Sometimes I wish I were that fortunate person all over again! Tuchman, who passed away in 1989, not only wrote an outstanding book, but her own family's history is intertwined with the early events of World War I: she was two years old when she and her parents were crossing the Mediterranean en route to Constantinople to visit her grandfather Henry Morgenthau, Sr., who was then ambassador to Turkey (her uncle was Henry Morgenthau, Jr., Roosevelt's secretary of the Treasury for over twelve years). They witnessed British cruisers in pursuit of the German battleship *Goeben,* which successfully eluded the British, reached Constantinople, "and brought Turkey and with it the whole Ottoman Empire of the Middle East into the war, determining the course of the history of that area from that day to this." Among the many references to France, the ones pertaining to Sedan, where the Prussian army captured Napoléon III on September 1, 1870, are especially memorable. Sedan, Tuchman notes, on the eve of war, was still very much in the French consciousness: " *'N'en parlez jamais; pensez-y toujours'* (Never speak of it; think of it always) had counseled [Minister of the Interior Léon] Gambetta. For more than forty years the thought of 'Again' was the single most fundamental factor of French policy."

Paris 1919: Six Months That Changed the World, Margaret MacMillan (Random House, 2002). This multiple-award-winning book opens with this sentence: "For six months in 1919, Paris was the capital of the world." Indeed it was, as the peacemakers—from

the Big Four countries (Britain, France, Italy, and the United States) and Japan—met there every day to create the terms of the peace treaty concluding World War I. (Others who came to Paris as peacemakers included Lawrence of Arabia and Ho Chi Minh.) As Richard Holbrooke writes in his foreword, "The road from the Hall of Mirrors to the German invasion of Poland only twenty years later is usually presented as a straight line"; MacMillan, however, refutes this, arguing that the peacemakers have been unfairly blamed for mistakes that were made later. This is a fascinating and ultimately timely book for the twenty-first century, as some of the major problems we face today have their roots in decisions made in Paris in 1919: the Balkan wars between 1991 and 1999; the war in Iraq, whose borders reflect the rivalry between France and Britain; a homeland for the Kurds; tension between Greece and Turkey; and a severe situation between Arabs and Jews "over land that each thought had been promised them."

The Second World War, Winston Churchill (Houghton Mifflin, 1948). When my husband walked into the room as I was compiling this bibliography, he asked, "Why don't you just tell everyone to read Churchill's work and be done with it?" He and I are both enormous fans of Churchill, and his question makes a good point. This six-volume work is Churchill's masterpiece, and Churchill was honored with the Nobel Prize in 1953. A boxed set of the volumes in paperback was published by Mariner Books in 1986.

A Soldier's Story, Omar N. Bradley (Modern Library War Series, 1999; originally published in 1951 by Henry Holt). Novelist Caleb Carr is editor of this fine series—other volumes include Ulysses S. Grant's *Personal Memoirs* and Theodore Roosevelt's *The Naval War of 1812*—and in his introduction to the series he makes several notable points about military history. He reminds us of the general attitude in the United States during the sixties and early seventies, when admitting to an interest in human conflict was most unpopular. Military history enthusiasts, he points out as well, are often among the most well-read people we'll ever meet, and they are also usually quite knowledgeable in discussions of political and social history. "The reason for this," he explains, "is simple: the history of war represents fully half the tale of mankind's social interactions," and one cannot understand war without also understanding the political situation, cultural developments, and social issues of the time. Military history, Carr notes, "is neither an obscure nor a peculiar subject, but one critical to any understanding of the development of human civilization. That warfare itself is violent is true and unfortunate; that it has been a central method through which every nation in the world has established and maintained its independence, however, makes it a critical field of study." Omar Bradley—better known as the "GI General"—is often referred to as the greatest military tactician of our time, and though this classic isn't limited to World War II in France, the D-Day assault and the liberation of Paris are treated at length.

Strange Defeat: A Statement of Evidence Written in 1940, Marc Bloch (Norton, 1968). "Much has been, and will be, written in explanation of the defeat of France in 1940, but it seems unlikely that the truth of the matter will ever be more accurately and more vividly presented than in this statement of evidence," wrote the *New York Times Book Review.* Bloch gives a personal, firsthand account of why France fell when faced by the Nazi invasion. This was written in the three months after the fall of France, before Bloch was captured, tortured, and executed by the Nazis.

An Uncertain Hour: The French, the Germans, the Jews, the Klaus Barbie Trial, and the City of Lyon, 1940–1945, Ted Morgan

(William Morrow, 1990). Morgan is a Pulitzer Prize–winning journalist who was a young boy in Paris at the time of the armistice, when he and his family left for Spain and then the United States. He returned to France in 1987 to cover the Barbie trial for the *New York Times Magazine,* and he had access to thousands of pages of secret documents prepared for the trial, including hundreds of depositions that were never made public. Due to these documents, Morgan is able to provide much detail about major events and the everyday lives of residents under occupation. Morgan notes that there were more journalists in Lyon for the Barbie trial than for the Nuremberg trials, and that younger people, mostly students, stood in line every day for hours hoping to get one of the one hundred seats set aside for the public. He wondered why, and he answered, "Because the French had to look into this particular mirror, however distorted. Because there was a generation of young people that was still picking up the tab for World War II."

Vichy France: Old Guard and New Order, 1940–1944, Robert O. Paxton (Knopf, 1972). Paxton's is the single definitive volume on Vichy, and if you're only going to read one, read this one. Paxton documents the inner workings of the Vichy government, the politics between Philippe Pétain, Pierre Laval, and François Darlan, and the surprisingly slow growth of the Resistance. The revelation that the Vichy government enjoyed such mass support came as somewhat of a shock upon the book's publication in 1972, though it is accepted knowledge that the French wanted to avoid the destruction of France at all costs. Paris remains a beautiful city in part because of accommodation and collaboration, but the history of this period is far more complicated than that. As Paxton writes, "It is tempting to identify with Resistance and to say, 'That is what I would have done.' Alas, we are far more likely to act, in parallel situations, like the Vichy majority. . . . The deeds of occupier and occupied alike suggest that there come cruel times when to save a nation's deepest values, one must disobey the state. France after 1940 was one of those times."

The War Memoirs of Charles de Gaulle: The Call to Honour: 1940–1942 (Simon & Schuster, 1955); *Unity: 1942–1944* (Simon & Schuster, 1959); *Salvation: 1944–1946* (Simon & Schuster, 1960). I bought these hardcover volumes at a used-book store about fifteen years ago and I hadn't even realized that De Gaulle had written them, probably because they do pale in comparison to Churchill's volumes. I was sure they would be pure puffery, but I was only partially right—no one ever said De Gaulle was modest, after all—and I was quickly swept up in his *certaine idée de la France* (which included a certain place for him). De Gaulle's voice was the voice of occupied France, and his memoirs stand alone. Carroll & Graf published a single paperback volume of this work in 1998.

World War II: The Encyclopedia of the War Years, 1941–1945, Norman Polmar and Thomas B. Allen (Random House, 1996). This is a great reference with more than twenty-four hundred entries by two military historians who are also coauthors of a number of other books and articles. The book is definitive, but its uniqueness lies in the fact that it "looks at World War II through American eyes," which is why it begins in 1941. (Events that happened before December 7, 1941, are covered in a chapter entitled "Prologue to War.")

FRANCE AND THE FRENCH

There are a staggering number of books available about France and the French, and I own a great many of them. To review them fully would require a separate volume, so I have kept my comments about them brief due to page-count considerations, and from time to time I will remark on them in greater detail on my blog.

Creating French Culture: Treasures from the Bibliothèque Nationale de France, edited by Marie-Hélène Tesnière and Prosser Gifford (Yale University Press in association with the Library of Congress and the Bibliothèque Nationale de France, 1995). The theme for the exhibit this book accompanied was to explore the relationship between culture and power in France, but I see this as nothing less than a history of France as told through its documents, manuscripts, books, orchestra scores, photographs, prints, drawings, maps, medals, and coins. Covering twelve centuries, these treasures are quite extensive, and include such offerings as: the "Letter of Suleyman the Magnificent to Francis I, King of France"; the first edition of *The New Justine, or The Misfortunes of Virtue* by the Marquis de Sade; the constitution of the "Thirteen United States of America" in French, printed at the behest of Benjamin Franklin; a map of the battle

4544. PARIS — La Madeleine
Cette Église a été commencée en 1764 sous Louis XV, par Constant d'Ivry. Transformée en Temple romain en 1806 et rendue au Culte en 1842. Le fronton, par Lemaire, représente le Jugement Dernier.

Madeleine Church
This Church was begun y ear 1764, during the reign of Lewis XV by Constant d'Ivry. Transformed into a Roman Temple y 1806 are and restored to Worship y ear 1842. The pediment represents the Last Judgment

of Austerlitz; the handwritten "*J'accuse*" letter by Émile Zola in defense of Captain Alfred Dreyfus, before it was printed on the front page of *L'Aurore;* and five issues of *Resistance: Official Bulletin of the National Committee for Public Safety,* published from December 1940 to March 1941. A masterpiece.

Atlas Pocket Classics: France

This handsome boxed set is the inaugural edition in a series of travel classics published by Atlas & Company (2008). Novelist Diane Johnson introduces *Travels with a Donkey* by Robert Louis Stevenson, based on a notebook he kept while traveling in the Cévennes; *Gleanings in France* by James Fenimore Cooper, a rare work based on a collection of his letters home that detailed France in its last days of monarchy; and *A Motor-flight Through France* by Edith Wharton, who lived in Paris from 1911 until her death in 1937 (this is one of my favorite works).

The Discovery of France, Graham Robb (Norton, 2007). I wasn't sure I needed to read *another* book about the history of France when this one was published, but I couldn't ignore the praise it received: winner of the Royal Society of Literature Ondaatje Prize, *Publishers Weekly* Best Book of the Year, *Slate* Best Book of the Year, *New York Times* Notable Book of the Year, and comments like this one from the *Mail on Sunday:* "Certain books strain the patience of those close to you. How many times can you demand: 'Look at this! Can you imagine? Did you know that?' without actually handing over the volume? This is such a book. . . . It's not so much a cool linear account as a mosaic, like the patchwork *pays* of France herself." When I picked up a copy and learned that it was the result "of fourteen thousand miles in the saddle and four years in the library" and that "this was supposed to be the historical guidebook I wanted to read when setting out to discover France," I positively knew I *needed* to read it. It is authoritative and dense (in a good way), but is not for the casual reader. Best of all is that, as Robb notes, the book "shows how much remains to be discovered."

Fragile Glory: A Portrait of France and the French, Richard Bernstein (Knopf, 1990). To my mind, this is the best overall book about France after Fernand Braudel's *The Identity of France* (below). Bernstein was the Paris correspondent for the *New York Times* from 1984 to 1987, and his book explores Paris and such broader topics as *la France profonde* ("deep France"), French children's names, the myth of the anti-American, immigrants, politics, and the French struggle with their past. He concludes that France is still a nation greater than the sum of its parts, but that the French people are becoming more like everyone else, losing many qualities that made them different.

France on the Brink: A Great Civilization Faces the New Century, Jonathan Fenby (Arcade, 1999). Journalist Fenby has written for the *Economist,* the *Christian Science Monitor,* and the *Times* of London, and he was named a Chevalier of the French Ordre du Mérite in 1990. He's been reporting on France for over thirty years, and in this work he presents a full array of the country's ills and contradictions. Readers who haven't kept up with the France of today may be alarmed to discover that some classic French icons—berets, baguettes, accordions, cafés, foie gras—are fading.

Harriet Welty Rochefort

French Toast: An American in Paris Celebrates the Maddening Mysteries of the French (1997) and *French Fried: The Culinary Capers of an American in Paris* (2001), both by Harriet Welty Rochefort and published by St. Martin's, are two excellent books that approach the cultural differences between the French and Americans with wit and wisdom. Welty Rochefort, an American from the Midwest who is married to a Frenchman and holds both an American and a French passport, has lived in Paris for more than three decades. She is a journalist, having written for the *International Herald Tribune, Time,* and others, and is a journalism professor at the Institut d'Études Politiques de Paris (known simply as Sciences Po). She also writes a great online column, "Letter from Paris," for the Paris Pages (paris.org).

Welty Rochefort's position in a Franco-American couple allows her to be both a participant and an outside observer in French life. "Being neither fish nor fowl," she writes, "has given me a constant comparative view of both life in the United States and life in France, as well as perceptions about the French that tourists rarely acquire. For example, life with the French has put a whole new meaning on the word *complicated*. The simplest situation in France suddenly becomes something extremely complex and detailed. The French attention to detail—from the way one cuts cheese to the color of one's panty hose—has never ceased to fascinate me." She relates in *French Toast* how she feels "rather more at home" with the French because of their refreshing lack of Puritanism while, on the other hand, when she visits the States she really appreciates the "civility of people who aren't afraid to be nice to one another even if their families haven't known one another for the past two hundred years."

Also in *French Toast* she interviews her husband, Philippe, to share his points of view, which are sometimes eye-opening. And though *French Fried* is dedicated (mostly) to food, since "the most awesome experiences in France revolve around cuisine," it is an equally revealing read. Harriet and Philippe maintain their own Web site (understand france.org), which I also highly recommend—it's packed with suggestions for places to stay and eat, sites to see, dozens of tips, and just-like-home places in Paris for homesick Americans.

The French, Theodore Zeldin (Pantheon, 1983). Zeldin is better known for his major work *France: 1848–1945,* which I've not yet seen, but in this book he explains that he puts a lot of stock in humor because "nothing separates people more than their sense of humor." As a result this book is filled with dozens of caricatures and cartoons, which help illustrate various themes. The final chapter, "What It Means to Be French," is worth reading on its own. At its conclusion, Zeldin leaves readers who are determined to cling to a more grandiose definition of France with a remark by Pierre Dac, at the time one of France's most popular comedians: "To the eternal triple question which has always remained unanswered, Who are we? Where do we come from? Where are we going? I reply: As far as I, personally, am concerned, I am me; I come from just down the road; and I am now going home."

The French: Portrait of a People, Sanche de Gramont (Putnam, 1969). Sanche de Gramont, whose family is a very distinguished one in France, became an American citizen in 1977 and legally changed his name to Ted Morgan, an anagram of de Gramont. In addition to *An Uncertain Hour,* recommended previously, he is the author of more than a dozen books, including biographies of Churchill (a Pulitzer Prize finalist in biography in 1983) and William Somerset Maugham (a National Book Award finalist in 1982). Whether he's writing under the name de Gramont or Morgan, his articles and books are

engaging and he's an astute binational observer. Though this book on France is more than forty years old, it's still meaningful and accurate. "France," de Gramont writes, "like Adam, had been modeled by the finger of God, and was thus perfectly proportioned and balanced (at equal distance between the equator and the Pole), fertile of soil, and temperate of climate." By virtue of living there the people were chosen, and *l'hexagone* had everything the people needed or desired. "This was the European Eden, as the Germans knew when they coined the expression 'As happy as God in France.' "

The Identity of France in two volumes, *History and Environment* and *People and Production,* Fernand Braudel (HarperCollins, 1988, 1989) Braudel, who passed away in 1985, has been referred to as the "greatest of Europe's historians." He believed strongly in the necessity of world history, and his genius was in his ability to link people and events across all time periods in a single sentence. He once came up with the phrase "economic geography" to describe his approach to history. Braudel is better known for his monumental work *The Mediterranean and the Mediterranean World in the Age of Philip II* (Harper & Row, 1972, 1974), one of my favorite books of all time, but this book on France is equally unprecedented and fascinating.

Alistair Horne

Author and historian Sir Alistair Horne, who was awarded the French Légion d'Honneur in 1993 and received a knighthood in Britain in 2003 for his works on French history, has so brilliantly and engagingly written about France that I felt he deserved a space all his own here. His trilogy of books devoted to the three Franco-German conflicts over a seventy-year period are unmatched. The first volume in the series is *The Fall of Paris: The Siege and the Commune 1870–71;* the second is *The Price of Glory: Verdun 1916,* which has been continuously in print for nearly fifty years; and the third is *To Lose a Battle: France 1940.* All were originally published in hardcover in the sixties but are now available in paperback editions by Penguin. A read of just one of these outstanding books is revealing, but all three provide an eye-opening view of how the events were all related.

La Belle France: A Short History (Knopf, 2005; Vintage, 2006) is the book I would recommend on the history of France if forced to name only one. As Horne wisely notes in his introduction, "The pursuit of harmony, though by no means always attainable, is what France is about." *La Belle France* is enormously engaging and comprehensive, and happily both the paperback and hardcover editions include color illustrations. Horne acknowledges that ever since he wrote the *Price of Glory* trilogy, he's been enticed by the "dangerously ambitious project of attempting a full-scale History of that complex, sometimes exasperating, but always fascinating country—France." However dangerous the ambition, readers of this short history will be grateful for his effort.

A Savage War of Peace: Algeria 1954–1962 (Viking, 1978) is equally thorough yet conversational, and Horne again proves his ability to portray the big picture and the major players as well as the everyday lives of ordinary people living through events.

Mission to Civilize: The French Way, Mort Rosenblum (Harcourt, 1986). Rosenblum was a senior foreign correspondent for the Associated Press in Paris when he wrote this enlightening book. He now lives on a houseboat on the Seine and has writ-

ten a number of other very good books on French topics. This
work is specifically devoted to the importance of *la mission
civilisatrice*—i.e. the "civilizing mission" of colonization—to
the French. Rosenblum explains many aspects of the seemingly
contradictory French foreign policy: the difference between a
mauvaise foi and *mauvais caractère;* the *Rainbow Warrior bavure*
(*bavure* being a hitch or foul-up, notably by officials or police,
which was so common that a smooth operation was referred to
as *sans bavure*); *beurs* and *beaufs*; Algeria; Vietnam; and *le fast-food*.

Portraits of France, Robert Daley (Little, Brown, 1991). As a naive
   étudiante in Paris in 1979, I did not realize why the rue Lauriston, where Hollins Abroad Paris had its school for thirty-plus
   years, was referred to as *sinistre* until I read Daley's chapter
   "The Gestapo of the Rue Lauriston." There I learned that 93
   rue Lauriston was the site of an infamous den of torture and in-
   quisition during World War II—not by the Nazis but by a gang
   of French convicts organized by Pierre Bonny and Henri La-
   font. (Happily, although I have nothing but fond memories of
   my classes at no. 16, Hollins has since moved its school out of
   the sixteenth arrondissement altogether.) Daley has put together a miniature tour of French history and culture in this
   collection of twenty essays. While his portraits take readers to
   all corners of *l'hexagone,* even dedicated students of France may
   find some surprises here, as he preferred to find his stories in
   places where most readers haven't looked before.

When in France . . .

Different from the lengthier tomes featured in this section
are the following sources on France and the French. These
are more like guidebooks, though the subjects are dealt with
in more detail than in a traditional guidebook.

Culture Shock! France: A Survival Guide to Customs and Etiquette, Sally Adamson Taylor (Marshall Cavendish, 2008). Similar to—but not quite as thorough as—Polly Platt's books below, this guide covers such topics as the French attitude toward pets, the "no" syndrome, dos and don'ts in restaurants, visas and work permits, queuing, office relationships, why businesses close for lunch, etc. Although some of the topics pertain more to people who plan to be in France for an extended stay, this is a really useful book even for short visits. Note that there is also a *Culture Shock! Paris* guide by Frances Gendlin (Marshall Cavendish, 2007).

France: Instructions for Use, Alison Culliford and Nan McElroy (Illustrata, 2007). Hands down, this is the best book of its kind and is indisputably indispensable. And it measures about 5½ × 4 inches, so it's perfect to bring along and carry around with you every day. It is rather remarkable that a book so small in size has so much packed into it, but there is truly not a practical topic missing. The little book's subtitle says it all: *The Practical, On-site Assistant for the Enthusiastic (Even Experienced) Traveler.* Nan McElroy is the founder of the *Instructions* series (there are also volumes on Italy and Greece that are equally indispensable), each book being the publication she wished she'd had on her first trip. *Instructions* books have two components: the little handbook and the free "Planning Your Adventure" download (in this case from franceinstructions.com), which is most applicable in preparing for your trip, as opposed to consulting it once you've arrived at your destination. I love everything about this book, but I especially like the "Ten Tips for the Traveler Abroad," which include some *Collected Traveler* pearls of wisdom: leave home sweet home behind; however much luggage you're taking, it's too much; don't try to see too much in too short a time, whether in one day or ten;

plan ahead for those experiences that are really important to you; and it can help to remember the Stones' famous words "You can't always get what you want." Don't visit Paris, or anywhere in France, without this portable handbook.

French or Foe? Getting the Most Out of Visiting, Living and Working in France (1994, revised 2003) and *Savoir Flair!: 211 Tips for Enjoying France and the French* (2000), both by Polly Platt and published by Culture Crossings, the company Platt founded in 1986 as a training organization for corporate managers and executives and their spouses. Both of these on-the-mark books are indispensable for anyone planning to live, work, or study in France, but they're also essential for anyone who wants to really, really understand the ways of the French. No other books are as comprehensive as Platt's, and in addition to hundreds of explanations, Platt offers her own personal tips, such as the Ten Magic Words (*Excusez-moi de vous déranger, monsieur, mais j'ai un problème*) and her philosophy of Persistent Personal Operating.

Speak the Culture: France: Be Fluent in French Life and Culture (Thorogood, London, 2008). *Speak the Culture* (speakthe culture.co.uk) is a new series that's terrific, and the France edition was the debut title in the series. History, society, and lifestyle; literature and philosophy; art and architecture; cinema, photography, and fashion; music and drama; food and drink; media and sport—these are all covered impressively well, "so that you might get to know the country as one of its own citizens."

Realms of Memory: The Construction of the French Past in three volumes, *Volume I: Conflicts and Visions* (1996), *Volume II: Traditions* (1997), *Volume III: Symbols* (1998), Pierre Nora (Columbia University Press). Originally published in France in seven vol-

umes as *Les Lieux de mémoire* (Places of Memory), this stunning
collection is easily at the top of my *de rigueur* reading list. The
series is a singular publishing event, and was hailed by the *Times
Literary Supplement* in London as "a magisterial attempt to define what it is to be French."

The Road from the Past: Traveling Through History in France, Ina Caro
(Nan A. Talese, 1994). What a grand and sensible plan Caro
presents in her marvelous book: travel through France in a
"time machine" (a car), from Provence to Paris, chronologically, and experience numerous centuries of French history in
one trip. I envy her and her husband, Robert Caro (the award-
winning biographer of Robert Moses and Lyndon Johnson),
for making such an unforgettable journey. As we progress
chronologically, we visit the sites she has selected, which best
represent a particular age and are also the most beautiful examples within each historical period. Seeing each period separately, and then all of them together in Paris, is "an
incomparable experience," as she concludes.

Sixty Million Frenchmen Can't Be Wrong: Why We Love France but Not the French, Jean-Benoît Nadeau and Julie Barlow (Sourcebooks, 2003). The husband and wife authors of this excellent book reveal new insights about the French on nearly every page, and I consider this *de rigueur* reading for every visitor to France. Nadeau and Barlow went to live in Paris for two years as correspondents for the New Hampshire–based Institute of Current World Affairs. They were focusing on globalization, specifically why the French were (seemingly) resisting globalization. But after one year, they realized that asking why the French were resisting globalization "was the wrong question about the right topic. The French were globalizing in their own way. But France needed to be understood in its own terms." Their first breakthrough in reaching this fact was that it's impossible to separate the past from the present in France. The French live very modern lives, but *simultaneously* they hold on to respected traditions, and they have proved that this works. Roquefort cheese is still made in caves according to a tradition that dates back twelve centuries; Napoléon introduced the Civil Code, which is currently used by most European nations; the metric system, high-speed trains, and the Concorde were developed in France; fourteenth-century châteaux and cutting-edge architecture both have a home in France; and when you make a purchase at just about any kind of shop, the staff will carefully and painstakingly wrap it up like a gift, even if it isn't and even if there is a long line of customers behind you. Plenty more examples abound. Read this book and discover more, as well as a whole lot else about France and the French.

Travel + Leisure's Unexpected France (Dorling Kindersley, 2007). This is an anthology of articles that have appeared in *Travel + Leisure* over the years, introduced by editor in chief Nancy Novogrod. (A separate volume on Italy has been published as well.)

Novogrod describes the book as presenting "a view of the country's pleasures that is at once panoramic and highly selective—pastoral, coastal, urban, encompassing both the old and the new." If you clip articles like I do, you might not feel you need this book, but even though I have all these original articles in my files, I'm still glad I bought this volume—it's far handier than searching through my massive files and, as I don't often save an article's accompanying photographs, it's nice to see them here. Included in this collection are pieces on Paris, Versailles, the Loire Valley, the Paris Ritz, Normandy, and Coco Chanel.

FICTION

The Anchor Anthology of French Poetry: From Nerval to Valéry in English Translation, edited by Angel Flores, with an introduction by Patti Smith (Anchor, 2000).

The Blessing, Don't Tell Alfred, and *The Pursuit of Love,* all by Nancy Mitford, all recently published in paperback editions by Vintage (2010). As Zoe Heller writes in her foreword to *The Pursuit of Love,* "It was, of course, Nancy who started it all. Without her, there would be no Mitford industry." Mitford's legendary British family is truly the stuff of novels, and she often based the characters in her eight novels on members of her family. She was the eldest of six sisters, one of whom was notoriously smitten with Hitler and who committed suicide shortly after Britain declared war against Germany, so Mitford had no shortage of intimate material. She was born in 1904, and in the 1920s, when she began writing novels, she was friends with Evelyn Waugh and others in his literary circle. Mitford moved to France in 1946 and remained there for the rest of her life, and her novels remind me of those by Barbara Pym, whose books I also love, in that the characters are so eccentric, quirky, and very British; but the reason these novels appear here is because each has a French or Parisian connection. Mitford's biographies of Madame de Pompadour, Voltaire, and Louis XIV are held in high regard (though I'm sorry to say I have yet to read them). More details about her work and her life may be found at Nancymitford.com.

Complete Poems: Blaise Cendrars (University of California Press, 1993). Fans of Cendrars (né Frédéric Louis Sauser) will be pleased to know about a unique and wonderful book published by Yale University Press in 2009: a facsimile of *La Prose du Transsibérien,* a poem originally published in 1913 with accompanying artwork by a favorite painter of mine, Sonia Delaunay. This facsimile comes in a little package with a booklet of the English translation and a foldout of the poem (in French), and is modeled after an original copy of the work held at Yale's Beinecke Rare Book and Manuscript Library. The original edition unfolds to over six feet in length, and as translator Timothy Young notes, "If 150 copies were laid end to end they would be as tall as the Eiffel Tower." Young explains this work "is noted today as much for its lyric beauty as for its unmatched composition of colors by Sonia Delaunay (née Terk)," and the intensity of the pigments survive in the Beinecke copy "with an astonishing vibrancy."

The Château, William Maxwell (Knopf, 1961).

French Folktales, Henri Pourrat, selected by C. G. Bjurström, translated and with an introduction by Royall Tyler (Pantheon, 1989). One hundred and five legends culled from the rural provinces of France, which are, as Tyler writes in the introduction, "stories to eat with your pocketknife, among friends. They are delicious, and the days they taste of will never come again."

France: A Traveler's Literary Companion

Whereabouts Press, based in Berkeley, California, has recently introduced a series I'm crazy about called the Traveler's Literary Companions. As travel writer Jan Morris asks, "What could be more instructive for the traveler—and more fun!—than to see a country through the eyes of its own most imaginative writers?" And the neat people at Whereabouts (I just *know* they're neat) remind us that "good stories reveal as much, or more, about a locale as any map or guidebook." (Incidentally, the name of the press also reminds me of a book called *Whereabouts: Notes on Being a Foreigner* by Alastair Reid [White Pine Press, 1995]. Reid, who lived for many years in Spain, wrote that "coming newly into Spanish, I lacked two essentials—a childhood in the language, which I could never acquire, and a sense of its literature, which I could.")

What I especially enjoy about this series is that the writers whose fiction is featured are mostly all contemporary, so we are introduced to writers we might not find otherwise. The France volume (published in 2008) is edited by William Rodarmor and Anna Livia, and they include a most diverse group of writers in this edition, among them Christian Lehmann, Samuel Benchetrit, Frédéric Fajardie, Jacques Réda, Colette, Annie Saumont, Eric Holder, and Andrée Chedid. Rodarmor concludes that "these pieces are neither bonbons nor full-course meals. They're more like hearty appetizers. You're at a bountiful buffet, and you should feel free to come back for more."

Madame Bovary, Gustave Flaubert (various editions).

One Hundred Great French Books: From the Middle Ages to the Present, Lance Donaldson-Evans (BlueBridge, 2010). French literature, the author notes in the introduction, has been an inspiration to readers around the world for the simple reason that it is "one of the great literatures on the planet and would surely be offered World Heritage status if such a category existed in the literary sphere." Donaldson-Evans, professor of Romance languages at the University of Pennsylvania, has written a unique and worthy book, and I wish there were hundreds more just like this one for other countries in the world. This book is not necessarily an introduction to the *best* one hundred French books, but rather the emphasis is on the word "great." The book is also not for specialists of French literature, but rather for the general reader who would like to learn about, or renew acquaintance with, some noteworthy books published in French. Additionally, the books selected had to be available in English translation, and lastly Donaldson-Evans admits to having a hidden agenda: to "whet your appetite to read or reread some or all of the works presented." A number of the writers represented were born outside metropolitan France but have French as their primary language, such as authors from the Caribbean, Canada, Belgium, Switzerland, and African nations. And what a selection this is—everything from *The Song of Roland, The Romance of the Rose, The Letters of Madame de Sévigné,* and *The Count of Monte Cristo* to *The Journal of Eugène Delacroix, The Flowers of Evil, Astérix, So Long a Letter* by Mariama Bâ, *The Sand Child* by Tahar Ben Jelloun, and *Monsieur Ibrahim and The Flowers of the Koran* by Éric-Emmanuel Schmitt. (Plus, there are fifty other great titles recommended at the back of the book.) I, for one, discovered at least a dozen books I want to track down, but I like this book also for providing me with good outlines of titles I'd known of but haven't read, which is sometimes enough, though not nearly as satisfying as what Roland Barthes calls "*le plaisir du texte,* the pleasure that comes from reading a great book and being stirred to the core by it."

Reckless Appetites: A Culinary Romance, Jacqueline Deval (Ecco, 1993). One of my favorite quirky books, blending the fictional story of Pomme and Jeremy with literary history and almost one hundred recipes.

Scaramouche: A Romance of the French Revolution, Rafael Sabatini (originally published in 1921; various editions available). The opening line of this truly swashbuckling book is among the great opening lines of all time: "He was born with a gift of laughter and a sense that the world was mad."

Literary Traveler

A unique and dangerously interesting Web site—it's easy to start browsing and completely lose track of time—that I love is Literary Traveler (literarytraveler.com). Founders Linda and Francis McGovern say their mission is "to inspire readers and travelers to explore their literary imagination. We uncover the connections between great literature and great places, to inspire our readers to pursue their passions and help them become part of what they have read." It's a wonderful concept, and the site has been referred to as a "bookworm's delight" by the *Wall Street Journal*.

Since 1998, Literary Traveler has been featuring great travel writing, and the online archive is quite large. I've found some really wonderful pieces on Paris and other parts of France and beyond. A basic subscription is free, although access to some content is limited; there is a monthly fee for a premium subscription, which offers full access to the site's content. The Web site is very well done and was named to *Forbes*'s Best of the Web. Literary Traveler also offers tours, such as a Lost Generation literary tour in Paris and a French Resistance tour in Lyon.

Somewhere in France, John Rolfe Gardiner (Knopf, 1999).

Suite Française (2006) and *Fire in the Blood* (2007), both by Irène Némirovsky and published by Knopf. If Némirovsky's fiction inspires you to want to know more about her real life, you may also like *The Life of Irène Némirovsky, 1903–1942* by Olivier Philipponnat and Patrick Lienhardt (Knopf, 2010), as well as *Shadows of a Childhood* by Elisabeth Gille (New Press, 1998). Gille, Némirovsky's daughter, was five years old when her mother was deported to Auschwitz, and she and her sister were hidden in the French countryside until the war was over. This novel—her third, and the first to appear in English—won the Grand Prix des Lectrices de *Elle* in 1997. Gille died in Paris in 1996.

That Mad Ache, Françoise Sagan (Basic Books, 2009). This unique edition also includes a tandem work, *Translator, Trader: An Essay on the Pleasantly Pervasive Paradoxes of Translation* by Douglas Hofstadter, the translator of the Sagan work. Printed in the reverse from the novel (starting at the last page), Hofstadter reveals some of his own thoughts about translations in general as well as revelations he had while translating Sagan's novel, which was originally published in 1965 under the title *La Chamade.*

KEEPING THE *ART DE VIVRE* IN YOUR LIFE

A trip anywhere in the world can be transforming, but there's no doubt that Paris (or *anywhere* in France, for that matter) is a particularly inspiring destination. France is seductive, and many people—myself included—have a great desire to incorporate many French lifestyle details into their lives. Happily, there are some great resources to help us Francophiles re-create a French spirit in our homes.

Bringing France Home: Creating the Feeling of France in Your Home Room by Room, Cheryl MacLachlan with photographs by Ivan Terestchenko (Clarkson Potter, 1995). MacLachlan worked for *Esquire* a few decades ago and traveled to Paris on business four to five times a year. Each time she returned to New York, she felt that she was missing something, though it wasn't a case of wanting to move to France—she loved her job and her life. "The answer," she decided, "perhaps was to try to make France a part of my day-to-day life back home." So she did, but then she took this answer one step further, and examined the French lifestyle and explored just what it was that made France France. Discovering that "French life was in the details," MacLachlan found it possible to bring France home to America. She takes readers on a tour of every room in a French

house and offers tips galore; there are also chapters on the pleasures of the table and on resources.

Bringing Paris Home, Penny Drue Baird (Monacelli Press, 2008).
"Step outside the door, glance around, and you know you are
in Paris," writes Baird, founder of the design firm Dessins and
one of *Architectural Digest*'s top one hundred designers. "What
is it about just being there that creates a stir within us? All at
once, we are surrounded by physical beauty and by ethereal
stimuli—the smell of the streets, the sky, the street signs, the
light. Can the air really be that different? . . . This heightened
sensual experience stays with us throughout our visit. Can we
bring it home?" In chapters detailing architecture, fireplaces,
furniture, paint and wall treatments, lighting, cafés and table-
tops, flea markets, and collecting, Baird answers this question
with a resounding yes. She spent every summer for many years
in a region of France, but one year she and her family decided
to stay in Paris for an entire year. They found an apartment
in the seventh near her favorite Paris café, Bar de la Croix
Rouge, which she refers to as "completely typical by French
standards and outrageous by American" (it has fourteen-foot
ceilings and eight fireplaces). She decorated her Paris apartment the way the French do: if you see something you really
like, you buy it first and figure out where to put it later. The
chapter on flea markets is particularly useful for anyone interested in buying items that require shipping—the *transiteur*
(shipper), she notes, is as essential to the flea market as the vendors, and he or she will pick up your merchandise, pack, ship,
insure, clear customs, and deliver. Baird wisely warns that
bringing Paris home "is not as simple as adding lace curtains
or provincial pottery to your décor. It is something much
more subtle and much more personal. It has to do with the
philosophy of European living and many characteristics." By

turning these pages readers embark on a stroll through Paris identifying both the tangible and intangible gems that may be brought home.

And a duo of titles published by Clarkson Potter from French style specialist Linda Dannenberg:

French Country Kitchens: Authentic French Kitchen Design from Simple to Spectacular, with photographs by Guy Bouchet (2008). When she thinks back on all the hundreds of homes she's visited in France over the last twenty-five years, Dannenberg says, it's almost always the kitchens she remembers most clearly and with the most affection. In these pages readers glimpse several kitchens in Paris and its surrounding regions as well as in other parts of France. These include Patricia Wells's kitchen in her Provençal home, Chanteduc, and the kitchen of Michel Biehn, owner of La Maison Biehn, a renowned shop specializing in Provençal quilts, antiques, and tabletop items in L'Isle-sur-la-Sorgue. Among the most distinctive characteristics of the French country kitchens Dannenberg visits "is the acknowledgment of the past in some way, either as inspiration or to respect the kitchen's 'old bones'—the walls, the beams, the floors, the volumes—or to use old vintage elements, cooking tools, or art, even in a very contemporary kitchen design." For nearly every kitchen featured there is an accompanying recipe that is representative of the region and was prepared in the kitchen. "It may be one humble, functional room," notes Dannenberg, "but the French country kitchen reveals all you need to know about the art and joy of living in France."

Pierre Deux's Paris Country: A Style and Source Book of the Île-de-France, with Pierre Levec and Pierre Moulin, and photographs by Guy Bouchet (1991). This book appeared a few years after the groundbreaking and hugely successful *Pierre Deux's French Country*, and it is as essential to Paris and the Île-de-France as its sister volume is to Provence. In addition to the design and decorating tips there is useful information for visitors. (Though some of the restaurant and hotel information may be outdated, these details may be researched online, as is the case for the shops, antique fairs, museums, and festivals.)

Readers who may be traveling on to Provence will want to read *New French Country: A Style and Source Book* (2004), in

which Dannenberg picks up where she left off with *Pierre Deux's French Country* more than twenty years ago, with homes, gardens, fabrics, furniture, pottery, architectural elements, decorative accents, and an excellent directory of French country sources in Provence.

The Age of Comfort: When Paris Discovered Casual—And the Modern Home Began, Joan DeJean (Bloomsbury, 2009). Though not the same kind of book as the others here, this is *de rigueur* reading about the fundamental ideas about homes and homelife in what the author calls the "Age of Comfort," 1670 to 1765. DeJean notes that the architects, craftsmen, and inhabitants of Paris during this century "can be said to have created a blueprint for today's home and the way we live in it." The English words "comfort" and "comfortable" derive from the French word *réconfort*, help or assistance, and they only took on their modern meaning in the late eighteenth century (before this time they signified help or consolation, as in today's "comforting"). Thomas Jefferson, DeJean tells us, longtime resident of Paris and great admirer of the eighteenth-century French way of life, was among the first to use "comfortable" in the new way.

DeJean relates a truly fascinating history of the first sofas, private bedrooms, bathrooms, and living rooms that could not have been accepted and embraced without visionary architects and interior designers, as well as the influence of two women, the Marquise de Maintenon (Louis XIV's mistress) and the Marquise de Pompadour (Louis XV's mistress). Interestingly, she relates that although the French have been recognized as style leaders for centuries, the phrase *art de vivre* "is no longer much in use." DeJean is the author of nine other books on French literature, history, and culture of the seventeenth and eighteenth centuries, all of which have somehow escaped my reading list. Among the titles is *The Essence of Style: How the French Invented High Fashion, Fine Food, Chic Cafés, Style, Sophistication, and Glamour* (Free Press, 2005), about which I will report on my blog.

This is the France the French know best and love best, their private France, the one they grow up with and have pictures of and instantly turn the clock to when no one's looking, the France they'd like nothing better than to hand over to their children in the twenty-first century, the way it was just barely handed over to them after two world wars from those who inherited it from the nineteenth century—a France that, for all its turmoil at home and elsewhere, and for all the changes brought on by the Information Age and the Age of Anxiety, has managed to safeguard the daily rhythm and precious rituals of its day-to-day life, a France that always seems to trust it will be there tomorrow, a France that is always open for business and infallibly closes at very set hours. It is a France that, all told, is never bigger than a city block but that, within its narrow purview, easily explains why so many Parisians have never ventured beyond their own *arrondissement* or why so few have ever bothered to learn another language. They know every conceivable shade of the French subjunctive and know every meandering anonymous lane near home—and that's good enough. Walk the block from the *fromagerie* to the *boulangerie,* to the *boucherie,* to the *traiteur,* to the *marchand de tabacs,* to the *fruitier, crémerie,* and *charcuterie,* and, come to think of it, you have walked the world.

—André Aciman, *Entrez: Signs of France*

LE PENSEVR
DE RODIN OFFERT
PAR SOVSCRIPTION
PVBLIQVE AV PEVPLE
DE PARIS MCMVI

PARIS

We think of Paris as *la ville lumière,* and it is unthinkable that the word could be attached to London, Rome or even Athens.

—ROBERT PAYNE,
The Splendor of France

I thought everyone should see Paris, if just once. Paris galvanizes you, makes you think of better things, be a better person.

—DEIRDRE KELLY,
Paris Times Eight

On a corner the smell of fresh croissants wafts from a patisserie. Time to get dressed. In a greengrocer's shop two men are arranging fruit and vegetables as if they were millinery. An uncle in a café is looking through a magnifying glass at the stock prices in the morning paper. He doesn't have to ask for the cup of coffee which is brought to him. The last street is being washed. Where's the towel, Maman? This strange question floats into the mind because the heart of Paris is like nothing so much as the unending interior of a house. Buildings become furniture, courtyards become carpets and arrases, the streets are like galleries, the boulevards conservatories. It is a house, one or two centuries old, rich, bourgeois, distinguished . . . Paris is a mansion. Its dreams are the most urban and the most furnished in the world.

—JOHN BERGER,
"IMAGINE PARIS,"
Keeping a Rendezvous

Foreword to John Russell's *Paris*

ROSAMOND BERNIER

YEARS AGO, DURING the summer between my junior and senior years of college, a classmate and I were in the employ of an elderly couple who owned a large, rambling country house in Connecticut and a stunning apartment in one of New York City's premier apartment buildings. Our job was to cook, clean, and otherwise help maintain the country house, at which there were dinners, parties, and house guests all summer long. As a result, we had the opportunity to meet a number of notable people, including some neighbors, two of whom were John Russell, former art critic of the *New York Times,* and his wife, Rosamond Bernier, cofounder of the prestigious French art magazine *L'Œil,* author, and lecturer.

Exactly thirty years later, when I was working on this manuscript, I contacted Rosamond. I was thrilled to be corresponding with her—I'd attended a few of her wonderful lectures at the Metropolitan Museum of Art over the years (though I was too shy to introduce myself, *certaine* that she would not remember me)—and I still marvel at the joys of six degrees of separation; you just never know who you will meet again in your life. I asked Rosamond if I might include an article she wrote about Braque in my book, but she said she was saving that one for inclusion in her own memoir. While I was considering what else I had in my files by her, I began paging through John Russell's *Paris* (Harry N. Abrams, 1983, 1994), and I read for the five hundredth time Rosamond's foreword. I said to myself, *Ça y est!*—that's it!—why not feature this in full in the book? Rosamond granted me permission, and it is with great pleasure that I include her foreword to my favorite book on Paris ever written.

ROSAMOND BERNIER was a contributing editor for *Vogue* for many years and is the author of *Matisse, Picasso, Miró: As I Knew Them* (Knopf, 1991). She was decorated by the French government in 1980 and 1999 when she received the Chevalier de la Légion d'Honneur in recognition of her contribution to French culture. Bernier was honored (along with her husband, John) as a National Treasure by the Municipal Art Society of New York in 2004, and she has given more than two hundred lectures at the Metropolitan Museum of Art. *Town & Country* has referred to Bernier as "the Met's living treasure," and Leonard Bernstein wrote of her that "Madame Bernier has the gift of instant communication to a degree which I have rarely encountered." Videos of her Met lectures are available exclusively through Kultur (kultur.com) and of these a great number feature French art topics, such as "French Impressionism: An Accessible Paradise" and "French Impressionism: Paris by Day and by Night." Bernier is currently working on a memoir.

WHEN I first read John Russell's *Paris*, I remembered particularly a very small room halfway to the sky in what was then my favorite Left Bank hotel. The rooms on the top floor of the Pont Royal are not as large as the ones lower down, but after trying some of the others I decided to perch above, where each room had a small balcony and you could step out through the French windows, and there in front of you was a clear view across Paris.

You could look down to the right and follow the rue du Bac on its straight reach for the Seine. Eighteenth-century town houses with flat stone façades—not yet sluiced clean on André Malraux's orders—and elegant doorways lined one side of the street, rising to steep, humped roofs (gray tile, usually) bitten into by mansard windows with projecting triangular hoods. Across the river was the cluttered mount of Montmartre topped by the ridiculous but endearing white fantasy of the Sacré-Coeur. To the left was the Eiffel Tower and, still further, the gold-ribbed dome of the Invalides. Paris in my pocket.

This is where I came to live in the late 1940s when an American magazine sent me to Paris to report on the arts. The Pont Royal was cheap in those days, and it was near to everything that I wanted.

I was extraordinarily lucky to be starting a career at that time, when Paris was still a great center of intellectual and artistic energy. Art and life were beginning again after the long dark night of the German occupation. As Cyril Connolly once wrote about French writers, "Intelligence flows through them like a fast river." The river was indeed flowing fast. The great figures of twentieth-century art were still in full activity. There were new magazines, new books, new art galleries, new plays, new hopes. Even new music was beginning to make its way.

Writers, publishers, art dealers from all over stayed at the Pont Royal or met there. Fred, the Swiss concierge, knew them all and kept a fatherly eye out for me. When I came home from work he might tell me, "Monsieur Skira left this morning to visit Monsieur Matisse in Vence. Monsieur Matisse didn't sound a bit pleased when he telephoned." (The Swiss publisher Albert Skira was chronically late and never answered letters, which infuriated the supermethodical Matisse.) Or he might say, "Monsieur and Madame Miró are arriving tomorrow from Barcelona for a week. Monsieur Curt Valentin is expected from New York Tuesday." (Curt Valentin was the most imaginative New York art dealer of the day.) "Monsieur Stephen Spender came in from London and was looking for you."

My room with its turkey-red carpet, brass bed, and nubbly white coverlet offered few amenities: one chair; an old-fashioned

stand-up wardrobe; watery lights. The telephone was cradled un-
easily on two metal prongs. Its function was mainly symbolic.
Even the most exasperated jiggling rarely caught the attention of
the *standardiste*. Often it was quicker to go out, buy *jetons,* and call
from a café. Once, in a rage of frustration, I stormed down to
confront the telephone operator face to face, only to find her
standing in her cubicle, tape measure in hand, intently fitting a
friend for a dress while her switchboard flashed futile appeals.

The bar, downstairs from the lobby, was conspiratorially dark,
and filled with deep and overstuffed brown leather armchairs and
sofas. This was my club, a quintessentially Parisian listening post
where you went to find out who's in, who's out, and who's gone
away and will never come back. Publishers and authors negotiated
over the new fashionable drink in France: "le Scotch." The
painter Balthus, more Byronic than Byron himself, would drop by
and give me news of Picasso. Jean-Paul Sartre and Simone de
Beauvoir were regulars. At that time their fame and the provocative aura that surrounded the word "Existentialist" (practically
nobody knew what it meant) had made them objects of universal
curiosity, and they had abandoned their previous headquarters at
the Café de Flore for the less exposed Pont Royal.

Later, when I had an apartment, I continued to see Jean-Paul
Sartre and Simone de Beauvoir, though neither of them cared
much for Americans in general. Once when Sartre came to lunch
he gave an offhand demonstration of mental agility: without stopping the general conversation he deciphered, one after another,
the formidably difficult word-and-picture puzzles on my dessert
plates.

Although I moved from the Pont Royal I never left the quar-
ter. It was, and is, a neighborhood of bookstores and publishing
houses. The grandest, Gallimard, is a few steps from the Pont
Royal. I used to go to its Thursday afternoon garden parties every
June; they were long on petits fours and short on liquor. Alice B.
Toklas lived around the corner from my office and was always

ready to receive the favored visitor with enormous teas. She was exquisitely polite, and even when very old she would insist on serving the guest herself. When I did her some small favor, she sent a charming note of thanks in such minute handwriting that I had to take out a magnifying glass to read it. Although her dress was monastic, she loved elaborately flowered hats, and would appear at my apartment, a diminutive figure under a herbaceous border that not even Russell Page himself would have imagined. She bought one such hat every year, she told me.

In Paris, you are on easy terms with the past. I would nod to Apollinaire, a favorite poet, as I went by 202 boulevard Saint-Germain, where he lived after coming back wounded from the front in World War I. I liked going by the Jesuit-style Église de Saint-Thomas-d'Aquin, set back from the boulevard, where Apollinaire was married, with Picasso as witness. On my way to Nancy Mitford's I would go by 120 rue du Bac, a handsome house from which Chateaubriand set off every afternoon to visit Madame Récamier. Ingres, Delacroix, Corot, George Sand, Madame de Staël, Voltaire, Wagner (he finished *Die Meistersinger* in Paris) were among the friendly neighborhood ghosts.

It is often said, and with some reason, that Parisians are not hospitable to the foreigner. But what an abundance of generosity and hospitality came my way! I remember Picasso rummaging through the indescribable chaos of his vast studio on the rue des Grands-Augustins to try and dig up some drawings I wanted to publish. (He found them, I gave them back, and he never could find them again.) Fernand Léger lined up his recent work for me and asked which canvases I liked best. Pleased with my choice he whacked me jovially across the back: "You're a good girl, you have a good strong stomach." Matisse received me with all the books he had illustrated meticulously opened out so that he could explain in each case what problems he had solved, and how. The admirable, austere Nadia Boulanger (who taught so many American composers, beginning with Aaron Copland) invited me to her icy apartment on the rue Ballu to hear her latest protégé. The composer, Francis Poulenc, a bulky pear-shaped figure, was droll beyond words and yet indescribably poignant as he accompanied himself on a small upright piano and sang the soprano solo—that of a woman desperately trying to hold on to her lover—from his *La Voix humaine.* President Vincent Auriol took me on a tour of the Palais de l'Élysée after a press conference to point out the famous Gobelin tapestry. And I remember the ultimate Parisian accolade: a great French chef, the late René Viaux of the restaurant in the Gare de l'Est, named a dish after me.

A few years after my Pont Royal days I was starting my own art magazine, *L'Œil,* in a minute office at the back of a cobbled courtyard on the rue des Saints-Pères. It was sparsely furnished— no pictures yet. The wall behind me was painted a shade of blue I like particularly, the color of a package of Gauloise cigarettes. When Alberto Giacometti came by for a chat, I said a bit apologetically that it must seem odd—an art magazine office with no art around. "Not at all," he answered, looking at me across my desk. "You are a *personnage sur fond bleu,* that's all you need." (Giacometti characteristically tried to discourage us from running an article on him in the first issue. "It will ruin the chances of your magazine. No one will buy it if it shows my work." Naturally, we paid no attention.)

For the magazine, we needed good writers and got in touch with a young English art critic whose weekly column in the London *Sunday Times* was indispensable reading if you wanted to know not only what was going on in England but on the Continent as well. It was clear that, unlike many critics, he loved art; he wrote about it with informed enthusiasm, and he wrote in crystalline prose. There was not a dull phrase to be weeded out in translation (French translation did wonders for some of our German, Dutch, Italian, and English-language contributors) and, what is more, he knew France and the French language very well.

We corresponded. He sent in his articles—on time. We met.

Our conversations centered on ideas for features and deadlines. I had the intense seriousness of the young and the harassed, and I was producing a monthly publication on a shoestring as thin as the one Man Ray wore in lieu of a tie. In private life both of us were programmed, to use computer language, in other directions. Unlikely as it seems, I had no idea that while I was discovering Paris and the Parisians he was working on a book about Paris.

Some twenty years later, Reader, I married him. Only then did I discover John Russell's book *Paris* (originally published in 1960). Here was sustained delight. No one else could combine the feel and the look, the heart and the mind, the stones and the trees, the past and the present, the wits, the eccentrics, and the geniuses of my favorite city with such easy grace.

Reading this book, for me, was like sauntering through the city where I had lived so long. By my side was a most civilized companion who casually brought all the strands together and made them gleam—not forgetting to stop for an *apéritif* and a delicious meal en route. The book was long out of print, and I felt it unfair to keep this to myself. I showed it to a publisher friend. He immediately agreed that others would enjoy John Russell's *Paris* as much as we did. He suggested it be brought up to date, in an illustrated edition.

The author and I went to Paris to gather the illustrations. There was some confusion about our hotel reservation, and the receptionist at the Pont Royal apologized for giving us a small room on the top floor. Here the circle closes in the most satisfactory of ways: it was the identical room, no. 125, in which I had lived when I first came to Paris. The turkey-red carpet was now royal blue, the furniture was spruced-up modern, there was—is this possible?—a minibar. And there was a pushbutton telephone that clicked all of Europe and America into the streamlined receiver.

We stepped out onto the little balcony. Deyrolle the naturalist's, where I used to buy crystals and butterflies, was still across the street. There were some new chic boutiques, but the noble eighteenth-century façades still stood guard over the past. We looked around happily: there they were, our cherished landmarks—the Invalides, the Église de Sainte-Clotilde, and the Eiffel Tower on the left, and on the right the former Gare d'Orsay, soon to be a museum of late nineteenth-century art, the Sacré-Coeur, and the Grand Palais.

The huge open sky overhead had drifted in from the Île-de-France. The bottle-green bus bumbled down the rue du Bac. The tricolor flew the way it flies in Delacroix's *Liberty Guiding the People*. I was back again, this time in John Russell's Paris.

"One of my favorite things to do in Paris is to go to the movies. Now, some may blame this on my Southern California upbringing, but to me it's a true cultural immersion. Seeing a film there feels like a capital-*E* Event. Parisians relish films as they would a meal, paying close attention and settling in for their little rituals (which used to include uniformed ushers escorting everyone to their seats). Parisian film buffs continue to cherish the old while chasing the new: you might find a classic Hollywood screwball comedy, the latest blockbuster, a brooding new Euro-indie flick, and *Les Enfants du paradis* playing in a ten-block radius.

"Most of all, I love seeing a film at La Pagode in the seventh arrondissement. A grassroots effort saved this Belle Époque cinema from demolition, and the last time I went there it still had an atmospheric whisper of decay. It's a delirious Far East fantasy of a building, with a curving roof and a shaggy, mysterious garden. Grauman's Chinese Theatre has nothing on this!"

—Jennifer Paull,
freelance writer and
former Fodor's editor

According to Plan—Maps of Paris

CATHARINE REYNOLDS

ॐ

ALL PARISIAN HOUSEHOLDS have at least one well-worn *plan de Paris,* and I cannot imagine, even for a second, being in Paris without my own well-worn edition. In recent years I've actually been bringing this old edition, which dates from 1979, with me instead of the newer versions I have because it's far preferable: there are numbered tabs for the arrondissements, making it faster to find what you're looking for; I like the cover better; and the individual maps are larger and therefore easier to read. But a few years ago I discovered a large version (measuring about fifteen inches by fifteen) of the *plan de Paris,* and now I am completely prepared (if a bit compulsive)—I make copies of the arrondissements I know I will visit, and before I set out each day I mark my route with a highlighter. (And of course I also carry my small *plan de Paris* in my bag.) I am not necessarily advocating that you do the same, but I will advise that even if you have only a few days in the city, investing in a *plan* is essential for moving about skillfully and understanding Paris. "For in Paris," as noted in this piece, which appeared in the July 1990 issue of *Gourmet,* "geography and history are inseparably entwined."

CATHARINE REYNOLDS, who was most recently a contributing editor at the former *Gourmet,* also wrote the magazine's "Paris Journal" column—which was honored with a James Beard Foundation Award in 1998—for more than twenty years. Reynolds is currently working on a biography of Nicolas Fouquet, Louis XIV's finance minister.

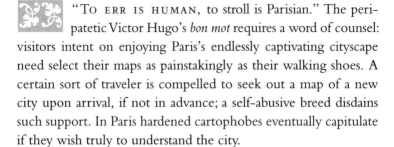"TO ERR IS HUMAN, to stroll is Parisian." The peripatetic Victor Hugo's *bon mot* requires a word of counsel: visitors intent on enjoying Paris's endlessly captivating cityscape need select their maps as painstakingly as their walking shoes. A certain sort of traveler is compelled to seek out a map of a new city upon arrival, if not in advance; a self-abusive breed disdains such support. In Paris hardened cartophobes eventually capitulate if they wish truly to understand the city.

Only pseudo-sophisticates recoil at the sight of "site seekers" squinting at unfurled foldouts, struggling to trace the path from picture gallery to supper. In Paris, map toting is no newcomer's proclamation of ignorance. The most knowledgeable taxi drivers cannot know each of the city's 6,417 streets offhand; instead they pack copies of *Paris par Arrondissement* in their glove compartments. (Those who don't, warrant the curses of their hapless customers.)

But what constitutes a good map? Stationers and bookstores overflow with options. Flat maps tend to be cumbersome, and so small map volumes, albeit more expensive, are a sound investment. A straightforward choice for a short stay is the classic *L'Indispensable,* a 7 by 4½ inch navy volume that for the past fifty years has lived up to its name, with omnibus lists of government offices, embassies, schools, hospitals, museums, churches, department stores, theaters, movie houses, et cetera. *L'Indispensable* offers a thumb-indexed alphabetical list of streets followed by maps of each of the city's twenty arrondissements, with some of the larger ones meriting two maps, as well as plans of the bewildering Défense business complex. A large folded map at the back allows an overview of the city and suburbs.

The privately owned L'Indispensable publishing house brings out thirty-five different map formats in five languages, but its maps suffer on the whole from old-fashioned graphics, which, however evocative, can be less than easy to read, as are most of the maps produced by the firm of A. Leconte.

Many Parisians prefer the maps put out by the thirty-year-old firm of Ponchet, most of which wear practical black plastic covers. Ponchet produces a volume similar to the standard, midsize *Indispensable,* as well as a 12 by 8½ inch *Grand Paris,* ideal for those daunted by the challenge of map reading in jackrabbiting vehicles. Their numbers must be growing, as this map has been a runaway success among Parisian motorists struggling to find either restaurants or friends living on obscure streets.

The beige ink favored by the firm of Plans-Guide Blay renders its maps less appropriate for walkers and drivers than for cipher clerks, who might also relish the challenge of the miniature typefaces and creative abbreviations in the staple-bound map booklets. These volumes offer the attraction of being compact, but they prove ultimately disappointing.

On the other hand, Michelin, whose yellow-clad road maps are models of the genre, puts out an exemplary if large 12¼ by 9¼ inch *Atlas Paris par Arrondissements.* Unhappily, Michelin's smaller Paris map book does not divide its maps by arrondissement, which is slightly bewildering. The firm's other Paris *plans* are of the bedsheet variety: They may facilitate plain sailing on the open road, but their expanse sends puzzled pedestrians flying.

Visitors might welcome a few bits of information that a born Parisian is assumed to have learned at his or her mother's knee. For example, none of Paris's popular *plans* explains the disarmingly simple formula according to which buildings are numbered—a formula that can orient one in the most unfamiliar neighborhood. Since February 4, 1805, Parisian houses have been numbered serially, with odd numbers on one side and evens on the opposite. On streets running at right or oblique angles to the Seine the numbers rise from the river; on streets running parallel to the river the numbers start from the upstream, or eastern, side.

Nor do map books alert visitors to bear in mind that their street indices are alphabetized by the streets' full names. Thus the rue Édith-Piaf is found under *E* not *P.* But the rue Washington is called just that, so it is listed under *W.* Equally, a title is in some cases part and parcel of a street's name, as in the case of the avenue du Général-Leclerc, and is therefore alphabetized under *G.* Streets named for saints demand special attention as well: in some rosters the rue Saint-Yves is listed before the rue Saint*e*-Anne; in others all the saints are heaped willy-nilly at the end of the *S* entries. Know your map—and, until you do, practice lateral thinking.

And don't try to make do with a dated map. Existing street names can no longer be changed, but an average of twenty-five additions appear each year, if only to honor deceased local worthies with tree-shaded crossroads. In a busy year Paris has been known to gain as many as forty-two new streets—and Murphy's Law decrees that the address you are seeking will be among the parvenus.

All of the maps here recommended rely on an arrondissement-to-the-double-page format that is both practical and culturally informative. The snail curl of the arrondissements is easily grasped, but the character of each *quartier* must then be mastered. By focusing the map reader's attention on the individuality of each arrondissement—the haughty, established style of the 7ème, still known by its denizens as the Faubourg Saint-Germain; the *louche* air of much of the 9ème; the gritty charms of the 20ème, which set one to wondering how it came to be called Belleville; and the interminable turn-of-the-century sculpted masonry of the 16ème, largest of all the arrondissements—the maps offer a painless history lesson, for in Paris geography and history are inseparably entwined.

Geography provides Frenchmen another field in which to exercise their Cartesian heritage: their earliest lessons teach them to call their republic the *hexagone* because the French landmass conveniently corresponds to that shape. This uncanny adherence to geometry applies to the capital as well, for Paris has managed to maintain a near-circular shape for more than two millennia. Settled on a damp island in the Seine, Lutetia initially relied on the river for defense. As Paris expanded along the adjacent banks, its citizens realized that topography offered little protection; where it failed, geology came to the rescue, providing abundant local limestone for walls.

The Romans built the first wall; the early Capetians are thought to have built a second. These seemed inadequate to King Philippe-Auguste on the eve of his departure for the Third Crusade, so in 1190 he began to girdle his capital's 625 acres with a thirty-foot rampart. It took twenty-three years to build but was very solid; vestiges still dot the older portions of the city.

A century and a half later the fortifications along the Right Bank were extended by Charles V to shield the city from the English; some three hundred years later additional works extended them to encompass more than twenty-five hundred acres until, in 1670, Louis XIV concluded that his victories were sufficient to guarantee Paris's security and ordered Charles V's walls demolished. The land thus freed was planted with trees, creating a "boulevard," a word deriving, ironically, from the Teutonic word for "bulwark."

But the kings of France had not had done with walls. Goods entering Paris had long been taxed at the gates of the city, but the new boulevards proved too permeable to fraudsters. In 1784 the tax collectors, or *fermiers généraux,* obtained royal permission to build a ten-foot wall around the capital:

Pour augmenter son numéraire
Et raccourcir notre horizon,
La Ferme a jugé nécessaire
De mettre Paris en prison.

To fill their coffers
And lower our horizon,
The taxmen have judged it necessary
To imprison Paris.

grumbled the wordsmiths of the Pont Neuf, who quickly assessed the popular resistance in near-palindrome, quipping that
the fourteen-mile *"mur murant Paris rend Paris murmurant"* (the

wall circling Paris renders Paris rebellious). Come the Revolution, no observer was startled when the forty-five strange and wonderful tax gates, designed by Claude-Nicolas Ledoux, figured among the mob's first targets.

The *fermiers généraux*'s wall was only a tax barrier. In 1814 Louis-Philippe, the Citizen King, was persuaded to build a twenty-five-mile fortification encircling the tax wall and encompassing twenty-four suburban villages. The annexation of these villages and their nearly twenty square miles in 1860 nearly doubled Paris's size.

In the twentieth century the walls finally came tumbling down (to the wrecker's ball), and the Bois de Vincennes and the Bois de Boulogne were incorporated into the city limits. Each successive wall had corseted the capital's growth. Having occupied less than five acres two thousand years previously, Paris had grown to a city of more than forty square miles, without much altering her rotund figure. Traces of each expansion, like the rings of a tree, can be seen in the street plan—in spite of Baron Georges Haussmann's radial thoroughfares. The nineteenth-century wall was demolished in the 1920s, but its circuit yielded the land for the *boulevards extérieurs* that speed (or fail to speed) traffic around Paris's periphery.

Baudelaire bemoaned the fact that "the shape of a city / Changes faster, alas, than the heart of a mortal." The historical maps of Paris chronicle those changes, reaching beyond language to recount their times; as a bonus they are often masterworks of the woodcut maker's and engraver's arts. Thus it is not surprising that those caught up in a passion for Paris are seduced by the siren charms of these historical maps, many of which have been reproduced and some of which can be purchased for reasonable sums.

The Archives Nationales, at 11 rue des Quatre-Fils, catalogs tens of thousands of maps, but the earliest recognized contemporary map of Paris is the Plan de Munster, which declares itself "The Portrait of the City." Produced, probably partially from memory, by a Franciscan monk named Sébastien Munster, this rather crude woodcut shows the Paris of about 1530, when François I was busy bringing the Renaissance to France. Like most maps in that era, Munster's map served as a kind of civic ego trip, enhancing the fame of the city and its monarch in both French and Latin.

A decade later an enormous tapestry incorporated a map of the late-medieval city in a style derived from illuminated manuscripts, with the place names inscribed on curious, beguiling banners. In the eighteenth century the tapestry, purchased by the city, was hung to adorn the façade of city hall on the Feast of Corpus Christi and was used to cushion the floor at a ball celebrating the advent of a dauphin in 1782. By 1787 it was in tatters. Fortunately the Plan de la Tapisserie had been copied, and engraving plates made. The latter are today part of the sumptuous collection of the Chalcographie, a unique department of the Louvre's Cabinet des Dessins, where fine engravings restruck from the original plates are available at quite affordable prices.

About 1551 another woodcut map appeared, the Plan de Truschet et Hoyau. This was an ambitious work covering eight sheets and cataloging the city's 287 streets and 104 churches—which served a population of roughly 350,000 souls. Like most sixteenth-century cartographers, Olivier Truschet and Germain Hoyau could not content themselves with two dimensions; they were forever trying to provide a third dimension, to limn the elevations and to add a human element. Guilt must have affected the cartographers' minds, because their cityscape included six cautionary gallows—occupied—not to mention plump-cheeked cupids blowing wind from the four corners of the map and drawing attention to the map's river axis rather than compass orientation. The precision sacrificed to figuration was almost always art's gain. The Plan de Truschet et Hoyau is often called the Plan de Bâle because the only extant original was discovered in the mid-nineteenth century in a library in Basel, where it had likely been carried by a traveler.

No modern chamber of commerce advised by the most go-go ad agency could outdo the purple prose of early map cartouche writers, as witness the etched Plan de Braun, published about 1572, on which a verse declares that "Paris is truly the royal house / Of the god Apollo." Even more naive, the Plan de Saint-Victor is usually attributed to the engraver of architect Jacques Androuet du Cerceau. Only a single copy exists, but fortunately another engraver, Guillaume d'Heulland, copied it between 1755 and 1760 onto a copper plate that continues to yield purchasable re-strikes at the Chalcographie. In 1609 both François Quesnel and Vassalieu produced *plans* for France's first urbanist king, Henri IV; each was long on praise for both the monarch and the "marvels" of his capital, and short on accuracy, often depicting construction projects that were still on the drawing boards. Many such projects progressed no further, due to Henri's assassination by the mad monk François Ravaillac, a crime that might never have succeeded—the king had eluded seventeen earlier attempts—but for the fact that the royal carriage was caught in a traffic jam on a narrow street.

Produced six years later, the splendidly engraved Plan de Mathieu Mérian includes an image of Henri's successor, the young Louis XIII, as well as a number of his subjects. Jacques Gomboust's 1647 nine-sheet map, peopled by 509 figures, decorated with engravings of six royal residences and the grander aristocratic seats, and framed by descriptive text, was a roll-up guide to the city and its environs. It omitted elevations of all but the most important structures and, overall, was considerably more accurate than its predecessors.

The Plan de Bullet et Blondel, drawn less than two decades later, reveals the city's tremendous growth under Louis XIV and demonstrates the error in thinking that the Sun King neglected

Paris in favor of Versailles. Drafted at the king's behest and surrounded with long-winded text, this map features its authors' own works, for architect François Blondel and his pupil Pierre Bullet had designed the triumphal gates at the Porte Saint-Denis, the Porte Saint-Martin, the Porte Saint-Antoine, and the Porte Saint-Bernard. Their architectural training is evident in their renditions of the gardens of the Louvre and Palais Royal; these lacy engravings define the term *parterre en broderie.* An inset map of the environs of Paris points to the court's imminent transfer to Versailles.

The Plan d'Albert Jouvin de Rochefort is the most absorbing of all the seventeenth-century maps, alive with more than six hundred figures caught up in their daily lives: trudging to work, tilling the fields surrounding the city, hunting stag on the Plaine Monceau, dueling on Montparnasse, swimming in the river. For all its animation, Rochefort's map, dated 1690, is remarkably scientific, oriented perpendicular to the meridian, that is, with the north at the top.

In the succeeding century, maps came into their own as administrative tools. In 1714 Marc-René, Marquis d'Argenson, lieutenant general of the Paris police, commissioned the Plan de Jean de la Caille, which enumerates every feature, from the 896 streets and 22,000 houses down to the city's 25 horse troughs. This was the first map of Paris to divide the city into sections, illustrating each on a separate sheet.

The perceived value of such maps decided the city fathers to pioneer a municipal map office. The Abbé Delagrive, renowned for his devoted work with "rod, chain, and theodolite" and for the handsome geometric map that had resulted, was named Géographe de la Ville and quickly undertook studies of urban water distribution. Delagrive marketed his own map "in the Rue Saint-Jacques . . . at a wigmaker's"; today we can purchase a restrike of it at the Chalcographie.

The historic map of Paris best known to the world, the Plan Turgot, recalls to me the New York City of the seventies, when I frequented Le Cygne not only to feast on its raspberry soufflé but to thrill to eighteenth-century Paris, for the restaurant's walls were papered with blowups of the map.

The Plan Turgot is shrouded in misconceptions. First of all, unlike most maps of its time, it is known by the name of the man who commissioned it, Michel-Étienne Turgot, not the man who surveyed it, Louis Bretez. Descended from Norman nobility, Turgot was the capital's *prévôt des marchands,* a royal appointee responsible for administration, which office he held for an unusually long eleven years. Little surprise that he decided to blow his city's horn and commission a splendid *plan.* (Turgot's third son, Anne-Robert-Jacques, for whom Michel-Étienne is often mistaken, was to become Louis XVI's reforming minister of finance.)

The Plan Turgot was a map out of sync with its time, drawn in the great seventeenth-century tradition of the bird's-eye view. By 1734 Delagrive and his imitators had already accustomed the map-reading public to precise renderings on which one could number the very pillars of the churches. And the Cassinis, the family who put French cartography on the map, were just about to begin triangulating for their famed topographical map of the kingdom.

The purpose of Turgot's map—which it serves to this day— was as retrograde, and eternal, as its style: to broadcast the wealth and beauty of Paris. If Delagrive could draft sanitation plans worthy of the council chamber, Bretez would execute a vast plan worthy of the drawing room. Promised a fee of ten thousand *livres* and armed with a permit that granted him ready access to all the city's buildings to make sketches, Bretez, a member of the Académie de Sculpture et de Peinture and onetime professor of architecture and perspective, blazoned the capital across twenty sheets, which, end to end, measure 10½ by 8 feet. Bretez knew full well that he was bucking the trend and perhaps betraying his training in perspective, for he apologized in print for his license, explaining that without forcing the perspective he would have lost some of the most interesting monuments of the city. At a time when maps had come to be oriented perpendicular to the meridian, the Plan Turgot has the east at the top, to allow Bretez the bravura chance to detail the façades of the churches, almost all of which face east. Sadly, Bretez didn't live to see the final engraved product of his labors.

The Plan Turgot is the least rare of eighteenth-century maps because twenty-six hundred copies were run off. Some of them were mounted on linen; the remainder were bound. These were sent as presents to destinations as distant as Constantinople and China. Further copies have been (and remain) available, as the copper plates ended up at the Chalcographie. However inaccurate topographically, Bretez's map, which attempted to portray each and every building, makes this a fascinating architectural study— and enormously decorative.

Purists criticized the Plan Turgot from the moment of its appearance, but the public loved it, drawn in by the lack of topographical progression and left happily lost in the city. The map's popularity continues today, with reduced-scale facsimiles eagerly purchased from the Bibliothèque Nationale's shop in the rue des Petits-Champs, as well as from myriad souvenir shops.

But in the Age of Enlightenment scientific mapping necessarily had to triumph over figurative mapping, however artful. In Paris the apostle of the former was a Burgundian architect named Edme Verniquet, who, having purchased the venal office of road surveyor, discovered that none of the available maps was accurate enough to allow him to align buildings. He devoted half his adult life to devising such a mathematically exact plan. From 1783 until the royal purse grew too empty in 1788, Verniquet enjoyed Louis XVI's patronage in paying the sixty surveyors and two hundred helpers who charted the city at night by torchlight to avoid disrupting traffic. The project captured the imagination of *le tout-*

Paris, who flocked to gape at the draftsmen laboring in the gallery of the Couvent des Cordeliers on a seventy-two-sheet map that, assembled, measures 16½ by 13 feet. The Plan Verniquet captures the last portrait of the Paris of the *ancien régime* before so many of its convents and churches were demolished and Napoléon's *gloire* was imprinted on the urban fabric.

Verniquet was a hard act to follow. His *plan* was the basis of almost all Paris maps in the first half of the nineteenth century until Baron Georges Haussmann commissioned a new survey in 1853. But that is not to say that nineteenth-century maps are not fascinating and charming. Engineer Aristide-Michel Perrot's 1834 *Petit Atlas Pittoresque des Quarante-Huit Quartiers de la Ville de Paris* offers alongside its maps delectable *aperçus* of the life of the city; the map of the twelfth arrondissement, the Quartier du Jardin du Roi, which became the Jardin des Plantes, is accompanied by an illustration of its caged giraffe, which drew all Paris in wonderment.

Haussmann definitively established the Office of the Plan de Paris in 1853, appointing Deschamps to head it. The maps he and his colleagues produced were accurate and full of purpose, if perhaps less romantic than their predecessors. Literacy and cheap, colorful reproduction spread maps far and wide—but did not devalue them; as the Plan de Munster indicates, maps, regardless of design, production technique, or purpose, are "Portraits of the City."

Those bitten by the historical-map bug should repair to the Chalcographie, handsomely installed under the Louvre's pyramid, for restrikes or to the Bibliothèque Nationale's smart boutique at 6 rue des Petits-Champs, 2ème, for reduced-size facsimiles. Those seeking period maps might address themselves to one or another of the specialist map dealers, firms like Louis Loeb-Larocque, at 31 rue de Tolbiac, 13ème, or Sartoni-Cerveau, at 15 quai Saint-Michel, 5ème—both streets of which they can locate in their *Paris par Arrondissement*.

Il connaît Paris comme sa poche (he knows Paris like the back of his hand or, literally, like his pocket) is high praise indeed. Those who merit such praise will have often whipped a map from pocket or pocketbook to find their way.

Why I Love My *Quincaillerie*

BARBARA WILDE

෴

THIS IS ANOTHER Paris Postcard that Barbara Wilde shared on her great Web site, L'Atelier Vert, introduced previously (on page 16). I, too, love the French *quincaillerie,* and I'll repeat how I also love Wilde's postcard missives. Each one is unique, containing some wonderfully written passages. Here's a superb one from one of her earliest postcards, "What Am I Doing Here?": "I love to think that after I am gone, Paris will remain the same, imperceptibly absorbing the drop of my life into the river of humanity that has flowed through it for so long. The permanence of Paris comforts me."

"VOUS DÉSIREZ, MADAME?" I felt like rubbing my eyes. I had just walked through the door of my local hardware store, and this most professional of shopkeeper greetings had just been uttered by a pixieish nine-year-old in long braids. She regarded me through the lenses of her glasses with every bit as much aplomb as the sixty-something matron who usually minded the store. Her serious demeanor bespoke the gravity and importance of the interaction we were about to embark upon, while her courteous phrasing implied the profound respect she held for me, her customer. In short, at age nine, she already had a perfect grasp on the quintessence of the complex socio-professional skills that comprise the Parisian shopkeeper's art.

In fact, she turned out to be the daughter of the owner of this wonderful shop. Dad was behind a different counter, busy with another customer. Daughter was already on holiday break (it was

just before Christmas) and was apparently in training to inherit the family business. The manager of the shop, the lady I was familiar with, was present but remained discreetly in the background of my interaction with the young lady.

I duly explained that I was looking for an oval Le Creuset casserole to give as a gift to a friend who had admired mine. The young miss led me over to a pyramid of these very casseroles stacked in diminishing sizes. Then she courteously stood aside to allow me to inspect them at close range. (I delicately refrained from asking her name for a host of complex French reasons. If I asked her name, I would be forced to *tutoyer* her, using the familiar form of address, as she is a child, and I didn't want to spoil our roles with this familiarity. Also, one would never ask a shopkeeper one had just encountered for the first time for her name.)

When I'd made my choice, the junior shopkeeper expertly extracted it, took my credit card, and plugged it into the electronic transmitter, then, discreetly averting her eyes, handed me the gizmo so that I could enter my PIN. Meanwhile, the manager wrapped up my purchase. Before I departed, I congratulated the owner of the shop on the impeccable professionalism and courtesy of his daughter. And I left musing about how much I love this store, and why.

Paris has two types of hardware stores: the *quincaillerie,* specialized in actual hardware, and the *droguerie,* not a drugstore but a shop specialized in paints, cleaning products, glues, and other household potions. My neighborhood store combines both these product lines. Merchandise is densely stacked and hung floor to ceiling and must often be sought with a ladder. Overstock is housed in the cellar, which is accessed by a trapdoor and its attached steep steps.

So what's so unusual and wonderful about these stores? The first thing is the incredibly diverse variety of products they stock. My store has everything from oilcloth to shopping caddies, picture-hanging supplies, cleaning supplies, myriads of lightbulbs (a nightmare in France because there are about twenty different noninterchangeable types), an excellent cookware line, candles, shoe-care products, trash cans . . . it just goes on and on. I'm sure they must stock thousands of different items, and all this in an area smaller than the average American master bedroom.

The diversity of cleaning supplies alone is mind-boggling. A product exists for every imaginable purpose—and for many purposes that you have never imagined. Did you have a laundry accident and now all your husband's white T-shirts are pink? Not to worry, the *détacheur pour linge teint par accident* will get them white again. Are lime deposits clogging your washing machine? Here's just what you need. . . . You have a spot on a leather handbag? Well, what kind of leather is it? Ah, here's the correct product to solve the problem. . . .

The French householder is by nature profoundly frugal. She prefers never to throw anything away, and considers it a serious responsibility to take excellent care of what she has. Doing this in the French manner—that is, with a mania for complication, specificity, and diversity—requires thousands and thousands of different products. Of course, no one but the shopkeeper could possibly know which of them to recommend for a particular situation.

This fact leads to the second thing I love about my *quincaillerie/droguerie,* an aspect that is part of the very definition of this type of store in Paris. I can walk in with the most bizarre problem—stain on clothing, spot on my wood parquet floors, whatever—and the shopkeeper will listen patiently and attentively to my plaint. Then she will climb her ladder and extract one of her thousands of products, the one which has been designed to take care of *just* my problem. She will then explain to me in a most serious and authoritative manner *precisely* how to use the product, admonishing against common pitfalls along the way.

Meanwhile, I'm feeling comforted because 1) I thought I was the only person dumb enough to have this problem, and it turns out I'm not; and 2) I've just been presented with a clear solution. When the shopkeeper looks at me to see if I want to buy the product, of course I do! I absolutely love this process of knowing that when I walk into my hardware store, my problem will be solved—kindly and professionally.

The second reason I love this store is that it meets all my imaginable needs. My store is never out of a product. Whenever I occasionally summon the courage to venture into a "superstore" (*grande surface*), that dehumanizingly vast acreage of mostly useless junk imported from China, and have wandered the endless aisles in my demoralizing quest—all my senses bombarded with garishness—invariably the item I'm looking for is out of stock.

So how do these small, independent wonder-stores manage to persist in Paris? The answer is simple, and yet unthinkable in the United States: superstores are not allowed to exist within the city limits. This is a measure deliberately taken to protect the diversity of the thousands of small shops that make Paris the place we love, as well as the livelihoods of all those shopkeepers. In the provinces, the effects of the superstore metastasis have been just as devastating as in the United States. It's becoming difficult to find an old-time *quincaillerie* in French country towns. Sadly, village squares are often marked by the vestige of a storefront, where once— before the appearance of the local Brico Dépôt—thrived a magnificent country hardware store densely stocked with all the accoutrements of daily country life, including a smiling, knowledgeable, and courteous shopkeeper familiar to all.

Do the products at my local hardware store cost more than the mass-market junk in the *grande surface*? Of course they do! But I can't even *find* these products in the mass-market stores, let alone find someone who will explain to me how to use them. I'm oh so happy to know that, just a three-minute walk away, I'm sure to be able to solve my latest household catastrophe, in a calm, orderly, stressless atmosphere, surrounded by interesting, quality products, and administered to in a courteous and highly personalized way by a shopkeeper I know. In short, I happily pay more to preserve this intensely human and agreeable experience of my daily life. Call it the price of civilization.

Thirza's Take on Paris

THIRZA VALLOIS

Iғ—*MON DIEU!*—I was told I could bring only three books with me to Paris, I'd choose the trio of *Around and About Paris* guides by Thirza Vallois, who has lived in Paris for more than forty years. To quote from her author bio, "She knows Paris stone by stone and has read every book of note about its history and development." I knew when I picked up volume one, *From the Dawn of Time to the Eiffel Tower* (which covers the first through seventh arrondissements), that *this* was what I wanted to accompany me around the city.

Each volume in this hugely informative series—the other two are *From the Guillotine to the Bastille Opera* (eighth through twelfth arrondissements) and *New Horizons: Haussmann's Annexation* (thirteenth through twentieth)—is organized numerically by arrondissement, representing the way the city grew, and each arrondissement is presented with an overall introduction followed by a detailed walk. Readers and walkers will experience the major sights and special out-of-the-way places and will learn what makes each *quartier* distinct. *Vraiment,* these books are remarkable for the details Vallois imparts—and even if you use just one volume and follow just one walk, you will be amazed by how much you'll learn.

THIRZA VALLOIS contributed this piece to the Web site Bonjour Paris (bonjourparis.com; see the Bonjour Paris entry in the Miscellany for more details). She is also the author of *Romantic Paris* (Interlink, 2003) and *Aveyron: A Bridge to French Arcadia* (Iliad, 2007).

For those among you who don't know my writing, some background information may be of some interest. Contrary to what my readers and interviewers tend to assume, my involvement with Paris was not born out of passionate love for the city but out of exasperation, and writing about it was a therapy of sorts. As a matter of fact, Paris was a huge letdown when I first disembarked at the Gare du Nord: as a naive teenager I expected a *Vogue* magazine Paris, not a grotty working-class neighborhood! Besides, nobody had prepared me for the ill-tempered city it was in those days. Given my distaste for the place on my first visit, I cannot for the life of me say why I came back and why I never left. I am not quite sure what magnetic force drew me in, but having mulled over this for so many years, I believe it was the amplified density of human experiences that ultimately makes Paris the unique city it is and eventually gets under our skin.

I started writing about Paris in order to figure out the place and its people and thus get them out of my system. Rather than tackle them frontally, which would have kept me in a confrontational mode, it occurred to me that by exploring the city I might reach the same objective in a more fun way. This led to an overwhelming, fifteen-year project which I had not anticipated, by the end of which time I had been living in Paris for over thirty years. As I traveled deeper and deeper into its different facets, it got hold of me insidiously and I became increasingly indulgent towards its flaws and appreciative of its virtues. Rather than writing about it as therapy, I found myself embarked on a lifelong quest, because although I know it very well compared with most people, one never knows Paris fully, which is one of its beauties. There is always more to dig and probe into, which to me is part of the addiction. To quote the ultimate Paris lover, Victor Hugo, "He who looks into the depths of Paris grows giddy," the epigraph I chose for my books because I could think of no other that would sum it up better.

Paris has opened up to the world since the days of Victor Hugo, and in the last ten or fifteen years has engendered a pleasanter and more laid-back species of denizens. Thus, for example, although the *Bonjour* greeting is still very much alive, the more formal *Madame, Monsieur,* or *Mademoiselle* bits are used more loosely. Most Parisians speak at least some English, making the city more user-friendly to foreigners. In short, present-day Paris is less blunt but increasingly bland, no longer polluted by the smoke of Gauloises but watered down instead by Starbucks coffee. . . . (Remember, the first McDonald's made its appearance already back in the 1970s.) You can't have it both ways.

The gentrification of Paris, however, is not a recent phenomenon. As a matter of fact, the regeneration of Paris was on the agenda of the French Revolution. It was tackled timidly by the following regimes and radically under Haussmann. Haussmann, however, did not eradicate the entire existing urban fabric. Much more of the old city was preserved than people realize. His genius consisted in weaving together the old and the new seamlessly, thus preserving an overall cohesion. Although the bustling medieval flavor was destroyed in some places, elsewhere it survived. Closer to us it was helped by the fact that, unlike London, Paris was not bombed by the Germans. Nevertheless and inevitably, old neighborhoods do get cleared over time, either because they genuinely threaten ruin or because of the pressure of the speculation market. In twentieth-century Paris such regenerations began in the 1960s and would have begun earlier if it hadn't been for the war years. One must bear in mind, however, that the younger generations have no reference to the past, they do not bemoan (unlike me), and they live comfortably in the present environment, spending time at Starbucks preferably to traditional French cafés.

I am currently preparing an electronic version of *Around and About Paris* and rewalking Paris for that purpose. It's a mixed experience of joy and sadness: the joy of seeing an old courtyard, bistro, or artisan's shop still standing unchanged; the sadness over those that have disappeared. Such is life. Besides, this was also the case in the 1980s when I began to write my books. Like all organic life, Paris is a city in the making and in constant mutation, and some of it is good. Renewal also brings hope and freshness. Some places look better than they used to, some new gardens are exquisite, here and there a shabby wall has been embellished by an artist unknown to me. And despite the reign of commerce and electronics, there are still so many bookshops in Paris! It is heartwarming to see that it remains a place of intellectual pursuit and debate, inhabited by a population that actively cares about politics and societal issues. Have no fear—the constant aggravation caused by strikes and protest demonstrations is proof enough that the passionate Gallic spirit is still very much alive in its capital city as well as in the rest of the national territory.

Proust's Paris

SANCHE DE GRAMONT

MARCEL PROUST SEEMS to be more celebrated now than he ever was, and the publication of recent books such as *Marcel Proust's Search for Lost Time* by Patrick Alexander (Vintage, 2009), *The Year of Reading Proust* by Phyllis Rose (Scribner, 1997), and *How Proust Can Change Your Life* by Alain de Botton (Pantheon, 1997) attests to the popularity of Proustomania. Many Proust fans who visit Paris also make a pilgrimage to Illiers–Combray, just south of Chartres, where Proust's celebrated tome, *In Search of Lost Time* is set. Readers of my first Paris edition may recall a *New Yorker* piece I included in that book called "In Search of Proust" by André Aciman. In it, Aciman refers to the "Prousto-tourists" who come to the *former* town of Illiers, which added Combray to its name officially in 1971, on the centennial of Proust's birth. Aciman also notes that the town of Illiers–Combray sells about two thousand madeleines, the famed cake at the heart of Proust's story, every month. The village also has a very lovely Marcel Proust museum, which was originally the home of Proust's paternal uncle and aunt and in fact is also known as Aunt Léonie's House. In her excellent account of the museum's restoration and history, "Marcel Proust at Illiers–Combray" (*Architectural Digest,* October 2000), Judith Thurman accurately notes that "all great writers have an exceptionally fine-tuned sense of place, but none, surely, has ever been finer than Marcel Proust's. The architect of that sublime memory palace, *In Search of Lost Time,* is inseparable from his own décors, real and imagined."

But, as anyone who's read Proust's literary masterpiece knows, Belle Époque Paris is at the center of the story. Here is a unique piece, originally appearing in *Horizon*, that is both a brilliant encapsulation of the novel and an annotated geographical legend to the city of Paris just before and after the turn of the twentieth century. The original article was accompanied by a map, because as the *Horizon* editors noted, the sense of reality in Proust's novel is so compelling that "its characters seem as authentic as the Paris streets in which they come and go." I encourage readers to look at a detailed map of Paris and locate the sites that Sanche de Gramont has pinpointed below. Again to quote the *Horizon* editors, "Such a mixture of the imagined and the actual would surely have pleased Proust. His own central character, in love with Gilberte Swann, once his childhood playmate, 'had always, within reach, a plan of Paris, which . . . seemed to [him] to contain a secret treasure'—for in it he can find the street where his beloved lives." Readers can imagine that they have "been allowed to glance at Proust's *carnet,* or address book, where the novelist has jotted down some of the prominent landmarks of his vast work."

SANCHE DE GRAMONT, introduced previously, is also the author of many books under the name Ted Morgan. Morgan is the author of, among others, *Valley of Death: The Tragedy at Dien Bien Phu That Led America into the Vietnam War* (Random House, 2010), *FDR: A Biography* (Simon & Schuster, 1985), *My Battle of Algiers: A Memoir* (Smithsonian, 2006), *A Shovel of Stars: The Making of the American West, 1800 to the Present* (Simon & Schuster, 1995), and *Maugham: A Biography* (Simon & Schuster, 1980).

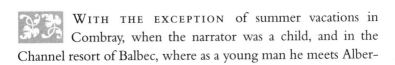 WITH THE EXCEPTION of summer vacations in Combray, when the narrator was a child, and in the Channel resort of Balbec, where as a young man he meets Alber-

tine, later his fiancée, and of a short trip to Venice with his mother, all of *Remembrance of Things Past* takes place in Paris. The presence of the city saturates the novel the way moisture saturates the air and determines its atmospheric pressure.

I can think of one other city so present in a great modern novel, and that is Joyce's Dublin. But unlike Joyce, who delivers Dublin in a single day, Proust makes Paris unfold over a period of roughly forty-five years, from 1875 to 1920. To read Proust is to observe the flowering and decline of a period in the capital's history, for the debacle of 1870 and the horrors of the Commune were followed by years of determined amusement known as *la belle époque*. Those who had expected a wake found, instead, a celebration that was interrupted only by another war.

Proust was born in 1871 in a Paris already physically transformed by the Baron Haussmann, who destroyed entire neighborhoods to build long, straight thoroughfares like the rue de Rivoli, who crossed the Seine with five new bridges, and who built the Halles central market. The transformation continued during Proust's life. The avenue of the Opéra linked the rue de Rivoli with Garnier's opera house, inaugurated in 1874. The young Proust saw the Eiffel Tower go up, its four perforated iron legs rising from the green meadow of the Champ de Mars. In 1900 the Petit and Grand Palais were opened to the public. In the same year the first line of the Métro was inaugurated, and the fanciful wrought-iron entrances, with their orange lights and insectlike appearance, contributed to what became known as the "firefly" style of decoration.

And yet the capital of two and a half million people still resembled a collection of villages. The Champs-Élysées remained unpaved until the twentieth century. The houses on the avenue du Bois (today's avenue Foch) still had private stables. Passy was a rustic suburb. Public transportation consisted mainly of horse-drawn omnibuses, despite the Métro, which Proust mentions only once.

Electric street lighting was still a novelty, so that the narrator, going to visit Mme Swann, the mother of Gilberte, was guided by the light in her living room, which shone like a beacon in the dark. Houses, even the houses of the rich, were badly heated. In the early spring Mme Swann received visitors with an ermine wrap over her shoulders and her hands in an ermine muff, like "the last patches of the snows of winter, more persistent than the rest, which neither the heat of the fire nor the advancing season had succeeded in melting."

The traditional coexistence of luxury and discomfort was tempered by new inventions. Thus, the narrator acquires a telephone. As he waits for a call from Albertine, he remarks: "The advance of civilisation enables each of us to display unsuspected merits or fresh defects which make him dearer or more insupportable to his friends. Thus Dr. Bell's invention had enabled Françoise [his maid] to acquire an additional defect, which was that of refusing, however important, however urgent the occasion might be, to make use of the telephone. She would manage to disappear whenever anybody was going to teach her how to use it, as people disappear when it is time for them to be vaccinated."

This, then, was the city the narrator inhabited, not a mere setting, or a series of useful addresses, but a source of daily nourishment for his senses. Its sounds reached him as he lay ill in his room: "On certain fine days, the weather was so cold, one was in such full communication with the street, that it seemed as though a breach had been made in the outer walls of the house, and, whenever a tramcar passed, the sound of its bell throbbed like that of a silver knife striking a wall of glass."

The street hawkers outside his window were "an orchestra that returned every morning to charm me." Their cries seemed like a recitative in an opera, "where an initial intonation is barely altered by the inflexion of one note which rests upon another . . ." When he heard the cry *Les escargots, ils sont frais, ils sont beaux . . . On les vend six sous la douzaine,*" it reminded him of parts of Debussy's *Pelléas et Mélisande.* The practical Albertine interrupted his reverie to say: "Do make Françoise go out and buy some. . . . It will be all the sounds that we hear, transformed into a good dinner."

In counterpoint to the aristocracy with which *Remembrance* is mainly concerned, Proust shows us the little people of Paris, like the street vendors and the rouged lady called the "Marquise," who operates the public toilet on the Champs-Élysées. Someone asks the Marquise why she does not retire, and she replies: "Will you kindly tell me where I shall be better off than here . . . my little Paris, I call it; my customers keep me in touch with everything that's going on. Just to give you an example, there's one of them who went out not more than five minutes ago; he's a magistrate, in the very highest position there is . . . for the last eight years . . . regularly on the stroke of three he's been here, always polite . . . never making any mess; and he stays half an hour and more to read his papers and do his little jobs. . . . And besides . . . I choose my customers, I don't let everyone into my little parlours . . ." The instinct for social stratification, Proust shows us, exists at every level.

Another of Paris's multiple functions is to evoke distant places where the narrator has never been, canceling the need to travel. He imagines "that the Seine, flowing between the twin semicircles of the span and the reflection of its bridges, must look like the Bosporus." There was a room from which he saw "across a first, a second, and even a third layer of jumbled roofs . . . a violet bell, sometimes ruddy, sometimes too, in the finest 'prints' which the atmosphere makes of it, of an ashy solution of black; which is, in fact, nothing else than the dome of Saint-Augustin, and which imparts to this view of Paris the character of some of the Piranesi views of Rome."

This room was Proust's own bedroom on the boulevard Haussmann, but the narrator, more elegant, and for the requirements of the plot, lives in a wing of the Duc de Guermantes's town house, the address of which is never specified. "It was one of those old town houses, a few of which are perhaps still to be found, in which the court of honour—whether they were alluvial deposits washed there by the rising tide of democracy, or a legacy from a more primitive time when the different trades were clustered round the overlord—is flanked by little shops and workrooms, a shoemaker's for instance, or a tailor's . . ."

Just as Proust's Paris is more than a city, the Duc de Guermantes's town house is more than an address—it is the symbolic fortress of an inaccessible caste, for the Duc and Duchesse de Guermantes are the social leaders of the Faubourg Saint-Germain, which is less a location than a state of mind. It is not limited to the fine old houses clustered around the boulevard Saint-Germain. The Guermantes town house, for instance, is on the other side of the river, on the right bank. It has everything to do with belonging to the *ancien régime* aristocracy, still conscious of its privileges, still royalist, certain of its superiority and contemptuous of outsiders, surviving thanks to an exclusiveness that makes it seem the custodian of a rare and desirable way of life, and to the rigid enforcement of a complicated social code.

The Baron de Charlus, the Duc de Guermantes's younger brother (that brothers should have different family names is one of the arcana of the Faubourg), says: "I know nothing outside the Faubourg Saint-Germain." Like the forbidden city of Peking, it is a closed, self-contained, self-sufficient society. Albertine, jealous of her fiancé's Faubourg friends (whom she will never meet), says: "Of course, whoever comes from the Faubourg Saint-Germain possesses all the virtues."

To the narrator, viewing it at first from afar, the Faubourg is a sublime enigma. He is incapable of imagining what it can be like, what these remote minor deities say to one another, what language they use. The guests arriving at the Duc de Guermantes's house "might have been made of some precious matter; they are the columns that hold up the temple." "Alas," he says, "those picturesque sites . . . I must content myself with a shiver of excitement as I sighted, from the deep sea (and without the least hope of ever landing there) like an outstanding minaret, like the first palm, like the first signs of some exotic industry or vegetation, the well-trodden doormat of its shore."

The narrator discovers, however, that the boundaries of the Faubourg are more flexible than he thought. A few outsiders are given "naturalization papers," little ways in which they know they have become accepted. Proust, like his narrator, gained access to the reputedly unapproachable world of the Faubourg because he was witty, kind, and solicitous, and above all, because he passionately wanted to. It is hard to resist true passion. After having been its distant admirer, the narrator becomes the chronicler of the Faubourg. The focus of Proust's Paris shifts, and centers on this tiny minority with an inflated sense of its own importance, absorbed in matters of rank and social exclusion, indifferent to the world outside its gates.

Familiarity makes the narrator lose the sense of ecstasy he felt when the Faubourg was out of reach. He becomes aware of the malice and foolishness that exclusiveness conceals. He tests the walls of the temple, and they give a hollow sound. The exquisite politeness is calculated: "The ladies of the Faubourg build up a credit of amiability in anticipation of the dinner and garden party where they will not invite you, and are particularly nice in prevision of the day when they will overlook you." The men are convinced that no greater honor exists than that of being accepted by them. Charles Swann, an outsider who has been thus honored, is by birth neither an aristocrat nor a Gentile. When the fate of Captain Dreyfus intrudes on the smugness of the Faubourg Saint-Germain, the Duc de Guermantes cannot understand how Swann, after having received a friendly reception from the Faubourg, can be sympathetic to the Jewish officer convicted of treason.

The elegance, the refinement, the courtliness are screens that mask unfeeling hearts. The narrator, although still awed by the Faubourg's splendor, exposes its callousness, as in the famous scene where Swann arrives at the Guermantes town house and announces that he is dying to the Duchesse, who is late for dinner. " 'What's that you say?' cried the Duchess, stopping for a moment on her way to the carriage, and raising her fine eyes, their melancholy blue clouded by uncertainty. Placed for the first time in her life between two duties as incompatible as getting into her carriage to go out to dinner and shewing pity for a man who was about to die, she could find nothing in the code of conventions that indicated the right line to follow, and, not knowing which to choose, felt it better to make a show of not believing that the latter alternative need be seriously considered, so as to follow the first, which demanded of her at the moment less effort, and thought that the best way of settling the conflict would be to deny that any existed. 'You're joking,' she said to Swann."

The Faubourg carries within it the seeds of its decline. The narrator watches it founder, the victim of external circumstances such as the war, as well as of its inability to defend itself against the principal cause of infiltration—misalliances. When Robert de Saint-Loup, the Duc de Guermantes's nephew, marries Gilberte, the daughter of Odette and Swann, the Princesse de Silistrie complains that "there is no more Faubourg, Saint-Loup is marrying a Jew's daughter." The narrator, returning to Paris after a long absence, finds the Faubourg no longer exclusive: ". . . a thousand alien elements made their way in and all homogeneity, all consistency of form and color was lost. The Faubourg Saint-Germain was like some senile dowager now, who replies only with timid smiles to the insolent servants who invade her drawing rooms, drink her orangeade, present their mistresses to her."

Stunning reversals have hastened the Faubourg's decline. The Prince de Guermantes (cousin of the Duc), ruined by the war, his wife dead, has married the rich Mme Verdurin, the incarnation of bourgeois pretentiousness, whom no lady of the Faubourg, a few years earlier, would have received. The Faubourg's standard-bearers, the Duc and Duchesse de Guermantes, have more or less abandoned it. The Duchesse now frequents social groups much further down the social scale, and has become particularly fond of the company of actresses. The Duc has become hopelessly infatuated with Swann's widow, Odette, who has in the meantime been married to the Baron de Forcheville.

Thus Odette, who starts out a common courtesan, becomes in the end the wife of one member of the Faubourg and the mistress of another. The doddering Duc de Guermantes is so taken with Odette that he accepts in her home the presence of people he would in the past have disdained. Social boundaries have crumbled, and Odette shows off her relic of the Faubourg like a collector showing an antique. "All that seemed to be forever fixed is constantly being refashioned . . ." the narrator remarks.

Running parallel to the decline of the Faubourg as a social bastion is the decline of the narrator's friends caused by advancing years, and the transformation of the city owing to the war. On his way to a musical matinee at the Prince de Guermantes's, the narrator sees Charlus in the street, recovering from an attack of apoplexy, bent, his hair and beard gone completely white, his eyes glazed, hardly able to walk. At the matinee, he sees the men and women he had known young arriving like phantoms, imprisoned in the thousand bonds of the past, age having marked their faces the way geologic change marks the surface of the earth.

The men were now elderly white-haired hermits. Women's faces were crumbling like those of statues. Women who still seemed young from afar grew older as they were approached and one saw the wrinkles and the greasy spots on their skins, the deep erosion along their noses, the alluvial deposits on the edge of cheeks that filled the face with their opaque mass. Some faces seem covered by a plaster mask, others by a gauze veil. Gilberte, the narrator's first love, has become a fat lady whom he fails to recognize, and then mistakes for her mother, Odette.

Wartime Paris causes the same sense of dislocation. Planes circle the city, little brown specks against the sky. The museums are closed, and from the doors of shops hang handwritten signs saying they will be open at some remote time in the future. The blackout begins at nine-thirty. Soldiers on leave fill the streets, looking into the windows of crowded restaurants and saying: "You'd never know there was a war on here." Sirens announcing a Zeppelin raid seem to the narrator "Wagnerian, so natural to announce the arrival of the Germans."

Although the Germans are an hour's drive from Paris, receptions and dinners continue to be given, and fashionable women attend them wearing bracelets made from shell fragments, while the men carry cigarette cases made from English coins. The narrator feels "the surprise of a foreigner who knows Paris well but does not live there, and who, upon returning to the city for a few weeks, sees in the place of a little theatre where he has spent pleasant evenings, that a bank has been built in its place."

The city's permanence is merely another illusion, for nothing lasts, in cities as well as in hearts, and the very streets can alter as quickly as a face ages. Paris's final function is to serve as the setting for Proust's inquiry upon the passage of time. As the narrator enters the Guermantes courtyard on his way to the matinee and trips on uneven paving stones, he experiences the happy rush of involuntary memory. Just as, earlier, the shell-shaped pastry called a madeleine brought back his childhood, the paving stones bring back his trip to Venice, for he had walked over uneven paving stones in the St. Mark's baptistery. Instead of joining the other guests, he retires to a library to savor this "veritable moment of the past."

He has stepped outside the flow of time and experienced a sensation that is not disappointing, for it is given to him whole, recaptured. Reality was disappointing because at the moment he perceived it he could not imagine it, "by virtue of the inevitable law that we can only imagine what is absent," and it was only through his imagination that he was capable of grasping beauty.

But now, thanks to the physical sensation in the present that has restored the past, reality and imagination are fused and allow the narrator to apprehend "a fragment of time in the pure state . . . A minute freed from the order of time has re-created in us, to feel it, the man freed from the order of time. And one can understand that this man should have confidence in his joy, even if the simple taste of a madeleine does not seem logically to contain within it the reasons for this joy, one can understand that the word 'death' should have no meaning for him; situated outside time, why should he fear the future?"

The privileged moment is brief, and once over, the narrator must return to the aging faces and the eroding landscape. And this is the final, melancholy lesson taught not only by Proust's characters but by the city streets they walk on and the buildings they live in, by the restless spirit of the great city: "The places that we have known belong now not only to the little world of space on which we map them for our own convenience. None of them was ever more than a thin slice, held between the contiguous impressions that composed our life at that time; remembrance of a particular form is but regret for a particular moment; and houses, roads, avenues are as fugitive, alas, as the years."

THE CITY THAT PROUST KNEW

The **Champs-Élysées** is where the narrator as a child becomes the playmate of Gilberte, daughter of Charles Swann and Odette de Crécy—themselves major characters in the novel. The children play on the lawns near the **Alcazar d'Été**. Under century-old cedars, candy and soft drinks are sold from wooden booths. A little farther down stands the cast-iron public lavatory where the

narrator's grandmother suffers the stroke that leads to her death. On the corner of the Champs-Élysées, above the **rue de Berri**, the narrator, now grown up, sells a family vase to a Chinese curio shop for ten thousand francs, in order to buy flowers for Gilberte. On his way back from the shop, he sees Gilberte with a young man he cannot identify, and suffers pangs of jealous uncertainty. On the corner of the **rue Royale** stands a photographer's stall, where the narrator's servant, Françoise, buys a snapshot of Pope Pius IX, while the narrator chooses one of the actress La Berma.

Swann, the rich aesthete, is invited to lunch at the **Élysée Palace**, on the rue du Faubourg Saint-Honoré, with the president of France, Jules Grévy. It is an invitation that astonishes Doctor Cottard, one of the members of the "little clan," as Mme Verdurin's tacky, bourgeois salon is known. "What's that you say? M. Grévy? Do you know M. Grévy?" asks Cottard, finding it hard to believe that someone he was having dinner with, and who held no official post, could be on friendly enough terms with the head of state to be invited for lunch at the Élysée.

The old **Trocadéro** is described as a gingerbread castle "whose towers at twilight glowed so that they seemed covered with currant jelly like the towers pastrycooks make." It was torn down in 1937 to make way for the present Palais de Chaillot.

The musician Morel, who becomes the lover of the Baron de Charlus (the Duc de Guermantes's homosexual brother) and of Robert de Saint-Loup (Guermantes's nephew), is a member of the Conservatory on the **rue Bergère.**

On the **rue de Bourgogne**, the narrator's butler observes the Baron de Charlus spending an hour in a *pissotière,* recognizing him by his bright yellow trousers.

Mme Verdurin holds her salon on the **Quai de Conti**, in a building she claims is the former residence of the Venetian ambassadors.

The **Quai d'Orléans** is where Swann lives as a bachelor. Odette, the lovely courtesan who will become his wife, considers the apartment musty and old-fashioned and the neighborhood inelegant because it is close to the Halle aux Vins, the wine market.

On the **avenue Gabriel** a homosexual propositions the narrator's friend Saint-Loup, who is dressed in his officer's uniform. Saint-Loup, shocked at the audacity of the "clique," pummels the accoster savagely, but is later found to be himself a member.

To the **Halles**, or central market, the narrator's servant, Françoise, goes to choose the ingredients for her famous *boeuf en gelée,* "as Michelangelo passed eight months in the mountains of Carrara choosing the most perfect blocks of marble for the monument of Jules II."

The **rue Rabelais** is where the Jockey Club still stands. Swann is a member, as is the Baron de Charlus, who goes there every evening at six. When the obscure Chaussepierre is elected president over the Duc de Guermantes, the Duc concludes that the reason is his friendship with Swann, a Jew, at a time when the Jewish Captain Dreyfus had been accused of treason and anti-Semitism was raging. Guermantes would refer to the Dreyfus case, " 'which has been responsible for so many disasters,' albeit he was really conscious of one and one only; his own failure to become president of the Jockey [Club]."

The **Invalides** is the tomb of Napoléon I, to which the government invites the Princesse Mathilde, his niece, to welcome the visiting Czar Nicholas of Russia. She sends the card back, saying that she needs no invitation to go to the Invalides, since her place in the crypt, next to the emperor, is reserved.

The pious Françoise has never been to the cathedral of **Notre-Dame**. "In all the years she had been living in Paris, Françoise had never had the curiosity to visit Notre-Dame. That was because Notre-Dame was part of Paris, a city in which her daily life unfolded, and in which, consequently, it was difficult for our old servant to place the object of her dreams."

From the **Gare Saint-Lazare**, the narrator takes the train for the resort of Balbec, where he spent the summers as a young man and where he meets Albertine, his next love after Gilberte. He enters "one of those vast, glass-roofed sheds . . . into which I must go to find the train for Balbec, and which extended over the rent bowels of the city one of those bleak and boundless skies, heavy with an accumulation of dramatic menaces, like certain skies painted with an almost Parisian modernity by Mantegna or Veronese, beneath which could be accomplished only some solemn and tremendous act, such as a departure by train or the Elevation of the Cross."

Before her marriage, Odette has a small house on the **rue La Pérouse**. Swann is courting her, and the mere mention of the street is enough to start his heart fluttering. In a conversation with an army general Swann says: " 'Some fine lives have been lost . . . There was, you remember, that explorer whose remains Dumont d'Urville brought back, La Pérouse . . .' (and he was at once happy again, as though he had named Odette). . . .

" 'Oh, yes, of course, La Pérouse,' said the General. . . . 'There's a street called that.'

" 'Do you know anyone in the rue La Pérouse?' asked Swann excitedly.

" 'Only Mme. de Chanlivault, the sister of that good fellow Chaussepierre. . . .'

" 'Oh, so she lives in the rue La Pérouse. It's attractive; I like that street; it's so sombre.'

" 'Indeed it isn't. You can't have been in it for a long time; it's not at all sombre now; they're beginning to build all round there.' "

The narrator remarks on people "who look like their neighborhood, who carried on their persons the reflections of the rue de l'Arcade, or the avenue du Bois, or the rue de l'Élysée." The passing reference to the **rue de l'Arcade** is particularly interesting, for the male brothel that the Baron de Charlus frequents was based on Proust's experience in a similar establishment at 11 rue de l'Arcade, run by a former footman, Albert le Cuziat. Proust here is indulging his habit of dropping veiled hints about his secret aberrations. It was in Le Cuziat's brothel that young men posing as butchers' apprentices were brought for Proust, and that he watched rats being tortured. These activities are implicit in the innocent-appearing reference to the rue de l'Arcade.

The **rue Saint-Augustin** is a reminder of the Baron de Charlus's complaint that Jews live in streets bearing saints' names, which he considers a sacrilege. He suggests they ought to live in a street "which is entirely conceded to the Jews, there are Hebrew characters over the shops, bakeries for unleavened bread, kosher butcheries, it is positively the Judengasse of Paris."

The **rue de Rivoli** is the street of the Louvre. The Duchesse de Guermantes visits the museum to see Manet's *Olympia,* and comments: "Nowadays nobody is in the least surprised by it. It looks just like an Ingres! And yet, heaven only knows how many spears I've had to break for that picture, which I don't altogether like but which is unquestionably the work of *somebody.*"

The narrator sees the **Eiffel Tower** covered with searchlights, lit over wartime Paris in 1914 to detect German planes.

The **rue de Varenne** is where the Prince and Princesse de Guermantes live, until they move to a new mansion on the **avenue du Bois**, today's avenue Foch.

To the **Orangerie**, in the Tuileries gardens, the writer Bergotte, suffering from an attack of uremia, goes to see Vermeer's *Street in Delft,* on loan from The Hague Museum. A critic has written that a fragment of yellow wall in the painting could be considered a thing of perfect beauty, and against the advice of doctors, Bergotte goes out to see this fragment. "His giddiness increased; he fixed his eyes, like a child upon a yellow butterfly . . . upon the precious little patch of wall. 'That is how I ought to have written. . . . My last books are too dry, I ought to have gone over them with several coats of paint, made my language exquisite in itself, like this little patch of yellow wall.' . . . he sank down upon a circular divan . . . he rolled from the divan to the floor, as visitors and attendants came hurrying to his assistance. He was dead."

This scene parallels one in Proust's life. Although mortally ill, Proust left his apartment for the last time, on the arm of his friend Jean-Louis Vaudoyer, to see this very Vermeer painting, which he considered "the most beautiful in the world." The exhibit opened in May 1921. Proust died in November of the following year after finishing *Remembrance of Things Past*.

G. Y. Dryansky

Gerald Dryansky may not be a writer whose name is known in every household, but for readers of *Condé Nast Traveler* his name is very well known indeed. Dryansky has been writing for *Traveler* since, I think, its inception in 1987, and I have long admired his well-written and thought-provoking pieces. I regret I was unable to include one of the very best articles ever written about Paris here, but I urge readers to go online to search for the article, which appeared in February 2003: "The Secret Life of Paris," by Gerald Dryansky and with photos by William Abranowicz (one of my favorite photographers). Among a number of perceptive passages in his piece is this one: "There is something special in the material beauty of a city whose contribution to civilization is not so much vistas and monuments as it is the local approach to a civilized life. To understand Paris, you have to start with Parisians." Dryansky's daughter Larisa has also written for *Condé Nast Traveler,* and one of her articles, "The Villages of Paris" (February 1995), is also one of my favorites. It focuses particularly on the neighborhoods of Auteuil, Montsouris, Passy, Plaisance, Butte-aux-Cailles, Rhin-et-Danube, Batignolles, Charonne, Belleville, Ménilmontant, La Goutte-d'Or, and Montmartre.

In my correspondence with Gerald, he mentioned in passing that one of his *Traveler* pieces *he* likes best is "True Glitz," about Monte Carlo (May 2007). In addition, he and his wife, Joanne, are the coauthors of *Fatima's Good Fortune* (Hyperion, 2003), a novel set in Paris.

We'll Always Have . . . Questions

ANN BURACK-WEISS

I LAUGHED OUT loud when I read this piece, especially when I got to the part about the handheld shower head. I, too, have never understood what, if any, logic there is in this device. If the shower stall has a built-in bench, you can sit down, which is easier and makes some sense, but most of the time there is no bench—and often there is no shower door or curtain, so the water goes all over the floor, the walls, the sink, everywhere.

ANN BURACK-WEISS, who claims to have never progressed beyond high school French, is also the author of *The Caregiver's Tale: Loss and Renewal in Memoirs of Family Life* (Columbia University Press, 2006). This piece originally appeared as the back-page essay in the travel section of the *New York Times* in 1996.

THE JOHN TRAVOLTA character in *Pulp Fiction* had it right about Paris—things there are the same as here, "just a *little* bit different." His interest was piqued by the McDonald's special (a quarter-pounder transformed by the metric system and nostalgia for the monarchy into The Royal). Having just returned from a month in France, I share his quotidian observations. Mine, however, are awash in puzzlement. Would a French person take pity on me and answer the following:

Do you really save money on those timers?

Paris was probably dubbed the City of Light in irony—by a victim of the timer (aptly called a *minuterie*) that is attached to many lights in hallways and bathrooms. I picture this person midway up a winding staircase, or perhaps otherwise involved in a sealed six-by-six room, when the light clicked off. The French have combined their twin passions for privacy and frugality into the diabolical construction of Les Toilettes. The stall has a floor-to-ceiling door and a light that invites you to enter and fasten the intricate lock before the light suddenly turns off, leaving you to grope through a succession of awkward acts in total darkness.

Do you carry flashlights? Candles?

Doesn't it get expensive plastering up those holes in the wall?

Is there an expression for "penny wise and pound foolish" in French?

What do you do with the shower head while you soap and shampoo?

The French had to invent the shower *à deux,* not for its romantic possibilities but as a practical solution to an enduring national problem—the handheld shower. Alas, a shower partner is not always available. I have mastered the trick of never getting between the handheld shower and the wall in the curtainless tub. I accept that I will be standing in a foot of water, as tubs are short and deep and drains take their time. But I still don't know what to do with the shower head when I need both hands.

Do you hold it between your teeth? Under your neck?

Do you have special knee-toning exercises at the gym to work up your grasping strength?

Are you free mornings at seven?

Is attendance at scarf-tying classes mandatory in the public schools?

Every woman in France, nymphet to granny, wears a scarf. Squares, tiny and huge. Streamers, thick and thin. Silk, polyester, chiffon, wool—with everything from jeans to gowns—all tied with insouciant elegance. Not for them our continuous instructional videos at the scarf counter illustrating three obvious maneuvers: the shoulder triangle, the twice around the neck, and the sailor's knot. They intertwine two or more long scarves, they drape lightly and tightly, sling high and low. They wear scarves as hats, as belts, as hair bows. The men have only one style. And it is grand—very long, very trailing, very sexy.

Do you take off your scarves when you get home or do you keep them on till bedtime?

Are there any French people who just can't get the hang of it?

Are you free mornings at eight?

Is la caisse *a cultural icon?*

I am in a department store and see a soap dish that I like. I have the one hundred francs right here, the package will fit into my knapsack, and on to dinner—not. The salesclerk takes the dish from my hand and gives me a piece of paper. With it I go to the opposite end of the floor and wait as the empty-handed shoppers ahead of me converse earnestly and at length with La Caisse. The French are not a superficial people. Several modes of payment are possible and the meanings attendant to each must be explored. Payment concluded, claim ticket in hand, I cross the floor once again to the bath accessories department and these possibilities: the clerk who holds the dish is nowhere to be found, the clerk who holds the dish has never seen me before in her life and can't imagine what dish I'm talking about, the clerk who holds the dish remembers everything but where she put it. *Pas de problème,* here is another just like it. Well, almost—it is a bit larger and twenty francs more. A notation on the chit, another trip to La Caisse, a return to her and . . . *voilà,* the soap dish is mine.

Is this why the French dine late?

Are the motionless people in cafés recuperating from shopping expeditions?

How do you say "efficiency expert" in French?

Were the coquilles Saint-Jacques *that Alice and Brad Hinkel of Des Moines enjoyed at Chez Claude (and asked* Gourmet *to get the recipe for) in fact . . . frozen?*

Don't deny that it is possible. The evidence is, as with Poe's

purloined letter, hidden in plain sight—260 Picard stores full of frozen food lining the streets of France. Oh, they are wily. They have named the stores Les Surgelés—one glance through the window at the white-clad salespeople and low, long cases that you can't see into enhances the uneasy feeling that medical implements that you'd rather not think about are on sale there. Chef Claude may well have studied with Paul Bocuse—but don't tell me that when he has one of those nonstop days, he doesn't sneak into Picard for everything from *soupe* to *noix*. When the guests, ravenous from museum walking, rush in asking, "What's for dinner?" he puts on his signature touch, a tomato rose, and produces the plate with a flourish. When they heap praises upon him, he stifles a knowing smile and thinks, "Just the way *I'd* do it myself, if I had the time."

Can a dish consisting of potato noodles, cheese, and ham (*gnocchi-jambon-fromage*) really be Weight Watchers?

What's the *real* story behind Croque Monsieur and Croque Madame?

Have you ever eaten a bad meal?

Can I come and live with you?

Your age, gender, and appearance are, as they say in the personals, not important. Oh, French person, I want to live your life. I want to walk kilometer upon kilometer every day—single file down narrow, curving streets and six abreast on large boulevards. I want to pay three dollars for a tablespoon of coffee with a chocolate wafer on the side. I want to order a *tartine avec confiture* (bread and jam) at a different café every morning and notice how the bread is always a different length and consistency, the butter thick or thin, salted or sweet, the jam apricot or strawberry, already spread on or in a dish to the side, the price never twice the same. I want to pay confidently with money I no longer have to put on my glasses to check the denomination of. I want to shop where the bottle with the red cap is whole milk and the bottle with the blue cap is double *crème*. I want to go to a dry cleaner who calls a suit a costume and returns the pants done up in gift-wrapping paper. I want to eat yogurt that sometimes tastes like sour cream and sometimes like sweet cream and is filled with fruits like rhubarb and figs. I want to stand in line for an ice cream cone where each scoop comes nestled in its own compartment.

I want to live where sitting is an activity that people get dressed up and go outside to do. I want to live where people who smoke don't cough and people who eat fat aren't fat and everyone looks as if they have secrets. I want to buy pierced earrings with those nifty European clasps.

I want to put my hand in my pocket and come up with a fistful of Métro stubs that were not required to leave the station last week and shuffle through them until I come up with the one needed for my release today. I want to stand midpoint on any bridge at any time of day, and store the sensations in every pore.

RECOMMENDED READING

As Terrance Gelenter notes on his Web site Paris Through Expatriate Eyes (paris-expat.com), "If Helen of Troy was the face that launched a thousand ships, then Paris is the city that launched tens of thousands of books." Believe it or not, this list was edited—there are some (very good) titles I decided to save for my blog—but it simply isn't possible for me to shorten this list of recommendations any further.

Living in Paris, José Alvarez with photography by Christian Sarramon and Nicolas Bruant (Flammarion, 2006). Originally published in French as *L'Art de vivre à Paris,* this is one of those rare coffee-table books that is filled with great photos *and* substantive text. It's one of my very favorite books, and the eighteen-page visitor's guide at the back of the book is excellent.

Paris, Julian Green (Marion Boyars, 2000). A wonderful, brilliant little book printed in both French (on the left-hand pages) and English (on the right-hand pages). Green (his first name is usually spelled Julien) was born in Paris in 1900 and died there in 1998, and he left only during World War II. He thus knew the city more intimately and far longer than many others. This is his very personal love poem to Paris, which begins with an inviting opening line: "I have often dreamed of writing a book about Paris that would be like one of those lazy, aimless strolls on which you find none of the things you are looking for but many that you were not looking for." Having the French text side by side with the English presents a unique language-learning opportunity. Twenty-four of Green's own black-and-white photos are included.

Paris: The Biography of a City, Colin Jones (Viking, 2005). In his introduction, Jones notes that one Piganiol de la Force, author of an early visitor's guide in 1765, stated that "one would be very wrong if, seeing the vast number of books devoted to the history of Paris . . . one imagined that there was nothing more to be said." The vast number of books about Paris is indeed staggering, but Jones sets out to encompass the city's history in a single volume anyway, what he refers to as an "impossible" history of Paris. He's done quite an admirable job—though, at nearly five hundred pages, this is not for the casual reader—and he hopes that, for all its omissions, the book "will contain enough of interest to manage a *Michelin Guide* recommendation: *vaut le détour.*" I think it is a worthy detour indeed.

Paris Inside Out: The Insider's Handbook to Life in Paris, David Applefield (Globe Pequot, 2005). Applefield arrived in Paris in 1978 "at the Gare du Nord in the somber grayness of a typical Parisian October," and he's still there. This is a guide geared mostly for those who plan to live in Paris, but I find it very useful even for visitors who simply want to know Paris on a deeper level. "The Author's Credo for Survival in Paris" is of value to both short- and long-term visitors, as are a great number of other topics.

Paris *en poche* (in your pocket)

An entertaining and ridiculously fun book to bring along is *Paris Quiz: How Well Do You Know Paris?* by Dominique Lesbros (Little Bookroom, 2009). With four hundred "provocative, curious, and humorous questions" about Paris arranged from the first through twentieth arrondissements, this little paperback (it fits in a pocket or small handbag) is not only interesting but perfect for those times when you might be waiting for a train or a subway, or just have some time to kill. I find the questions incredibly addictive, and even those who think they know a lot about Paris may be surprised.

Paris: Buildings and Monuments, Michel Poisson (Harry N. Abrams, 1998). This (heavy) hardcover is not one to bring along, but is very much worth reading before you go. Architect Poisson guides readers on a personal tour of 535 buildings and monuments in every arrondissement. There are no photographs but rather line drawings and hand-drawn maps that can be useful for arranging one's own walking tour. Poisson has included a number of buildings that don't appear in most other books and he has provided an illustrated index of Paris architects.

Paris Web sites

Some sites about Paris that I regularly browse include:

Bonjour Paris (bonjourparis.com), run by American expat Karen Fawcett. Regular subscribers receive a complimentary weekly missive, but only with a paid premium subscription do users have access to all the articles on the site (see more details in the Miscellany).

Paris Through Expatriate Eyes (paris-expat.com), created by "Anglophonic, Francophonic Francophiliac" Terrance Gelenter. The site not only includes a great list of recommended reading, but also includes information on Gelenter's travel-planning service and airport transfers, insider tours, restaurant reservations, etc. *And* he offers several apartment rentals that look terrific. As author Pete Hamill has said, "If you believe that Paris is the most beautiful city in the world . . . if you want to better understand the mysteries of the Parisian character, then Paris Through Expatriate Eyes is the place to be." Subscribers receive a biweekly newsletter, The Paris Insider, and for twenty euros you can be a prestige member and receive a number of benefits. Gelenter is also the author of *Paris par Hasard: From Bagels to Brioche,* which I've not yet read but am looking forward to. He also organizes swell gatherings in Paris—one of these days I will make it to one of them.

Secrets of Paris (secretsofparis.com), maintained by Heather Stimmler-Hall, who has written for a number of periodicals and travel guides (*Fodor's, Michelin, Time Out,* etc.). She is also the author of a nifty guide called *Naughty Paris: A Lady's Guide to the Sexy City* (Fleur de Lire, 2008). Hall has been writing a Secrets of Paris newsletter since 2001, and she covers a wide variety of topics for first-time and repeat visitors. She is also available as a tour guide for half- and full-day tours, and plans customized itineraries and self-guided tours.

Paris: History, Architecture, Art, Lifestyle, in Detail, edited by Gilles Plazy (Flammarion, 2003). "The ambition of this book is to prepare you for Paris, to remind you of the city when you reluctantly return home, or to console you if a journey to the City of Light proves an impossible dream." That passage, from the foreword, accurately describes this very large, heavy (about eight pounds!), and gorgeous book. I positively love it, mostly because it's so big that I feel it goes on forever. Each time I open it I discover there is so much I haven't seen previously.

This book is heavy enough to *be* a coffee table, but it is a very worthy (coffee-table) book indeed, and I do believe it is worth the price (list price about $95) for those who are insanely passionate about Paris. With contributions by eight writers and hundreds of color and black-and-white photographs and reproductions, this is a true tour de force.

Paris to the Moon, Adam Gopnik (Random House, 2000). I have my own story about when this wonderful book of Gopnik's "Paris Journal" columns from the *New Yorker* was still a manuscript: I was working on the first edition of this book and I had earmarked two of Gopnik's columns for inclusion. These were "The Rules of the Sport"—a hilarious account of the time Gopnik tried to join a Parisian gym—and "Papon's Paper Trail," about the 1998 trial of Maurice Papon, who was charged with complicity in crimes against humanity during the German occupation of France in World War II. (The trial was, according to Gopnik, "the longest, the most discouraging, the most moving, at times the most ridiculous, and certainly the most fraught trial in postwar French history"—all reasons why I wanted to include the piece.) Through a permissions representative, I learned that Gopnik had in fact included both of these pieces in his manuscript, and he felt that since our books would be appearing at approximately the same time, it wouldn't be appropriate for me to include them. I was disappointed, but also reassured that I had chosen well!

Paris Traditions (Watson-Guptill, 1999). This lavishly illustrated hardcover features contributions by eight writers on architecture, art, fashion, festivals, food and drink, music, sports, and stage and film. The photographs and illustrations are really wonderful and I find this book to be great for whetting one's appetite for Paris. A four-page directory of addresses appears at the back of the book.

Paris: Wish You Were Here!, edited by Christopher Measom (Welcome Books, 2008). This chunky, hugely appealing book is organized by arrondissement, and sandwiched in between sections are excerpts from works by Mark Twain, Anita Loos, Ernest Hemingway, Ben Franklin, David Sedaris, Ludwig Bemelmans, and more; song lyrics; notes on *les Américains à Paris* (Charles Lindbergh, Josephine Baker, Mary Cassatt, etc.); recommendations for historic monuments, places to eat, and cultural offerings; and wonderful illustrations, reproductions, and photographs in black and white and color. Measom's own first trip to Paris was when he was a student in Spain, where it was so hot and dry that by November he had running water only a few hours day. When he got to Paris, it was overcast, cool, and there was plenty of running water, and he's been smitten with the city ever since. This is a great book to give as a gift if you could ever part with it.

Quiet Corners of Paris, Jean-Christophe Napias with photographs by Christophe Lefébure (Little Bookroom, 2007). This wonderful little gem of a book will ensure you see many of the lesser-known corners of Paris, including parks, gardens, squares, villas, cul-de-sacs, *places, rues,* backstreets, *passages,* art galleries, hills, *buttes,* cloisters, courtyards, churches, cemeteries, museums, international cultural centers, and libraries. Plus there's one *hôtel,* the Hôtel des Grandes Écoles (75 rue du Cardinal-Lemoine, 5ème), which is also one that I recommend. The author informs us that this book's job is "to lead questers to the city's magical islands—famous or unknown— where their thirst for silent escapes can be slaked." It positively succeeds. Just a few *coins* (corners) this book led me to are the Jardin Saint-Gilles-Grand-Veneur (3ème), Butte-aux-Cailles (13ème), Square d'Orléans (9ème), and Square Récamier (7ème).

Remembrance of Things Paris: Sixty Years of Writing from Gourmet, edited and with an introduction by Ruth Reichl (Modern Library, 2004). For those readers who are clippers (like me), you will want to read this terrific anthology even if you already have most of the original articles from *Gourmet* in your files (as I do). As Reichl notes in the introduction, "For a true gourmet in the first few decades of the twentieth century, Paris was the heart's home, the place that mattered, a shrine for everyone who believed that eating well was the best revenge. It was where Hemingway's

Moveable Feast took place, where Liebling spent his time *Between Meals,* where M. F. K. Fisher's *Gastronomical Me* was born." But *Gourmet* was founded in 1941, when Paris was impossible to visit, so it took a few years for Paris to be properly featured in its pages. The book is divided into ten sections—including "Remembering Paris," "Feeding a City," "Americans in Paris," and "The Bistro Scene"—and some of my favorite articles ever written about the city are here: "Paris in the Twenties" by Irene Corbally Kuhn; "The Old Flower Market" by Joseph Wechsberg; "Noël à Paris" by Judith and Evan Jones; "It's What's for Dinner" by François Simon; and *all* the pieces by Naomi Barry (there are ten here). This book, like the magazine I very much miss, reminds us that food is linked in so many ways to place; in reading about one you also learn a lot about the other.

Seven Ages of Paris, Alistair Horne (Knopf, 2002). In his foreword, Maurice Druon, of the Académie Française, writes that "Horne is everywhere and knows everything. . . . Nothing escapes his paintbrush"—which indeed appears to be true when reading this magnificent book. Druon also calls the book "in itself, a monument," an endorsement with which I wholeheartedly agree. Horne explains in the preface that in the course of working on nine previous books on French history over three decades, he kept a "discard box" of little details on Paris (as Churchill is said to have done during World War II), and that box became a scrapbook of sorts as well as the origin of this book. With inserts of photographs and reproductions, this is a *de rigueur* read.

The Locals' *Point de Vue*

"There is a world of difference between the Paris of tourism and Parisians' Paris," notes Bill Gillham in **Parisians' Paris** (Pallas Athene, 2008), which is a great book for *anyone* visiting Paris but especially so perhaps for repeat visitors, as Gillham has purposefully made only summary reference to the obvious sights. However, he does include such topics as making hotel reservations, bathrooms, special trips for children, and free concerts and classic films. He really does cover all the bases. He also wisely urges caution when reading articles that have titles like "Secret Paris" and "Hidden Paris." The Saint-Germain quarter, for example, "is the most intensively scrutinized sector of Paris. Even outside the main tourist areas, can anything have escaped the city's five or six million visitors a month and those who write guides for them? The answer is that Paris is always changing, at the same time always contriving to remain the same. The cliché is right: the process of getting to know the city is never finished. And so the first-time visitor is only to a degree at a disadvantage, as guide writers driven by the demon of updating know to their cost."

A Parisian's Paris by Philippe Meyer (Flammarion, 1999) is, despite the similar title, not a guidebook but a "wish" for anyone who picks it up to decide to visit Paris in what he refers to as the "fifth season," known as *la rentrée,* the time of year at the end of summer when Parisians return home from wherever they've been for the month of August. *La rentrée,* as Meyer defines it for this book, exists only in Paris; it lasts for an unpredictable length of time—he's witnessed it for a full ten days or for a mere forty-eight hours—and it ends without warning. It's identified by subtle, unexpected changes, such as: "If someone runs toward a bus stop just as the bus is leaving, the driver waits and reopens the door." It is a time when Parisians "reclaim possession and awareness of their city, once again struck by a beauty they had managed to overlook, by the realization that Paris is still a miracle. Filled with pleasure and pride, Parisians delight in sharing their contentment. They know full well they couldn't live anywhere else. That's the time to visit the capital, because it's the one moment when Paris and the Parisians show themselves at their best." Meyer, a well-known radio commentator, presents an urban chronicle that is critical, affectionate, and revealing.

A Traveller's History of Paris, Robert Cole (Interlink, 1998). This edition is one in a great series for which I have much enthusiasm. It's a mini "what you should know" guide that's small enough and light enough to carry around every day, and every edition in the series highlights the significant events and people with which all visitors should be familiar.

Vie et Histoire

I first read about the *Vie et Histoire* series—a twenty-volume encyclopedia about the city of Paris, one volume for each arrondissement—in *Travelers' Tales Guides: Paris.* I've been slowly collecting the volumes over the years—though I'm still missing the seventh arrondissement, which is the one I most covet—and I hope I'm fortunate enough to acquire them all. These hardcover books, all in print in French (so it takes me a while to read them, dictionary in hand), each include these categories: *histoire, anecdotes, célébrités, curiosités, monuments, musées, promenades, jardins, dictionnaire des rues,* and *vie pratique.* Each is filled with color and black-and-white illustrations, reproductions, and photographs.

A Writer's Paris: A Guided Journey for the Creative Soul, Eric Maisel (Writer's Digest, 2005). "You feel at home in Paris," writes Maisel, "because the things that you care about—strolling, thinking, loving, creating—are built into the fabric of the city. Despite its negatives—eighteen million tourists annually, eleven percent unemployment, large numbers of homeless people—Paris remains the place where you can feel comfortable decked out as a dreamy artist." This little book is not for everyone—Maisel really has written it for writers, notably those who plot to go to Paris to write—but there are nonetheless wonderful passages in it that would appeal to anyone with a smidgen of creativity and a deep devotion to the City of Light.

Janet Flanner

Readers of my first Paris edition may recall that I included an obituary of Janet Flanner that appeared in the *New Yorker*. Flanner—who wrote under the *nom de correspondance* Genêt—wrote a regular "Letter from Paris" for the *New Yorker* from 1925 to 1975. Readers of the magazine before the 1990s know that it was a long-standing policy not to print bylines. Not until I requested permission to reprint the obituary did I learn it had been written by William Shawn, distinguished editor of the magazine for nearly forty years. Of Flanner, he wrote, "She loved the people of France among whom she lived so much of her life, and she loved no less the American people for whom she wrote," and "her estimates of people and events, her perceptions and illuminations, were rarely embarrassed by time."

I love all of Flanner's books, which include *Janet Flanner's World: Uncollected Writings, 1932–1975* (1979), *Paris Journal, 1944–1965* (1977), and *Paris Was Yesterday, 1925–1939* (1972), all published by Harcourt. These collections are for both those of us old enough to remember her missives and young Francophiles about to discover her. We are most fortunate, not only as readers but as human beings, to have such a vast and perceptive record of Parisian life and times. She was *there* for much of the twentieth century's momentous events.

Equally interesting is Flanner's personal life. In *Janet, My Mother, and Me: A Memoir of Growing Up with Janet Flanner and Natalia Danesi Murray* (Simon & Schuster, 2000), William Murray explains how his mother, Natalia, met Flanner—at a cocktail party given by Natalia in 1940 at her apartment on East Forty-ninth Street in Manhattan. The encounter, Murray relates, was a *coup de foudre.* His account illustrates what life was like for him growing up with these women in New York and Rome. Murray's book is fascinating on several levels—we learn about his own career at the *New Yorker,* where he was a staff writer for thirty-three years—but it is perhaps most valuable in its portrayal of what it was like for gay professional women during a time when it was not accepted. In the introduction to *Darlinghissima,* a book of letters between the two, Natalia writes, "I hope that my grandchildren, and other young women like them, born in a freer, more liberated society, more knowledgeable about relationships between the sexes and without the inhibitions or taboos of an earlier era, will understand and value our experiences and efforts to be, above all, decent human beings."

PARIS MEMOIRS

It's a toss-up if there are more memoirs written of Paris, Provence, or Tuscany, which is to say there are an awful lot about each of these hugely appealing destinations. It's hard for me to pass up reading a Paris memoir, so, yes, I've read all of these, and can report that each is unique and worthwhile. I think you'll agree that any one (or five) is an enjoyable read.

Almost French: Love and a New Life in Paris, Sarah Turnbull (Gotham, 2003). "Like an Aussie backpacker in need of a bath, probably," is how Turnbull describes her appearance when she meets Frédéric, her French boyfriend, at Charles de Gaulle airport. "I'm not the sort of girl who crosses continents to meet up with a man she hardly knows," she reveals, yet there she is, indeed meeting up with a Frenchman she's only conversed with for approximately forty-five minutes. Thus begins this wonderful love story and memoir, in which you find yourself cheering for Turnbull at every step of her sometimes rough way. One aspect I especially like is that she shares a great number of French phrases that are quite useful: instead of ordering a *verre de vin* (glass of wine) at a café or restaurant, ask for a *coup de pif* (which she says is slang and untranslatable)—I did the last time I was in Paris and I just *know* the raised eyebrows of the waiter signified he was surprised I knew such a phrase.

C'est la Vie, Suzy Gershman (Viking, 2004). "I always knew that one day I would live in France," Gershman writes on the first page of her memoir. "This was not a dream on my part, but a fact of life, not whispered in the winds of chance, but firmly written on the mistral of my life." She had me right away with that, but she sealed it when she further explained that when she heard Billy Joel sing, "Vienna waits for you," she knew exactly what he meant: Paris was her Vienna, and it was waiting for her. Trite as that may sound, I was completely on board—I identify enormously with song lyrics. Without giving away the details, the stage of Gershman's life that is the subject of this book is sad, funny, and uplifting all at once, which is reason enough to read it. But she also reveals a lot of details about French traditions and daily life in Paris. One custom is the *crémaillère,* a party to show off a new home. The word derives from the expression *pendre la crémaillère*—to hang the saucepan on a hook over the fire. At the time the expression was coined, people cooked only on open fires, so when the saucepan was hung the house was ready. Today, in their version of a housewarming, "French people [invite] all their friends for the *crémaillère,* given as soon as the new home is set up and functioning—usually at a point just under one year after arrival."

French Lessons, Alice Kaplan (University of Chicago Press, 1993). This well-written book was selected as a Notable Book of 1993 by the *New York Times Book Review* and was a National Book Critics Circle Award nominee. It's an unusual memoir and an insightful work about language. I love the way she writes about learning and teaching French, her French summer camp in 1968, where if you were caught speaking one word of English you got a *mauvais point,* and her love affair with André on her junior year abroad. I also found her research on French fascist intellectuals—and her interview with the only one still living at the time, Maurice Bardèche (who has since passed away)—fascinating and unsettling.

I'll Always Have Paris!, Art Buchwald (Putnam, 1996). I fully expected this memoir to be funny (it was), but I was unprepared for it also to be a bit sad. I should explain: I am the sort of person who still gets choked up when the Tin Man tells Dorothy his heart is breaking at the end of *The Wizard of Oz,* so you may not get as teary-eyed as I did when reading about Buchwald's wife, Ann, who passed away before this book was published. She is present on nearly every page even when she's not part of the narrative. But it's hard for anyone not to laugh at Buchwald's press-junket adventures with the *International Herald Tribune* and the VIPs he meets over the years. Very entertaining, with eight pages of black-and-white photos.

A Girl in Paris: A Persian Encounter with the West, Shusha Guppy (Tauris Parke, 2007). In his preface, Philip Mansel, author of one of my favorite books (*Constantinople: City of the World's Desire, 1453–1924*), writes that "if there was one area of the world for which Paris, France and the French language possessed particular magnetism, it was the Middle East. In the Ottoman Empire in the 1830s, French became the second language of the governing classes. By the 1850s an Ottoman poet could write: 'Go to Paris, young sir, if you have any wish; if you have not been to Paris, you have not come into the world.' " Guppy, born in Iran and now London editor of the *Paris Review,* arrived in Paris in the 1950s at age seventeen to attend the Sorbonne. I love her personal story of living "on the top floor of a seven-story building" on the Left Bank as well as hearing about Paris shortly after World War II. But most of all I love how she writes about exile, weaving Persian memories and vignettes into her French experience.

A Homemade Life: Stories and Recipes from my Kitchen Table, Molly Wizenberg (Simon & Schuster, 2009). The title of this wonderful, wonderful book does not give any clue that it has to do with Paris, and certainly when I picked it up I had no idea that the word "Paris" would appear in it even once. But it turns out that Paris is a very special city for Wizenberg, as she has spent lengths of time there over the years, studying, living, visiting, and eating. She lived in the eleventh arrondissement after college, in a "petite piece of paradise," and in that year she learned she loved to cook. Wizenberg says that the only reason she travels is for an excuse to eat more than usual. "I couldn't tell you what the inside of Notre-Dame looks like, but I do know how to get from the greengrocer on rue Oberkampf, the one with the green awning, to that terrific *fromagerie* way down in the seventh, near Le Bon Marché." Though she clearly has a sense of humor, it's not humor that sustains this book. Wizenberg cares deeply about food—browse her blog (orangette.blogspot.com) and read her monthly column in *Bon Appétit*—but also about family. When she tells the story of her father dying and I got teary-eyed (on the train, no less), I was crying not only because I was thinking of my own wonderful father (who also has passed away) but because I truly cared about Molly and what happened in her life. She has a winning way of drawing people to her, and when you finish the book you feel like you could pick up the phone and call her. She shares a number of recipes at the end of each chapter, which are among the very few that have appeared in a book like this and that I actually tried—with super results. I don't believe I will spoil anyone's pleasure in reading this book by sharing some lines from the final chapter. What life comes down to, Wizenberg says, is winning hearts and minds. "Underneath everything else, all the plans and goals and hopes, that's why we get up in the morning, why we believe, why we try, why we bake chocolate cakes. That's the best we can ever hope to do: to win hearts and minds, to love and be loved." *Read this book!*

Immoveable Feast: A Paris Christmas (2008) and *We'll Always Have Paris: Sex and Love in the City of Light* (2006), both by John Baxter and published by Harper Perennial. Of these two, I enjoyed *Immoveable Feast* best, and not only because I learned that Baxter had been a visiting professor at my alma mater, Hollins College (now University), in 1974. He writes that Hemingway meant the title of his famous book (*A Moveable Feast*) to allude to periods in the Christian calendar—notably Lent and Pentecost—that change their dates depending on when Easter falls. Similarly, as Baxter explains, there is more than one "right" time to discover Paris. "Its pleasures can be relished at any moment in one's life. But the phrase is subject to another interpretation. At certain times of year, the spirit of Paris moves elsewhere. Its soul migrates, and this most beautiful of cities briefly falls empty." The two times of year when this happens are during the month of August and at Christmas. Baxter, who is married to a French woman, delightfully and humorously recounts a Christmas meal he made for his French family while revealing much about French customs and traditions.

Lunch in Paris: A Love Story, with Recipes, Elizabeth Bard (Little, Brown, 2010). I was prepared to *like* this book but was surprised to really *love* it. From the first few pages, I felt Bard could also have been describing me. I felt a kindred spirit when I read, "Wherever I've been in the world, museums have been my second homes," and "When the age for dress-up was over, I immersed myself in novels, diving into other peoples' imaginary worlds. The streets of Dickens's London were much easier for me to get my head around than fractions." But when she admits to despising mayonnaise, I knew I'd practically met my twin (for the record, we're talking supermarket mayonnaise, not the homemade variety). Gwendal, the love in Bard's life, is a dream of a boyfriend/husband. Without giving too much away, I'll just note that when he spruces up the apartment while Bard is away in New York, he immediately secured the top spot on my list of World's Best Husbands (knocking to second place Richard Dreyfus's character in *The Goodbye Girl* when he sets a dinner table for two on a New York rooftop). It is Bard herself, however, for whom we're cheering. She is in-

spiring, warm, funny, wise, and lucky, this last for figuring out sooner than most what truly matters in life. And her passage about the "promised land" in the conclusion is the best I've ever read about embracing the values that France offers while retaining the best ones from the U.S.A.

My Life in France, Julia Child with Alex Prud'homme (Knopf, 2006). In her introduction to this wonderful memoir, published not long after her death in 2004, Child describes the book as being "about some of the things I have loved most in life: my husband, Paul Child; *la belle France;* and the many pleasures of cooking and eating." It was a new experience for her, writing a series of linked autobiographical stories instead of a collection of recipes, and it focuses mostly on the years she lived in Paris and Marseille, 1948 through 1954. "Those early years in France were among the best in my life," she writes, and you can feel her excitement about being in Paris on the page. By now everyone knows that the movie *Julie & Julia* was based on this book and Julie Powell's book *Julie & Julia* (Little, Brown, 2005), which I enjoyed mostly because I loved that Powell was so inspired by Child to start her blog and work her way through *Mastering the Art of French Cooking.*

Paris in the Fifties, Stanley Karnow (Times Books, 1997). Before he was honored with a Pulitzer Prize for *In Our Image: America's Empire in the Philippines* and before the bestselling *Vietnam,* Karnow went to Paris in 1947 intending to stay for the sum-

mer. He stayed for ten years, landing a job as a foreign correspondent for *Time,* and happily for the rest of us he saved carbon copies of all his original dispatches, a revised selection of
which form the basis of this engaging look into a noteworthy
decade.

Paris Personal, Naomi Barry (Dutton, 1963). "Fortunately," Barry
writes in her introduction, "the story of I Love You has no
end. It can stand being retold over and over and over again.
Otherwise, I ask you, how could anyone dare to write still another book about Paris? So, with love as the excuse, I dared."
And thank God she did, even if it's now more than forty years
old. What is amazing is that a number of restaurants Barry
recommends are still with us—La Tour d'Argent, Prunier, La
Closerie des Lilas, Maxim's, Le Grand Vefour—as well as some
shops, antiques galleries, museums, etc. In his endorsement,
Art Buchwald writes, "Naomi Barry knows Paris better than
any American woman I know." Having had the supreme pleasure of meeting Barry on several occasions, I completely concur. I treasure this volume.

Paris: Places and Pleasures, Kate Simon (Capricorn Books, 1971).
There are few travel writers like Simon around anymore, so if
you run across a copy of this out-of-print volume, buy it without hesitation. "An Uncommon Guidebook" is how it's described on the cover, and indeed this is much more like a
memoir than a guidebook. Though there are recommendations for things to see and do, they aren't approached in a predictable fashion, and it's the essays—"How Come the Angry
Parisian?," "Est-ce Que Vous Parlez Anglais?," and "Parisian
Contours and Stances"—that really make the book worthwhile
and still apropos. Simon wisely notes that, with few exceptions,
every neighborhood in Paris has some treasure or other to
offer.

Paris Times Eight: Finding Myself in the City of Dreams, Deirdre Kelly (Greystone, 2009). Kelly's book is such a good read because she is truthful and self-deprecating and she has a passion for Paris that is utterly infectious. The "eight" in the title refers to eight life-changing and/or momentous visits to Paris, some of them made while on assignment for Toronto's *Globe and Mail,* where she still works as a reporter at large.

The People of Paris, Joseph Barry (Doubleday, 1966). Though many references in this book, by a former correspondent for the *New York Post,* are dated, it's still a good read, especially as a record of Paris just after World War II and in the 1950s and '60s. It is indeed the *people* that Barry focuses on, as they are what interest him most. "France is never more French than when it is universal," Barry writes. "When I am most exasperated with De Gaulle's nationalism, I think of the *beau geste* of this Frenchman. One of the big people? One of the little people? One of the people of Paris."

Petite Anglaise, Catherine Sanderson (Spiegel & Grau, 2008). The words "A True Story" appear at the bottom of this book's cover, which is probably wise as the book looks and reads like a novel. Englishwoman Sanderson was realizing a dream when she moved to Paris, though not far into her teaching stint she recognized that something was missing from her experience. "I was living alongside the French, not among them. Observing French life, but never truly living it. A hairbreadth away from fulfilling my dreams. And yet sometimes this tiny gap seemed so unbridgeable." But when she met a French man (Mr. Frog) at the Café Charbon and had a daughter with him (Tadpole), all this changed. She also started a blog (petiteanglaise.com), and her life changed again. Without revealing the rest of the story, I admit Sanderson's tale didn't end the way I wanted it to, but she didn't then, and doesn't now, ever want to leave Paris.

(Sanderson now also has a son, and I was happy to read that she has "moved on" and no longer feels the need to document every detail of her personal life on her blog.)

The Piano Shop on the Left Bank, Thad Carhart (Random House, 2001). The title of this gem of a book appealed to me immediately because I took piano lessons for seven years when I was young. But you don't have to know anything about pianos to love this memoir, inspired by a sign—DESFORGES PIANOS—on an ordinary storefront in Carhart's Paris neighborhood. The people Carhart introduces us to, and their relationships to music and to each other, tell another, little-known story of Paris.

Return to Paris, Colette Rossant (Atria, 2003). If you, like me, are a fan of Rossant's *Memories of a Lost Egypt* (Clarkson Potter, 1999) you will be predisposed to like this memoir as well. Rossant's own family story is of interest, but the Paris she returns to in 1947—she was born there but spent eight years in Cairo—is an interesting subject as well. Early in her life,

Rossant paid attention to food, and she shares a number of recipes here, some of which I've tried and liked. Rossant lives in New York now, but a large part of her will always be French.

The Sweet Life in Paris: Delicious Adventures in the World's Most Glorious—and Perplexing—City, David Lebovitz (Broadway, 2009). This book includes more than forty recipes as well as a directory of culinary *bonnes adresses,* making it useful and valuable, but it's also a great memoir of the years since Lebovitz, a dessert cookbook author and former pastry chef at Berkeley's Chez Panisse, moved to Paris. It's positively filled with insights, expressions, and new vocabulary words (my favorite: *les bousculeurs,* from the verb *bousculer,* meaning "to push abruptly in all directions" and referring to the habit Parisians have of cutting people off in line or walking on a sidewalk and expecting you to move out of their way; as Lebovitz notes, "they just refuse to be herded into straight lines"). I've made a handful of the recipes and they all turned out great; the real star was Spiced Nut Mix, which combines nuts with, among other ingredients, chili powder or smoked paprika (I used Spanish pimentón), maple syrup, cocoa powder, and pretzel twists, and it is *d-é-l-i-c-i-e-u-x.* Lebovitz also maintains an award-winning blog (davidlebovitz.com), which is a good resource for visitors to Paris—not only is it chock full of culinary recommendations, but he's compiled a great list of travel tips. (See page 306.)

A Town Like Paris: Falling in Love in the City of Light, Bryce Corbett (Broadway, 2007). When I first learned of this memoir, by a (then) twenty-eight-year-old Australian guy who'd been living and working in London before moving to Paris, I was inclined to dismiss it—I feared it would be little more than a Drinker's Guide to the City of Light. I'm glad I read it, because even though there are plenty of references to bars and drinking I am, after all, a wine-loving writer, and Corbett is a lovable man with whom I share a (perhaps) over-the-top infatuation with Paris. I found myself smiling—if not laughing out loud—at many passages, especially in the hilarious "Get 27" chapter, which refers to, usually, a not very popular mint liqueur available in French bars. Corbett and some friends form a motley band by the same name, Get 27, spoken *jet vingt-sept* in French, "a name that rolled easily off the tongue," and perform at a Marais bar called Le Connétable. Regardless of how many glasses of beer and wine you vicariously consume while reading the book, you find yourself completely agreeing with Corbett about the reasons he is in Paris in the first place, chief among them "because having a modest yet comfortable lifestyle is more important than acquiring and aspiring."

Paris en Photo

Of the many, many books filled with photographs of Paris, here is a selection of titles whose pages I never tire of turning:

À Propos de Paris, Henri Cartier-Bresson and with texts by Vera Feyder and André Pieyre de Mandiargues (Bulfinch, 1994). More than 130 black-and-white photos by a photographer whose name is virtually synonymous with Paris.

Métropolitain: A Portrait of Paris, Matthew Weinreb and Fiona Biddulph (Phaidon, 1994). I like this photography book because none of the images are typical; Weinreb has focused on the smallest details, which, he says, "are so often missed by the hurried walker in the street." The photo of the Institut du Monde Arabe is especially nice as the building is quite difficult for an amateur to capture on film, and the photo of Chagall's ceiling in the Opéra is magnificent—if you somehow miss seeing the real thing, this is a good consolation prize.

Paris (Assouline, 2004). I am crazy for Assouline's books, and this one, in its own slipcase, features good text with hundreds of photos.

Paris: 500 Photos, Maurice Subervie with a foreword by Bertrand Delanoë, (Flammarion, 2003). "How many people," Paris mayor Delanoë asks in his foreword, "during an aimless stroll through our city, have felt the urge to seize a color, an instant, a piece of the azure sky, or a fragment of the night?" An awful lot, surely, but there's no question that most of us cannot possibly capture that color, instant, or piece of sky as seductively as Subervie.

Paris: The City and Its Photographers, Patrick Deedes-Vincke (Bulfinch, 1992). A fascinating look at the history of photography and the role Paris played in its development, featuring the work of Lee Miller, Brassaï, Robert Capa, Cartier-Bresson, Robert Doisneau, and others. There are no photographs after 1968 because, as the author states, "with the student riots of that year and the ensuing disruption, and with the urban upheaval of the mid-1960s, came the end of an era."

Paris Vertical, Horst Hamann (teNeues, 2006). In order to photograph Paris vertically, Hamann notes, he had to rethink how he looked at things. "The visual challenge was not the search for the top, the vanishing points in the sky, but the inconspicuous, the details at eye level." Hamann's black-and-white photos are paired with great quotations in both French and English.

FICTION

For classics titles listed here, multiple editions are generally available.

Babylon Revisited, F. Scott Fitzgerald.

The Blessing, Nancy Mitford (Vintage, 2010).

Birdsong, Charlotte Gray, and *The Girl at the Lion d'Or,* a trilogy by Sebastian Faulks, available from Vintage.

The Book of Salt, Monique Truong (Mariner, 2003).

The Children's War, Monique Charlesworth (Knopf, 2004).

City of Darkness, City of Light: A Novel, Marge Piercy (Ballantine, 1996).

Claude & Camille: A Novel of Monet, Stephanie Cowell (Crown, 2010).

The Club Dumas, Arturo Pérez-Reverte (Harcourt, 1996).

Le Divorce (1997), *Le Mariage* (2000), *L'Affaire* (2003), all by Diane Johnson and published by Dutton.

Don't Tell Alfred, Nancy Mitford (Vintage, 2010).

Fields of Glory, Jean Rouaud (Arcade, 1992). This is a beautifully written, slender little novel that was awarded the 1990 Prix Goncourt for best work of fiction in France.

The Hunchback of Notre-Dame, Victor Hugo.

Is Paris Burning?, Larry Collins and Dominique Lapierre (Simon & Schuster, 1965).

Honoré de Balzac

Balzac (1799–1850) was the first novelist to place Paris at the heart of his fiction, and travelers have a number of Balzac novels from which to choose: *Cousine Bette, Eugénie Grandet, Old Goriot, Lost Illusions, The Unknown Masterpiece, The Wrong Side of Paris.*

Balzac's Paris: A Guided Tour (balzacsparis.ucr.edu) is an outstanding online resource that I stumbled upon while working on this manuscript. It's a promenade through the heart of Paris in the time of Balzac, described through some of his works and accompanied by maps and engravings, and it's wonderful. The site is composed of materials from the Vernon Duke Collection in the special collections department of the University of California Riverside library. Duke was the songwriter who composed "April in Paris," and his collection includes eight hundred books, rare maps, and other documents that present life and manners in Paris from the reign of Louis XVI to the end of the Belle Époque. To quote from the site, "One would have to go to the Musée Carnavalet in Paris to find a more comprehensive collection of original documents from this crucial time in the development of Paris."

Many of the Parisian scenes that feature in Balzac's novels take place along a route that's very popular with tourists today—from the Arc de Triomphe to the Concorde, the rue de Rivoli and Palais Royal, the Louvre, and on to the Île de la Cité and the Latin Quarter. This route was the scene, to quote Balzac, of the greatest "splendors" and "miseries" of Parisian life during his time.

Alan Furst

"Astonishingly," wrote Janet Maslin in the *New York Times* in 2000, "Alan Furst is not yet a household name." If you don't yet recognize his name, I urge you to read one of his very good thrillers (I doubt you will stop with just one), and if you *do* already know Furst's name, I know you will agree with Maslin's remark. I am not generally a reader of thrillers, and I even hesitate to refer to Furst's books as thrillers, because they're so much more—I prefer to think of them as espionage novels that are amazingly evocative and atmospheric. Paris is the backdrop, major or minor, in nearly all of his books. These include *The World at Night* (1996), *Red Gold* (1999), *The Polish Officer* (1995), *Dark Star* (1991), *Night Soldiers* (1988), *The Foreign Correspondent* (2006), and *The Spies of Warsaw* (2008), all currently available in Random House paperback editions. (*Spies of the Balkans*, published in 2010, is Furst's most recent book, though the action takes place in Greece.)

Furst told *New York Times* writer Rachel Donadio that after he wrote a few desultory novels, "I suddenly realized there could be such a thing as a historical spy novel . . . but I went looking to read one and I couldn't find one." So he set out to write one, and the result was *Night Soldiers.* In a 2008 interview with Charles McGrath, also at the *Times,* Furst explained that the Europe he describes so perfectly in his books is largely a place he carries around in his head and visits at will—he referred to it as being like teleportation. "The first time it happened," the piece reports, "was in the early '90s, when he was listening to a tape he had bought of Django Reinhardt and Stéphane Grappelli playing in Paris with the Hot Club of France in 1937." Furst said, "I went right there, to that nightclub in Paris, with war coming on, and the Spanish Civil War in the background, and the purges going on in Moscow. . . . I smelled the smoke, the cheap perfume. The whole thing just came to me, and I knew I wanted to put it in a novel."

Literary Paris, Jeffrey Kraft (Watson-Guptill, 1999). Though this book includes passages that are the author's own very real observations and opinions, the inspiration for it is wholly literary, which is why I have included it in this section. As Kraft states, "My choice of text is just that, my own. I am only a devoted student of French literature," and he has chosen choice lines from works by Apollinaire, Barthes, Baudelaire, Brillat-Savarin, Hugo, James, Joyce, Rimbaud, Saint-Exupéry, Sand, Stein, and Zola, just to name a few. Kraft's black-and-white photos are quite nice, and his literary selections steered me toward a few works I was eager to read in full. I like the way he describes Paris as characterized by both *grandeur* and *décadence* (decline), Balzac and Proust: "While we are there it is the city of Balzac . . . yet in memory Paris is Proustian, a gradual unfolding backward."

Mademoiselle Victorine, Debra Finerman (Three Rivers, 2007).

The Mark of the Angel, Nancy Huston (Vintage, 2000).

Mavis Gallant

Most of Gallant's short stories are set in Paris or are about Parisians, or both, and her characters and scenes are unforgettable. In my favorite, "Across the Bridge," Sylvie's mother turns her leather bag, filled with Sylvie and Arnaud's wedding invitations, upside down over the Seine—one of the most memorable short story images I've ever encountered. Other memorable stories are gathered in *The Collected Stories of Mavis Gallant* (1996) and *Overhead in a Balloon: Twelve Stories of Paris* (1987), both published by Random House. These volumes are out of print—though very much worth tracking down—but New York Review of Books Classics has recently published two great editions, *Paris Stories* (2002) and *The Cost of Living: Early and Uncollected Stories* (2009).

Ernest Hemingway

I will always remember how reading Hemingway made me feel when I was a student in Paris—I loved reading his books and I was bursting with happiness. Years later, I came across the following quote in an article in *Gourmet* by Gene Bourg, and was relieved that someone else had "got it" and set things straight: "In *A Moveable Feast* Hemingway postulated that once a man has been young and happy in Paris, he can never be truly happy again. Agreeing with him would be very dangerous indeed. But agreeing and understanding are entirely different things."

Over the years I went on to read just about everything Hemingway wrote, but it all began with *A Moveable Feast* and *The Sun Also Rises*. Both are set wholly or partly in Paris and both, I'm happy to say, are just as good in the rereading as they were thirty-two years ago.

Les Misérables, Victor Hugo.

The Moon and Sixpence, W. Somerset Maugham.

A Paris Hangover, Kirsten Lobe (St. Martin's, 2006).

Pictures at an Exhibition, Sara Houghteling (Knopf, 2009).

Sarah's Key, Tatiana de Rosnay (St. Martin's, 2007).

A Tale of Two Cities, Charles Dickens.

The Year Is '42, Nella Bielski (Pantheon, 2004).

Muriel Barbery

It was the title of Barbery's novel *The Elegance of the Hedgehog* (Europa, 2008) that got my attention first, and then when I read that Renée, one of the main characters, is the concierge of twenty-seven years at "number 7, rue de Grenelle, a fine *hôtel particulier* with a courtyard and private gardens," I was completely hooked. As a student *I* lived with a French family in a *hôtel particulier* also on the rue de Grenelle, also with a courtyard and private garden. The book turned out to be one of the best books I've ever read. Really. I have stuffed so many little papers in it to mark so many memorable and beautiful passages, like this one: "We have to live with the certainty that we'll get old and that it won't look nice or be good or feel happy. And tell ourselves that it's now that matters: to build something, now, at any price, using all our strength. Always remember that there's a retirement home waiting somewhere and so we have to surpass ourselves every day, make every day undying. Climb our own personal Everest and do it in such a way that every step is a little bit of eternity. That's what the future is for: to build the present, with real plans, made by living people."

Gourmet Rhapsody (Europa, 2009) is equally brilliant and unique, and takes place in the same building. The "greatest food critic in the world," Pierre Arthens, is dying, and his last wish is to identify a flavor that he can't remember. He knows that "this particular flavor is the first and ultimate truth of my entire life," and he knows that the flavor dates back to child-hood or adolescence, predating his vocation as a food critic. In alternating chapters we meet members of Arthens's family and others in the building, and after Arthens relates some of the best eating experiences of his life, we do finally learn the flavor he's searching for in the final chapter. (I didn't guess it, and I will only say that it comes as a bit of a surprise.)

Novel Ideas

"Novel Ideas" was the title of a March 2009 article written by David Burke in the (wonderful) former *Paris Notes* newsletter. In it, Burke—who moved to Paris in 1986 intending to stay for a year but has now been there twenty-five—shares a quote by Italian writer Leonardo Sciascia that I love: "Paris is a book city, a written city, a printed city. A book city made of thousands of books. A city that might be called a library's dream, if a library had the ability to dream." And Burke had the envious task of living that dream while he worked on his unique and engaging book *Writers in Paris: Literary Lives in the City of Light* (Counterpoint, 2008). He had the opportunity to page through books, study maps, paintings, and photographs, and walk all over the city tracking down literary sites. "All of this was rich and rewarding," he notes, "but what really brought Paris to life for me were the great Paris novels and the lives of their characters, who illuminated the soul of the city."

His book is filled with dozens and dozens of authors and works of fiction, as well as maps, so readers may craft literary itineraries of their own. Burke writes that "immersion creates its rewards," a statement with which I wholeheartedly agree, and he aptly observes that our appreciation of writers' lives and work, and Paris itself, "is heightened by following them from place to place in our imaginations or, even better, in our walking shoes."

WALKING TOURS

There are many ways to walk around Paris. You can set yourself precise destinations, or just drift along. With a guidebook in hand, you can try to systematically explore a neighborhood, or else you can just take the first bus that comes along and ride it to the end of the line, or you can try to go places by taking a different route from the one you normally take. Or else you can devise a route by deliberately imposing arbitrary rules that will restrict matters even more, such as, for example, taking streets whose names begin with the same letter, or going exclusively in alphabetical order, or in some particular chronology. In practice, these itineraries are extremely difficult to work out. During the course of one's walks, with the aid of guidebooks and maps, one can follow them more or less in their entirety. For the stroller who restricts himself like that, Paris becomes a giant labyrinth that during the course of his peregrinations gives him the feeling of having left the beaten path.

—Georges Perec, *Paris*

While it's always nice to simply wander aimlessly, have a day or two on your trip without a single plan or reservation, it's equally important that other days be more structured, with sites to see, architecture to admire, and cafés to linger at. As I noted in the introduction, the more you plan, the more free time you have, and walking tours give you just that. Sometimes, a plan to just amble along the *rues* is structure enough, as François Baudot, in the introduction to *Paris* (Assouline, 2004), wisely notes: "You drift in Venice, you meander in Rome, you wander in Madrid. In New York, you go from point A to point B. You often get lost in Tokyo. You always find your way in Marrakesh. In London, you catch a taxi; in Seville, a sunstroke. But only in Paris do you stroll." Along with Thirza Vallois's trio of *Around and About Paris,* the following are my favorite walking tour books. I continue to use these even though I know exactly what I will encounter and where I will end up.

Impressionist Paris: The Essential Guide to the City of Light, Julian More (Pavilion, 1999). This illustrated hardcover isn't particularly hard to pack, but it's a little hard to conceive of carrying it around while walking, as it's thick and heavy. I recommend making photocopies of the pages you want to bring along. It is a very good and interesting (if not quite "essential") guide, and More, who has lived in France for many years, is also the author of some of my favorite books, including *Views from a French Farmhouse.* In eight chapters, More proposes walks and drives within Paris proper as well as in Fontainebleau, Giverny, and along the Seine and Oise rivers. Each is more of a "contemplative ramble" than a heavy hike or tour, "to be taken at your own speed and leisure." Visits outside Paris can be done within a day, and walks are full-day or half-day adventures. More describes his book as being "mainly about looking. Looking at paintings, looking at town and country, absorbing a distinct atmosphere that still exists."

The Impressionists' Paris:Walking Tours of the Artists' Studios, Homes, and the Sites They Painted, Ellen Williams (Little Bookroom, 1997). With twenty color reproductions of artworks, period café and restaurant recommendations, maps, and vintage photographs, this great little (about 5¼ × 7¼ inches) hardcover features the works of Manet, Degas, Monet, Renoir, Bazille, and Caillebotte. (Pissarro, whose Parisian street scenes seem to beg inclusion, is left out since, as Williams notes in the afterword, he didn't begin painting his *grands boulevards* canvases until the 1880s, whereas this book focuses on the 1860s and 1870s.) I've used this book (and the Picasso one below) several times, following each route to the letter, and I continue to be amazed at how many sites depicted in the paintings remain the same. The author's recommendations for cafés and restaurants have all turned out to be memorable spots.

A Paris Walking Guide: 20 Charming Strolls through the Streets, Courtyards, and Gardens of Paris, translated by David Cox (Parigramme, 2009). This is a more compact edition of Parigramme's twenty-volume guide to the arrondissements of Paris, the *Guides du Promeneur,* and it is a must-have book, but only available in France. I bought it in Paris and saw it in many bookstores and museum shops there. There are two guiding premises for the series: "We never see—or only poorly see—things that have not been pointed out" and "Seeing and learning changes our lives." There is much in this edition that does not appear in any other English-language guidebook, and the walks are terrific.

Pariswalks, Sonia, Alison, and Rebecca Landes (Henry Holt, 2005, sixth edition). The *Walks* series has been a favorite of mine since it first appeared in 1981, originating with the Paris guide. This edition features walks through five of the oldest neighborhoods of Paris: Saint-Julien-le-Pauvre, La Huchette, Saint-Germain-des-Prés, Mouffetard, and Place des Vosges. Each walk is about two and a half hours, and after each one you'll be "a friend and possessor of the *quartier* forever." I share the authors' enthusiasm for getting to know a part of the city intimately, what they call "close-up tourism." Two useful tips: morning walks are recommended because courtyard doors in both business and residential buildings remain open for mail and other deliveries, and sitting on the grass is not *interdit* in the Square René-Viviani, next to little Saint-Julien-le-Pauvre. However, recommendations for cafés, restaurants, hotels, and shops are covered better in other books.

Picasso's Paris: Walking Tours of the Artist's Life in the City, Ellen Williams (Little Bookroom, 1999). This sister volume to the Impressionists guide above is equally appealing, and it's not just for first-time visitors. As Williams notes, "Following in the footsteps of this one extraordinary inhabitant can reveal entirely new aspects of the city even to those familiar with it." Picasso lived in four neighborhoods in Paris—Montmartre, Montparnasse, Étoile, and Saint-Germain-des-Prés—and happily, as Williams discovered, most of his Paris still exists today. The four museums in Paris that display his work are included in this volume. As with the Impressionists guide, this one also has a red ribbon marker, a thoughtful touch for walkers who want to easily mark a page while looking around or stopping for a *vin ordinaire*.

Secret Paris: Walking Off the Beaten Track, Jacques Garance and Maud Ratton (Jonglez, 2007). I bought this in Paris and in North America it's probably available only online, but wherever you see it buy it *tout de suite!* This slender paperback is filled with things to see in Paris that, almost exclusively, do not appear in any other book. Take, *par example,* the first arrondissement: until I picked up this book, I had never even heard of the strange image of Napoléon at the Colonnade de Perrault at the Louvre, the Galerie Dorée of the Banque de France, or the Colonne Médicis on the rue de Viarmes . . . not to mention the Cercle Suédois, the Swedish club where Alfred Nobel created the Nobel Prize in 1895 and where you can, twice a month on Wednesdays, see the desk he sat at and have a drink in rooms that overlook the Jardin des Tuileries . . . or the commemorative plaque of the Texas embassy at the corner of rue de Castiglione and Place Vendôme (the state of Texas established its own embassy in Paris after it gained its independence from Mexico in 1836 and before it became a U.S. state in 1845). This book is an eye-opener and a gem.

Walks Through Napoléon & Joséphine's Paris, Diana Reid Haig (Little Bookroom, 2004). I bought this book because of the affection my daughter has for Napoléon—as she's only eleven, she's not quite an expert (yet). But when we were in Ajaccio, on the island of Corsica, we visited Napoléon's childhood home and saw statues aplenty of him—so many that Alyssa began referring to him as "you know who." I thought the book would be fun and interesting for her, and indeed it has proven to be so. The four walks detailed here—and the itineraries for Malmaison and Fontainebleau—are wonderful for me, too.

If you prefer guided walking tours, here are a few that I highly recommend:

★ Context Travel (contexttravel.com) offers very in-depth walking tours for small groups (no more than six) of "intellectually curious travelers." The walks are led by scholars and specialists in such fields as archaeology, art history, cuisine, urban planning, history, environmental science, and classics. What initally drew me to Context was its stated mission, which sounds very compatible with *The Collected Traveler*: "We are committed to the character of the city—its built environment, cultural heritage, and living fabric." Just a few of the company's Paris tours are Paris by Riverboat, Louvre French Masters, Modernist Architecture, and Marais Mansions; there are family walks specifically geared to kids as well. Context, based in Philadelphia, offers equally terrific tours in eleven other cities, including Athens, Istanbul, Rome, Venice, New York, Boston, and Philadelphia.

★ Isabelle Hauller, a *conférencière officielle* and *docteur en histoire de l'art,* has tours listed on the Paris Balades Web site (parisbalades.com/hauller). Her tours are in French, and she sends monthly e-mail updates of her offerings so you may reserve in advance.

★ Centre des Monuments Nationaux (monuments-nationaux .fr). This government organization offers guided tours of many well-known monuments and gardens in all regions of France.

Before you depart on a walk, remember to bring something to record the names of interesting spots you pass that you may want to return to later. Unless they state otherwise, guides appreciate tips, so if you feel yours was particularly good, give him or her a few extra euros. Guides are also good sources of information and typically enjoy sharing the names of some favorite places (often little visited by tourists). They're there to answer your questions, so don't hesitate to query them after your tour.

INTERVIEW

Patricia Wells

Like many other people, when I first picked up The Food Lover's Guide to Paris *by Patricia Wells, I knew I was holding a significant book in my hands, a book positively like no other, one I just knew was going to change my life, the way Paris itself had. Indeed it did, and to this day I count the guide among my favorite books in the world. The* Food Lover's Guide *"cracked the code," as Patricia notes in* We've Always Had Paris . . . and Provence: *"We made it possible for every American who came to the city to feel comfortable, knowledgeable in ordering that steak rare, daring to sample that warm foie gras, willing to take the Métro out to the twentieth arrondissement to sample Bernard Ganachaud's crusty sourdough bread, or confident that they knew what to swoon over when they could get a table at Jamin, the new hit restaurant." And here's the remarkable thing: even though the guide's last edition was published in 1999 (Workman), it is still indispensable. Many of the places to eat, purveyors, and shops are still in business today; Patricia's notes and tips are still accurate; the recipes she provides are still winners (whenever I bake madeleines and* financiers *I turn to this book); and the French-English culinary glossary at the back of the book is the most extensive you'll find in any similar book (I made a copy of it years ago and still bring it with me to France).*

Of course, since she compiled this book, Wells went on to write The Food Lover's Guide to France *(Workman, 1987), which I also still use, and eight cookbooks, including* Bistro Cooking *(Workman, 1989),* Simply French: Patricia Wells Presents the Cuisine of Joël Robuchon *(William Morrow, 1991), and* The Paris Cookbook *(HarperCollins, 2001). She also served as restaurant critic for the French newsweekly* L'Express, *the only woman and only foreigner ever to have held the post. Additionally, Wells teaches cooking classes both in Paris and at her eighteenth-century home in Provence, Chanteduc. More recently, in 2008, she and her husband, Walter, wrote* We've Always Had Paris . . . and Provence: A Scrapbook of Our Life in France *(Harper), which I read in two days because I just couldn't stop reading about their thirty years together in France. It was Walter's career move from the* New York Times *to the* International Herald Tribune *that*

brought the couple to Paris. He recalls in the book that, with hindsight, the decision to go to Paris was right, but he asks: "Why Paris? What was it about the city that pulled us there and kept us? Well, how high is the sky? It's not that the answer is elusive, or the answers, because there are millions of them in words and images and none of them are more adequate than grunts and blurs. The ones that are adequate are personal and intense and they have grown and changed over thirty years. I don't remember now how many of my own answers were obvious in 1980. But both as a new arrival and as a longtime resident, a hundred times a day if not a thousand I found something that brought passing delight."

I missed meeting Patricia and Walter when I was last in Paris, and I look forward to the day when I will (hopefully) meet them. But in the meantime, I caught up with Patricia via e-mail in between cooking classes:

Q: Had you visited Paris before you moved to the city in the first week of January 1980?
A: I first visited in January of 1972 and it was love at first sight!

Q: Some years after you moved to Paris you also bought a house in Provence. How much time do you spend now in Paris?
A: We basically spend from May to October in Provence and in Paris, with frequent trips back to Provence and the United States, in the fall and winter months.

Q: *The Food Lover's Guide to Paris* was updated four times. Did you anticipate how successful it would be?
A: I always feel that if I am crazy in love with something and write about it, there will be enough people that feel the way I do. It turned out that way, and it was a wonderful way to launch a book career.

Q: There really is no other book like the *Food Lover's Guide,* before or since. Why did you decide not to continue updating it?

A: As the world became more and more digital and Paris began to change more and more quickly it seemed that, by the time I updated it, it would be out of date. Keep in mind that the book was written before home computers, sticky notes, faxes, e-mail, Federal Express, etc.—we wrote our notes on carbon paper and had to mail in the copy! I also felt that all the time I spent updating the guide would take me away from other writing and researching.

Q: Can you name a handful of places that appeared in the first edition that you still frequent today?

A: So many places. Of course, the grand restaurants that were small ones when the first guide came out, such as Guy Savoy (18 rue Troyon, 17ème) and Robuchon (La Table de Joël Robuchon, 16 avenue Bugeaud, 16ème; L'Atelier de Joël Robuchon, 5 rue de Montalembert, 7ème). The great majority of the restaurants in the first guide either don't exist anymore or have changed hands many times over. We may go back to many of the originals—such as Chez les Anges (54 rue de la Tour Maubourg, 7ème) and Le Chiberta (3 rue Aresène-Houssaye, 8ème), which kept the name but is a totally different restaurant now. For cafés of course we still go to Café de Flore (172 boulevard Saint-Germain, 6ème) and Le Dôme Café (108 boulevard du Montparnasse, 14ème); for wine bars, Willi's (13 rue des Petits-Champs, 1er) and Au Sauvignon (80 rue des Saints-Pères, 7ème); and all of the markets, which of course have changed the least over the years in terms of stability. We still get coffee at La Brûlerie des Ternes (10 rue Poncelet, 17ème), chocolate at La Maison du Chocolat (original location at 52 rue François 1er, 8ème, and other locations), bread at Poilâne (8 rue du Cherche-Midi, 6ème).

Q: In an essay you wrote for *Bon Appétit* (May 2001), you noted that the number of female chefs in Paris seemed to have declined by that time. You also noted that Parisians were still rather reluctant about global cuisine, that "the French flirtation with foreign influences is so light as to be nonexistent." Are there more female chefs in Paris today, and have Parisians more fully embraced outside culinary influences?

A: I don't know the exact number of female chefs in Paris today but they still are very small in number. It is still a very physical job and one that is difficult for anyone who wants to raise a family. Parisians today certainly embrace all manner of cuisines but stay faithful to their own since there is so much variety.

Q: How many classes do you offer in Paris in a calendar year, and how quickly do they fill up? How far in advance do you recommend interested participants confirm?

A: We announce our classes in November two years in advance, so that in November 2010, for example, we announce the class schedule for 2012. Almost all classes fill up completely, but it is hard to say how far in advance people should reserve. The best is to watch the Web site (patriciawells.com), which always gives an idea of spaces available.

Q: I see that you've recently offered Tastes of Vietnam classes. What inspired you to teach there?

A: A student who has ties to Vietnam asked if we wanted to do it and it seemed like a perfect challenge. And it was. We have also taught classes in Florence, Venice, and Verona.

Q: What is your favorite time of year in Paris?

A: I always offer classes in Paris in the spring. I love the first-of-season asparagus, peas, baby artichokes, spring lamb, strawberries, and even great tomatoes from Sicily.

Q: Which arrondissement do you live in, and what are some of your most frequent stops in your neighborhood?

A: We live in the seventh and I have my office in the sixth. Favorite haunts are of course Bon Marché (24 rue de Sèvres, 7ème) for both the department store and food hall; Fish La Boissonnerie (69 rue de Seine, 6ème) for dinner; Fromagerie Quatrehomme (62 rue de Sèvres, 7ème) for cheese; the boulevard Raspail street market on Tuesday, Friday, and Sunday; La Dernière Goutte (6 rue Bourbon le Château, 6ème) for wine; Huilerie Leblanc (6 rue Jacob, 6ème) for oil; and Poilâne for bread.

Q: How long were you working at the *International Herald Tribune*?

A: I worked there from 1980 on, and still do some occasional writing, but gave up my restaurant critic job in 2007.

Q: You've obviously experienced a lot of changes in Paris over the last thirty years. Have some things remained the same? And in what ways do you feel Paris changed you?

A: As I said earlier, the markets are the one constant, though the increased availability of produce is one big change. When we moved to Paris, people dressed up, men in sport coats on weekends, women in dresses. Now it seems everyone dresses the same all over the world. Stores are open longer hours. Many small places have gone out of business, but I am pleased to see that there are still so many independent shopkeepers with great boutiques.

Q: I suspect that your wine Clos Chanteduc—a Côtes-du-Rhône that received a score of 89 from Robert Parker—is the one that occupies the most space in your wine cellar. Is it available in the States?

A: Eric Solomon of Eric Solomon Selections (european cellars.com) is now our importer.

Q: Are you working on a new book?

A: Yes! Two books, to be out in 2011: *Salad as a Meal* and *Simply Truffles,* both published by William Morrow.

Q: Will you ever move back to the States?

A: Never say never, but we have no plans to return for good.

At any season, and all year long, in the evening the view of the city from the bridges was always exquisitely pictorial. One's eyes became the eyes of a painter, because the sight itself approximated art, with the narrow, pallid façades of the buildings lining the river; with the tall trees growing down by the water's edge; with, behind them, the vast chiaroscuro of the palatial Louvre, lightened by the luminous lemon color of the Paris sunset off toward the west; with the great square, pale stone silhouette of Notre-Dame to the east. The stance from which to see Paris was any one of the bridges at the close of the day. The Pont Neuf still looked as we had known it on the canvases of Sisley and Pissarro.

Paris then seemed immutably French. The quasi-American atmosphere which we had tentatively established around Saint-Germain had not yet infringed onto the rest of the city. In the early twenties, when I was new there, Paris was still yesterday.

—Janet Flanner, *Paris Was Yesterday: 1925–1939*

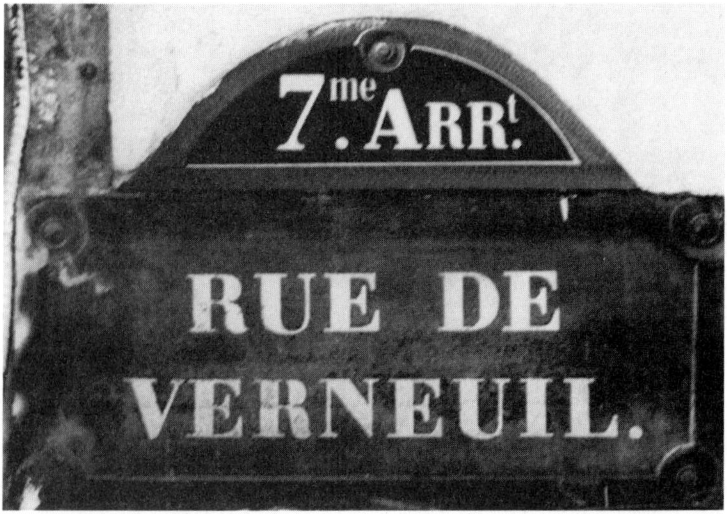
7me ARRt.
RUE DE
VERNEUIL.

LES QUARTIERS

It would take volumes and libraries to tell the story of the Marais, so profoundly French is it in every stone, so tied to the wandering of History that human forgetfulness and urban development could do it no harm.

—LÉON-PAUL FARGUE,
Le Piéton de Paris

In spite of its glamorous appearance, Paris is a hidden, private city. You only get to see inside when Parisians decide to let you in. And they only let you in when they know who you are.

—JEAN-BENOÎT NADEAU AND JULIE BARLOW,
Sixty Million Frenchmen Can't Be Wrong

The New Left Bank

ALEXANDER LOBRANO

꧁꧂

As THE AUTHOR of this piece aptly notes, it's really been only recently that the tenth arrondissement was considered worthy of locating in your *plan de Paris,* let alone considered hip. Yet that is what it has definitely become, along with neighborhoods in the eleventh and twelfth.

ALEXANDER LOBRANO lives in Paris and was European correspondent for ten years for the former *Gourmet,* where this piece originally appeared in a longer version. He is also the author of *Hungry for Paris* (Random House, 2010, second edition) and was an editor of the Zagat guide to Paris restaurants. Readers may follow Lobrano's restaurant adventures at his Diner's Journal postings on his Web site (hungry forparis.squarespace.com).

WHEN MY FRIEND Catherine moved from the Marais to the tenth arrondissement eleven years ago, I needed a map to get to her housewarming party. Even though I'd lived in Paris for decades, the only reason I'd ever been in the tenth was to catch a train. Back then, most Parisians would have told you the same. But as I emerged from the Métro on that crisp Indian-summer night, I found myself bowled over by a charming new city.

High wrought-iron footbridges arched over the gray waters of the stone-lined Canal Saint-Martin, dotted here and there with vivid spots of color from a few fallen leaves. The whole area was peaceful and pretty and suggested a poignancy I'd not before experienced in this city. Catherine's apartment turned out to be terrific, too. After selling her small place in the Marais, she'd landed a sunny loft with oak floors and casement windows. Best of all, she no longer had a mortgage. This real estate grand slam was the talk of the party, but even though I envied my friend, I couldn't imagine giving up my place in Saint-Germain-des-Prés. Besides, there was no place to shop or eat in the tenth.

A couple of weeks later, I found myself back in the tenth, at a new restaurant called Chez Michel. Chef Thierry Breton's food was brilliant, but my dining companion and I agreed that the poor guy had made a big mistake with the location. Needless to say, Chez Michel is now packed nightly, and these days Catherine has an admirable choice of restaurants practically at her doorstep. If those first change-of-address cards announcing new homes in unfamiliar arrondissements were an occasional curiosity back then, these days I'm surprised when I notice a move that hasn't landed someone in the tenth, eleventh, twelfth, nineteenth, or twentieth arrondissement. The ninth, a central neighborhood once known as La Nouvelle Athènes because of its neoclassical architecture, is on the upswing, too, for those priced out of prime areas like Saint-Germain.

Affordable real estate partly explains the accelerating migration into these formerly down-at-the-heels neighborhoods, but many also choose them for their old-fashioned ambience, at once relaxed and convivial. "It was such a relief to escape the bourgeois prissiness of the seventh," another friend told me after finding an apartment overlooking the Parc des Buttes-Chaumont, in the nineteenth, a still-gritty area but one brimming with wonderfully quirky shops (and entirely free of the international brands and chain stores back in Saint-Germain).

I'll always love the Left Bank (it's still where you'll find the best hotels), but like almost all of my Parisian friends, I head deep into the double-digit arrondissements so often now that I no longer need a map. If you do the same, you'll be rewarded not just with good food but also with a fascinating glimpse of the *quartiers* the French consider the Paris of the twenty-first century.

TENTH ARRONDISSEMENT

Think of this area as a developing photograph, an image progressing from blurred first impression to materialization in detail. Until very recently, this neighborhood was one of the more anonymous parts of Paris—rootless and slightly forlorn, thanks to the fact that its main business has always been getting people in and out of town, through either the Gare du Nord or the Gare de l'Est. It doesn't help that the grid of streets here is slashed crosswise by two pounding arteries (the boulevard de Magenta and the rue La Fayette) whose sole purpose is whisking passengers between the stations and the rest of the city. That snapshot of indeterminacy has changed, though; today, the tenth has been reborn as one of the most dramatic neighborhoods in the city.

Good bones helped: The Canal Saint-Martin, a glorious nineteenth-century waterway, connects to the Seine through a path of leafy planes, poplars, and chestnuts, begging you to wander along its banks, catching some sun by day or lingering over a bottle of wine in the evening. It finally occurred to young hipsters how supremely desirable—not to mention how affordable—it might be to live beside a onetime working canal. This aquatic spine of the quartier began to gentrify a few years ago (it's no longer such a bargain), but if you stroll down any of its side streets, you'll still find one of the most unusual urban oases anywhere in the world.

The rue du Château-d'Eau, for example, is the epicenter of African hairdressing, almost entirely lined with brightly colored barber shops and beauty parlors. But every now and then, something else sneaks in. Something like **Globus France**, a shop that sells charcuterie from Bosnia, Serbia, Croatia, Romania, Poland,

and Hungary. On the rue Cail, everything is Indian, including the wonderful vegetarian restaurant **Krishna-Bhavan**, tucked amid shops and clothing stores. The jewel of the rue du Faubourg-Saint-Martin is the foppishly opulent Mairie du 10ème Arrondissement, or town hall, a massive mock–Loire Valley château, finished in 1896, that rather comically lords it over the neighboring clutch of Turkish cafés. Nearby is the pedestrian Passage Brady, a glass-roofed nineteenth-century arcade that's become a legendary destination for backpackers, stuffed as it is with cheap Indian and Pakistani restaurants. (Try **Le Passage de Pondichéry**.) Just a few blocks over, on the rue de Marseille, branches of chic clothiers are sprouting up, and you'll also find **Du Pain et des Idées**, one of the best new bakeries in Paris.

Generations of privileged Parisian brides have chosen their porcelain, stemware, and silver on the irresistibly named rue de Paradis, where most of the major French crystal manufacturers had their showrooms. (It's a convenient walk from the Gare de l'Est, which serves the province of Lorraine, where the crystal factories of Baccarat and Saint-Louis are still located.) Today most of the crystal showrooms have moved to more conventionally stylish precincts, but there's still some great tabletop shopping in the area. At no. 18, you'll find the stop-you-in-your-tracks-grandiose **Magasins de Vente des Faïenceries de Choisy-le-Roi**, the former showroom of the ceramic works that supplied the tiles for the Paris Métro. Intended to broadcast the company's *savoir-faire*, the interior is elaborately decorated in an odd neoclassical theme complete with urns and busts.

Is it my imagination, or are the paving stones outside the Gare du Nord almost eternally damp, an *avant-goût* of life under gray northern skies? But there's also grandeur here, in the façade of female statues, each representing a destination served (Amsterdam, Berlin, Warsaw), that look down from pedestals with goddesslike hauteur. Of course, Paris towers above them all. The Gare de l'Est, on the other hand, reflects Alsace's Germanic aspect and quietly bristles with regional pride, as reflected by **En Passant par la Lorraine**, which sells Alsatian eaux-de-vie and eight-packs of boutique brewers suds.

Around the corner, the rue des Récollets (punctuated by an unexpected breath of fresh air from the gardens of a medieval convent) leads to the Canal Saint-Martin, a hardscrabble precinct of workshops and small factories turned dreamy enclave of the city. Originally commissioned by Napoléon, the canal was built between 1805 and 1825 by engineer Pierre-Simon Girard, who had studied the hydraulics of the Nile during Napoléon's Egyptian campaign. It became a major freight route into central Paris and commercialized what had been a relatively rural part of town beyond the city walls.

Linger near the canal and you'll also pick up on the tenth's particularly twenty-first-century gestalt, one that puts a premium on art and leisure over money and work, with an aesthetic soft spot for the sort of ironic retro gear on display in the windows of shops like **Antoine et Lili**. Not surprisingly, the streets on and around the canal have experienced a café boom. Spots like **Chez Prune** and **Le Poisson Rouge** are packed around the clock, and while there's no *grande dame* like Saint-Germain's fabled Café de Flore, the tenth can hold its own with the bar at the **Hôtel du Nord**, familiar to many thanks to Marcel Carné's memorable film of the same name. Stylish restaurants like **Ploum** and **La Cantine de Quentin** let you see what the cool crowd likes to eat these days, from Ploum's spinach in sesame cream to the Parmesan risotto served by Guy Savoy alum Johann Baron at La Cantine.

Away from the canal, the tenth harbors appealing modern places like Odile Guyader's laid-back **Café Panique** and Thierry Breton's brilliant **Chez Michel**. There are also wonderful fly-in-amber places, most specifically the delightful **La Grille,** which may serve the best *turbot au beurre blanc* in Paris. But to borrow a line of Arletty, the star of *Hôtel du Nord,* what all these places have most in common is simply "*Atmosphère! Atmosphère!*"

Tenth Arrondissement Address Book

Antoine et Lili (95 quai de Valmy / +33 01 40 37 41 55).

Café Panique (12 rue des Messageries / +33 01 47 70 06 84).

La Cantine de Quentin (52 rue Bichat / +33 01 42 02 40 32).

Chez Jeannette (47 rue du Faubourg-Saint-Denis / +33 01 47 70 30 89). Hugely popular café offers a perfect snapshot of the tenth's laid-back style.

Chez Michel (10 rue de Belzunce / +33 01 44 53 06 20).

Chez Prune (71 quai de Valmy / +33 01 42 41 30 47).

Coin Canal (1 rue de Marseille / +33 01 42 38 00 30). Furniture from the fifties, sixties, and seventies.

Du Pain et des Idées (34 rue Yves-Toudic / +33 01 42 40 44 52).

En Passant par la Lorraine (Gare de l'Est / +33 01 40 35 47 80).

Furet Tanrade (63 rue de Chabrol / +33 01 47 70 48 34). Fabulous small-batch jams and savory éclairs.

Globus France (74 rue du Château-d'Eau / +33 01 42 47 00 58).

La Grille (80 rue du Faubourg-Poissonnière / +33 01 47 70 89 73).

Hôtel du Nord (102 quai de Jemmapes / +33 01 40 40 78 78).

Le Jemmapes (82 quai de Jemmapes / +33 01 40 40 02 35). Stylish café-restaurant with a casual menu.

Krishna-Bhavan (24 rue Cail / +33 01 42 05 78 34).

Le Look (17 rue Martel / +33 01 50 10 20 31). Hipster canteen, busy all day long.

Maria Luisa (2 rue Marie-et-Louise / +33 01 44 84 04 01). Brick walls, seventies funk, and the best pizza in Paris.

Le Martel (3 rue Martel / +33 01 47 70 67 56). A hip crowd and great French and North African food.

Le Passage de Pondichéry (84 passage Brady / +33 01 53 34 63 10).

Philippe Chaume (9 rue de Marseille / +33 01 42 39 12 60). An intriguing photo gallery.

Ploum (20 rue Alibert / +33 01 42 00 11 90).

Le Poisson Rouge (112 quai de Jemmapes / +33 01 40 40 07 11).

Urbane (12 rue Arthur-Groussier / +33 01 42 40 74 75). Relaxed canteen with a popular Sunday brunch.

Le Verre Volé (67 rue de Lancry / +33 01 48 03 17 34). Wonderful wine bar.

Wowo (11 rue de Marseille / +33 01 53 40 84 80).

Aux Zingots (12 rue de la Fidélité / +33 01 47 70 19 34). Friendly service, excellent wine list, and appealing bistro staples.

ELEVENTH AND TWELFTH ARRONDISSEMENTS

Anyone who goes to Paris to eat will tell you that the city has been steadily tilting east, specifically toward the eleventh and twelfth arrondissements. This is why I find myself staring at an exhibit of the potato-producing countries of the world inside a display case in the Parmentier Métro station. A wonderful expression of the French penchant for public edification, this stop was named in honor of Antoine-Augustin Parmentier, the agronomist who convinced his countrymen that potatoes were indeed edible (they were originally cultivated in France only as animal feed, and it was assumed their tubers were toxic to humans). The honor is appropriate, not only because of the shared subterranean bond between the subway and the elegantly named *pomme de terre* ("apple of the earth"), but also because the denizens of this venerable working-class district subsisted on a steady diet of potatoes for a long time.

Who knows what Parmentier would have made of the sudden popularity of daikon, wasabi, and all the other exotic root vegetables that have become a mainstay on menus in the eleventh and twelfth? My guess is he'd be dumbstruck to find that this slice of the city has become its trendiest gourmet destination, especially for those who want to taste what's new without spending a small fortune.

L'est populaire, which encompasses the old, proletarian neighborhoods of Oberkampf, Ménilmontant, Bastille, Faubourg Saint-Antoine, Daumesnil, and Bercy, has gone gastro in a major way. It's here that countless young chefs have chosen to set up shop, due in no small part to the low rents, but also to the demographic turnover that's seen an influx of well-heeled *bobos* (bourgeois bohemians) with adventurous palates and a love of good food.

It was, curiously enough, the Opéra Bastille that got the ball rolling. This much derided building (many still compare it to a lavatory thanks to its glass blocks and skin of pale green tiles)—

commissioned by President François Mitterrand as a symbol of his Socialist party's devotion to making the performing arts accessible to working people—opened on July 13, 1989, to commemorate the two hundredth anniversary of the storming of the Bastille. Ironically, by drawing thousands of affluent Parisians to this part of the city for the first time (many of the locals found the programming uninteresting and the ticket prices too high), he set the stage for a real estate revolution.

Hot spots like the pioneering (but now defunct) China Club, a Shanghai-in-the-thirties-themed bar and restaurant, opened to cater to the fashionable culture vultures who discovered the charm of this old-fashioned neighborhood, which had been the center of furniture making in Paris for centuries (and which had already acquired a gloss of bohemian glamour from the free spirits who'd seized upon the low rents along the rue de Lappe and the rue Saint-Sabin a few years earlier). Following the completion of a second set of public works in the mid-nineties, these arrondissements—which had previously lacked any major attractions (even the perennially trendy Père-Lachaise cemetery is just across the street, in the twentieth)—became a destination for a broader public. The change began fourteen years ago with the conversion of a long-abandoned railway viaduct into the Promenade Plantée, a greenbelt walkway that runs all the way to the edge of the city. Underneath it, in a series of brick arches that were the support for the tracks themselves, the Viaduc des Arts became a street-level parade of shops devoted to arts and artisans. (Check out the handmade copper cookware at **L'Atelier des Arts Culinaires**.) In nearby Bercy, the transformation of the handsome brick warehouses that formerly served the wholesale wine trade (barges from Burgundy unloaded their cargo here) into shops, cafés, and restaurants gave way to a whole new neighborhood. *Et voilà,* eastern Paris, once snobbishly dismissed by the bourgeoisie, was suddenly hot, even fashionable.

But aside from a few old bistro standbys like **Le Quincy** and

À la Biche au Bois, these neighborhoods didn't have many restaurants to boast about. That situation has changed dramatically.

Rodolphe Paquin was one of the first chefs to take advantage of this vacuum when he opened **Le Repaire de Cartouche**, not far from the Place de la Bastille, more than ten years ago. "It was obvious the neighborhood was getting younger and more affluent," he says. "The rent was half of what I'd have paid in the seventh or the eighth." Inventive dishes like his carpaccio of calf's head with oyster vinaigrette and his *côte de sanglier* (wild boar) with pickled beets have been packing them in ever since.

Paquin was a pioneer, but today this patch of Paris teems with destination restaurants, including **Le Chateaubriand**, one of the city's best contemporary bistros and certainly its most popular. The talented young chef Inaki Aizpitarte first attracted attention at **La Famille**, in Montmartre. And since he moved to the Oberkampf section of the eleventh two years ago, his food has become even more intriguing. He does a single menu nightly, and it reflects both his background—he's from the Basque country and traveled in Latin America and Israel before moving to Paris—and his sometime fascination with Japan. "Everything I do is intended to tease as much of the natural taste out of my produce as possible," he says, and dishes like mackerel ceviche with Tabasco and slow-cooked tuna belly with asparagus and chorizo deliciously prove his point. His grilled pork belly with a sauce of *réglisse* (licorice root) and a small salad of grated celery root offers a brilliant contrast of textures and flavors.

Oberkampf is also a great bet for wine lovers. **Le Marsangy**, a relaxed and friendly bistro with very good food, has an excellent wine list, as does the consistently good **Le Villaret**. And there are regular wine tastings at **La Cave de l'Insolite**, one of the city's most interesting new wine shops. (Nearby, **La Bague de Kenza**, on the rue Saint-Maur, sells the best Algerian pastries in Paris.)

In the Faubourg Saint-Antoine, the neighborhood that straddles the eleventh and twelfth arrondissements along the street of the same name, **Le Bistrot Paul Bert** has become so popular it can be tough to score a table. What drives this trio of cozy dining rooms decorated with flea market bric-a-brac is some of the best traditional bistro cooking to be found in Paris today. The chalkboard menu changes often but runs to dishes like coddled eggs with *cèpes, coucou de Rennes* (a Breton breed of chicken prized for its delicate flesh) in a sauce of morels and *vin jaune,* and their much loved signature dessert, a sublime Paris-Brest, the praline-buttercream-filled round *choux* pastry created to commemorate a bicycle race between the two cities from which it takes its name. **L'Écailler du Bistrot**, run by the same owners as Le Bistrot Paul Bert, is a terrific address for seafood lovers, and on the same street the hip **La Cocotte**, Argentinean-born Andrea Wainer's wonderfully eclectic gastroshop, sells everything from cookbooks and table linens to kitchen equipment and the world's best *dulce de leche.* Next door is **Crus et Découvertes**, a first-rate new wine shop.

Other excellent restaurants in the area include **Au Vieux Chêne**, serving up a delicious market-driven menu; **Chez Ramu-laud**, a relaxed bistro with an inventive menu, a stylish crowd, and a great wine list; and **La Gazzetta**, where young Swedish chef Petter Nilsson has generated major word of mouth with dishes that are variously of Scandinavian, French, and Italian inspiration. With its loftlike décor, La Gazzetta has something of a New York City vibe, along with a menu that changes all the time. One night, roasted endive with dill, horseradish, lemon, and puréed almonds proved a parade of bitterness, acidity, sweetness, and heat; grilled cod with a side of Brussels sprout purée, fresh tarragon, and capers had a quiet elegance; and ricotta ice cream with ewe's-milk cheese, hazelnuts, and olives made for an unexpectedly sexy grand finale.

The latest contender in eastern Paris's new gastro sweepstakes is **Le Cotte Rôti**, a tiny place not far from the eminently gastro-nomic **Marché d'Aligre**. Despite the fact that he describes his restaurant as a bistro, young chef Michel Nicolas puts a lot more creativity into the menu than such a label would imply. His cooking veers between such surprises as an oyster milkshake and *nougat de volaille* (a sweet riff on chicken terrine) and homier dishes like pork loin roasted in hay and served with *gratin dauphinois*. Nicolas's classical training (he worked with Marc Meneau at L'Espérance, in Burgundy) and respect for the best French produce are the perfect springboard for the kind of creativity found throughout the eleventh and twelfth, a part of the city that treasures the past as ardently as it loves discovering the new.

Eleventh/Twelfth Arrondissements Address Book

Astier (44 rue Jean-Pierre-Timbaud, 11ème / +33 01 43 57 16 35). Traditional bistro with a fantastic cheese tray.

L'Atelier des Arts Culinaires (111 avenue Daumesnil, 12ème / +33 01 43 40 20 20).

La Bague de Kenza (106 rue Saint-Maur, 11ème / +33 01 43 14 93 15).

Le Baron Rouge (1 rue Théophile-Roussel, 12ème / +33 01 43 43 14 32). A terrific neighborhood wine bar that's packed with a young crowd.

À la Biche au Bois (45 avenue Ledru-Rollin, 12ème / +33 01 43 43 34 38).

Le Bistrot Paul Bert (18 rue Paul-Bert, 11ème / +33 01 43 72 24 01).

Le Bistrot du Peintre (116 avenue Ledru-Rollin, 12ème / +33 01 47 00 34 39). Art Nouveau café with decent food and a fun crowd.

Café Place Verte (105 rue Oberkampf, 11ème / +33 01 43 57 34 10). With an hors d'oeuvres bar and delicious *plats du jour*.

Café Titon (34 rue Titon, 11ème / +33 01 43 71 74 51). Where the shopkeepers and restaurateurs of the fashionable rue Paul-Bert hang out. Good for quick lunches; on Saturday, there's a Sri Lankan spread.

La Cave de l'Insolite (30 rue de la Folie-Méricourt, 11ème / +33 01 53 36 08 33).

Le Chateaubriand (129 avenue Parmentier, 11ème / +33 01 43 57 45 95).

Chez Ramulaud (269 rue du Faubourg-Saint-Antoine, 11ème / +33 01 43 72 23 29).

La Cocotte (5 rue Paul-Bert, 11ème / +33 01 43 73 04 02).

Le Cotte Rôti (1 rue de Cotte, 12ème / +33 01 43 45 06 37).

Crus et Découvertes (7 rue Paul-Bert, 11ème / +33 01 43 71 56 79).

Le Duc de Richelieu (5 rue Parrot, 12ème / +33 01 43 43 05 64). Steps from the Gare de Lyon; a best bet for a hearty meal before or after traveling.

L'Écailler du Bistrot (22 rue Paul-Bert, 11ème / +33 01 43 72 76 77).

L'Équateur (151 rue Saint-Maur, 11ème / +33 01 43 57 99 22). Delicious Cameroonian and Senegalese cooking.

Eurotra (119 boulevard Richard-Lenoir, 11ème / +33 01 43 38 48 48). A sort of discount version of Dehillerin, the famous cookware store in Les Halles.

La Gazzetta (29 rue de Cotte, 12ème / +33 01 43 47 47 05).

Marché d'Aligre and *Marché Beauvau* (the covered market in the middle of the open-air Marché d'Aligre), two of the greatest and least-known markets of Paris, both with a distinctly neighborhood feel. (Place d'Aligre, 12ème.)

Le Marsangy (73 avenue Parmentier, 11ème / +33 01 47 00 94 25).

Le Pause Café (41 rue de Charonne, 11ème / +33 01 48 06 80 33). Trendy, with nice, simple food.

La Pharmacie (22 rue Jean-Pierre-Timbaud, 11ème / +33 01 48 06 28 33). A former drugstore; now a grocery store, organic tea salon, restaurant, and bookshop.

Le Quincy (28 avenue Ledru-Rollin, 12ème / +33 01 46 28 46 76).

Le Réfectoire (80 boulevard Richard-Lenoir, 11ème / +33 01 48 06 74 85). Hip little bistro specializing in nostalgic retro dishes.

Le Repaire de Cartouche (8 boulevard des Filles-du-Calvaire, 11ème / +33 01 47 00 25 86).

Au Vieux Chêne (7 rue du Dahomey, 11ème / +33 01 43 71 67 69).

Le Villaret (13 rue Ternaux, 11ème / +33 01 43 57 89 76).

"Paris gives me a *frisson* every time I arrive. Nowhere else affects me so physically and spiritually. Perhaps it is partly because I was not born a *Parisienne* but grew it into the fabric of my garments when spending my college years there and then visiting frequently every year all my life. I'm definitely a Left Bank lover, and my secret gardens are parts of the Luco (Luxembourg Gardens), especially around the Fontaine de Médicis and the upper southwest corner near rue Vavin. Square Paul-Painlevé, a tiny garden near the Sorbonne and the Cluny museum, and Place Dauphine, both of which I discovered while a student and used to sit in for hours reviewing for exams, still beckon me and the latest book I am reading. *Flâner* in Paris is another treat as there is so much beauty: buildings, shops, the *bords de la Seine,* inner courtyards, markets (particularly boulevard Raspail)—the aesthetic they transmit is signature Paris. Walks, walks, walks are Paris—say, on the way to a visit to the Rodin museum. These are a few of my favorite things. And then there's the iconic sitting at the terrace of a café. I love it, whether on a main boulevard or on a small street. Eating out is me and whether eating a sandwich at a café, dining at a bistro, or celebrating New Year's Eve at the Tour d'Argent, it is like nowhere else and, oh, so good. Paris for me is also going to the movies and the theater with friends and following with a discussion and deconstruction around a seafood platter."

—Mireille Guiliano, author of
French Women Don't Get Fat

On the Île Saint-Louis

HERBERT GOLD

THIS IS MY FAVORITE piece written about the lovely Île Saint-Louis.

HERBERT GOLD is the author of more than twenty books, including the memoir *Still Alive: A Temporary Condition* (Arcade, 2008), *Best Nightmare on Earth: A Life in Haiti* (Prentice Hall, 1991), *Fathers* (Random House, 1967), *Daughter Mine* (St. Martin's, 2000), and my favorite, *Bohemia: Where Art, Angst, Love, and Strong Coffee Meet* (Simon & Schuster, 1993). I share the following passage from *Bohemia* that I particularly love not because it is about the Île Saint-Louis but because of the singular Parisian spirit it portrays, which residents of the Île would appreciate:

A fellow Fulbright scholar, studying in Belgium, happened to arrive for his first visit to Paris on July 14, Bastille Day, when the entire city was strung with colored lights. Bands played on every corner, or at least flutes and musettes; people were dancing, singing, embracing, inviting us and anyone else nearby to join them for their wine and food. It recalled the *soupers fraternels* of revolutionary times, when the people of Paris set their tables outside, lay extra places for hungry or convivial passersby who wished to share bread, wine, and cheese. This Bastille Day mood, after war and Nazi occupation, was one of spiritual orgy, a festival nourished by deep griefs. My friend saw only the gaiety. He looked about at the hubbub, sighed, and said, "I always knew Paris would be like this." Paris, of course, is not really like this. But we know it must be, therefore it is; the Paris of our dreams is a required course.

AN ISLAND PRIME, an island at the secret heart of Paris, floating in time and space across a footbridge on the shady side of the cathedral of Notre-Dame de Paris, the Île Saint-Louis may also be the most ambiguous orphan island there is—city and not a city, village and metropolis, provincial and centrally urban, serene and hyped by hundreds of years of noisy lovers of solitude.

Unique it is, possessed of itself, even self-congratulatory, yet available to all who choose to stroll from the population sink of contemporary Paris to a place that has no Métro stop or depressed highway. One could live there forever and do it in a short span of time, and I did.

Just after World War II, I came to study philosophy amid the existentialists of Saint-Germain-des-Prés. The first winter was bitter cold, with food rationing and no heat, and we philosophers—that is, admirers of Juliette Greco with her long nose, hoarse voice, black jeans, and sweaters—had to find cafés to do our deep thinking in.

In existential pursuit of the largest *café au lait* and most tooth-rotting but warming chocolate, I bought a bicycle to widen my field of operations, showing a certain Cleveland shrewdness by paying eight dollars for the rustiest, most battered bicycle I could find so that I could leave it unlocked.

Behind Notre-Dame, across the narrow footbridge of the Pont Saint-Louis, on the tranquil Île Saint-Louis, which did little business and did it negligently, I leaned my bike against a café that served large coffees, rich chocolate, and few customers. I remember it as Aux Alsaciennes, because it served Alsatian sausage, corned beef and cabbage, *choucroute garnie* at lunchtime; but for many years, now that the place has been discovered, it has been called the Brasserie de Saint-Louis-en-l'Île.

Somehow, here I couldn't think about Bergson and Diderot and the hyphen between them, a little-known idea-smith named Maine de Biran, my thesis. Maybe it was the action of pumping a rusty bicycle; maybe it was the red-faced waiters, the black-dressed postwar girls with bruised eyes; but on the Île Saint-Louis I graciously allowed the history of philosophy to continue on its way without me.

My bike had no carrier for books; instead, I could stick a notebook under the seat. While warming myself at Aux Alsaciennes, I began to write a novel.

Nearly two years later, when the stationery store lady wrapped the package for mailing to Viking Press, she figured out what it was and gave it a sharp slap, crying out, "*Merde!*" I was startled because I thought I knew what that word meant and took it as a judgment of my coffee-and-*choucroute*-fueled, eighteen-month creative frenzy, but she explained that it meant "Good luck!"

(The book, *Birth of a Hero*, about a Resistance hero who happened to be stuck all his life in Cleveland, was published. I went home to Cleveland to buy the three-cent stamp with my picture on it but they were still using George Washington. I like that first novel now mostly because it instructed me that I had the right to do it.)

At some point in the creative process, I left a GI overcoat—the vestmental equivalent of my bicycle—on a rack at the brasserie. The waiters kept asking when I would take it again, but spring came, the birds sang on the Île Saint-Louis, and other birds allowed me to buy them hot chocolate; I was too overwrought.

Later, I decided to see how long the coat would live on the coatrack. As the years went by, I committed more novels, visited Paris as a tourist, and came to the Île Saint-Louis to check on my coat. It was still there. "Soon," I promised the waiters.

One May in the early sixties, I noticed that the narrow, swaying footbridge across which I used to wheel my rustmobile had been replaced by a wider, stabler cement product, although it was still blocked to automobiles. And my coat was gone from the café, which had changed its name to the Brasserie de Saint-Louis-en-l'Île. And that *tout Paris* had discovered the happy place that in my secret mustard-loving heart will always be Aux Alsaciennes.

Anciently, the Île Saint-Louis was two islands, Île Notre-Dame and Île-aux-Vaches (Cow Island). You can buy old maps that show the walls of medieval Paris and this tiny pasture in the Seine, from which cows and milk were brought by dinghy into the city. In the seventeenth century the places were joined, and in a burst of elegant speculation, bankruptcies, and respeculation, a dense web of *hôtels* (fine mansions) were spun.

The Hôtel Lambert and the Hôtel de Lauzun are two noble examples, but the entire island, its narrow pre-Detroit and even pre-Citroën streets, its encircling quays for strolling and breeze-taking by the Seine, has a comfortingly unified classical pattern.

The decoration and architecture date from a single period of French elegance and are protected by fanatic preservationists, among whom was former president Georges Pompidou, who helped stuff other districts of Paris with freeways and skyscrapers. (Pompidou lived on the Île Saint-Louis.)

There is an ice cream shop, Berthillon, with perhaps the best and certainly the most chic sherbets in France. Usually the lines stretch out onto the street—people waiting for their *glace café, sorbet, crème*—as others in other places wait in line to pay taxes or to see if their portrait is on the three-cent stamp.

There is but one church on the island, Saint-Louis-en-l'Île—lovely, tranquil, softly flowing, with devout deacons scrubbing the stone with straw brooms from a stock that seems to have been purchased by some seventeenth-century financial genius of a priest who feared inflation in the straw-broom market.

Contemporary Paris discovered it could find quadruple use for the Île Saint-Louis: as an elegant residential quarter of the fourth arrondissement; as a strolling museum neighborhood, a sort of Tricolorland with no parking meters, no movie house, or cemetery (if people die, they have to be taken to the Continent); as a quiet corner for small restaurants, antiquaries, bars, bookshops, hotels, Mme Blanvillain's 160-year-old olive shop (she was not the founder), and a pheasant-plucker named

Turpin in case you need your pheasant plucked; and the fourth use is optional.

On my most recent visit, the spirit of the place was expressed by the aforementioned Berthillon, the studio for ice cream masterpieces with the seventeenth-century aspect. It was early July. A cheerful sign said: "Open Wednesday, 14 September." Where else would an ice cream shop close for the hot months?

I was relieved by this assurance of little change in the weekend-maddened, vacation-crazed spirit of the French *commerçant*. No matter how greedy he might seem to mere mortals, plucking money from the air and sewing it into his mattress, the flight to seaside or country cottage remains sacred.

Throwing duffel on bed, not even glancing at the exchange rate, I seized a notebook in jet-lagged claws and made a quick tour of the few streets and circumnavigating quays of the island, trying to find what had changed, what had remained the same, and what might persuade my body that it was time to sleep. The fact that I had cleverly scheduled my visit to come near the July 14 celebration, when France dances and drinks and makes new friends in the street till dawn—all because their ancestors tore down the Bastille—did not induce thoughts of prudent shut-eye.

(In my student days, when an American friend studying in Belgium bicycled into Paris for the first time, he happened to arrive on Bastille Day and found colorful lights strung from everywhere, accordions, embraces, a fierce festival glitter in every eye. He fell upon my little room crying, "Oh, I always knew Paris would be like this!")

A street sweeper with the timid face of a peasant come to the metropolis was scrubbing down the stones in front of the Saint-Louis-en-l'Île. No change here.

Libella, the Polish bookstore on the rue Saint-Louis-en-l'Île, reminded me that Paris has always been everyone's other home. The wall above Libella bears a stone plaque telling us that in 1799 the engineer Philippe Lebon discovered, in this building, the principle of lighting and heating with gas—the word "principle" and past experience suggest that the French did not actually get around to doing it for a while.

The island is crowded with such notices—tributes to poets, advisers to kings, soldier heroes, men of God, and even a film critic immortalized on a plaque affixed to the place where he analyzed Jerry Lewis as *auteur*.

There is also a plaque on the wall of the Fernand Halphen Foundation in the rue des Deux-Ponts:

> **To the Memory**
> **Of the 112 Inhabitants**
> **Of This Building**
> **Including 40 Children**
> **Deported and Killed**
> **In the Concentration Camps in 1942.**

No island is entire of itself, exempt from history. Across the street, in the ice cream shops, bistros, the Bateau Bar—fifty brands of beer from all nations—gratification proceeds on its necessary course.

It was time to sit at a café table for the island equivalent of my typical San Francisco after-racquetball vitamin and health hi-pro yogurt shake; in this case, a coffee with "yak"—cognac.

Two helmeted Vespa people came skidding to a stop in front of me. Like space warriors, they were encased in huge plastic headgear. Evidently they knew each other, because they fell to kissing, their helmets thudding together. I peeked at their faces when they came apart. They were both about sixty years old and hadn't seen each other in hours.

A fisherman nearby, when I asked what he caught with all his equipment, assured me that trout hover near the fresh underground springs at the head of the island.

"And what else?"

"A moment of meditation. A view of Notre-Dame. There are gargoyles, sir. At this season, there are roses."

During the morning, a fisherman was catching roses; that night in front of the footbridge leading to Aux Alsaciennes, the Communist Party sponsored a rock celebration of Bastille Day. A girl in a "Wichita University Long Island" T-shirt danced to a French knockoff of "Lady Jane" and other Rolling Stones hits. Instead of a male partner, she held a contribution box for *Humanité,* the party newspaper.

The little park at the end of the island where the Pont de Sully links the Left and Right Banks of Paris—leading to the workers' quarter of Bastille in one direction, the Quartier Latin in the other—has a grand stone monument to "Barye 1795–1875" at its entrance. The sculptor seems to be telling a busy story, including naked lads, heroes, a foot on a screaming animal, a sword, a staff, a few less boyish youths. Who the heck was Barye 1795–1875?

He may be there to provide a little relaxation from all the really famous people who lived and live on the Île Saint-Louis. (He turns out to have been a watercolorist.)

The square Barye, surrounded by the Seine on three sides, is quiet, peaceful, scholarly, artistic, with occasional summer concerts; kids sleeping on their backpacks, workmen with bottles of *rouge;* Swedish au pair girls watching the babies and sunning themselves with that passionate solar intensity only Swedish girls achieve—happy sunbathers when it's hot and moonbathing when it's not; haggard widows in black, wincing with their memories; birds chirping and barbered bushes and peeling-bark trees and neat cinder paths: all honor to Barye 1795–1875!

Three small hotels on the island located on the rue Saint-Louis-en-l'Île, a few steps from each other, have been converted from seventeenth-century houses: the Lutèce, the Deux-Îles, and the Saint-Louis.

When I telephoned the Lutèce from San Francisco for a reservation, the place was booked, but the good madame leaned out the window and yelled next door to the Deux-Îles to ask if they had a place. Also booked. So was the Saint-Louis. But on my arrival, I managed to persuade the daughter of the proprietor of the Saint-Louis to find me a corner room.

On the short walk home—saying "home" comes quickly in this island universe—I noticed that Hippolyte Taine and Georges Sadoul did their work in the same building. Marc Chagall and Charles Baudelaire, Voltaire and Mme Pompidou, dukes and barons, and *chanteurs de charme,* plus a stray prince or princess, an inventor or hero—who didn't have a connection with the Île Saint-Louis?

The Île Saint-Louis is like France itself—an ideal of grace and proportion—but it differs from the rest of France in that it lives up to itself. Under constant repair and renovation, it remains intact. It is a small place derived from long experience. It has strength enough, and isolation enough, to endure with a certain smugness the troubles of the city and the world at whose center it rests.

The self-love is mitigated partly by success at guarding itself and partly by the ironic shrugs of its inhabitants, who, despite whatever aristocratic names or glamorous professions, live among broken-veined *clochards* (hoboes) with unbagged bottles, tourists with unbagged guidebooks, Bohemians with bagged eyes.

The actual troubles of the world do not miss the Île Saint-Louis—one doesn't string hammocks between the plane trees here—but the air seems to contain fewer mites and less nefarious Paris ozone.

The lack of buses, the narrow streets, the breeze down the Seine help. And as to perhaps the most dangerous variety of Paris smog, the Île Saint-Louis seems to have discovered the unanswerable French reply to babble, noise, advice, and theory—*silence.*

One can, of course, easily get off this island, either by walking on the water of the Seine or, in a less saintly way, by taking a stroll of about two minutes across the slim bridges to the Left Bank, the Right Bank, or the bustling and official neighbor, the Île de la Cité.

Island fever is not a great danger, despite the insular pleasures of neatness, shape, control. Some people even say they never go to "Paris." (In 1924, there was an attempt to secede from Paris and France, and Île Saint-Louis passports were issued.) Monsieur Filleui, the fishmonger, used to advertise: "Deliveries on the Island and on the Continent."

The Île Saint-Louis, an elsewhere village universe,

happens also to be an island by the merest accident of being surrounded by water. Its bridges reach inward to shadow worlds of history and dream, and outward toward the furor of contemporary Paris.

Shaded and sunny, surrounded by the waters of the Seine like a moat, it remains a kind of castle keep that is powerful enough in its own identity to hold Paris at bridge's length, a breath away. Amazingly, it has occurred to no one powerful enough to do anything about it that this place, too, could be high-rised, filthied, thoroughfared, developed. There is no Métro station. The breezes down the Seine keep busy, sweeping and caressing.

Despite the claims of metropolis on all sides, the Île Saint-Louis still expresses the shadow presence of the Île Notre-Dame and the Île-aux-Vaches. The ancestor islands make a claim to be remembered because they have been forgotten, and both the aristocratic and the chic who live here, and the *gratteurs de guitare,* who occasionally come to serenade the ghosts of counts and courtesans, know that they tread in a palimpsest of footsteps, including ancient Gauls, Romans, and now, chirping and clicking beneath the willows, the occasional polyester-clad, camera-breasted tourist.

A more characteristic sight is that of the professional anguish of a French intellectual walking his dog. The rich tend to live like Bohemians here. (Only the poor, as Anatole France said, are forbidden to beg.)

The Île Saint-Louis is one of the places where a postwar generation of Americans in Paris loosened its military discipline—if we happened to have any—studied peace and art and history and depravity (called it freedom, called it fulfilling ourselves), lived in awe before our fantasy of France (still do just a little).

We bought old bicycles and new notebooks. We pretended to be students, artists, philosophers, and lovers, and, out of our pretensions, sometimes learned to be a little of these things.

Remarks are not literature, Gertrude Stein said, and islands are not the world. But some remarks can tell us what literature is about, some islands can tell us what a sweeter, more defined world might be. In Spinoza's view, freedom consists of knowing what the limits are. I came to Paris as a philosophy student but left it as a novelist. On the Île Saint-Louis, I am still home free, watching the Seine flow and eddy and flow again.

The Paris of Parisians

CATHARINE REYNOLDS

ᘜᘓᘔ

IT HAS BEEN noted by many observers of Paris that the city is essentially a collection of villages. The five *quartiers* featured here—in the third, sixth, twelfth, thirteenth, and seventeenth arrondissements—have still retained their neighborhood feel, and a visit to any one of them will reveal dimensions of Paris well beyond its more famous *grands boulevards*, *rues*, and *places*.

CATHARINE REYNOLDS, introduced previously, was a contributing editor at *Gourmet,* where this piece originally appeared in 2001.

YOU'VE PROBABLY CLIMBED the Eiffel Tower and checked out the stained glass at the Sainte-Chapelle. But have you really seen Paris? Beyond its set-piece monuments and cultural icons, the Paris of Parisians is a collage of villages. And visitors who venture outside the Eiffel–Concorde–Notre-Dame triangle to explore these enclaves will discover another dimension of the city.

It's something of a miracle that so many distinct neighborhoods survive. And it's Baron Haussmann, often condemned for the uniformity he imposed on Paris and for the broad boulevards he cut through medieval areas in the mid-nineteenth century, who may, ironically, be indirectly responsible. Today, the boulevards carry the worst of the city's traffic, leaving the byways to the locals. Nor can you discount the role of what might be called the tyranny of the baguette. This staple goes stale quickly, making daily provisioning essential and thus encouraging the survival of local food shops along with the street life they promote.

The five *quartiers* featured here, many of them recent additions to Parisians' "hot" list, have all retained that neighborhood feel. They are as varied as their inhabitants—and seem to us perfect examples of what makes the city one of the world's liveliest and most livable.

IN THE THIRD

In spite of its location in this central arrondissement, **Temple**, a tangled skein of streets north of the Picasso Museum and south of the Place de la République, has been largely overlooked in the dramatic gentrification that has renewed the Marais over the past thirty years.

At least until recently. The narrow streets—many of them named after the provinces of France—are still lined with handsome seventeenth- and eighteenth-century *hôtels particuliers,* not all of which have been restored. The generous spaces and sleepy, very Parisian aura here have attracted artists, young professionals, in-the-know foreigners, and a burgeoning gay community. Most of these new arrivals come armed with more panache than cash, and today they share the sidewalks with the artisans who have long sustained the area.

The *quartier* remains identified with a building that is no longer there: the Temple, a priory whose name derived from that of the Knights Templars, a military and religious order founded during the First Crusade. The organization once controlled a walled city covering much of both the third and fourth arrondissements. Midway through the Revolution, the Temple became a prison, and en route to the guillotine, Louis XVI and his family were some of its first inmates. In an effort to erase memories of the pitiful child king, Louis XVII, who died there, Napoléon demolished the tower where the family had been held.

Today, this peaceful area is one of the most forward-looking in Paris. The young lovers who wheel their firstborn around the duck pond in the Square du Temple are likely as not dues-paid members of the Net set who flock to the ultracool Web Bar to surf and salsa. This neighborhood invites the pedestrian: the one-way system discourages through traffic, so you can zigzag back and forth, here admiring an ivy-hung courtyard, there sizing up a produce display. Shops and galleries are gradually displacing the ateliers of wholesale jewelers, who have populated the *quartier* for centuries, but the newcomers are somehow more low-key than those who have taken over the streets adjacent to the Place des Vosges.

Perhaps this is because the Temple remains a vibrant residential neighborhood. Afternoons see youngsters, testing the limits of their *trottinettes* (scooters)—and of their parents' patience—just avoiding collision with dealers shuttling fifties furniture into their boutiques and graphic artists piloting portfolios into taxis. And households supply their tables along the rue de Bretagne, where butchers, fishmongers, and greengrocers compete with merchants in the newly restored Marché des Enfants Rouges, the capital's oldest market.

IN THE THIRTEENTH

In the Parisian lexicon, *stressé* is the all-purpose adjective. And for many young urban professionals, the human scale of neighborhood life in the villagy *quartiers* on the city's periphery is the sovereign antidote. Originally hamlets in their own right that were annexed wholesale to Paris on January 1, 1860, these enclaves come by their bucolic manners honestly.

Just a few short years ago, an address *aux Cailles,* as the **Butte-aux-Cailles** is lovingly called, would have taken some explaining.

These days, however, it excites raw envy, as more and more people discover this pocket of intimacy deep in the western section of the thirteenth, only a short Métro ride from the humming heart of the city. *Butte* means "knoll," and in Paris is more commonly applied to the Butte Montmartre. The Butte-aux-Cailles has Montmartre's charm, but, being less publicized, it is less visited. And its residents are determined to keep it that way, trumpeting that the Cailles *has* no attractions—perhaps forgetting that this is precisely what explains its appeal. This forgotten part of Paris, with its cobbled streets and old-fashioned streetlamps, exudes a provincial atmosphere of permanence.

The Butte-aux-Cailles earned a place in history in 1783, when the world's first hot-air balloon landed there after a twenty-five-minute journey from the western side of the city. The area remained sparsely populated until the middle of the nineteenth century, when the poorest of Parisians, dispossessed by Baron Haussmann's slum clearances, took refuge there. Ragpickers soon joined them, but infrastructure was slow in coming.

Today, the area tempts you to wander aimlessly: to discover a litter of kittens snoozing on a windowsill of one of the gabled houses at 10 rue Daviel, known appropriately as Petite Alsace. Or to trip down the cobbled rue Samson as it nears the rue de la Butte-aux-Cailles, racking your brain to recall which Jean Renoir film must have been set here. The architecture is modest, with none of the furbelows of monumental Paris, but it's easy to imagine—or is it hear?—Georges Brassens melodies cooing from radios. Some of the Cailles's streets perpetuate good country names—"Mill in the Meadows," "Poplars"—seeming to defy the misguided urban planners of the sixties and seventies who permitted high-rises to be built not far away, like grim reality checks.

In your wanderings, you may sight residents loping with laptops to nearby lofts bowered by chestnuts, or backpack-encumbered Madelines sailing home from school unaccompanied in the quiet streets. In fine weather, the pharmacist, who elsewhere in the city would spend his quiet time officiously tidying, here takes the air, leaning against his doorframe, gossiping until a customer appears. And in a city that has at least three restaurants called Chez Paul, the Butte-aux-Cailles's Paul, with its lace curtains and traditional *grand-mère* food, may be the most appealing. But then neighborhood standards are high, hoisted there by the inventive cooking of Christophe Beaufront of L'Avant-Goût.

IN THE SEVENTEENTH

Clear on the other side of town, **Les Batignolles** also began life beyond the city's walls, on barely cultivated land. Here, in the 1820s and 1830s, developers constructed modest country retreats with patches of garden for the growing class of prosperous Parisian shopkeepers, who were soon joined by petty bureaucrats and washerwomen.

Everything and nothing changed with the coming of the railroads. The Paris–Le Pecq line, completed in 1837, cut the area off from the west. When Les Batignolles was annexed to Paris, Baron Haussmann's engineering alter ego added a handsome park, the Square des Batignolles, but did little else to knit the backwater into the wider urban fabric. Low rents and an ample supply of laundresses and seamstresses willing to model attracted painters like Manet and Renoir. From 1865, they made the Café Guerbois and the Cabaret du Père Lathuille, on what is now the avenue de Clichy, the crossroads of artistic café culture, attracting Bazille, Degas, Pissarro, and Monet. But painterly Paris soon moved on, leaving Les Batignolles very much to itself.

Until lately. These days, two-career couples, delighted by its retro rents and sleepy, shabby-chic atmosphere, are snapping up apartments here. The neighborhood's easy rhythms seem a world removed from the pressures of the Place de l'Opéra, little more than a mile away. Many residents find they can even walk to their law offices and banks. The organic market, held every Saturday just nearby, is yet another draw.

Like any French village worth its salt, Les Batignolles has a fine church standing at its heart. A semicircle of buildings frames the pretty *place* around neoclassic Sainte-Marie des Batignolles. The corner café boasts the confident name of L'Endroit and, within its varnished concrete walls, is every bit as edgy as the Café Guerbois was in its day. The trees along the southwest side of the church shelter a handful of timeless shops: a florist, a dealer in pretty bibelots, and a children's outfitter with the sanguine name of Merci Maman. (Truth told, the children playing in the shadow of the *boules* game in the square beyond do look as though they mind their manners—but then more than a few of the newer Batignolles parents grew up in the strict and starched purlieus of the sixteenth arrondissement.)

The rue des Batignolles is the main drag, lined with pleasant boutiques, the local town hall, and restaurants. Then there's the tree-lined rue Brochant, where you can admire the gilded curlicues on the Boucherie du Square, sample Christian Rizzotto's ethereal cinnamon *ganaches,* and investigate the antique dolls at L'Atelier de Maïté. And at afternoon's end, when the food shops reopen, you can eye supper along the rue des Moines, stopping at the tiny Fromagerie des Moines to nibble Saint-Marcellins and Pont-l'Évêques. In this neighborhood, even doing chores is a sensory delight.

IN THE TWELFTH

Trend spotters say the Bastille is over as the mecca of haute hip, but their divinations cut no mustard at the **Marché d'Aligre.** Tucked away just a bit east of Carlos Ott's behemoth opera house, the market has been the hub of a skilled artisans' quarter for centuries. Newcomers may be more of-the-moment, but as far as the stallholders are concerned, last year's pashmina passion will provide next year's stock for the secondhand clothes dealers—and everybody will have to go on eating.

In a city of legendary markets, the Marché d'Aligre is unique in that it includes a street market, a covered market, and an open-air flea market (open six days a week). Named for the wife of Étienne d'Aligre, a worthy seventeenth-century chancellor, the market once rivaled the old Les Halles.

Today this is one of the city's most integrated neighborhoods. And the next new thing—be it in blown glass, *strié* velvet, or neon

tubing—will likely emerge from the workshops in the small passages that honeycomb the area. A handful of the cabinetmaking trades that were the backbone of the area remain, but many of the workshops are now ateliers for a new breed of supercharged creators. By day they hunker down at work; at night they play. The modern street section of the market, strung along the rue d'Aligre, is reputed to offer the city's best values. Which, to an extent, explains the diversity of the crowd: graceful Malian women haggle with Tunisians over plantains, *comme il faut* students from the nearby law school stock up on apples and vintage frocks, and gay couples fill their shopping carts. Some of the merchants are specialists, like the fellow who deals only in garlic, shallots, and onions, or the mother and daughter who have for decades pyramided the north corner of the *place* with lettuce and herbs.

The covered market, the Marché Beauvau, might as well be in *la France profonde.* Here, a suckling pig turns on a butcher's spit, and the scent of spices and fragrant oils floats out from the stall known as Sur les Quais. Outside, on the eastern edge of the square, secondhand dealers spread life's castoffs. The merchandise looks little different from that on offer in a 1911 Atget photo of the area, save for the fact that a brutalist concrete apartment-building-cum-ground-floor-supermarket has replaced the *triperie* and greengrocer. And there are treasures to be unearthed. Occasionally there is a trove of flirty thirties bias-cut dresses in silk crêpe. Snapped up, they may soon clothe a lithe form sambaing at one of the area's many hot nightspots. At noon, market habitués often heap their bags in a corner at a nearby wine bar or head for the hypercool Le Square Trousseau. This centenarian bistro hasn't allowed its head to be turned by its new, big-name clientele. That may be Jean-Paul Gaultier tucking into *petit salé* (salt pork with lentils) over there, but that's only reasonable: his Faubourg Saint-Antoine store, installed in a former furniture showroom, is just around the corner.

IN THE SIXTH

The rue du Cherche-Midi, on the western edge of the sixth arrondissement, is not laid-back. Here, rail-thin blondes swing leather-clad hips out of tiny Mercedes Smart cars and bolt into Eres to scoop up bikinis. More conservative types saunter from boutique to boutique, weighing the merits of saddle-stitched handbags from Il Bisonte against the frivolity of fur-trimmed microfiber *sacs* from Ginkgo. Down the street, every passerby lusts after the Andrée Putman armchairs at Hugues Chevalier, and there are nouveau-rustic wrought-iron lamps and door furniture at La Maison de Brune, not to mention every manner of stylish footgear at the ultrahip Lundi Bleu.

Following the route of a Roman road that once led from Lutèce to Vaugirard, the **rue du Cherche-Midi** today serves as a new kind of link. It bridges two styles, serving both the fashionistas who flock to Saint-Germain and the BCBGs, a hardy breed of French preppies, many of whom nest in the seventh arrondissement. Whatever their fashion icons, this shopping sorority can't resist the siren allure of the Cherche-Midi vitrines.

The street's retail charms are so conspicuous that they almost obscure what is one of the city's most sought-after neighborhoods. Some of the capital's most gracious apartments sit above the boutiques, carved from eighteenth- and nineteenth-century private houses. The "happy few" occupy aristocratic family mansions—some have been in the same hands for two hundred years. Other inhabitants, whom we might call limousine liberals but whom the French refer to as *gauche caviar,* choose the *quartier* for the grandeur of its fine houses and its access to the Collège de France and the other cultured haunts of the Left Bank.

The handsome balconies at no. 11 merely hint at the gilded splendor of the Louis XV paneling in its second-story reception rooms, and the nearby rue du Regard typifies the best of the se-date eighteenth-century limestone façades of the neighborhood, with elegant pediments and *portes cochères* that spark fantasy.

But the real magic of the neighborhood, what brings us back, is the people—the Little Blue Riding Hood employing Cartesian arguments to persuade Maman that the bear beanbag in the window really requires immediate adoption; the tailored gentleman looking the part of a retired diplomat, emerging from his bookbinder with a leather volume under his arm.

And amid all the fashion temptations, there are food shops (this is Paris, after all). The neighborhood baker is the internationally known Poilâne, the city's largest organic market is held on the boulevard Raspail each Sunday, and the Grande Épicerie de Paris is only streets away. There are restaurants and cafés, too, though visitors are well advised to reserve if they hope to claim a table at L'Épi Dupin. Alternatively, they can join the ladies who don't really lunch for a sandwich at Cuisine de Bar, where there's even a diet choice. In this *quartier,* it's important to be able to slither into a bodysuit from Feelgood.

IN THE NEIGHBORHOODS

Temple

Recently remodeled, the **Musée des Arts et Métiers** showcases French inventions, among them Pascal's adding machine, Foucault's pendulum, Ader's airplane, and the Lumière brothers' movie camera. (60 rue Réaumur / +33 01 53 01 82 00.)

Chez Omar is something of a hybrid: a nicotine-soaked brasserie specializing in couscous. Its clientele is equally eclectic, with models waiting for tables alongside locals, and cutting-edge moviemakers as pleased with the *merguez* as the wanna-bes. (47 rue de Bretagne / +33 01 42 72 36 26.)

The fare at **Au Bascou** is as good as Basque food gets: chestnut soup, stuffed *piquillo* peppers, and roasted squab, enjoyed with whatever little-known bottles Jean-Guy Loustou, the restaurant's owner and host, may suggest. (38 rue Réaumur / +33 01 42 72 69 25.)

Le Pamphlet's prix-fixe menu includes happy innovations such as squid risotto, crab ravioli sauced with pea emulsion, and licorice ice cream. (38 rue Debelleyme / +33 01 42 72 39 24.)

A huge, flat-screen monitor greets arrivals at **Web Bar**. With its concrete tables, velvet banquettes, and wired workstations, this is a grown-up cybercafé. (32 rue de Picardie / +33 01 42 72 66 55.)

Behind a shabby façade, **DOT** (Diffusion d'Objets de Table) sells reproductions of bistro tablewares. (47 rue de Saintonge / +33 01 40 29 90 34.)

There's nothing shy about **Philippe Ferrandis**'s fantastical *bijoux*. Once an accessorist for Oscar de la Renta, today he makes and sells his bold and bright *objets* from this showroom-atelier. (2 rue Froissart / +33 01 48 87 87 24.)

In Franck Delmarcelle's **Et Caetera**, you'll find huge garden urns alongside eighteenth-century tables, and lanterns and mantel-pieces alongside sideboards and chandeliers. Everything in this long, narrow boutique is gutsy and slightly overscale. (40 rue de Poitou / +33 01 42 71 37 11.)

L'Habilleur stocks last season's merchandise, but the men's and women's duds all reflect the most wearable trends and are dis-played in handsome, civilized surroundings. (44 rue de Poitou / +33 01 48 87 77 12.)

Agence Opale, a photo agency that specializes in portraits of au-thors, stocks prints of period photos of literary heroes. (8 rue Charlot / +33 01 40 29 93 33.)

Picquier et Protière sells its Marimekko-style fabrics by the yard but also makes them into cushions and stunning shopping bags with stout leather handles. (10 rue Charlot / +33 01 42 72 39 14.)

Galerie Yvon Lambert has been ahead of the curve since the late sixties, spotting Cy Twombly and Richard Long early on. It represents, among others, Nan Goldin. (108 rue Vieille-du-Temple / +33 01 42 71 09 33.)

Butte-aux-Cailles

The **Place de la Commune de Paris** commemorates the Butte-aux-Cailles's role as headquarters for the insurgents in May 1871. Its bloody history is curiously at odds with the graceful, green cast-iron Fontaine Wallace that today stands in the middle of the tiny *place.*

A brick façade with late Art Nouveau sinuosities disguises the **Piscine de la Butte-aux-Cailles**, a municipal swimming pool fed by a bubbling artesian well. Roofed in then-innovative reinforced concrete, the pool, surprisingly, was built at the same time as the façade—in 1924. (5 place Paul-Verlaine / +33 01 45 89 60 05.)

At **L'Avant-Goût**, Christophe Beaufront's luncheon menu, often featuring a luscious pig's-cheek stew, has raised the bar for Paris's *néo-bistros.* (26 rue Bobillot / +33 01 53 80 24 00.)

Chez Paul's traditional French cuisine attracts people from all over the city. (22 rue de la Butte-aux-Cailles / +33 01 45 89 22 11.)

Les Abeilles sells dozens of honeys, along with supplies for bee-keepers. (21 rue de la Butte-aux-Cailles / +33 01 45 81 43 48.)

Aux Délices de la Butte is the quintessential neighborhood bakery, with *cannelés de Bordeaux* and baguettes worth seeking out. (48 rue Bobillot / +33 01 45 89 45 55.)

La Cave du Moulin Vieux specializes in wines from small producers. (4 rue de la Butte-aux-Cailles / +33 01 45 80 42 38.)

You don't have to be Italian to appreciate the salamis and aged Parmigiano-Reggiano at the Bologna-comes-to-Paris grocery **Cipolli**. (81 rue Bobillot / +33 01 45 88 26 06.)

Les Batignolles

Foursquare yet understated behind its four Doric columns, **Sainte-Marie des Batignolles** has stood since 1830 at the heart of the village of Batignolles. (77 place du Dr.-Félix-Lobligeois / +33 01 46 27 57 67.)

At **L'Endroit**, the of-the-moment hangout across from the church, the food tends to be as high design as much of the crowd, and the music crescendoes well into the night. (67 place du Dr.-Félix-Lobligeois / +33 01 42 29 50 00.)

It's wise to reserve one of the twenty-odd seats at **La P'tite Lili**, where locals go to chill out. The menu is limited, but the sausages are flavorful, the salads sassy, and the meat and fish excellent. (8 rue des Batignolles / +33 01 45 22 54 22.)

Families sate their pasta passions at **Arcimboldo**, where they go en masse to share gnocchi and ravioli and wash it all down with Chianti. (7 rue Brochant / +33 01 42 29 37 62.)

The market-fresh food at the **Cinnamon Café**—tomatoes stuffed with whiting *mousseline,* apple crumble—is the stuff of memories. (5 rue des Batignolles / +33 01 43 87 64 51.)

Merci Maman carries the sort of handsome, sturdy clothes you see on Paris schoolchildren. (73 place du Dr.-Félix-Lobligeois / +33 01 42 29 11 62.)

The tiny candleholder that will make a table sparkle, the little present worth stashing for next December—such bibelots are the stock-in-trade of **La Vie en Rose**. (73 place du Dr.-Félix-Lobligeois / +33 01 42 63 70 71.)

The jury's out on which is better: **Christian Rizzotto**'s cinnamon *ganaches* or his *rocailles*. (14 rue Brochant / +33 01 42 63 18 70.)

The **Fromagerie des Moines** is particularly strong on Norman cheeses like Camembert and Pont-l'Évêque. (47 rue des Moines / +33 01 46 27 69 24.)

For thirty-three years, **L'Atelier de Maïté** has specialized in buying, selling, and repairing dolls made between 1860 and 1930. (8 rue Brochant / +33 01 42 63 23 93.)

By the Marché d'Aligre

Opera fans thrill to visits backstage at **Carlos Ott's Opéra Bastille**. The workrooms and full-scale rehearsal studios kindle lyric fascination. (120 rue de Lyon / +33 01 40 01 19 70.)

The **Marché d'Aligre** is the only Paris market open six days a week. It includes a street market, a covered market, and a flea market. Open Tuesday to Sunday, 8 a.m. to 1 p.m. (Place d'Aligre.)

Le Square Trousseau is headquarters for many of the Bastille area's trendies. The food runs from comfort (terrines and tarts) to winds-of-change world food (risotto, chicken *b'stilla*). (1 rue Antoine-Vollon / +33 01 43 43 06 00.)

Sunday mornings are the choicest time at the wine bar **Le Baron Rouge**. Where else can you eat Arcachon oysters off the hood of a parked car while tasting Cairanne from Richaud? (1 rue Théophile-Roussel / +33 01 43 43 14 32.)

After a hard morning's trade, shoppers and merchants collapse at **La Table d'Aligre** to savor sophisticated country cooking. (Place d'Aligre / +33 01 43 07 84 88.)

Whether you need a plum-colored sou'wester or a sequined pink beret, **La Sartan** is the Mad Hatter's Parisian outpost. (24 rue de Charenton / +33 01 53 33 09 09.)

Michel Moisan has made his name as an organic baker; his walnut-hazelnut bread brings many across town. (5 place d'Aligre / +33 01 43 45 46 60.)

Spices and oils scent the entire Marché Beauvau thanks to **Sur les Quais**, which stocks at least a dozen vintages of olive oil—from Marché Beauvau, Sicily, Andalusia, and the Peloponnese. (place d'Aligre / +33 01 43 43 21 09.)

À la Providence is the place to buy French-style furniture hardware. (151 rue du Faubourg St.-Antoine / +33 01 43 43 06 41.)

Unlike some cutting-edge designers, **Nathalie Dumeix** creates for the less-than-anorexic. Zip into a vampy, bias-cut crêpe dress. (10 rue Théophile-Roussel / +33 01 43 46 00 22.)

Rue du Cherche-Midi

Lionized by Second Empire hostesses for his flattering portraits, Ernest Hébert would largely be forgotten today but for the handsome eighteenth-century Petit Hôtel de Montmorency-Bours, which houses the **Musée Hébert**, dedicated to his works. (85 rue du Cherche-Midi / +33 01 42 22 23 82.)

The lunchtime crush at **L'Épi Dupin** is real, but so is the lunch, rich with chef François Pasteau's inventions. Try the lamb enveloped in thin slices of eggplant. (11 rue Dupin / +33 01 42 22 64 56.)

Cuisine de Bar makes open-faced sandwiches of foie gras and shrimp on Poilâne's famed sourdough, to be washed down with a fruit-juice cocktail. (8 rue du Cherche-Midi / +33 01 45 48 45 69.)

Finely finished leather handles top the bright microfiber handbags at **Ginkgo**. Some even sport fur collars. (4 ter rue du Cherche-Midi / +33 01 45 44 90 87.)

Feelgood lives up to its name, selling flirty dresses and good-value bodysuits, made of low-shine microfiber, that sculpt the shape. All emerge from suitcases looking as well rested as the wearers would like to be. (9 rue du Cherche-Midi / +33 01 45 44 88 66.)

At **Elena Cantacuzène**, ethnic styling meets catwalk chic. A handful of her beady "jools" are available in special American stores, but here you select from the full range. (47 rue du Cherche-Midi / +33 01 45 44 95 94.)

Under the gaze of passersby, **Pierre Marsaleix** binds books. He's pleased to fill special orders based on sketches, and stamps volumes in elaborate designs. (113–115 rue du Cherche-Midi / +33 01 42 22 12 13.)

Célimène Pompon deals in what the French quaintly call *travaux de dames,* or needlework. Among the handsome original cross-stitch canvases, you'll also find beguiling stuffed animals. (41 rue du Cherche-Midi / +33 01 45 44 53 95.)

Taken with sleek Normandie-inspired furnishings? **Hugues Chevalier** displays a tempting array. (17 rue du Cherche-Midi / +33 01 45 48 69 55.)

RECOMMENDED READING

A Corner in the Marais: Memoir of a Paris Neighborhood, Alex Karmel (Godine, 1998). At the center of Karmel's memoir is a specific building in the Marais, a building that "has no special distinction apart from the fact that it has been standing for centuries"—and that he and his wife bought an apartment in it some years before this book was published. Though his (French) wife would prefer to live in an apartment overlooking the Place des Vosges "to any other place on earth," the pied-à-terre they buy is on the notable Marais street of the rue des Rosiers, then, as now, too cold in the winter and too hot in the summer. But they love it, and they love this neighborhood. Karmel ends this well-written and fascinating book with a chapter entitled "Neighbors," which is a walking tour that begins on the rue Vieille-du-Temple and ends in the Place des Vosges. Lastly, he includes a wonderful excerpt from *Le Piéton de Paris* (The Walker of Paris) by poet and writer Léon-Paul Fargue (1876–1947), who was an avid wanderer best known for his evocative depictions of Paris. In this three-page excerpt alone, one learns quite a bit about the Marais, which is "not merely the past," as Karmel notes, but "also a vibrant, living neighborhood in the present."

Into a Paris Quartier: Reine Margot's Chapel and Other Haunts of St.-Germain, Diane Johnson (National Geographic Directions, 2005). Paris has haunted the American imagination from the days of Franklin and Jefferson, Johnson notes in her introduction to this interesting and quirky book, and the city has also occupied an important place in American literature, from Henry James to Hemingway. "And, like Jefferson's, like Gertrude Stein's, the American imagination has tended to fasten on a particular part of Paris: the Left Bank around the church of Saint-Germain-des-Prés." As Johnson also notes, the Saint-Germain neighborhood may just be the most visited and written about of all Parisian neighborhoods, so it was an unlikely candidate for her to write a book about. But something Johnson sees every day outside her kitchen window stood out to her, symbolizing her present connection to Saint-Germain: "the back of a little chapel built by Queen Marguerite de Valois in 1608." (Valois was the first wife of Henri IV.) Johnson not only reveals the story of this chapel but essentially the stories of a Paris most visitors walk right past and never notice. Though I eagerly devoured these stories of a favorite *quartier,* it was a remark in Johnson's introduction that really made me want to read this book. As she was writing an introduction to a collection of short stories about Paris by American writers, she was struck by how many of the stories were about personal defeat—the Americans in almost all the stories go home "to face real life in the States, and will think wistfully forever after about what might have been, if only they had stayed, or had learned how to stay, in Paris. We are moved to ask: What is it about Paris? And what is eluding us at home?"

Man Ray's Montparnasse, Herbert Lottman (Harry N. Abrams, 2001). Lottman first went to Paris in 1949 as a Fulbright fellow and has spent most of his life since then in France. He's also the author of a number of French-themed books, including biographies of Philippe Pétain, Gustave Flaubert, Colette, and Jules Verne, and *The Left Bank: Writers, Artists, and Politics from the Popular Front to the Cold War* (Houghton Mifflin, 1982). But it was Montparnasse that Lottman had wanted to write about for a long time—"ever since I settled in Paris in the late 1950s and began my explorations into its cultural life." He couldn't quite figure out how to connect the dots between the Dada artists, the Surrealists, the École de Paris painters, the Anglo-Americans, heirs and heiresses, Gertrude Stein's weekly open house—until he realized that American photographer Man Ray was the link. "Man Ray could talk to everybody, and he made it a point to do so. And not surprisingly, everybody was ready to talk to this friendly New Yorker, not necessarily for his conversation but for his camera, which he was eager to use." Lottman vividly evokes the first thirty years of Paris in the twentieth century, when the streets surrounding boulevard du Montparnasse and the boulevard Raspail were the center of the avant-garde in Europe. By 1934, however, France was in a depression, there was much strife between political parties, and in Paris there was a general air of pessimism. When Marcel Duchamp was asked to sum up the glories of Montparnasse, he replied that, though Montparnasse was the first international colony of artists, superior to Montmartre, Greenwich Village, or Chelsea, "Montparnasse is dead, of course, and it may take twenty, fifty, or a hundred years to develop a new Montparnasse, and even then it is bound to take an entirely different form." Later, as Lottman notes, when the Nazis occupied Paris in 1940 and Man Ray left Montparnasse, he could not have known that "the Quarter as he had come to know it would cease to exist." Man Ray documented an extraordinary time and extraordinary people; this book includes fifty-three of his unforgettable black-and-white photographs.

Paris has been so beautiful for so long that, with few exceptions, every neighborhood has some treasure or other to show. It might be a well-designed antique water pump in a forbidding alley in the Glacière section of the thirteenth, a handsome fountain and a street of curiously designed apartment houses not far from the nondescript rue Monge, an old court, wrinkled and molten and still a *grande dame,* in the fur district—and everywhere, the rhythms of old streets meeting, proliferating, branching like the veins of a leaf.

—Kate Simon, *Paris: Places and Pleasures*

Habit de Cuisinier

LA CUISINE FRANÇAISE

Everyone who has visited France knows that it is a nation of hardy, persistent individualists. The French simply refuse to conform to type, whether it be a question of dress, of manners, or of politics, particularly the last. This quality of independence manifests itself with unusual emphasis in the matter of food and wine. This may seem surprising to those who have formed a conception of typical French fare. The genuine French cuisine, however, is an absolute tapestry of individualism, varying abruptly from one province to another, to the fascination of food-minded travelers. There is nothing "typical" about it.

—SAMUEL CHAMBERLAIN,
FROM THE INTRODUCTION TO
The Food of France BY WAVERLEY ROOT

Over centuries, the dinner table has remained an anchor for families and friendships, the heart of what is finest about France. Each course requires separate effort, part of a whole. Children learn their values and their manners at mealtime. Nothing important gets signed, sealed, or delivered without the clinking of glasses and the rattling of cutlery.

—MORT ROSENBLUM,
A Goose in Toulouse

A Saga of Bread

NAOMI BARRY

WHEN I INCLUDED this piece in my first Paris edition, Barry told me the only baguette in all of France that she liked was *la flûte Gana* from Ganachaud, a legendary *boulangerie* in the twentieth arrondissement. After she first tried it, she immediately thought of a French advertising slogan of the time, *Voilà un préjugé qui m'a coûté cher,* which translates as "And that's a prejudice that cost me dearly." If she once thought all baguettes were alike—dull and tasteless—she didn't anymore. I happen to be fond of the crispy, airy baguette in general, but I grant that the *flûte Gana* is one of the most perfect baguettes on earth. The original Ganachaud (rue de Ménilmontant) was presided over by master baker Bernard Ganachaud, who has since retired. That original shop is now closed, but Ganachaud's daughters, Valérie, Isabelle, and Marianne, have opened their own *boulangerie* nearby (226 rue des Pyrénées), which appears to be thriving. The family also now oversees a network of *boulangeries* with the Gana brand throughout France.

My husband and I once had the supreme great fortune to meet Bernard before he retired, although it happened quite by accident. I mentioned to the cashier at Ganachaud that I was visiting from the States and had learned of the bakery in Patricia Wells's b— But before I could say the word book, she excitedly summoned Bernard, who led us upstairs to his office, where we were served coffee and *bostock,* slices of slightly stale and toasted brioche flavored with kirsch and almonds (which is very yummy). All the while I was explaining that we didn't really *know* Patricia Wells—we had only read her book—but he didn't seem to mind as he shared some publicity clippings with us and chattered on about his recent venture in Japan.

There are a number of other outstanding *boulangeries* in Paris, and you will discover your own, some famous and others perhaps known only within your *quartier*, but a trip out to the twentieth (the neighborhood is Gambetta) is very much *vaut le détour*—it's worth the trip, to quote the *Guide Michelin*. I recommend making the journey a full-fledged excursion, also visiting the Père-Lachaise cemetery and Le Saint-Amour café (on the edge of the cemetery, at the corner of avenue Gambetta and boulevard de Ménilmontant). Le Saint-Amour was recommended by Patricia Wells years ago, and I've since visited several times, downing glasses of good Burgundy and enjoying the abundant *bonhomie*.

NAOMI BARRY wrote for many years for *Gourmet*. She is also the author of *Paris Personal* (Dutton, 1963), *Adorable Zucchini* (Brick Tower, 2005), and *Food alla Florentine* (Doubleday, 1972).

CHRISTINE, A BANK of information about her city, gave me the address of "the best bread place in Paris." Of course I made the trip since you don't find great bread on every corner anymore, even in France where the national image used to be a pair of crossed baguettes under a Basque beret.

The bakery was at 150 rue de Ménilmontant in the working-class district of the far-out twentieth arrondissement. Maurice Chevalier, who had been a child of the neighborhood, used to sing about Ménilmontant and he infused it with a titillating glamour, which has lingered.

The farther we progressed up the steep hill on our first foray into the territory, the more unpromising it seemed as the site of "the best bread in Paris." I was mentally accusing Christine of a bum steer when up loomed Bernard Ganachaud's bakery with the sudden brightness of a big ferry station in an otherwise darkened landscape.

It was huge with six times the frontage of any shop in the vicinity. Breads of assorted shapes and sizes were artfully displayed behind the gleaming windows. Thirty varieties are available in a Tour de France of regional breads. Some are better than others because in the down-home original versions, some simply are better than others. A *pain d'Auvergne* had a real style but it turned out to be disappointing, for instance.

On one window a girl employee was writing in large white letters the hit parade of specialties due to come forth from the visible ovens. The odors tantalizingly evoked a glorious farmhouse kitchen even if your childhood had not been that lucky. Although the French are notorious for the way they jump queues, in Ganachaud's bread line they were a model of decorum, proving that good behavior is determined by what is worth waiting for.

Ganachaud refuses to deliver and he doesn't care who you are. The chef of the Crillon was crazy about the deluxe baguette baptized *flûte Gana* and wanted it for the hotel. He was told to come and get it. Ganachaud insists on quality control of his product until the moment it is handed over to the customer. That means on the premises. Were it to spend a couple of hours in the back of a delivery van . . . He shudders. So the Crillon accepted to do its own fetch and carry. At the end of a year, the chef moaned, "*Mon cher,* do you realize that my taxi bill to get to you has been even greater than my bread bill?"

The complaint pleased Ganachaud no end. To go from the Crillon on the Place de la Concorde to the rue de Ménilmontant is like going from Eighty-first Street and Fifth Avenue in Manhattan to New Lots Avenue in Brooklyn. Individual customers from the chic arrondissements miles away have worked out a pool system. Whoever makes the trek is honor bound to bring back a supply for the others.

I immediately recognized the *maître-boulanger,* who was wearing the white work jacket with the tricolor ribbon collar and his name embroidered on the breast pocket that Bragard has made for most of the top chefs of France, giving them the uniformed look of an Olympic team. Despite a fluff of white hair and mustaches, Ganachaud's movements were quick and youthful and he was light on the balls of his feet like a bantamweight boxer. He interrupted a staccato monologue he was delivering to a young man in a corner, invited me to his organized little office, and—*toc-toc*—ordered me a coffee and a *flûte Gana.*

I have never been much of a fan of the baguette, the long skinny loaf usually known abroad as French bread, but I became a fanatic of Ganachaud's upmarket version. It is not only the best I have ever eaten but I am scared of it because once started I can't stop. It is twice the price of a regulation baguette, which has been no deterrent to the sales.

There was a delicious chewiness to the crust and a pleasing consistency to the crumb and, much as I love butter, it didn't need any. The *flûte* was no mere support for cheese but could stand very nicely on its own.

"No serious artisan need ever worry about competition from

the factory," said Ganachaud, "although if technology can make a bread with the same savor, I am not against it. However, the industrial bakery cannot furnish a bread that is really fresh."

He was referring mainly to the baguette whose short but happy life is responsible for those bread lines throughout France three times a day. The round loaf that was the peasant's staff of life could be counted upon to remain edibly fresh for several days. Big as a pillow, it took a while for all the moisture to evaporate from the crumb. The svelte baguette has comparatively little crumb and it goes dry in no time flat. Ganachaud's *flûte* has a crust porous enough for the moisture to come in as well as go out and consequently it remains fresh for a few hours more than the average. As long as you don't ask the perishable to be forever, a quality baguette at its peak can be memorable.

The Japanese, anxious to acquire the best of the West, wanted to franchise his *flûte*. Ganachaud gave them his usual "On my conditions or No Go." Not only would the bread have to be made according to his rigorous specifications, but the ovens had to be adjacent to every point of sale. They agreed and now there are sixteen outlets in Japan where you can buy an authentic *flûte Gana* thousands of miles from the rue de Ménilmontant.

Meanwhile Ganachaud has created an artisanal network throughout France. Twenty independent young bakers have three-year contracts with him that allow baking and advertising the *flûte Gana* in their establishments. The contracts are renewable for another three-year period after which the bakers can go on producing the *flûte* with no more commitment to him. It is an odd financial arrangement and rather like six years in holy orders, but profitable.

At breakneck speed, Ganachaud related a little of his past. He was born in southwest France in 1930. His father was a small farmer who plumped up the family income by baking and delivering big loaves of bread to other farm families around the countryside. Bernard supplied a helping hand from the age of eight, both at the kneading trough and on the delivery wagon.

While studying at a stern Jesuit academy in Bordeaux he continued to aid his father prepare the dough and make the dawn deliveries. He was an excellent student, wanted to become a lawyer, and somehow found time to be active in the Scouts. But a daily schedule of five a.m. until midnight was too much for his health to sustain. He dropped his studies and concentrated on being a baker, applying all his intelligence and intensity to one of the oldest métiers in the world.

The real killer was lack of sleep. For the customer to have fresh bread in the morning, the baker must observe the fermentation at a fixed period in the night pretty much like a sailor on the watch who can sleep for a few hours only before the next stretch of duty.

Ganachaud decided to break the servitude by harnessing cold to slow down the fermentation and thus allow himself an eight-hour night without interruption. It was a freedom he had never known. At present he has young bakers working under his rule but thanks to the scientific application of cold the deadly night shift is no longer necessary.

The harshness of his early youth had left a permanent toll and he felt he would have to sell his now flourishing business. His attractive young daughters, Valérie and Isabelle, were aghast. "Papa, you simply can't do it. We will carry on for you."

They enrolled in a professional school and finished the three-year course with top honors. As far as I know, Ganachaud's girls are the first professional women bakers in France and the first to earn the tough CAP (*Certificat d'Aptitude Professionnelle*) in what is regarded as one of the most macho of the artisan trades.

Slender and full of grace, they admit to consuming at least a half pound of bread a day regularly, proof that it is not bread that makes you fat but what you put on it. Except for the respite offered by the slowing down of the night fermentation through cold, they watch the clock like hawks, for good bread making demands chronometer precision.

In most other ways the Ganachauds work by the old-fashioned precepts. "A true baker," says Papa, "mixes his own flours." (Any loaf that disobeys his commands is rushed to a laboratory to find out the reason why.) The true baker chooses his combination of flours the way a great tea blender selects leaves of different strains. He uses natural leavenings instead of factory-produced yeasts and baking powders and shuns the preservatives that give added shelf life.

In Paris an alarming number of bakers are buying prepared mixes or frozen dough from industrial plants. With the latter they need but shape it into the desired form and slide it into the oven for baking. Bread from these terminal stations is rarely better than average. Bake shops are springing up with charming décors that suggest a world as it used to be, but the décors are deceptive stage sets masking chain operations.

Lucien Pergeline, a director of the Grands Moulins de Paris, revealed that certain bakers have cut down on the traditional fermentation period with the astute use of commercial baking powders, thus saving themselves an hour or more of time. In addition, with the powders they can achieve a short-weight loaf of 200 grams that has the size of a 250-gram baguette and sell it for the price of the latter.

"Hmm," I said. "Sounds like watered stock—when the drovers of upper New York State used to walk their cattle to market forcing them to drink a maximum on the long march, thus upping the price on the hoof."

The purists of the profession are up in arms and there are debates, symposiums, and articles on saving the Good Bread of France. An alerted segment of the public passes around the names of honest bakers the way they pass on the name of a good bistro discovery. Jean-Michel Bédier, chef of Le Chiberta in Paris, tells me there is a worthy baker in Saint-Sauveur-en-Puisaye, the Burgundy town where Colette was born. We may drive down. It is only seventy-five miles away.

The more I learned, the more choosy I found myself becoming. Strolling in Paris, I noticed Gérard Mulot's sign at 2 rue Lobineau, a step from the rue de Seine in the sixth arrondissement. *Fabrication Maison depuis 1976.* I liked this proud proclamation of the date as if it went back two centuries. What caught me, however, was the mention of *pain au levain,* which meant that Mulot was using a starter dough as his leavening. His *pain de campagne* was excellent with a faint and pleasant note of acidity, more to my liking than any I have found in my neighborhood of the seventh arrondissement.

On a recent Sunday afternoon I went to the big book fair at the Porte de Versailles because Paul Guth, whose *Moi, Joséphine, impératrice* (I, Joséphine, the Empress) is one of my favorite biographies, was to autograph his latest work. The delightful Mr. Guth has written more than fifty books and is one of the few contemporary French authors who has been able to live by his pen.

He turned out to be a fervent partisan of honest bread. I went to see him a few days later in his sixteenth arrondissement apartment where he writes with a pen at a small table looking out on what could be a small walled garden in the provinces.

At the request of other partisans, he had written a pamphlet entitled *Le Pain en majesté,* or Bread Enthroned, in which he called bread "God's representative of his flesh and soul, born in the secret of the night during the night of time." Like a troubadour of old, Guth proclaimed the virtues of bread battling against our delirium for speed, which was ruining our sensations and sentiments and leading to the downfall of the Occident. "With its eternal values, bread attaches us to the earth from which we are being torn by an industrial civilization."

In his childhood in a peasant house in the Bigorre, a pretending-to-be-asleep little boy watched his aunt Amandine knead the dough. "Writhing, she lifted it in strips, stretched it, threw it, punched it down. All the while, she groaned softly with the wails of love, of birth, of death."

After my next trip to Ganachaud, I dropped off a loaf at Guth's door.

My friend Maxine, who eats out at a different Paris restaurant every night, told me excitedly, "I found two great new ones. And they are baking their own bread."

Alain Passard is the chef-owner of l'Arpège at rue de Varenne in the locale that used to be l'Archestrate. The youthful Passard has two stars from Michelin. At Arpège, the bread is baked in the morning for the lunch service and in the afternoon for the evening service.

"Bread is very important in a restaurant and I love to make it. The customers are very surprised. Almost the first thing they say is, 'Where do you buy this bread? It is fabulous. We don't find it in Paris.' Some of the women ask me, 'Oh, if only I could have some with my coffee in the morning.' If any is left over, I give it to them for toast." His hundred clients a day manage to put away four kilos of Arpège's individual rolls and six kilos of country bread, which is a lot of bread for a fashionable crowd.

Alain grew up with the taste of good bread. It was made by a farmer friend of his father. When he was twenty and already trained as a pastry chef, he said to his father's friend, "May I spend two weeks and learn to make bread the way you do?" One of its secrets is sea salt from Guérande in Brittany, *sel de Guérande,* considered the Flower of Salt.

The fine bread accompanies a cuisine that is refined and restrained, genuine and unpretentious and never banal. An example is a simple and charming entrée consisting of cabbage leaves stuffed with crab meat in a light mustard sauce. The combination of rusticity and sophistication is characteristic of Alain Passard.

Like Passard, Gilles Epié of Le Miraville is a young Breton. His approach to food is much the same—imaginative and inventive without excess or affectation. His little restaurant was barely six months old when it received the accolade of a star from the Michelin.

He started baking bread while working in Brussels, and could find none that seemed suitable to partner his style of cuisine. The public's reception convinced him to do the same when he came to Paris. Not an insipid bread but a forthright loaf with the fermentation set off by beer and grapes. Into his dough goes a touch of honey and the honorable *sel de Guérande*. There is never any bread left over to give the customers to take home.

At Charenton-le-Pont on the edge of Paris, an address as unprepossessing as the rue de Ménilmontant, is the small Musée Français du Pain. Occupying a floor in the head office of a flour-milling company that supplies most of the leading pastry chefs in France, it is an endearing place.

The museum is the dada of the company's owner, Jacques Lorch. For twenty-five years M. Lorch has been ferreting out artifacts pertaining to the subject that is his passion. The collection now numbers more than a thousand pieces, and to obtain some of them he had to beat out offers from big museums around Europe.

"The story of bread is the story of the life of man," said M. Lorch.

The oldest exhibit in the museum is a model of a granary in Egypt, dating back to approximately 2000 BC. We know that the ancient Egyptians already had leavened bread because when the Hebrews fled the country they went in such a hurry they left their starter dough behind. As a result the Exodus had to be effected on matzos.

On a fourth century AD Roman mold of the Goddess of Victory are the letters DULC, which, according to Lorch, was the abbreviation of the Roman confectioner Dulciarius. There are seals from many countries. During the ages when bread was brought to communal ovens for baking, it was the custom to mark the loaves. Thanks to these brands, an individual could claim his bread once it was baked.

Of the many documents on display, the one that captivated me most was a proclamation of November 15, 1793, announcing that only one type of bread could be sold, the *Pain d'Égalité*. Henceforth, there was to be no more white bread for the rich and black bread for the poor. The future did not promise Pie in the Sky but a compromise loaf for all alike.

"Can you find out more for me about the *Pain d'Égalité?*" I asked Lucien Pergeline of the Grands Moulins de Paris.

White flour is the ultimate refinement of the whole grain of wheat. According to the articles of the revolutionary decree, no more than fifteen pounds of bran could be extracted from one hundred kilos of any kind of grain. The order specified that all bread would be composed of three-fourths wheat flour and one-fourth rye flour. In localities lacking sufficient rye, barley flour was to be substituted.

In Article 9 the bakers were warned that they faced imprisonment if they made anything other than a single type of bread to be known as the "Bread of Equality."

The law didn't last for long. Under the empire of Napoléon I, the new aristocrats went right back to white bread. Society shifts. Now it is the well-to-do who cherish the virtues of the bread once spurned by the less well-off. If it came to a choice today, the former would rather give up cake.

Whether it is white or black, leavened or unleavened, bread is the food common to all mankind.

In Turkey, a land of long-respected traditions, any piece of bread seen lying upon the ground is to be raised, pressed against the heart, the lips, and the forehead, and then placed on a high ledge. One does not walk upon bread. It would be a sacrilege to the Creator.

As the poet sang, "A jug of wine, a loaf of bread—and Thou."

Bread Box

"Bread is located at the crossroads between the material and the symbolic, between economics and culture," notes Steven Kaplan in his excellent book *Good Bread Is Back: A Contemporary History of French Bread, the Way It Is Made, and the People Who Make It* (Duke University Press, 2006). Kaplan also points out various phrases and proverbs that feature bread in France: a person who is very ill has lost "the taste for bread"; a marvelous individual is "better than good bread"; and a tiresome experience is "as long as a day without bread."

In short, bread matters in France. Kaplan, himself French, notes that "even if consumers eat much less bread than in the past, they see themselves in bread, which continues to contribute to their identity as French people. In public opinion, bread remains deeply bound up with the basic values of sociability and well-being, with sacred and secular communion." In addition to Kaplan's book, two other noteworthy bread reads are *Bread of Three Rivers: The Story of a French Loaf* by Sara Mansfield Taber (Beacon Press, 2001) and *Boulangerie! Pocket Guide to Paris's Famous Bakeries* by Jack Armstrong and Delores Wilson (Ten Speed, 1999). In the first, Taber travels initially to Brittany to "understand bread in a deep way, beyond even the capacity of my tongue." We follow her to master bakers elsewhere—while delving into salt, wheat, water, and yeast—and find that though Taber set out in search of something as simple as a loaf of bread, she instead found herself "sitting down to a rich, five-course French meal." She acknowledges that it was sometimes difficult to learn about the way eating habits have changed the role of bread in French life, and that, as one baker told her, "the French bread the Japanese make is much better than the average French!" But she concludes that "romance based on ignorance and fantasy and unconscious prejudice is not as satisfying or rich as romance grounded in the truth. Maybe one can include fairy tales in the range of possibilities, and consciously choose to be romantic sometimes and just stick to the opinion that you are eating the world's most glorious loaf of bread." It's a wonderfully written book that's also an eye-opener. *Boulangerie!* is a paperback guide, a little bigger than an index card so you can easily carry it around with you, featuring 223 establishments in every arrondissement. A primary consideration for inclusion was the response to the question "*Faites-vous le pain vous-même?*" (Is your bread baked here in your shop?) The authors listed only *boulangeries* whose answer was yes; in 1997, the French government's small business ministry stipulated that only bakeries that selected their own flour, kneaded their own dough, and baked the loaves on their premises may be called *boulangeries*. The *boulangeries* are not rated, but the author team assures readers that the selected listings will not disappoint.

Since 1993, there has been an annual Grand Prix de la Baguette de Tradition Française de la Ville de Paris contest, which is a long way of saying a Best Baguette in Paris contest. In March of 2010, 141 baguettes were sampled by fifteen judges, who included Franck Tombarel of Le Grenier de Félix (64 avenue Félix Faure, 15ème, and the 2009 winner) and Benjamin Turquier of Boulangerie 134 RDT (134 rue de Turenne, 3ème, and the 2009 runner-up). The 2010 winner was Djibril Bodian of Le Grenier à Pain Abbesses (38 rue des Abbesses, 18ème). (To learn the names of other honorees, try Googling "best baguette in Paris" and a year.) The editors at a great site called Paris by Mouth (parisby mouth.com) had a different list in 2010 (with some overlap); in their Five Great Baguettes, Eric Kayser (8 rue Monge,

5ème) took the number one spot, followed by Gosselin (258 boulevard Saint-Germain, 7ème), Du Pain et des Idées (34 rue Yves-Toudic, 10ème), Coquelicot (24 rue des Abbesses, 18ème), and Julien (75 rue Saint-Honoré, 1er). The contributing editors at Paris by Mouth, by the way, are a discerning bunch—they include head editor Meg Zimbeck as well as Alexander Lobrano, Clotilde Dusoulier, Dorie Greenspan, Patricia Wells, and Wendy Lyn. In their profiles on the site, they each share their Top 3 Paris Tastes, a valuable little guide by itself.

Culinary Paintings

Years ago, when I was looking through a large box of postcards I'd accumulated from various museums and galleries, I noticed that I had a great number of still life images, and these all depicted food and drink: walnuts, silver goblets, brioches, cherries, melons, apricots, beautiful bowls, coffeepots, wine, bread, apples, onions, picnics, fancy feasts . . . I had them all and I loved them and I didn't want them hidden in a box anymore. But I had entirely too many to do something meaningful with them *all,* so I selected those I loved the best and had them framed. Some of these were actually high-quality cards suitable for framing, and they really do look fine under glass. These are now in my dining room and kitchen, and I'm so glad I can look at them often.

So, naturally, I love the Poilâne *boulangerie*, not only for the bread, which is outstanding, but for the little room in the back that is essentially a museum of paintings, all depicting loaves of bread. It seems not everyone knows about this room, but anyone is welcome to walk in—it's just behind the cash register. I think it's wonderful. The paintings were collected by Pierre Poilâne, who founded the original bakery in 1932. Lionel, Pierre's son, later ran the business until he died tragically in a plane crash in 2002; Pierre's daughter Apollonia is now carrying on the family tradition. The elder Poilâne exchanged his bread for paintings, and though I don't believe they are particularly rare or valuable, they're quite beautiful. As Pierre Rival explains in *Gourmet Shops of Paris,* the presence of the paintings "is testament to the strength of the link between Poilâne bread and art. Against the odds, the artists in Saint-Germain-des-Prés succeeded in making pain Poilâne fashionable." Other favorites of mine at Poilâne are the *punitions,* unbelievably simple but delicious cookies, and the special decorated loaves—don't miss these! At the Poilâne store online (poilane.fr), there are also wonderful French breakfast bowls and a bread knife that is to die for.

When I saw a book called *Food in the Louvre* (Flammarion, 2009), I knew I had to have it. What a combination: color reproductions of artworks in the Louvre with a preface by Paul Bocuse and recipes by Yves Pinard, head chef at the Grand Louvre restaurant. The artworks featured are by Jean-Siméon Chardin, Francken the Younger, Louise Moillon, Jan Steen, Murillo, Eugène Delacroix, François Boucher, and others; images also include a Roman floor mosaic, Egyptian crockery, and a Greek red figure cup. Bocuse writes that "for a chef, turning the pages of this book is a singularly rewarding experience." He observes that many of the works have a festive aspect that illustrates his idea of what cooking should be: "Seated around a table with friends, time no longer means anything. For eating is above all sharing in the pleasure of other people's company and many is the time in my restaurant I have noticed how a great meal depends first and foremost on the diners and on the interaction between them. An alchemical process seems to take place whenever people sit round a dining table."

Liquid Gold

SUSAN HERRMANN LOOMIS

⟨⟨⟩⟩

OLIVE TREES IN France thrive in regions far south of Paris, but in nearby Burgundy, the Huilerie Artisanale J. Leblanc et Fils specializes in another culinary item of note: nut oils. Though I've not visited the mill, I've been regularly visiting the tiny Leblanc shop in Paris's sixth arrondissement for many years (6 rue Jacob). In addition to a variety of nut oils (I always select my favorite, hazelnut), there are very good mustards and vinegars, and the service is always friendly and helpful.

SUSAN HERRMANN LOOMIS is the author of numerous books, including *On Rue Tatin: Living and Cooking in a French Town* (Broadway, 2001), *Cooking at Home on Rue Tatin* (William Morrow, 2005), and *French Farmhouse Cookbook* (Workman, 1996). Most recently, she published *Nuts in the Kitchen: More than 100 Recipes for Every Taste and Occasion* (Morrow, 2010), which is filled with creative, uncommon recipes from around the world. (I particularly like the Parmigiano-Reggiano Seed Sticks, Mushroom and Walnut Tarte Tatin, and the hazelnut *financiers,* based on the recipe she helped develop when she was working on *The Food Lover's Guide to Paris* with Patricia Wells.) She includes an essay in her book devoted to the Leblanc family.

Loomis founded and runs the On Rue Tatin cooking school (see page 259) at her home in Normandy, and for several weeks each year the school moves to Paris, where she offers "another dimension of my passion for France." One-day classes are also offered in Paris, as well as French country lunches in Louviers. Loomis maintains a blog, Life Is Nuts (nutsin.wordpress.com), and is a partner in NoTakeOut.com, a nifty Web site that helps users plan, prep, and cook an entire meal with fresh, seasonal ingredients.

PLACED BEFORE YOU is that exquisitely simple French creation: a mélange of fresh, tender lettuce leaves dressed lightly in a tangy vinaigrette. The buttery aroma of hazelnuts wafts up from the crisp green salad, yet there isn't a nut to be seen. Where oh where is that divine smell coming from?

Jean-Charles Leblanc, from the village of Iguerande in Burgundy, is the sorcerer behind this olfactory trick. Head of the family enterprise Huilerie Artisanale J. Leblanc et Fils, he supplies France and beyond with some of the world's finest nut oils. Their products, which come from just about every nut in the world including the rare Moroccan argan nut, make their way into more than just salads: almond oil may be drizzled over a tender fish fillet, walnut oil incorporated into a moist cake, pine nut oil added to a bowl of pasta, pistachio oil tossed with avocado and grapefruit.

The Leblancs are far from being the only nut oil producers in France—indeed, there are too many to count, given that nearly every region that grows nuts has small mills that produce oil for local consumption. But Leblanc oils are considered the pinnacle of this culinary art.

Jean-Charles follows in the footsteps of his great-grandfather, who started the mill in 1878. Back then, local farmers brought their walnuts and rapeseed to the mill, which sits in the family barn located on the D982. Jean-Charles's sister Anne—who grew up in the house next to the barn and now runs the family shop in Paris—describes Iguerande as *paumé,* or lost, in the middle of nowhere. But nowhere has become somewhere because of the family oil mill.

The minute you turn onto the D982, you know you've arrived—the air is redolent of toasted nuts. Jean-Charles's mother minds the boutique, which was recently expanded, while his brother handles accounting and communications. The business has grown, but once inside the mill, you realize that the heart of this operation has changed little since great-grandfather Leblanc's day. The only significant difference is that the huge stone that slowly grinds nuts beneath its bulk is no longer powered by a horse; a system of pulleys and belts suspended from the ceiling now keeps it turning. These many years later, that old stone wheel is still the best way to crush nuts without compacting them.

Daniel Demours, one of the company's two employees who aren't family members, scoops the coarsely ground nuts into a blackened kettle that sits over a gas flame. "We cook them to add flavor and allow the oil to separate," he explains.

Demours checks the cooking nuts every few minutes—timing is everything. "These are pine nuts, and they cook fast," he says, opening the lid and deftly stirring the mash, which has already turned from solid to almost liquid in the heat. "Most nuts should be cooked for about twenty minutes, but you've got to watch these carefully—they're ready in about five."

He walks over to the presses and checks the flow of oil coming from them. It has slowed to a mere trickle, signaling that it is time to add more nuts. He runs back to the kettle, takes off the lid, and inhales, tipping the runny mass into a container. He opens a press and removes the flat disks of compressed, nearly dry nut paste left after the oil is extracted. Each is separated by a woven mat used to filter the oil. "Mats used to be made of human hair," notes Demours. "Now they are woven from synthetic fibers."

He pours more pine nuts into the press, covers them with a filter, and repeats the process until the press is nearly full. He then cinches it closed, puts a barrel under the spigot, and waits for the golden liquid to flow. "We press in small batches—no more than twenty-five kilos," says Jean-Charles. "That is the only way to get the highest quality."

Once a barrel is full, it sits in the cool barn long enough for the oil to decant, a period of several days. It is then bottled, labeled, and stocked in a warehouse behind the mill. At least in theory. "We don't really have any stock because we sell everything as quickly as we make it," laughs Jean-Charles.

As if on cue, a farmer and his wife walk into the barn with a sack of walnuts. Jean-Charles weighs it on an old scale. "This is the last of this year's harvest," the farmer says. "I bring them in when I need more oil." The couple leaves with a gallon jug.

The Leblancs now get only one-third of their walnuts locally; the rest come from the Périgord region. As for the other nuts that go into the dozen or so varieties of oils they produce, their provenance reads like a map of the world. Hazelnuts are from Italy and Turkey, pine nuts from China (the ones from Italy don't yield as much oil), almonds and pecans from California, pistachios from Iran, poppy and squash seeds from Austria, peanuts from the southern United States. But only the highest quality nuts make it into the Leblanc presses.

The mill produces about three hundred liters of oil per day, 365 days a year. Leblanc *père*, now eighty-two, still delivers to clients within a fifty-mile radius. One is Franck Lesaige, chef and owner of Le Relais de Saint Julien in nearby Saint-Julien-de-Jonzy.

"I use Leblanc oils primarily in first courses," says Lesaige. "One of my favorites now is a *royale de foie gras.* I dress artichoke hearts in pistachio oil, balsamic vinegar, shallots, and chives, then top it all with a foie gras cream." He adds hazelnut oil to *tête de veau,* or boiled head cheese, and generally slips nut oils in whenever he has the inspiration.

Given their delicate flavor, nut oils are generally used for seasoning rather than cooking, although they are sometimes used in baking. Once opened, they must be refrigerated and will keep for about three months. Unopened bottles will wait indefinitely as long as they are kept in a cool dry place.

Huilerie Artisanale J. Leblanc et Fils, Le Bas, Iguerande, Burgundy (+33 03 85 84 07 83 / huile-leblanc.com). The Paris shop is located at 6 rue Jacob, 6ème / (+3301 46 34 61 55).

Chocolat

The great correspondent of the seventeenth century Madame de Sévigné counseled, "Take chocolate in order that even the most tiresome company seems acceptable to you," which is also sound advice today! For me, fine chocolate is one of life's supreme pleasures, and when I wanted to learn more about it I turned to what I think is the best book ever published on the subject: *Chocolate: A Bittersweet Saga of Dark and Light* by Mort Rosenblum (North Point, 2004), which was honored with an International Association of Culinary Professionals Award for literary food writing in 2006. The historic and contemporary story of chocolate is global, but how sweet for visitors to France that much of it is written in the chocolate shops of Paris. Rosenblum pleads that "if anyone ever banishes me to a desert island with only one style of chocolate, please make it French." He also recommends *The Chocolate Connoisseur* by Chloé Doutre-Roussel (Tarcher, 2006), which I of course had to read as well.

For me, no trip to Paris is complete without visits to as many *chocolatiers* as I can fit in my schedule. Each boutique is different from the next, selling varied and often inventive creations, so each visit is a fresh experience.

My number one favorite chocolate stop is Pierre Hermé (72 rue Bonaparte, 6ème / 185 rue de Vaugirard, 15ème /

pierreherme.com), which is a *pâtisserie* that also offers an out-standing selection of chocolates. Hermé began his career as an apprentice to Gaston Lenôtre, and he went on to stints at Fauchon and Ladurée before earning such accolades as "the Picasso of Pastry" (*Vogue*), "pastry provocateur" (*Food & Wine*), "the Kitchen Emperor" (*New York Times*), and "an avant-garde pastry chef and magician with tastes" (*Paris Match*). He was awarded the Chevalier de la Légion d'Honneur in 2007, and is the youngest person ever to be named France's pastry chef of the year. If you have a reason to buy pastries—you've been invited to someone's house, you're renting an apartment and you've invited friends for dinner, you're putting together a *pique-nique,* or simply that it's Monday—Hermé is a great stop as you can buy both pastry and chocolate, as well as other gifts. The pastries here are stunning and really stand out, especially in the sleek sliver of a space at the rue Bonaparte location. There are several chocolate assortments in various-sized boxes, and the knowledgeable staff can help you decide among them. (And don't hesitate to try the *délicieuses gourmandises à croquer*—chocolate-covered candied grapefruit peels, my favorite!) I even love the bags your purchases come in: sturdy white paper with a die-cut design. Ambitious home bakers may want to try their hand at some of Hermé's recipes in *Desserts by Pierre Hermé* (1998) and *Chocolate Desserts by Pierre Hermé* (2001), both written by Dorie Greenspan and published by Little, Brown.

As much as I love Pierre Hermé, I also love the chocolates at other Parisian shops:

Jean-Paul Hévin (231 rue Saint-Honoré, 1er / 3 rue Vavin, 6ème / 23 bis avenue de la Motte-Picquet, 7ème / jphevin .com). At the rue Saint-Honoré shop chocolates may be purchased to take away or enjoyed in the *salon de thé* upstairs.

Aoki (25 rue Pérignon, 15ème / 35 rue de Vaugirard, 6ème / 56 boulevard de Port-Royal, 5ème, with a *salon de thé* / Lafayette Gourmet, 40 boulevard Haussmann, 9ème, sada haruaoki.com). Like Pierre Hermé, Sadaharu Aoki is also a pastry chef, and he brings a matchless Japanese sense of order and aesthetics to classic French *pâtissier.*

La Maison du Chocolat (nine locations; its first, since 1977, is at 52 rue François-1er, 1er / lamaisonduchocolat.com). Though Maison now has stores elsewhere in the world, including New York, I still think the quality of the chocolates is excellent, and Maison hot chocolate is still the best. (Many folks say the best is at Angelina, 226 rue de Rivoli, but they've probably just never had it at La Maison du Chocolat.)

Debauve & Gallais (30 rue des Saint-Pères, 7ème / 33 rue Vivienne, 2ème / debauve-et-gallais.com). Paris's oldest chocolate maker retains a soft spot in my heart even though I prefer the other *chocolatiers* here—I love the interior of the rue des Saint-Pères shop, dating from 1800. The old-fashioned, though exquisite, selections and packaging make better gifts for more traditional palates.

La Chocolaterie de Jacques Genin (133 rue de Turenne, 3ème). Genin's creations were praised by Mort Rosenblum in *Chocolate* as his favorite chocolates in the world.) Before Genin's Marais shop opened in 2008, he supplied Alain Ducasse's restaurants, hotels like the George V and Le Crillon, and shops like Hédiard. Anyone else who wanted to try his chocolates had to make an appointment at his fifteenth arrondissement lab and agree to purchase a minimum order of one kilogram. In an interview with Lennox Morrison for the *Wall Street Journal,* Genin described himself as a rebel. "I don't even want to be called a master chocolate maker. I call myself a foundry man who works with chocolate because that is what I do. I melt down chocolate to create fresh products." In 1991 he went to La Maison du Chocolat and worked as head *pâtissier*, then left five years later to go off on his own. I know I'm not alone in being grateful for the new shop. Many people rave about the caramels, but I myself am partial to the chestnut-flavored *sucre d'or,* and I *love* the JG-monogrammed silver boxes—very classy.

The Anatomy of Success
Rémi Flachard, International Specialist in Vintage Cookbooks

NAOMI BARRY

I HAD NEVER heard of Rémi Flachard before I read this piece, and I cannot wait to visit his bookshop the next time I am in Paris. Only Naomi Barry would describe it as a "gallimaufry," which sent me to the dictionary, where I learned it means a hodgepodge or jumble. Perfect! Just my kind of shop. Though I'm of course interested to look at the "uncharted sea of books," I'm even more interested in the menus marking historic occasions.

THE SUBJECT OF gastronomy, like the subject of love, has been the stuff of literature for thousands of years. To read about food is to extend the pleasure of actually eating it. To read the menu of an inspired meal is enough to set the taste buds quivering. The market expert in this mouthwatering domain of bibliophilia is Rémi Flachard, who for the past twenty years has been supplying collectors around the world with works pertaining to their passion.

Flachard's headquarters is a modest bookshop at 9 rue du Bac in the seventh arrondissement of Paris. His little shop, furnished in False Gothic, is a gallimaufry of vintage cookbooks ranging from rare to *rarissime,* plus a selection of quality titles from the twentieth century. Those from earlier centuries are splendidly leather-bound and generously tooled in gold. An important section of the stock is devoted to wine and vineyard culture. Another group deals with bread and bread making. The collection of historic menus is exceptional.

Most of the books are in French, which is not surprising since for centuries French chefs headed the kitchens of most of the royal courts of Europe and managed to write down what was going on. Just as French was the lingua franca in the world of the diplomats, French was the lingua franca in the world of the summit cooks, a world unmarked by borders.

Flachard is an exceptionally tall, thin fellow who sports exquisite shoes, boots, and *bottines;* speaks in a measured *vieille France* manner; and rain or shine bicycles twenty minutes to work each morning across Paris from the seventeenth to the seventh arrondissement. His ivory-tower shop maintains an active mailing list reaching into eight countries, where the collectors are avid to grab Flachard's latest finds. Flachard's high-end finds are not kitchen home companions—one does not risk gravy on an 1823 edition of a work by the legendary Antonin Carême or a treatise on the economic viability of the potato by the agronomist and army apothecary Antoine-Augustin Parmentier.

The other day I dropped in on Flachard, a way stop I enjoy every few months because it feels like a trip into a literary Paris of Once Upon a Time that I happen to adore. He was hunched over a table piled with ledgers, papers, index cards, and other paraphernalia. If Dumas or Balzac had walked in we probably would have said hello without surprise. The crowded scene is deceptive. Although the narrow premises appear to be an uncharted sea of books, Flachard, who knows his stuff, can locate in an instant any requested volume even when it is hidden deep behind two others. Thoughtfully, he has spirited the most valuable items out of sight. Thus one can feel free to browse without succumbing to a wave of excessive temptation.

Flachard was finishing preparation on his catalog (Number 39), a lovingly produced illustrated booklet describing exceptional items currently available. He mails out several thousand of his catalogs twice a year. Requests to purchase the catalog are frequent. He turns them down, saying, "The catalog is not for sale. Buy a book and I give you the catalog for free."

With books priced in the hundreds and thousands of euros, the response at first sounds disdainfully lofty. Actually it is not as high-handed as it first might seem. The shop offers a considerable selection of quality books more digestibly priced from twenty to sixty euros. Consequently, obtaining Flachard's gift catalog is not completely beyond reach. Serious collectors keep the catalog on their shelves as a source of reference.

Flachard was excitedly poring over a recently acquired set of fifty-five official menus commemorating banquets, dinners, and receptions that had taken place between 1900 and 1960. The precious trove represented the private collection of Pierre de Fouquières, who had been the French foreign office's chief of protocol during what obviously was a highly entertaining period. On many occasions it was Fouquières who represented France at the party.

The stunningly designed menus in the Fouquières collection that Flachard was cataloging evoked the social history of an era. The wedding of the crown prince of Iran to Fawzia, the ravishing sister of Farouk of Egypt, was a lavish affair. Fifteen elaborately illuminated menus attest to the fifteen banquets that celebrated the ceremony. Fawzia eventually was repudiated for having produced only a daughter.

The elegant Fouquières, who from his photo was the quintessence of Fifty Million Frenchmen Can't Be Wrong, had impresarioed glorious official receptions for delegations of Italians, Swiss, Belgians, Americans, English, and Norwegians. In 1911, Fouquières was an official guest at the festive dinner at the Calcutta Club for the marriage of Tikka Sahib, the son of the maharajah of Kapurthala, the mythically rich family whose fief was one of the princely states of India. According to the menu, the

Kapurthala wedding dinner was as dazzling as anything dreamed up by Bollywood decades later.

The Franco-Russian Alliance, 1893 to 1909, can be followed through Flachard's fascinating series of eleven beautifully decorated menus of meals that punctuated its many events. It was party time much of the way. The excitement began on October 19, 1893, when the municipality of Paris honored the officers of the Russian squadron with a sumptuous banquet at the Hôtel de Ville. Luminaries among the 564 guests were the mayors of Lyon, Marseille, Bordeaux, Lille, Toulouse, Le Havre, Nantes, and Reims. The illustrious catering firm of Potel et Chabot was engaged to serve the luxurious banquet.

The menus read like a diary of an embassy attaché.

On October 5, 1896, at two p.m., the Russian imperial yacht *Polar Star* arrived in Cherbourg on a courtesy visit. Aboard were Tzar Nicholas II and Tzarina Alexandra Feodorovna. They were greeted by President Félix Faure, who that night hosted a dinner in their honor at the Préfecture Maritime.

Nicholas and Alexandra were back in France again on September 18, 1901, this time steaming into Dunkerque on the imperial yacht *Standart*. President Émile Loubet hosted the welcoming lunch. Two days later the French president and the Russian tzar cohosted a gala dinner at the Château de Compiègne. Escoffier, in his *Livre des menus,* cited the dinner at Compiègne as a model for a grand presidential reception.

The menus from the years of the Franco-Russian Alliance are a footnote of history. The relationship obviously was warm. On July 28, 1908, the tzar and tzarina had dinner on the French warship *Vérité,* anchored in the roadstead off Cherbourg. A year later they returned to Cherbourg aboard the imperial yacht *Standart,* and were greeted like old friends. On the night of July 31, 1909, dinner on the *Vérité* was an eighteen-course royal gala.

The fête continued. Lunch aboard the *Vérité* on August 1, 1909, had been scaled down to a happy informal family affair.

The tzar and tzarina had brought their children along on the trip, the four young archduchesses Olga, Marie, Tatiana, and Anastasia.

In his specialized *librairie,* Flachard has for sale a few memorabilia with gastronomic connections. I was captivated by a pencil portrait of the endearing Édouard de Pomiane, scientist, gastronome, and author of several delightful books always in demand.

At tony dinner parties in nineteenth-century Paris, the menu was passed around in a handheld *porte-menu*. Flachard has two examples of these elegant little accessories. One with a frame and handle in sterling silver was by the firm Charles-Nicolas Odiot (ca. 1850–1860). The other, in silver plate and marked by the firm Christofale, dates from 1900. Either one would add a charming grace note to any dinner party today.

Cooking Classes

There are a number of cooking classes in Paris (and nearby) for students at all levels of comfort in the kitchen, including:

Ritz Escoffier School (click École Ritz Escoffier at ritz paris.com).

Patricia Wells (patriciawells.com); see interview page 169 for more details.

On Rue Tatin (onruetatin.com), in Normandy and in Paris with Susan Herrmann Loomis; see page 247 for more details.

Promenades Gourmandes (promenadesgourmandes.com) with Paule Caillat.

Le Cordon Bleu (cordonbleu.edu).

See the **Shaw Guides** (cookforfun.shawguides.com) for many more listings.

If you've ever harbored thoughts about taking cooking classes in Paris, you've probably seen *Sabrina* (the original, of course, with Audrey Hepburn), and you'll also likely devour *The Sharper Your Knife, the Less You Cry* by Kathleen Flinn (Viking, 2007), a book I very much love about the author's bold decision to earn a full cuisine diploma from Le Cordon Bleu. On Flinn's second day of the course, she looks at her bloodstained apron, "gray bits still clinging to parts of it. This isn't like *Sabrina* at all. Audrey Hepburn would never have ended up covered in fish guts." I laughed out loud, got teary-eyed, and cheered all the way for Flinn, and now I don't have any desire to attend classes at Le Cordon Bleu, because it's *really* hard, as Flinn will tell you. Anyone who completes a Cordon Bleu course deserves our praise and admiration. She includes many recipes from her course in the book, but to me these are quite secondary to her own story—about Paris, about cooking school, about friendship, love, and life.

Why We Love French Wine

PETER HELLMAN

I DON'T KNOW all the reasons that other people love French wine, but I know why *I* love it: in comparison to similar wines from other countries, French wine is almost always, over 95 percent of the time, better, in any type of vessel from which it's drunk.

PETER HELLMAN is a journalist who has written for *Wine Spectator, New York,* the *New York Times, Atlantic Monthly, Food & Wine,* and other publications. He wrote the "Urban Vintage" wine and food column for the *New York Sun* until 2008, and is the author of *The American Wine Handbook* (Ballantine, 1987) and *When Courage Was Stronger Than Fear: Remarkable Stories of Christians and Muslims Who Saved Jews from the Holocaust* (Marlowe & Company, 2004).

THE FRENCH INSIST that the unique glory of their wines originates in the soil—*le terroir.* For once, these rather immodest people are shortchanging themselves. The true source of French wines issues from their very own heads, hearts, and finicky palates. Otherwise, any batch of happy peasants could have invented Champagne, or determined that it takes thirteen different grapes to make a proper Châteauneuf-du-Pape, or managed to classify the great red wines of Burgundy (all made from the same Pinot Noir grape, mind you) into more than 250 *grands crus* and *premiers crus.*

This last fact struck home years ago as I drove along a tiny country road that hugged the vine-draped Côte de Nuits—a first pilgrimage to the region of my favorite wine. A sign marked the spot where the commune of Morey-Saint-Denis ended and Chambolle-Musigny began, fabled names to anyone who adores red Burgundy. The wine map in my head told me that the vines sloping gently upward to my right had to be the *grand cru* of Bonnes-Mares, a thirty-seven-acre appellation that straddles the two communes. (Full yet delicate, meaty yet refined, a well-aged Bonnes-Mares is my dream of red Burgundy.)

A woman was pruning vines near the road. I pulled over. "This must be Bonnes-Mares," I said to her confidently.

"*Mais non, monsieur,*" she said reproachfully. "This is only plain commune wine."

I told her about the wine map in my head.

"Bonnes-Mares is not here," she repeated firmly. "It's over there."

She pointed to a spot no more than half a dozen rows away. No undulation, dip, or break of any kind that I could see separated the vines of the *grand cru* of Bonnes-Mares from the communal stuff. Yet one wine fetches triple the price of the other. If you are lucky enough to drink a twenty-year-old bottle of Bonnes-Mares from a good vintage, I'll lay odds that you won't find it overpriced.

How serious are the French about *le terroir*? It's said that the members of the INAO (Institut National des Appellations d'Origine des Vins et Eaux-de-Vie), entrusted with dividing the Côte d'Or into appellations as small as two acres (La Romanée), wouldn't hesitate to actually taste the soil. How else to detect subtle differences between similar-appearing plots? Perhaps such differences accounted for the otherwise undetectable boundary between Bonnes-Mares and the lesser stuff.

Burgundy is the extreme example of the French compulsion to divide up territory. There are hundreds of appellations and an astounding number of place names. Charles de Gaulle once noted how difficult it is to govern a country that has a different cheese for every day of the year. How about a choice of wines for every cheese, *mon cher général*?

You'd think that so many wines would be a source of rampant confusion for the poor consumer. Actually, there's comfort in the rigidly monitored appellation system. That's because the French—an individualistic people in some ways—don't try to create an individual statement with their wines the way so many New World winemakers do. They are best satisfied when they make a wine that conforms to the standards of their appellation. On the Médoc peninsula of Bordeaux, for example, wines from the southernmost commune of Margaux are typically highly perfumed and delicate. Wines from Saint-Estèphe, at the Médoc's northern end, tend to be hard edged and meaty. You might say that Margaux draws curves and Saint-Estèphe right angles.

Here in Bordeaux, as in Burgundy, lines are sharply drawn in the soil. Just beyond the priceless vineyards of Château Lafite

Rothschild in the commune of Paulliac, for instance, is land where no grapes deserving of the name Bordeaux may be grown. It's only a stone's throw from the most esteemed vineyard land in the world to the domain of reeds and bullfrogs.

If all French wines, Bordeaux in particular, were born beautiful, they'd be less wondrous when they come of age. In fact, there's nothing meaner in the mouth than young Bordeaux from a strong vintage. In my own cellar is a *cru bourgeois* called Château Marsac-Séguineau, from the intense 1975 vintage, bought when it was young. A brilliant royal purple, it ripped my gums with its tannin—the vinous equivalent of an assault rifle. The wine stayed that way for more than a decade, and I gave up hope that it would ever mellow. But then, after a long hiatus, I gingerly tried another bottle. Eureka! That snarl had turned to silk. Well, almost. At sixteen years of age, the wine was still angular enough to provide the classic contrast to the rich taste of roast leg of lamb.

As we get older, there's something deeply affirmative about the progress of well-aged Bordeaux. We hope that as the sap of our youth is left behind, we will show greater depth of character, soften our sharp edges, and become more interesting people. In short, we want to believe that with age we can still bloom. That's precisely the path of a fine claret from youth to the fullness of age. We drink it overtly for pleasure. But we also drink it as a reminder that we can get not just older but better.

Usually it's red wines and such sweet wines as Sauternes that we save for aging. A very few dry white wines can also improve with age. My memory settles on a dusty case of 1964 Corton-Charlemagne, a *grand cru* Burgundy from the esteemed shipper Robert Drouhin, that a friend and I found forgotten in the back of a wine shop in 1977. The proprietor, happy to get rid of wine he presumed to be over the hill after thirteen years, sold us the case at a bargain. We'd planned to hold off until dinner before trying a bottle, knowing that the wine might indeed be over the hill. Instead, on the way home, we pulled over to a shaded roadside picnic table. Out of the glove compartment came clear plastic cups and a corkscrew.

The smell of that wine mingled oak, freshly toasted country bread, and an elusive tang of lime. In the mouth came a rush of flavors and a texture that was simultaneously stony and unctuous. I'd be more specific, except that it is better to marvel at a great old white Burgundy—or red, for that matter—than to dissect it.

A year or so later, during a visit to Burgundy, I mentioned this marvelously youthful Corton-Charlemagne to a winemaker working in the Roman-era cellars of Drouhin located in Beaune. We were only a few miles from the hill of Corton.

His eyes lit up. "Ah, yes," he exclaimed. "In 1964, you know, the secondary aromas never really gave way to the tertiaries. It was most unusual."

The winemaker was alluding to the three phases into which French enologists divide a wine's evolution—as perceived by *le nez*. Primary aromas are those of the fresh juice of the grape. Secondary aromas develop with fermentation, the smell of young wine. The best wines go on to develop a bouquet in which multiple scents perform a dance as complex and as evanescent as a Balanchine ballet.

You needn't speak wine techno-talk to appreciate a wine like that '64 Corton-Charlemagne. But the precise terminology does drive home a point: the best French wines are not produced by happy little peasants. They are an expression of the unique French blend of sensuality and science. It wasn't by chance that fermentation was demystified by a wine-loving Frenchman named Pasteur.

We think of formal meals as the only way to properly honor a great wine in its prime. But that's not necessarily so. I once carried home from Paris a single magnificent bottle of Burgundy, a 1961 Musigny from the Comte de Vogüé. I don't mind saying that I have never, before or since, paid so much for a single bottle of wine. It awaited only a suitably lofty occasion to open it. For a long time, that opportunity never presented itself.

Then, for a birthday dinner, my wife prepared a favorite dish, potato and salt-cod purée, or what the French call *brandade de morue*. Its smell flowed from the oven and filled the house. As it came out of the oven, I heard a crash. Dashing in from the dining room, I found our beautiful old oval ceramic dish on the floor in shards, the *brandade* splashed everywhere and my wife in tears.

"This calls for the best bottle in the house," I said as we cleaned up.

Our abbreviated birthday dinner consisted of a salad, some good country bread, a wedge of Gruyère—and that Musigny. It gave me the greatest pleasure of any wine I'd ever uncorked. Except, perhaps, for that Corton-Charlemagne drunk at roadside from a plastic cup.

Radishes

I *love* radishes, especially the long and slender kind known as French breakfast radishes, which are a little less sharp than the regular variety. I love radishes with a big blob of tapenade; I also like them alongside hard-boiled eggs, aioli, and slices of pumpernickel; I like them thinly sliced on a buttered baguette as a sort of *tartine;* and I even like them sautéed. But my favorite way to eat radishes is to dip chunks in softened, unsalted butter (preferably French) and then in flakes of *fleur de sel*—wow.

Molly Wizenberg loves radishes, too, as anyone who's read *A Homemade Life* already knows, and recently I was happy to discover that Kate McDonough, editor of one of my favorite Web sites, the City Cook (thecitycook.com), and author of *The City Cook* (Simon & Schuster, 2010), does as well. After I read McDonough's essay "Spring Cooking" on her site, I asked her if she would permit me to share it with readers of this book. She kindly agreed:

While radishes may not be the first ingredient you think of when it comes to spring cooking, they are for me.

On my first trip to Italy, a trip filled with memory-searing experiences, I tasted my first risotto. It was in Florence, at a small ristorante located alongside the Arno, about two bridges down from the Ponte Vecchio. The chef had spent a few years living in California and loved to guide Americans through his menu, and he convinced me to try a spring radish risotto. About thirty minutes later (every risotto was cooked to order; none of this half-cooked-then-finished-later risotto done by most U.S. restaurants) the waiter brought me a plate filled with almost soupy, pale pink rice. Its flavor combined the sweetness of butter and garlic with Parmesan's salt and the pepper of spring radishes. The pink, of course, was from the radishes' red skins. And the tender rice, combined with the crunchy cooked radish, was the chef's genius.

A few years later my now husband and I were again traveling, this time to the Normandy region of France. We had rented a car to drive the coastal towns where the Battle of Normandy was fought and where, nearly nine hundred years earlier, plans were laid for the Battle of Hastings depicted in the extraordinary Bayeux Tapestry. Today Normandy is home to some of the best apple groves and dairy farms in all of Europe, a kind of bucolic disconnect from the area's violent past; it is common to see cows roaming among the remains of concrete artillery pillboxes in the grass-covered hills over Omaha Beach.

We arrived in Bayeux just in time for lunch and spotted its weekly farmers' market under way in a parking lot not far from the Bayeux Tapestry museum. Since we always traveled with basic picnic tools, we headed to the market with a corkscrew and a Swiss army knife. We spread our lunch on the hood of our rented Peugeot, making sandwiches from pieces torn from a just-baked baguette, a smear of sweet butter (could any other butter taste as wonderful as one sold by a Normandy dairy farmer at his local market?), and white-tipped spring radishes that we had rinsed with bottled water. Dessert was a wedge of an apple tart cut crudely with the knife's small blade. No meal has ever tasted better.

I've long promised to try to make that pink risotto. I never have. I suspect I don't want to disrupt the remembrance of that dinner along the Arno with my then boyfriend, now dear husband.

But as for that radish sandwich—it is a favorite that I crave every spring and summer. A baguette is perfect but radishes will stand up to any bread you like, including a whole grain. Spread the bread with good sweet butter, maybe an imported Irish or French butter because they usually have a higher butterfat content than those made in the U.S. For the radish, the slightly sweeter, elongated white-tipped radish is a great choice, but these can be difficult to find, even at farmers' markets. So select round, firm red radishes that have a little waxy shine to their surface and minus any signs that they may have spent the last few weeks in a warehouse. Snip off the stems and roots, give a rinse, and cut each into thick slices. Arrange the slices— be generous—on the buttered bread and add a tiny pinch of your best salt (this is a time to use a precious fleur de sel if you have it).

Add a glass of cold, chalky Sancerre and it's a perfect lunch or first course of a spring dinner.

RECOMMENDED READING

ABOUT FRENCH CUISINE

At Home in France: Eating and Entertaining with the French, Christopher Petkanas with photographs by Jean-Bernard Naudin (Phoenix, 1999). Four of the tables and *maisons* featured in this lovely book are in northern France—two in Paris, one in Beaujolais, and another in Brittany.

Between Meals: An Appetite for Paris, A. J. Liebling (North Point, 1986). This is one of those books that had reached legendary proportions in my mind before I even read it. It seemed to be mentioned in nearly everything I read about Paris. Predisposed as I was to like this book, it exceeded my expectations. With Liebling as a guide, I can taste the wine, hear the cutlery clanking, smell the Gitanes, and believe I'm sitting in a cane wicker chair at a Paris café.

The Cooking of Provincial France, M. F. K. Fisher with Julia Child (Time-Life, 1968). The collaborative effort to produce this book, one of the volumes in the *Foods of the World* series, was extraordinary, the likes of which we'll probably never see again. (For a fascinating behind-the-scenes look at the series, see "Viola, the Soufflé!," *Gourmet,* January 2006.) Though long out of print, this and other *Foods of the World* editions turn up regularly at yard sales, in used-book stores, and on the Web.

Culinaria France, André Domine (HF Ullmann/Tandem Verlag, 2008). This thick volume is one in the very good *Culinaria* series, great for travelers: each book is filled with beautiful color photographs and the culinary specialties of each region are presented in depth, so that visitors will know what to expect to see at markets and on local menus. One chapter is devoted to Paris and the Île-de-France, covering such topics as Les Halles, Parisian breakfast, Jewish breads and other specialties, and everyday Parisian fare, while others focus on the surrounding areas of Champagne, Lorraine, Alsace, Nord-Pas-de-Calais, Picardy, Normandy, Brittany, the Loire Valley, and Burgundy. Some recipes are included, but the *Culinaria* books are more informational than practical.

The Food of France, Waverley Root (Knopf, 1958; Vintage, 1992). "Eating habits," says Root in the first chapter, "are part of our social habits, part of our culture, part of the environment, mental and physical, in which we live." If your only vision of "French" food is limited to heavy sauces and butter, this definitive volume will open your eyes to the true diversity of France's culinary map. There are separate chapters on the Île-de-France, Normandy, and Burgundy, where much of the food

and wine served in Paris restaurants and offered in shops originates.

French Country Cooking, Elizabeth David (John Lehmann, 1951;
various reissues available). The combination of David's text and
the beautiful color reproductions of artworks depicting food by
Bonnard, Gauguin, Chardin, Signac, Monet, Renoir, and others makes this one of my most treasured volumes.

French Lessons: Adventures with Knife, Fork, and Corkscrew, Peter
Mayle (Knopf, 2001). Mayle claims he can't pretend to have
done more than scratch the surface of French gastronomy, but
the surface he did scratch is enlightening and entertaining. For
this culinary journey Mayle traveled to all corners of France to
attend the sort of wonderful gastronomic *fêtes et foires* that make
visiting France so rewarding. He was surprised about "the high
level of enthusiasm for any event, however bizarre, that sought
to turn eating and drinking into a celebration. The amount of
effort put in by the organizers, the stall holders, and the general
public (who, in some cases, had traveled halfway across France)
was astonishing. I cannot imagine any other race prepared to
devote an entire weekend to frogs' legs or snails or the critical
assessment of chickens." Four events are within two hours of
Paris: Les Glorieuses, the most important chicken event of the
year; the Foire aux Escargots in Martigny-les-Bains; Les Trois
Glorieuses, a wine auction held every November in Beaune;
and the *boudin* festival in Monthureux, north of Dijon. Best of
all for travelers is the final chapter, "Last Course," a detailed list
of all the fairs, festivals, restaurants, and places featured, with
contact information for each.

The Physiology of Taste, or Meditations on Transcendental Gastronomy,
Jean-Anthelme Brillat-Savarin, translated by M. F. K. Fisher
and with illustrations by Wayne Thiebaud (Counterpoint,

1994; originally published by Heritage Press, 1949; available in a new Everyman's Library edition, 2009). *Physiology* is also available in several other editions, but this illustrated hardcover from Counterpoint is *the* edition to have (if you can find it). Brillat-Savarin (1755–1826) is right up there with Apicius as one of the world's greatest gastronomes, and he is the one we have to thank for such observations as "The discovery of a new dish does more for human happiness than the discovery of a new star." (Or, to quote Mort Rosenblum in *A Goose in Toulouse*, "Great human events are fine, Anthelme Brillat-Savarin observed, but let's not forget lunch.") I will surely be condemned for admitting that I'm a bit bored by some of the essays, but overall this is a masterpiece.

A Special Ensemble

Two books that I treasure and that I feel deserve to be noted separately are *Bouquet de France: An Epicurean Tour of the French Provinces* by Samuel Chamberlain with recipes translated and adapted by Narcissa Chamberlain (Gourmet Books, 1952) and *Gourmet's Paris* (Gourmet Books, no copyright date appears anywhere in the volume I own, but I believe the book dates from the late 1970s or early 1980s).

Bouquet de France is a guidebook, restaurant directory, and cookbook, and even though the restaurant listings are obviously out of date (though a few are still open!) this is a terrific read. The Chamberlains lived for more than twelve years in pre–World War II France, and they contributed many articles to *Gourmet*. Narcissa's passion was gastronomy while Samuel's was illustration, and the illustrations in this book are what really set it apart.

Gourmet's Paris does not feature illustrations but rather color photographs and a number of contributions from several writers, notably Naomi Barry, who opens her very good and still apropos essay with the observation that "everybody—consciously or subconsciously—comes to Paris looking for an extension of himself, for a talent not yet fully expressed, for a romance not yet realized, for a new way to look, a *joie de vivre* with vitamins plus, a heightened sense of identity, and sometimes just for Fun. Unless you are an ascetic by conviction, part of the fun will be eating, because Paris has a greater density of good restaurants than any other place on earth." Like *Bouquet de France,* this is also a guidebook and a cookbook, a collection of love letters from a journey through "this best garden of the world."

COOKBOOKS

I have long felt that you cannot separate the history of food from the history of a city or a country—they are intertwined, especially in France. Consider: Henri IV's famous pronouncement that every family in his realm should be able to afford stewed chicken—*poule au pot*—every Sunday; the fate of chef François Vatel, who supposedly invented *crème chantilly* for a banquet in honor of Louis XIV at the Château de Chantilly, but then, after several mishaps including a late fish delivery, committed suicide before the *crème* was ever served; or the origin of the word "bistro," possibly derived from Russian soldiers (occupying Paris in 1814 after the defeat of Napoléon) who felt food service was too slow, so they pounded their fists on tables and shouted, "Bistro!" meaning "Hurry!" Really great cookbooks—the kind with both authentic, tried-and-true recipes and detailed commentary on food traditions and unique ingredients—are just as essential to travel as guidebooks. The books below are my favorites for French and/or Parisian

recipes. All I really need to note about them is that I turn to these often—I consider most to be as worthy as classic novels.

60-Minute Gourmet (Times Books, 1979) and *More 60-Minute Gourmet* (Ballantine, 1986), both by Pierre Franey. Franey's column for the *New York Times,* featuring recipes that would take less than an hour to prepare, was a nationwide sensation when it appeared in 1975. Franey ushered in a new era of American cooking, but in the French style: all these recipes are French inspired, with titles in French, and all are reliable winners—many suited to weeknight cooking—for serving to family and friends.

Barefoot in Paris, Ina Garten (Clarkson Potter, 2004).

Bistro Cooking, Patricia Wells (Workman, 1989).

The Cook and the Gardener: A Year of Recipes and Writings from the French Countryside, Amanda Hesser (Norton, 1999). Hesser cooked for Anne Willan, founder of L'École de Cuisine La Varenne, for a year in Burgundy. (The school [lavarenne.com] is now located in California.) Hesser reminds readers that the stuff of a garden should never be very far away from a kitchen.

French Cooking en Famille, Jacques Burdick (Ballantine, 1989).

Mastering the Art of French Cooking, Volume I by Julia Child, Louisette Bertholle, and Simone Beck (1961) and *Volume II* by Julia Child and Simone Beck (1970), both published by Knopf. When I want to make the most classic of French dishes, I turn repeatedly to this set. I have never, ever been disappointed, though unlike the spirited Julie Powell (of *Julie and Julia* fame), I have *not* cooked every single recipe in these two exemplary volumes.

Saveur Cooks Authentic French, the editors of *Saveur* magazine (Chronicle, 1999). "French food," as noted in the introduction, "is rich, its flavors concentrated, but it can satisfy in small amounts. No one eats cassoulet every day, and none but the most voracious have a second helping. But that one serving, once in a while, is a treasure house of flavors resonant of good living; it feeds the soul as well as the body." This book is also valuable for "Our French Restaurants," a great province-by-province guide to favorite places throughout the country.

The Taste of France, Robert Freson (Stewart, Tabori & Chang, 1983). This is that rare volume, one hundred great recipes paired with 375 fabulous photographs by Freson, plus outstanding contributions by Anne Willan, Alan Davidson, Jill Norman, and Richard Olney. A twenty-fifth anniversary edition was published in 2007.

Baking

I became a home baker because I was so inspired by the French art of *pâtissier,* but also because it seemed that every time I was invited to someone's house for dinner, dessert was always· an afterthought, some preservative-laden cake or pie purchased from the freezer section of a supermarket. I couldn't understand why such attention was placed on the appetizer, the main course, and the wine, but not the dessert—so I started making them myself, and I might say I am now quite accomplished. Perhaps some of my favorite baking books will become favorites of yours:

The Cake Bible (William Morrow, 1988) and *The Pie and Pastry Bible* (Scribner, 1998), Rose Levy Berenbaum. The use of the word "bible" is not misplaced here as these are the most definitive books on the subject. For novices and seasoned bakers alike, featuring many cakes, pies, and tarts in the French tradition.

Great Pies & Tarts (1998) and *Great Cakes* (1999), both by Carole Walter and published by Clarkson Potter. The pies and tarts volume has more recipes for French-style creations than the cakes volume, but both are excellent.

La Maison du Chocolat, Robert Linxe (Rizzoli, 2001). I'm intimidated by some of these recipes from the legendary Paris chocolatier, but the Moist Chocolate Almond Cake and the Chocolate Almond Macarons are not complicated and wildly delicious.

Martha Stewart's Pies & Tarts (Clarkson Potter, 1985). I plowed through this in much the same way that Julie Powell steadfastly made her way through *Mastering the Art of French Cooking.* (Okay, I can't take quite as much credit as Julie, as there are three recipes I just never made.) Martha's recipes for *pâte brisée* and *pâte sucrée* crusts are the ones I turn to still, and her recipe for *tarte tatin* is flawless.

Paris Boulangerie-Pâtisserie, Linda Dannenberg (Clarkson Potter, 1994). This fine book features recipes from thirteen legendary Paris bakeries; the *pain d'épices* honey cake from Pâtisserie Lerch is a staple at my house. The directory of mail-order sources in the United States and restaurant supply stores in Paris is great.

Ready for Dessert: My Best Recipes, David Lebovitz (Ten Speed, 2010). A revision of his *Room for Dessert*—which was an International Association of Culinary Professionals award nominee—and with a dozen new recipes, this wonderful book is filled with many French-inspired treats.

SINGLE-SUBJECT CULINARY BOOKS

I love to delve into books devoted to one culinary specialty, and here's an assortment of some on specialties near and dear to the French:

Absinthe: History in a Bottle, Barnaby Conrad III (Chronicle, 1988). This is an alluring history of the infamous anise-flavored libation also known as *la fée verte* (the green fairy). The production, distribution, and sale of absinthe was banned in France on March 16, 1915, as it was believed to be the cause of alcoholism, suicide, general insanity, and epilepsy. Wormwood and its essence, thujone, was the ruinous and dangerous ingredient. Absinthe had its supporters, but they had no sway over the army: absinthe promoted drunkenness among soldiers, and it was crucial for the troops to be sober and united against Germany. In 1922, the government allowed the sale of wormwood-free absinthe, known today as *pastis,* available from producers such as Pernod and Ricard.

Cheese: A Connoisseur's Guide to the World's Best, Max McCalman (Clarkson Potter, 2005). This beautifully photographed and useful book features cheeses from around the world, but, naturally, many of them are French. I like it especially for the wine-pairing tips; the book makes a great gift when accompanied by selected cheeses and the recommended paired wines.

The Joy of Coffee: The Essential Guide to Buying, Brewing and Enjoying, Corby Kummer (Houghton Mifflin, 1995; revised 2003). A comment I often hear from people who visit France is that the coffee is so much better there. I believe it's not the coffee that's better but the quality of the preparation and the dairy products. (Coffee, after all, does not grow in France, and good-quality beans are available to coffee roasters around the world.) Coffee lovers will find this book enlightening as it addresses plantations, cupping, roasting, grinding, and storing (the best place for storing, if you drink it every day, is not in the freezer, as many people mistakenly believe). But even better are the recipes for baked goods that pair particularly well with coffee. I've made almost all of them and can vouch that they are especially yummy; the Unbeatable Biscotti are just that.

Olives: The Life and Lore of a Noble Fruit, Mort Rosenblum (North Point, 1996). Rosenblum tackled olives before he got to chocolate, and for those of us who love olives this is an essential read. Olives symbolize "everything happy and holy in the Mediterranean," and though there is nary an olive tree growing around Paris, it matters not. "Next time the sun is bright and the tomatoes are ripe," Rosenblum advises us, "take a hunk of bread, sprinkle it with fresh thyme, and think about where to dunk it. I rest my case."

Salt: A World History, Mark Kurlansky (Walker, 2002). Did you know that salt makes ice cream freeze, removes rust, seals cracks, cleans bamboo furniture, kills poison ivy, and treats dyspepsia, sprains, sore throats, and earaches? Salt is believed by Muslims and Jews alike to ward off the evil eye, and bringing bread and salt to a new home is a Jewish tradition dating back to the Middle Ages. I was humbled to learn that the La Baleine sea salt I've been buying for years is owned by Morton, and I was surprised to learn that most of the salt mined today is destined for deicing roads in cold-weather places around the world. (Readers interested in more myriad uses for salt should get the nifty *Solve It with Salt: 110 Surprising and Ingenious Household Uses for Table Salt* by Patty Moosbrugger.)

Wine Box

True wine lovers want to know about *all* the wines of the world, even if they may prefer French wines over others. The following books are all good general resources for wine and include sections on French wine. (And wine in a box, by the way, *is* decent if not good in France. Though I have yet to try an American boxed wine that's a match for any of the French brands—if you come across one, please let me know.)

Great Wines Made Simple: Straight Talk from a Master Sommelier, Andrea Immer Robinson (Broadway, 2005, revised edition).

Jancis Robinson's Wine Course: A Guide to the World of Wine (Abbeville, 2006, revised edition).

Michael Broadbent's Vintage Wine: Fifty Years of Tasting Three Centuries of Wine (Harcourt, 2002).

The Oxford Companion to Wine, Jancis Robinson (Oxford University Press, 2006, third edition).

The Pleasures of Wine (2002) and *Vineyard Tales* (1996), both by Gerald Asher, wine editor at *Gourmet* for more than thirty years, and published by Chronicle.

What to Drink with What You Eat: The Definitive Guide to Pairing Food with Wine, Beer, Spirits, Coffee, Tea—Even Water—Based on Expert Advice from America's Best Sommeliers, Andrew Dornenburg and Karen Page (Bulfinch, 2006).

Windows on the World Complete Wine Course, Kevin Zraly (Sterling, 2009, updated edition).

The Wine Bible, Karen MacNeil (Workman, 2001).

Wine People, Stephen Brook (Vendome, 2001). This is a unique collection of forty portraits of individuals involved in all aspects of wine production and consumption. The profiles are not limited to proprietors and producers, but also include wine merchants and traders, wine writers, a collector, an auctioneer, and a sommelier—and the majority are French. Brook reminds us that wine is a fascinating subject, "a culture that binds together the aristocrat and the peasant, the producer wedded to his soil and the sharp-eyed city merchant, the cautious grower and the extravagant consumer. It is a major source of conviviality. A raised glass can bring down, if only temporarily, national boundaries."

The World Atlas of Wine, Hugh Johnson and Jancis Robinson (Mitchell Beazley, 2007).

ABOUT FRENCH WINE

Adventures on the Wine Route: A Wine Buyer's Tour of France, Kermit Lynch (Farrar, Straus and Giroux, 1988). Lynch, a wine merchant based in Berkeley, California, has earned a reputation for championing very good wines from smaller, sometimes eccentric producers that might never be found in the United States were it not for his efforts to import them. Lynch's journeys around France, on routes and in cellars, are truly fascinating, as are the men and women who make the wine he loves. The late noted food and wine writer Richard Olney has it exactly right when he opines in the preface, "No book on wine and the people who make it has ever been written that remotely resembles *Adventures on the Wine Route.*" Regions near Paris that Lynch visits include the Loire, Beaujolais, Côte-d'Or, Chablis, and Mâconnais-Chalonnais. This book was the winner of the Veuve Clicquot Wine Book of the Year award.

Alexis Lichine's Guide to the Wines and Vineyards of France (Knopf, 1989, fourth edition). Lichine, a former wine exporter, grower, and winemaker (Château Prieuré-Lichine), notes that "from time immemorial, the world's greatest wines have come from France. Though not large in size, for the diversity and quantity of wine it produces France could be a continent. . . . There is hardly a corner of the country that does not offer its own distinctive wines and cuisine, history and scenery, in almost equal measure." Though this wonderful book is out of print, it can still be found and is still very much worth reading for context.

Hachette Atlas of French Wines & Vineyards, edited by Pascal Ribéreau-Gayon (Hachette, 2000). I defer to Robert Parker in his foreword for the best endorsement of this fine book: "This comprehensive book splendidly chronicles and describes the wines of France. It is to be applauded loudly by anyone with a fondness for that country's diverse and dynamic viticulture."

Reflections of a Wine Merchant: On a Lifetime in the Vineyards of France and Italy, Neal Rosenthal (North Point, 2008). Rosenthal began working in the wine business in 1978, and with his partner, Kerry Madigan, formed Rosenthal Wine Merchant and Mad Rose Group (madrose.com), an "umbrella for a close-knit group of people who understand that wine is an agricultural product and that in its best and purest form wine must reflect a specific sense of place." *Terroir,* then, is of the utmost importance to Rosenthal. He notes on his Web site the two rules that guide Rosenthal Wine Merchant: "Ninety percent of the ultimate wine is created in the vineyard, and the role of the winemaker is to let the wine make itself." Today Rosenthal's company represents approximately seventy-five producers, and he shares stories about some of them in this engaging book.

Rosenthal endeared himself to me when I read, "I am curious about the new and different, but I am most at home with the tried and true. Ultimately, my portfolio of growers and their wines reflects my search for wines that are part of classical tradition. As a result, we may be out of the mainstream." I feel the same way about the wines I prefer. I also like his answer to this interview question on WineLibrary.com: "What advice would you give a novice wine drinker to help him or her deepen his/her appreciation of wine?" Rosenthal's advice is to "find a wonderful, passionate, generous retail merchant who is willing to share his/her knowledge. Then, most important of all, be a curious consumer." Rosenthal Wine Merchant represents producers throughout France, and profiles of them are available on the Mad Rose Web site.

Wine and War: The French, the Nazis, and the Battle for France's Greatest Treasure, Don and Petie Kladstrup (Broadway, 2001). Journalists Don and Petie Kladstrup made a fascinating discovery while working on a story about the French government's plan to dig a tunnel through the Loire Valley for the high-speed TGV train network. In the course of their interview with Vouvray vintner Gaston Huet, who opposed the plan, the Kladstrups learned "one of the most amazing stories we have ever heard, a story about courage, loneliness, despair and, in the end, how a tiny bit of wine helped Huet and his fellow POWs survive five years of imprisonment." The writers met other winemakers and heard other stories, and quickly realized that they deserved to be shared and remembered in a book. Some readers may not be aware that the Germans drew the demarcation line between France's occupied and unoccupied zones quite deliberately: the prized vineyards of Bordeaux, Champagne, and Burgundy were not by accident part of the occupied zone. The Kladstrups reveal some truly extraordinary tales about the resourcefulness of wine producers and the villainy of collaborators. Three years of research and interviews aided the Kladstrups in unraveling this previously untold chapter of history, which often reads like a thriller and which I highly recommend.

The Wines of France: The Essential Guide for Savvy Shoppers, Jacqueline Friedrich (Ten Speed, 2006). Friedrich's "Norman Rockwell block" in South Orange, New Jersey, was wine-free when she was growing up, and her first wine loves were Riunite Lambrusco, Lancers, and Mateus. But Friedrich has since become a wine maven, and she is really passionate about French wine. She's not afraid to assert that "France is the greatest wine-making country in the world. And it always will be, at least in our lifetime." (I agree.) This is a hugely helpful book both for visitors to France and wine-buying readers at home.

INTERVIEW

Kermit Lynch

Kermit Lynch, author of Adventures on the Wine Route *(noted above), opened a retail wine shop in Berkeley, California, in 1972 and later began importing and distributing wines nationwide. Among the noteworthy wines he imports is Domaine Tempier Bandol, which I discovered by reading* Adventures *and is now one of my favorite wines on earth (a bottle is even featured on the cover of my previous book on Provence, the Côte d'Azur, and Monaco).*

"Wine is, above all, pleasure," notes Lynch, and this tenet is abundantly clear in his writing. Though I've not yet met him, I believe his enthusiasm for wine is infectious; when his talented staff members write about wine in the store newsletters, they, too, enthuse with unrestrained pleasure in their tasting notes. The store's online newsletter, by the way, is fantastic, educational, and somewhat legendary—if you like wine, you

will want to subscribe (kermitlynch.com), but you can also read Lynch's
Inspiring Thirst: Vintage Selections from the Kermit Lynch Wine
Brochure *(Ten Speed, 2004). Nearly all the notes make me want to run
out and buy a bottle faster than I can say* vin. *For example, of the 2007
Château Roûmieu-Lacoste Sauternes Cuvée André, the review states, "I
believe that if you don't drink some of this monumental Sauternes—
well, only a masochist would miss the experience this wine provides. It is
one of the great bottles of the past few years—an essence of peach, apricot, and orange peel, one of the most delicious things your mouth will ever
have the pleasure to contain. A work of art, I say, noble rot and noble
sweetness." And of a 2009 Régis Minet Pouilly-Fumé from the Loire:
"You'll rarely see rounder, plumper Sauvignon Blanc. Thankfully there is
freshness and nerve to keep it standing up straight and you have the best
of both worlds. This is not quaffin' Sauv Blanc, it is serious food wine."*

*In 1998, Lynch was honored with a Chevalier de l'Ordre du Mérite
Agricole; in 2000 he was named Wine Professional of the Year by the
James Beard Foundation; and in 2005 he received the Chevalier de la Légion d'Honneur. In 1998 Lynch purchased Domaine Les Pallières—
founded in the fifteenth century and remaining in the Roux family for
nearly six hundred years—in Gigondas, Provence, with the Brunier family of Vieux Télégraphe. He and his family live part of the year in
Provence, "near enough to Domaine Tempier that I can fill up the trunk
of my car whenever I need to."*

Q: When did you first visit France, and what did you find inspiring?
A: My first trip was in 1971. I spent time in Paris and Cassis, and
   also a lot of time in Salzburg and Barcelona. In all three countries I admired the food and wine cultures.

Q: You often cite your visit to Jean-Baptiste Chaudet's wine shop
   in Paris on a trip to France in 1974 as "enlightening." At the
   time you had a French vocabulary of about twenty words. How
   was Chaudet helpful to you, and is his shop still in business?

A: Chaudet's store is closed, unfortunately, but he taught me
that there were great wines in
the little-known AOCs (Appellation d'Origine Contrôlée,
the French system of designat-
ing, controlling, and protect-
ing the geography and quality
of wines, liquors, and foods,
notably cheese).

Q: What are some Loire and
Chablis wineries that you rec-
ommend for visitors, and are reservations necessary?

A: A lot of wineries in Chablis receive visitors. It is best to go
and knock on the door. Most will be welcoming, but not
Bernard at Domaine Raveneau. He's closed to the public. In
the Loire, same story, but all my producers there will receive
visitors. My staff can help, or people can just call or have their
hotel arrange for a visit.

Q: Do you often get invited for meals at the homes of winemakers?

A: I am often invited to dine at my producers' homes and have
known some great home cooks like Lulu Peyraud of Domaine Tempier, Gérard Chave, Maguey Brunier, and many
others. Some particularly memorable pairings have included
bouillabaisse with a cool young red Bandol, leg of lamb with
a red Châteauneuf-du-Pape, asparagus with Cheverny, and
oysters and grilled sausages with Chablis.

Q: What's considered your "house wine" at your home, wine
that you pour for everyday drinking?

A: I drink white Burgundy often: Pouilly-Fuissé from Domaine

Robert-Denogent is a recent favorite around the house. My wife always looks for a glass of Bandol rosé as an apéritif. We drink a lot from my winery, Domaine Les Pallières in Gigondas, which I make to my own taste: a full-bodied red but not heavy, oaky, or aggressive.

Kermit Lynch Wine Merchant is located at 1605 San Pablo Avenue in Berkeley (510 524 1524). Browse the Web site (kermitlynch.com) to search the newsletter archive and to learn more about the wines represented.

INTERVIEW

Ina Garten

Readers who may have met Ina Garten at one of her many book signings know that she is as gracious and enthusiastic in person as she appears on her Food Network show, Barefoot Contessa. *I feel fortunate to know her, and I can confirm that her warm personality isn't just confined to her work: Ina is a real down-to-earth, thoughtful, fun-loving person. Plus, she's gaga for Paris! In her seven bestselling cookbooks (all published by Clarkson Potter), she has boosted the confidence of many home cooks to tackle dishes they might otherwise never have tried, and she firmly believes cooks should have fun at their own parties. Her book* Barefoot in Paris *(2004) is devoted to simplified versions—but without loss of flavor—of many classic French dishes. Note that even if you don't cook, you should take a look at her list of recommended Parisian places at the back of the book.*

I recently caught up with Ina by telephone as she was in the final stages of completing her most recent book, How Easy Is That? *(2010).*

Q: When did you first know you wanted to visit Paris?

A: When I was three years old, my grandparents brought me back a dress they'd bought in Paris. I *loved* that dress, which I always referred to as my Paris dress, even though I had no concept of what Paris was—I'm not sure I even knew it was a city. I just knew it had to be a special place.

Q: When did you finally get to Paris?

A: When I was growing up, my parents thought that traveling to Europe was something you had to do in your life. But, according to my father, it was something you did only with a husband, along with acquiring cashmere and pearls. I was twenty-three when I married Jeffrey, and during the first week we were married he gave me pearls and cashmere. A year later we went on an American Express tour to Rome, Paris, and London. Recently, I discovered a box of letters Jeffrey wrote to me in high school—I met him when I was fifteen. He wrote one letter in particular that neither of us remembered. In it, he wrote, "Someday I'd like to take you to Paris. We won't have much money at first, and we'll have to rough it, but maybe one day we could stay in a nice hotel. And maybe one day we could buy an apartment there." It was really a wonderful surprise to find this letter.

Q: The wonderful cities of Rome and London aside, what did you think of Paris when you got there?

A: How can you go to Paris and not think it's the most fantastic place you've ever been? I don't remember a lot of specific details about that first trip, though I do remember going to the outdoor food markets, which I loved. I remember going to the Poilâne *boulangerie*. I think I loved to cook—that's another thing I never did until I married. But clearly that's what I was interested in, even though in college, at Syracuse University, I started out in fashion design and I also studied business.

Q: You bought an apartment in Paris in 2000. What arrondissement is it in, and what are some of your favorite things about your *quartier*?

A: I was very specific about where I wanted to live in Paris. I told several real estate agents that I wanted an apartment that was within walking distance of the boulevard Raspail market, the cheese purveyor Barthélemy (51 rue de Grenelle), La Grande Épicerie in the Bon Marché department store (38 rue de Sèvres), and Poilâne (8 rue du Cherche-Midi). I went to Paris for one week per month for a year to look at apartments. There was one agent that I just knew was going to find the right apartment—he didn't forget about me after I left, and one day he called me in New York and said, "I have the apartment for you. It's in the seventh arrondissement. Come see it." I asked Jeffrey, "What should I do?" and he said, "Go quickly!" So I flew to Paris that night. I remember that I only had a handbag with me. I looked at the apartment, and it was the most god-awful apartment I'd ever seen in my life. The kitchen was gray and pink. I really couldn't see myself living there, so I told the agent I was sorry but I couldn't possibly buy this apartment. He suggested we go have lunch and then come back and see the apartment again. He probably thought it would look better after a big bottle of wine. But it didn't—it was dreadful. So I left Paris, but I dreamt about the apartment on the plane flight home. I just couldn't decide. It needed major renovation. But a friend said to me, "You can fix the apartment but not the location." And that was it. The price *was* reasonable (the franc was low then) and so I bought it and have never looked back. Jeffrey never saw the "before"—we had an implicit deal: I could do whatever I wanted with the apartment as long as he didn't have to be involved with the renovation. So we walked in together when it was all finished and it was so exciting.

In my neighborhood I love to have a picnic in the Luxembourg Gardens, I love going to the movies, and I love an omelette and a glass of Champagne at Flore. There's a wonderful Italian restaurant called Marco Polo (8 rue de Condé) and another one called Le Cherche Midi (22 rue du Cherche-Midi). [Note to readers: this is a favorite restaurant of mine as well!] Also, the Café de la Croix-Rouge (Carrefour de la Croix-Rouge, near Saint-Sulpice) is a favorite. The Village Voice (6 rue Princesse) is my local bookstore and it's great. I'm lucky to live near the most extraordinary florist, Marianne Robic (39 rue de Babylone). Her shop is so amazing! She creates unexpected bouquets, like pairing big bunches of fresh mint with white roses—she's a genius. New to the neighborhood is Pâtisserie des Rêves (93 rue du

Bac)—my taste goes more toward Poilâne, but Rêves is really
lovely.

Q: How often do you get to Paris?
A: Four times a year.

Q: When you have guests, what are some things you recommend
   they add to their itineraries?
A: Most of my guests have been to Paris before, so I don't recommend the Louvre, for example, or a lot of the well-known
   highlights. Most of the things I know everybody knows, but I
   do love the Musée Nissim de Camondo (63 rue de Monceau,
   8ème). The kitchen there is amazing. It was renovated by
   Shoré Dupuy, who was the head designer for the prestigious
   La Cornue stove company, founded by Albert Dupuy in 1908
   (she also renovated my kitchen). The dining room—with the
   table all set—is also great, and the museum really gives you a
   sense of how people lived in the early to mid-1900s.

Q: Now that you've been in Paris for ten-plus years and have
   seen all the major sites, how do you most like to spend your
   time?
A: In the beginning we used to just wander around our neighborhood. We felt then, and still do, that the thing about Paris
   is that it's the world: you can go just about everywhere in the
   world and never leave the sixth and seventh arrondissements!
   We're terrible tourists—though I do go to Belgium quite a
   bit and take some overnight trips to London and Milan, we
   pretty much stay close to home. For us Paris is really vacation
   time. We have a lot of really good friends who live there, and
   we spend time with them and we go to the park and read
   books. Recently, I did see an Yves Saint Laurent exhibit at
   the Petit Palais, which was one of the greatest shows of all
   time, but that was more an exception than the rule.

Q: Do you take trips outside of Paris, and if so where do you go?

A: We're really just starting to explore the rest of France. Near Paris, the Champagne district is fabulous. I'm a huge Veuve Clicquot fan—we had lunch there with a winemaker, and every course was paired with a different sparkling wine, including a demi-sec Champagne that I'd never had before. It was sweet and was paired with a choclate cake. The history of Veuve Clicquot is fascinating, and Madame Clicquot was too: she was widowed at the age of twenty-seven with no experience in business of any kind, as she came from a wealthy *ancien régime* family. In her private life she was conservative and conventional, but she was willing to take risks in the vineyard and she was a brilliant businesswoman. We've also enjoyed visiting Normandy, where we have a friend who has a château on the coast with an incredible garden. And we've traveled a lot in the south, throughout Provence and to Nice on the Côte d'Azur. I do anticipate that we'll plan more travels within France.

Q: How do you incorporate Paris into your life here in New York?

A: Actually, I deliberately don't. It would be very easy to bring back, say, Mariage Frères teas and Poilâne bread, but I like to leave them in Paris so that they're special for the times when I'm there. In New York, I frequent La Maison du Chocolat (1018 Madison Avenue, 30 Rockefeller Center, and 63 Wall Street), and I do enjoy a nice treat from Hermès (691 Madison Avenue and other locations). I'm so happy that Frédéric Malle has just opened here in New York (898 Madi-

son Avenue). It's a fabulous space—in a beautiful Art Deco building with 1930s French art and furniture from his own collection—and the Malle fragrance I wear is Une Fleur de Cassie.

Q: What do you miss when you're away from Paris?

A: I miss the way French people entertain. When they entertain it's really special. Every time you get invited for dinner the meal is incredible and everyone talks about interesting things, and everyone stays up until two in the morning (somehow, in Paris, you just do it) and I love sleeping in until ten. I also miss the more leisurely pace of French life, which is completely different from here. But I think the thing I miss the most there is that people really appreciate the food. The food here in the States has been so altered, and everything you taste is so watered down, with no true flavor. When you taste a strawberry in France—which of course, at the outdoor markets, would be available only in the spring—you're reminded more of strawberry jam. It's bursting with true strawberry flavor and tastes like the best strawberry you've ever had, because it is. There is also more than one *variety* of strawberry. Take raspberries as another example—they're available year-round in North America, so they're not special, and also they have no taste. There's a real sense of the seasons in France.

Q: When I was working on my travel journal *En Route* (Potter Style, 2007), you were one of several travelers I asked about what books inspired your wanderlust over the years. Like me, you said that you always read books based on the place you're going, and for you this is mostly France. At the time, you mentioned your favorites were *Paris to the Moon* by Adam Gopnik, *A Moveable Feast* by Ernest Hemingway, *The World at Night* by Alan Furst, *Mastering the Art of French Cooking* by Julia Child, and *The Wirtz Gardens* by Patrick Taylor (which is about the Belgian landscape gardener Jacques Wirtz, who believes very strongly in preserving the spirit of a place in his work). What books might you add to the list today?

A: I also love all of Janet Flanner's writing about Paris and *The Flâneur* by Edmund White.

Q: You have such a busy schedule, yet you seem to balance everything really well. Have you picked up any tips about organizing from the time you spend in Paris?

A: I haven't picked up any tips in France, but I'm very disciplined about how I spend my time. It's very easy to get carried away with all the things people want you to do. We plan our trips a year in advance, and France is like the circuit breaker. It's inviolate, to the point where, for example, a friend of ours had a bar mitzvah and we flew home for it and we flew right back. Paris equals time off for me. It's a really important part of my really busy life.

Fear of food, indulgences, and small helpings. Because of media hype and woefully inadequate information, too many people nowadays are deathly afraid of their food, and what does fear of food do to the digestive system? I am sure that an unhappy or suspicious stomach, constricted and uneasy with worry, cannot digest properly. And if digestion is poor, the whole body politic suffers. . . . The pleasures of the table—that lovely old-fashioned phrase—depict food as an art form, as a delightful part of civilized life. In spite of food fads, fitness programs, and health concerns, we must never lose sight of a beautifully conceived meal.

—Julia Child, *The Way to Cook*

BISTRO

Le Pré
aux
Clercs

BRASSERIE

STELLA

café   res

À TABLE!

I can hear the glass door of the café grate on the sand as I open it. I can recall the smell of every hour. In the morning that of eggs frizzling in butter, the pungent cigarette, coffee and bad cognac; at five o'clock the fragrant odor of absinthe; and soon after the steaming soup ascends from the kitchen; and as the evening advances, the mingled smells of cigarettes, coffee, and weak beer.

—GEORGE MOORE,
Confessions of a Young Man

There's no city in the world where you eat better. Period.

—ALEXANDER LOBRANO,
Hungry for Paris

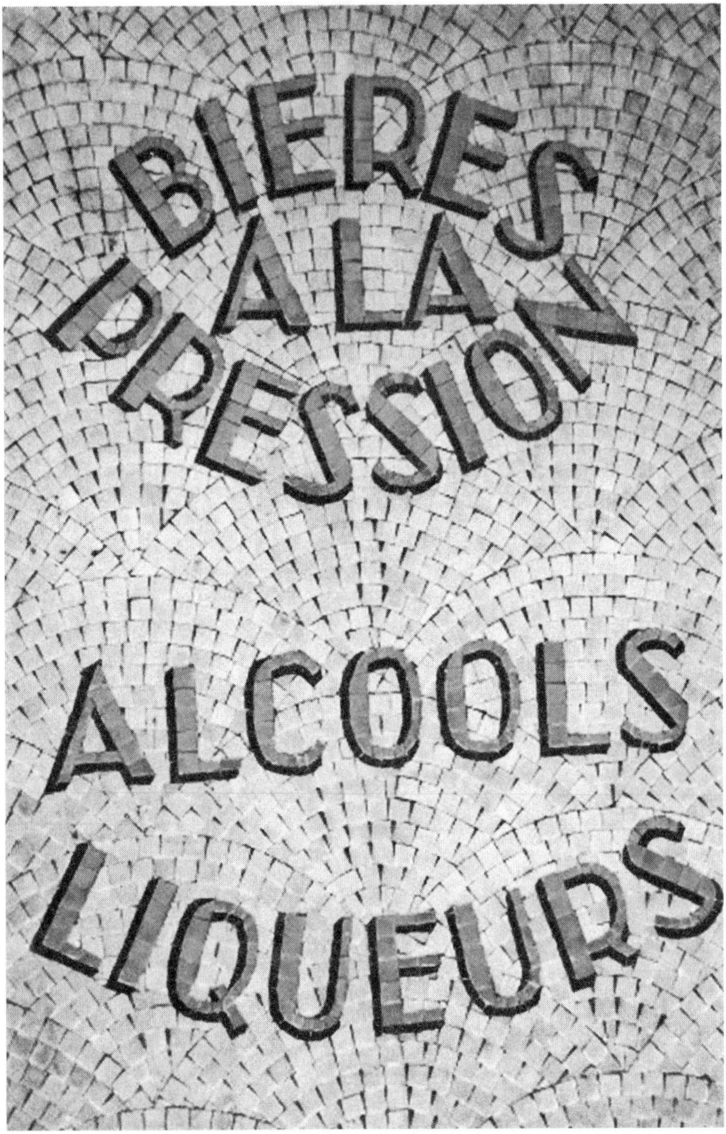
BIERES
A LA
PRESSION
ALCOOLS
LIQUEURS

A Clean, Well-Lighted Café in Montparnasse

ADAIR LARA

I HAVE BEEN a fan of this essay since its original appearance in the *San Francisco Chronicle* in 1991, and it continues to bring a big smile to my face.

ADAIR LARA wrote a popular (and often very funny) twice-weekly column for the *Chronicle* for twelve years, and her award-winning columns have been published in several collections: *Welcome to Earth, Mom: Tales of a Single Mother* (Chronicle, 1992), *At Adair's House: More Columns by America's Formerly Single Mom* (Chronicle, 1995), and *Slowing Down in a Speeded-Up World* (Conari, 1994). Lara is also the author of *Naked, Drunk, and Writing* (Ten Speed, 2010), *You Know You're a Writer When . . .* (Chronicle, 2007), *Hold Me Close, Let Me Go* (Broadway, 2001), *The Granny Diaries* (Chronicle, 2007), and *Normal Is Just a Setting on the Dryer and Other Lessons from the Real, Real World* (Chronicle, 2003), among others. She has contributed to numerous magazines, including *Cosmopolitan, Departures, Glamour, Redbook, Ladies' Home Journal,* and *Good Housekeeping.* San Francisco mayor Willie Brown declared May 17, 2002, Adair Lara Day.

PARIS—IT WAS a pleasant café in Montparnasse, the famous artists' quarter of Paris. An American sat at a small table, took out a yellow pad, and began to write. A cup of coffee steamed at her elbow. It was good to sit in a café and watch the people go in and out.

Before coming to Paris, she had read *A Moveable Feast* by Ernest Hemingway, who lived here in the 1920s and wrote in the cafés. Her friend Bill had hated the book, in which Hemingway wrote terrible things about people who were nice to him in Paris but had the poor timing to die before he did. Bill was afraid she would start stringing all her sentences together with *and* too, but it was Paris in the warm summer, and she did not care what Bill said. He had gone to the American Library without her and would stay carefully away all morning to let her write.

She had chosen her café after some deliberation. It was a clean, well-lighted place on the Avenue du Général-Leclerc, near where Hemingway had penned his short stories at the Closerie des Lilas, where F. Scott Fitzgerald had written at the Dôme, and where stacks of other authors had written at the Deux Magots.

All the writers had horrid cheap flats—that's why they went to cafés. The American and her friend had a cheap flat too, owned by a depressed Frenchwoman named Marie-Claude, who nailed all the shutters closed, turned off the gas, took the TV, and told a friend to rent it if he could.

So conditions were perfect to nudge the American with the very overdue novel and the tiny, dark flat into the cafés, where, she thought, if she sat where Hemingway sat and drank what he drank (though it seemed a tad early for a rum Saint James), she might write a novel too.

She would sip the good Parisian coffee and watch the French hurry to the Métro to work, and write about the way the lady-bugs had swarmed on the bush in the sea-damped hollows of Lagunitas when she was eight and afraid of her father.

"Write one true sentence," Hemingway said, and the American thought, then wrote, "I hate that kind of advice."

She liked better what Steinbeck said: "Don't start by trying to make the book chronological. Just take a period. Then try to remember it so clearly that you can see things: what colors and how warm or cold and how you got there. Then try to remember people. And then just tell what happened. It is important to tell what people looked like, how they walked, what they wore, what they ate."

Next to her an elegant young couple were chatting and smoking. The French know that smoking is bad for you, but they don't care. The American, temporarily at a standstill with the ladybugs, wrote down everything they were wearing, her shiny black flats and his pink tie, and everything they ate and drank. Then she nibbled the end of her pen.

After a while the American put away her yellow pad. She was tired and sad and happy, as she always was after trying to write, and though she felt she had done some very bad writing indeed, she would not know how bad until she read it over the next day.

She sipped her cold coffee and looked around. Mozart and jazz played softly in the background, and a good cup of coffee cost four francs, and they left you alone, not even coming to wipe the table, but maybe it was not the right place for inspiration to come. She frowned. What was wrong?

It was pleasant. It was clean. It was in the heart of Montparnasse. It was McDonald's.

The *Art of Eating*

One of my favorite food magazines is the *Art of Eating,* an excellent, critical, superbly written quarterly newsletter by Edward Behr. It's been referred to as "the must-have foodie quarterly" by National Public Radio, and by me as one of the best publications of any kind, ever. I can't resist sharing some other accolades it has received: "A publication of great class and pedigree. It is worth every dollar" (World Class

Wines); "He could care less about cover notes, entertaining his readers, or providing vicarious thrills to make them renew. If you want an in-depth look, it's one-of-a-kind stuff. He's not pandering to anybody but [only to] his own curiosity" (Chris Kimball, quoted in the *Boston Globe*); and "I'm a devoted reader" (Corby Kummer, *Atlantic Monthly*).

Behr founded the quarterly in 1986, and although it's not exclusively about France, over the years Behr has devoted several issues to various aspects of French food and restaurants, each of them worth the effort to special order. All of these below are still available for purchase, and don't let the fact that some of them are more than a decade old deter you: this is top-notch food writing and is still very much relevant.

Paris (Again) (Number 60, Winter 2002) features a fantastic and interesting annotated address book that covers Paris and examines French food, land, culture, the parable of the sauce spoon, the advantages of fashion, bread, charcuterie, cheese, chocolate, kitchen tools, meat, open-air markets, pastry, restaurants formal and informal, spices, and wine—with an in-depth look at croissants.

In *Paris (or What is French Food?), Part I: Posing the Question and the Classic Parisian Baguette* (Number 45, Winter 1998), Behr asks, "What today remains distinctly French about the food in Paris?" and he embarks on a search for real French bread. *Part II: More Answers and Places that Are Truly French* (Number 46, Spring 1998) offers recommendations for some good food-related addresses in Paris and poses a final question: "How long will French food last?"

Check out the *Art of Eating* Web site (artofeating.com) to learn more about interesting topics such as dark chocolate in Paris, new Paris bistros, wines of the Loire and of Anjou, Champagne, and foie gras, and more. A subscription is the best way to regularly get the magazine, but copies are sold at some retail stores, such as Whole Foods and Kitchen Arts & Letters.

"If you're an oyster eater, the first thing to do is head for Huîtrerie Régis. It's at 3 rue Montfaucon in the sixth arrondissement, a short walk from the Mabillon Métro station. Paris is filled with restaurants and cafés selling oysters, but this one is special. It's tiny, decorated in all white, and dead serious: the minimum order allowed is a dozen oysters per person. Whether you walk in the door liking oysters or loving them, you will walk out feeling like you *understand* them. They're impeccable here, fat and shiny with a flavor that rings in your mouth like a bell.

"After you eat your oysters, if it's nice outside, take a walk. I love the smell of Paris, and walking is the best way to catch it. It changes from season to season, but it's particularly fine in late spring, before the heat comes, when the air is light and quick. The city smells then like a mix of croissants in mid-bake, car exhaust, new grass, and roses, the ones waiting on the sidewalk outside every flower shop. It's not a perfect smell, and sometimes it's not even a good smell, but it's resolutely Paris. It's the first thing I notice when I arrive and the thing I miss the most when I leave."

—Molly Wizenberg,
food writer, author of
A Homemade Life,
columnist for *Bon Appétit,*
and co-owner of the restaurant
Delancey, in Seattle

David Lebovitz

As mentioned earlier, David Lebovitz's award-winning blog (davidlebovitz.com) is a great resource for travelers to Paris, especially those with culinary interests. Lebovitz is a former pastry chef at Chez Panisse in Berkeley and the author of *The Great Book of Chocolate* (2004), *The Perfect Scoop* (2007), and *Ready for Dessert* (2010), all published by Ten Speed Press, and *The Sweet Life in Paris* (Broadway, 2009). His blog includes listings for his favorite places to eat in Paris as well as his favorite dining and travel guides; even better, he offers some excellent essays that I highly recommend (type these into the search feature): "10 Common Ordering Mistakes People Make in Paris," "10 Insanely Delicious Things You Shouldn't Miss in Paris," "Tipping in France and Paris," "Romantic Restaurants in Paris," "Where Is the Best Duck Confit in Paris?" and "Tips for Vegetarian Dining in Paris." Lebovitz also conducts chocolate and gastronomy tours in Paris, which sell out immediately (or so it seems). I wish he offered these more frequently; if you've been fortunate enough to secure a reservation, I'm sure you'll agree!

Counter Culture
The Success of Breaking the Rules

NAOMI BARRY

NAOMI BARRY WAS *Gourmet*'s first resident correspondent in Paris, and in *Remembrance of Things Paris,* Ruth Reichl opines that Barry "may be the most underappreciated restaurant writer of all time." Reichl continues by saying, "Reading fifty-year-old restaurant reviews would not normally be much fun; it takes a writer of extraordinary abilities to make you care about meals that you will never be able to eat. But with each review Barry offers up such a rich slice of life that you feel you are sitting at the next table, eavesdropping on your neighbors chatting with the chef."

I completely agree with Reichl's remarks, and I feel I am one of the luckiest people on the planet to know Barry, who still lives in Paris, in the seventh arrondissement. She has kindly invited me to her beautiful apartment on two occasions—once with my daughter, Alyssa, and once with my friend Amy—and good food, laughter, and great conversation were in abundance each time.

Barry wrote the piece below for the newsletter of the Chef Culinary Network, which provides legal support and business development services for entrepreneurial chefs, top restaurants, and luxury hotels in the gourmet culinary market. The restaurant she reviews here, L'Atelier de Joël Robuchon (5 rue de Montalembert, 7ème / +33 01 42 22 56 56 / joel-robuchon.net), has been described by the *Louis Vuitton*

City Guide as "an experience you must not miss. . . . Absolutely everything is excellent and exquisitely refined."

After eight years, Joël Robuchon's trailblazing l'Atelier is still the most sought-after restaurant in Paris. There have to be reasons why. In 2003 Robuchon's return from retirement was awaited with the interest of Mlle Chanel's return from retirement two decades before. Curiosity was intense but the buzz was mostly negative.

"He won't last two months" was the prediction.

One day in August, feeling lonesome because all my friends were out of town, I decided to treat myself to lunch at l'Atelier, which operates full steam seven days a week, twelve months a year. Incredible, in a town where vacation is sacred.

Paris in August is wonderful or awful. Business is down to a flutter. Butcher, baker, and most of the neighborhood restaurants are *en vacances* until September. In the shuttered, quasi-abandoned city, l'Atelier was blessedly open and full as usual: hep visitors from half the world and the odd Parisian in town for one reason or another. The atmosphere was a relaxed We Happy Few. The place was packed.

"Amazing," I said to Éric Lecerf, one of the chef-partners who was at the helm that day. "I thought nobody was in Paris. What is your secret formula?"

"Our figures are 15 percent higher than this time last year. In fact our figures have been going up steadily since the beginning. Before we opened we were nervous. It was a risk. We had staked our entire savings and our future on this radical concept." Lecerf sounded gratefully surprised.

The success of the pioneer team has led to the string of Ateliers Robuchon has since opened on three continents.

Philippe Braun, Robuchon's trusted lieutenant, leaves Paris from time to time to analyze and to control the details of each new Robuchon property. After we spoke he would soon be off to Taipei for a final look at the latest in the group.

Under the Robuchon umbrella, the Paris Atelier is a working partnership of four members of the brigade at Robuchon's former restaurant, Jamin. The quartet—Philippe Braun, Éric Lecerf, Éric Bouchenoir, Antonio Hernandes—had earned its stripes. Working at Jamin had been tough as a marine boot camp. At l'Atelier, one of them is always on active service, ensuring there is never a lapse in performance. The customer does not detect it, but the discipline is almost military. These days the group has added another chef to its galaxy, the talented, rosy-cheeked young Axel Manes.

Today the public has accepted everything that the gloom-and-doom prophets of 2003 had predicted they would never accept.

1. You still can't walk into l'Atelier unless someone opens the door for you from the inside, a technique reminiscent of Manhattan's speakeasy era.
2. No reservations. The howl was so great the house compromised. You can now reserve for the eleven-thirty a.m. lunch service and the six-thirty p.m. supper service. Otherwise you have to take your chances. Let's face it. Being a regular does help, whenever there is a possibility.
3. Whether you are feeble or fat, you have no choice but to perch on a high stool (there are forty-one of them), elbows on the counter. There are no tables.

More people than not accept the game plan. The quality of the food has won out. Every plate placed before you on the counter is a summit of *haute gastronomie.*

"We have the products," said Philippe in partial explanation of what is so special about this particular Atelier. "France has everything, if we look for it."

Baby lamb chops from a breed discovered in the Pyrénées are an exquisite staple on the Paris bill of fare. They are unlike any I have ever tasted . . . tender and subtly flavored with thyme from mountain meadows: the tiny chops are dainty enough for a party hosted by Alice in Wonderland.

"Part of our secret lies with our network of suppliers," said Éric Lecerf. "Over the years I have built a list of over two hundred. In the morning I can phone a fisherman on the coast and ask for fifty sea perch. That evening I will have my fifty sea perch, fresh from the sea. Our customers know that never do we serve a fish that has been farm raised."

Guests and staff, face-to-face on either side of a counter, have undergone an altered humanized relationship. The waiter is no longer an anonymous servitor but a key figure in the ritual between kitchen and client. The waiters, an exceptionally appealing bunch, admit to loving the chance for brief conversation with the customers. You may not notice that surreptitiously everyone is giving a wipe and a polish. The high maintenance is part of the rigorous discipline.

In a limited way, the Paris Atelier tries to emulate the ethic of the traditional Japanese inn, the *ryokan,* which aims to satisfy the desire of the guest before the guest has had the chance to even voice his desire.

Recently a waitress overheard a trio of regulars discussing the imminent birthday plans of one of their number. She alerted the pastry kitchen. At the meal's end a surprise birthday cake was presented before the trio.

Clients, thawed by the affable atmosphere, frequently chat with the strangers sitting next to them. "A couple of nights later," said Éric, "I've seen these same strangers back again together—this time as friends."

French fries are an icon of France. Some *frites* are good, some are better, some are terrible. The very very best have a maximum of crusty exterior. L'Atelier wanted to produce a superlative French fry to serve with its steak tartare.

The solution turned up in the drawer of a farmhouse kitchen cabinet in Poitou. Someone remembered the purpose of the housewifely gadget of corrugated tin, which resembled a toy-size Pipes of Pan.

"I saw my grandmother use one," he said. "She would press it into the sides of a large potato. The potato became a mass of spirals, doubling the surface of a conventional French fry."

The naive kitchen aid probably sold for next to nothing during the thirties. Armed with the prototype, the Atelier team located an artisan willing to reproduce it by hand.

"We need ten of them," said Philippe. "The gadgets cost us one hundred euros each. More than one thousand euros for a few platters of *pommes frites* as we like them."

You have to be crazy.

"We're crazy," said Philippe with an irresistible smile.

Simplicity at l'Atelier in Paris is the simplicity of Marie Antoinette playing elegant milkmaid at Versailles. The luxury is still there but stripped of its more elaborate trappings. The charm is in the paradox.

My lunch at l'Atelier was a jolly affair. I had a giant prawn clasped in a delicate, paper-thin crust presented like a jewel on a rectangular plate of artistically troubled glass, accompanied by a small pool of emerald-green basil sauce. There were three of the irresistible baby lamb chops and a little iron pot of Robuchon's signature mashed potatoes.

I talked with a pair of *chocolatiers* from Belgium on my left and a couple from Ireland on my right. The Belgians offered me a glass of Champagne. Giovanni, the sommelier who looks as if he stepped out of a painting by Veronese, filled it half again. I couldn't have had a better time.

NOTES ON EATING OUT

In North America, we don't have very strict definitions for places to eat—besides specific categories like diners, drive-ins, fast-food places, and seafood shacks, every eating establishment is really a restaurant, whether modest or elaborate. The restaurant may specialize in a single type of cuisine or feature a variety of foods, but the name of a place doesn't always indicate how expensive it is or what diners will find there. In France, there is a basic understanding of what diners can expect whether at a *café, brasserie, salon de thé, bar à vin,* and so forth, and visitors who don't already know these differences may find them very helpful, not only for the price ranges but for the types of food on offer. Here's a brief list of what you'll find in Paris:

Bar à vin: Wine bars are numerous in Paris, and I love them. For me, they are almost always where I prefer to eat because I can try many great wines by the glass that I can't afford by the bottle and eat light fare chosen specifically to pair well with the wine. Most wine bars are casual, though a few offer actual meals, and are generally inexpensive to moderately priced.

Bistro: Traditionally *un bistro* is a small, casual restaurant that's family owned and operated. The menu selections change daily, though only a few dishes are offered, and wine comes in one red and one white variety, usually by the carafe. Prices tend to be modest. However, note that other bistros are quite fancy establishments, with prices to match.

Boulangerie: Though of course a *boulangerie* stocks bread, many also bake savory items filled with cheese, herbs, olives, slices of ham, or pâté that are terrific for eating *en plein air* (outdoors), so don't overlook a *boulangerie*—or a *pâtisserie* for that matter. Though known primarily for desserts, *pâtisseries* often also bake savory items that are easily transported to a picnic blanket or park bench.

Brasserie: The word *brasserie* derives from *brasseur* (brewer), so you can be sure beer will be on the menu. It's typically offered as *une pression* (on tap) or *un demi* (about a third of a liter), but you may also find *un formidable,* a very large glass like those served at the Hofbräuhaus in Munich. Most Parisian brasseries also serve specialties from the region of Alsace, which means you'll find lots of sausages, wursts, sauerkraut, and delicious Alsatian white wine.

Café: Daniel Young, in *The Paris Café Cookbook,* defines a *café* as "any establishment where you can stop in for nothing more than a beverage and stay for as long as you like." This is why both a bistro and a brasserie may also be considered cafés. It is worth repeating that you can order nothing more than a coffee or a glass of beer or wine and sit at a café for many hours and no one will hurry you along. (Though your waiter may ask you to settle the bill if he or she is going off duty.) Light fare, such as sandwiches, omelettes, salads, and baked goods in the morning, is what to generally expect at a café.

Charcuterie: Like a *boulangerie, fromagerie* (cheese shop), or *pâtisserie,* a *charcuterie*—which offers prepared foods—is good to remember for putting together a *pique-nique* or any meal on the go. A typical charcuterie might have an assortment of cooked hams, sausages, duck confit, and pâté as well as breads, cheeses, smoked fish, quiche, pizza, salads, and terrines. Most everything may be eaten at room temperature, or you can ask them to heat it up.

Restaurant: Though a bistro can sometimes be a restaurant, and a good restaurant can be inexpensive, generally *un restaurant* is a fancier establishment with a printed menu (as opposed to one handwritten on a chalkboard) and usually costs more. Some Parisian restaurants specialize in seafood or vegetarian cuisine, or the cooking from a particular region of France, or simply a style that is creative and contemporary.

Salon de thé: Tea salons in Paris bear only a slight resemblance to those in England. As Patricia Wells has noted: "Parisians don't fool around with frail cucumber sandwiches and dry currant buns—they get right to the heart of the matter, dessert." A few lunch or dinner selections may be offered at tea salons, but they are light, and may not be nearly as good as the sweet selections.

And some tips to remember:

* At many cafés and casual places to eat, the price for food and drink is different depending on where you sit. If you stand at the bar (known as a *comptoir* or *zinc*) the price is cheaper than if you sit in the *salle* (dining room), which is cheaper than *à la terrasse,* the prime people-watching spot outside on a sidewalk, garden, or *place.*

* *Haute cuisine* is, to my mind, not simply a dining experience; it's nothing less than an elaborate stage production of the highest caliber. True, it's very expensive, but properly executed, the experience is sublime and unforgettable—and worth every euro. Ruth Reichl, during her tenure as restaurant critic for the *New York Times,* frequently reminded readers to keep several points in mind when considering the price of fine dining in France: *haute cuisine* is extremely labor intensive and requires enormously expensive ingredients; you never have to wait for a table in France because you effectively "buy" a table for the afternoon or evening; economically speaking, French restaurants are completely different from American restaurants, which concentrate on turning as many tables as possible during mealtimes; and prices on French menus include tax and tip, both of which add up to a hefty sum for a nice meal.

* In October 1998, *Wine Spectator* devoted one entire issue to Paris, and though this was some time ago, I still think the edition included some of the best advice for Americans dining in France today. It remains true that Americans *are* welcome at the

great restaurants of France—as long as they are small in number. The writer explained, "The maître d' at one three-star restaurant told me, 'When an American calls, I put him on the waiting list until I see how the reservations are balanced. The French don't like to eat in a dining room full of Americans, and neither do the Americans.' " Americans are often seated at the worst tables, and as many of us are unlikely to return to a particular gastronomic temple and it's presumed we don't know much about food, we remain low on many restaurants' priority list. It helps to know all this, but as the writer reminds us, "Don't be intimidated; remember who's paying the bill."

★ If you're not comfortable making a restaurant reservation by telephone, why not stop in and do it in person? This way, you will be certain that the details are all correct, you'll have the opportunity to see the restaurant and take a look at the menu, and you'll establish an early relationship with the staff.

★ Odd as it may seem to our capitalist sensibility, many restaurants in Paris, including some high temples of gastronomy, are closed on Saturday for lunch and/or dinner and on Sunday. Be sure to plan accordingly if there is a particular restaurant you have your heart set on visiting. Note, also, that many eating establishments of any type are closed for part or all of August.

★ Under the category of "knew it but forgot" is tipping: nearly every bill you receive anywhere in France at any type of eating establishment will include the tip, which is indicated by the words *service compris*. If you feel you have received exceptional service and you want to tip extra, it is customary to leave no more than a few euros, or 5 percent of the bill's total. At bars, cafés, and elsewhere, it is also customary to round up your bill to the next euro. Note that if you are paying with a credit card, usually the bill will be brought to you with the total already filled in with no opportunity to leave a tip. If you must put the tip on your card, tell your waiter in advance that you'd like to add a tip to the total, but otherwise just leave the tip in cash. (I once had to leave a wine bar, search for an ATM, and return with the tip, which I felt was necessary because the waiter had really been terrific. The beam on his face when I returned was worth the twenty minutes it took to retrieve the cash.)

★ As noted in the introduction, mealtimes in France—whether at restaurants or in food shops—are generally well established and adhered to, even in Paris. Other than at cafés and brasseries, which typically serve food and drink continuously, by two in the afternoon lunch service is over and patrons will not be admitted (or if they are, there won't be much food left to offer). This is easy enough to grasp, but less clear is when lunchtime officially *begins*. Mark Greenside, in *I'll Never Be French (No Matter What I Do)*, recounts the following: "At 12:00 virtually every French person not serving food in Gare Montparnasse stops whatever he or she is doing and starts to eat. By 12:05 not

a single chair, table, bench, or horizontal surface is empty. There are lines—actually wedges, the French don't make lines—thirty and forty people deep waiting to buy a sandwich or a Coke or their ubiquitous bottle of water. . . . At 11:55 we could have sat anywhere and bought anything. By 12:05 there's no place to go. I haven't seen anything like it since the piranha tank at the Brooklyn Aquarium." This is not unique to France—I've had very similar and more stark experiences in Greece, for example—but is nonetheless worth noting.

A Passion for *Pâtisseries*

When I was a student, I established a Sunday routine that I loved: go to the Louvre at opening time (it was free on Sundays), stay for about three hours, and go to a *pâtisserie*, preferably a different one each week. As I couldn't afford to eat both lunch *and* dessert, on Sundays I would eschew lunch for the full *pâtisserie* experience, which for me was a *café crème* and a treat (or sometimes two) of my choice. My only rule was that I couldn't repeat the treat I ordered for at least one month, which ensured I would try all the *pâtisserie* classics: *Paris-Brest, religieuses, macarons, croissants, brioches, profiteroles, financiers, éclairs, kugelhopf, Napoléons,* etc. (I felt it was important that I be familiar with the classics, since at that time the only French pastries I'd ever heard of, or eaten, were *éclairs,* which of course everyone back home pronounced with a long *e*.) I often think longingly of this Sunday tradition, and though at my age now I'm no longer able to enjoy *pâtisserie* treats so frequently, I usually try to sample a *pâtisserie* a day when I visit Paris—by eating sensibly, this is really not a weight-gaining indulgence.

The pastries at even the most humble *pâtisseries* in Paris are an art. Even if you use your waistline as an excuse not to indulge at all (such a shame, I say), at least admire the pastry creations in the windows. And don't forget that most of these *pâtisseries* all have beautifully packaged treats that make great gifts (just be careful what you choose in the hot summer months). I find many *pâtisseries* to be truly intoxicating, and I am equally fond of legendary places and less exalted pastry shops. I seek these out and incorporate them into my daily itineraries the same way I plan visits to restaurants and cafés. You'll make your own discoveries, of course, but for a good selection of memorable *pâtisseries* in one source, I think the best book is *Paris Pâtisseries: History, Shops, Recipes* (Flammarion, 2010)—I use the word "best" because, as the editor notes, "in this book we only show the best, the truly exceptional." And so you'll find Pâtisserie Stohrer, Pain du Sucre, Fauchon, Ladurée, Gérard Mulot, Lenôtre, Laurent Duchêne, Dalloyau, Du Pain et des Idées, Blé Sucré, Pierre Hermé, and others. The book includes the history of each bakery, up-close photographs of some desserts that give the word "mouthwatering" new meaning, and the *pâtisseries'* specialties, ranging from classics to newfangled favorites destined to become classics; plus there are twenty-five recipes and other favorite addresses. "The stories conveyed by desserts," the editor notes, "are stories of nostalgic affection that become part of family lore. . . . Parisians are always ready to cross the city from one end to the other to fetch *the* cake whose mere mention makes their mouths water."

I have completely filled a little notebook I've dutifully kept for many years with my notes from all of the *pâtisseries* I've ever visited in Paris. As you might imagine, it's quite extensive, and sharing all the lengthy descriptions with you

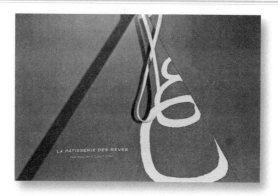

here is not my intent. I have too much difficulty paring down my list of favorite *pâtisseries* to only a few, so instead, I will share only two that are rather new to Paris. I'm really excited about them and they are completely different from the city's classic, Old World *pâtisseries* (but by coincidence happen to be in the same arrondissement).

Pâtisserie des Rêves (93 rue du Bac, 7ème, and 111 rue de Longchamp, 16ème / lapatisseriedesreves.com). Chef and cookbook author Philippe Conticini, who was also *chef de cuisine* at Petrossian in New York, is the *créateur* behind this bakery, which is definitely the stuff of *rêves*—dreams. This is a far cry from a homespun bake shop; it's *beyond* sophisticated, hip and bright. Though plenty of classic pastries are on offer, it's the *ré-créations* and *gâteaux de saison* that are really eye-popping. The *créations gourmandes* are featured under glass domes—I like to refer to them as *cloches* (bells)—on a two-tiered circular display table in the center of the boutique, and when you want one a staff member brings you a fresh one from the kitchen in the back. In addition, there are nicely packaged tins of nuts, cocoa, and brown sugar, as well as a wonderful boxed set of gorgeous paperback recipe books—they all make great gifts.

Hugo & Victor (40 boulevard Raspail, 7ème / hugo victor.com). Hugues Pouget, who worked as pastry chef for Guy Savoy for six years and was honored as Champion of Desserts of France in 2003, is the founder of this extraordinary shop, along with his partner, Sylvain Blanc. Though descriptions of *pâtisseries* often characterize the treats as rare gems in a jewelry store, nowhere is this more true than here at Hugo & Victor. *Everything* is too dazzling to eat! But eat you must from this *cabinet de curiosités sucrées* (cabinet of sweet curiosities), and I really don't believe anything would be a disappointment. I am partial to the *pétales de pamplemousse* tart (grapefruit) and *le bonbon chocolat demi-sphère,* but I still have ten flavors of *macarons* to try, fourteen chocolates, and some wonderful concoctions that look like colored shards of glass called "the five seasons of Hugo & Victor." When asked in an interview if he would share a pastry-making trick, Pouget replied, "Use sugar as seasoning rather than ingredient, as you do with salt. In my pastries, there is on average 5 percent sugar rather than the usual 15 percent." Asked if he considered creating pastries an art form, he replied, "*Oui*. When creating a pastry you think about the flavor combinations, color, texture, volume; there is a feeling, an emotion, and a creation"—all of which is on lavish display when you walk into Hugo & Victor.

A Few of My Favorites

Here are some places to eat a meal or a snack that I have particularly enjoyed in recent years—but it is by no means a complete list of *every* place I've enjoyed eating at in Paris. The establishments that appear below have been among my favorites for the past five years.

* **Au 35** (35 rue Jacob, 6ème / +33 01 42 60 23 24). Au 35 is a small—only about a dozen tables, plus a few upstairs reached by a narrow staircase—neighborhood place that turns out very good, uncomplicated dishes seven days a week for satisfied diners, who happen to be mostly locals. Daily choices are limited, but they're seasonal and prepared with care; the staff members are very *gentil* and full of smiles.

* **Berthillon** (31 rue Saint-Louis-en-l'Île / +33 01 43 54 31 61 / berthillon.fr). Founded in 1954, this legendary *glacier* (ice cream shop) on the Île Saint-Louis is noteworthy for its luscious, truly memorable flavors, as well as for the long lines of people waiting to order—the wait is worth it—and for the fact that it's closed for the month of August (and on Mondays and Tuesdays as well). Plan accordingly!

* **Bistrot Melac** (42 rue Léon-Frot, 11ème / +33 01 43 70 59 27 / melac.fr). Named after the owner, Jacques Melac, this wine bar is a favorite of many locals and tourists and is "a place where people can meet, eat, and drink wine." Indeed, a sign hanging from the ceiling notes, "*L'eau est ici reservée pour faire cuire les pommes de terre*" (The water here is reserved for cooking potatoes). Melac is from the Aveyron and most of the food served here is from that region, while

most of the wines poured are little-known varieties from Languedoc and the Loire. It's hard not to make new friends here as most of the tables are communal style.

★ **Cafés Verlet** (256 rue Saint-Honoré, 1er / +33 01 42 60 67 39 / cafesverlet.com). The Verlet is good to know about for purchasing excellent coffee beans, loose tea, candied fruit, cakes, *confiture,* peppercorns, vanilla, and more, but sitting down and enjoying a cup or something to eat is a great pleasure. Verlet was founded in 1880, and in 1995 Éric Duchossoy purchased the business from Pierre Verlet, grandson of the founder. In an interview, Duchossoy noted, "You should know I was born in a coffee bean," referring to the fact that his father and grandfather were in the coffee-roasting business, and his father still roasts at the family business in Le Havre. Duchossoy travels frequently and meets the farmers who supply the company's beans. At Verlet there are four house blends and twenty single-origin coffees—all of which are roasted fresh daily—as well as nearly fifty different kinds of tea. My friend Lorraine and I enjoyed cups of cappuccino here that were outstanding, served in beautiful olive-green stoneware mugs on leaf-shaped saucers and with a little square of Paul Hévin chocolate on the side. Whether you sit downstairs or upstairs, the café is cozy and filled with lots of Parisians. And though it's on a chic street, the prices are quite reasonable.

★ **Ladurée** (21 rue Bonaparte, 6ème / +33 01 44 07 64 87 / laduree.fr). There is no question that the older Ladurée outposts in the eighth arrondissement (16 rue Royale and 75 avenue des Champs-Élysées) are more grand and more beautiful than the smaller boutique in the sixth, but I prefer it, both for its smaller scale and for the fact that the neighborhood doesn't have any other place quite like it. After some serious retail activity at the enticing shops on rue Bonaparte near the cross street rue Jacob, it is nice to know you can relax in Ladurée's pretty tea salon. My favorite items to buy in the shop are the *guimauves* (marshmallows), cocoa powder in that distinctive pale green and gold tin, and jars of *caramel au beurre salé,* which usually ends up being consumed with a spoon right out of the jar.

★ **L'Absinthe** (24 place du Marché Saint-Honoré, 1er / +33 01 49 26 90 04 / restaurantabsinthe.com). This modern French bistro has a great, animated atmosphere and really good food to match. The kitchen is under the direction of Caroline Rostang, daughter of noted chef Michel, and dishes are solidly classic but with some updated, not to say wildly creative, touches. The upstairs room is a little quieter than downstairs, and in warm weather tables spill out onto the *place.* The wine list is good and, yes, there are a number of absinthe options on the menu.

★ **L'As du Fallafel** (34 rue des Rosiers, 4ème / +33 01 48 87 63 60). I've eaten and cooked my fair share of falafel, so I can say with some authority that the falafel here is truly "ace," as its name purports. Many people have told me that the best falafel in the world is found in Israel, but as I haven't been there yet to investigate the claim, I just tell everyone who will listen that the best falafel is here in Paris. It is truly a gastronomic delight that puts any other falafel you've ever had to shame. Clotilde Dusoulier, in *Edible Adventures in Paris,* advises that if the line is too long at L'As, head down the street to Mi-Va-Mi, at 23 rue des Rosiers, for a falafel she describes as "just as good as that of their celebrity neighbor." Duly noted!

* **Le Grand Véfour** (17 rue de Beaujolais, 1er / +33 01 42 96 56 27 / grand-vefour.com). This beautiful, beautiful restaurant, set in the arcades of the Palais Royal, opened as the Café de Chartres in 1784 and was bought by one Jean Véfour in 1820. Guests have been illustrious: Napoléon and Joséphine, Voltaire, Dumas, Fragonard, and Simone de

Joyau de l'art décoratif du XVIIIᵉ siècle, dans un écrin - Les jardins du Palais-Royal - Le Grand Véfour est le haut lieu gastronomique de la vie politique, artistique et littéraire de Paris depuis plus de 200 ans.

Tucked away in the Palais-Royal Gardens Le Grand Véfour - one of the gems of 18th century decorative art - has been a temple of Parisian gastronomy for politicians, artists and writers for over 200 years.

Beauvoir and Jean-Paul Sartre, to name a few. The restaurant was closed from 1905 to 1947; after the liberation of Paris it was bought by the owner of Maxim's and reopened in 1948 under the direction of chef Raymond Oliver (Jean Cocteau designed the reopening menu). Today Le Grand Véfour is a Michelin-starred establishment, a member of the Relais & Chateaux group, and owned by the Taittinger Champagne family. The chef is Guy Martin, also the author of a number of cookbooks, and though some say the food lacks sparkle, the lunch I had there with my friends Amy and Arlene was very, very good. (My only complaint was the exorbitant price for glasses of Taittinger, which we were not informed of in advance!) The three and a half hours I spent there were among the most memorable I've ever had in Paris.

★ **Le Pré aux Clercs** (30 rue Bonaparte, 6ème / +33 01 43 54 41 73). This is the kind of neighborhood place, with consistently good but not amazing food, that has long been common in France but not so in the States. On my last visit I went three times. The owner, who seems to know a great number of his patrons—he gives nearly everyone who enters two kisses and a hug—is incredibly friendly and welcoming, and the staff is equally friendly and efficient. The overall vibe of the place is one of great conviviality, with eclectic and appealing music playing.

★ **Le Train Bleu** (20 boulevard Diderot, Gare de Lyon, 12ème / +33 01 43 43 03 06 / le-train-bleu.com). Listed as a national historical monument in 1972 after its restoration in 1968, this special restaurant was created by the Paris-Lyon-Mediterranée Company and opened in 1900 on the occasion of the Exposition Universelle in Paris.

Originally called the Buffet de la Gare de Lyon, it was renamed Le Train Bleu in 1963 as a tribute to the legendary
train service from Paris to the south. The reason to come
here is really not for the food, which is average, but for one
of the most atmospheric dining spaces in the world. The
forty-one paintings which cover all the walls and ceilings
feature the sunny Provençal and Côte d'Azur destinations
of the original *train bleu,* as well as some of the Alps. On
my short list of goals in life is to have dinner at Le Train
Bleu and then stroll down to the tracks to board a night
train for Menton. I just know it will be splendid.

★ **Paul** chain of bakeries (approximately forty locations in
Paris / paul.fr). Founded in Lille by a family of bakers dating back four generations to 1889, Paul celebrated its

Le Train Bleu

gare de Lyon

120th anniversary in 2009. In 1958, after his father passed away, Francis Holder and his mother took over the family bakery and expanded it. Today there are 360 outlets in France alone and some in numerous other countries (in the United States, there are a handful of bakeries, only in Florida). Such growth doesn't normally appeal to me, but what I like about Paul is that I can get a nice salad, better than decent bread, and a glass of wine for a reasonable price within a short period of time and be on my way. I'm not positive I would frequent Paul if it were in New York, but the truth is, this chain is far better than any American food chain. I'd welcome it here, and I like knowing it's an option when I'm in France.

★ **Willi's Wine Bar** (13 rue des Petits-Champs, 1er / +33 01 42 61 05 09 / williswinebar.com). I will always have a warm spot in my heart reserved for Willi's, named after William Foster Simpson Browning III, the basset hound of owner Mark Williamson (the much-loved dog passed away in the mid-eighties). Williamson specializes in Côtes-du-Rhône wines, which are paired with a great range of dishes small and large—I've really enjoyed everything I've eaten here. There are tables in the back, but I prefer the seats at the long bar in front, which is where I had my special Willi's moment: On a fall day in 1995 I was the only person at the bar at about five p.m., so I had the privilege of talking to the bartender with no distractions and could listen in on his conversations with other staff members. There was a lot of anxious chatter because it was Williamson's birthday (or maybe it was his partner's; my memory of this detail isn't entirely clear, but it doesn't really matter). The staff had arranged for T-shirts to be imprinted marking the occasion, and I was shown one and asked for my opinion (it was great!). Everything about the birthday was a surprise, so there was lots of whispering and numerous calls placed between Willi's and nearby Juvéniles (47 rue de Richelieu), owned at the time by Williamson and then-partner Tim Johnston (and still a good place for tapas and wine). I had this insider's view for only about an hour and a half, because by that time the seats at the bar started to fill up. I had to leave, but the staff members sent me on my way with a warm farewell and hugs all around. Willi's never disappoints, and its limited-edition posters make fine souvenirs. Note: Macéo (15 rue des Petits-Champs) is Williamson's other venture, a contemporary restaurant named after saxophonist Maceo Parker, which I also very much like.

* **Ziryab** (on the top floor of L'Institut du Monde Arabe, 1 rue des Fossés-Saint-Bernard, 5ème / +33 01 53 10 10 20). I've never actually eaten a meal at Ziryab, which specializes in mostly Lebanese cuisine that I hear is quite good. But I have sipped delicious *thé a la menthe* on the outdoor terrace, where I looked out at the fabulous view and felt I was in one of the best spots on earth.

French Restaurant and Food Guides

If you are a real culinary nut, you may like to review a number of sources to find places to eat, drink, and buy provisions. Let me stress that all these guides are fairly subjective, so if you determine you trust a particular author or team of writers, that seems as sure a guide as any to lead you to places that won't let you down, be it a modest eatery or a Michelin-starred temple. I generally eat and drink well when I'm in France, if not always fabulously. You will, too, by following trusted advice, understanding the difference between the varieties of French eateries (detailed previously), and reading about regional specialties. You'll also undoubtedly discover some good places on your own that I hope you'll share with me!

Regarding the well-known *Guide Michelin* and *Pudlo Paris,* I like consulting both. (Though there is a Zagat edition devoted to Paris, I am not generally a fan of Zagat, as I feel the descriptions are not thorough enough, and I concur with *Art of Eating* publisher Edward Behr, who remarked that Zagat "has all the defects of democracy. It's a poll. It's like an average. It's too smoothed out. . . . I would prefer to hear a little more in-depth from someone with one point of view.")

The mighty Michelin has battled some criticism over the last few years, and though it may not be as scrupulously unbiased as the staff likes to claim, I think it has emerged relatively unscathed. For me, the best reason to consult the Red Guide (not to be confused with the Green Guides, which are for touring) is for the Bib Gourmand places, which are awarded this accolade for serving very good food at a reasonable price. Peter Mayle has described these places as not very fashionable and rarely eulogized by the guidebooks. "But they have something about them that I—not to mention a few hundred thousand French customers—find irresistible. A very distinct character, the comforting feeling that you and your appetite couldn't possibly be in better hands."

Le Guide Pudlo, compiled by Gilles Pudlowski, restaurant

critic and journalist for the French weekly newsmagazine *Le Point,* is very comprehensive and only recently available in English (distributed by Little Bookroom). It's organized by arrondissement and features not only the *grandes tables* but also hundreds of recommendations for specialty gourmet shops, bars, cafés, wine bars, and tea salons. Additionally, the Pudlo includes a number of places with the best value for money or best foreign cuisine, and listings for places open on Sundays and others that are open past eleven p.m. Note that there are also separate Pudlo guides for Alsace; Normandy and Brittany; and Provence, Côte d'Azur, and Monaco.

Other guides I frequently consult include:

Authentic Bistros of Paris, François Thomazeau and Sylvain Ageorges (Little Bookroom, 2005). The authors quote some lyrics from the song "Le Bistro" by Georges Brassens: "On a run-down old square / In a poor part of Paris / Some angel took this dive / And made it / A palace." Each of the fifty-one bistros profiled in this handy little book (about the size of an old Baedeker's guide) is indeed a palace of sorts. Though it's true that Parisian bistros are facing possible extinction, there are enough of them left to warm the hearts of locals and visitors alike. The authors' criteria in making their selections included testing the classic ham sandwich, *le jambon-beurre.* "It was an arbitrary decision," they note, "but it turned out to be revelatory. Good bars make a good *jambon-beurre.* That's just the way it is. And their beers are the right temperature. And the espresso is neither too hot nor too cold, no matter what time you order it. And the house red is never harsh." Interestingly, they also discovered that a large number of the establishments featured are or were owned by natives of the Auvergne region. Only a few of these favorite bistros appear in other books, and I had the opportunity a few autumns ago to discover some new places, including the bar in the film *Amélie* and the Charbon Escalier, the last *café-charbon* of Paris (*charbon* is French for coal and signifies that a café is heated by a coal stove and not gas or electricity).

Clotilde's Edible Adventures in Paris, Clotilde Dusoulier (Broadway, 2008). I echo Nach Waxman and Matt Sartwell's enthusiasm for this book (see page 351), and I will add something else that's appealing about Clotilde: she is a self-described "enthusiastic list-maker" and keeps lists of books she wants to read, places she wants to visit, stories to write, and projects to tackle. This great read is a window onto Clotilde's Paris that can be yours, too.

The Food Lover's Guide to the Gourmet Secrets of Paris, Kate Whiteman (Universe, 2006). Organized by neighborhood in nine chapters, this fully illustrated volume is not only lovely to look at but is great for planning neighborhood itineraries that are filled with lots of culinary stops (plus there are forty recipes). Restaurants, cafés, markets, and specialty shops are noted side by side with each *quartier's* landmarks, museums, and sights, making this a great planning guide and souvenir.

Gourmet Paris: What You Want to Eat, Where, Dish by Dish, Emmanuel Rubin (Flammarion, 2002, revised edition). Here's a guide "for dipping into, buffet style" and it's quite unlike any other: it's organized by type of food—andouillette, crème brûlée, foie gras, fondues, game, potatoes, rum baba, snails, and tajines, for example—and offers readers a selection of good places to find these specific foods. Additionally, there are recommendations for places in museums, along the Seine, with a view, or with terraces, as well as good bets for dining solo, in a large group, or with children.

Gourmet Shops of Paris: An Epicurean Tour, Pierre Rival with photographs by Christian Sarramon (Flammarion, 2005). I love this book because it's organized by chapters entitled "Sweet Paris," "Savory Paris," "Paris in a Glass," and "Paris on the Go," with both longtime well-known addresses and trendy, but worthwhile, new ones. The photographs are enticing and the six-page "Gourmet's Notebook"—covering confectionery and chocolates, cakes large and small, ice cream and sorbet, bread and cheese, fine food stores, wine shops (and one for whiskey), and cafés and sandwich shops—is an estimable epicurean guide.

The Historic Restaurants of Paris: A Guide to Century-Old Cafés, Bistros and Gourmet Food Shops, Ellen Williams (Little Bookroom, 2001). Perhaps not surprisingly, Williams notes, "Paris abounds in restaurants and gourmet shops that have been in business for more than a hundred years," and this is a perfect little guide for seeking out these unique establishments. This is a hardcover volume but is small enough to bring along.

"I think one thing that I appreciate the most when I go to Paris is renting an apartment. You look it up on the Internet and you see pictures of rooms and make all the arrangements, and it's like walking into a novel—an Anne Tyler novel: What would happen if . . . ?—and suddenly you become Madame Jones on rue Hachette or something like that—you just take on the French life. I like it particularly, of course, because you can do some of your own cooking, and it's such fun to go to the markets and buy things—it's not enough just to go and look. You live kind of an enchanted life, and for me it takes me back to the years I lived in Paris, from 1948 to 1951. I had my first job at Doubleday as an assistant editor and I went to Europe for a three-week vacation, to Italy and the Côte d'Azur and then to Paris. After three weeks I just couldn't bear to come back home, so I got my vacation extended for another three or four weeks. Then literally the day before I was to go home I was sitting in the Tuileries Gardens and I was watching the sun set over the city and it was so beautiful and I thought, 'What am I doing going home? This is where I belong!' And then I got up and walked away, leaving my purse hanging on the bench. I'm sure Freud would say this was not an accident. When I got around the corner, I realized that my passport, my passage home, my whole identity was in that purse. And it was all gone. When I went back to my hotel I decided it was an act of fate and I'm supposed to be here. So instead of crying to my mama begging for a ticket home, I stayed in Paris and tried to get a job.

"Eventually I picked various things up—that's a long story that I tell in my book—and then I met Evan, my future husband, who was there because he started a weekend magazine with *Stars and Stripes* after the war. These were wonderful years, particularly in the beginning, when the French loved us so. We were their saviors, after all. It was so touching to watch this country still recovering from the war and the occupation . . . some of the shame, some of the pride, and all of these things. One example I think of was the time I was in a *boulangerie* and we were all standing in line to get a fresh baguette and a man up front cracked open a baguette and cried out, then passed the loaf all around and people started shouting and clapping. I asked someone what this was all about and he exclaimed, "The flour is white!" To me that just tells you multitudes about the French people, their love of food, their pride in it, the time they will take to make a meal. I've seen people wearing carpet slippers buying three times the amount of pâté that I could afford! It just was such a priority in their lives. I must have some French genes hidden in me because I always respond to that. And it's *sensible* eating, you know. You eat at least three courses and they're small amounts, you linger and you spend at least an hour and a half at the table instead of this grab-a-bite-and-run that is the American philosophy.

"So, I sort of feel that my soul, or my tummy, needs that refreshment every year. I try to go to Paris almost every year for a few weeks. I find a little apartment and live a totally different life. A few times I will change the arrondissement I rent in, particularly if someone like Claudia Roden is staying at her apartment in the rue Saint-Dominique and I want to be close by there. Recently I've found that the old Saint-Germain district—fun as it is to go and have a drink there— is *so* touristy. You don't find the wonderful little shops—the little *fromagerie* and the little *boulangerie*—that you do in the more family-oriented neighborhoods, particularly around the area of the rue Cler, where there's a market on the weekends that I love."

> —Judith Jones, editor to Julia Child, Edna Lewis,
> Claudia Roden, Penelope Casas, and Marion
> Cunningham, among others, and author of
> *The Tenth Muse: My Life in Food* (Knopf, 2007)
> and *The Pleasures of Cooking for One* (Knopf, 2009)

Dorie Greenspan

Cookbook author Dorie Greenspan—whose books include *Paris Sweets: Great Desserts from the City's Best Pastry Shops* (Broadway, 2002), *Baking: From My Home to Yours* (Houghton Mifflin, 2006), *Desserts by Pierre Hermé* (Little, Brown, 1998), and *Around My French Table: More Than 300 Recipes from My Home to Yours* (Houghton Mifflin, 2010)—has lived in Paris part-time for over twelve years. She maintains an excellent blog, In the Kitchen and On the Road with Dorie (doriegreenspan.com), which is a worthwhile resource for travelers. Greenspan writes very clearly and passionately and cares deeply about getting the details right.

One memorable post from her is "The Paris Ten: Must-Tastes," a list of ten iconic foods of Paris, "the tastes a visitor, perhaps a first-timer, shouldn't miss in the city." In another post, about Hugues Pouget and the bakery Hugo & Victor (see page 320), she writes, "I think I know a little about what makes chefs great. There's their talent, that's almost a given; there's their energy—they're built with superchargers that aren't standard equipment among us ordinary mortals; there's their skill at organization and production (not a glam quality, but a really important one); and there's their intelligence, a kind of intelligence that includes creativity, but that also includes the ability to express, share, explain that creativity, and, in doing that, inspire and teach others." Log on and subscribe to Greenspan's monthly newsletter!

Thanksgiving in Paris

LAURA CHAMARET

CHAMARET WORKS IN book publishing in New York, and I feel fortunate to know her because she's as crazy for Paris, and France, as I am. But it wasn't always so: she was smitten with Italy and Spain (she spoke both Italian and Spanish) and had never studied French nor set foot in France. "I never had a care in the world to know anything about France," she told me, "until the night I went to a bar with my best friend on West Fifty-first Street and I met a French man at the bar, and married him not long after." Chamaret's husband, Sébastien, is from a very small town in the *département* of Mayenne in the Loire Valley next to Normandy, where his family has lived on the same farm for four generations. When he first brought Chamaret there, she related, "It was one of the most foreign cultural experiences of my life. I'm very adaptable—I was born overseas, I've lived in a number of different places, and I'm pretty good at adapting to my surroundings—but I've never felt so much like a fish out of water. Me, a New York City girl in the middle of nowhere in France where things don't get done the way they get done here, and Sébastien's parents don't speak a word of English. They were so welcoming, so inviting, and just incredibly lovely. Everything we ate was grown or made right there on the farm, from the pâté to the pears and everything in between. The house was simple and clean and it didn't matter that it hadn't been redecorated in many, many years—the chairs were the same ones they'd had for fifty years. It was a whole different kind of thing and couldn't have been further from my life up to that point."

Laura and Sébastien never had any intention of living in Paris, but on a trip around France to see where they *did* want to live, they ended up stranded in Paris on September 11, 2001. A good friend offered to stay at his girlfriend's and gave them his apartment until they could get home, which wasn't until a week later. "We fell in love with the city," says Chamaret. "And I'm sure some of that love was due to the situation, our emotions, and how wonderful the Parisians were to us, but we knew we were staying for at least a few years." And they did. (Though they eventually returned to New York to start a family, they plan to move back to France one day.)

Trips and sojourns in France over the intervening twelve years have led many friends and colleagues to seek the travel advice of the Chamarets. "You have no idea how many people ask my husband and me for advice on what to do when they're going to France," Chamaret told me. "I assume that they have read a guidebook or two, and I tell them what my three favorite museums are—the Musée d'Orsay, the Centre Georges Pompidou, and the Orangerie. A lot of people don't know that at the Pompidou there's a restaurant with a beautiful terrace on top that has one of the most lovely views of Paris you've ever seen—the food's not great but it's a great place to go for a drink after you've seen the fabulous collection." But she adds, "No one realizes how much work goes into requests like these, because you have to consider what people hope to get out of their trip, you have to think of what things to recommend for first-time visitors versus those who're visiting again, you have to know how familiar they are with the language and culture, and you have to create an itinerary—it's time-consuming and it's work, which is why the services of a good travel consultant are so valuable!"

LAURA CHAMARET, who is not a writer by profession, won first prize for this piece in a 2006 *Food & Wine* essay contest entitled Tell Us About Your Most Memorable Thanksgiving. She kindly edited her essay slightly for this book. Her husband, former *chef de cuisine* at Manhattan's legendary La Goulue and pastry chef at Orsay, is co-owner, with Adrien Angelvy, of the new restaurant Le Comptoir (251 Grand Street / 718 486 3300 / lecomptoirny.com) in the Williamsburg neighborhood of Brooklyn.

MY FATHER'S BIRTHDAY always fell near or on Thanksgiving. So while I was growing up, it was considered an important holiday for our family. It was a time that, no matter where my parents or siblings were on the globe, we would reunite at one table and break bread. It was an enjoyable time that gave me a fleeting notion of stability that I longed for.

At the end of my twenties, I still had a globe-trotting lifestyle and in 2002, I moved to Paris with Sébastien, my French boyfriend—now husband. He became a chef at an early age and was the executive chef at Perry Bistro (since closed) in New York City when we met in 1999. We moved to the City of Light so I could learn to speak French fluently. His parents were milk farmers in the countryside and didn't speak a word of English. If this relationship was going to continue, it was high time I could have a conversation with them. When we made the leap, we didn't have much money, so we found a one-bedroom apartment in a seventh-floor walk-up. We didn't care because it had a terrace, and who needs an elevator when you have a terrace to dine on and a view of the rooftops of Paris? It was in the nineteenth arrondissement, in the northeast section of the city by the mystical Canal Saint-Martin.

We made fast friends with people Sébastien knew through the New York restaurant scene. Our friend's brother Louis didn't live far from our *quartier,* and his girlfriend, Virginie, became my best friend. Our network grew and when autumn came I missed the simple yet crucial event of carving a turkey with family—and with my father now gone, my childhood tradition had become a memory. But these people over time had become my family— a strong support so far from home. When I told Virginie how much I longed for Thanksgiving, she was fascinated, and she wanted to know what this holiday was all about. Many Parisians had heard of it and wondered about it, she told me. We should plan our "French Thanksgiving," she said, and as she's gregarious, she told all our friends. What began as a dinner for eight turned into a banquet for twenty-eight like wildfire. Some of our friends weren't French but were, like me, expatriates from other parts of the world who were attracted to Paris and all it had to offer. They, too, had wondered about this Thanksgiving phenomenon.

A week before Thanksgiving, Sébastien informed me we needed to order the turkey from the butcher now. I thought this was absurd. Surely if people were this curious about our holiday, turkeys would be everywhere in anticipation of a stray American in their neighborhood—ethnocentric thinking indeed. As instructed, I went to our butcher—a kind, large, jolly man who we came to know well during our time living on avenue Secrétan. I asked him for a ten- or twelve-kilo *dinde* and he laughed in my face. Surely I was joking. That would be nearly impossible to find in time for my dinner next week. It's simply not the time for turkeys, he informed me. Could he get me a goose instead? Then he stopped and remembered vaguely about that American tradition of killing turkeys in the middle of November, and could I explain why we do this? At every turn, I found myself recounting a quick version of American history and how Thanksgiving has transformed into a time for food and family more than anything else. He was happy to go above and beyond and get my *dinde.* It would be here by Tuesday.

Two days before Thanksgiving, our friends were over for *apéritifs* and we looked around our 650-square-foot apartment trying

to figure out exactly how we were going to fit twenty-eight people for dinner—and at one table, no less. The one table we had
could seat six at most. They called themselves into action immediately, determined to make the dinner a success. Louis would
bring two extra tables from his parents' house and folding chairs.
We would move the armoire and couch out of the living room
and line the table up diagonally through the center of the room to
fit everyone together. Lionel would bring at least twenty plates;
Virginie would ask Alona and Thérèse to bring extra silverware.
We would go out tomorrow morning together to buy cheap wine
glasses from the catchall five-and-dime shop down the street. We
were all quite thankful that the liquor store was only across the
street!

The hard part was getting all the food. The French apartment
lifestyle has yet to incorporate a Sub-Zero. Our apartment didn't
come with an oven, either. We only had a large tabletop rotisserie
oven in which to make turkey, popovers, and stuffing in. The timing had to be perfect. We had a tiny two-shelf fridge under our
counter. Everything that needed to be refrigerated would have to
be bought Thursday morning. Thankfully it was a chilly November, because the turkey would have to live on the terrace in the
small shed for a while to keep cold. Wednesday was spent prepping vegetables, as well as making *pain surprise* for the *apéritifs* and,
of course, the pies—two pumpkin and two of grandma's apple
pies.

You might be asking yourself what a *pain surprise* is. Quite simply, hollow out the bread, make a mix of sandwich flavors, and
put them back in! I made salted cucumber with chive *crème fraîche,
jambon de Serrano* with olive tapenade, *brandade de morue* (a spreadable codfish concoction that is quite delicious), and mousse of
duck foie gras with sea salt and fig jam. It's a surprise because you
don't know what sandwich you will get—a terrible plan for an
American party of picky eaters, but the French don't seem to
have that in their blood.

PAIN SURPRISE

Cut off the top of a large round bread loaf, or *boule*. For this dish, *pain de mie* is the best bread option.

Cut a circle inside the crust sides and very strategically cut out the bottom to lift out the bread.

Slice those into sandwich-size pieces and make various flavors of small tea sandwiches.

As I prepped away, various people climbed up and down seven flights of stairs with supplies or stuffed our bedroom with the living room furniture to make extra room. They were literally working for their meal. It was grand. Everyone was having a fantastic time and making Thanksgiving possible. It had become a quest.

❧   ❧   ❧

The morning of Thanksgiving, our fridge decided not to cooperate and the door fell off. I called Sébastien at the restaurant where he worked not knowing what to do, and he assured me that everything would be fine. He got the evening off and would fix it when he returned home. In the meantime, he told me, "Improvise." Hadn't I been doing that all along? Well, when you are already dealing with the size of a fridge I had, the challenge was keeping everything cold. To make matters worse, when I took the turkey out of the little porch shed, I knew it wouldn't be enough meat for the size of our group, so I ran to the butcher and got three turkey roulades—basically, breasts rolled and tied by the butcher. I was panicked because I had no idea how I would fit them into the fridge or the cooking schedule. Things were packed in the fridge as it was (*crème fraîche*, butter, cheese, herbs, leeks, sausage . . . to name a few), so my biggest obstacles were keeping everything from spilling out and finding a good place to put the door while I awaited technical assistance!

Timing the cooking order to make this whole thing possible was a multitasking achievement. The morning of our big event, the turkey was the first thing to go in, at about eight-thirty a.m. It would take at least six to seven hours on the highest setting, better known as number 8 on French ovens, to cook. It's an everyday challenge figuring out the conversion temperatures when you have the American ones in your head. This time, eight was easy! The sausage and chestnut stuffing was the next to cook, taking about an hour and a half to two hours. The potatoes and *haricots verts* were done on the stove top, lightening up the oven schedule considerably. You may be asking yourself how so many hours were possible before a Thanksgiving meal but it is not a holiday in France, so we weren't going to sit down much before seven o'clock in the evening. The tough part was toward the late afternoon. You have to make the popovers last (they deflate, and who wants to eat a cold popover?) and I had three turkey roulades to roast. What I ended up doing was roasting them once everyone had arrived. They baked through the cocktail hour(s) and the beginning of dinner. They were meant to serve as seconds to everyone, so the timing was great. Sure enough, everything worked out. I managed to have centerpieces, flowers, candles, and enough wine to make it complete.

When all was said and done, we sat down with twenty-three of our friends and shared our first real Thanksgiving overseas. Although it's an American tradition, I tried to incorporate tastes of my new homeland. We feasted on *herbs de Provence* turkey, sausage and chestnut stuffing, leek and *crème fraîche* mashed potatoes, *haricots verts amandine,* and Roquefort popovers. In turn, they were served with true Americana authenticities like cranberry sauce and grandma's apple pie. Unlike our other typical meals in France, we stuffed ourselves, as is the custom after all. I told stories about the origins of Thanksgiving and realized in the middle of all this that the people at my table represented a multitude of places: France, England, Russia, Sweden, Norway, South Korea, and others. They had gathered together and made the effort to make it special. These were my overseas brothers and sisters. I experienced not only a wonderful Thanksgiving Day so many miles from home in Paris, but the *feeling* of home and stability that I'd missed.

Salons de Thé

As popular as coffee is in Paris, tea has become very *au courant* over the last twenty years or so, and there are many more *salons de thé* than there once were. As Sebastian Beckwith, a cofounder of my favorite tea company, In Pursuit of Tea (inpursuitoftea.com), mentioned to me, "Paris is a city that respects tea. Compared to England, where tea is really comfort food, France elevates tea to a higher level—the French are masters at scenting and flavoring tea, adding flavors and oils and herbs to make their blends. And I like that *salons de thé* offer a meeting place for Parisians as well as travelers."

Among the most venerable *salons* is Mariage Frères, notably its outpost at 30 rue du Bourg-Tibourg in the Marais (+33 01 42 72 28 11 / mariagefreres.com). There are other Mariage Frères outposts and tea counters in Paris—as well as in other French cities, in Germany, and in Japan—but none of them, in my opinion, are as grand and Old World as this one. It's quite an impressive space, and you really feel like you've stepped into another world, which in fact you have. As Alain Stella describes it in *Mariage Frères French Tea: Three Centuries of Savoir-Faire* (Flammarion, 2003): "Open the door of the Mariage Frères tea house, and a mysterious fragrance slyly declares itself. This fragrance comes forward first to greet you, then embrace you. . . . You might be tempted to say, like everyone else who vainly attempts to describe it, that it's the scent of paradise. To a certain extent, this fragrance incarnates the spirit of Mariage Frères. The French tea merchant launches you on a sensual voyage to a dreamlike place, unique in the world, full of endless delights. Mariage Frères invites you to discover its wealth of five hundred teas, each of which, on being served, yields up a few molecules of scent certain to surprise and charm you."

Founded as a tea and vanilla import firm in 1854, Mariage Frères remained a family business until 1982, when it was sold to Richard Bueno and Kitti Cha Sangmanee. Marthe Cottin, the only family member who was still with the company at the time, shared her knowledge of the tea trade (which was considerable) with Bueno and Sangmanee, as well as her "priceless asset—an extraordinary address book rich with one hundred years of suppliers as well as clients." Franck Desains, who created the company's distinctive black and pale yellow packaging, joined the company in 1987, and he continues guiding the company with Sangmanee (Bueno passed away in 1995). (The family name Mariage has nothing to do with marriage or nuptials: the word comes from the old French verb *maréier,* "to run the seas." In a nautical context, a *maréage* referred to a sailor's contract for the run, a set wage for a voyage no matter how long it lasted. Before 1650 the family name was spelled in several different ways, but after 1650 Mariage was adopted as its official spelling.)

At the time Bueno and Sangmanee came to Mariage Frères, tea was barely noticed in France. But even when Sangmanee visited England to learn more about tea, he discovered that tea there was mostly sold in tea bags found in supermarkets. At fancy hotels that offered proper afternoon tea service the selection of teas was limited to five or six varieties, and Sangmanee realized that the quality and variety of tea he and Bueno were offering was far greater than that commonly found in England. Tea was woven into the fabric of British life but it was not considered a fine, high-quality product. Sangmanee realized then that the future of Mariage Frères lay in a "gourmet" direction: offering a large range of teas and seeking out the very best leaves and harvests in the world.

If Mariage Frères has since become somewhat ubiquitous (you can buy Mariage Frères tea at a number of stores in New York alone, for example), its rue du Bourg-Tibourg shop remains distinctive, not only for its interior but for its Musée du Thé, upstairs, which is filled with exquisite *objets.* Fans both of tea in general and of Mariage Frères in particular will want to immediately obtain a copy of the book noted above—it's a gorgeously produced volume in its own slipcase, and its author Alain Stella, is "an enthusiastic connoisseur of the everyday pleasures that define cultures and civilizations." (Don't you just love that?)

Cafés

"Cafés are central to Parisian life," writes Noël Riley Fitch in *Paris Café: The Select Crowd* (Soft Skull, 2007), which is a wonderful read both about the famous Select café of Montparnasse—in the immediate vicinity of Paris's other legendary cafés, Le Dôme, La Coupole, and La Rotonde—and about the role of cafés in French life. "They have been called the salons of democracy because we are all free to choose our own café. Once you have cast your lot with a particular café, you in a sense 'own' the café (and it owns you!). Loyalty binds. 'It is easier to change one's mind,' as one wag said, 'than it is to change one's café.' " Fitch and the illustrator of the book, Rick Tulka, are so fond of Le Select because it remains the least changed and has retained its authenticity by not becoming a restaurant and not catering to tour buses. All reasons, they believe (and I agree), that Le Select is not often frequented by tourists.

The Paris Café Cookbook: Rendezvous and Recipes from 50 Best Cafés (William Morrow, 1998) and *The Bistros, Brasseries, and Wine Bars of Paris: Everyday Recipes from the Real Paris* (William Morrow, 2006), both by Daniel Young, are two books I *really* like, along with Young's more recent *Coffee Love: 50 Ways to Drink Your Java* (Wiley, 2009), a photo- and fact-filled little book with fifty recipes for a wide variety of coffee drinks worldwide. Young is no stranger to the culinary world—he's also the author of *Made in Marseille: Food and Flavors from France's Mediterranean Seaport* (William Morrow, 2002) and he served as food critic and columnist for the *New York Daily News* from 1985 to 1996. He also maintains a great Web site, Young & Foodish (youngandfoodish.com). Young obviously really knows his *cafés,* both the kind you drink and the kind you frequent. I highly recommend readers note Young's list of "Café Do's and Don't's" in *The Paris Café Cookbook,* a few of which are: "Don't assume a café that carries *pain Poilâne* has good food. Do ask for *pain Poilâne* when you order a *croque-monsieur*" (though note that you will pay a premium for it); "Don't plan a café lunch for noon. Do plan a lunch at a popular café for 12:55" (despite Mark Greenside's observation on page 316, one o'clock is a popular time for lunch, and the best way to snag a table among locals is to show up just before office workers fill up the best cafés); and "Don't order a *café au lait* at any Parisian *café, brasserie, bistro,* or *tabac.* Do order a *café crème* or, better yet, a *petit crème*" (at some point in the early nineties, *café au lait* became *café crème,* and if you order a *café au lait* you will immediately be identified as a tourist who is about thirty years behind the times).

To Young's guide to Parisian café decorum, I would add the following reminders: waiters command respect in France, even at cafés, and men and women typically have serving jobs as a profession. Consult the menu posted outside the café before you sit down; Parisians usually know what they want before they take a seat. Cafés (and many restaurants) may have three seating areas, each commanding a different price: at the bar (or *au comptoir*), where there might be seats but customers usually stand (least expensive); indoor tables (more expensive than the bar); and outside tables, known as *à la terrasse* (most expensive). If you see tables set with napkins and silverware, don't sit at one unless you plan on eating a meal. Don't expect *service rapide;* allow at least thirty to forty-five minutes to place your order, eat or drink, and pay. If you're really in a hurry, stand at the bar, where it will be faster and cheaper. If your waiter asks you to pay the bill before you've finished, it's because he or she is going off duty and is required to settle the bill first. Finally, don't complain about the price of your thimble-sized cup of espresso. You're in Paris, after all, and you're paying for the pleasant privilege of obtaining a seat at a table where you can linger—even if your tiny cup is long depleted—for hours.

Though cafés may no longer hold quite the central place in the lives of the French as they once did—according to Harriet Welty Rochefort in an article she wrote for *France Today,* the number of cafés in France has fallen from two hundred thousand in 1960 to little more than forty thousand today—they are by no means out of fashion. If you frequent the same café on a string of mornings, you may find, as I have, that you see the same people in it, usually sitting in the same spots. As André Aciman notes in *Entréz: Signs of France,* "Cozy, snug, warm, and secure, a café is not only a second home in a country where homes are always too small, or where being alone is unthinkable; it is a place where one draws closer to others. In *La Bohème,* everyone would sooner go to a cabaret than stay at home, for one is more comfortable out than in."

RECOMMENDED READING

Beginning with my Tuscany and Umbria book, I invited Nach Waxman and Matt Sartwell, of New York's Kitchen Arts & Letters, to recommend cookbooks and culinary titles to *Collected Traveler* readers. Kitchen Arts opened in 1983 and is the largest store in the United States devoted exclusively to books on food and wine, with more than thirteen thousand titles in English and other languages. I previously spent two sessions with Nach and Matt and filled up three hours on my tape recorder, which proved to be great for my Tuscany and Umbria book but hugely time-consuming for Nach and Matt. So for this Paris edition, they took a different tack and came up with a list they've entitled "Ten Great Ways to Prepare for a Trip to Paris." Their excellent picks are as follows:

The Food of France, Waverley Root (Knopf, 1958; Vintage, 1992). Root puts French cooking into historical context and tells readers what the culinary specialties are in each region of France.

He says, this is what they eat in this place, and therefore this is what you want to look for when you're in local restaurants. And since everything in France ends up in Paris in one way or another, this book is eminently helpful.

Marling Menu Master for France, William Marling (Altarinda, 1971). This is perfect for the traveler who wants a quick and easy, get-me-out-of-trouble, what-am-I-eating? book. It's arranged by course and it provides handy descriptions of items you'd find on a menu.

The A–Z of French Food, edited by Geneviève de Temmerman (Scribo Editions, 1995) is for the more ambitious culinary traveler. This slender guide is the most comprehensive French-to-English food dictionary we've ever seen. In addition to menu items, it covers cooking terminology, which is especially helpful if you're having a conversation with a waiter or chef or even a home cook. We always keep on hand a standard English–French dictionary, but it just doesn't cover a significant number of food words. This A to Z guide is very popular with American cooks who are going to work in French kitchens.

Clotilde's Edible Adventures in Paris, Clotilde Dusoulier (Broadway, 2008). The advantage with this book is that Clotilde is Parisian but she lived in the United States for some years, so she understands Paris the way an American might see it. She's both realistic and serious in her approach. And though she covers some of the standard places, she also treats the neighborhood places that a Parisian would know but that are not likely to turn up in a guidebook.

The Brasseries of Paris, François Thomazeau and Sylvain Ageorges (Little Bookroom, 2007). The brasserie is the kind of more casual experience that we think most Americans are looking for when they come to Paris, and this modestly sized portable book is filled with attractive profiles of appealing places for every type of traveler.

The Ethnic Paris Cookbook, Charlotte Puckette and Olivia Kiang-Snaije (Dorling Kindersley, 2007). This book is unlike any other we've seen and it brings together the full range of France's former colonies and beyond. The French have touched the whole world, after all, and it's natural that all of these cuisines are to be found in Paris. Organized by the ethnic communities in Paris, with chapters on North Africa, Southeast Asia, sub-Saharan Africa, the Middle East, and Japan, it contains recipes, of course, but it is also a guide to some terrific restaurants, corner shops, and ethnic markets. The kinds of ethnic foods on offer in Paris aren't the same as those to be found in the States, so this is a good book to read before you depart.

Paris Pâtisseries: History, Shops, Recipes (Flammarion, 2010). With this book you have complete fantasy fulfillment! It's very dangerous to page through, and if you're wondering about whether it's worth going to Paris, it could change your mind. Legendary *pâtissier* Pierre Hermé wrote the foreword, and as each chapter is devoted to a type of *pâtisserie*—chocolate, contemporary, *viennoiseries,* cakes from childhood—it's easy to find something in particular you might be craving. There are some recipes included in the last chapter, but the addresses of the *pâtisseries* and the stories behind the sweet creations are much more valuable.

Paris in a Basket: Markets—The Food and the People, Nicolle Aimee Meyer and Amanda Pilar Smith, with a foreword by Paul Bocuse (Könemann, 2000). The focus of this book is on outdoor food markets and it's organized by arrondissement, so you can really see what everyday food shopping is like in each neighborhood. Paris just has so many more markets than we do here in the States, and there is a detailed market guide (indicating the days of the week the markets are set up) at the back of the book. This is especially helpful to those travelers who may be renting an apartment or who are staying in a place with a little kitchen.

Parisian Home Cooking: Conversations, Recipes, and Tips from the Cooks and Food Merchants of Paris, Michael Roberts (William Morrow, 1999). This is Nach's favorite French cookbook, written by a former American chef and restaurant consultant who moved to Paris. It's basically a book about what French people eat when they come home from work, everyday cooking by people who are not professional chefs but who share the French love of very good food. The recipes are for weeknight cooking, and this is the book for anyone who comes away from Paris vowing to make a difference in the way they cook. Roberts will help remind them how simple it is to cook ordinary French food.

Related Culinary Books of Interest

A Meal Observed, Andrew Todhunter (Knopf, 2004). This wonderful little book is a seductive account of a long, luxurious dinner at Paris's celebrated Michelin-starred restaurant Taillevent (named after the cook to Charles V and Charles VI, alias Guillaume Tirel, who allegedly wrote the first French cookbook, *Le Viandier*) and an account of what went on in the restaurant's kitchen. Todhunter was in the enviable role of apprenctice-cum-reporter and spent several months working in the kitchen, which, though highly orchestrated, was "less an atelier than a gun deck on a ship of war, a place of shouts and fire." He is a likable guide and a fair observer. Whether a traveler has the good fortune to dine at Taillevent or another Michelin temple, this book is a superb insider's introduction to *haute cuisine* in France. (And the single recipe included, for Marquise au Chocolat et à la Pistache, is delicious!)

Au Revoir to All That: Food, Wine, and the End of France, Michael Steinberger (Bloomsbury, 2009). In 1997, Steinberger believed that "nothing left me feeling more in love with life than a sensational meal in Paris. I refused to entertain the possibility that French cuisine had run aground." He knew that "it was now pretty easy to find bad food in France if you went looking for it," but as far as he was concerned, "France remained the first nation of food, and anyone suggesting otherwise either was being willfully contrarian or was eating in the wrong places." But just after the turn of the millennium he reached the same conclusion as Adam Gopnik, who suggested in "Is There a Crisis in French Cooking?" (*The New Yorker,* April 28, 1997) that "the muse of cooking" had moved on to restaurants in New York, San Francisco, Sydney, and London, and that it was increasingly difficult to find places to eat in Paris that exuded the same dynamism. In chapters detailing a brief history of French cuisine, the enormous bureaucracy involved in owning a restaurant in France, the meteoric rise of Spanish cuisine (in 2008 the fabulous seaside town of San Sebastián boasted eighteen Michelin-starred restaurants—more per capita than any other city in the world)—the suicide of Burgundy chef Bernard Loiseau, the dining guides and ratings, fast food, cheese and wine, Alain Ducasse, the lack of multicultural staff, and more, Steinberger has written a convincing and eye-opening account of the decline of French cuisine. There were, and are, bright spots, however, in his tale, which is very much worth reading by anyone with an interest in cuisine.

INTERVIEW

Alexander Lobrano

Travel and food writer Alec Lobrano likes to say he has a "bipolar food background," which he explains by the fact that his parents hail from Boston and New Orleans, two American cities with two very different food traditions. Growing up in Connecticut and spending summers with two great-aunts in New Orleans provided him with a very broad gastronomic background, but this didn't prepare him for Paris, which he first visited in 1972. He'd just spent six weeks elsewhere in Europe, and he, his mother, and two brothers were meeting his father and sister in Paris. The family had more than one meal at the noteworthy restaurant Androuët, which specializes in cheese, and were even taken down into the cheese cellar by flashlight, an experience he says "hit me right over the head like a hammer." When, on his last night in the city, he ate boeuf bourguignon *and onion soup at a little subterranean place in the Latin* Quarter, *he savored every drop and craved more. And as he notes in* Hungry for Paris, *"Little did I know then that this addiction would become the compass by which I would live my life." Not surprisingly, Alec burst into tears when his family left Paris on that first trip.*

Thirty-eight years later, Alec no longer has to wonder when he'll be back in Paris or plan elaborate schemes to get himself there, as he's been living in the city since 1986. He served as Gourmet's *European correspondent for ten years and was an editor of the* Zagat Paris Restaurants *guide, and he feels he sees Paris from the level of the tabletop. In 2008 the first edition of* Hungry for Paris *was published (Random House), and in 2010 an updated edition was issued. In utter honesty, I can't imagine anyone visiting Paris, for the first or fiftieth time, and not consulting this guide. It is discriminating without being haughty or ruthless; it is well written, interesting, fun to read, practical, and indispensable. As Alec informs us, he tries a half dozen new restaurants and returns to old favorites each week, and all the restaurants he recommends are places he's frequented many times. Though this obviously isn't a guarantee for the visitor—anyone can try a place on an off night, and tastes do differ—he vouches for the "seriousness, reliability, and quality of their cooking." In addition to the reviews, I especially like the essays, notably "The French Foreign Legion: The Parisian Passion for North African Cooking," "Table for One," and "The Rise and Fall of the Parisian Brasserie." It's equally valuable to read the section "But What About? Or Why Certain Famous Restaurants Aren't Included in This Book," and the section listing places open all or part of the weekend is perhaps alone worth the price of the book. Whether you use the book to search for modest establishments or grand Michelin-starred temples, you will find, as Alec does, "singularly spectacular eating" in the City of Light.*

After some years of corresponding only by e-mail, I finally met Alec, in Paris, on an overcast, drizzly day at a café called Le Nemrod. We sat outside on the covered terrace, but after the raindrops began to fall on our table and my notebook was getting wet, I asked if there was another culinary haunt in the area that Alec particularly liked where we could go and take

a few photos. As luck would have it, Alec said there was a new pâtisserie that had recently opened that he'd only briefly seen and wanted to revisit, so we walked a short distance to La Pâtisserie des Rêves (see page 319). And, yes, for me at least, it most definitely is a pâtisserie worthy of rêves. The photos here of Alec inside the bakery are in black and white, so you'll have to use your imagination to envision the bright and airy interior and the mod colors of hot pink, lime green, and orange. Rêves is the creation of chef and cookbook author Philippe Conticini, and it is without doubt one of the most creative pâtisseries anywhere in the world. Alec and I found time to chat in between my many oohs and ahhs.

Q: The subtitle of your book is *The Ultimate Guide to the City's 102 Best Restaurants.* Why 102?

A: The original number was 101, but that sounded too much like a college intro course, so I added another one. I arrived at the choice of a hundred restaurants because I wanted to offer a broad selection of excellent tables in all parts of the city and in all different restaurant classes and categories without becoming encyclopedic. When I look at a restaurant book with a thousand restaurants, I always find myself wondering, "But which ones are really good?" In *Hungry for Paris,* they're *all* really good—these are the places I'd send close friends who love good food.

Q: I understand that you only replaced about a dozen restaurants for the second edition of your book, which seems to me to be a statement about the consistent quality of places to eat in Paris—after all, it's possible that you could have had to replace many more. Do you find that the level of quality is generally higher, and that places don't open and close with such rapidity as often happens in the States?

A: There are fifteen new or revised restaurants in the updated edition of *Hungry for Paris,* which is indeed a reflection of the fact that the Paris restaurant scene is less novelty driven than that in other major cities on the one hand, and also a reflection of the fact that the best-quality restaurants in Paris are much more enduring than similar tables in, say, London or New York.

Q: When you first moved to Paris, in 1986, you bought three restaurant guidebooks. Which ones were they, and what were their shortcomings?

A: I bought Patricia Wells's *The Food Lover's Guide to Paris,* the Michelin guide, and the Gault Millau guide. The one I used the most was Patricia Wells's book, because it offered a complete portrait of every restaurant in terms of cuisine, history, décor, and clientele and had a friendly, reliable tone. The Michelin guide in those days was still a sphinx (this was before they started adding a few tag lines of copy) so it wasn't very helpful, and I found Gault Millau rather too Gaullist and self-congratulatory in tone. I travel a great deal for my work as a food and travel writer, and so I often avail myself of guidebooks, Web sites, etc., as a consumer. With this experience, I wrote the Paris restaurant book I'd be hoping to find if I were visiting Paris as an adventurous and intrepid food lover, or looking for a subjective survey of the city's best restaurants with write-ups that would fully prepare me for the experience I'd have if I chose this place—Where is it? What's the atmosphere like? Who goes there? And so on. I want all of this information in addition to an erudite judgment of the kitchen, and if I'm going to carry a pound or two of paper with me on a trip these days, I also want something that will be fun to read.

Q: Is there a food guide to another city in the world that you thought was well done and that might have inspired you for your own book?

A: The restaurant guide that first made me aware of the literary possibilities of restaurant guides was Seymour Britchky's *The Restaurants of New York* (1977), which offered witty, amusing, useful portraits of a constellation of New York City restaurants that this author, a very good writer, liked. It was published by Random House and the editor was Joe Fox.

Q: When you were growing up, what were some books or movies that inspired a love of travel? And similarly, what have been some of your favorite books about Paris or France that you treasure as an adult?

A: My love of travel began as soon as I learned to walk, a curiosity that was profoundly nourished by my paternal grandmother, Jean, who was one of the most intrepid travelers I've ever known and who fanned the flames with black-and-white postcards from Egypt, India, Persia, Peru, and many other places. As soon as I learned to read, I devoured a series of books called *The Land and the People of . . .* that I found at the Westport, Connecticut, public library. These nonfiction books presented the history, geography, etc., of a variety of different countries and I couldn't get enough of them. I also had an aunt who worked as an editor for a New York publisher, and she gave me a series of books that were the portraits of the lives of a little boy and a little girl in a variety of different European countries. I read the French book so many times it fell apart, but still remember it vividly—the kids lived in Paris but went to Nice to visit their grandparents, who owned a hotel. Their grandmother put a vase of mimosa on the night table in their room and fed them *petits farcis*. I was desperately jealous. Since reading, eating, and traveling are my compass points, it's hard to think of a book that hasn't inspired me, but I especially love Henry James, Proust, Cervantes, and Thomas Hardy, all of whom provoked a fierce desire to inhabit the worlds they described, and I also love Elizabeth David, A. J. Liebling, M. F. K. Fisher, Richard Olney, and Julia Child, in terms of falling in love with French food. I'd also tip my hat to *The Cuisine of the Sun* (Random House, 1976), a wonderful Niçoise cookbook by Mireille Johnston, and *The Belly of Paris* by Émile Zola, in the new translation by Mark Kurlansky (Modern Library, 2009), which is still the best gastronomic pornography I've ever come across.

Q: As there are quite a number of American expatriates living in Paris, do you see them often, or get together for, say, Thanksgiving?

A: The American community in Paris is smaller now than it once was, because Paris is an expensive city in terms of housing and Asia seems to be attracting a lot of those footloose young types who want to experience another culture these days. Since my partner is French, I live a more French life than many of my expat American friends, some of whom have a tendency to stick together. Thanksgiving is one occasion that we Yanks will get together, and not one of them goes by without a grateful discussion as to why French turkeys are so much better than American ones—they're not overbred and are raised free-range on a healthy diet that does not include antibiotics or growth hormones. Most American turkey is pretty terrifying. Most American foods are available in Paris these days, but there are still some things I lug back with me from any trip to the United States, including chipotles in adobo sauce, fire-roasted jalapeño peppers, California raisins, cornmeal, and Lipton onion soup mix (for dip).

Q: Which arrondissement do you call home, and if forced to name your favorite café or *bistro du coin,* what would it be?

A: I live in the ninth arrondissement between the church of La Trinité and Saint-Georges, and the best little bistro in the area is the wonderful Chez Georgette (29 rue Saint-Georges / +33 01 42 80 39 13), a friendly place that does wonderful French home cooking and is very reasonably priced. The café I go to most often is the Café La Rotonde (2 place d'Estienne d'Orves), because it's just downstairs, the people watching is terrific, and the staff is nice. My two favorite cafés are Le Nemrod (51 rue du Cherche-Midi, in the sixth—they do superb *croques-monsieur* and *-madame,* great steak tartare, and their Morgon Vieille Vignes is one of my favorite wines—and the Le Nemours (Place Colette, in the first), because it has a great terrace, good coffee, and is right next to the gorgeous gardens of the Palais Royal.

Q: How often do you cook at home, and what are the cookbooks you use most often?

A: I love to cook and don't see how anyone can write about food without being a passionate cook. The cookbooks I refer to most often include *La Cuisine du marché* by Paul Bocuse, Marcella Hazan's two Italian cookbooks, and James Beard's *American Cookery.*

Q: What are some of your favorite day-trip destinations outside of Paris?

A: The medieval city of Troyes, which has the most spectacular collection of stained glass in France, is a superb overnight trip from Paris, and it also has two truly delightful hotels: Le Champ des Oiseaux (champdesoiseaux.com) and La Maison de Rhodes (maisonderhodes.com). La Mignardise in Troyes (lamignardise.net) is a very good contemporary French bistro, too. As long as it's not high season, when it gets too crowded, I also love Barbizon in the Seine-et-Marne region south of Paris. The brasserie at Les Pléiades hotel (hotel-les -pleiades.com) is excellent, and the Boucherie de l'Angélus (64 Grande Rue, Barbizon, / +33 01

60 66 40 27) is one of the best all-purpose grocers in France—their meat is superb, they have a terrific assortment of cheese and charcuterie, a small but good selection of vegetables, and even a nicely stocked wine department. When I crave a quick trip to the seaside, I head for Le Touquet on the English Channel in Picardy. The Hôtel Westminster (westminster.fr) is a polite, affordable old-fashioned hotel, and I love the fish soup at Perard (restau rantperard.com), a popular long-running fish house there. I also never miss a meal at La Grenouillère (lagrenouillere.fr) in nearby Madeleine-sous-Montreuil—Alexandre Gauthier is one of the most interesting young chefs in France, and I can't think about his poached lobster tail served in a smoldering juniper branch (for the perfume) without my mouth watering.

Q: Do you envision expanding *Hungry for Paris* to include other culinary-related favorites such as *pâtisseries, boulangeries, charcuteries,* ice cream shops, coffee and tea salons, chocolate purveyors, bookstores, street markets, florists, and tabletop stores?

A: Since I don't want to make *Hungry for Paris* too much of an armload, I am planning to expand my Web site (hungryfor paris.com) to include write-ups and listings of my favorite cafés, *charcuteries,* tea shops, etc. In my experience, most people only go to one or two of these places—whereas they'll go to many restaurants—so I'd rather offer this information online and let people cut and paste from my site before they travel.

Q: At the risk of becoming outdated, what are some restaurants you've recently discovered that you're particularly impressed by?

A: In Paris, I love Frenchie, La Cave Beauvau, Jadis, and Yam'Tcha, all of which I include in the updated version of *Hungry for Paris.* Outside of Paris, the best meal I've had recently was at Sa.Qua.Na in Honfleur—superb fish cookery in a really charming Zen-style dining room. During a recent trip to Istanbul, I fell head over heels for Çiya—I had no idea that the Turkish kitchen was so brilliantly diverse, and I loved some of the sour-savory tastes of the dishes I tasted there.

Q: When you're not thinking about or writing about food in Paris, what are some of your favorite ways to spend time in the city?

A: Whenever I have a few minutes free, I head for the Louvre, the Musée d'Orsay, or one of the city's many other wonderful museums—and always by foot, since Paris is one of the world's great walking cities. I love walking along the stone-paved banks of the Seine, and I love strolling through the city's food markets, too. And there's no better way to spend a sunny afternoon than to head for the Jardin du Luxembourg, the world's most perfect urban park, with a good book. For me, the Jardin du Luxembourg offers the ultimate unself-conscious display of European civilization, with all of its grandeur, beauty, endearing flaws, and petty hidebound codes.

You got very hungry when you did not eat enough in Paris because all the bakery shops had such good things in the windows and people ate outside at tables on the sidewalk so that you saw and smelled the food.

—Ernest Hemingway, *A Moveable Feast*

MUSEUMS, MONUMENTS, AND GARDENS

I threw myself on a bench and began to wonder if there was anything better in the world worth doing than to sit in an alley of clipped limes smoking, thinking of Paris and of myself.

—George Moore,
"In the Luxembourg Gardens,"
Memoirs of My Dead Life

I stand for a long time on the Place de la Concorde, where there is as much sky as in a Russian rye field or a corn field in Kansas.

—Nina Berberova, *The Italics Are Mine*

In Paris the past is always with you: you look at it, walk over it, sit on it. I had to stop myself from grabbing Gwendal's arm as we walked up the narrow passage to the entrance: *Pardon me, sir, I couldn't help but notice; the cobblestones outside your door are older than my country.*

—Elizabeth Bard, *Lunch in Paris*

I had never really wanted a photograph of a picture before I saw Millet's *Man with the Hoe*. I was about twelve or thirteen years old, I had read *Eugénie Grandet* of Balzac, and I did have some feelings about what French country was like but *The Man with the Hoe* made it different, it made it ground not country, and France has been that to me ever since.

—Gertrude Stein, *Paris France*

The Walls of Paris

MARY McAULIFFE

ᘓᘛᘔ

AS READERS OF my previous books may recall, I love stone walls. I don't remember when I became consciously aware that I loved stone walls, but I know I have admired them for a long time. Actually, I love stone in general—whether smooth or rough; whether a building, walkway, tower, stairway, archway, bridge, aqueduct, whatever.

Paris is not necessarily a city that immediately comes to mind when thinking about walls, but in fact the city has had several walls built around it—to keep invaders out, to hold the plague at bay, and to foil tax evaders. I'm especially fascinated by the fifty-five *barrières* (tollhouses) conceived in 1784 by the *fermiers généraux,* or independent contractors who collected taxes for the king. The *barrières* were designed by Claude-Nicolas Ledoux, and according to an article by Stephen Costello that appeared in the *New York Times* (June 11, 1995), were meant to be rather modest customs offices. Ledoux, however, "imagined a monumental system of gateways worthy of ancient Babylon or Memphis. Audaciously, he called these *barrières Les Propylées de Paris,* from Propylaea, the monumental entrance at the west end of the Acropolis in Athens." Ledoux apparently constructed more buildings than any other architect of his time (though most of his work has since been destroyed) and the *barrières* "would be his most extensive and costly."

Readers especially interested in Ledoux may want to know about the Saline Royale—royal salt works—located about three hours from Paris in Arc-et-Senans, in the Franche-Comté region. The complex was built in a unique semicircle per Ledoux's plans, and it became a UNESCO World Heritage Site in 1963. All of Ledoux's models for the Paris *barrières* are displayed in a museum dedicated to him there, the Institut Claude-Nicolas Ledoux.

MARY McAULIFFE was a regular contributor for more than a decade to *Paris Notes* and is the author of *Paris Discovered: Explorations in the City of Light* (Princeton Book Company, 2006), where this piece, adapted from a *Paris Notes* article, originally appeared. She holds a PhD in history and is working on a book about the dawn of the Belle Époque in Paris, including Monet, Zola, Bernhardt, Eiffel, Debussy, Clemenceau, and their friends.

IT MAY SEEM ODD, but not all that many years ago, Paris did indeed have walls—real, working walls, meant to keep out an enemy. And although it may seem strange to think of the City of Light enveloped by bristling defenses, this has been exactly the case for much of its long history.

In fact, Paris has had many walls, each encircling the city like so many rings on a tree. Just as rings tell the story of a tree's growth, these walls tell the story of a city's growth. For Paris's walls, or series of walls, have given the city its distinctive shape— not only the outwardly spiraling outline of its arrondissements, but the arch of its Grands Boulevards, the curvature of its No. 2 and No. 6 Métro lines (circling Paris from the Arc de Triomphe to the Place de la Nation), and the familiar path of its beltway, the Périphérique.

The earliest of this long string of fortifications dates from almost two millennia ago, the third century AD, when the Romans forged a stout set of defenses to protect Gallo-Roman Paris (Lutetia) from barbarian attacks. Erecting sturdy walls around the Île de la Cité as well as their nearby forum, the Romans turned the entire town into a military outpost.

Nothing remains aboveground of the forum or its defensive walls, which encompassed the entire Left Bank area from rue Soufflot to rue Cujas, between rue Saint-Jacques and boulevard Saint-Michel (5th). But a visit to the Crypte Archéologique, beneath the Place du Parvis that fronts Notre-Dame, brings you face-to-face with the remains of the third-century Gallo-Roman wall that once encircled the Île de la Cité. (Remember that the Cité was a far smaller and lower place two millennia ago, before Seine silt and human landfill did their work.) You can find another trace of Roman wall at 6 rue de la Colombe, on the Cité's northern side.

Centuries after the Romans, when Paris was struggling with yet another onslaught—this time from the Norse—Eudes, Count of Paris, built a wooden precursor to Louis VI's Châtelet at the entrance to the wooden bridge linking the Right Bank to the Île de la Cité. (Eudes wisely built a similar defense on the Left Bank as well.) Not only did this Châtelet and its stone successor protect the Cité, but by the twelfth century it anchored a wooden stockade that some historians believe encircled a portion of the Right Bank, which by then was emerging as the city's commercial quarter.

Nothing remains of this stockade, of course, although you can find hints of its former presence. Its eastern gate, Porte Baudoyer, bestowed its name on Place Baudoyer (4th). Winding its way across the quarter, rue François-Miron follows the path of an ancient road that entered the stockade through Porte Baudoyer, linking Paris to the east.

Wooden defenses and the crumbling remains of Roman walls seemed to have done the job for a while, but by the late twelfth century a new threat—this time from the king of England—set the French to building a far sturdier set of fortifications. Philip II (later called Philip Augustus) responded vigorously to the fact that the English monarch (the famed Richard the Lionheart) was also the duke of Normandy and half of France besides. Philip surrounded Paris with stone ramparts ten feet wide and thirty feet high, punctuated by a battery of towers and reinforced with a deep ditch. He also erected a formidable riverside castle, the Louvre, to the immediate west of these fortifications, providing extra muscle in the direction from which the enemy was expected to attack.

Neither Lionheart nor his immediate successors put Philip's fortifications to the test, but you can still see this fortress's massive foundations, recently excavated and now dramatically displayed beneath the Louvre's Cour Carrée.

You can also find fragments of Philip's eight-hundred-year-old wall. The best known of these are the section near the Panthéon (rue Clovis at rue du Cardinal-Lemoine, 5th) and the impressive tower-to-tower stretch along rue des Jardins-Saint-Paul (4th).

There are other lesser-known remnants of this ancient fortification, some of which turn up in surprising places. On the Right Bank, for example, take a look at the stunning fifteenth-century Tour Jean-sans-Peur (now open to the public at 20 rue Étienne-Marcel in the second), which incorporates a portion of Philip's wall, including the base of one of its many towers. On nearby rue des Francs-Bourgeois (4th), Crédit Municipal's inner courtyard contains a splendid tower base (with newer top) plus an outline of the diagonal course the wall took through these parts, en route to the river.

On the Left Bank, at 4 cour du Commerce Saint-André (6th), the Catalonian tourist office has preserved a magnificent three-story tower from Philip's wall, incorporating it into a chic renovation. Closer to the river, at 27 rue Mazarine (adjoining Passage Dauphine, 6th), you will find a beautifully restored wall section plus a tower base on the first and second subterranean levels of a parking garage.

Once you get the hang of it, you'll know where to look. Philip repeated his monumental towers every sixty meters along the wall, which extended from the Louvre and a matching Left Bank tower on the west to the rue des Jardins-Saint-Paul segment and its Left Bank counterpart to the east. The Tour Jean-sans-Peur portion stands close to the wall's northernmost point, while the piece near the Panthéon is about as far south as the fortifications got before curving back toward the river (the Place de la Contrescarpe, in the fifth, marked the southern point of the counterscarp, or sloping outer side of the ditch surrounding the wall). Also remember that any nearby street incorporating the word *fossé* (moat or ditch) in its name is a good clue to follow. Rue Mazarine, by the way, was once called rue des Fossés-de-Nesle, while rue Monsieur-le-Prince was once rue des Fossés-Monsieur-le-Prince.

Having completed his massive fortification, Philip is said to have embraced his architect and announced, "There is now a king, and a France." Unquestionably Paris was now far more secure, and it was not until almost two centuries later, after major hostilities once again broke out between France and England, that a French king decided to update his capital's defenses.

By this time (the late fourteenth century), the burgeoning city had grown into a cramped metropolis that was pushing hard against the confines of Philip's outdated wall. Given England's crushing victories on French soil, France's king Charles V determined to do something about the antiquated ramparts that so indifferently defended—and so grievously constrained—his people.

His solution was to build a new wall, encircling a far larger area. But unlike Philip, he chose to place this bristling new fortification around only the commercial Right Bank, which by this time had far outstripped the university-centered Left Bank in growth and prosperity. Leaving the Left Bank to whatever protection Philip's ramparts could still provide, Charles flung his bulwarks in a wide arc from approximately the site of the present Place du Carrousel (in the midst of today's Louvre) in the west to his formidable new fortress, the Bastille, in the east.

Moving the old city gates outward along such major thoroughfares as rue Saint-Denis and rue Saint-Martin to the north, and
rue Saint-Antoine and rue Saint-Honoré to the east and west, he
in effect created a new and larger shell for the prospering Right
Bank city within. He also provided protection for the new royal
palace at the Hôtel Saint-Paul (the site now bounded by rue
Saint-Paul, rue Saint-Antoine, and rue du Petit-Musc in the
fourth, near the Bastille) and the Louvre, which he now converted into a royal residence.

Some two centuries later, as religious and civil warfare engulfed
France, yet another Charles (Charles IX) and a Louis (Louis XIII)
extended this wall in an arc from the Saint-Denis gate westward, to
encompass the city's growing Right Bank. The wall now stretched
from the Bastille in the east to a point ending between the present-
day Place de la Concorde and the Tuileries in the west.

Remnants of this wall unexpectedly came to light during recent renovations of the Musée de l'Orangerie (Place de la Concorde, 1st), where a lengthy section has now been preserved. You
can also find vestiges of the Bastille's counterscarp (in the Bastille

station of the No. 5 Métro line) as well as the site of Charles V's Saint-Honoré gate, marked by a bas-relief of Jeanne d'Arc's head (161–163 rue Saint-Honoré, 1st).

Most importantly, though, you can still trace the course of Louis XIII's wall as you stroll down the Grands Boulevards, from the Place de la Madeleine (8th) in the west all the way to the Place de la Bastille in the east, for the Sun King himself, Louis XIV, laid out these most Parisian of all promenades along the course of his father's defensive wall, which he pulled down in the wake of satisfying victories over all his enemies. The word "boulevard" itself, historians remind us, derives from an old Germanic word for "bulwark."

Louis XIV, who never did things by halves, also demolished the old fortified entry gates of Saint-Martin and Saint-Denis, erecting in their place the triumphal arches that still remain (bordering the tenth). These arches framed ceremonial entries into the city until the nineteenth century, when the Arc de Triomphe took their place.

Until the Sun King sent out his demolition crews, the successive walls of Paris had served for centuries to keep out danger, whether enemy troops or—as in the case of the Hôpital Saint-Louis, built just outside city walls—the plague. (Now a greatly expanded full-time hospital, Hôpital Saint-Louis still retains its seventeenth-century core, at 2 place du Docteur-Alfred-Fournier, in the 10th.)

But since Philip's time, the walls of Paris had also served the king in quite another capacity—that of foiling smugglers intent on evading the traditionally steep royal tariffs on incoming goods. The disappearance of Louis XIII's wall left the royal tax collectors in the lurch, giving resourceful Parisians a major assist in bypassing the tollgates.

The royal solution was simple and dramatic: a new wall around Paris, this time one whose sole purpose was to buttress the royal tax collectors, or tax farmers, called the *fermiers généraux*. This wall, known as the Fermiers Généraux wall, went up in a hurry in the 1780s, ringing Paris with more than fifty tollhouses linked by a wall ten feet high and more than fifteen miles in circumference. Much of Paris's population was devastated by this turn of events, which sent prices soaring.

Oddly, those responsible for the wall seemed to think that Parisians would find their new constraint more acceptable—even a matter of pride—if it appeared to be a magnificent work of art, a kind of "garland" around Paris. They could not have been more mistaken. Instead, the very grandness of the numerous neoclassical tollhouses designed by Claude-Nicolas Ledoux, one of the foremost architects of his day, stirred up an extraordinary degree of anger and resentment. Even aficionados of neoclassical architecture, such as Thomas Jefferson (who served as American minister to France during the 1780s), heartily despised them. Not surprisingly, the people of Paris destroyed many of these hated "temples of commerce" during the opening clashes of the Revolution.

Only four of these controversial tollhouses have survived. On the Left Bank, twin buildings—the remains of the old tollgate the Barrière d'Enfer—still stand at Place Denfert-Rochereau (14th), where one now serves as an entrance to the Catacombs. On the Right Bank, a small rotunda (capped by a nineteenth-century dome) graces the northern entrance to Parc Monceau (8th), marking what once was the Monceau toll barrier. Far to the east, in the Place de la Nation (11th and 12th), two columns dramatically mark the old Barrière du Trône tollgate. (The statues that top these columns, added later, are of Philip Augustus and Saint-Louis.) Twin buildings flanking these columns once served as offices and lodgings.

Most striking by far is the Rotonde de la Villette (19th), at the foot of the Bassin de la Villette by Place de la Bataille-de-Stalingrad. The largest of the surviving tollhouses and the centerpiece of the misjudged "garland" that Ledoux cast around Paris, this massive rotunda (based on Palladio's Villa Rotonda) guarded a convergence of northern routes into Paris, including the old

Roman road to the sea. A strange relic of the *ancien régime* in this working-class neighborhood, the rotunda—set in a pleasant park—survives the indignities of the nearby Métro (which here streams past aboveground), just as it somehow managed to survive the revolutionary mobs two centuries ago.

The Fermiers Généraux wall itself managed to survive for many years, owing to the fact that Napoléon Bonaparte and subsequent regimes found both it—and the income it collected—useful. But in 1860 the government at last took it down, leaving only the boulevards that had run beside it and, eventually, the No. 2 and No. 6 Métro lines to mark its course.

By this time Paris had continued its surge outward into areas such as Passy, Montmartre, and Belleville. Reflecting this new ring of growth, the government had already enclosed Paris within yet a larger and more bristling wall. Named after France's then premier Adolphe Thiers, the Thiers fortifications (built from 1841 to 1845) eventually marked Baron Haussmann's administrative limits for Paris, complete with the arrondissements as they exist today. In time, the Thiers wall also replaced the Fermiers Généraux wall as a tax barrier. But from the outset its chief function was defensive, reflecting concern for Paris's security in the post-Napoleonic world.

The enemy no longer was England but Prussia and a reunited Germany. Yet the Thiers fortifications did little to stop the Germans during the 1870 Franco-Prussian War, and never saw action during World War I. One of the first things the French did to inaugurate the peace in 1919 was to pull down these outdated ramparts.

Originally, in addition to the unlamented wall, the Thiers fortifications included sixteen forts built outside the wall's perimeter. Despite heavy bombardment and destruction during the Franco-Prussian War and the subsequent Commune uprising, many of these forts still survive and now serve as nuclei for more modern military installations.

Little else of the Thiers fortifications now remains except for the names of its many gates. But you can easily trace the wall's general course by driving the Périphérique. Defining Paris's current city limits (with the exception of the adjacent Bois de Boulogne and Bois de Vincennes), the Périphérique provides yet another shell around a city that has outgrown and cast off a remarkable series of ever-larger shells.

Perhaps you will remember this the next time you inch your way through bumper-to-bumper Périphérique traffic. You may indeed be gridlocked, but you are also following—albeit slowly—the latest in a succession of rings marking two grand millennia of growth for this remarkable city.

Affordable Gothic Thrills

ANNE PRAH-PEROCHON

꧁꧂

"How to Look at a Gothic Cathedral" would be a good subtitle for this piece. For the uninitiated, the three major elements of Gothic architecture are *l'arc brisé* (pointed arch), *la voûte sur croisées d'ogives* (vaulted arches which cross diagonally), and *les arcs-boutants* (flying buttresses).

If you read a little French and have a passion for architecture, look for the *Grammaire des Styles* series in Latin Quarter bookshops. (Gibert Jeune, gibertjeune.fr, is the best known, with eight locations around the Place Saint-Michel—the general-interest bookstore is at 5 place Saint-Michel—and one in the Grands Boulevards neighborhood.) The series, published by Flammarion and popular among students, covers architectural styles from all over the world; the three most useful titles for France are *L'Art roman, L'Art gothique,* and *La Renaissance française.* Each volume is an inexpensive, slender paperback featuring black-and-white photos and drawings.

ANNE PRAH-PEROCHON is an art historian, lecturer, and former editor in chief of *France Today,* where this piece originally appeared. She has been decorated by the French government as a Chevalier de la Légion d'Honneur and Officier des Palmes Académiques. She also writes the history section of *France-Amérique: Le Journal français des Etats-Unis,* a monthly founded in 1943 by World War II France Libre exiles that became the international weekly edition of *Le Figaro* in the 1960s. In 2007, *France-Amérique* was bought by *Journal français,* the largest French-language journal published in America since 1978.

 The sheer number of major churches that rose in France between 1170 and 1270 (six hundred of them!) is awe-inspiring. Even more impressive is the fact that they are still standing to this day, through numerous wars and hundreds of years. It is impossible to visit France without stumbling upon these lofty monuments in which you can appreciate, for free, masterpieces of just about any art form.

However, you might sometimes be perplexed about the best way to visit these awesome buildings. I hope the following tips and recommendations, based on personal experience, will contribute to your enjoyment.

Take along warm clothing—even in the middle of summer, a cathedral is usually chilly and drafty (the crypts are particularly icy). Also, wear comfortable shoes, because you will probably be doing a lot of pacing in one spot as you admire your surroundings. Inside the church, beware of uneven flagstones, worn over many centuries by millions of feet. Because you walk most of the time with your eyes up, it is easy to make a misstep or even twist your ankle.

If you are tempted to climb the stairs leading to the towers or the steeple to enjoy a panoramic view, remember that there are hundreds of them—narrow, hollowed in the center, very steep, and in spirals. Climbing cathedral steps is not for the weak of heart; Notre-Dame de Paris, for one, counts 387 steps in its northern tower!

Sunlight streaming through the *verrières* (stained-glass windows) of large cathedrals such as Chartres, Amiens, and Bourges offers a kaleidoscopic effect, so select a sunny day for your visit if possible. If not, try to visit each cathedral at its optimal time of day. For example, Notre-Dame de Paris is very dark inside, so if you must visit on an overcast day, do so at midday. Chartres and Amiens, on the other hand, are naturally bright, so you can visit them later in the day. Different parts of the churches—all oriented the same way—are also best seen at particular moments of the day: the light through the windows of the apse (behind the altar) is at its most joyous in the morning, whereas the sunset light creates very dramatic effects on the rose windows of the western façade.

Even if you are not religious, you will have an enriching experience if you attend high mass on Sunday mornings, because a cathedral is fully alive during mass. Attend a service to experience the organ music, the vapors of the incense, the flowers, and the liturgical chants. Times are posted at the entrance or marked in your guidebook. In summer, large cathedrals offer free concerts of sacred music on Sunday afternoons. Until his death a few years ago, the celebrated organist Cochereau was often found rehearsing or performing in Notre-Dame de Paris.

A guided tour is only as interesting as its guide. If you spot a priest or a monk explaining the details of the church, follow him! They are the best guides, because they live on the premises, take part in local excavations, and often have authored scholarly books on their church; in short, they are passionately in love with their topic. In the absence of a tour guide, a region-specific Michelin guidebook (with the green cover) offers a good balance of explanations and useful tips.

Before entering the cathedral, walk around it to appreciate its architecture and the relationship of the steeple and the towers to the rest of the building. Remember that builders always started with the choir (where the altar stands), because without a choir the church was useless. Because it often took several generations to build, a cathedral could become a stylistic hodgepodge as architects of different eras came and went. The average building time was about eighty years and life expectancy was thirty years, so a child born in Reims around 1210, when its cathedral was begun, could hardly have hoped to see it finished. This privilege was reserved for the child's great-grandchildren. This hodge-podge effect can be seen in Chartres cathedral, although it was built remarkably fast. On the north portal of Chartres, the statues have stylized hieratic heads seemingly stuck on stiff candlelike bodies, whereas the statues of the Royal Portal are graceful and free, representative of a later style.

When looking at a Gothic cathedral, you are at a disadvantage over your medieval counterpart, who, upon entering a church, automatically knew where to find a symbolic scene and the reason for its placement. Keep in mind that all cathedrals, at least until the sixteenth century, were enormous compasses oriented from the rising to the setting sun, a custom dating from early Christian days. It was customary to enter from the western side, which is where sculptors lavished their creativity, particularly on the tympanum above the main portal. Medieval theologians and artists confused the meaning of the word *occidens* (the western side) with the verb *occidere,* meaning "to kill," so it seemed natural to them to represent the end of the world on the western façade (the western façades of many cathedrals, including Notre-Dame de Paris, La Sainte-Chapelle, Bourges, and Chartres depict Last Judgment or Apocalypse scenes).

Once inside, look at the relationship between the length of the church, the height of its ceiling vault, and the dominating presence of windows. Before looking at the numerous details of the interior, take a quick tour of the cathedral, following the *bas-côté* (right aisle) all the way to the *abside* (apse) and then come back to the main portal by the left aisle. Stop at the *croisée du transept* (transept crossing), where the north-south and east-west axes meet. This is the best place from which to evaluate the daring of the medieval engineers and architects, who erected vaults up to 140 feet high. Leaning against one of the four angle pillars, look up to the vault or the tower in the transept. It is dizzying, especially in Bourges or Amiens. Try to imagine the cathedral as it looked originally, when every inch of space was covered with color—paint, tapestry, embroidery, Byzantine brocades, or Oriental rugs.

Depending on the time you have and the interest you feel for details of architecture and iconography, you may want to tour the cathedral again, this time following the description of Michelin or a more specialized book. To better appreciate the beauty and picturesque details of the pillars and tall stained-glass windows, bring a pair of binoculars. Without them, you might not realize that the beautiful stained-glass windows are not just displays of color, but long narrations that usually can be read from bottom to top and from left to right. In Chartres, the famous Charlemagne window (on the left in the ambulatory, behind the main altar) traces Charlemagne's story from the vision of Emperor Constantine to Charlemagne's deliverance of Jerusalem through Roland's battle with the Infidels and subsequent death.

Chartres's windows also reflect the wide range of donors, those individuals with sufficient power and wealth to make donations independently of the ecclesiastical authorities. A full panorama of medieval society (some four thousand royalty, nobility, tradesmen, and craftsmen) is shown in figurative medallions depicting seventy guilds or corporations (bakers, shoemakers, water carriers, butchers, money changers, wine merchants, and tailors, among others) hard at work.

The Charlemagne window was paid for by the corporation of fur merchants, whose "signature" stands at the bottom, where a merchant shows a fur-lined cloak to his customer. Some signatures were displayed in prominent locations (the medieval equivalent of advertising): the newly baked bread of the bakers who donated the window of the Prodigal Son can be seen in the central window of the central chapel, whereas the portrait of another donor, Thibault, Count of Chartres, was put in a dark corner next to the Notre-Dame de la Belle Verrière window to the right of the choir.

The art of identifying seemingly anonymous characters or saints in stained-glass windows or other art forms lies in the recognition of their distinctive emblems, used in art since the sixth century CE. These clear and expressive images enabled even illiterate people to understand abstract ideas. Not only do we recognize them because of their appropriate dress (bishops in robes, kings crowned and robed, soldiers in armor) but also by the instrument of their death (the wheel for Saint Catherine, the knife for Saint Bartholomew, stones for Saint Stephen, arrows for Saint Sebastian . . .).

Equally important is the relative position of the saints in relation to Christ, because the closer to God, the saintlier the character is assumed to be. On the portal of the Last Judgment in Notre-Dame de Paris, the saints are presented in orderly concentric bands below the patriarchs, prophets, confessors, martyrs, and virgins surrounding the figure of Christ.

Symmetry was also regarded as the expression of heaven's inner harmony, so artists juxtaposed the twelve patriarchs of the Old Testament with the twelve apostles of the New Testament (each with the emblem of his former occupation, such as the fish for Peter, the fisherman, and a purse for Matthew, the tax gatherer), and the four major prophets (Isaiah, Ezekiel, Daniel, and Jeremiah) with the four evangelists (Matthew, Mark, Luke, and John). In the saintly hierarchy, next came the four archangels. Naturally, Mary held the prime location, very close to Christ on the right-hand side.

Once you have identified the carved scenes in one cathedral, you will be able to apply this knowledge to most churches, because no medieval artist would be rash enough to modify the appearance of figures and the arrangement of the great scenes from the Gospels or to group figures according to individual fancy. Similarly, you won't need long to identify the church iconography and to recognize many characters and scenes, even if you weren't born into the Christian religion. King David is always shown playing the harp, and the three magi are invariably wearing crowns, even while they sleep! Seeing a tiny naked child, you will recognize the image of a soul; seeing a mature woman clasping a young girl, you'll know it is Anne, holding her daughter, the Virgin Mary.

Now, after arming yourself with the appropriate clothing, a good guidebook, binoculars, and a little knowledge and endurance, you can fully appreciate this free and edifying pastime of visiting cathedrals.

TO REFRESH YOUR MEMORY

So many great books have been written about Gothic cathedrals that they form an inexhaustible supply. Two of the oldest studies remain the best:

Mont-Saint-Michel and Chartres, Henry Adams (Houghton Mifflin, 1933).

Notre-Dame de Paris, Allan Temko (Viking, 1959).

THE ROAD TO DISCOVERY

Paris

Notre-Dame de Paris (Place du Parvis Notre-Dame, 4ème / notre damedeparis.fr). Open every day 8 a.m.–6:45 p.m.

Crypt of Notre-Dame de Paris. Open April to September daily 10 a.m.–6:30 p.m.; October to March, 10 a.m.–5:30 p.m. The crypt contains vestiges of two-thousand-year-old houses.

Musée de Notre-Dame de Paris (10 rue du Cloître Notre-Dame, 4ème). This museum retraces the great moments in the history of the cathedral.

La Sainte-Chapelle (4 boulevard du Palais, 4ème / sainte-chapelle .monuments-nationaux.fr). Open March to October, 9:30 a.m.– 6 p.m.; November to February 9 a.m.–5 p.m.

Amiens (Somme)

Cathédrale Notre-Dame (Place Notre-Dame / cathedrale-amiens .monuments-nationaux.fr). Open April to October, 8:30 a.m.– noon, 2–7 p.m.; November to March, 8:30 a.m.–noon, 2–5 p.m. Its nave rises 138 feet with the support of 126 slender pillars.

Beauvais (Oise)

Cathédrale Saint-Pierre (rue Saint-Pierre / cathedrale-beauvais.fr).

Bourges (Cher)

Cathédrale Saint-Étienne (Place Étienne Dolet / cathedrale -bourges.monuments-nationaux.fr). This is the widest Gothic French cathedral and the most similar to Notre-Dame de Paris. Its western façade has five sculpted portals. Beautiful stained-glass windows.

Chartres (Eure-et-Loir)

Cathédrale Notre-Dame (Place de la Cathédrale / diocesechartres .com/cathedrale).

Reims (Marne)

Cathédrale Notre-Dame (Place du Cardinal Luçon / cathedrale -reims.com). Open 7:30 a.m.–7 p.m.; closed November 1–March 14. This cathedral has been the backdrop of French kings' coronations from medieval times to 1825 (King Charles X). Its western façade has two thousand statues. In its apse, there is a lovely Chagall window showing the Crucifixion and the sacrifice of Isaac.

Rouen (Seine-Maritime)

Cathédrale Notre-Dame (Place de la Cathédrale / cathedrale -rouen.net). This Gothic masterpiece was painted thirty times by Monet in the 1890s; several of the paintings are in the Musée d'Orsay in Paris.

Steven Barclay

Steven Barclay is the author of one of my favorite books, *A Place in the World Called Paris,* with a foreword by Susan Sontag and illustrations by Miles Hyman (Chronicle, 1994). Here Barclay has gathered wonderful excerpts from twentieth-century fiction, poems, essays, and memoirs and organized them under such compelling categories as "Conditions of Its Greatness," "Presence of the Past," "Seasons, Rain, Light," "Means of Transport," "Love and Solace," and "A City to Die In." Among the writers included are Patric Kuh, V. S. Pritchett, Djuna Barnes, Henry Miller, Maya Angelou, Ludwig Bemelmans, Mavis Gallant, James Wright, Ned Rorem,

Cyril Connolly, Jean Rhys, Nina Berberova, and Françoise Gilot. For those who want a book of short passages to be picked up at random, this is the *livre* for you!

Barclay holds dual French and American citizenship—he was born in Los Angeles, but when he was four, his father, who worked for Bank of America, was transferred to Europe and the family landed in Paris in 1965. His maternal grandmother was French, and his mother now lives in Paris year-round. (Barclay lives in San Francisco but owns a place in Paris that happens to have the address of the original Shakespeare and Company bookstore.) "France was always home," he told me, "and today I go to Paris every two months and I stay for ten days or so, and then I go in the summer and stay a month."

Working on his book enabled Barclay to reconstruct his Paris. When he reached adolescence, he read "anything and everything to do with Paris. I read authors who had travel essays about Paris, diaries and memoirs, everything. And I collected them all. I photocopied them and I would reread them and I put them all in a box. And so the contents of that box became a book. Just as I tend to avoid books on the bestseller lists, I tried to find writings that hadn't become clichéd. The book was the purest form of Paris for me—it's the Paris that exists in your head and you can have it at any moment when you turn the pages of my book."

I asked Barclay to share some of his Paris favorites. He loves "the Deux Magots at seven a.m., when there are no Americans there. You can read the *Trib* or *Le Monde* and it's wonderful. I love it. The same four people wait on you. Give me pavement and a café any day! I do not long for a park or a forest or a beach. The *Place des Vosges* at eight in the morning is also nice, because there's no one there."

But Barclay's favorite Parisian spot is the Musée Albert-Kahn and its garden, in a suburb just west of the city (14 rue du Port, Boulogne-Billancourt / albert-kahn.fr). "I can't remember how I first heard about it, but I'm always interested in anything new. I was stunned by its beauty, and I have an affinity for small museums that used to be private residences. Kahn was a wealthy banker who lost everything in 1929, but for ten to fifteen years preceding that, he had, with his money, enabled young people—not professional photographers—to use his state-of-the-art equipment to create a color photographic record of, and for, the people of the world. He wanted to show the French people that we were all the same. The photos are now considered to be the most important collection of early color photographs in the world, and the gardens are beautiful and well maintained. It's a complete secret—no one really seems to know about it, even the French. People say things like, 'My aunt took me there when I was ten—what's it like now?'"

A Tale of Two Artists

CATHARINE REYNOLDS

HERE'S A GOOD piece on two artists, Eugène Delacroix and Aristide Maillol, and their eponymous museums in Paris. Neither museum is ever especially crowded, but each is rewarding. I am an especially big fan of Maillol's 1905 *La Méditerranée* bronze in the Musée Maillol. Happily you can also see this sculpture in the Musée d'Orsay, which has both a marble version (a copy made during Maillol's lifetime) and a bronze (a recent cast). The original limestone statue is in Switzerland.

CATHARINE REYNOLDS, introduced previously, was a contributing editor at *Gourmet,* where this piece originally appeared. Reynolds recently wrote to give me a great recommendation for a restaurant near both museums profiled here: Café Varenne (36 rue de Varenne, 7ème / +33 01 45 48 62 72). "Diane Johnson has been spotted there more than once, alongside all the pols from the Matignon. The food's the best of home and the regional wines well chosen and sometimes surprising."

EVEN THE MOST devoted art connoisseurs can find the Grand Louvre and its ilk just that: big, not to say exhausting. Paris's small museums—often devoted to the works of a single artist—come as a welcome antidote, offering a keyhole view of creators and their creations.

For me, none is more evocative than the Musée National Eugène Delacroix, tucked in the square on the leafy rue de Furstenberg, a backwater of the sixth arrondissement north of the Église Saint-Germain. Visitors quickly recognize it as the location chosen by director Martin Scorsese for the final, bittersweet scene in *The Age of Innocence.*

The setting admirably suited Eugène Delacroix, that prolific Romantic giant of mid-nineteenth-century painting, whom Théophile Gautier lauded as a fiery, savage, passionate artist who "depicted the anxieties and aspirations of our period." Delacroix lived the last five years of his life behind the green gates in the northwest corner of the square.

Delacroix's color merchant, Étienne-François Haro, had in 1857 located the apartment, with its parade of six rooms caught between an eighteenth-century inner courtyard and a pretty back garden shaded by a chestnut tree. The land had once belonged to the nearby abbey church. It provided a "hermitage" of monastic quiet yet was only a few blocks from the work that had episodically absorbed much of the painter's creative energy since 1849: the Chapelle des Saints-Anges at the Église Saint-Sulpice. At the side of the garden the landlord had built a pretty studio with a north-facing skylight and lofty walls to the artist's specifications.

When he moved from the Right Bank into his new abode after Christmas 1857, the ailing fifty-nine-year-old painter found it "decidedly charming," writing in his *Journal* that "the view of my small garden and the cheerful appearance of my studio inspire elation."

The forty thousand annual visitors to the recently spruced-up museum share that response. Although not very many of the furnishings were Delacroix's own, his spirit pervades the peaceful, domestic-scale rooms. Drawings, small oil sketches—mostly on loan from the Louvre—and holograph letters line the walls and vitrines of the square sage green salon and the adjacent library and bedroom, illustrating the threads of his life: his friendships with George

Sand and Gautier; his fashionable philhellenism; and his taste for Shakespeare, Byron, and Sir Walter Scott. His self-portrait in the guise of Ravenswood, hero of *The Bride of Lammermoor,* exemplifies Romanticism as well as any other image, revealing the twinkling eyes that Odilon Redon claimed "seemed to outshine chandeliers."

The library's four hundred volumes were dispersed. Delacroix's delightful *Journal*—chockablock with thoughtful musings and extracts from his interests—demonstrates the breadth of his interests and literary gifts that rival his painterly talents. He was an enormously likable man: acute, analytical, affectionate, handsome, wry, courageous, intense, and loyal.

The airy garden studio, with its tall easel and his palettes and paint tables alongside bowls and leather goods he brought back from Morocco, Algeria, and Spain, inspires fantasies. Delacroix had been the rallying point for an art more passionate than David's and Ingres's neoclassicism. He exalted imagination. The classical, literary, and biblical vocabulary of his works is today less familiar to many of us and the colors in which he gloried have often proved unstable, yet the sweep and gusto that caused him to break with the era's prevailing academic canon leave us captivated.

Later in his life, a self-appointed cerberus—a sensible Breton named Jenny Le Guillou—dominated Delacroix's domestic life. Her portrait, painted shortly after she became his housekeeper in the mid-1830s, today hangs in the bedroom, looking out with keen, thoughtful eyes. At once mother and confidante, Jenny was devoted to his genius, massaging his confidence and providing an unruffled influence, a contrast to the erratic attentions of his worldly mistresses and flirtatious models. Jenny even accompanied him to the seaside and to museums, where Charles Baudelaire once observed them, "he, so elegant, refined and learned," though not one to disdain explaining "the mysteries of Assyrian sculpture to this excellent woman."

The Musée Delacroix faithfully evokes these personalities but possesses none of the artist's great canvases. A half hour's wandering through its rooms serves as an *aide-mémoire,* inspiring one to track Delacroix's paintings across Paris, the museum's map in hand: from *La Barque de Dante,* which made his name at the 1822 Salon, to the flamboyant ceiling in the Galerie d'Apollon, both at the Louvre, to the canvases at the Musée d'Orsay; from the Musée Carnavalet to the Petit Palais. Of course, one should see the lyrical yet austere wall paintings at Saint-Sulpice. Their power is apparent, in spite of bad lighting and damage from damp. Take the time to seek out the splendid if troubling *Pietà* at Saint-Denys-du-Saint-Sacrement in the Marais and to venture an hour's tour of the Assemblée Nationale to admire the magnificent décors of the Salon du Roi (located off the left side of the debating chamber and therefore, ironically, the principal writing room for French Socialist deputies) and the Bibliothèque.

The art critic Robert Pincus-Witten writes, "Aristide Maillol's place among the great sculptors has been secure for nearly a century." Others who are less aesthetically attuned dismiss this nineteenth-century artist's work with "Seen one, seen 'em all."

Whatever your predispositions, you should plan a visit to the Fondation Dina Vierny–Musée Maillol. You can't help but walk away convinced of the genius of this man whose *oeuvre* focused almost exclusively on the female form but who found in it the means of expressing endless near-abstract reflections.

The museum nestles discreetly beside a ninety-foot-wide fountain created by one of the eighteenth century's leading sculptors, Edme Bouchardon. Little matter that the rue de Grenelle is only sixteen feet wide. The pure theatricality of the grand Fontaine des Quatre-Saisons endears it to Parisians.

First-time visitors to the Musée Maillol determined to gain insight into the artist's work should head directly upstairs, and seek out the early paintings. For, to the surprise of many, Aristide Maillol came to sculpture via painting and tapestry design.

Born in 1861, this son of a cloth salesman had passed a lonely childhood in Banyuls-sur-Mer—a coastal town not far from the Spanish border in what is called French Catalonia—first distinguishing himself in art at secondary school. At twenty he prevailed on his impoverished family to assure him a twenty-franc monthly stipend and took off for Paris. Initial rejection by the Académie des Beaux-Arts discouraged but did not defeat him. He eventually gained admittance, but the courses proved disappointing, providing little more than technical grounding.

Maillol was more shaped by the friends he made, among them members of the Nabis, a group whose name means "Prophets" in Hebrew. These Neoplatonic artists, who included Maurice Denis, Édouard Vuillard, and Pierre Bonnard, sought to express "Ideas" through their creations, lending substance to their interior visions. Georges Seurat's color theories also appealed to Maillol, but the artist's greatest single inspiration seems to have been Paul Gauguin. The museum's early Maillol canvases, *L'Enfant couronné* and *Le Portrait de Tante Lucie,* which date from 1890, glow with backgrounds of Gauguin's much-favored cadmium yellow.

A chance visit to the Musée de Cluny sparked Maillol's interest in tapestry. Two years' feverish tapestry design—the handsome products of which are arrayed at the museum—wrought mayhem with the artist's eyesight, so he turned to wood carving and then to monumental sculpture.

At the time, Rodin still dominated the latter field. Unlike most of his contemporaries, the Catalan consciously avoided the master's studio, convinced, in the words of Constantin Brancusi, that "nothing grows in the shade of great trees." Which is not to suggest that the two did not respect one another; indeed, Rodin actively promoted Maillol's career.

Paralleling Cézanne's growth as a painter toward abstraction through simplified volumes, Maillol predicated his sculpture on geometry. He cast aside the nineteenth-century lexicon of classical allegory and symbolism (and the exaggerated sentiment it sustained), seeking to express abstract truths through distilled mass, specifically, the female body. Already in 1896 a bronze such as *La Vague* reveals the characteristic sumptuous reserve that would mark Maillol's subsequent work.

The Salon of 1905 proved a turning point in Maillol's career. Amid the sensation created by the Fauves, Maillol's *La Méditerranée* garnered André Gide's praise and announced the themes that forty years' work would amplify. Examples of many of Maillol's monumental sculptures occupy a room on the south end of the museum's second story. The artist called on the female figure to express a whole range of human thought: the fecundity of *Pomone;* grief for the dead of World War I; and homage to men as disparate as Cézanne, Debussy, and a French revolutionary, Auguste Blanqui. No Kate Mosses here; sturdy limbs and apple breasts characterize Maillol's earthy women.

The most familiar face within the museum is also its creator, Dina Vierny. In 1934, the fifteen-year-old Russian-born Ms. Vierny became Maillol's model and Egeria, inspiring a final decade of creativity: bronzes, sanguines, and oils—some of which are on view in the museum. Still others were produced by Maillol's friends, for he was in the habit of lending Dina to them, as in the spring of 1941, when he sent her to his lifelong friend Matisse with the message: "I am lending you the inspiration for my work, you will render her in a single line." The resultant drawings still hang in the museum. His gift for friendship indirectly cost him his life, when, at the age of eighty-three, he set off from Banyuls to visit Raoul Dufy. The car veered off the road, and Maillol died a few weeks later of his injuries.

The Musée Maillol's very existence is a tribute to his model's tenacity. As the residual legatee of the Maillol estate, Ms. Vierny set up the foundation, assembled the buildings to house the museum, and installed the works, orchestrating every detail down to the (exquisite) doorknobs and the (brilliantly conceived) lighting and framing.

Ms. Vierny is an unapologetic collector. The museum exhibits some of her French primitives and works by a number of Soviet painters—many of them artists her rue Jacob gallery represented in the postwar period. The rooms are also sprinkled with Degases, Redons, Picassos, and Duchamps.

In the mid-sixties Dina Vierny, not a woman to be gainsaid, gave the state eighteen of Maillol's monumental sculptures to be displayed in the Jardin du Carrousel west of the Louvre. The area—only ten minutes' walk away—has recently been replanted to great effect.

Musée National Eugène Delacroix

(6 rue de Furstenberg, 6ème / +33 01 44 41 86 50 / musee -delacroix.fr). Open daily 9:30 a.m. to 5 p.m. except Tuesdays.

Fondation Dina Vierny—Musée Maillol

(59–61 rue de Grenelle, 7ème / +33 01 42 22 59 58 / musee maillol.com). Open daily 11 a.m. to 6 p.m. except Tuesdays.

Saint-Denys-Du-Saint-Sacrement

(68 bis rue de Turenne, 3ème / +33 01 44 54 35 88).

Assemblée Nationale

(33 bis quai d'Orsay, 7ème / +33 01 40 63 99 99 / assemblee
-nationale.fr).

Of Cobbles, Bikes, and *Bobos*

❧❦❧

AFTER MY RECENT profession of my fondness for stone, it should come as no surprise that I love the cobblestones of Paris. And as this piece attests, cobblestones are as much a part of Paris's identity as the Eiffel Tower; old as the city itself, they are also a sign of change.

DAVID DOWNIE lives in Paris with his wife, the talented photographer Alison Harris. Together, they have collaborated on a number of books, including *Paris, Paris: Journey into the City of Light* (Broadway, 2011) and several Little Bookroom *Terroir Guides,* such as *Food Wine: Burgundy* (2010), *Food Wine: The Italian Riviera & Genoa* (2008), and *Food Wine: Rome* (2009). Downie is also the author of *Quiet Corners of Paris* (Little Bookroom, 2007) and *Paris, City of Night* (MEP Foreign, 2009), and he wrote for many years for the former *Paris Notes,* where this piece first appeared (see interview with Downie on page 563).

Sous les pavés, la plage.
Under the paving stones lies a beach.
—Slogan of Paris student rioters in 1968

WHAT CITY'S STREETS are paved with dreams and peacock-tail mosaics—thousands of them? No prize if you guessed. The classic Paris cobble is an eight- or ten-centimeter granite cube, a *pavé mosaïque,* laid down in patterns road builders call *queues de paön*. Many of the capital's 5,993 streets—totaling over one thousand miles—are cobbled, and cover a quarter of Paris's surface area. That translates to millions of cobbles, often unseen under the asphalt, and always unsung.

Cobblestones are as much a part of Paris's identity as the Eiffel Tower. Read a classic from Anatole France to Émile Zola, find a riot or revolution, and cobbles will star in the show. The pavements rose in righteous wrath in 1789, 1830, 1848, 1870–71, and again in 1944, when the Nazis decamped. There's nothing better than cobbles for barricade building or shot-putting. *Aux barricades, camarades!* And there lies the irony. Cobbles did not disappear when Paris streets were widened, paved, and modernized. Modernization—"Haussmannization"—aimed to rid Paris of medieval alleys, where rioters could ambush troops. The cobbles merely went underground—under the asphalt.

Sound like ancient history? Click forward to times recent enough for hoary fiftysomethings like me to remember. Behind the cobblestone barricades of 1968, rioters shouted not only *Aux*

barricades but also *Sous les pavés, la plage*—under the paving stones lies a beach. The cryptic chant egged on students to tear up stones as their forebears had, but also hinted at a different world, a beach in the big city.

In reality that "beach" was the sandy layer the cobbles are embedded in—or were. Nowadays sand is mixed with mortar, and joints between cobbles are grouted. Rioters would be hard-pressed to pry them out. That's telling of our times. So, too, is the current positive value attached to the humble cobblestone, at least for those with green credentials, meaning green politics or a swelling wallet full of greenbacks.

The sometimes idealistic Soixante-huitards of '68 are as dead today as the barricade builders of rue Royale in 1848. Everyone but commuters, it seems, is embracing cobbles and their petrified relatives as heralds of low-carbon prosperity. Wherever the peacock's tail is laid down anew or exposed by *débitumation*—the stripping of bitumen, meaning asphalt—real estate values soar. Neighborhoods are revolutionized not by rioters tearing up cobbles, but by cobble-prone developers, new-paradigm moguls, Greens, and *bobos*—Paris's celebrated bohemian bourgeois.

"Cobbleification" is an integral part of pedestrianization and means that streets or neighborhoods are car-free or benefit from restricted traffic flow. In Paris, these areas go by the designations *zone piétonnière, aire piétonne, quartier vert,* and, most recently, Réseau Vert—a specific pedestrian-cyclist roadway network.

Like other attempts at social engineering through urban planning, Europe's first and biggest pedestrian zone was created in the 1960s. The Strøget area turned historic Copenhagen into a giant mall, complete with fast-food joints, roughneck street fauna, men dressed as Vikings, and what boosters called "street entertainers"—musicians, performers, artists, jugglers, and fire-swallowers. They've become a permanent feature of pedestrian zones worldwide, and a powerful argument against building more of them.

Given the motor-mania of the sixties, Paris was slow to follow Denmark's lead. The City of Light's first—and still its largest—pedestrianized area was begun in the mid-1970s. It spread around the former wholesale markets at Les Halles, and the Centre Pompidou at Place Beaubourg. The idea was to redesign European cities such as Paris for cars, creating safe havens for tourists, especially shoppers, in traffic-clogged historic neighborhoods. After the Les Halles/Beaubourg experiment came the Saint-Séverin/Saint-Michel precinct and its wall-to-wall couscous joints and Greek tavernas, an object lesson in how not to master plan a city.

Mallification continued under pro-automobile mayor Jacques Chirac, and the policy only began to morph during the reign of his successor, Jean Tiberi. But with traffic, noise, and air pollution untenable, instead of beginning the process of limiting cars throughout town, Tiberi initiated more refuges. These weren't the malls of the seventies and eighties, but they maintained the fiction that Paris and cars could live together. The Les Halles/Beaubourg enclave grew, and more were planned and built.

Throughout the late eighties and nineties near rue Montorgueil, northwest of Les Halles, the barricades against traffic went up, creating a fortified city-within-the-city, this time with cobbled streets in white Carrara marble. On the periphery, pneumatically activated telescopic piston bollards—called *bornes télescopiques*—do today what drawbridges did in the past. They're linked via audio and video to a remote police squad in a centralized *poste de contrôle* security HQ, with a 24/7 maintenance crew. Only residents, delivery trucks, and emergency vehicles are allowed into the citadel.

In recent years, the Montorgueil zone has spread to rue Saint-Denis and abutting streets, extending as far as rue Montmartre. Running across it is the first section of Réseau Vert, an experimental linear network of semi-pedestrianized, partly cobbled streets with limited car access. To slow traffic, cobbles also mark intersections and pedestrian crossings elsewhere. For now, Réseau Vert runs from Châtelet to Canal Saint-Martin. It may well prove the twenty-first-century answer to twentieth-century citadel pedestrianization.

Though invented by Green Party planners nearly twenty years ago, Réseau Vert is a weapon in Socialist mayor Bertrand Delanoë's anti-vehicular arsenal. The days of denial are over. The mayor's "de-Haussmannization" campaign to keep cars out of town means pain to drivers will increase until they switch to public transportation, bicycles, and walking.

Aptly, a few hundred yards west of the Les Halles/Beaubourg/Montorgueil/Saint-Denis pedestrian zone–cum–Réseau Vert, in rue du Louvre, is Paris's Direction de la Voirie et des Déplacements. The roadworks department is on the front line in the war against automotive oppression. Here I met architect Yann Le Toumelin, in charge of the Réseau Vert. Mild-mannered, Le Toumelin is too young to remember Les Halles before the wholesale market became a mall. For Parisians under fifty, Les Halles and the Saint-Séverin/Saint-Michel pedestrian zone "have always been there."

Longevity isn't always a measure of success. The mistakes of past pedestrianization—lack of access, increased street noise from cafés and musicians, radical demographic shifts, aggravated congestion on perimeter streets—are being studied from the ground up. "Starting with the cobbles," said Le Toumelin mildly. "Nothing makes a pedestrian area look and feel more seedy than broken or missing paving stones."

Some stones crack under the weight of a single delivery truck, he explained, adjusting his frameless designer glasses. While sketching on an A3 sheet, he described the various cobbles and flagstones found in Paris. There are the classic *pavés mosaïques* in peacock-tail patterns. The best are granite—other stones wear too fast. Second most popular is the *pavé échantillon,* shaped like a bread loaf in a variety—a Whitman's Sampler—of colors. They're rectangular, measuring $20 \times 14 \times 14$ centimeters, and laid out side by side. The *dalle* is a flat, rectangular flagstone and varies widely in size. Usually gray, heavy, and expensive, *dalles* are used not only on streets but also on sidewalks, such as those of rue de Rivoli or the Île Saint-Louis. A novelty is the *dallette,* a smaller flagstone measuring 20 × 30 × 15 centimeters. "They're tricky to keep in place," Le Toumelin admitted, citing recent problems in the Marais's rue Saint-Antoine, fronting the celebrated Baroque church of Saint-Paul.

I left the affable architect's office having learned a new vocabulary, from *débitumer* and *dépoteletisation* to *axes civilisés, rallentisseur, dos d'ânes,* and *gendarme endormie.* Whether stripping bitumen off cobbles and removing poles from sidewalks, trying to teach civility to Parisian drivers, or installing cobbled speed bumps and sleeping policemen, Le Toumelin and his department have their work cut out. They can design a pedestrian-friendly world with low sidewalks, handsome paving, ingenious one-ways, and dead ends, plus limited, snail's pace traffic, but the city of Paris lacks police authority to enforce driving and parking regulations. That's the job of the Préfecture, which controls the Police d'État, often at odds with the mayor. Paris is the only city in France without its own police force.

The oddity of the situation continues: a major source of revenue for the French government is the tax on gasoline. It varies with petroleum prices and exchange rates, but generally yields about a euro per liter, meaning four to six dollars per gallon. So how much does the government really want to reduce car use? Bankruptcy would probably follow if green policies were ever adopted. On the other hand, the city of Paris depends on revenues from parking violations, so the anti-car war the mayor is waging is not only virtuous, it's profitable.

Curiouser still, city planners have yet to commission studies to determine whether residents in pedestrianized areas are satisfied and whether, as anecdotal evidence clearly suggests, cobbles lead to gentrification—meaning higher real estate prices and radical shifts in resident profiles, street-level business, and noise problems.

Once a policy has been adopted on high, the man in the street either adapts or moves out. Why are there no statistics showing how the demographics of cobbled neighborhoods shift? It's hard to get eye-witness reports before and after cobbling, for a simple reason: locals of pre-cobble days disappear.

At the top of rue Montorgueil near the Sentier Métro station, the date 1991 is spelled out in cobbles. I remember watching the road workers laying them down, and wondering what Carrara marble had to do with Paris. Back then Alison and I used a ragtag gym in a tumbledown building off this street. Reportedly it was the oldest gym in Paris. We wagered ourselves how long it would be before the *bobos* showed up. We've lived in Paris for decades, in the Marais for over twenty-five years, and have witnessed the changes cobbles bring.

As I strolled down rue Montorgueil on a recent visit, heading toward Les Halles, I couldn't help being impressed by the chain store bakeries and cafés, designer boutiques, and trendy restaurants, not to mention the offices of Web consultants, artists' studios, and real estate agencies, most on side streets. Never mind that the Carrara marble pavements wouldn't stick, and have been replaced by classic cobbles.

It was reassuring to find a handful of traditional places—among them the landmark pastry shop Stohrer, at 51 rue Montorgueil, with a nineteenth-century storefront and painted ceilings. They invented the *baba au rhum* and *puits d'amour*. I always bought sweets here after a workout—the gym was next door. The gym is no longer. A luxury apartment complex has replaced it.

The landmark oyster eatery from the mid-1800s, Au Rocher de Cancale (at no. 78), still has its wonderful murals of birds and boozers, and carved wooden oyster decorations outside. Lounging on sidewalk tables, thirtysomethings half hidden by cigarette smoke pecked at their laptops, hooked up via Wi-Fi. Indoors a couple of codgers rustled newspapers and looked distinctly out of place.

The totally un-PC façade of Au Beau Noir (no. 59) is still around, and new neighborhood regulars I buttonholed find the establishment's dry-cleaning services handy. Further down the road, historic restaurant L'Escargot Montorgueil appears little changed, with its private dining rooms and cozy décor, though most of the snails are imported from eastern Europe nowadays, and the longtime clientele is gone.

For better or worse, the feel of the neighborhood has changed, utterly. As one curmudgeonly butcher told me, Montorgueil has gone from a rough-and-ready "authentic" market street to a certified *bobo* playground, preferred, it's claimed, by the *gauche caviar*. It's a fact that the Socialist party's local HQ is on the corner of rues Montorgueil and Léopold-Bellan, but, ironically, given the rents, you have to wonder how much longer the PS will be able to afford it. Real estate sells for 7,500 euros per square meter in the Montorgueil citadel, up tenfold since pre-cobble days, and a thousand euros a month to rent a closet-size studio is typical, among Paris's highest. There's no question of chicken or egg. As with Les Halles/Beaubourg/Saint-Denis, the cobbles came first.

Closer to home, I toured the Marais's newest pocket-size pedestrianized areas, my eyes on the peacocks' tails and Whitman's Samplers of cobblestones, not to mention the *dalles* and *dallettes*. Most of the Marais was gentrified in the 1980s and '90s without the help of cobbleification—exception made for streets and squares like Place du Marché Sainte-Catherine. But it took the recent repaving and semi-pedestrianization of the old Jewish neighborhood on and around rue des Rosiers, and on rue Saint-Antoine, to complete the process. The boutiques stand cheek by jowl and real estate prices have spiraled up, apparently unaffected by the Great Recession of 2008–10. So far, some longtime residents have held on, anchored by religion, family, and culture. More walkers and bikers than ever crowd in, yet complaints about increased noise are few: the street has always been chaotic.

After months of jackhammering and snarled traffic, another semi-pedestrianized zone was born in 2008 on rue Saint-Antoine, fronting Saint-Paul. If Yann Le Toumelin is right, rues des Rosiers and Saint-Antoine are the way of the future. They're part of Réseau Vert. Instead of a citadel with piston bollards—which often malfunction, damaging vehicles—other means will be used. They include easy and cheap traffic signals, 15 kph signage, cobbles, and traffic cops to bar the unauthorized. Sidewalks have been widened and lowered, and the poles that keep cars at bay—but hinder strolling—have been removed. No parking is allowed—in theory. Civic sense is key and plainly doesn't always work. The Saint-Paul experiment and the Réseau Vert in general often feel like war zones, with frustrated drivers facing outraged bikers and pedestrians. Perhaps war is part of the process.

New-generation cobbled areas can only work in tandem with car-hostile roads flanking them, and bikes are essential. The Vélib rental scheme—in which riders pick up and drop off bikes at dozens of parking areas—is astonishingly popular, peaking at over one hundred thousand users a day. With armies of walkers and bikers, drivers will have to yield—or so the theory goes. War? *Aux barricades, camarades!*

Cobbled, semi-pedestrianized areas continue to crop up around town, from rue Cler in the seventh arrondissement to rue de la Forge-Royale in the eleventh and rue Cavallotti in the eighteenth. If—a big "if"—it is fully implemented, the Réseau Vert roadway network will link these green islands. Much depends on who sits in the mayor's office. Another irony is, were the whole of Paris to be de-Haussmannized as Mayor Delanoë plans, the first generation of pedestrian citadels might morph back toward normality. They would be absorbed into a saner, gentler, less car-clogged cityscape. No one expects real estate prices to go down within them, or *bobos* to move out. Once the old-timers have left, they do not return. Meanwhile, investors are watching to see where the cobbles—and bike lanes—are headed next.

Perfection Squared

LIKE THE AUTHOR, I, too, think the Place des Vosges may be the world's most harmonious urban spot. It is also a spot where I recommend first-time visitors go on their first day in Paris, combined with a visit to the nearby Musée Carnavalet, the official museum of the history of Paris. Though the *place* was originally called Place Royale, it acquired the name Vosges after the first French *département* to pay its taxes.

The best ways to enjoy the *place* are to walk all around it under the arcades and to sit for a while on one of the benches—both methods are, in fact, essential to grasping the rhythm of the space, as each reveals different aspects. After you've strolled and sat, then you may eat, shop, and browse. I have enjoyed many happy hours at Ma Bourgogne under the arcades (no credit cards accepted; ma-bourgogne.fr), I love the Maison de Victor Hugo (at 6 place des Vosges, and there is never anyone else there), and I have parted with many euros at the Librairie du Patrimoine in the Hôtel de Sully (reached from the southwest corner of the *place* and filled with unique items, cards, and books about Paris, France, and beyond).

ANDRÉ ACIMAN is a professor of literature and the author of many books, including the novels *Eight White Nights* (2010) and *Call Me by Your Name* (2007), the memoir *Out of Egypt* (1994), and *False Papers: Essays on Exile and Memory* (2000), all published by Farrar, Straus and Giroux. He edited

Letters of Transit: Reflections on Exile, Identity, Language, and Loss (New Press, 1999) and contributed to *Condé Nast Traveler's Room with a View* (Assouline, 2010).

Even today, after many years, there are moments when your eyes could almost be fooled—when they'll still believe that however you wandered into this huge quadrangle called the Place des Vosges, you'll never find your way out. Wherever you turn your gaze, this mini-Paris in the heart of old Paris, and perhaps the most beautiful urban spot in the world, seems to turn its back not just on the rest of the world but on the rest of Paris as well. You step in—and time stops.

At night, when the Place des Vosges grows quiet and traffic comes to a halt, the arched entrances under the Pavillons du Roi and de la Reine blend into the darkness, as do the two narrow side streets tucked to the northeast and northwest of the Place, the rue des Francs-Bourgeois and the rue du Pas-de-la-Mule. With no apparent means out, it is impossible not to feel that you are indeed back in this self-contained, self-sufficient seventeenth-century enclave, just as the original founders of the square, four hundred years ago, wished to be locked in a Paris of their own devising—a Paris that had the very best of Paris, a Paris that hadn't quite been invented yet and of which this was a promise. Recent restoration has been so successful that the Place looks better today than it has in three centuries and gives a very good picture of the Paris its *ancien régime* founders envisioned.

On the Place des Vosges, you can almost touch old Paris. At midnight, upon leaving L'Ambroisie (at no. 9)—among the best and most expensive restaurants in Paris, in the building where Louis XIII stayed during the 1612 inauguration of the square—you don't just step into seventeenth-century Paris but into a Paris where the eighteenth and nineteenth centuries are superimposed over earlier and later times no less beguilingly than Atget's *vieux Paris* photos can still cast albuminous sepia tones over Y2K Paris. The footsteps heard along the dark arcades may not even belong to a living soul but to shadows from the past—say, Victor Hugo, who lived at 6 place des Vosges between 1832 and 1848, or Cardinal Richelieu, who two centuries earlier lived diagonally across the square (at no. 21), or the occasional ruffian who would turn up in this affluent enclave and terrorize the ladies. Turn around and you might just as easily spot the fleeting silhouette of the notorious seventeenth-century courtesan Marion Delorme (at no. 11), heading home under the cover of the arcades; or of France's most illustrious preacher, Bossuet (at no. 17); or of Madame de Rambouillet (at no. 15), whose salon was a who's who of seventeenth-century France. Marion had been Cardinal Richelieu's mistress once but was now accompanied by Cardinal de Retz, one of France's most devoted ladies' men. An habitué of the Place des Vosges, Retz, the turbulent antimonarchist, had been the lover of both Marie-Charlotte de Balzac d'Entragues (at no. 23) and the Princesse de Guéméné (at no. 6).

Many aristocratic ladies who lived on the square and around the Marais were known as *précieuses:* women who adopted an overrefined, highly conceited form of speech that, despite their cultivated delicacy in attitude and taste, by no means entailed an equally cultivated sense of morality. They frequently had several lovers, and the Princesse de Guéméné was no exception. She loved the unruly Count of Montmorency-Boutteville, who had also been the lover of Madame de Sablé (at no. 5) and who, following a terrible *duel à six* in 1627 in front of no. 21, the home of Cardinal Richelieu (who had made dueling a capital offense in France), was subsequently captured and beheaded. Such would be the fate of two of the Princesse's other lovers.

Nothing better illustrates these crisscrossed, overlapping, and at times simultaneous passions than the loves of another *précieuse,*

Marguerite de Béthune (at no. 18). She was the daughter of the Duc de Sully, King Henry IV's superintendent of finances, who was instrumental in planning the Place des Vosges (his Hôtel de Sully still feeds into the Place through a tiny, near-inconspicuous door at no. 7). Marguerite had been the mistress of both the Duc de Candale (at no. 12) and the Marquis d'Aumont (at no. 13). Since the even numbers on the Place des Vosges are located to the east of the Pavillon du Roi, and the odd to the west, it is possible to suppose that when she was with one she could easily manage to think of, if not spy on, the other.

Throughout its history, the very thought of the Place des Vosges has instantly conjured images of grand passion and grand intrigue. The importance that the Place des Vosges has in the French imagination, like that of Versailles, may explain why French literature, from the seventeenth century on, has never quite been able to disentangle love from its surrogate, double-dealing, or courtship from diplomacy, underscored as they all are by the cruelest and crudest form of self-interest. Such irony escaped no one, and certainly not the disabused courtiers of *précieux* society.

Few of them had anything kind to say about love or about the women they loved. Cardinal de Retz's racy and tempestuous *Mémoires* were most exquisitely vicious in this regard. (Of his ex-mistress Madame de Montbazon, he wrote, "I have never known anyone who, in her vices, managed to have so little regard for virtue.") And yet his *Mémoires* are dedicated to one of the *précieux* world's busiest writers, his good friend Madame de Sévigné, born at 1 bis place des Vosges. Sévigné was herself a very close friend of the Duchesse de Longueville, Madame de Sablé, the Duc de La Rochefoucauld, and Madame de La Fayette, the author of Europe's first modern novel, *La Princesse de Clèves.* To show how intricately interwoven this world was, one has only to recall that La Rochefoucauld may have had a platonic relationship with La Fayette but he most certainly did not with the Duchesse de Longueville, with whom he had a son and for whom the disillusioned and embittered La Rochefoucauld probably continued to ache until the very end of his days. Known as one of the most beautiful women of the period, the fair-haired Duchesse led as blustery a life as Cardinal de Retz—first as a lover, then as a warrior, and finally as a religious woman. It was because of her bitter feud with her rival, Madame de Montbazon, that another duel took place on the square, between descendants of the Guise and the Coligny families. Each man may have gallantly taken the side of one of the two women, but after about a century of feuding between the Catholic Guises and the Protestant Colignys there was enough gall for another duel. It took Coligny almost five months to die of his wounds.

It is said that the Duchesse de Longueville watched the duel from the windows of 18 place des Vosges, the home of Marguerite de Béthune, the woman whose lovers' pavilions faced each other. The quarrel between the Duchesse de Longueville and Madame de Montbazon reads like a novel filled with slander, malice, jealousy, and spite. Scandalmongering was a favorite occupation, and the preferred weapon was not so much the sword as the letter: dropped, intercepted, recopied, falsely attributed, and purloined letters were ferried back and forth, leaving a trail that invariably led to the loss of reputations and, just as frequently, of life—Coligny's in this instance—and ultimately to civil unrest. At the risk of oversimplifying, tensions mounted to such a pitch that many of those who had anything to do with the Place des Vosges before the middle of the seventeenth century eventually joined the Fronde, the antimonarchist aristocratic campaign of 1648–53. It was the last aristocratic revolt against the monarchy, and Louis XIV, the Sun King, never forgot it. To ensure that the aristocracy never again rose against him, he made certain that almost every one of its members moved to Versailles.

Like its storied residents, the Place des Vosges remains a tangle of the most capricious twists in urban memory. Known initially as the Place Royale in 1605, it became the Place des Fédérés after the Revolution in 1792; the Place de l'Indivisibilité in 1793; and then the Place des Vosges in 1800, under Napoléon. It resumed its first name in 1814, after the restoration of the monarchy, and lost it once more to the Place des Vosges in 1831. After yet another revolution, it became once again the Place Royale in 1852, and finally the Place des Vosges in 1870. The Place teemed with intellectuals, writers, aristocrats, salons, and courtesans. It witnessed generations of schemes, rivalries, and duels, the most famous of these being the duel of 1614, known as "the night of the torches," between the Marquis de Rouillac and Philippe Hurault, each flanked by his second, everyone wielding a sword in one hand and a blazing torch in the other. Three were killed; Rouillac alone survived, and lived thereafter at 2 place des Vosges.

I come to the Place des Vosges to make believe that I belong, that this could easily become my home. Paris is too large a city, and time is too scarce for me to ever become a full resident—but this square is just right. After a few days, I am at home. I know every corner, every restaurant, and every grocer and bookstore beyond the square. Even faces grow familiar, as does the repertoire of the high-end street entertainers and singers who come to perform under the arcades every Saturday: the pair singing duets by Mozart, the tango and fox-trot dancers, the Baroque ensembles, the pseudo-Django jazz guitarist, and the eeriest countertenor–mock castrato bel canto singer I've ever heard, each standing be-hind stacks of their own CDs.

For lunch, I've grown to like La Mule du Pape on the rue du Pas-de-la-Mule, scarcely off the square: light fare, fresh salads, ex-cellent desserts. And early in the morning, I like to come to Ma Bourgogne, on the northwest corner of the square, and have breakfast outside, under the arcades. I've been here three times al-ready, and I am always among the first to sit down. I think I have my table now, and the waiter knows I like *café crème* and a buttered baguette with today's jam. I even get here before the bread arrives from the baker's. I sit at the corner of this empty square and watch schoolboys plod their way diagonally across the park, one after the other, sometimes in pairs or clusters, each carrying a heavy satchel or a briefcase strapped around his shoulders. I can easily see my sons doing this. Yes, it does feel right.

Then, just as I am getting used to the square and am busily making it my home—tarts, salads, fresh produce, baguette, jam, coffee—I look up, spot the imposing row of redbrick pavilions with their large French windows and slate roofs, and realize that this, as I always knew but had managed to forget, is the most beautiful spot in the civilized world.

Parisians, of course, have always known this, and during the seventeenth and eighteenth centuries routinely overwhelmed foreign dignitaries by escorting them to the Place before returning them to the business of their visit. What must have struck these foreigners was something perhaps more dazzling and arresting than French magnificence or French architecture. For the Place des Vosges is not magnificent in the way, say, Versailles, or the Louvre, or the Palais Royal are magnificent. And the thirty-six cloned, slate-roofed, red-brick and white-stone "row house" pavilions—with the interconnecting arcades, or *promenoir,* running the length of all four sidewalks of a square no larger than the size of a Manhattan city block—can by no stretch of the imagination be called a miracle of seventeenth-century architecture. As with any *cour carrée,* what is striking is not necessarily each unit but the repetition thirty-six times of the same unit, many of which already boast a small square courtyard within. It is the symmetry of the square that casts a spell, not each segment—except that here the symmetry is projected on so grand a scale that it ends up being as disorienting and as humbling as quadratic symmetry is in Descartes or contrapuntal harmonies are in Bach. If the French have nursed an unflagging fondness for Cartesian models, it is not because they thought nature was framed in quadrants but, rather, because their desire to fathom it, to harness it, and ultimately to explain it as best they could led them to chop up everything into pairs and units of two. Drawing and quartering may have been one of the worst forms of execution, but the French mania for symmetry has also given us palaces and gardens and the most spectacular urban planning imaginable, the way it gave us something that the French have treasured since long before the Enlightenment and of which they are still unable to divest themselves even when they pretend to try: a passion for clarity.

It is hard to think of anyone who lived on or around the Place des Vosges during the first half of the seventeenth century who didn't treasure this one passion above all others. Even in their loves—hapless and tumultuous and so profoundly tragic as they almost always turned out to be—the French displayed intense levelheadedness when they came to write about them. They had to dissect what they felt, or what they remembered feeling, or what they feared others thought about their feelings. They were intellectuals in the purest—and perhaps coarsest—sense of the word. It was not what they saw that was clear; human passions seldom are. It was how they expressed what they saw that was so fiercely lucid. In the end, they preferred dissecting human foibles to doing anything about them. They chatted their way from one salon to the next, and on the Place des Vosges this was not difficult to do. Almost every pavilion on the square had a *précieuse* eager to host her little salon, or *ruelle,* in her bedroom. It is difficult to know whether there was more action than talk in these intimate *ruelles.* What is known is that everyone excelled at turning everything into talk. They intellectualized everything.

And it shows everywhere. Charles Le Brun, an ardent disciple of Descartes, remains one of the principal decorators of the Place des Vosges. His style is frequently considered Baroque; yet few would argue that if anything was alien to the Baroque sensibility it was Cartesian thinking. On the Place des Vosges, the dominance of intellect over excess is never hard to detect. Yet there are still telltale signs of sublimated trouble. The street level and first and second floors of every pavilion may have been the picture of architectural harmony and were built according to very strict specification; there were to be no deviations from the model supplied by King Henry IV's designers (often thought to be Androuet du Cerceau and Claude Chastillon). But the dormer windows on the top floors do not always match; they are each builder's tiny insurrection against the master plan.

Henry IV, who favored the building of the Place, remains the most beloved French king: *le bon roi* or *le vert galant* (the ladies' man), as he is traditionally called, famous for his wit, good cheer, sound judgment, and all-around hearty appetite. Every French peasant, he said, would have a chicken in his pot each Sunday. When told that he could become a French king provided he converted from Protestantism to Catholicism, he did not bat an eyelash. Paris, he declared, was well worth a Mass. Like the Place Dauphine, the square's cousin on Île de la Cité, the Place des Vosges is built in a style that is recognizably Henry IV: all brick and stone facings, brick being, like the personality of Henry IV, down-to-earth, practical, basic, made for all times and all seasons. Though the Place des Vosges is elegant and posh, and is hardly spare, there is nothing palatial here. It also reflects the spirit of the high-ranking officials, entrepreneurs, and financiers to whom the king and his finance minister, Sully, had parceled out the land in 1605 on condition that each build a home, at his own expense, according to a predetermined design. Some of them were born rich; others had made vast fortunes and, no doubt, intended both to keep them and to flaunt them. But like their king, they were neither garish nor gaudy; wealth hadn't gone to their heads, just as power hadn't gone to their king's. Both forms of intoxication were due to happen, of course, but in another generation and under a very different monarch: Henry IV's grandson Louis XIV, the Sun King.

The grounds on which Henry IV decided to build the new square had once been the site of the Hôtel des Tournelles, famous for its turrets, where King Henry II had died in 1559 as a result of a wound inflicted during a friendly joust with a man bearing the rather foreign-sounding name of Gabriel de Montgomery. Following Henry II's death, his wife, Catherine de Médicis, had the Hôtel des Tournelles razed. To this day, Catherine is regarded as a mean, cunning, and vindictive queen, whose ugliest deed was the

St. Bartholomew's Day Massacre of 1572, during which hundreds of French Protestants were put to the sword. It is another one of those ironies of history that the Protestant Henry IV, who had hoped to placate French Catholics by marrying Catherine and Henry II's daughter Queen Margot, was not only unable to forestall the massacre, which erupted immediately after his wedding, but would himself be felled by a religious fanatic forty years later, a few blocks from where Henry II had died. He thus did not live to see his square completed.

Henry IV and Sully were far too practical to be called visionaries, but surely there must have been something of the visionary in each. They had originally intended the arcades to house common tradesmen, cloth manufacturers, and skilled foreign workers, most likely subsidized by the government. The idea was a good one, since Sully, like France's other finance ministers, had had the wisdom to attract foreign workers to help France produce domestically and ultimately export what it would otherwise have had to purchase abroad. But in this case it proved too impractical. This, after all, was prime real estate. It was so exclusive an area that, rather than design a square whose buildings would boast façades looking out on the rest of Paris, the planners turned these elegant forefronts in on themselves—as though the enjoyment of façades were reserved not for the passerby, who might never even suspect the existence of this secluded Place, but strictly for the happy few.

The Place des Vosges has all the makings of a luxurious inner courtyard turned outside in, which is exactly what Corneille saw in his comedy *La Place Royale*. Everyone lives close together, everyone moves in the same circles, and everyone knows everyone else's business. Look out your window and you'll spy everyone's dirty laundry. And yet don't be so sure, either: as Madame de La Fayette said of life at court, here nothing is ever as it seems. The Place des Vosges was, as Corneille had instantly guessed, not just the ideal gold coast but the ideal stage.

None of the residents, however, had any doubt that they be-

longed at the center of the universe. They were prickly, caustic, arrogant, querulous, spiteful, frivolous, urbane, and, above all things, as self-centered as they ultimately turned out to be self-hating. Like the square itself, this world was so turned in on itself that if it was consumed by artifice, it was just as driven by the most corrosive and disquieting forms of introspection. No society, not even the ancient Greeks, had ever sliced itself open so neatly, so squarely, to peek into the mouth of the volcano, and then stood there frozen, gaping at its worst chimeras. They may have frolicked in public, but most were pessimists through and through. The irony that they shot at the world was nothing compared with that which they saved for themselves.

La Rochefoucauld, who wrote in the most chiseled sentences known to history, expressed this better than any of his contemporaries. His maxims are short, penetrating, and damning. "Our virtues are most frequently nothing but vices disguised." "We always like those who admire us; we do not always like those whom we admire." "If we had no faults, we would not take so much pleasure in noticing them in others." "We only confess our little faults to conceal our larger ones." "In the misfortune of our best friends, we find something that is not unpleasing."

It is hard to hear the echo of so much pessimism or intrigue on the square today. Art galleries, shops, restaurants, and even a tiny synagogue and a nursery school line the arcades. Access to the Place des Vosges is no longer restricted to those who possess a key—which used to be the case. Now, on a warm summer afternoon, one of the four manicured lawns—French gardens are always divided into four parts—is made available to the public, and here, lovers and parents with strollers can lounge about on the green in a manner that is still not quite characteristically Parisian. The Place lies at the heart of cultural activity in the Marais. Two blocks away is the Bastille Opéra; a few blocks west is the Musée Carnavalet; to the north, the Jewish Museum and the Picasso Museum. The rue Vieille-du-Temple, one of the most picturesque streets in the Marais, crosses what is still a Jewish neighborhood.

In the evening, the square teems with people who remind me that the SoHo look is either originally French or the latest export from New York. In either case, it suggests that everything is instantly globalized in today's world. And yet, scratch the surface . . . and it's still all there.

Which is why I wait until night. For then, sitting at one of the tables at the restaurant Coconnas, under the quiet arcades of the Pavillon du Roi, one can watch the whole square slip back a few centuries. Everyone comes alive—all the great men and women who walked the same pavement: Marion Delorme, Cardinal de Retz, the Duchesse de Longueville, and especially La Rochefoucauld, who would arrive at the Place des Vosges in the evening, his gouty body trundling ever so cautiously under the arcades as he headed toward no. 5 to visit Madame de Sablé. No doubt his gaze wandered to no. 18, where more than a decade earlier his former mistress, the Duchesse de Longueville, had watched from her window as Coligny championed her cause and then died for it. He and Cardinal de Retz and the Duchesse de Longueville had joined the Fronde in their younger days, only to end up writing lacerating character assassinations of one another. Now the most defeated and disenchanted man in the world—putting up a front, calling his mask a mask, which is how he hid his sorrows in love, in politics, and in everything else—La Rochefoucauld would arrive here to try to put a less sinister spin on his tragic view of life by chiseling maxim after maxim in the company of friends. "True love is like ghosts, which everybody talks about and few have seen." "If we judge love by the majority of its consequences, it is more like hatred than like friendship." "No disguise can forever hide love when it exists, or simulate it when it doesn't."

I think I hear the clatter of horses' hooves bringing salon guests in their carriage, the brawling and catcalling of hooligans wandering into the square, the yelp of stray dogs, the squeak of doors opened halfway and then just as swiftly shut. I can see lights behind the French windows. Then I must imagine these lights going out, one by one, followed by the sound of doors and of footsteps and carriage wheels on the cobblestones again, not everyone eager to run into anyone else, yet everyone forced to exchange perfunctory pleasantries under the arcades, as some head home two or three doors away or pretend to head home but head elsewhere instead.

An hour later the square is quiet.

On my last evening in Paris, I drop by L'Ambroisie. It's almost closing time. I have come to inquire about the name of the dessert whiskey they had offered us at the end of our previous evening's meal. The waiter does not recall.

He summons the sommelier, who appears, like an actor, from behind a thick curtain. The man seems pleased by the question. The whiskey's name is Poit Dhubh, aged twenty-one years. Before I know it he brings out two bottles, pours a generous amount from one, and then asks me to sample the other. These, it occurs to me, are the best things I've drunk during a week in France. I find it strange, I say, that I should end my visit by discovering something Scottish and not French. One of the waiters standing nearby comes forward and says it is not entirely surprising. Why so, I ask? "Had it not been for the Scotsman Montgomery, who by accident killed Henry II during a joust, the Hôtel des Tournelles would never have been leveled and therefore the Place des Vosges would never have been built!"

I leave the restaurant. There are people awaiting taxis outside. Everyone is speaking English. Suddenly, from nowhere, four youths appear on skateboards, speeding along the gallery, yelling at one another amid the deafening rattle of their wheels, mindless of everyone and everything in their path as they course through the arcades. As though on cue, all bend their knees at the same time and, with their palms outstretched like surfers about to take a dangerously high wave, they tip their skateboards, jumping over the curb and onto the street, riding all the way past the cruel Rouillac's house, past the bend around Victor Hugo's, finally disappearing into the night.

Only then can I imagine the sound of another group of young men. They are shouting—some cursing, some urging one another on, still others hastily ganging up for the kill. I can hear the ring of rapiers being drawn, the yells of the frightened, everyone on the Place suddenly alert, peering out their windows, petrified. I look out and try to imagine how the torches of the four swordsmen must have swung in pitch darkness on that cold night in January 1614. How very, very long ago it all seems, and yet—as I look at the lights across the park—it feels like yesterday. And like all visitors to the Place des Vosges, I wonder whether this is an instance of the present intruding on the past or of the past forever repeated in the present. But then, it occurs to me, this is also why one comes to stay here for a week: not to forget the present, or to restore the past, but to forget that they are so profoundly different.

Solar-Powered Timekeeping in Paris

SUSAN ALLPORT

JUST AS MUCH as I love stone, I also love sundials and I love that the author of this piece went in search of some with her husband in Paris. I've seen two that she mentions, and I intend to track down the others, but not mentioned here is one of my favorites, at 19 rue du Cherche-Midi. It is actually a stone bas-relief of a man with a beard holding a tablet of a sundial. On the other side of the tablet, helping to hold it up, is a cupid. The man's right hand has come to rest at a spot where the line for noon and the figure XII are missing, and the inscription below this reads, "Je Cherche Midi" (I seek noon). One description I've read explains that this is a reference to the Italian hours, which were once counted from sunset to sunset, and an allusion to the phrase *"chercher midi à quatorze heures."* The phrase implies that to waste time in a ridiculous venture is to seek the impossible: though the hour of noon might fall at sixteen, seventeen, or eighteen o'clock depending on the hour of sunset and the time of year, it could never be at fourteen in Paris due to its northern latitude. The rue du Cherche-Midi has had this name since 1595, likely due to the sundial.

SUSAN ALLPORT is the author of *The Primal Feast: Food, Sex, Foraging, and Love* (Crown, 2000), *A Natural History of Parenting* (Harmony, 1997), and *Sermons in Stone: the Stone Walls of New England and New York* (Norton, 1990), among others. She contributed this piece to the travel section of the *New York Times*.

I CAN'T IMAGINE that the Musée Carnavalet in Paris sells too many copies of the book *Cadrans solaires de Paris*—Sundials of Paris—an inventory of more than one hundred of the city's sundials. But when it sold one to my husband, David, he was immediately hooked. And so David and I began tracking down these timekeepers of old when we celebrated our twenty-fifth wedding anniversary in February 2002, continuing the mission in January the following year.

There are many ways to look at Paris—through its architecture, history, museums, cafés, or street life. Sundials are one of the most esoteric. But somehow it was fitting to be thinking about time on an anniversary that few would ever count on celebrating. Moreover, searching for sundials required skills of each of us: my husband's excellent sense of direction and my high school French, which allowed us to make sense of the tome that was our guide.

As I discovered when I sallied out alone to revisit a nearby sundial and found myself walking in confused circles—or as David discovered when he arrived at the location of a sundial to learn that access required written authorization—we both were absolutely necessary for this hunt, a mutual dependence that is reflective (but that we often chafe at!) of the rest of our life.

And a hunt it was, a citywide scavenger hunt, taking us to places we would not otherwise have gone: a corner of the Jardin des Plantes, the botanical garden in the fifth arrondissement where the architect, Edme Verniquet, had placed a folly of a sundial within a maze on top of a hill; or the center of the Place de la Concorde, where we saw from the bronze lines radiating out into the busy roundabout and from the numerals embedded into the sidewalks that the obelisk, transported from Egypt in 1833, had been transformed by the French into the gnomon of a giant sundial, a project that was started in 1939, then abandoned during the war and never completed.

David loved this part of the business, finding our quarry, in which I felt like a small, obedient child, clueless as to where I was heading. But even I was taken by the Alice in Wonderland aspect of the sundial at the Hôtel de Sully in the Marais, examined on our second visit. We entered the building, the home of the Ancient Monuments and Historic Buildings Commission, from the busy rue Saint-Antoine and walked through one courtyard into a quieter, interior courtyard with a lovely parterre garden. Then, after viewing the simple sundial on the handsome seventeenth-century rear façade, we popped into the Place des Vosges through a small door in the garden's outside wall. Without this excuse of a sundial, we might never have discovered this delightful shortcut through the Marais.

Without question, however, the sundials themselves are fascinating, and many are inscribed with such apt reflections on the nature of time that they were worth seeking out for those snippets of truth alone. One might already be familiar with the inscription on top of the recently regilded sundial in the center court of the Sorbonne, Sicut Umbra Dies Nostri—Our Days Pass Like a Shadow—but standing below that dial as the shadow of its style moves slowly from one Roman numeral to the next really does give one that feeling.

The afternoon dial on the Convent of Mercy on the rue des Archives in the third arrondissement advises Utere Dum Lyceat, to make the most of your time. And at the Palais de Justice, on the side of the building on the Quai des Orfèvres, a bas-relief of Time with his scythe and Justice with her sword and scales proclaims Hora Fugit Stat Jus—The Hour Flees; Justice Stays—a reminder of both the strength and the fragility of the law, given the sham trials that occurred inside this same building during the French Revolution.

Not all the inscriptions are somber. A whimsical blue chicken on a sundial at 4 rue de l'Abreuvoir in Montmartre clucks, "*Quand tu sonneras, je chanteray*"—"When you ring, I sing," a humorous reference to the time when chickens were alarm clocks. Sundials ask us to contemplate not only time and its passage, but also when and why humans began to divide time into hours, a development that was not, at first, universally embraced, as the Roman comic playwright Plautus (circa 200 BC) made clear, condemning the man who set up a sundial in the marketplace "to cut and hack my day so wretchedly into small pieces."

Yet surely it was inevitable that humans would associate the movement of shadows with the passing of time, then use those shadows both to understand the earth's place in the universe (some sundials show the signs of the zodiac and the months of the year) and mark the hours. And inevitable, too, that those who knew the time (the word "gnomon" is derived from a Greek word meaning "one who knows") would use that knowledge to control the actions of others.

In Paris, the earliest sundials are on churches, where they have long enabled passersby to know the time of prayers. One of the simplest but most dramatic is the noon mark on the fifteenth-

century Église Saint-Étienne-du-Mont on the rue Clovis in the Latin Quarter. On one of the church's flying buttresses, it falls like a plumb line from the gargoyle above.

What I found most interesting about sundials, though, came to me only gradually as David and I crisscrossed the city this January. First, there is the fact that it is mighty hard to tell time this way. (And not just because sundials are useless at night.) Three out of four of our days in Paris were cloudy, so no shadows were cast. And many sundials are, by necessity of their locations, either morning or afternoon dials. So even when we had successfully found a dial—and were blessed with the sun—it was often the wrong dial for that time of day.

I don't know what the Parisians of old did when they happened upon a sundial that was actually "ringing" the hour, but when my husband and I had our first sighting, at the Sorbonne, where an obliging guard had allowed us into the courtyard, we celebrated with a long lunch of *céleri rémoulade* and *steak frites* nearby at Le Balzar. We missed out on more sightings that afternoon, but Paris is, after all, much more than the sum of its dials.

Clouds are one reason clocks quickly replaced sundials once clocks became reliable (for hundreds of years the two coexisted because sundials were necessary to check and reset mechanical timepieces). But there's another, far subtler reason that has to do with accuracy. Sundials, as it turns out, are too accurate for human affairs. They tell the true time, the exact time, as the sun passes overhead. This sounds like a virtue, and it was until people began to travel greater and greater distances in shorter and shorter amounts of time. Then they needed a less exact time, a mean or *moyen* time, where noon is noon for an entire city or country. Later, they needed a daylight saving time to get the most out of summer's long days. Clocks and watches can tell these fictional times, inventions of humans for humans, but sundials can't.

The last sundial we saw on these esoteric visits, perfect for two individuals who hadn't quite settled yet on a *moyen* time, was one of our favorites. It was a bas-relief of a girl's face placed on the side of a building near the Sorbonne at 27 rue Saint-Jacques by Salvador Dalí in 1968. At first, we walked right by this blue-eyed girl with her flaming eyebrows and simple gnomon, but then we remembered to *lever le nez,* as our book says—look up—and this charming face told us her time.

Station to Station

BARBARA DINERMAN

I PREFER TRAVELING by train above all other modes of transportation, and arriving in or departing from a grand train station is much more exciting to me than any airport. A tour of Paris's train stations is also a tour of the city in the years around the turn of the twentieth century. If you have time to see only one, you won't be disappointed in choosing the Gare de Lyon, home of the beautiful and evocative Le Train Bleu restaurant.

BARBARA DINERMAN is a former resident of Paris and returns frequently. She has written regularly on interior design, travel, and art for *Veranda, Robb Report,* and *Art & Antiques.* In 1997, she won an annual journalism award from the American Society of Interior Designers. Dinerman is also the author of award-winning short stories and a novel, *H* (iUniverse, 2007). The following piece was originally published in 1999.

WE DON'T USUALLY think of such utilitarian buildings as train stations when we plan our explorations of Paris. But the six great stations extant today are certainly worth our inspection. They're as much a history lesson as the noted monuments, as rewarding an architectural study as Baron Georges-Eugène Haussmann's façades of the Grands Boulevards, and as much fun as a visit to any of the flower-laden parks.

With the exception of the Gare Montparnasse, which soars

eighteen stories in its familiar late-twentieth-century structural form, Paris's train stations reflect the exuberant faith in industrial progress that marked the end of the nineteenth century. The great architects of the day conceived these remarkable structures, and Impressionist artists such as Édouard Manet, Claude Monet, Gustave Caillebotte, Jean Beraud, and Norbert Goeneutte competed to properly record the dramatic impact of the stations on the Parisian landscape and its citizenry.

Just three years after the Paris Salon of 1874 (where Manet's *The Railway,* now known as *The Gare Saint-Lazare,* brought down a storm of ridicule), Émile Zola took up the cause. "That is where painting is today," he wrote in defense of new paintings by Monet. "Our artists have to find the poetry in train stations, the way their fathers found the poetry in forests and rivers."

In fact, Monet's group of eleven works depicting the Gare Saint-Lazare became the basis for an art exhibition titled Manet, Monet, and the Gare Saint-Lazare at the Musée d'Orsay last spring. The successful exhibition then moved to the National Gallery in Washington, D.C. For modern-day audiences, these artistic efforts are powerful reminders that the trains, along with the cuttings and tracks that transformed their neighborhoods, were nothing less than a wondrous symbol of change.

As the stations made grand architectural statements, we can admire them today as a glimpse back at the turn of *that* century, and for what they still are today. Enter any station, and the crowds—not to mention the restaurant facilities and even the poster art—will amaze you. This dazzling network of railways is alive and well, despite the preponderance of air travel. Compare the SNCF (Société Nationale des Chemins de Fer) with Amtrak: not exactly a contest.

Of course, the sense of nostalgia is strong, and marketing efforts have been surprisingly aggressive. Having adopted the slogan *À nous de vous faire préférer le train* (We'll make you want to take the train) on its brochures, schedules, and ubiquitous ads, the company's officials are aware of the sentimental value of rail travel.

Vintage posters show the legendary trains such as the 1925 Sud Express steaming out of the Gare de Lyon for the Riviera, and the Boîte à Sel delivering elegantly dressed and coiffed passengers to the Gare d'Austerlitz from Biarritz.

With the stations recently cleaned up and vigorously updating their amenities, it can be richly rewarding to devote a few days to them. Think of them as a historical collection, a phenomenon unleashed by industrialization, and particularly as a glamorous symbol of mobility. For the first time, people could hop a train and ride in comfort to the south of France, the southwest, the north, the east. The possibilities seemed endless, and the opportunity to house these revolutionary steam railways gave architects a bold new form of expression.

At first, architects balked at the new engineering techniques, such as using iron beams or vaults to create the broad spans needed to construct the ticket halls and train sheds. As Anthony Sutcliffe notes in *Paris: An Architectural History,* an entirely new kind of structure was needed in nineteenth-century Paris—one that would accommodate "large-scale manufacturing, steam railways and high-volume commerce. These buildings started to appear in and around Paris in about 1840."

Iron and glass were becoming less expensive, but architects feared that aesthetic appeal might suffer. Respected names such as Labrouste, who designed the Sainte-Geneviève Library in 1842, made efforts to build with the new materials. In the 1850s, the Les Halles food market area (designed by eminent architect Baltard) pleased the emperor with its extensive system of roofs and clerestories. Still, the first two railway stations—Gare d'Orléans (1840), now Gare d'Austerlitz, and Gare du Nord (1846)—used modest railway architects. The Gare du Nord was originally an arcaded classical design "reflecting the horizontality of the trains and looking like *orangeries* or market buildings in the pre-Baltard style," notes Sutcliffe. But as the more fashionable architects showed that the new materials could be applied to fine architecture, the stations began to look like showplaces.

GARE DU NORD

After the Gare du Nord's modest beginning as a railway-company design in a then remote area of the city, railway chairman Baron James de Rothschild took another look at the neoclassical structures that dotted the city—notably Jakob Ignaz Hittorff's nearby church of Saint-Vincent-de-Paul. Rothschild commissioned the German-born architect to give the Gare du Nord a facelift in 1859. Hittorff created a neoclassical frontage with giant Ionic pilasters that define the central pavilion; the gables on the end pavilions reflect the wide pitched roof of the train shed. Huge statues stand on the façade, so that the structure "combined a practical design for a railway station and the classical features of a self-conscious Parisian public monument."

The interior is considered cathedral-like in its vastness, the original green columns supporting the roof of the train shed. Hittorff complained about a lack of "monumental street access," though Haussmann supplied two short approach streets. Access has further improved with the recent addition of a service road and drop-off area at the front entrance. From the upper level, you can see the bullet-shaped TGV trains to northern towns and the Thalys line to Belgium, Holland, and Germany waiting to speed away.

The Gare du Nord is also the starting point for Eurostar, the Channel Tunnel (Chunnel) line, and the upper level has been transformed into a plush service-area-cum-waiting lounge. To inaugurate the Euro Tunnel in May 1994, François Mitterrand commissioned a sculpture. Europa Operanda's futuristic bronze figures of an adult and child dominate the parapet overlooking the Grandes Lignes.

GARE DE L'EST

Built three years after the original Gare du Nord, this station inspired all the others. As Sutcliffe notes, the stations "offered the chance to create completely new spaces and circulation systems, using iron and glass in a more creative way than was normally possible in Parisian architecture." Stations also had "monumental potential at the head of the approach streets." Architect F. A. Duquesney emphasized the semicircular vault of the train shed, "which sprang above an arcaded frontage and was flanked by two three-story pavilions, topped by a balustrade, in the formal style of railway offices of the day." The large, glazed arch had radiating iron tracery and glass that formed a striking wheel symbol. As in the Gare du Nord, statues graced the façade, each representing a town served by the network.

The boulevard de Strasbourg, linking the Gare de l'Est and the Grands Boulevards, would not be completed until the early 1850s, but Duquesney designed the structure with the future vista in mind. Although—or perhaps because—the immediate neighborhood today is a bit down-at-the-heel, the station makes an imposing sight as it dominates Place Napoléon III.

What is perhaps most striking about the Gare de l'Est, however, is its haunting history as the point of departure for the Nazi concentration camps of World War II. If you don't have this history in mind at first (as you contemplate such eastern destinations as Strasbourg and Bâle, plus the newly completed TGV line to Strasbourg and Germany), you will soon be reminded by at least four large plaques. "*N'oublions jamais,*" the plaques implore visitors. "*De cette gare partirent des milliers des patriotes français pour le tragique voyage.*" Let us never forget . . .

GARE SAINT-LAZARE

Farther west and serving the western region of the country, including Normandy as well as extensive Paris suburbs, this more

centrally located station didn't stand at the head of a great vista. Sutcliffe dismisses the Gare Saint-Lazare as "a conforming Parisian façade architecture, virtually unrecognizable as a station." However, in its newly sandblasted state, connected by a blue fili-greed skywalk from the Hôtel Concorde Saint-Lazare, this mid-nineteenth-century structure has a definite glamour; its neighbors include the splendid Second Empire department stores Printemps and Galeries Lafayette.

The Gare Saint-Lazare was redesigned in the 1860s as the Second Empire made its mark under Napoléon III. Hauss-mann's street improvements were in full swing, and the Hôtel Terminus (now the Concorde Saint-Lazare) coincided with the remodeling of the station. Today, this bustling area is entertain-ing. The 1895 seafood restaurant Mollard is across the street, decorated with fabulous mosaic murals, and the posh 1889 Paul *boulangerie* is located at boulevard Haussmann and rue Tronchet (where lines form for turtle-shaped loaves and gourmet sand-wiches).

The most striking feature of the Gare Saint-Lazare is the range of its amenities. On the ground floor is the vast Galerie Marchande. This ultra-mall sells everything from fresh vegetables to Swarovski crystal. You can get your umbrella repaired at Maroquinerie à la Pierrette. ("*Même les plus malades,*" a sign promises—even the worst of them.) And when was the last time you were in a station that had an antiques shop? Oh, yes, you can get glasses in an hour and your photos developed at the same time.

The Galerie Marchande has undergone a massive renovation. This is also now the site of the new RER Haussmann-Saint-Lazare commuter rail station. Up the escalator to the main ticket hall, two huge brasseries are doing a brisk business, and the hot-dog-shaped stainless-steel stands on rubber tires—a whimsical presence in every station—serve all sorts of refreshments to go. Meanwhile signs boast of on-time performance and *wagons-lits* posters exhort us to "discover the new cuisine on board—for the pleasure of the taste and the trip."

GARE D'AUSTERLITZ

After our virtual journeys to the north, east, and west from these Right Bank stations, let's move south to the Left Bank for the southern routes. If the Gare Saint-Lazare and its environs recall city life in the late nineteenth century, the Gare d'Austerlitz reflects the era of travel to the posh watering holes of the southwest, notably Biarritz and Saint-Jean-de-Luz.

Though the station itself is rather nondescript due to its early origins, it offers a fine glimpse into a leisurely era, when travelers disported themselves in the formal restaurant upstairs, seen from outside as a row of bright blue awnings over flowered window boxes. In the restaurant, Le Grenadier, you will be given its history (named for a neighborhood soldier in Napoléon's army) and a daily changing menu offered with private-label wine. Salons display paintings of the campaigns.

In the ticket hall, banners announce a new link with the city of Bourges. Travelers can buy packages that include guided visits to the Cathédrale Saint-Étienne and other sights; in the early 1990s, Jacques Chirac launched the Seine-Rive-Gauche project, a pleasant riverside strip that runs southeast from the station.

Many Parisians dismiss the Gare d'Austerlitz as architecturally dull. However, the sight of the Métro trains entering on an overpass (the huge archway on the upper level of the station) is compelling, like watching a train disappear into a mountain.

GARE DE LYON

Just across the Seine (technically the Right Bank), the station's fanciful clock tower dominates the rue de Bercy area, which has been revitalized, particularly with the opening of the new Bibliothèque Nationale de France in the late nineties. But when the Gare de Lyon was being built, in 1902, the area was poor and the site awkward.

The Paris Exposition of 1900 had created a climate for change. Railway companies felt "a strong obligation to enhance the cityscape," notes Sutcliffe. Both the Gare de Lyon and the Gare d'Orsay (now the Musée d'Orsay) were "variants of the classical style, though the Gare de Lyon, standing at the gateway to the east end, was more daring, using symbolism, the picturesque, expressionism and height. . . . [It] epitomizes public architecture in Paris at the height of the Belle Époque."

Architect Marius Toudoire created, says Sutcliffe, "languorous sculpture springing directly from the walls, and the colorful decoration recalled the architecture of luxury hotels and casinos on the Côte d'Azur." For present-day visitors, the legendary Train Bleu restaurant is "the world's most palatial station restaurant in a lush neo-rococo." Lunch or dinner is a feast for the senses, and

though reviews of the cuisine vary, I found the food to be delicious, and the service elegant (*pommes gaufrettes* served in a silver bowl, for example.) My rack of lamb arrived on a Christofle slicing trolley, which had a hood of embossed silver.

Le Train Bleu's fabulous murals of high society enjoying themselves in Lyon and the Riviera, its richly carved moldings, crystal chandeliers, and velvet drapes make even a cup of coffee memorable in the adjoining bar, Le Club Américain. The restaurant is listed as a historic site. In an elegant glass case are mementos, from the signature china to the Train Bleu watch.

GARE MONTPARNASSE

This startlingly modern station on boulevard Montparnasse was rebuilt to serve the TGV to the Atlantic coast, including Nantes and Quimper as of 1990. It forms a glass and concrete complex with the 1973 Tour Montparnasse, which soars to fifty-nine stories over the once-Bohemian district. Sutcliffe calls the Gare Montparnasse nothing more than a "modest practicality," but it appeals with its broad arched views of the surrounding area, its restaurants judiciously placed on the perimeter of the upper level.

Whether or not the charms and unexpected comforts of the train stations persuade you to *"préférer le train,"* you can savor the pleasures of the journey—past and present—simply by visiting the stations themselves.

Streets of Desire

VIVIAN THOMAS

As Vivian Thomas notes below, "Anyone who's been to Paris knows that it's possible to fall in love with a street." By extension, I am absolutely in love with this piece. And as you might guess, few other pleasures are as wonderful to me as accidentally discovering an old book (especially one in a series) with as much detail in it as the one Thomas describes. I have complete book envy! In an online search, I have found a variety of paperback and hardcover editions of *Évocation du vieux Paris,* and it is just a matter of choosing which one I prefer before a copy comes into my possession.

VIVIAN THOMAS is assistant editor of *France Today.* She also contributed numerous articles to the former *Paris Notes,* where this piece originally appeared.

Sometimes opening a book is like opening a door. For me, the door to the streets of Paris was opened by my friend Charles, a professor in the south of France. Scanning his bookshelves one day when I was visiting, he pulled down a slightly tattered copy of Jacques Hillairet's *Évocation du vieux Paris.*

"Here's a book you'd like. You can keep this one—I have another copy."

Although published in 1953, the book looked older, with yellowed, brittle pages. Too bulky to be a guidebook, it was the second volume (*Les Faubourgs*) of a three-volume set. But leafing

through it, I found myself mentally walking through Paris, street by street and house by house, looking at it through the eyes of a historian who seemed to know not just every building, but every balcony, courtyard, and doorknocker.

I couldn't wait to get back to Paris and start walking with Hillairet as my guide. Now, many years later, I've walked most of Paris with him. I found an abridged one-volume edition called *Connaissance du vieux Paris* in a secondhand bookstore, and although it's even heavier, I happily lug it with me as I explore unfamiliar streets and learn new stories about old favorites.

Anyone who's been to Paris knows that it's possible to fall in love with a street. It may be a tiny *impasse* or a spacious *boulevard,* but it's so full of history, beauty, sweet memories, or pure Parisian charm that it becomes "your" street. It's the one you head for first when you arrive, the one you dream about when you're away from the city too long, the one you imagine yourself living on when you let your fantasies run wild. These are a few of mine.

RUE MOUFFETARD

I first walked down the rue Mouffetard just before Christmas when Paris was mostly unknown to me. It was early evening, dark and cold, but festive shop windows and groups of scurrying pedestrians enticed me all the way to the end of the street where a brightly lit market spilled into the street. Suddenly hungry, I was overwhelmed by the aroma of spit-roasted chickens stuffed with rosemary and the sight of a hundred cheeses with names new to me, vegetables arranged like Byzantine mosaics, and heaps of glittering fish so fresh they still smelled of the sea. The *pièce de résistance* was lying in state on a table in front of the *boucherie:* a huge bearlike animal that was, I was told, a *sanglier,* or wild boar.

Since that first eye-opening walk, I must have strolled down the Mouffe' hundreds of times, always finding it the very essence of Paris. This is at once the youngest and oldest of streets. Youngest because, close to the Sorbonne, it's full of students who make a cheap dinner from the panini or crêpes sold on the street, and linger with their friends for hours of discussion over one beer in the Place de la Contrescarpe. Oldest because the street itself goes back to Roman times.

Once the start of the main road that led from Paris to Italy, the rue Mouffetard was also the main street of the village of Saint-Médard, clustered around the church that still stands near the rue Censier. From the bank of the Bièvre River, the village grew until it reached the walls of Paris in the fourteenth century and was annexed in 1724.

The Bièvre was eventually polluted by wastes dumped by the weavers and tanners who lined its banks, and some historians claim that the name Mouffetard came from the stench that lingered here—*mouffette* means skunk.

The Bièvre now runs underground and the smell is history, but relics of the past remain. At the top of the street, the Place de la Contrescarpe has been a popular meeting place since Rabelais and his friends frequented the Pomme de Pin cabaret, whose carved sign remains, now above a butcher shop. Today the *place* is ringed with cafés like the Delmas, once La Chope, a favorite of Hemingway, who lived around the corner.

The street is lined with mansard-roofed houses, one of which contained a real buried treasure. When a house at no. 53 was demolished in 1938, workmen found over three thousand gold coins stamped with the image of Louis XV, along with a note stating that Louis Nivelle, a royal counselor, left them to his daughter. The money went to his descendants, the city of Paris, and the lucky workmen.

A sculpted oak tree decorates the façade of a tavern at no. 69—Le Vieux Chêne was the meeting place of a revolutionary group in 1848. And down the hill at no. 122, À la Bonne Source has the street's oldest sign, a classified monument from the late 1500s showing water carriers at a well.

The market, which has operated since 1350, teems with basket-toting Parisians every day but Monday. And although the church of Saint-Médard is now an oasis of calm in the tumult, it was once the scene of religious hysteria so frenzied that the king was forced to intervene. When the death of a pious young deacon named François de Paris was followed by seemingly miraculous cures, unruly crowds mobbed the cemetery until Louis XV ordered it closed. The locked gates carried a stern message: "By order of the King, God is forbidden to perform miracles in this place."

COUR DU COMMERCE SAINT-ANDRÉ

A wide arch at 130 boulevard Saint-Germain flanked by figures of Hermes and Hephaestus is the gateway to a time warp, the Cour du Commerce Saint-André.

This cobblestone passage is steeped in history. At no. 8, Marat ran a printing press that produced his revolutionary tabloid *L'Ami du peuple.* Standing in the narrow *rue piétonne,* I wonder if his press was loud enough to drown out the thumps coming from no. 9, where a carpenter was using sheep to test a new device he had built for its inventor, Dr. Ignace Guillotin. A year after Charlotte Corday murdered Marat in his bath, the guillotine would end the days of another famous resident. Danton, who moved into no. 20 in 1789, was arrested there in 1794 and executed six days later.

Benjamin Franklin and Thomas Jefferson frequented this street as patrons of the Café Procope, where Parisians first tasted coffee. Opened in 1686 by Sicilian Francesco Procopio dei Coltelli (and still open today), Le Procope was also a haunt of the Encyclopédistes—you'll see some of their portraits in the windows. The restaurant's A-list literary clientele has included everyone from La Fontaine and Voltaire to Jean-Paul Sartre and Simone de Beauvoir.

Today's *cour* is half as long as it was before Haussmann created the boulevard Saint-Germain in 1866; Danton's home stood roughly where his statue now stands, on the boulevard across from the entrance to the *cour.*

Although short, this street is full of lovely secrets. It originally followed the *contrescarpe* of Philippe Auguste's wall, part of which still exists at no. 4. Inside the Catalonia tourist office's gift shop are the impressive remains of a round tower, one of many that once studded the twelfth-century wall.

Another hidden treasure is the Cour de Rohan. This series of vine-draped courtyards linking the *cour* with the rue du Jardinet is where the bishops of Rouen once had their Parisian *pied-à-terre.* Its entrance is across from Le Procope.

No sleepy backwater, the *cour* is lively by day with shoppers and lunchers and by night with restaurants catering to the movie-going crowd of the Odéon *quartier.*

HAMEAU BOILEAU

> *Paris est pour un riche un pays de Cocagne:*
> *Sans sortir de la ville, il trouve la campagne.*
>
> —**Boileau**

In one of my favorite fantasies, the one where I can live wherever I like and money is no object, I head straight for the sixteenth arrondissement and pick out a house in the Hameau Boileau. Not really a street, the *hameau* is a cluster of quiet, leafy cul-de-sacs full of butterflies and birds, where pretty homes nestle in gardens far from traffic but close to upscale amenities.

Back when Auteuil was a country village, poet Nicolas Boileau-Despréaux bought property here, seeking relief from the city he considered too crowded, noisy, and dangerous (in the seventeenth century!). Describing it caustically in *Les Embarras de Paris,* quoted above, he complains that the rich can buy peace and quiet in the city:

> *Mais moi, grâce au destin, qui n'ai ni feu ni lieu,*
> *Je me loge où je puis, et comme il plaît à Dieu.*

When that was written in 1660, Boileau had not yet attained literary fame, although it was not quite true that he had "neither hearth nor home," having inherited a small fortune from his solidly bourgeois father.

Twenty-five years later, when he was received into the Académie, he bought his long-desired sanctuary—a little country house picturesquely covered in vines, with gardens stretching to the *hameau*'s present-day entrance at 38 rue Boileau. He frequently entertained guests here, and Racine, a frequent visitor, wrote, "He's happy as a king in his solitude, or rather in his inn at Auteuil."

In the early nineteenth century, when financial speculators discovered Auteuil, Boileau's former property was subdivided. Today's houses, in a private community surrounded by woods, range from neoclassic to Art Deco in style, but most have the look of luxurious country homes. The most striking one is a turreted Gothic-style fantasy that dominates the avenue Despréaux.

Strolling along those tranquil roads under massive chestnut trees, I found it hard to believe that a short walk would take me to the Michel-Ange-Molitor Métro stop. The cynical Boileau would not be surprised to learn that, over three hundred years later, money still buys country calm in the city.

RUE LEPIC

The magic of Montmartre is easy to miss. It disappears in the traffic and tourist traps, especially in the Place du Tertre. But the *butte* has old, romantic streets that are well worth seeing, and rue Lepic brings together all that is characteristic and captivating in this former village.

Before this street was built, Montmartre was a leafy hill covered in vineyards and topped with windmills. A hamlet at the top clustered around the *place* and its church—not Sacré-Coeur, but the much older Saint-Pierre—and thatched cottages on narrow lanes housed millers, workmen, artists, and quarry workers who dug the gypsum that made plaster of Paris.

One steep road, today's rue Ravignan, linked the village to Paris for centuries, until the day in 1809 when Napoléon I rode out to inspect a new telegraph apparatus. Forced to dismount halfway up the hill and continue on foot, the emperor was not amused. Construction soon began on the rue de l'Empereur (now rue Lepic), which climbs the hill in a gentle curve.

It starts down at the Place Blanche, named for the permanent blanket of white powder left by plaster carts. Just off the *place* stands the famous Montmartre institution called the Moulin Rouge, where high-kicking dancers displayed petticoat ruffles, shapely legs, and occasionally a total lack of underwear.

Opened in 1889 (and still kicking, with several shows nightly), the Moulin Rouge in its glory days is shown on a mural near the theater's entrance at 82 boulevard de Clichy. Toulouse-Lautrec sits at his usual table sketching dancers including slender Valentin le Désossé (the Boneless) and chubby Louise Weber, nicknamed La Goulue (the Glutton).

From Place Blanche, rue Lepic climbs through a lively market into a residential *quartier* where another artist once lived. Vincent van Gogh spent two years at no. 54 with his brother Theo, an art dealer who introduced him to Toulouse-Lautrec, Pissarro, and Gauguin. Under their influence his palette evolved from somber neutrals to brighter colors before he left for Arles in 1888. Artists' studios still stand on rue Lepic and neighboring streets like rue de l'Armée-d'Orient—look for buildings with large north-facing windows and skylights.

Van Gogh may have climbed this same stretch of rue Lepic when he was painting *Le Moulin à Montmartre*. At no. 77, I find his model. An arched gateway carries the name Moulin de la Galette, and looking up through the trees I see the windmill, tantalizingly inaccessible since it is now on private property. Of all the sites in Montmartre, this may be the one most loaded with history.

By the Middle Ages, Paris's highest hill, where the Romans once had a temple to Mars, supported some thirty windmills. This one, built in 1621, stands on the site of a thirteenth-century predecessor. So famous were these mills that in 1570 the Italian poet Tasso wrote that two things struck him most about Paris: the stained-glass windows of Notre-Dame and the windmills of Montmartre.

Although carts usually lumbered up the hill loaded with wheat to be ground into flour or grapes to be pressed for wine, some wagons brought grimmer burdens. Montmartre's height made it a strategic point whenever the city was attacked, and cannons mounted here fired on the Russians in 1814 and the Prussians during the Commune of 1871.

Peace restored, the Moulin de la Galette became a popular *guinguette.* Parisians loved Sunday *promenades* to the *butte,* where millers and their wives offered fresh milk and *galettes,* or cakes, made from their flour. Now they could spend the afternoon at an outdoor dance hall. In 1876, Renoir immortalized the *moulin* in his joyous painting of Parisians in their Sunday best, dancing and flirting in the dappled sunshine.

The *guinguette* is gone now—replaced by an apartment building. And of Montmartre's many mills, just one other remains—you'll pass the Moulin Radet at the next corner, several blocks before rue Lepic ends at the Place Jean-Baptiste-Clément.

Paul Verlaine, who knew both the glory and misery of the city's streets, described them poetically in *La Bonne chanson:*

> *Le bruit des cabarets, la fange des trottoirs,*
> *Les platanes déchus s'effeuillant dans l'air,*
> *Toits qui dégouttent, murs suintants, pavé qui glisse,*
> *Bitume défoncé, ruisseaux comblant l'égout,*
> *Voilà ma route, avec le paradis au bout.*

With Verlaine's verse in mind and Hillairet in hand, I look forward to discovering many more streets of desire.

Paint the Town

PARIS MUSE

࿇࿇࿇

THIS TERRIFIC PIECE—about three paintings that tell the story of Paris in three episodes: Regency, Revolution, and Republic—is adapted from two tours, the History of Paris in Paintings at the Louvre, and the Age of the Impressionists at the Musée d'Orsay, offered by Paris Muse. This unique company offers private tours in Paris museums that have been described as "small and delicious" as opposed to "an all-you-can-eat buffet." Founded in 2002, Paris Muse is the complete opposite of a large-group tour operator, never booking more than four people to a museum tour (but larger walking tours are also available). Guides, who are trained and experienced art historians, are native English speakers living in Paris doing graduate work or preparing publications related to art history. Tours are offered in about a dozen Paris museums, and there are two great tours for families. Visit the Paris Muse Web site, parismuse.com, for more details and to sign up for its *Quoi de Neuf?* newsletter. I subscribe and really enjoy it.

THE HISTORY OF Paris is often told as a story of rulers, the monuments they built, and the wars that knocked them down. In the painted visions of its artists, there is another, subtler version of that history. Before the late nineteenth century, very few Paris painters turned their eye on the actual city itself. They painted their cultural moment instead, capturing the spirit and ideas of their age in much the same way movies or popular novels do today. That's why, when we visit the city's museums today, if we are not always looking at paintings of Paris, we are often looking at paintings about Paris. The gilded frames that hang in the Louvre and Musée d'Orsay are windows into the minds of its past residents. With a little background we can begin to read them, to see how three paintings in particular speak to the preoccupations and desires of Parisians who lived during key episodes in the city's history: Regency, Revolution, and Republic.

At first blush nothing could seem further removed from eighteenth-century Paris than the idyllic country setting in Jean-Antoine Watteau's *Pilgrimage to the Island of Cythera* (1717, Louvre, Sully Wing, 2nd floor, Gallery 36). Eight couples are making their way to a gilded boat that readies for sail. Each pair enacts a stage in the progress of seduction, their bodies forming an undulating ribbon across the surface of Watteau's luminous landscape. At one end, a man in a blue cape strenuously woos his partner, who gazes away at her fan, feigning indifference. Another suitor gently tugs his lover down the hill to the shore. She looks back over her shoulder wistfully. Closer to the boat, the women no longer need to be cajoled. These maidens cling exuberantly to their suitors' arms. The discreet eroticism of this flirtation is underscored by chubby "putti" soaring high above the couples, some of them engaged in suggestive, even risqué, gymnastics.

The scene may have been conjured by Watteau's imagination, but it reflects a real form of elite entertainment enjoyed by the *ancien régime*. A *fête galante*—an elaborate outdoor party involving role-playing and theater performances—allowed courtiers to try out new identities and gallant seductions. This party is taking place on the island of Cythera, however, believed to be the sacred birthplace of Aphrodite, the ancient Greek goddess of love. That's why we also see a statue of her, festooned with roses (her signature flower), watching over the couples. Her son Cupid is here, too. His arrows have been laid to rest, his mission accomplished.

Watteau came to painting by way of eighteenth-century

Parisian theater, where this theme of a mythic voyage to Cythera was already very popular, especially in the opera-ballet. It's no accident that his carefully choreographed couples appear to be performing some kind of minuet. A "pilgrimage to Cythera" was also contemporary slang for a trip to the suburb of Saint-Cloud, where on the extensive grounds of the royal palace there (destroyed in 1870), Parisian lovers enjoyed many a fresh-air Sunday outing. A boat departed for Saint-Cloud from the present-day Samaritaine department store (recently closed). Because eighteenth-century subversive writers used Cythera as a phony publication locale, Venus's mythical isle also became synonymous with the underground libertine press.

That's why, despite the otherworldly mood of amorous reverie in Watteau's painting, it was later understood to literally document the degeneracy of a morally bankrupt elite, a class whose most pressing concern appeared to be how long the party would last. In the aftermath of the 1789 Revolution, Watteau's seemingly apolitical painting looked both reactionary and royal, sparking such an outrage that the Louvre's curator placed it in storage.

Back in 1717, however, Watteau's *Cythera* was a new kind of painting for a new age. Louis XIV's long absolutist reign had come to a close just two years before. His nephew, Philippe II, was now ruling as regent for the child-king Louis XV. A well-read, tolerant ruler, Philippe reversed many of his uncle's absolutist policies, ending his wars and closing the worst of the Parisian prisons. Censored books that had once been banned were now in print. Around Philippe's primary residence at the Palais Royal a more relaxed court life set in, once again in Paris after a long Versailles exile.

His regency's cultural détente blew fresh air into Watteau's vaporous painting, which shows people enjoying themselves informally, not following some strict court ritual. That's also evident in the intermingling of classes. Eighteenth-century peasant blouses and straw hats mix freely with shimmering, aristocratic silks.

These textures and delicately colored details are intended to be savored up close, with a relaxed and roving eye. Watteau's intimate
painting is more at home in a Parisian *hôtel particulier* than in some
grand hallway at Versailles.

In stunning contrast, the massive scale of Jacques-Louis David's
The Lictors Bring to Brutus the Bodies of His Sons (1789—over ten
by thirteen feet!—Louvre, Denon Wing, 1st floor, Gallery 75)
commands our attention more urgently. Like Watteau, David
took his story from the Parisian stage, specifically Voltaire's *Brutus,*
first performed in 1730. But the two works' similarities end there.
In place of pleasure, we have a tragic story told in a style more
cerebral than sensual. This suited the stern moral climate of Paris
during the last days of the *ancien régime.*

David transports us to the home of Junius Brutus, first consul
of Rome, who had rid the republic of its last king, Tarquin.
Shrouded in metaphorical darkness, Brutus turns his back on the
horrible sight of his two dead sons, executed for their involvement in a treasonous plot to restore the very monarchy Brutus
had brought down. David believed that painting should ask its
viewers tough ethical questions. Is Brutus above humanity, for his
personal sacrifice to the republic, or below it, for allowing his
own sons to be killed?

The painting received rave reviews at the Louvre's annual
Salon, opening just weeks within the 1789 storming of the Bastille. In the months that followed, its main theme—of measuring
the interests of a society against those of an individual—was no
longer a remote concern for ancient Roman leaders. Parisians
subsequently adopted David's Brutus as a heroic antiroyalist, the
kind of dutiful father to the nation that France needed. It is
doubtful, however, that David's original client for the painting,
the king himself, saw Brutus the same way. It was one of Louis
XVI's last acquisitions before the entire royal collection was seized
by the new government.

David's technique was by far the most Revolutionary aspect of his painting. He developed an austere neoclassical style that could be grasped immediately by the throngs visiting the Salon, held in the Louvre's still-crowded Salon Carré. The grace and delicacy of Watteau might be lost in this shuffle, but David's crisp lines guaranteed his painting maximum visibility. His figures' pantomime of gestures—Brutus's tight clutch on the letter revealing his sons' treachery versus his wife's mournfully extended arm—magnifies their emotional conflict across the space of a noisy gallery (the effect still works today). David wanted his paintings to speak directly to a motley Parisian public. It was, arguably, an audience that painters were thinking about for the very first time in history.

Parisian women were soon emulating Roman fashion, wearing the same corset-free looser shifts with high-waisted belts as the women in *Brutus*. David's nearby *Portrait of Madame Récamier* (1800) is an excellent example of this Parisian fashion *à l'antique*. *Brutus* helped launch a taste for Roman-inspired furniture, too. Jacob Frères began their careers by creating historical replicas for David to paint (he was a stickler for accurate interiors in his paintings). Later, they would produce similar Empire-style furniture for Napoléon I.

David was not just setting fashion and decorating trends in Paris, however. He played an active role in the new government. As elected deputy to the Convention, he voted for the execution of his former royal patron. Since his radical ideas had failed to win him many friends at the Royal Academy of Painting, when the new government put him in charge of it, he had it abolished. He organized more egalitarian *salons* open to submission from all artists. David was also given the job of glorifying Revolutionary martyrs in paint, and organizing government-sponsored pageants—like the Festival of the Supreme Being in 1794—which transformed Paris into a stage set of patriotic spectacle.

All of this Revolutionary handiwork got him into serious trouble during the post-Terror crackdown. David was arrested and briefly imprisoned at the Palais du Luxembourg. While in his prison room, he painted a self-portrait, which the Louvre now owns as well. Although promising to follow principles rather than men from now on in, David began painting for Napoléon in 1798, just a year shy of the coup d'état that would make him, like Brutus, first consul of France. The work that now draws David's biggest crowds at the Louvre is his *Coronation,* a marvelous piece of Napoleonic propaganda that signals both the end of David's radical challenges to his audience and the return of absolutist power to Paris.

One can imagine why later generations of Parisian artists might want to steer clear of politics and power, and focus more on the act of painting itself. By Auguste Renoir's time, the Impressionists weren't interested in reaching the Parisian public—*le peuple*—as David had tried to do. Paris was now a teeming metropolis with many different publics, each with their own idea of what French art should look like. Renoir's *Bal du Moulin de la Galette* (1876) was shown in what we might now call an "alternative art space" because his work was banished from the mainstream Salon (David's egalitarian policies didn't last too long).

Today, there's usually a crowd in front of Renoir's painting at the Musée d'Orsay (Level 5, Gallery 32), but in 1877 most Parisians weren't ready to accept that contemporary scenes from their daily life were worthy enough for something as lasting and high-minded as fine art. Renoir felt differently. He painted his boyhood friends, sipping their grenadine, on a scale normally reserved for heroes. Instead of to a Roman interior, we are transported to a recognizable locale in Paris, the Moulin de la Galette *guinguette* at the foot of the Montmartre mill that gave it its name.

Although the merrymakers are relaxed, the painting itself is a complex piece of craft, a large composition with several figures moving under changing conditions of light, filtered through the courtyard's acacia trees. While David used light to help tell his story (Brutus in darkness, his wife and daughters in the harsh light of reality), for Renoir light is the story. And in place of David's clearly outlined figures, Renoir's softly fuse with one another and their surroundings.

The impression of ease and spontaneity this new technique created was hard won. It took Renoir over a summer, working in his nearby atelier on rue Cortot, to finish the painting. His friends later claimed that Renoir painted the whole thing right there at the Moulin de la Galette, but in view of its large dimensions that's unlikely. Plus, he also had a fair amount of editing to do back at the studio. During Renoir's time, Montmartre was outside the official city limits, so it was an especially freewheeling, some might say seedy, place. The Moulin de la Galette in particular was not exactly respectable, which was precisely its attraction for bourgeois Parisians who went up there to "slum" on the weekends. Besides struggling artists, it was frequented by pimps, prostitutes, and local toughs. Renoir's idealized vision hints at none of that. He's more interested in the pleasurable surfaces of things, not their complicated substances.

When the painting was exhibited in 1877 Paris was not as peaceful as Renoir's painting would have us believe. In an effort to revive the monarchy that year, President MacMahon dismissed his Republican-minded prime minister and put a monarchist in charge. He then dissolved the parliament. His constitutional coup d'état, known as *le seize mai* after the date on which it happened, nearly brought the rocky Third Republic down for good, just seven years into its existence. Renoir remained focused on light and color throughout. "For me, a picture should be something likable, joyous, and pretty—yes, pretty," he said. "There are enough ugly things in life for us not to add to them."

Like Renoir himself, the urbane figures in his painting are turning away, taking a day off from the ugly hassles of modern life. This form of escapist leisure for the masses was born in Renoir's Paris. But most of it was taking place in new glitzy attractions on the boulevards. By 1877 the Moulin de la Galette was the last remaining *guinguette* in Paris. Visitors to the Orsay tend to get nostalgic over Renoir's painting now, but there was already a good deal of nostalgia—for the simple life that once was—when it was painted.

Eventually Renoir became a successful, even wealthy painter in his old age. He and his Impressionist friends were the first generation of artists who managed to do this from the bohemian margins, without ascending the traditional hierarchy of the Parisian art world. Unlike Watteau and David, for example, Renoir did not have lengthy academic training. He went to the École des Beaux-Arts (what the Royal Academy became after the Revolution), but he didn't stay for long. Copying plaster casts of antique sculpture bored him; he was anxious to start painting outdoors. While this new path for the arts may represent a triumph of innovation over tradition (no more Greeks and Romans!), Renoir was looking to the past, specifically to Watteau. His *Bal* is an Impressionist update of the *fête galante* theme, with its animated couples acting out the stages of seduction, drawing us back into the space of the picture. Renoir rediscovers Watteau's mythic Island of Cythera right here in his own city.

Future generations of Parisian artists will continue to keep the past greats in mind, too, but the good ones will always try to capture what defines their moment.

Passages

CATHARINE REYNOLDS

✿❀✿

IF THE REMAINING few *passages* in Paris are said to be predecessors of our shopping malls of today, we have much to be thankful for in that there are at least some left, but much to lament in that their modern versions are such poor imitations.

I find it fascinating to visit these old *passages,* beautiful shopping arcades built of iron and glass in the mid–1800s. Each one has its own character—no two are alike—and I've found some of the contemporary shops in them to be among the most enticing in Paris. (Visitors may also recognize the *passage* known as the Galerie Vivienne from Luis Buñuel's film *That Obscure Object of Desire.*) Try to include a walk through at least one *passage* as you explore Paris—we really do not have the architectural equivalent in North America. Some of the places mentioned in this article may no longer exist; as always, if you have your heart set on visiting a particular restaurant or shop, check ahead of time that it is still open.

CATHARINE REYNOLDS, introduced previously, went to live in Paris as a student in 1964 and has lived and traveled there off and on ever since. This piece appeared in the January 1988 issue of *Gourmet.*

"WINTER *WILL* COME, and then Paris is the devil," lamented the Irish poet Thomas Moore in 1820. His moan remains relevant: last winter brought ample evidence of just how filthy January weather in Paris could get—it took the army, equipped with trench spades, to dig the city out of the snow. Yet for visitors and residents all is not forlorn if the weather turns nasty. No need to lock oneself in, deprived of the city's pleasures. Clearly Moore didn't, for he went on to write:

> *Where shall I begin with the endless delights*
> *Of this Eden of milliners, monkies and sights—*
> *This dear busy place, where there's nothing transacting*
> *But dressing and dinnering, dancing and acting?*

Together with affluent Parisians of his time, Moore would have taken refuge from the weather in the *passages* that were lacing together Restoration Paris. The *Petit Larousse* tells us that a *passage* is "a covered walkway where only pedestrians go," a definition that disregards the narrow boutiques that have traditionally lined the *passages* of Paris and excludes the glazed roofs that were and are essential to the enchantment of Paris's *passages.*

Paris is hardly alone in possessing such glassed-in commercial walkways. Milan and Naples have their *gallerie,* London has its arcades, Brussels has its *galeries;* so do Leningrad and Moscow. All are the ancestors of our modern shopping malls, but Paris's nineteenth-century *passages* possess bags more charm.

The origins of the *passages* are not clear. The commercial success of Philippe-Égalité's late-eighteenth-century wooden arcades in the Palais Royal no doubt attracted the attention of speculators. Inspiration may have come from descriptions of Oriental bazaars by veterans returning from Napoléon's Egyptian campaign. Demand coincided with technology, for engineers had perfected systems that permitted economical overhead glazing of large, long areas.

The money-spinning appeals of the *passages* were obvious: post-Napoleonic France was reveling in the fruits of her belated industrial revolution. Her citizens were all too delighted to be able to spend their money in the dry warmth of the *passages,* sheltered from the hurly-burly of unwieldy carriages, fractious horses, and earthy odors. Developers were not slow to see the opportunities; between the battles of Waterloo and Sedan *passages* mushroomed in the area from the Palais Royal north to the Grands Boulevards.

In their heyday the *passages* were places to see and to be seen. Most were located near coach transport depots and theaters. *Mondaines* hastened there to visit their glovemakers, engravers, milliners, and jewelers, and then to gush over their prizes at the nearby cafés and restaurants. As time went on the attractions were multiplied with the growth of the entertainments of the Boulevards. As John Russell says so aptly, "A hundred years ago . . . the Grands Boulevards were Cosmopolis itself," and the *passages* functioned as a vital element in that sophistication. Where else were the *boulevardier*'s wife and mistress to buy their fripperies?

Then came the nearly fatal hiatus. In the intervening century the epicenter of the city moved west, and trains altered the transport habits of the capital, leaving the Boulevards to molder—often not very genteelly. Baron Haussmann mercilessly cut streets through some of the finest *passages,* like the Passage de l'Opéra. Fashionable Third Republicans deserted the small, specialized shops of the *passages* for the *grands magasins.*

Of the 137 *passages* enumerated by the *Véritable conducteur parisien* of 1828, only about twenty worthy of the name remain. Until just a few years ago even the handsomest of those were tenanted chiefly by sex shops, cut-rate clothes outlets, unpedigreed stamp dealers and numismatists, pedicurists, cobblers, printers, and a handful of old-fashioned deluxe *commerçants,* who were bravely determined to rise above the rainwater spilling through the broken panes of the skylights that had once been the glory of these very *passages.*

All that is changing. Demand for central Paris real estate has made it increasingly attractive to restore and refurbish many of the city's nineteenth-century *passages.* Fueled by the prosperity of Paris's born-again Bourse, renovation is rife, and the *passages* nearest the stock exchange have been the first to benefit. What with this pressure on central Paris real estate values, many of the city's nineteenth-century *passages* are undergoing a resurrection—which is a boon to the nostalgic; the curious; students of urbanism; admirers of nineteenth-century cast-iron architecture; chronic *lèche-vitrines,* that is, those suffering from that most extreme, Gallic form of window shopping; and Parisian and visitor alike caught by winter's weather. Rain or shine, an expedition, map in hand, through the three kilometers of Paris's *passages* (which need not be undertaken of a piece!) offers a seasonable opportunity to see what's old and new in Paris.

Just to the east of the Palais Royal, running off the tiny rue du Bouloi behind a tree-bedecked square, lies one of the lesser-known *passages,* the Galerie Véro-Dodat, developed in 1826 by a pair of savvy pork butchers who built opposite the terminus of the Messageries-Générales, the line of horse-drawn carriages that brought provincials to Paris from all of eastern France. Messrs. Véro and Dodat must have been tasteful butchers as well, for the identical mahogany shop fronts, with narrow brass-framed windows outlined with *faux marbre* columns topped with gilded bronze capitals and cherubs, are a model of grace and sobriety.

A dally along the diagonal black-and-white checkerboard-floored *passage* overhung with ivies dangling from the second-story window boxes can yield all manner of surprises. The bright, chic hats and trendy sweaters at Jean-Claude Brousseau catch the eye immediately. His is an address treasured by misses in search of a turban or an outrageously oversize velvet beret that will turn the heads of race-goers at Chantilly and Gauloises-puffing Breton fishermen alike. Il Bisonte at the other end of the *galerie* can provide the same misses with solid Florentine-made handbags and satchels. In between are the specialist *antiquaires,* dealers like Robert Capia, Paris's leading expert on antique dolls and the very man to see for those in search of a doll marked Bru, Jumeau, Steiner, or Schmitt. M. Capia is equally pleased to take on repairs or simply to chat about the history of the *passage.* His neighbors, Alain Fassier, R. and F. Charles, Eric Philippe, and Bernard Gauguin, trade in nineteenth-century rustic furniture, stringed instruments, early-twentieth-century furniture, and books respectively. M. Gauguin has some particularly fine old cookbooks, which are said to attract Alain Senderens, who is forever on the lookout for new dishes for Lucas-Carton. Nor is the *passage* without its restaurant, Le Véro-Dodat, behind whose lace curtains chef Yannick Ouvrard serves up tempting fare.

A few blocks to the northeast a pair of linked *passages* runs off the rue des Petits-Champs. The Galerie Vivienne and the Galerie Colbert are perhaps the best-restored and most lively of Paris's *passages.* They share neoclassical decors, though in fact the Vivienne was built in 1823, three years before the Colbert. Goddesses and nymphs disport themselves under the Vivienne's arched roof and around its rotunda, while young models people its length below. They wander across the swirling pastel mosaics from shops like Catherine Vernoux, run by a former casting director with a penchant for colorful geometric knits; to Yuki Torii, a bold Japanese designer who seems to have broken away from the somber palette of most of his countrymen; to Camille Blin, a lady given to shapely jersey dresses and daring jewelry; to Jean-Paul Gaultier, whose clothes an exhibitionist can wear with confidence. The more domestic then tuck into Casa Lopez to ogle its splendid custom-made rugs or Si Tu Veux for a magician's hat or an old-fashioned wooden pull toy for a godchild. Then they collapse into one of the wicker chairs spread before À Priori Thé, a tea shop started by three Americans, which explains the superiority of the brownies and pecan pie.

The more pensive can stop at the Librairie Petit-Siroux,

founded in 1826 and still redolent of the provincial, timeless atmosphere that has long drawn writers to the *passages*. Surrealist Louis Aragon was a regular there and a great champion of the outright louche and secret aura of the *passages*, eloquently limning their spell in *Le Paysan de Paris*. Small wonder that this bookshop does a good business in volumes about Paris.

A door leads into the glittering rotunda of the Galerie Colbert, which has just undergone a total face-lift. The Bibliothèque Nationale owns the Colbert and has installed its comely Musée des Arts du Spectacle and the Musée Charles Cros between the *faux marbre* columns, along with the winning boutique Colbert, selling well-reproduced postcards and posters drawn from the library's collection. The museums mount changing exhibits of posters and costumes related to theater, opera, and dance, and a dazzling collection of antique phonographs.

The Passage Choiseul stands five blocks down the rue des Petits-Champs. Restoration is more of an intention than a reality there, yet the Choiseul merits a visit. Betwixt the neon bedizenments, general sleaze, and shops selling unlabeled clothes purported to come from leading manufacturers, one can enjoy the graceful tribune supported on Ionic columns and savor what Paul Verlaine called *"les passages Choiseul aux odeurs de jadis . . ."*

This is the most literary of the *passages*, for here Alphonse Lemerre, the publishing genie of the Parnassiens, had his offices at nos. 27–31 from the 1860s onward. Paul Verlaine, Sully Prudhomme, Leconte de Lisle, and José-Maria de Heredia met in his shop regularly. Louis-Ferdinand Céline, author of *Mort à crédit*, lived there also. His mother kept a lace shop over which he spent sixteen years inhabiting "three rooms linked by a corkscrew." The nineteenth-century atmosphere is extended by the captivating office and artists' suppliers Lavrut, whose oaken drawers overflow with pastels and a bounteous selection of my favorite Clairefontaine notebooks with ultrasmooth paper designed for those who appreciate the pleasures of writing with a fountain pen. Not to break the spell, one can slip into the *café au lait* box called Pandora to sip some of Paul Corcellet's ethereally flavored teas, perhaps accompanied by the house's poppy-seed-studded quiche lorraine and a salad.

The Passage des Princes, running off the rue de Richelieu to the north, was another hangout of the Parnassiens, whose poetry magazine, the *Revue fantaisiste,* published works of Charles Baudelaire, Catulle Mendès, and others. Built in 1860, the elbow-shaped Passage des Princes is the last subsisting Second Empire *passage,* yet it looks very tired, which seems a terrible pity, especially when one reflects on the glitter its airy, lantern-hung coral arches once knew as the home of Peter's restaurant. French gastronome Courtine credits the eponymous Pierre Fraysse, who had worked in Chicago, with naming *homard à l'américaine,* a variation on a lobster preparation of his native Sète, to flatter a table of late-arriving Americans.

Today the Passage des Princes's most visitable shop is Sommer, a pipe-making concern five years older than the *passage* itself and long-standing supplier to serious smokers like Georges Simenon. Even the most dedicated antitobacco lobbyist cannot help but admire the workmanship in the antiques for sale or stand fascinated before the craftsmen creating small works of art in the window, using brier and the firm's specialty, *écume de mer,* a silicate said to purify the noxious elements in tobacco.

Perhaps the most evocative if not the tidiest of Paris's *passages* are the three spanning the boulevard Montmartre, the Passage des Panoramas, the Passage Jouffroy, and the Passage Verdeau. The oldest, the Panoramas, is named for the two giant panoramas that were installed to either side of its entrance by an American speculator named James Thayer. Thayer had purchased the French patent for painted perspectives, or panoramas, from countryman Robert Fulton, who used the proceeds to fund his experiments with steamboats. Meanwhile Thayer developed the *passage* to cash in on the crowds come to see the sixty-two-foot-high canvases of Paris and Toulon.

And his success was great. The Passage des Panoramas was a center of fashionable shopping right up to the fall of the Second Empire. *Modistes* vied with stylish cafés. Jean-Marie Farina perfumed the air with his *véritable* eau de Cologne. Marquis's chocolate brought top-hatted dandies sprinting. There the *antiquaire* Susse sold Alexandre Dumas *père* Eugène Delacroix's *Le Tasse dans la prison des fous* for six hundred francs, little suspecting that the wily Dumas would go on to sell it for fifty thousand.

The Passage des Panoramas was extended repeatedly, eventually providing access to the stage door of the Théâtre des Variétés, the theater where Zola's Nana held men spellbound. Here is Zola's description of the Panoramas, where poor Comte Muffat waited:

> Under the glass panes, white with reflected light, the *passage* was brilliantly illuminated. A stream of light emanated from white globes, red lanterns, blue transparencies, lines of gas jets, and gigantic watches and fans outlined in flame, all burning in the open; and the splash of window displays, the gold of the jewelers, the crystal jars of the confectioners, the pale silks of the milliners, glittered in the shock of mirrored light behind the plate-glass windows.

However bogus Nana's art, real talent was encouraged there after 1868, when the Académie Julian was installed in the Passage des Panoramas. The Académie tutored many painters, including Americans Childe Hassam and Charles Dana Gibson.

Today the Passage des Panoramas has more memories than glamour, but it seems to be bootstrapping its way up, led in no small part by Stern, the capital's grandest *graveur,* which since 1840 has served a clientele of emperors, grandees, miscellaneous aristocrats, diplomats, and just plain folk with painstakingly engraved *bristols* (calling cards), bookplates, signet rings, invitations, and letterheads from its ravishing shop paneled with dark oak heavy with caryatids and curlicues.

The neighborhood is mixed. The less said about the Sauna Hamman Euro Men's Club the better. The food shops are generally fast, though L'Arbre à Cannelle serves an amiable tea amid potted palms; the stamp dealers tout themselves as *maisons de confiance,* which always leaves me wondering; and the newer shops— like Maknorth, the outlet for a Cambodian designer of the bold school, and Trompe l'Œil, the place for obelisks and for fruit not intended for eating—are signs that things are looking up.

Across the boulevard Montmartre the Passage Jouffroy, dating from 1845, beckons from beneath the weight of the Hôtel Ronceray. It has an Oriental flavor, thanks to two of its largest shops, the Palais Oriental and La Tour des Délices. The former is ideal if you have to cancel a trip to Marrakech, stocking almost everything to be found in the souks. The latter is full of delectable sweetmeats made of honey and almonds and coconut, which it serves up with mint tea.

France takes over farther down under the skylight with Pain d'Épice, a shop specializing in tiny, shiny toys to fill a stocking as well as the miniature *batterie de cuisine* and provisions for the larder of a dollhouse Cordon Bleu. Galerie 34 and Abel are treasure houses of parasols, umbrellas, walking sticks, and canes, dating from the seventeenth century to the end of World War II. And I never fail to stop at La Boîte à Joujoux at the bend of the *passage* opposite the exit of the Musée Grévin to select a fifteen-franc bag of *bonbons à l'ail* (garlic hard candies) from among the jokes.

The Librairie Vulin operates in a more serious vein, promising "*toujours de belles occasions*" (always good bargains). The shop's bins of books line the *passage,* making Vulin a *bouquiniste* without the hazards of Seine-side rainstorms. Opposite stands Cinédoc, a mecca for film fanatics questing for posters, postcards, magazines, black-and-white studio stills, and books, including biographies of stars from Bud Abbott to Loretta Young.

Across the rue de la Grange-Batelière the Passage Verdeau entices from between Corinthian columns. Its skylights, divided into small squares, its peeling cream paint, and its stony floor make the *passage* seem more tenebrous and bleak, but its restaurant and specialist shops assure it a following. Most prominent among the boutiques is Photo Verdeau, the source for rare cameras. Its ample stock of nineteenth-century matériel—objects like stereopticons—is complemented by a selection of silent films starring Harold Lloyd and Charlie Chaplin. Cheek by jowl, two good bookstores, the Librairie Farfouille and the Librairie Le Comédien, offer delicious scents to the bookhound. Postcard collectors flock to La France Ancienne. A good postsearch lunch is available at either the Restaurant Martin Malburet (aka Drouot Verdeau) or Les Menus Plaisirs. The first is more ambitious, with its collection of enameled promotional signs spread over two stories. I spied one vaunting Brasseries du Katanga while enjoying the *gigotin d'agneau en croûte* (lamb in pastry) and the *marquise au chocolat extra bitter et moka* (dense bitter chocolate and mocha mousse).

Another day I sampled Les Menus Plaisirs, a restaurant name with a double entendre, referring to both the pleasures of the *carte* and the small pleasures enjoyed by a king when he ruled the land. In the case of this small restaurant the pleasures take the form of such offerings as good salads and pastas with smoked salmon, foie gras, basil, or garlic.

The fate of some of the other *passages* has been less happy. Some, like the Passage du Caire and the Passage du Havre, have capitulated to the worst excesses of commerce. In the case of the Passage du Caire this is a shame, for it is the oldest extant, with an exceptionally elegant, bright glass skylight. Its entrance on the rue du Caire still bears three stylized *retour d'Egypte* pharaohs. Unfortunately the wholesale garment district seized the neighborhood, and today the poor *passage* is hostage to neon-lit tenants who supply display wares, mannequins, and wrapping materials to small shops across France. I have long bought Christmas wrapping paper in hundred-meter rolls there. One need only brave the lack of service in this whole-sale world; the shopkeepers always seem pleased enough to deal in cash if one is prepared to purchase in bulk.

The Passage du Havre, located near the Gare Saint-Lazare, is even more honky-tonk, with the three well-stocked boutiques of La Maison du Train its only redeeming features. Little boys of all ages journey there to purchase rolling stock and to obtain spare parts and repairs.

Sadder still are those *passages,* like the Brady and the Prado, that have been grossly misused and not maintained, their identities swallowed up by neighborhoods grown tacky around them. The Brady was truncated by the cutting of the boulevard de Sébastopol and never really recovered. Today its name is hardly discernible in the broken floor tiles, and holes in the glazing gush rainwater on the merchants of ginger and manioc. The only shop front worth a pause—for the young and brave—is Allô-stop, a unique organization that for a minimal fee introduces would-be hitchhikers to drivers who are bound in the same direction.

But there is hope. With the examples of the Galerie Colbert and the Galerie Vivienne to inspire them, Paris's architectural watch-dogs appear to have persuaded the Assistance Publique, which owns the boarded-up Passage du Grand Cerf, to restore this once lovely, airy *passage* located near the Forum des Halles. Its glass will be renewed and its aerial walkways under the skylights will again survey healthy *commerces.* Improvements in its neighbor, the Passage Bourg-l'Abbé, now chiefly devoted to wholesale underwear man-ufacture, will surely follow, because late-twentieth-century urban-ists have awakened to the amenity value of the *passage.*

But beware! There are *passages* and *passages.* Paris's contempo-rary property developers have appropriated the name but spurned the extravagance of the glazed roof. However glitzy the boutiques that line the *passages* and *galeries* of the Champs-Élysées, they can-not compete with the haunted and haunting charms of the nine-teenth-century *passages.*

The Secret Shops of the Palais Royal

BARBARA WILDE

WHEN I LIVED in Paris as a student, I rarely set food in the Palais Royal. "Too formal, too quiet," I sniffed, preferring instead the impromptu gatherings of guitar-playing young people in the little park next to Saint-Julien-le-Pauvre in the Latin Quarter. Returning to Paris over the years, however, I have come to prefer the Palais Royal, and it has earned an unequivocal favorite place in my heart.

I love equally the gardens and the arcades, especially the enormous glass lamps that hang from them, as well as the site-specific outdoor work created by Daniel Buren—black and white striped columns, of varying heights, are arranged in rows in front of a fountain filled with large silver spheres that reflect the surroundings. *Les Deux plateaux,* more often referred to as "Colonnes de Buren" (Buren's Columns), met with some resistance when it was mounted, but I think it's wonderful—the juxtaposition really works, and it's a great place for picture-taking. In 2007, Buren threatened to dismantle the whole project, claiming that the city had allowed it to deteriorate, but happily, a complete restoration effort began in 2009.

If you did nothing else than stroll the arcades and visit the retail shops within, that would be satisfying enough. The collection of shops in the Palais Royal is superb, utterly unique; there is positively no danger of buying something here that anyone back home will have. I, too, am a big fan of Mary Beyer (32–33 Galerie de Montpensier / marybeyer.com), and in addition to the other shops mentioned here I also recommend stepping into Dugrenot, a very beautiful *antiquaire-décorateur* founded in 1856 (21–22 Galerie de Montpensier).

BARBARA WILDE, introduced previously, is founder of L'Atelier Vert and writes a Paris Postcard blog, where this piece originally appeared.

FOR ABOUT A month now, I've been reading the complete novels of Colette, in French. At around seventeen hundred finely printed pages, this is quite an undertaking. But unlike some folks who groan or simply shy away from so many pages, I have the opposite reaction. If I find I like the author's writing, I feel a shiver of anticipation that I still have seventeen hundred pages' worth of discovery ahead of me. Plus, I feel a warm rush of being provided for, akin to what you might feel if you were socked in by a blizzard with a well-stocked larder and the firewood piled high and dry. A feeling of coziness and closeness—because nothing is going to come between me and that author for several weeks.

As part of my Colette obsession, I've recently spent a couple of afternoons drifting around the Palais Royal. Colette—born Sidonie Gabrielle Colette—lived in a number of houses during her life, as many as fifteen by some counts, almost all of them relatively humble dwellings chosen by the author for the beauty of their settings or gardens. When a journalist pointed out to her how many times she had moved, she replied that if she could only have an apartment in the Palais Royal, she would never move again. When a fan of hers read this article, he gave up his apartment in the Palais Royal to Colette, who stayed there until her death.

For me, Colette has always been an almost mystical figure of French literature. And now that I'm reading her in French, my fascination has only grown. So on my recent visits to the Palais Royal, I imagined Colette leaning out her window—as she so often de-

Ascension de la Tour Eiffel

scribes in her novels—and observing the quiet ambience that is so particular to the gardens and arcades of the Palais Royal. And I imagine seeing the vast courtyard that is the garden of the Palais Royal through her great, wise gray eyes.

But it's only relatively recently in its long history that the Palais Royal became tranquil. It was conceived tranquilly enough, between the years 1634 and 1639 by then minister Cardinal Richelieu, who wanted a residence near the Louvre where he could easily—by simply crossing his vast garden—minister to the royal family. The cardinal also had a pronounced taste for theater, and an entire wing of the palace was dedicated to theatrical productions. Louis IV, whose father inherited the palace from the cardinal, opened this theater to the public. It was in this theater that Molière acted all his plays and, in a sense, where he died, subsequent to losing consciousness while playing, ironically, *Le Malade imaginaire.* Today, the Théâtre du Palais Royal continues the tradition.

Subsequently, the palace was inhabited by various branches of the royal family and was the scene of many famously decadent parties. It was Philippe Égalité, the grandson of Philippe II of Orléans (regent after the death of Louis XIV), who gave the Palais Royal the atmosphere it still retains today. He lined the arcades with elite shops, which enraged the inhabitants of the palace, who no longer had a direct view of the gardens. He also, from 1786 to 1790, built the theater that became today's Théâtre du Palais Royal.

Then began a long period of upheavals and even violence, during which the Palais Royal witnessed three revolutions and was even partially burned. Poor Philippe Égalité was beheaded in the Palais Royal, and its elegant quarters became a mixture of gambling dens and brothels. It was then seized by the state and for a time harbored the tribunal of commerce and the stock exchange.

When King Louis XVIII was restored to power, he gave the Palais Royal to his cousin, Louis-Philippe, the duke of Orléans, who was also the eldest son of Philippe Égalité. The work he did on the palace gave it the façade we know today. In 1830, he became Louis-Philippe I, king of the *French*—a supposedly more democratic king, as distinguished from the former kings of *France*—and promptly moved to the Tuileries. Eighteen years later, the revolution of February 1848 sacked the Palais Royal and partly burned it. Finally, in 1854 Napoléon III claimed the Palais Royal and installed his uncle Jérôme in residence. After his death, Jérôme's son, Prince Napoléon (known as "Plon-Plon") lived in the palace with his wife, the princess Clothilde. That practically brings us up to the present day!

In 1986, Mitterrand's minister of culture hired Daniel Buren to create a three-thousand-square-meter sculpture of black and white columns in the courtyard of honor of the Palais Royal (at the south end of the gardens). The superposition of this highly contemporary work on such a traditional backdrop still generates controversy today. I don't mind it, actually, and children love playing among the columns.

So why have I bored you with this history lesson? Because I feel it is essential, as you walk under the arcades lining the gardens, to have a sense of the turbulent history of the place. And because it's probably the one place in Paris where you can get a sense of what that quintessential Paris experience—shopping—was like a couple of hundred years ago.

So let's stroll under these arcades, beginning with the entrance at the southwest end of the gardens.

One of the first shops you'll find is Au Duc de Chartres, which carries antique heraldry, medals, and coins. A very appropriate shop for the Palais Royal, don't you think? Just because its contents don't interest me very much doesn't mean this shop isn't heaven for fanatics of such things. I, for one, still enjoy peering through its windows and imagining the sort of people who are passionate about medals from bygone wars!

Perhaps instead of heraldry, you are fascinated by amber—that ancient tree sap metamorphosed into shimmeringly transparent golden yellow stone that sometimes contains insects or other fragments of past life trapped millennia ago in the sticky. La Maison de l'Ambre is a shop devoted exclusively to amber jewelry, with many pieces at affordable prices. So don't hesitate—walk right in!

Not long after La Maison de l'Ambre, you'll find the first of several shops on both sides of the garden belonging to Didier Ludot, Paris's number one purveyor of vintage designer clothing, shoes, bags, and other accessories. This isn't just any old second-hand store—*believe me!* If you're looking for a Chanel suit from the thirties or forties, this is your store. Or visit Ludot's shop, on the other side of the garden, dedicated uniquely to the "little black dress." You'll see examples of the genre from every decade.

All of the Palais Royal shops have a secretive air about them. First, they're inside a garden that is almost completely sealed off from the bustling Paris outside. Second, they're under the arcades,

René Lalique, collier noisettes, vers 1899-1900.

with big windows just made for peering through. But perhaps one shop carries this confidential theme a bit far: a sign in the curtained window just says "*Très confidentiel*" and lists a phone number. I haven't called it.

Just beyond it is a charming shop called L'Escalier d'Argent—the Silver Staircase. Now, just the name of this shop is enough to enchant me. The Silver Staircase offers small antiques and curios, as well as vests for men—very unusual, colorful vests, I might add. Now this is my idea of the perfect Palais Royal shop.

I also passed a shop specializing in antique pipes, both restoration and sales. Now, of course I don't smoke, but I can't help but appreciate that such an unusual shop exists.

The north end of the Palais Royal rectangle contains some jewels, the best known of which is Le Grand Véfour (apparently there used to be a Petit Véfour as well). Who can resist a restaurant that goes back to the late 1700s? Where Colette and Jean Cocteau rubbed elbows, where Sartre smoked and held forth, and before them, Bonaparte and Joséphine? The restaurant has one of the most beautiful interiors of any restaurant in Paris, resplendent with Belle Époque mosaics and frescoes. However many stars Chef Guy Martin may or may not have, according to the whims of the Seigneurs Michelin at the moment, the restaurant is worth an evening simply to soak in the ambience.

Continue along the northern boundary of the garden and you'll come to a narrow passage leading to the street outside, where you'll find two of my favorite three shops of the Palais Royal. First, there's a boutique dedicated to music boxes—nothing but music boxes [at Anna Joliet's]. I had a couple of music boxes as a child, and just catching the delicate strains of their music as someone enters the shop is enough to transport me back to my fascination with them.

Across from Anna Joliet's music boxes is a store called simply the Boutique du Palais Royal—and which is nothing less than the toy store of your—or at least my—dreams. Not one electronic or battery-operated toy mars the array of French-made children's playthings. Surely this is where Santa Claus does his shopping! The back of the store is crammed with beautiful dolls—I found just the baby doll to assuage my granddaughter Charlotte at the arrival of her new sibling, for example. (I'm just waiting to find out whether it's going to be a brother or a sister so I can buy the appropriate doll!) But while I'm waiting for that momentous news, I saw no reason not to send Charlotte some of the other fabulous toys from this store, particularly some of the wondrously imaginative wooden playthings (again, made in France). I bought her two sets of wooden magnets, one of which consists of different flower parts—many-colored petals, stamens, leaves—so she can compose her own French garden.

Turn the corner to descend the east arcade of the Palais Royal, and you'll come across at least two glove shops. I particularly love these shops because they hark back to a time when gloves were worn for elegance—and sex appeal. They were an intrinsic part of feminine mystique, and removing those beautiful, clinging gloves was more sensuous than any strip tease. The first of these shops is the Maison Mary Beyer. Here you'll find gloves that are literally *haute couture*. For instance, check out the fingerless glove, its wrist cloaked in plumes—clearly, we're talking gloves as pure fantasy here. And sorry, guys, this shop has only ladies' gloves. (Although the fantasies are all yours.)

A bit farther along the arcade is the shop of the French glove manufacturer Fabre. While you can find Fabre gloves in the big Paris department stores, you'll never find the full selection of this, their flagship boutique. Fabre makes gloves that are a bit more practical than Mary Beyer's, but still very sexy and *oh so* French. No woolly mittens here, but sleek, supple leathers, each model with its own quixotic touch of French fantasy. The design diversity of Fabre gloves is such a relief from the shopping mall–ified sameness of "designer" labels, whose gloves—like their eyeglasses—are probably all made by the same manufacturer in some

Asian country. In contrast, each pair of Fabre gloves seems to beckon to you, whispering, "Go on . . . express yourself!"

Now—drumroll. . . . I've saved the best for last. Like most gardener/cooks, I have a very sensitive nose and I love fragrances. That said, I find it nearly impossible to find a perfume that pleases me. The synthetic ingredients of today's perfumes are far too aggressive and cloying for me, and my reaction to department store perfume counters is to gag and run away. But in the Palais Royal is the perfume shop of Serge Lutens. Shiseido, which bought the line, has had the wisdom not to interfere with it. These are perfumes as you would have been able to buy more than two hundred years ago—or almost. Rich, subtle blends of natural fragrances, with an accent on the vegetal. Names like Bois de Violette, Chêne—oak, my favorite, evocative of leaves and moss—and Mandarine-Mandarin. These are fragrances that even *I* love to wear. Most are sold in a single formulation—a glass-stoppered flacon priced at 110 euros each.

A couple of modern designer lines—Stella McCartney is one of them—have trampled on the tradition of the Palais Royal's intimate shops by buying up several of them and converting them into one large space. But with those exceptions, the shops of the Palais Royal are a sort of living museum of the past. They evoke an era when "artisan" wasn't a catchy marketing term but simply the norm, an era when refinement, elegance, subtlety, and even idiosyncrasy were the predominant values of commerce.

Then, after you've made your round of the shops, take a stroll out into the garden itself, sit down on a sunny bench, and look up at the blank windows of the apartments lining the garden. Try to imagine the lives past and present within them. Think what it would have been like to inhabit the gardened landscapes so carefully traced and ever present in the novels of Colette. And let your mind take wing on this quote from the period of her life when she lived in the Palais Royal and no longer had a garden of her own: *"Vous n'avez pas de jardin? Moi non plus. Aimons celui que nous inventons.*"—You don't have a garden? Me either. So let's love the one we imagine.

Paris/New York

"Between the world wars, no two cities engaged in a more fertile conversation than Paris, de facto capital of the nineteenth century, and New York, its twentieth-century rival." So states Susan Henshaw Jones, president and director of the Museum of the City of New York, which in 2008–2009 organized a terrific exhibit, Paris/New York: Design, Fashion, Culture 1925–1940. An accompanying book by the same name and edited by Donald Albrecht (Monacelli, 2008) is a worthy guide to this fascinating relationship between the two cities. It's filled with gorgeous color and black-and-white photographs, drawings, and reproductions of artworks; these include some wonderful period photos of Art Deco masterpieces in New York's Bonwit Teller department store and in the Waldorf-Astoria Hotel, and (my favorite) one of Nelson Rockefeller's apartment, complete with a fireplace mural by Fernand Léger. The Paris Exposition of 1925 and the New York World's Fair of 1939 were enormously influential in linking the two cities.

Though the United States didn't participate in the 1925 Paris Exposition, thousands of American tourists visited the fair during its six-month run. Additionally, then secretary of commerce Herbert Hoover named an official commission to inform him "of ideas that would be valuable to American manufacturers," sending three commissioners and more than eighty delegates to represent American arts and architecture in Paris. The 1939 World's Fair, whose theme was "The World of Tomorrow," featured various pavilions and exhibitions celebrating America's industrial and corporate might. France, in contrast, sent its great ocean liner *Normandie* to New York—referred to in the book as "France afloat"—and its pavilion featured a first-class restaurant on the top floor that "brought *haute cuisine* to New York and would prove to be the training ground for the city's renowned post–World War II French restaurateurs." When Paris was invaded by the Nazis not one year later, the close links between Paris and New York were severed. "The relationship between America and France, New York and Paris, had already shifted into a new phase as Paris's role in world political and cultural affairs diminished and New York's expanded."

RECOMMENDED READING

❧

ART DEALERS

As much as I enjoyed the many art history classes I took in college and the many art museums I continue to visit, I find in many cases that even more interesting than the lives of artists of years ago are those of the dealers that represented them. When you see a painting in a museum, for example, there is usually a brief description of the work that includes the date it was completed and perhaps a lengthier story about it. But visitors are not typically informed of the work's provenance—who has owned it over the years since it was painted and how it came to be in the museum's collection. I am utterly *fascinated* with the provenance of artworks, and dealers are of course a big part of an artwork's journey. Just a few reads about legendary dealers are:

An Artful Life: A Biography of D. H. Kahnweiler, 1884–1979, Pierre Assouline (Grove/Atlantic, 1990). Daniel-Heinrich Kahnweiler formed the Bernheim-Jeune Gallery in Paris and represented, among others, Picasso, Braque, André Derain, and Maurice de Vlaminck. The twentieth century had more than one great art dealer, Assouline notes, "but of all those from Kahnweiler's generation who launched themselves on this adventure, he remains the only one whose name is inseparable from a decisive moment in modern art, the 'epic' of Cubism. The most important painters are indebted to this man, the greatest art dealer of his day."

Cézanne to Picasso: Ambroise Vollard, Patron of the Avant-Garde, edited by Rebecca Rainbow and published in conjunction with an exhibit of the same name at the Metropolitan Museum of Art, the Art Institute of Chicago, and the Musée d'Orsay (Metropolitan Museum of Art, 2006). Vollard (1866–1939), according to Philippe de Montebello in the foreword, "was without question the most influential art dealer in Paris at the turn of the twentieth century." Vollard is also particularly interesting because he was an author and a publisher.

MUSEUM GUIDES AND COLLECTIONS

Art Treasures of the Louvre: One Hundred Reproductions in Full Color, René Huyghe with Milton Fox (Abrams, 1951). This is a volume in the *Library of Great Museums* series, which I love. While not meant to be comprehensive, it's a special, selective collection of a variety of objects found at the Louvre. Though out of print, this and other editions in the series are readily found online and in used-book stores.

Artists in Residence: A Guide to the Homes and Studios of Eight 19th-Century Artists In and Around Paris, Dana Micucci with photographs by Marina Faust (Little Bookroom, 2001). This

LES BOURGEOIS DE CALAIS · 1884 · 1895

0091758

MUSÉE RODIN
77, rue de Varenne, 75007 PARIS

wonderful, must-have book comes in its own slipcase, but as it's a slender paperback it can easily be packed and brought along. Micucci notes that to explore artists' homes and studios is "to feel magically part of their history. . . . By visiting their homes, it is our privilege to meet them on terrain that nourishes a personal connection far beyond that afforded by an art museum." In addition to the very informative summaries of each artist's residence, Micucci has provided visitor information and suggestions for dining, accommodations, and short excursions.

A Fuller Understanding of the Paintings at Orsay, Françoise Bayle (Artlys, 2001). This *great* book, available at the Musée d'Orsay, is one of the best of its kind and I wish I had one just like it for about fifty other museums around the world. As Bayle states in the foreword, this publication "is not merely one more among the already numerous books" on the d'Orsay. "It takes a truly different, dual approach. It is a genuine guide that proposes both chronological pages and theme-based comparisons where the eyes of the various painters meet, sometimes glaringly."

Knopf Guides: The Louvre (Knopf, 1995). This book is a little heavy, so it might not be a good candidate to bring along, but I definitely recommend taking a look at it before you depart. Sections include "The Louvre through Visitors' Eyes" and "Origin of the Name Louvre" as well as many on the museum's collections, which have made it the largest museum in the world. Useful chapters also include possible itineraries, maps, and other practical information such as tours, lectures, activities, shopping, and family-oriented options.

Little-Known Museums in and Around Paris, Rachel Kaplan (Harry N. Abrams, 1996). If you are a museumgoer, you'll want and need this handy book. Some of the museums featured really are little known (and deserve to be better known) and the summaries are thorough and interesting. More than thirty museums—including six just outside of Paris, such as the wonderful Musée National de la Renaissance (Château d'Ecouen) and the Château de Monte Cristo—are highlighted and accompanied by ample color photographs.

Paintings in the Louvre, Lawrence Gowing (1994) and *Paintings in the Musée d'Orsay,* Robert Rosenblum (1989), both published by Stewart, Tabori & Chang. These gigantic companion volumes have no rivals when it comes to viewing the museums' paintings in a single volume.

GENERAL ART REFERENCE

There are of course dozens, if not hundreds, of resources for general art surveys, so I'll just share with you some of my favorites. I have consulted all of these below on many occasions.

Angels A to Z: A Who's Who of the Heavenly Host, Matthew Bunson (Three Rivers, 1996). This is a fascinating and useful reference you'll be glad to have, and it includes entries from Abaddon to Zutu'el with numerous black-and-white reproductions. Bunson gives several reasons for the popularity of angels, and explains, "Perhaps most important, throughout history one thought has proven powerfully constant and nearly universally accepted by Jewish writers, Christian saints, Muslim scholars, and followers of the New Age: The angel is one of the most beautiful expressions of the concern of God for all of his creations, an idea beautifully expressed by Tobias Palmer in *An Angel in My House:* 'The very presence of an angel is a communication. Even when an angel crosses our path in silence, God has said to us, "I am here. I am present in your life.'"

Gods and Heroes in Art, Lucia Impelluso (2003), and *Symbols and Allegories in Art,* Matilde Battistini (2005), both published by Getty. These two editions in the *Guide to Imagery* series have color reproductions throughout and note literary sources. I consider them to be essential.

Janson's Basic History of Western Art (Prentice Hall, 2008, eighth edition). *Janson's* was known for many years on every college and university campus and is still a classic for your home library. The original author, Horst W. Janson, passed away in 1982; his son Anthony took over authorship until 2004, and the book now has a new team of authors. There is also a volume for younger readers that is equally worthy.

The Museum Companion: Understanding Western Art, Marcus Lodwick (Harry N. Abrams, 2003). This portable volume is a guide to the biblical and classical subjects found in Western art masterpieces. Entries are alphabetical by name.

The Story of Art, E. H. Gombrich (Phaidon, 1995, sixteenth edition). Although Sir Ernst Gombrich has authored numerous

volumes on art, this is the one that really established his reputation. To quote from the jacket, "*The Story of Art* is one of the
most famous and popular books on art ever published. . . . It
has remained unrivalled as an introduction to the whole subject." Though a comprehensive book, French artists and those
who worked in France are well represented.

What Great Paintings Say, Rose-Marie Hagen and Rainer Hagen
(Taschen, in three volumes). Taken from articles originally
written for the magazine *Art* published in Hamburg, Germany,
these books are gems. The author team doesn't present
overviews of schools or periods of art history; rather, each
painting is introduced separately, almost as if no other existed.
"Pictures are windows," they believe, and "pictures offer adventure. . . . Those who return from a successful journey into a
picture are enriched by the experience." A great number of
works by French artists are included throughout.

FRENCH STYLES AND MOVEMENTS

The Barbizon School and the Origins of Impressionism, Steven Adams
(Phaidon, 1994). An important work highlighting some of the
still relatively unknown painters who greatly influenced the
Impressionists: Charles-Émile Jacque, Théodore Rousseau,
Narcisse Díaz de la Peña, and Georges Michel, followed by
Corot, Courbet, Daubigny, and Millet. These landscape
painters had been going to Barbizon, a small village on the
edge of the Forêt de Fontainebleau, where they forged a path
for the movement nearly fifty years before the word *Impression-
niste* was first uttered in Paris.

Dada: Zurich, Berlin, Hannover, Cologne, New York, Paris (National
Gallery of Art, 2008). Published to accompany an exhibit of

the same name, this is a definitive and leading work that highlights the cities in which the Dada movement excelled. Forty artists are covered, including André Breton, Marcel Duchamp, Man Ray, Tristan Tzara, and Kurt Schwitters.

French Art: Prehistory to the Middle Ages (1994), *The Renaissance, 1430–1620* (1995), and *The Ancien Régime: 1620–1775* (1996), all by André Chastel and published by Flammarion. Chastel was adviser to André Malraux, founder of the French Inventory of Historical Monuments, editor of the prestigious *Revue de l'art et de l'archéologie,* and a professor at the Sorbonne and the Collège de France. With more than four hundred exquisite color illustrations, these are simply the most detailed and most beautiful books on these periods of French art, unmatched in their thoroughness.

The History of Impressionism (1946) and *Post-Impressionism: From Van Gogh to Gauguin* (1956), both by John Rewald and published by the Museum of Modern Art. Rewald's first book was

published to universal acclaim, and he spent the rest of his life revising it in five subsequent editions. *Post-Impressionism* is widely acclaimed as well.

History of the Surrealist Movement, Gérard Durozoi (University of Chicago Press, 2002). This work is astounding in its depth and range, covering the years from 1919 to 1969, the year André Breton died, seen as the end of the movement.

The Judgement of Paris: The Revolutionary Decade That Gave the World Impressionism, Ross King (Walker, 2006). Fans of King's *Brunelleschi's Dome* will also like this in-depth look at the decade between the Salon des Refusés in 1863 and the first Impressionist exhibit in 1874. Though a number of artists are highlighted in this book, two in particular merit the most attention: Jean-Louis-Ernest Meissonier and Édouard Manet. King writes, "to overstate either Meissonier's reputation or his fortune would have been difficult in the year 1863." Meissonier's signature was said to be worth that of the Bank of France. Delacroix declared him "the incontestable master of our epoch," Alexandre Dumas *fils* called him "*the* painter of France," and a newspaper referred to him as "the most renowned artist of our time." But for all his renown and wealth, Meissonier was stuck in the eighteenth century, where he vastly preferred to be: Manet was about as opposite from Meissonier as imaginable. Though he, too, painted from the Old Masters in the Louvre and the Uffizi in Florence, with canvases such as *The Absinthe Drinker* and *Le Bain* he began to portray scenes of modern life. "More than a century after their deaths," writes King, "Meissonier gathers dust in museum storerooms" while Manet maintains his stature among the greats. A fascinating look not only at the art world of the time but at France, especially Paris, during a time of immense change and progress.

ART BOOKS OF RELATED INTEREST

Antoine's Alphabet:Watteau and His World, Jed Perl (Knopf, 2008). I love this little book because in many ways it reminds me of the A to Z Miscellany that appears in every volume of *The Collected Traveler.* Art critic Jed Perl covers items as varied as capriccio, fans, flirtation, London, Gérard de Nerval, and New York City, as well as ornament, party, qualities, religion, and youth, linking painter Jean-Antoine Watteau to each one. Perl brilliantly conveys how influential Watteau (1684–1721) was to numerous painters and writers, and "reaffirms the contemporary relevance of the greatest of all painters of young love and imperishable dreams." After I read this I had a burning desire to stand in front of Watteau's *Gersaint's Shopsign* (in Charlottenburg Palace, Berlin) and *The Holy Family* (in the Hermitage in Saint Petersburg), neither of which I've managed to see yet, unfortunately. I also had a renewed interest in *The Pilgrimage to the Isle of Cythera* in the Louvre (see "Paint the Town," page 445). It took five years for Watteau to complete this magnificent painting, which he submitted to the Royal Academy of Painting and Sculpture as his reception piece. With this work he became known as the painter of *fêtes galantes,* which translates as "gallant parties" and refers to the pursuits of the wealthy that Watteau portrayed so well. The Greek island of Cythera, birthplace of Aphrodite, goddess of love, is the subject of a debate over whether the lovers in the painting are about to set sail for the island or if they are returning. The Louvre's interpretative text panel notes that "without doubt, the mysterious hazy landscape in the distance is one of the most innovative features of the painting, reflecting the influence of the landscapes of Rubens and Leonardo da Vinci."

The Artist in His Studio, Alexander Liberman (Random House, 1988). This unique book is a splendid record of Liberman's visits to a number of artists—thirty-one of them, nearly all of whom were French or worked in France—in the 1940s after the war. He felt compelled to personally meet these artists and take photos in their studios because he feared, if he didn't, there would be no trace of the remarkable flowering of painting and sculpture the first half of the twentieth century had witnessed. No doubt he was also moved to do so by World War II's annihilation and destruction. Color and black-and-white photographs are paired with the text of Liberman's conversations with each artist.

The Banquet Years: The Origins of the Avant-Garde in France, 1885 to World War I, Roger Shattuck (Vintage, 1968). An original and thoroughly fascinating book linking playwright Alfred Jarry, painter Henri Rousseau, musician Erik Satie, and poet Guillaume Apollinaire as a group of artists representing significant aspects of la Belle Époque, or as he refers to it, "the Banquet Years." Shattuck believes that this group best reveals the period, and in this book he explores how the avant-garde took the arts into a period of "astonishingly varied renewal and accomplishment," which would change after the First World War.

Baudelaire's Voyages: The Poet and His Painters, Jeffrey Coven (Bulfinch, 1993). Companion volume to an exhibit of the same name mounted at the Heckscher Museum (Huntington, New York) and the Archer M. Huntington Gallery (University of Texas Austin), this is a unique package that allows for reading Baudelaire's poetry and viewing the art of his contemporaries together. It's the only time I've ever seen, for example, Matisse's *Luxe, calme et volupté* side by side with Baudelaire's "L'invitation au voyage." With sixty-five color and forty-nine black-and-white reproductions featuring Manet, Seurat, Rodin,

Gauguin, Daumier, Delacroix, Jongkind, Goya, Munch, Whistler, and others.

Pleasures of Paris: Daumier to Picasso, Barbara Stern Shapiro (Museum of Fine Arts, Boston/David R. Godine, 1991). Published to accompany an exhibit of the same name, which was organized to investigate the second half of the nineteenth century in Paris, famous as a time of frivolity and pleasure. But it was also a time of social injustice and political and military upheaval. The works of art included—by Manet, Daumier, Tissot, Toulouse-Lautrec, Degas, Renoir, Mucha, Vuillard, Cézanne, Pissarro, Bonnard, Picasso, and others—document both the more pleasant aspects of the period as well as some of its harsher realities.

Portrait of Dr. Gachet: The Story of a Van Gogh Masterpiece, Money, Politics, Collectors, Greed, and Loss, Cynthia Saltzman (Viking, 1998). A remarkable tale tracking the journey of one very famous painting and taking us behind the scenes of the art world and market. Although *Portrait of Dr. Gachet* is not the only work of art to have an interesting and many layered provenance, surely it has one of the most complex. The *Portrait* that hangs in the Musée d'Orsay, is not, as you might expect, the subject of this book. Van Gogh's usual practice was to paint two versions of his portraits, and as the title of the book suggests, one copy has seen quite a life of its own. The *Dr. Gachet* canvas at the center of this book was sold from the artist's estate in 1897, found homes with thirteen owners (one of whom was Hermann Göring, who had it for a brief time in 1938), and was eventually bought at auction in 1990 by Ryoei Saito of Tokyo for $82.5 million, the highest price ever paid at auction for a work of art to that point. Postcript: in August 1999, it was revealed that *Portrait of Dr. Gachet* had left Japan and may have been sold to an American investor.

SINGLE-ARTIST BOOKS

If there are hundreds of books published on general art surveys, there are *thousands* published on individual artists, and *so* very many of them are devoted to French artists. Due to the monumental volume of works, I can be of most help here by alerting you to particular series that are devoted to single artists. You may then easily research which artists you're most interested in, whether stepping into the shallow end of the pool by dabbling here and there or taking a plunge into the deep end, searching for more authoritative volumes. The point, after all, is to inspire you to turn a few pages of art books "to become reacquainted with names other than those of the luminous giants," to quote Kate Simon in *Italy: The Places in Between*.

Discoveries (Harry N. Abrams). Originally published in France by Gallimard, these colorful paperbacks are a terrific value. They're jammed with information, the quality of the reproductions is good, they're lightweight and easy to pack (approximately five by seven inches), and the price is right. *Discoveries* books offer a fairly detailed overview and there are more than one hundred titles in the series, many devoted to French art and artists.

Masters of Art (Harry N. Abrams). The *Masters of Art* series, with more than fifty titles, is great for readers who want a little more than *Discoveries* but not huge coffee-table tomes. Not all titles are still in print, but copies are generally available online. Note generally that Abrams, an early leader in the publication and distribution of art and illustrated books, has a number of quite comprehensive and scholarly titles, and readers who are serious about particular artists should browse its complete title list online (abramsbooks.com).

Pegasus Library (Prestel). *Pegasus* books are mostly hardcover and all beautifully produced. They're a little more scholarly than others and tend to have focused themes, such as *Edgar Degas: Dancers and Nudes, Renoir: Paris and the Belle Époque,* and *Picasso's World of Children.*

The Raft of the Medusa

In the winter of 1818, the Romantic painter Théodore Géricault began work on a large canvas (about twenty-three feet wide and sixteen feet high) that depicted what had by then become a thorn in the side of Louis XVIII and what remains today one of the uglier events in French history. After Napoléon was defeated at Waterloo, the British offered the new French king the port of Saint-Louis, on the coast of Senegal, considered to be an important trading post. A fleet of four ships was readied to take the new French governor of Senegal, Julien Schmaltz, and others—settlers, scientists, and some soldiers who had previously fought for Napoléon—to the port. The ships were the *Loire,* the *Argus,* the *Echo,* and lastly the *Medusa,* which was filled with nearly four hundred men, women, and children, including Schmaltz. The man appointed to lead this flotilla, Hugues Duroy de Chaumareys, had joined the English in the war against the revolutionaries in France and was awarded the post for his loyalty to the crown. He was, by all accounts, little prepared for this journey.

The *Medusa* proved to be the fastest ship, but it ran aground on July 2, 1816, on the Arguin Bank, off the coast of Senegal. Schmaltz suggested that they build lifeboats to transfer everyone to shore, but what transpired instead was that most of the "important" people were put on lifeboats, while almost everyone else (excepting those who elected to stay with the *Medusa*) was put on a crudely constructed raft. As the raft was so heavily overloaded and would overtake the lifeboats if it came close enough, De Chaumareys ordered that it be cut loose. What happened next was nothing short of a nightmare. "Horror after horror ensued," Albert Alhadeff recounts in his excellent book *The Raft of the Medusa: Géricault, Art, and Race* (Prestel, 2002). "When they were rescued thirteen days later, the raft was littered with human flesh, limbs of their fellow mariners waiting to be devoured."

Two survivors, Henri Savigny and Alexandre Corréard, both of whom appear in Géricault's painting next to the mast with the torn sail, wrote *Naufrage de la frégate la Mé-*

duse, which was published in November 1817, followed by an English translation, *A Voyage to Senegal.* Géricault was riveted by the story. He compiled a *"véritable dossier"* on the *Medusa,* "crammed with authentic papers, with documents of all sorts," noted his biographer, Charles Clément. Géricault studied the contents of this file with the greatest care, with "the persistence and minutiae a judge would apply to his docket"; he re-created the story on canvas, which was then exhibited at the Paris Salon on August 25, 1819.

The work created a national embarrassment for the Bourbon dynasty, as Captain de Chaumareys was seen as being associated with the monarchy. French historian Jules Michelet, Alhadeff explains, "saw represented in the painting 'the shipwreck of France.'" In Michelet's words: "It is France itself, it is our whole society that he put to sea on the raft of the *Medusa.*" After the stir caused by the painting, France ultimately reconsidered its involvement in the slave trade, and Schmaltz was dismissed in the summer of 1820.

The Raft of the Medusa, now in the Louvre, is on my short list of the world's most impressive paintings. If you visit the Père-Lachaise cemetery, you'll also find a relief of the painting on Géricault's tombstone. It was his magisterial work, largely synonymous with his name. Interestingly, Alhadeff notes that in 1997 the École Normale Supérieure des Beaux-Arts mounted an exhibition that included not only its numerous Géricault prints and drawings, but also a gigantic reconstruction of the raft. The replica rose more than two stories high and measured eight meters wide. This work was both a tribute to Géricault and a memorial to those lost in the tragedy.

MONUMENTS AND GARDENS

French Gardens: A Guide, Barbara Abbs with photographs by Deirdre Hall (Sagapress, 1994). The author divides this book geographically into four sections: north, the Paris region, the center, and the south; there are forty-one garden and park listings for Paris and the Île-de-France. Each entry includes directions with easy reference to the Michelin road atlas. Many private gardens are open to the public in June and sometimes during the first weekend of the month. These events—known as *journées des portes d'ouvertes*—are worth seeking out at local tourist offices or by using specific Web searches. Additionally, a day (or two) in September is reserved for the Fête des Jardins de Paris, allowing the public to access secluded gardens in the city that are normally closed.

The Garden Lover's Guide to France, Patrick Taylor (Princeton Architectural Press, 1998). This book is undoubtedly a prettier package than *French Gardens* just above—the color photographs help present the beauty and unique highlights of the

more than one hundred private and public gardens featured—though I don't find it as detailed. Taylor has organized the gardens by five regions covering all of France, and Paris and the Île-de-France are well represented. A serviceable map is found at each chapter opener, and there is a glossary of French garden terms at the back of the book.

Notre-Dame of Paris: The Biography of a Cathedral, Allan Temko (Viking, 1952). "The road—every road—has led to this moment and this place. Paris in the thirteenth century was one of the main stopping points in history, like Athens in the fifth century before Christ, and Byzantium in the sixth century after. Each had a social and political lesson for the world; each made the world a gift of architecture: the Parthenon, Sancta Sophia, the western façade of Notre-Dame." So opens one chapter in the most definitive book ever written on Paris's most famous cathedral. With black-and-white photographs, a foldout of the cathedral's plan, cross sections, and a great bibliography.

Doubtless you have your own Paris. It's not geographical; it's the place where life first came vividly to bloom for you, where you couldn't believe the exquisite beauty of the buildings, or the clouds, or the sun that shone after the rain.

—Don George, "Paris on My Mind"

THE SEINE

The Seine, at Paris, is more than beautiful. Poets and neo-impressionists shift their attention to it as the mood strikes. But it is also the main character in the lives of eight million people. Three-quarters of Parisians' drinking water comes from the river. And a lot of their industrial poison and raw sewage empties into it. You do not have to jump off a bridge to commit suicide, one engineer observed. The backstroke is enough.

—MORT ROSENBLUM, *The Secret Life of the Seine*

I could spend my whole life
Watching the Seine flow by . . .
It is a poem of Paris.

—BLAISE CENDRARS

Bridging the Seine

VIVIAN THOMAS

֍

OF COURSE EVERY visitor to Paris notices the Seine, but not every visitor pays the river's bridges the attention they deserve. Each Seine bridge is unique, and collectively the bridges are one of Paris's greatest monuments. Not *every* bridge in Paris is "worth eulogizing," as Eric Maisel aptly puts it in *A Writer's Paris*—many are simply ordinary, no different from bridges back home, nothing more than a way to go. "But a few of Paris's bridges are exceptional. They are worth the airfare and the languid hours I pray you devote to them. They are why you came." I am partial to the Pont des Arts and the Pont Alexandre III, but you will undoubtedly have favorites of your own.

VIVIAN THOMAS, introduced previously, has been an editor at *Where Paris* and is now assistant editor of *France Today*. She contributed numerous articles to the former *Paris Notes*, where this piece originally appeared.

MY HIGH SCHOOL French teacher changed my life one day by drawing a bird's-eye view of a boat on the blackboard. Two more sweeping lines, and the boat was in a river. "Here," she said, tapping her chalk on the boat, "is where Paris began. On the Île de la Cité." As she explained, the top half of the blackboard became the Right Bank, the bottom half the Left. "And this," she said, slicing a diagonal line straight through the boat's sharp prow, from bank to bank, "is the Pont Neuf, the oldest bridge in Paris." Her little drawing and the light that shone in her face as she talked about her favorite city planted the seeds of what would blossom into my lifelong passion for Paris.

Three years later I stood on that bridge, looking out over the island's pointed prow. I had stepped right into her picture, and ever since, I've had a special attachment to the island and its bridges.

No one knows exactly when a Gallic tribe called the Parisii first settled on the wooded island that would become Paris. But by 52 BC, they had already built between the island and the left bank of the Seine a five-arched wooden bridge that Julius Caesar found as he traveled south, seeking the shortest route from today's Amiens to Sens.

His decision to establish a camp in the village he called Lutetia Parisiorum reflected its strategic location, at the crossroads of the north-south trail he was traveling and the east-west water route of the Seine. The Parisii later fought the Romans but lost, and on fleeing the island burned the bridge behind them.

That first bridge, destroyed and rebuilt many times, became known as the Petit Pont when a second one, the Grand Pont, was built to the Right Bank, across the river's larger channel. Paris would have two bridges for over thirteen hundred years.

During the Gallo-Roman period, the city spilled over onto the Left Bank, only to retreat to the island again during the barbarian invasions. But by the end of the Middle Ages, Paris was booming. The swampy Right Bank was drained and cultivated, monasteries and abbeys were flourishing, and the city boasted ten bridges by the mid-1600s.

Parisians were not only crossing those bridges, but they were living and working on them. Houses and shops lined most of them, while beneath several bridges the Seine turned both huge waterwheels that supplied the city's water and noisy millstones that ground grain for its bread. Businesses flourished on bridges;

first fishermen, tanners, and millers, later luxury merchants like jewelers, booksellers, and *parfumeurs.* A bridge address became the pinnacle of chic.

The *ponts* were also lucrative sources of revenue for their builders. Before Colbert created the Ponts et Chaussées in 1716, not all bridges were financed by the state (or by the city, as they are today). The Church built some, recovering construction costs and making a profit from tolls. And developers built others. For instance, Christophe Marie built the Pont Marie in exchange for the right to sell lots on what is now the Île Saint-Louis.

The nineteenth century saw some twenty-one bridges built or reconstructed, many as a result of Haussmann's sweeping reconfiguration of the city. Today there are thirty-one *ponts routiers* and three *passerelles,* or footbridges (not counting Métro and railroad bridges), giving Paris one of the greatest densities of bridges in the world.

Every bridge in Paris has its own special charm. But some of my favorites are those that encircle the city's historic heart. Linking the Île de la Cité and the Île Saint-Louis to the rest of Paris, each one offers views worth stopping for. A walk around the islands, an easy and enjoyable promenade, is a perfect way to make their acquaintance.

Anyone who has opened a guidebook knows that the Pont Neuf (New Bridge) is the city's oldest. But when Henri IV inaugurated it in 1607, it was new in more ways than one. Its size was remarkable: the first bridge to straddle both branches of the Seine, it is still one of Paris's largest bridges. It was also the only stone bridge from which you could actually see the water, since it was never lined with houses. And it delighted Parisians by giving them the city's first sidewalks, separating them from the carriages and horsemen of the muddy roadway.

From the very beginning, the bridge became the heart of the city and the center of Paris street life. Part marketplace and part circus, it was the place to go to buy the latest ballad or bestseller, watch a medicine show, have a tooth pulled, or join the army. Each of the semicircular alcoves held a boutique; roving peddlers hawked their wares, musicians played and passed the hat, and purse-snatchers stalked the unwary in the noisy, colorful throng. Every so often, a royal procession would pass on the way from the Louvre to Saint-Germain.

Henri IV, who still reigns over the bridge in the form of a bronze equestrian statue facing the Place Dauphine, would doubtless be pleased to see the attention his bridge is getting today. A massive project to repair and strengthen it is at the same time artistically restoring this architectural treasure. It started with a nationwide search for materials, since the original sixteenth-century quarries are now closed. Once matching stones were found, master stonemasons began shaping and placing each stone, replacing worn and damaged sections. The 384 grotesque masks, nineteenth-century replacements for the originals, are also being cleaned and restored—no easy task, since no two *mascarons* are alike.

The result is resplendent. Now that the *petit bras,* or Left Bank segment, has been renovated, its gleaming white stone contrasts dramatically with the unfinished part, and the bridge looks new again. No wonder the bridge's name has entered the French language as a simile for ageless vigor (How is your father these days? *Solide comme le Pont Neuf!*)

Crossing the bridge to the Right Bank and turning right on the Quai de la Mégisserie, you pass the spot where the original Grand Pont once stood. Its exact site is unclear: some historians place it at the site of the Pont au Change, others at the Pont Notre-Dame. Both bridges may have been called the Grand Pont at different times. But the name Grand Pont had disappeared by the fifteenth century.

The Pont au Change is named for the moneychangers of Paris, ordered by Louis VII in 1441 to conduct business on this bridge. On Sundays, the fowlers of Paris held their live-bird market on the bridge, and to pay for the privilege, released flocks of white pigeons to celebrate royal entries into the city.

By the fifteenth century, the Pont Notre-Dame was known for its booksellers and armorers. Here, the spirit of the Italian Renaissance arrived when an architect from Verona built Paris's first stone-arch bridge, an elegant affair lined with identical arcaded brick houses. A subsequent version of this bridge caused so many boat accidents that it earned the nickname "Pont du Diable." Now one metal arch—flanked by two stone arches remaining from the 1853 bridge—spans the river.

Leading to the Place de l'Hôtel-de-Ville, the Pont d'Arcole is a serene-looking green iron bridge with a tumultuous history. It was built as a suspension footbridge in 1828, just in time for the 1830 Revolution. One story about its name is that a young revolutionary, under fire from the Hôtel de Ville, ran onto the bridge and planted the flag atop one of its towers, crying out before dying, "Remember, my friends, my name is Arcole!" A less romantic story is that it was named for Napoléon's 1796 victory over the Austrians. Whichever is correct, the bridge's destiny seems linked to war. It saw heavy fighting during the Commune in 1871 and, more happily, was the route the first troops of the Liberation took to the Hôtel de Ville in August 1944.

The Pont Louis-Philippe, named for the king who laid its first stone in 1833, leads to one of the loveliest spots in Paris, the Île Saint-Louis. Cross this bridge to the island, turning left onto the Quai de Bourbon, where splendid *hôtels particuliers* face the river.

First developed in the early seventeenth century by Christophe Marie, the largely residential Île Saint-Louis-boasts Paris's second-oldest bridge, named the Pont Marie after its builder. Completed in 1635, the bridge looks much the same today as it did when Paris's newly rich flocked here to build mansions that displayed their wealth. When part of it collapsed in 1658, twenty houses fell into the river and sixty lives were lost, a tragedy that led to the law banning all construction on the city's bridges. The Pont Marie's stone arches are decorated with empty niches complete with columns and pointed roofs, poignant reminders of the vanished houses.

Like the Pont Neuf, the Pont de Sully straddles both channels of the Seine. In the middle is a lovely garden, the last vestige of the former Hôtel de Bretonvilliers. This little park leads to the island's tip and a view of the busy east end of the Seine. This same bridge also has a traffic light for boats. To see it, cross to the Left Bank, turn left onto the Quai Saint-Bernard, and look back at the bridge's center arch. The Right Bank channel here is reserved for passenger craft; others must use the Left Bank side, and only at specific times. The light turns green for fifteen minutes every hour, from thirty-five to fifty minutes after the hour.

Retracing your steps, continue on the *quai* past the Pont de Sully to the next bridge, the Pont de la Tournelle. The original bridge, built in 1370, was the city's third (after the Petit Pont and Grand Pont). It was named for a turret of the twelfth-century city wall that stood near it. Today's graceful span dates from 1924, and its most notable feature is Paul Landowski's soaring white statue of Sainte Geneviève, keeping watch over Paris as she did here in 451, when her prayers protected the city from Attila.

If you take the steps down from the Pont de la Tournelle behind Sainte Geneviève, you'll find yourself at water level. From this wide quay, you can look between the islands to the bridge that joins them, the Pont Saint-Louis, a simple metal bridge that does not distract from the sight of Notre-Dame. But the best view of the cathedral is from the next bridge, the Pont de l'Archevêché; the classic view of its lovely curved nave and soaring flying buttresses.

The water-level promenade between the Pont de l'Archevêché and the Pont Saint-Michel is a magical place for bridge lovers. The traffic and energy of the city above seem very far away, the river is so narrow that the scale is very intimate, and your feet are almost in the water. Walking under the bridges gives you a new perspective—you can hear the soft splash of the river and feel its cool breath. And these bridges are so close together that at one point, the greenish copper arch of the Pont au Double frames the golden stone of the Petit Pont, which in turn reveals the Pont Saint-Michel's pale arch.

The history of the Pont au Double is closely linked to that of the charity hospital, the Hôtel-Dieu. When that establishment had run out of space and patients were crowded four to a bed, it received permission to build a wing that spanned the river. A two-story structure was built, and when Parisians asked if they could use the hospital's passageway to avoid the Petit Pont's traffic jams, officials recognized a moneymaker and started charging a toll. Horsemen paid double, hence the bridge's name. The hospital bridge and its replacement lasted until 1847, although the toll was abolished during the Revolution. Today's metal span dates from 1883.

Small, of course, the Petit Pont is great in historical importance, since a bridge of the same name has stood on its site for at least two thousand years. It was here that Caesar found the bridge he described in his *Commentary on the Gallic War*. And although centuries of building have widened and raised the Île de la Cité (only the Square du Vert-Galant at its tip shows the original level), today's Petit Pont is still, at 106 feet long, the shortest of Paris's bridges.

The Pont Saint-Michel, first built by prison labor in 1387, is the last of the island bridge circuit. Bridges on this spot have been lost to floods, ice, and boat accidents. Today's stone span dates from the Haussmann era, and as you pass under it the arch frames a lovely view of the sparkling new Pont Neuf.

The island bridges are just the first chapter in the saga of Parisian *ponts*. Beyond the Pont Neuf lie some of Paris's most beautiful bridges. There may be no more romantic bridge in the world than the graceful Pont des Arts, especially in the soft golden light of evening. The seventeenth-century Pont Royal is a dignified *monument historique,* while for sheer theatricality there's the Pont Alexandre III, its baroque splendor a fitting frame for the gilded dome of the Invalides.

And the bridge story is still being written. Jean Tiberi, the city's mayor from 1995 to 2001, made the beautification of the Seine a special mission. His ambitious program produced the Passerelle Léopold-Sédar-Senghor (formerly known as Passerelle Solférino) in 1999, bridging the Tuileries Gardens with the Left Bank, and initiated the project for another footbridge, the Passerelle Simone-de-Beauvoir near the Bibliothèque Nationale, which was completed in 2006. He also launched the project for the Seine promenade, an uninterrupted seven-mile riverwalk that will eventually make the river, its banks, and its bridges more accessible than ever.

So the next time you're in Paris, give the bridges more than a passing glance. Look at them, linger on them, lean on them a moment to watch the Seine roll by. This is where it all began, and there has never been a better time to discover, or rediscover, the bridges of Paris.

Boats

As the Seine flows right through the middle of Paris, it is impossible to avoid crossing over it, walking alongside it, viewing it from atop a monument or hill, or even riding upon it in a boat. To me, a Seine cruise is one of the most supreme pleasures of Paris, even if it's just for a short commute (some lucky Parisians really do get to work each day by boat). The best known, and oldest, of the tourist boats are the long, flat Bateaux-Mouches. The origins of these curiously named vessels come not from Paris but Lyon. In the nineteenth century, small boats that carried passengers on the Rhône and the Saône rivers were built in a part of town popularly known as Mouche—apparently the first engines on these boats made a whining sound like flies, or *mouches,* so the name stuck. Today in Paris visitors may choose between the Bateaux-Mouches (bateaux-mouches.fr), Bateaux Parisiens (bateauxparisiens.com), and Batobus (batobus.com). Not all of them operate year-round, nor traverse the same route, so check the details in a current guidebook, at the Paris tourist office, or on the Internet. They also differ in price, the Bateaux-Mouches being the most expensive. I prefer night-time trips, when all the monuments along the Seine are illuminated (generally until midnight during the week and a bit later on weekends). If possible, avoid the dinner cruises—the food tends to be mediocre and overpriced, and besides, these trips need no embellishment.

A Paris Afternoon

"No matter how many times you go to Paris, there is always something new to discover and savor. My husband, Lester, and I have been to Paris twenty, maybe twenty-five, times since our first visit in 1959. We often go during the last week in May to catch the first few days of the grand-slam French Open at Roland Garros stadium in the Bois de Boulogne. Last year, the two days we had tickets to the tennis tournament were broiling hot the first day and cold and rainy the second day. The next day we woke up to sunny blue skies. I felt like doing something outdoors and something that wouldn't require much energy—I was still a little jet-lagged and feeling a bit under the weather. We decided to have a picnic on the Seine and just take it easy.

"We picked up a couple of ham and Gruyère sandwiches on baguettes, some fresh apricots and cherries, and a bottle of water near our hotel in the Marais. We contemplated buying a bottle of wine but decided it wouldn't be a good idea with a Paris Opéra performance on the agenda for seven that evening. It was a short walk to the Île Saint-Louis and across to the Right Bank on the Pont de la Tournelle, from which the rear view of Notre-Dame with its magnificent flying buttresses and slender spire is one of my favorite sights in Paris.

"At the bottom of the ancient stone stair we walked along the river path in the direction of the next bridge, Pont de Sully, until we saw a grassy green knoll under a tree next to the retaining wall. We settled down there and had our picnic as we watched the Bateaux-Mouches and the working barges sail by, so close you felt like you could almost touch them. Suddenly two models, a bride and a groom, and a photographer with two assistants and various photographic equipment emerged from under the bridge and began posing and shooting the models with Notre-Dame in the background. They appeared to be Japanese, so we assumed the shoot was for a Japanese magazine. Then two young Parisians strolled by and stopped, as if on cue by the late street photographer Robert Doisneau, to entertain us with a passionate kiss. Meanwhile, as the afternoon wore on, our grassy picnic spot began attracting more than just us: A young woman reclined, I thought to take a nap, but she proceeded to carry on a long cell phone conversation, punctuated with many interjections of "*Mais oui.*" A family with a little boy made bubbles with a "magic" wand. A man arrived on his bicycle with a trumpet that he proceeded to play— jazz—and apparently for his own enjoyment, as when he finished he cycled off without passing his hat. A large family spread out their mouthwatering picnic treats on a stone bench and proceeded to gesticulate, shout, and eat all at once—no small feat. An elderly couple's cocker spaniel found our tree especially attractive.

"Eventually I opened the *International Herald Tribune* and began doing the crossword puzzle, until I dozed off. When I woke, we strolled back to our hotel feeling we had just experienced a wonderful afternoon. And it was absolutely free."

—Janet Schulman, former editor at large,
Random House Children's Books,
and former publisher, Random House
and Knopf Books for Young Readers

RECOMMENDED READING

Coming Down the Seine, Robert Gibbings (Dutton, 1953; Interlink, 2003). First published in 1953, this new edition includes Gibbings's original black-and-white engravings of Seine scenes. This is noteworthy since "however good his writing was, Robert Gibbings was primarily an artist and he attached equal importance to the wood-engraved illustrations in his books," Martin Andrews informs us in the 2003 foreword. Andrews believes Gibbings's love for *la France profonde*—the France of small villages, cafés, and good food—"will be shared by many modern-day readers, and for this reason, as well as for its delightful illustrations, this book should be essential reading for travellers in France today." I wholeheartedly agree, and I think you will share my opinion that this is a lyrical love letter to the river that has played a vital role in the history of France.

River of Light: Monet's Impressions of the Seine, Douglas Skeggs (Knopf, 1987). In this beautiful and interesting book, Skeggs presents a portrait of Monet and his lifelong connection to the Seine, but this is as much a story of the river as it is of Monet. As Skeggs writes in an early chapter, "The river Seine was Monet's landscape, his subject, and his home. The lessons that he learned from painting its water inadvertently altered the course of the arts. The vision that he imposed on it is still with us today." Chapters focus on different geographic points along the river, such as Sainte-Adresse, Paris, La Grenouillère, Argenteuil, Vétheuil, and Giverny, with nearly 150 reproductions of Monet's paintings and period photos.

The Secret Life of the Seine, Mort Rosenblum (Addison-Wesley, 1994). "There is not a river like it in the world," writes Rosenblum of the Seine, and he reveals just how unique it really is in this truly marvelous and engaging book. Rosenblum spent many years as a journalist in Paris, starting out at the Associated Press and eventually becoming editor in chief of the *International Herald Tribune.* He's written several other books on French-related topics that I've mentioned in these pages. Rosenblum's expert reporting sense is abundantly clear as he traces the Seine from its source, in Burgundy, to its mouth, at Le Havre, providing us along the way with a historical and present-day perspective on the river and the communities it serves. The geographic term for a river that flows into a sea is *fleuve,* he notes, but for the people who live and work on the Seine the river has always been just *la rivière,* which technically refers to inland waterways. He should know, as he lives aboard a fifty-four-foot boat moored in the center of Paris—talk about a room with a view!

Sundays by the River, Willy Ronis (Smithsonian Institution Press, 1999). Strolling or picnicking near water—oceans, rivers, lakes, streams, tributaries of any length—is a time-honored tradition in France. Sunday mornings and afternoons are still often reserved for this pastime, by residents and visitors alike. This favored *loisir* (leisure activity) is captured in this book by noted documentary photographer Willy Ronis. The forty-eight duotone images featured span nearly half a century, and they're reminiscent of scenes from Impressionist paintings.

Île de Chatou

When my friend Jay entered the room housing Renoir's *Déjeuner des canotiers* (*Luncheon of the Boating Party*) at the Phillips Collection (phillipscollection.org) in Washington, D.C., he actually gasped: he was simply unprepared for the effect this wonderful painting would have when seen up close. It is wildly popular, and long one of my favorites as well. Its history, including its acquisition by Duncan Phillips, is rather interesting. According to Susan Vreeland in her wonderful novel *Luncheon of the Boating Party* (Viking, 2007), Renoir finished the painting in 1881 and soon after it was purchased by the noted art dealer Paul Durand-Ruel, a champion of the Impressionists. Durand-Ruel sold it to a Parisian collector, but then reacquired it in 1882. Though originally against Renoir's wish, the painting was shown at the seventh Impressionist exhibition in March 1882, and also in London, Zurich, and New York, but was never shown at the Salon. In 1923, Duncan Phillips and his wife, Marjorie, were in Paris on an art-buying trip for what was then the Phillips Memorial Gallery. Duncan and Marjorie were invited to a lunch at the apartment of Joseph Durand-Ruel, son of Paul. According to the Phillips museum publication *Duncan Phillips Collects: Paris Between the Wars,* the couple, seated directly across the room from the painting, were so transfixed that the question of its purchase was not "if" but "how much." Just how much was soon revealed to be $125,000, a record price, even though it far exceeded Duncan's acquisitions account. But Duncan believed the painting would be a "cornerstone" of the museum and he bought it anyway. He explained to museum treasurer Dwight Clark that it was "one of the greatest paintings in the world . . . finer than any Rubens . . . as fine as any Titian or Giorgione. [It] will put us on the map as a collection of modern art second to none anywhere."

I absolutely love books devoted to single works of art, so I was thrilled when Scala published *Renoir: Luncheon of the Boating Party* (2003) in its *4-Fold* series, a great concept with

The Phillips Collection, Washington, D.C.

pages that fold out vertically and horizontally. A who's who of the figures in the painting reveals that painter Gustave Caillebotte is among the lively group on the terrace of the restaurant La Maison Fournaise, along with Charles Ephrussi, Baron Raoul Barbier, Aline Charigot—the seamstress Renoir met in 1880 and married ten years later—and Alphonsine and Alphonse Fournaise, daughter and son of the restaurateur, Alphonse Sr. The book refers to the work as "a clear attempt to match the achievement of some of the old masters Renoir admired in the Louvre"—notably Veronese's *Wedding at Cana* and Watteau's *Pilgrimage to the Isle of Cythera*—and "a *fête champêtre* set in a modern industrialized world."

La Maison Fournaise began on the Île de Chatou, a small island in the Seine just west of Paris, in 1857, when Alphonse realized there was an opportunity to cater to all the visitors the expanded railroad had brought to Chatou, beginning twenty years earlier. The train enabled working-class Parisians, who worked a six-day workweek with only Sundays free, to buy an inexpensive round-trip ticket to the Seine suburbs of Chatou, Argenteuil, Asnières, and Bougival. Alphonse started by renting out small boats and added a restaurant and hotel in 1860. La Grenouillère, the restaurant and swimming establishment in Bougival (made famous in paint by both Monet and Renoir), by this time had begun to be too crowded. Visitors looked farther afield to Fournaise. In 1877 a terrace and balcony were added, and Alphonse Jr. took over its operation in 1890. By the time he passed away in 1900, bicycling had outpaced boating as an attraction, but Alphonsine continued to run the restaurant until 1906. She offered lodging until she died in 1937, leaving La Maison Fournaise to cousins. In 1953 the property

was sold and became an apartment building; it fell into disre-
pair and was purchased by the town of Chatou in 1979.
After a lengthy renovation, it reopened in 1990 and, somewhat remarkably perhaps, La Maison Fournaise remains
much the same.

Chatou, which has been renamed the Île des Impression-
nistes, is easy to reach by car, RER, bus, and river transport.
Check out the Maison Fournaise Web site (restaurant
-fournaise.fr) for directions and more about its history, and
to compare before and after pictures of the restoration.

When crossing the Seine I repeat to myself: "My God, how beautiful Paris is!" as if I were the first one to say it. Beside Tarascon, I don't know where else I could live!

—Inès de la Fressange, *Paris*

GÉNÉRAL LECLERC
MARÉCHAL DE FRANCE

1944 - 1969
XXVᵉ ANNIVERSAIRE
DE LA LIBÉRATION
DE PARIS

PERSONALITIES

God invented Parisians so that foreigners would be unable to understand the French.

—ALEXANDRE DUMAS

Actually, it was the people, the streets, the life that brought me back to the city of the Seine. Above all, the people. They make the streets; they make the life; they make Paris. It should be obvious, but it isn't. "How," Gertrude Stein once asked, "can foreigners say they like France but not the French? It's the French who made the France they like—and keep it that way."

—JOSEPH BARRY, *The People of Paris*

The Master of the Machine

JOHN RUSSELL

ᎦᏃᏉ

THE MUSÉE NATIONAL Fernand Léger (musee-fernandleger.fr), in Biot, on the Côte d'Azur, is an excellent museum I recommend highly. There aren't a great number of works by Léger in Paris, but there are some to be found, notably at the Centre Pompidou (centrepompidou.fr), which holds a number of Léger works in its permanent collection. Not surprisingly, as Léger lived in exile in New York from 1940 to 1945, the Museum of Modern Art (moma.org) has some of Léger's most significant paintings. Readers wanting to delve further into the works of Léger may be interested in *Fernand Léger* (Museum of Modern Art, 2002) by Carolyn Lanchner, a former curator of painting and sculpture at MoMA, whose text accompanies each of the book's thirty-five color plates, and *Fernand Léger: Paris–New York* (Hatje Cantz, 2008) by Yve-Alain Bois and other contributors, which focuses on Léger's influence on major American artists, including Jasper Johns, Ellsworth Kelly, Roy Lichtenstein, Robert Rauschenberg, Frank Stella, and Andy Warhol.

JOHN RUSSELL was art critic for the *Sunday Times* of London and chief art critic for the *New York Times* from 1982 to 1990. He was also the author of *Paris* (Harry N. Abrams, 1983, 1994), *Reading Russell: Essays 1941–1988 on Ideas, Literature, Art, Theater, Music, Places, and Persons* (Harry N. Abrams, 1989), a number of monographs on artists such as Georges Seurat, Francis Bacon, Henry Moore, and Max Ernst, as well as *The Meanings of Modern Art* (Icon, 1991, revised edition), among others. Russell was renowned for avoiding the scathing form of art criticism and preferred to simply share his enthusiasm with his readers. As he wrote in *Reading Russell,* "It has never seemed to me much of an ambition to go through life snarling and spewing." His obituary in the *New York Times* in 2008 noted that art, for Russell, "remained a glorious love affair and a lifelong adventure. 'When art is made new, we are made new with it,' he wrote in the first volume of *The Meanings of Modern Art.* 'We have a sense of solidarity with our own time, and of psychic energies shared and redoubled, which is just about the most satisfying thing that life has to offer.' "

EVERY SO OFTEN there surfaces in art an image that is so compelling, so absolutely true to one particular moment in history, that it puts the historians out of business. One such image is evoked by *The Mechanic,* Fernand Léger's painting of 1920 that fixes once and for all the idea that the life of the industrialized masses need not be without dignity, nor the individual mass-man turned into a disinherited cipher.

Léger believed this, with all his heart. If he makes us believe it, too, it is because he was not only a master of plain statement but a man to whom doubt and compromise and equivocation were abhorrent. He believed that the conveyor belt and the assembly line had changed life for the better, and that the industrialized working man would have his full share of the benefits of his hard work. It was a matter of faith with him that the mechanic was the New Man, the man for whom the machine was not a tyrant but the instrument of social liberation.

This could have led to a sententious, Stalin-type imagery of the Heroic Worker. But Léger's mechanic is not at all like that, despite his bulging muscles. He is a man with a mind of his own. No faceless abstraction, he is distinctively a Frenchman of the 1920s, with his nautical tattoo, his sleeked-down hair and heavy mustache, his cigarette at the ready and rings on his well-fleshed finger. But there is also something very grand and quite timeless about him. Léger in 1919 had been in and out of the newly re-opened Egyptian and Assyrian rooms in the Louvre, and he gave his mechanic a look of ancient art in the severe frontal pose of the torso and the right-angled turn of the head on the neck. The mechanic meets us both head-on and in profile, as he might in an Assyrian relief.

Behind him, in terms of geometric flat planes and brilliant color, is the ideal place of work: the factory that never was. Looking at the casquelike cut of his forehead and cheekbones, we see immediately that this man is at one with his machines and could wish for no greater fulfillment than to be in charge of them.

Léger himself was not of industrial origins, and he never in his life worked in a factory. The son of a cattle breeder, he was born in 1881 and grew up on his father's farm in Normandy. His father was a giant of a man, and quick to come to blows when crossed. If he had not died suddenly while Fernand was still in school, there would never have been any question of his son being allowed to stray from the family business. Léger got started in Paris as an art student in 1903 and made a meager living as an architect's draftsman, to begin with, and as a retoucher for a portrait photographer. He impressed his friends in Paris by the inherited solidity of his build; with his abundant red hair, his countrified freckles, and his general air of rude health and good spirits, he was very much the farmer's son.

His was an accepting nature. He took change for granted, and welcomed it. That a new world should produce a new kind of art seemed to him not merely natural but axiomatic. Old-style aesthetes might wince to see red and yellow billboards set up among the halftones of the French countryside; Léger thought it was the best thing that could happen. New sights, new idioms, and new responses were what he lived by. "Modern man," he said in 1914, "has to take in a hundred times as many impressions as came his way in the eighteenth century. Is it surprising that our language is full of diminutives and abbreviations? If modern paintings are highly condensed, and if the forms with them are taken apart and redistributed, it's for the same reason."

Léger by that time was a friend of poets like Apollinaire and Cendrars, and a friend and prized colleague of painters like Robert Delaunay and Le Douanier Rousseau. Like Picasso, Braque, Derain, Vlaminck, and Juan Gris, he showed his work in Paris at D. H. Kahnweiler's little gallery near the Madeleine. He stood apart from the others, even so, in that when he tried his hand at a major work—the *Nudes in the Forest* of 1909–10—he instinctively chose a subject that involved people at work: naked woodsmen hacking away at tree trunks. It was a difficult, gloomy, almost monochromatic painting: the result of a long struggle, a "battle of volumes" as he said himself, to build the third dimension on flat canvas. "I wasn't ready for color," he said later.

Yet color was fundamental to modern life. The dynamic of that life, said Léger, was on the side of the poster in the street and the advertisement that lit up at night. "Post No Bills" was a ridiculous formula, well worthy of the society that sponsored it. "It's the taste of the middle class that's against posters," he went on. "The peasant is made of stronger stuff. Look how he likes a strong contrast of color in his clothes! A man like that isn't going to be scared by a billboard in a meadow."

Machinery had new color, too. Léger never forgot how he went to a pioneer aviation show in Paris with Marcel Duchamp and Brancusi. As they walked among the prehistoric aircraft, with their exposed machinery and huge wooden propellers, Duchamp grew more and more silent. Suddenly he said: "Painting's finished. How can we possibly compete with those propellers?" "I preferred the motors, myself," Léger would say as he told the story, "but then I always preferred metal to wood."

Léger had his fill of metal when he was drafted into the French army in 1914. Both as an artilleryman, from 1914 to 1916, and later as a stretcher bearer on the Verdun front, he saw as much as anyone of the horrors of war. But he never discussed them. What moved him was the human quality of his fellow soldiers and the immediate, unaffected beauty of the guns that he had to fire. He had been on the very edge, in 1912 and 1913, of a purely abstract art: an art based on contrasted forms that had no reference to the visible world. No sooner was he in the army than activity of that kind began to seem to him both petty and futile.

"There I was," he said later, "on an equal footing with the totality of the French people. My new comrades were miners, laborers, metalworkers, woodcutters. . . . What faces they had! What a shrewd, lively, and completely down-to-earth understanding of everything that went on! They were true poets in their everyday speech, so vivid and so inventive in their slang. And then the sight of the open breech of a 75mm cannon! The magic of the light on that white metal! One taste of all that, and I forgot about abstract art."

Léger was gassed at Verdun, and at the end of 1917 he was let out of the hospital and discharged from the army. But to the day of his death, in 1955, he never forgot the strength, the endurance, the total realism, the quick wit, and the uncomplaining good sense of his comrades-in-arms. Nor did he stop believing that civilian life would one day reward them for their offhand and undeceived heroism. If his paintings could bring that day nearer, or if they could indicate the conditions in which it would come about, so much the better. He was, however, very careful at the start not to sentimentalize the working man, or to assign him a more important place in the cities of the future than he would actually occupy.

In the great metropolitan paintings that Léger produced in 1919 and 1920—above all, in *The City*—human beings play a subordinate part. Objects among other objects, they are not individualized: individuality was kept for moments when, as in *The Mechanic,* the working man was off duty and could smoke a cigarette. But he was not diminished, in Léger's eyes, by his objecthood. Rather, it raised him to the same level—that of a functional elegance, a stripped-down beauty without precedent—that was the mark of every other element in the new metropolitan scene.

Not everyone, of course, looked with such favor on the first machine age. In the early 1920s Karl Čapek's *R.U.R.* was welcomed in theaters all over the world for its defeatist preview of robot society. In 1932 René Clair's *À nous la liberté* was enormously popular for its portrait of the dehumanizing effect of industrialization. Chaplin's *Modern Times* (1936) is a further and definitive example of this same disenchantment. But Léger did not stand alone in his optimistic approach to the problems of the postwar world. In the social strivings of the 1920s the machine had a fundamental, and it was hoped a benevolent, part to play.

Léger made new friends who agreed with him on these issues—especially the great architect Le Corbusier, who in 1925 gave him his first opportunity as a mural painter. Léger also involved himself in filmmaking, stage design, and book illustration. He had a sure instinct for the people with whom it would be most worthwhile to collaborate: Darius Milhaud in music, André Malraux as a beginner in literature, Abel Gance and Man Ray in the cinema. What he did in association with them reached, as often as not, only a small audience, but he never quite lost the expansionist dream—the notion of a world in which art would be for everyone and everyone would be for art.

By 1924, it seemed to him as though that world was almost in sight, if only people would acknowledge it. There was no limit to the potential of the machine as a creator of beauty. There was no reason why, not only the shopwindows and billboards, but the entire architecture of the city street should not be a carnival for the eye. The automobile shows of the mid-1920s would have emptied the museums and bankrupted the theaters, in Léger's view, if it were not for what he called "the hierarchical prejudice." "*There are no hierarchies in art,*" he said over and over again; it was for the skilled craftsman to realize that what he produced was more beautiful than most of what people went to see in the Louvre.

The role of color in all this was primordial, and Léger never lost an opportunity of listing the benefits that would follow from the liberation of color in everyday life. He told Trotsky about them, when he and Trotsky met in Montparnasse during World War I. He told his students about them, when he lectured at Yale in 1938. And, quite rightly, he took a great pride in the fact of his own influence in the matter. "In 1919, I painted *The City* with pure colors laid flat on the canvas. It was a revolutionary step. I proved that a painter could discard chiaroscuro and discard modulation and yet still have depth in the picture. The advertising agencies soon took my point. My pure blues and reds and yellows were lifted from *The City* and put to work in posters and store windows, and by the side of the road, and in signals of every kind. Color had been set free. It was a reality in itself. It could act in itself and by itself, independently of all the objects which had previously had to contain or to carry it. . . ."

Léger had been to the United States for the first time in 1931. By October 1940, when he arrived there as a refugee, he knew his way around. Adaptable by nature, he thoroughly enjoyed himself in New York, and in the country near Lake Champlain, and even at La Guardia Field, where he liked to watch the aircraft come and go. He was polite and constructive in all his comments on America, and he acknowledged that certain of his dreams for society as a whole had been fulfilled there: in the spectacle of New York by night, for example. But he was quick to get back to France, in the winter of 1945, and once there, he set about renewing his lifelong love match with the French working class. He also let it be known that he had joined the French Communist Party.

It would be difficult at the present time to find a more conservative body of men—one more dependent, that is, on the status quo—than the French Communist Party. (This was made particularly clear in May 1968, when it was palpable to all that the last thing the French Communists wanted was to get power.) But in 1945 Léger thought quite sincerely that his adherence to the Party might bring nearer the day when the working classes would have the leisure to develop the new style of life that was theirs for the asking—and, in fact, he remained a Party member for the rest of his life. It had been very disagreeable for Léger to stand up in front of working-class audiences at the time of the Popular Front, in 1936–37, and be greeted with shouts of "You only work for the rich! Who wants to listen to you?" (It was not, however, so traumatic as to cause him to refuse a commission from Nelson Rockefeller the next year.) Perhaps in a changed France all that could be changed, too?

It never was, really. If he was booed, it was no longer, admittedly, by the working class. I well remember the uproar that broke out in the stalls when Léger appeared in 1949 on the stage of the Opéra in Paris at the first performance of Milhaud's *Bolivar,* for which he had designed the scenery. Aesthetic prejudice no doubt played a part in this, but the basic sound was that of the propertied classes baying for the Party member's blood. The big commissions, however, still came from traditional sources: the Roman Catholic Church, above all. ("Nobody else asked me," he would say, when taxed with escapism, "and I did so want to make big decorations.") When he made paintings on the scale of epics, it was for himself primarily; and in his seventies he completed two huge complementary paintings on working-class themes—*The Constructors* in 1950 and *The Great Parade* in 1954.

These paintings do honor to Léger as a man: for his energy, his ambition, his largeness of heart. Léger had loved the circus all his life, and he tried to sum up his feelings for it in *The Great Parade; The Constructors* is a last salute to the children and grandchildren of the men with whom he had served in World War I. But there is a great difference between a painting that corresponds to an urgent social need—to something that *has* to be said—and one that does not. The two late paintings relate to a France that had already passed into history. They are descriptive, and by implication sentimental, in a way that Léger would never have permitted himself thirty years earlier. The style aspires to grandeur, but without the radical invention that marked the *Three Women* of 1921. "I'm a painter," Léger once said. "I'm not in the description business."

If in these two late paintings he ended up in "the description business," it was because that particular simplistic view of the working classes was no longer valid. The machine had not, after all, turned out to be the instrument of social liberation; and in just about every country in the world the hard-hat had become the henchman of reaction. Neither at work nor at play did the construction worker of the 1950s match up to the New Man Léger had put on canvas thirty years earlier. That specific impulse—and that specific art—had had its moment of validity in the 1920s. Art was the poorer for its disappearance; mankind, also.

The Message

AS THE AUTHOR notes elsewhere in *Out of the Kitchen: Adventures of a Food Writer,* from which this piece is excerpted, there are enough recipes in the first volume of *Mastering the Art of French Cooking* "to keep a person occupied, not to mention two people, for a lifetime of dinner parties," so she never expected to buy the second volume. And at the time (the early eighties), she had met writer Frances Mayes, who was still living in San Francisco and who had her own copy of the second volume, which she offered to lend (along with her *charlotte* mold) to Jeannette any time she wanted it.

Mayes and Ferrary signed up to join a cooking class taught by Simone Beck, one of the three original authors of *Mastering,* at her house in Provence, where they also had the opportunity to meet Julia Child at a cocktail party. "Julia greeted us with such embracing enthusiasm," Ferrary writes, "there was no time to be awe-stricken, and no need. Meeting her felt like a reunion with someone I'd known but hadn't quite met, a mere formality that had been overlooked until that moment."

Of all the many interviews and articles written about Julia Child, I am partial to this story, a chapter in *Out of the Kitchen* (John Daniel & Company, 2004), a warm and wonderful book that deserves to be better known, and in which Ferrary shares stories of her Brooklyn childhood and recounts her beliefs and values (sometimes contradictory), all of them having to do with food.

JEANNETTE FERRARY teaches food writing at Stanford University and the University of California Berkeley, and has been a columnist for the *New York Times* and a book and restaurant reviewer for the *San Francisco Chronicle*. She is also the author of *M. F. K. Fisher and Me* (Thomas Dunne, 1998) and is coauthor, with Louise Fiszer, of six cookbooks, including *A Good Day for Soup* (Chronicle, 1996) and *A Good Day for Salad* (Chronicle, 1999).

"YOU MADE *WHAT* for Julia Child's lunch?"

I couldn't believe my ears. The chef had been given the opportunity to prepare a box lunch for Julia Child. It was supposed to be casual and unfussy, just a little something before her afternoon appearance at Macy's San Francisco. He packed it in a football-sized gift box tied with blue ribbons and was delivering it to the sort of backstage dressing room where Julia, her sister Dorothy, and I were waiting. I only hoped they hadn't heard what he said. I took the boxes from him—there were three of them, one for each of us—and slid them onto a table by the door. Then I realized he was kidding; he must be kidding.

"Come on, tell me. What's in them?"

He looked frazzled, an appropriate response for someone who had invested all his creative energies into the challenging but intimidating task of whipping up a box lunch for Julia Child. He also looked annoyed.

"I told you. Tuna fish sandwiches."

Maybe he hadn't realized which Julia Child he'd been asked to make lunch for. He'd slapped together a couple of sandwiches for some ordinary Julia Child, an earthling who hadn't helped change the course of America's eating habits in her twenty-five years—it was 1985—of cookbook writing and television cooking shows. Surely he knew not what he did—or didn't do, as the case may be. Or perhaps the strain had been too much for him and he'd completely lost his mind. His eyes looked a bit jumpy, now that I peered more closely. Proof of his derangement surfaced almost immediately as Julia, attracted by the commotion, turned to greet him.

"Oh, hellooo, you're the chef, aren't you?" came the chortly tones, full of welcome and gratitude. The billowy abandon of her teal rayon blouse swarming with flickery white splotches contrasted with the workhorse immovability of a navy gabardine skirt. Cinnamon-orange hair, the same color as her lipstick, made thick, loopy curls across her forehead. She was smiling and talking, the metallic music of her voice pitched halfway between some kind of horn and a reed instrument not yet invented.

She shook the chef's hand, commending him for going to all the trouble, advising him he shouldn't have. She was right about the latter.

"I hope you like tuna fish sandwiches," he blurted out with no shame or embarrassment, clearly out of touch with reality.

"Why, yes. We love tuna fish, don't we, Dorothy?"

"Wonderful. I thought you would. Especially when I saw this magnificent specimen." He went on to describe how he'd gone down to the fish market at dawn, poking and slapping a dozen different fish before deciding on the nice fat one he brought back to poach for these sandwiches.

I felt foolish for thinking any chef in his right mind would present Julia Child with a StarKist chicken of the sea. Meanwhile Julia never flinched. She'd already dived right in, unperturbed about whether her sandwich had begun with a can opener or a court bouillon. (I remembered M. F. K. Fisher telling me, in her unique mélange of praise and condemnation, "Julia will eat anything.")

Over lunch, whenever I started to discuss the day's program, the tuna kept getting in the way.

"Isn't this just marvelous?" This a reference to the way the chef—"such a nice young man"—had cloaked the sweet chunks of fish with a creamy aioli that was "marvelously tart" and studded with chopped fennel instead of "ordinary old celery." As for the sourdough, fire and smoke trapped in its crusty ridges and curves, he must have taken the loaves directly off the baking stones: that was the consensus. A lull between sandwich and dessert gave me my chance.

"Is there anything in particular you want me to say out there?"

No, she was sure whatever I said would be fine.

I felt surprisingly at ease myself about the day's event, except for a disconcerting incident with the Macy's PR person, who had just whispered an infuriating instruction that Julia didn't know about. Whenever I interviewed Julia for an article, she always made it seem like we were friends, chatting. On a publicity tour for her previous book, *Julia Child and More Company,* she'd come to San Francisco to do a cooking demonstration and book signing, also at Macy's. I joined the welcoming committee at seven in the morning at her hotel, the Huntington on Nob Hill. With an amused grin, she watched the parade of sleepy-eyed but fit-looking businessmen emerge from the elevator in shorts, look at her sheepishly—even MBAs recognize Julia Child—and trot across the street for their morning jog. At the store, Julia and her entourage had been led down an alley and into some sort of service-entrance back door, presided over by a neckless security guard who eyed Julia suspiciously.

"Who is that woman?" he asked, his eyes following her every move. I was tempted to answer, "Why, that's the Lone Ranger," but I wasn't sure he'd see the humor in it, considering the hour.

One of Julia's friends and assistants, Rosemary Manell, had already started pulling rabbits and onions out of grocery bags, assisted by Pam Henstell from Knopf, the book's publisher. After taking a few pictures for my article, I offered to help, truly honored when Julia handed me a head of garlic and asked me to mince it finely. Determined to do an impeccable job, I carefully pried out two or three cloves. I rubbed them between my fingers in a massage-like motion, trying to coax off the papery covering. Instead of slipping off smoothly like a satin robe, it just crinkled and crumbled. What did come off glued itself onto my fingers; the rest of it didn't budge. Using my fingernails, I scraped and clawed around the stubborn little cloves to no avail. Still attempting to appear unruffled and competent, I reached for a nearby paring knife and began carving the surface of the clove, finally whittling it down to the size of an olive pit. This I cut into three or four slices on the bias, not unimpressed with my own handiwork. I became aware that Julia was standing perfectly still, watching my every move. Play your cards right, Julia, I was thinking of saying, and I shall reveal my secrets of garlic sculpting.

"Jeannette?" she called out as if it were a question. "What are you doing?" There was a suggestion in her tone of voice that there was a right way to mince a garlic and this wasn't it by an order of magnitude. I could protest that the method had definitely not been included in Simone Beck's course at L'École des Trois Gourmands, but this wasn't the time or the place.

Shaking her head as if in disbelief, she grabbed another clove and slammed down on it with the flat side of a giant saber, smashing it to a pulp. Then she worked the blade over it until it was practically liquid. As for the papery stuff, it lay on the chopping block in tatters.

"Thanks," I said, gathering up the remaining cloves. "Is there anything else I can help you with?"

She just laughed, unfazed by the crescendo of crowd-gathering sounds just outside the auditorium. Someone was adjusting the overhead mirrors so that those in the back could see her sautéing mushrooms and green onions and the garlic that Rosemary had kindly rescued me from. Once the doors were opened—the floodgates might be a more accurate term—people swarmed in. Most were women, all ages and descriptions, all with the same look of awe on their faces. As Julia's first squawky words trilled their way across the reverently silent throng, the group complexion softened into smiles, then grins and wide, throaty laughs. They were eating out of the palm of her hand and they weren't even eating.

After the demo, she signed about a million books and then she wanted to visit the cookware department. As we stepped into the elevator, a few people recognized her instantly. Hardly able to contain their excitement, they poked their friends or whoever was closest, rolling their eyes in Julia's direction, mouthing their message: "That's Julia Child." When the elevator opened, Julia noticed an in-store post office, walked over, and stood in line. Her height alone made her a presence, so it wasn't long before the person in front of her turned his head discreetly to take the measure of whatever was looming over him. He immediately began to babble.

"Oh, it's you. Oh my goodness. Julia Child. Please," he said, stepping aside with a bit of a flourish, begging her to go ahead. Seconds later, all the others became aware of the stir and then each of them in turn stepped aside in a kind of domino effect. She would have none of it.

"No. I'm in no hurry. Absolutely not," she protested, directing everyone back into line.

A few weeks after this event, she wrote me a postcard: "It was fun being with you that day, and I hope we can renew the experience with or without garlic!"

That wasn't the only time I'd seen Julia since meeting her at Simca's in 1978. I enjoyed writing about her gastrobatics, her jolly nature, and her contagious humor. She was eminently quotable: "If cooking is evanescent, well, so is the ballet"; men were often better cooks because they have a "what the hell attitude." And her advice to cooks, perhaps even more relevant to writers: "Above all, have a good time," she counseled, but "keep your knives sharp."

I'd written an article about her appearance at a benefit for the Children's Garden in San Francisco's Palace of Fine Arts; I'd reported on the evening she and René Verdon cooked dinner at his San Francisco restaurant, Le Trianon, as a benefit for KQED, the public television station. I'd even interviewed her about her favorite San Francisco restaurants: ". . . Once we went to Mike's Chinese Cuisine on the advice of Jack Shelton. I think it was over on Geary. We thought it was extremely good." She also mentioned, in passing, Campton Place, Le Trianon, L'Étoile, and Masa's, which "we found very ethereal."

For me, Julia embodied and resolved the enigma concerning women and food. She did so-called women's work and she liked it. Not only that but she derived success and fame from it, maybe even fortune. She'd harnessed her interest in food into a viable career if not a full-fledged mythology, and at an age when most women, and especially most men, aren't venturing into a new and extraordinarily public territory. She was almost fifty when *Mastering* was published, fifty-one when she first appeared on TV as the French Chef.

These accomplishments had seemed the perfect subject for an article for *Ms. Magazine.* Aware that there was a certain undeniable irony about *Ms. Magazine* honoring a woman's achievements in the field of cookery, I was confident the editor would see this as an opportunity to say that true liberation means a woman can pursue any field she chooses, even cooking!

The editors didn't see it that way. "Very nice but not particularly feminist" came the hand-scribbled verdict clipped to my returned manuscript. I was embarrassed by the *Ms.* rejection because, like so many women who greeted the very first issue, in 1971, with a sense of triumph and who had subscribed instantaneously, I considered the magazine my own. It spoke for me. It ranted and raved for me. It was strong enough and smart enough to counter all the demeaning and belittling and devaluing that went on in *Playboy* and *Esquire* and *Penthouse* put together. I couldn't explain the editors' appraisal, so I decided to send it to Julia, along with a copy of my review of her book, *Julia Child and More Company,* which had just been published in the *San Francisco Bay Guardian.* She wrote back that she "loved both those articles. . . . I thought the one rejected by *Ms.* was especially good and also very amusing. You certainly write well!"

And so, as Julia, Dorothy, and I sat there eating our tuna fish sandwiches, I was glad Macy's had asked me to interview her that day. The event celebrated her newest venture, a series of videotapes in which she explained and demonstrated basic cooking techniques, garlic mincing undoubtedly among them.

Nestled beside me was my own newest venture, a copy of *The California-American Cookbook,* just published by Simon & Schuster. I had already autographed this copy to Julia Child and had been waiting for the auspicious moment. And then, a few moments before, there had been this nasty business with the rules-are-rules, scowl-infested Macy's PR person. This was the same Macy's PR person who had promised that if I did this interview, it would be worth more than mere money, a commodity she insisted was in short supply at Macy's. I wasn't too savvy in the ways of book promotion, but I assumed one could do worse than to introduce one's new book in front of the Child-revering masses within buying distance of Macy's bookstore. Just a few sentences, I'd been told, but enough to give the audience the flavor of the book. This moment in the sun would, she whined apologetically, more than make up for the paltry sum Macy's was paying for doing the interview and might even result in the book's first avalanche of sales. Visions of cookbook-ravenous women stampeding down the aisles to lay claim to a copy of *The California-American Cookbook* had just stopped dancing in my head.

"You are not to mention your book today," the Macy's PR person commanded in scolding tones, her brow a landscape of petrified frowns. "This event is about Julia Child's new videotapes and we don't want anything to detract from that." When I protested that this was a breach of our agreement, she turned on her heel with a little smirk as if to say if I was dumb enough to trust Macy's, I had only myself to blame. I was wondering if any jury would convict me if I murdered her there on the spot when I noticed the gleam in Julia's eyes, her whole face in bloom. She was looking at my book.

"How beautiful!" she said, flipping through the pages. "You must be thrilled."

"Oh, I, well, yes, actually, and we, my coauthor and I, we autographed this copy to you."

"Thank you so much. Wonderful. Simon and Schuster, very good people. Tell me, how did you come to do the book?" I explained that I had not been enthusiastic when my agent first mentioned my writing a cookbook because, although I embraced any opportunity to write about food, I didn't consider myself a cook who could whip up two hundred original recipes. Julia nodded an all-too-understanding nod, possibly recalling my garlic butchery of a few years before. I kept scanning her face for signs of incipient yawning as I related probably too many details about developing a book about California's historical romance with food. As for the recipes, I'd chanced upon an article in the *New York Times* about a woman named Louise Fiszer who taught cooking in her own little cooking school/cookware shop in Menlo Park, about twenty minutes from me. I was captivated by the style and spirit of her recipes and the way they seemed to convey the kind of California message I wanted to write about.

I called Louise at her shop and she invited me over. We got along instantly, intrigued by the many parallels in our lives. We both came from Brooklyn, only miles from each other; we were two weeks apart in age; we both had recently bought a newfangled contraption called a computer that neither of us knew how to use.

Once we started to develop the book proposal, we worked

beautifully together, dividing tasks, respecting each other's opinions, resolving differences, of which there were incredibly few, if any, with no hurt feelings or wounded egos. We even learned, because it was essential to our project, how to work on the computer using the brain-straining word processing system called WordStar. Our agent received wildly enthusiastic responses to our proposal from several New York publishers—or more correctly put, he masterminded those responses by creating a bit of a frenzy and cultivating a bidding war mentality. To seal the deal, Simon & Schuster offered us a contract for $50,000. Not bad for 1983 and two unknown authors of their first book.

Strictly speaking, it was my third book proposal, the first being "The Last-Minute Epicure" with Frances Mayes. The second was a cookbook concept I developed with—or in spite of—Judy Rodgers, a young cook at the Union Hotel in the small Northern California town of Benicia. She insisted she had no time to work on the book proposal per se, so she gave me a sheaf of her menus which I used to create the table of contents. After I finished the proposal and began to receive enthusiastic responses from publishers, Judy decided she didn't want to do the book after all. It was too American, too Californian. She was afraid that a book about contemporary cooking would typecast her, that she'd lose credibility as a French chef before she even had any. I was crushed at the time, although I realized that if the book proceeded as it had to date, it would be a one-sided coauthorship.

"And so," Julia asked, bringing me out of this annoyingly vivid reverie, "is your collaboration with Louise a good one?"

"Yes. The best," is all I said, with a smile prompted by recalling my friend Frances's summing up of the situation: "The fact that it didn't work out with JR almost makes you believe in God."

"Well, this is a beautiful book indeed. You and Louise should be very proud."

A few minutes later, we walked onto Macy's makeshift stage greeted by the thunderous applause of a crowd that packed the airplane-hangar-sized room. I gave my little speech about Julia's impact on all of our lives and her venture into the new world of videotaped cooking lessons. When I passed the microphone to Julia, the walls seemed to be caving in from the room-rattling temblors of applause.

Holding up a copy of one of the videotapes, she waved to the cheering masses. The decibel level decrescendoed only when she started to speak. That's when I realized it wasn't a videotape she had in her hand: it was my book.

"Come on. Don't be shy. Show everyone this beautiful new book. This is Jeannette's new book, *The California-American Cookbook*," she called out, reading the cover to the audience. "It's full of absolutely marvelous recipes."

More clapping from the obedient Child-adorers, a bit subdued and possibly even confused (*Jeannette? Who's Jeannette?*), but an ovation nonetheless. On stage left, Macy's PR scowler was gnashing her teeth. I bestowed upon her one of my sweetest smiles.

Before Julia finished her talk, the audience was already furiously buying sets of her videotapes and mushrooming toward the stage to have her autograph them. I had to act fast. I pulled a big white apron out of a shopping bag and laid it before her.

"Would you please sign this to my four-year-old daughter, Natasha?"

"Of course," she said, scrawling all across the front, in bright blue ink, "To Natasha. Bon Appétit. Julia Child."

"Does she like to cook?" she asked, intently dotting all three *i*'s.

It was a logical question, considering the circumstances. It didn't seem to require deep philosophical reflection. But it made me wonder if I should be giving my daughter an apron after all, if this was one of those things that were "very nice but not particularly feminist." Would I be reinforcing the traditional girlie messages, blurring for Natasha the distinctions I'd tried to make clear for myself? Ideally I didn't want my daughter even to know that there was a time when women couldn't do whatever they wanted; and even though that time was still very much with us at her four-year mark in 1985, there were indications that her generation might feel its constrictions less strongly. Their talents and potential might flourish, if not unhampered at least less encumbered. That is, if they weren't confused by gifts of aprons and other such symbol-laden trinkets.

As I tucked the apron back into the bag, I took a last serious look at it. For a second I was startled. How could I have missed something so obvious? Of course this apron would make a fine present for my daughter, for anybody's daughter. Its message was not "Stand by the stove" or "This is your life" or "Anatomy is destiny." Far from it. Its message was "Bon Appétit."

We'll Always Have Paris

STACY SCHIFF

𝕲𝕾𝕾

WHEN THE AUTHOR of this piece and her family left Paris after a year there, they had more suitcases than they cared to count (though the number was significantly less than the 126 Benjamin Franklin reportedly had upon his departure in 1783). But even her then ten-year-old son had to admit the family had had an experience that couldn't be measured by suitcases.

STACY SCHIFF, a noted biographer, has received fellowships from the Guggenheim Foundation and the National Endowment for the Humanities. She's the author of *A Great Improvisation: Franklin, France, and the Birth of America* (Henry Holt, 2005), *Cleopatra: A Life* (Little, Brown, 2010), *Saint Exupéry: A Biography* (Knopf, 1994), and *Vera (Mrs. Vladimir Nabokov): Portrait of a Marriage* (Random House, 1999), which won a Pulitzer Prize for biography.

THE OBSESSION TOOK hold in New York, which posed a problem: what I wanted to write about next was Ben Franklin's eighteenth-century adventure in France. On some level, I knew from the start that the only way to research that book was to move our family, for some period of time, to Paris. And from the start—even as friends enviously asked if we would do so—I dreaded the prospect. Generally Paris is not considered a hardship posting, save to someone who values efficiency, candor, and Sichuan takeout. Nor was this to be a larky, lighthearted school year abroad. Paris means Angélina's *chocolat chaud* and the Tuileries at dusk and the Rodin Museum and Pierre Hermé, but it is also a city, I had come to learn, of phone repairmen, plumbers, and dentists, the vast majority of them French. With age, the dislocations tend to announce themselves less as bracing, extra-carbonated mental states than as crippling tornadoes of small details.

In part I suppose I dreaded what can only be termed my own devolution. Whereas at home I am organized, competent, and semiarticulate, I am in France awkward and incapable. I can be deaf to nuance; some frequencies elude me entirely. Franklin was very clear about the fact that a man sacrifices half his intelligence in a foreign language, but he had plenty of intelligence to spare. (He moaned especially that his humor fell flat on the page, as indeed it did.) Even without a language barrier, I knew myself to be handicapped. At any moment I am likely to revert to my Anglo-Saxon habits, to forget not to lay a finger on the greengrocer's tomatoes, not to reach for my *boulangerie* change before it is counted, not to order my sandwich before my *café crème*. (My husband falls in a different category. A Frenchman raised on foreign soil, he passes for a native until confronted with a cheese tray, at which juncture his passport is nearly revoked. He once left a Normandy innkeeper dumbstruck by asking, in unaccented French, what precisely *un potage jardinier* consisted of. Imagine a native New Englander inquiring after a definition of clam chowder.) There was one other deterrent, too, one that the biographer Richard Holmes has identified: "Writers of course are always slightly ashamed at not being at their desks, especially in Paris, where they might be out—having a good time, *mon dieu.*"

We figured that the one-year-old wouldn't object to the plan but assumed that some finessing might be in order for the eight- and ten-year-olds. Which may explain why we broke the news at the Café de Flore a semester beforehand, over *cafés liégeois* and

éclairs au chocolat, the blackmailing parent's best friends. The eight-year-old was an immediate convert. The ten-year-old succumbed neither to the sugar rush nor to the pandering. He made it clear that he would not be decamping to Paris until France fielded a major-league baseball team. And it was he who—on the August day we headed off to JFK with our fifteen suitcases—planted himself on the steaming sidewalk and refused to budge. It was also he who planted himself on the sidewalk and refused to budge a year later, when we headed to Charles de Gaulle with more bags than any of us bothered to count. They were at least fewer than the 126 with which Franklin headed home, baggage that included three Angora cats, a printing press, a sampling of mineral waters, and a variety of saplings.

By a happy quirk, we found an apartment in Franklin's old neighborhood, less hilly today than it was in the 1770s. There were other modern-day advantages as well. No fewer than six *boulangeries* stand along the mile that separated Franklin's home from that of John Adams. Franklin had to make that walk on an empty stomach, something I never did. There was, after all, pressing *pain au chocolat* research to be done. We lived fifteen minutes from Versailles, an expedition that took Franklin two dusty hours by carriage. When we bicycled in the Bois de Boulogne, we crossed the lawn where Franklin followed the first manned balloon as it rose into the sky in 1783, something he did with considerable anxiety. We were two very different Americans in Paris, but I delighted in the overlay of our lives. It did what a foreign adventure is supposed to do—it made the mundane thrilling. Along the route Franklin traveled twice every week, to the home of the woman he hoped to seduce (as opposed to the one he wanted to marry), was the lovely Congolese tailor who lengthened our son's pants before the start of the school year. Picking up the dry cleaning qualifies as less of a chore when you are doing so on ground you know Ben Franklin and John Adams have trodden before you. And I could always justify shopping at the pricey ice cream shop on the rue Bois-le-Vent. It seemed nearly obligatory to do so, given that the shop stands where the back door to Franklin's home once had. Moreover, it seemed dangerous not to, as the shop hours were erratic, a universal signal of artistic integrity but a guarantee of greatness in France.

To France America sent as her first emissary a man who confessed he was wholly indifferent to food. (And one who was ignorant about it in the extreme: it was his conviction that there was no butter in French sauces.) Franklin ate well but pined for a good Indian pudding, a piece of salt pork, Newton Pippin apples, walnuts. We had an easier time fending off homesickness. Never has our family eaten as many H&H bagels as we did in Paris; they could be had, frozen, at a little store on the rue de Grenelle, conveniently on my way home from the diplomatic archives. And so breakfast became an odd binational affair—bagels with Kiri, the French spreadable that most closely resembles Philadelphia cream cheese. One thing that immediately fell off our radar was Chinese food, much though the cravings for sesame noodles and pork dumplings continued. Just as the word *teamwork* is missing from the French language, so are the concepts "family style" and "for the table." To attempt a Sichuan or Hunan meal without sharing is to defeat the purpose of the exercise. Inevitably one is left to covet one's neighbor's plate.

On the other hand, Thanksgiving in Paris was a dead ringer for Thanksgiving at home, save for the much-missed butternut squash, and the fact that everything tasted better. I don't know whom we have to thank—I fear it may be Hallmark—but Parisian butchers have come a long way since the first time I ordered a *grosse dinde* in November, nearly twenty years ago. "Oh, is it for your American rite?" asked the butcher, with a squint of the eye generally reserved for Jewish-Masonic conspiracies. Now those *grosses dindes* come with a side order of miniature American flags. In New York we are Pilgrims, but in Paris we are Americans.

We had one great advantage over Franklin: we spoke French. Franklin rarely acknowledged that minor handicap, although he did refer to contracts that had been signed in his first year, when misapprehension was the order of the day. Even a bilingual family came in for its share of surprises, however. There was the hockey coach who chain-smoked on the ice. (There were also the unforgiving stares to be endured in the Métro when traveling with an eight-year-old in full hockey equipment, especially as that child was a girl.) School recess may well have taken place in the magnificent Parc Monceau, but one did not a) set foot on the grass, b) throw a ball, c) throw anything resembling a ball. In turn, the flying scarves, the chestnuts, the bottle caps were confiscated. The school week is cleverly configured to keep mothers from working (home for lunch; half-day Wednesday; four-hour birthday parties). The academic calendar is configured to keep teachers from having to work more than three weeks straight.

Some of the frustrations were maddeningly familiar. The problem is less one of language than of the sterling example set—and the expectations harbored—by North American efficiency. It is almost impossible to shake the Anglo-Saxon concern that you are holding up the line, a qualm that does not exist in France, where it is one's privilege and responsibility to do so. Quite simply, ours is a service economy. France's is not. A café waiter is meant to do his job, but that job is most decidedly not to guarantee the satisfaction of his customer. Rather it is the customer's job to admire the professionalism of the waiter, the expertise with which he can flick a baguette crumb into oblivion, his unerring capacity to make change. Stocking the larder is a full-time job, more so even than in Franklin's day, when the fruit seller and the *pâtissier* and the *laitier* delivered their goods to the door. (Judging from his household accounts, Franklin had a hearty and prescient taste for apple pie.) Early on the ten-year-old delivered up the paradox of Parisian life: in that city, one accomplishes precisely half of what one sets out that morning to accomplish. Which means that if one heads out with only one thing to do, one has a problem.

France is a country hidebound by regulations; the national sport consists of gracefully subverting them. The trick is not to follow the rules, but to avoid getting caught breaking them. It is *Casablanca* on a grand scale. One adapts quickly but sometimes ambivalently, especially since this is not necessarily the lesson one cares to impart to one's American children. 2002 was an election year in France, which meant several things. It meant there was a strike of some kind pretty much every minute; one might call the Louvre to confirm that the children's weekend class was in session, only to hike across town to discover that, indeed, class was not canceled, but that the building was locked tight. (The opposite might also be true. The post office was open, but the employees on strike.) The library staff might well be in place—except those who delivered titles from shelves L through S. Under the highly regulated exterior all is chaos: The order at a piano recital is whoever wants to go first. The TV news starts at a set time—and continues until the news is finished, a signal triumph of content over form. There may be a hockey bus to convey the team to Meudon, or there may not. (Naturally this non-truth requires three phone calls to establish.) There is no such thing as a Gallic work ethic, and in an election year there is no constituency that is too dignified, or too disenfranchised, to strike. In the course of the year, the emergency room doctors, the *gendarmerie,* the teachers, the unemployed—all walked out on strike. Everything is predicated on the crucial *except,* and *exceptionellement* quickly became our favorite word in the French language. The exception of the day became a staple of our dinner conversation.

Election year brought with it lessons apart from the political ones. As every Frenchman knows, all driving violations are promptly pardoned by the incoming Président de la République. It is his gift to the people of France; it is the modern-day version of royal prerogative; it is the tradition every candidate must vow to uphold. Which means that for the months leading up to any presidential election, all speed and traffic laws are de facto suspended. (Road fatalities rise accordingly.) Essentially what this means is that any piece of Parisian surface—sidewalk, driveway, bus stop—suddenly qualifies as a parking space. Quickly we went native; our children seemed ambivalent about what they termed our "rural parking." What kind of lesson, they asked, were we imparting? The lesson we were imparting was, should our children ever settle in France, they had better get with the program, or they will be circling the block eternally.

And then there is that staple of French life: the specious argument. After a full day's drive to the country, fully wilted, we inquire in a restaurant at five p.m. if there might be anything on hand to eat. No, is the answer. Not even an ice cream? Well, yes, of course, comes the reply. We got very good at playing Go Fish. Also at heading off the brand of logistical display we had encountered years earlier on an Air France flight, when we attempted to settle the firstborn in the airline's bassinet. He did not fit. The bassinet was for children under two. Ergo, reasoned the indignant stewardess, the child was not under the age of two. (As his passport duly attested, he was nine months old. Under other circumstances, my outsize American children have elicited plaudits, of the kind a Great Dane wins in a city of poodles. "*Ça, madame,*" offered a well-dressed gentleman in the Jardin du Ranelagh one day, pointing to a different nine-month-old, "*Ça, madame, c'est un bébé.*")

Go Fish is a game I can play. A different tournament will forever stand between me and French nationality. That is the sport essential to French life: I pontificate, therefore I am. Between Passy and Saint-Germain, a royalist taxi driver worked himself into a fever one night over Chirac's misdeeds and the pressing need to reinstall the Bourbon heir (rather than the Orléans pretender) to the throne of France. His diatribe, and his reliquary of a taxi, may be the last thing our children forget about the year abroad.

Some mysteries of our new life went unsolved. Is there anything the French can't advertise with cleavage? How is it possible that twenty-first-century Paris could still boast Turkish toilets? Why does the milk not need to be refrigerated? Why does the shampoo not lather? Certain things were best left unexplained, like the gaggle of short-skirted teenagers who congregated across the street from the apartment, rain or shine. "Have you ever wondered when those girls go to school?" asked the eight-year-old. Fortunately, she never noticed that those prodigies spent their day getting in and out of cars with out-of-town plates, cars which reliably delivered them back to the corner an hour later. At least they dressed respectably, as opposed to their sisters (and *faux* sisters) a block deeper into the Bois de Boulogne. There were two jogging itineraries: my Felliniesque own, and the less scenic route, which I took when running with the children.

In the end, though, the pleasures exceeded the familiar physical glories and culinary delights. One lives better in Europe, not only on account of the cheeses and the three-hour lunches and the enforced weekend. One does so thanks to SOS Couscous, whose deliverymen ladle dinner from dented metal casseroles; on account of pediatricians who pay house calls and orthodontists who take appointments until nine p.m.; because the playgrounds are vastly superior, free as they are from liability issues. There is good coffee and *steak frites* even at the hockey rink, where the adults are blessedly oblivious to the game. And the parent of a school-age child saves countless hours: there are no bake sales, no safety patrol, no home games. The last thing any French school administration cares to encounter in its hallways is a parent. We came nearly to take for granted those built-in privileges of a socialist country: when making travel arrangements, when buying shoes, when visiting a museum, we were entitled to a discount as a card-carrying "*famille nombreuse.*" (Woe to any *famille nombreuse* that attempts a dinner in a good French restaurant, however. At least until the two-year-old orders oysters.)

As it happened, we had something else in common with Franklin. While I waited to pick the children up from school one fall afternoon, my Parisian sister-in-law called to report that a plane had flown into the World Trade Center. I assumed she meant that a crazy student pilot had done so until I got home and turned on the television. From that moment on Americans in Paris were few on the ground. As she had been in the eighteenth century, America was naked and vulnerable again. "*Nous sommes tous Américains,*" blared the headlines, and any cabdriver who heard a whisper of English was happy not only to ask where we were from—for once New York was the proper answer, rather than California—but to offer sympathy and thanks for 1945. For the worst reasons imaginable, we enjoyed a taste of the fervor for the New World that Franklin had so effectively cultivated in the Old. A friend who was treated to a rare viewing of original Proust papers asked afterward why he had been so lucky. "Consider it repayment for June 6," he was told, just after the fiftieth anniversary of D-Day. Say the words "Benjamin Franklin" and you elicit a smile from a Frenchman. On days when I wasn't smiling, I made a point of coming home via the Place du Trocadéro, over which a bronze Franklin presides. Sometimes I felt closer to him there than I did in the archives. That is the blessed thing about France: the history is always close to the surface. I suppose it was why we went.

Le Père Tanguy

HENRI PERRUCHOT

HERE IS A piece about a person who, outside of art history circles, is little known to the museumgoing general public. But *le père* Tanguy—Father Tanguy—has long been one of my favorite personalities of the French Impressionist period, and he is the subject of one of my favorite paintings by Van Gogh, in the permanent collection of the Musée Rodin.

Van Gogh painted three portraits of Tanguy, with the canvas in the Musée Rodin (circa 1887) being the most famous. The portrait shows Tanguy as an elderly man wearing a Breton straw hat against a background of colorful Japanese prints. At this time in the late 1800s, Japan was just beginning to open up to the Western world, and Japanese porcelain was being exported to France. The porcelain was wrapped in tissue paper decorated with prints of Japanese art, and it was from these sheets of tissue paper that the Impressionists were inspired to adopt several Eastern techniques in their own works. Japanese prints became all the rage then in Paris. Not only Van Gogh but also Manet, Monet, Degas, and Toulouse-Lautrec—who signed his works with a stamp bearing the initials TL, borrowed from the Japanese tradition of *hanko,* seals of stone, horn, or wood used in lieu of signatures on personal and business documents—experimented with foreshortening and a flattening of figures portrayed in their canvases, borrowing from the Japanese style. In such works as *Portrait of*

Émile Zola by Degas (in the Musée d'Orsay), a Japanese screen and prints can be seen in the background of the seated Zola.

This piece also tells of how Tanguy's modest color-grinder's shop became a shrine of sorts of Impressionist and Post-impressionist painting.

HENRI PERRUCHOT was the author of many works on nineteenth-century painters, including Cézanne, Gauguin, Manet, Rousseau, Renoir, and Seurat, and contributed numerous essays to art publications. This piece originally appeared in the distinctive French art review *L'Œil,* and later, for the first time in English, in *Aspects of Modern Art: The Selective Eye III* (Reynal & Company, 1957).

ALL WITNESSES ARE agreed on the subject of "*le père Tanguy.*" He played a preponderant role in the dazzling renewal of French painting at the end of the nineteenth century. Just after he died Octave Mirbeau said of him that "the story of his humble and upright life is inseparable from the history of the Impressionist group . . . and when that history comes to be written, Tanguy will have his place in it." He couldn't have been more right. Maurice Denis once said that his little shop in the rue Clauzel was the "origin of the great gust of fresh air that blew new life into French art in and around the year 1890"; and Émile Bernard would have it that "the so-called Pont Aven school would be more accurately named the Rue Clauzel school."

Julien-François Tanguy was a Breton. He was born on June 28, 1825, half a dozen miles from Saint-Brieuc, in a village in the commune of Plédran, where his father was a weaver. The fifth child of a very poor, indeed almost penniless family, he went to Saint-Brieuc while still very young, and began life as a plasterer. In 1855, when he was thirty, he married a *charcutière,* abandoned his former trade, and helped his wife to market her ham and sausages. Whether he disliked being a pork butcher, or whether they just couldn't make a go of it, is not known: but in any case, in 1860, he and his wife, and the little daughter who had been born to them meanwhile, made off to Paris. There, Tanguy was employed by the Compagnie de l'Ouest until in 1865 he found work as a color-grinder with the firm of Édouard in the rue Clauzel, which at that time had a great reputation among artists. Soon after this he set up on his own, prepared his own colors, and hawked them himself in those parts of France which were becoming popular among open-air painters. So it was that he came to know Pissarro, Manet, Renoir, Monet, Cézanne—all of them then more or less un-known—at Barbizon, or Ecouen, or Argenteuil, or Sarcelles . . .

Unfortunately the war of 1870 interrupted all this and embroiled "Papa Tanguy" in a sequence of catastrophic adventures. What happened exactly is still a little obscure, but it's beyond question that at the time of the Commune Tanguy was one of the Fédérés. He was taken prisoner, sent to Satory, court-martialled and found guilty. He was sent to Brest, and there rotted until one of his fellow Bretons, the academic painter Jobbé-Duval, who was a member of the Paris Conseil Municipal, managed to get him a pardon.

He was back in Paris in 1873, or thereabouts, and reverted to color-grinding. As the firm of Édouard had just left the rue Clauzel he seized the opportunity of opening a shop in that very street, at no. 14.

The painters whom Papa Tanguy had known before the war, and who at once gave him their custom, were at that time in the thick of the fight. Their first group exhibition was to open on the boulevard des Capucines in the spring of 1874; and on that occa-sion an art critic, M. Louis Leroy, who saw himself as something of a humorist, gave them the name of "Impressionists" in the *Charivari;* and, as everyone knows, the name stuck. Papa Tanguy became the most fervent and loyal of the Impressionists' allies: as to just how this came about, a word of explanation is needed.

Papa Tanguy was a man of golden good nature. Heavy and dullish at first glance, he was in reality the most delicate, pure-minded and upright of men. He was easy-going almost to a fault: never did a painter appeal to him in vain for credit—and often this credit remained open indefinitely. Papa Tanguy was, in his own way, a stoic: "Anyone who spends more than fifty centimes a day is a blackguard," he liked to say, and the phrase fits the man in whom the kindness of an evangelist was allied to a natural sympathy for the revolutionary and the rebel.

For Tanguy had put himself on the side of the rebels ever since he had fought with the Fédérés and had a taste of prison life. The Impressionists, his friends, were making enemies on every hand; they must be fought for, tooth and nail. In his simple, tender-hearted way Tanguy thought that painting in a high key was Revolution itself. Anyone who fought for the victory of Impressionism and stood up for "the men of our *School*" (he liked to linger on the word) was fighting for a radiant, high-keyed to-morrow. And besides—Tanguy liked Impressionist painting for itself, and detested the "tobacco-juice" tonality which the middle classes of his time had taken to their hearts.

Unendingly generous by nature, Tanguy liked to assemble "his" painters around his frugal table. Paints and canvas he gave them gladly, and in return would take a picture or two: and what pictures, after all! No one else would look at them. Ribaldry and sarcasm met them on every side: the Pissarros, it seemed, were simply "palette-scrapings laid one after another on dirty canvas"; the Monets were painted "much as people touch up fountain-basins"; and as for the Cézannes, they were best not talked of: it would be many years before they were considered as anything but "painting as a drunken scavenger would see it," as someone remarked.

To get back some of his expenses—and, of course, to help his artists—Tanguy tried to sell some of the canvases which cluttered his shop in ever greater numbers; but only rarely did he succeed. His pictures were pledges that none could redeem. His collection grew steadily bigger and bigger until the shop became a real little avant-garde museum of contemporary art and a meeting-place for all those who supported the Impressionists and liked to know what was new in the world of art. It was Cézanne's work, above all, that they came to see. During the third Impressionist exhibition in 1877 Cézanne was attacked so violently, and suffered so deeply in consequence, that he decided that never again would he show his pictures in public. For nearly twenty years—until the famous exhibition organised by Vollard in 1895, which marked the beginnings of his great fame—he took no part in the activities of the art world. And during all that time, or at any rate until Tanguy died in 1894, the shop in the rue Clauzel (moved meanwhile from no. 14 to no. 9, by the way) was the only place in Paris where Cézannes could be seen.

"People went to Tanguy's as if to a museum," Émile Bernard tells us, "to see some studies by the unknown painter who lived at Aix . . . The unpretentious shop became, without knowing it, a Parisian legend. It was talked of in every studio. Members of the *Institut,* influential critics and writers who wanted to set everything to rights—all flocked there. Such was the unsettling effect of these canvases . . . the young people sensed that they were works of genius, their elders saw in them the madness of paradox, and the envious invoked the name of impotence."

Gauguin, Sérusier, Anquetin, Signac and Maurice Denis were among those who came to Papa Tanguy's shop to learn the lesson of Cézanne. (Later, as is well known, Cézanne, never the most conciliatory of men, was to accuse Gauguin of stealing from him his *petite sensation.*) But there were many other regular visitors, from Octave Mirbeau to Francis Jourdain and Léon-Paul Fargue, and from Toulouse-Lautrec to Dom Verkade and Jacques-Émile Blanche. It was also—and this is a remarkable fact—in Tanguy's window that in 1892 Ambroise Vollard saw a Cézanne for the first time. Nor, of course, must we forget Van Gogh who in 1886 and 1887 was a daily visitor to the shop. He had a profound admiration for Cézanne, and one day, to his great joy, he lunched with the Master of Aix at Tanguy's. The two artists set forth their ideas on painting: at the end of the meal Van Gogh gave Cézanne one of his pictures and Cézanne, abrupt as ever, looked hard at it and said: "No, but honestly—that's a madman's painting."

Tanguy held Cézanne in the deepest and most respectful regard; no less strong, for that matter, were his feelings for Van Gogh. And when, on returning from Provence in 1890, Van Gogh shot himself dead at Auvers-sur-Oise, Tanguy wept for him as if he had been his own son.

Octave Mirbeau once described a visit to Tanguy, not long after Van Gogh's death. "Ah, poor Vincent!" Tanguy lamented. "What a misfortune! Monsieur Mirbeau! What a misfortune! What a great misfortune! A genius like him! And such a delightful fellow! But wait—I'll show you some more of his masterpieces!" Papa Tanguy went off to fetch more Van Goghs from the back of his shop and came back with four or five in his arms and two in each hand. As he laid them lovingly against the backs of his chairs, shifting and turning them to get the best light, he went on groaning: "Poor Vincent! Are those masterpieces?—Or are they not? And there are so many of them, so many . . . And they're so beautiful that when I look at them it gives me a pain here, in my breast . . . Why should a man like that die? It's not right, it really isn't . . . Poor Vincent . . . I'll bet you don't know his *Pot of Gladiolus*? It's one of the last things he did. Marv—ellous, simply marv—ellous! I must show it to you—when it came to flowers there was no one to touch him, no one. He had such a feeling for everything . . ." And Papa drew a circle in the air, as painters do, as if to single out some part of a painting for particular notice. "Just look at that sky! And those trees! Aren't they just right? And the color! And the movement, I ask you!"

From time to time some lover of painting would buy a picture from the shop in the rue Clauzel. But Papa Tanguy's business methods were not at all those of the dealer-speculator. For his Cézannes he had a fixed price: a hundred francs for a large canvas, forty for a small one. The story is told of an enthusiast who asked the price of a Van Gogh: "Just a moment!" said Tanguy, and went and pored over his account book. "That'll be forty-eight francs," he said, finally. "Forty-eight? That's an odd figure—why not fifty? Or forty?" "Well," said Tanguy, "forty-eight francs is exactly what poor Van Gogh owed me when he died."

No, Papa Tanguy was not at all a speculator. "How he loved the pictures that he was obliged to sell!" Dom Verkade remembered. "Often he was in despair at seeing so fine a picture go out of his shop." And there was one picture that he would never consider selling: his own portrait by Van Gogh. (It is now in the Musée Rodin in Paris.) Vollard tells us that when anyone wanted to make a bid for it Tanguy would coldly ask a flat five hundred francs. This, at that time, was enough to put off any potential buyer at the start.

These idiosyncratic methods meant that Papa Tanguy never became rich—was never, indeed, even moderately well off. He remained to the day of his death frugal in the extreme and lived as sparingly as he possibly could. Yet fate had another hammer-blow in store for him: when he died, in 1894, it was of cancer of the stomach, and he had had to suffer appallingly. He had been taken to hospital, but when he sensed that the end was near he asked to be brought back to the rue Clauzel. "I want to die in my own home, with my wife beside me and my pictures all around." One evening he gave his wife his last instructions: "Life won't be easy for you when I'm not there. Our pictures are all we've got. You mustn't hesitate to sell them . . ." He was saying good-bye: the next morning, February 6, 1894, he died.

Madame Tanguy followed her husband's advice and made what money she could from the canvases which were still in the shop. The sale was held at the Hôtel Drouot on June 2, 1894. It brought in 14,621 francs—not a bad total, in itself, especially for people like the Tanguys who had been poor all their lives. But in relation to the masterpieces which came under the hammer it was pitiably small. The only picture that got anything like a good price was a Monet, a view of Bordighera, which fetched 3,000 francs. Six Cézannes (five went to Vollard and one to Victor Chocquet) went for 902 francs in all: their individual prices varied between 92 and 215 francs, and the auctioneer actually complimented Vollard on his "recklessness" in bidding up to the latter figure! The six Gauguins didn't average as much as 100 francs each. The Guillaumins went for between 80 and 160 apiece. Pissarro got up to more than 400, but a Seurat was knocked down for 50, and a Van Gogh for 30.

Papa Tanguy would have been deeply hurt, no doubt, to read of these prices. He had so longed to see his painters triumph—and that triumph, as it seemed, lay still in the distant future. But it was nearer than those concerned then dared to think. Only a year later Vollard was to hold his Cézanne exhibition, and in 1899, at the Chocquet sale, the painting by Cézanne which Chocquet had bought at the Tanguy sale (it was the *Pont de Maincy*) was to fetch 2,200 francs. Thereafter the prices rose continually—and not of Cézanne only, but of all Papa Tanguy's painters.

He never got rich, Papa Tanguy, but he wrote a fine page in the history of French art.

RECOMMENDED READING

BIOGRAPHIES

Rather than provide pages and pages of annotated biographies, I have simply provided below the titles of books representing a wide range of people, and I hope that you will be interested to know more about one or two of them. This list, by no means comprehensive, includes Parisian or French men and women as well as expatriates of several nationalities for whom Paris was a part of their lives.

Albert Camus: A Biography, Herbert Lottman (Doubleday, 1979).

Colette

Creating Colette, Volume I: From Ingénue to Libertine, 1873–1913 (1998) and *Volume II: From Baroness to Woman of Letters, 1912–1954* (1999), both by Claude Francis and Fernande Gontier and published by Steerforth.

Colette: Earthly Paradise: An Autobiography Drawn from Her Lifetime Writings (1966) and *Belles Saisons: A Colette Scrapbook* (1978), both by Robert Phelps and published by Farrar, Straus and Giroux.

Maurice Goudeket, Colette's third husband, whom she unsuccessfully hid from the Nazis but successfully managed to free from deportation to Auschwitz, wrote two of his own books about life with Colette: *The Delights of Growing Old: An Uncommon Biography* (Farrar, Straus and Giroux, 1968) and *Close to Colette: Intimate Portrait of a Woman of Genius* (Farrar, Straus and Cudahy, 1957; Greenwood, 1973).

Everybody Was So Young: Gerald and Sara Murphy: A Lost Generation Love Story, Amanda Vaill (Houghton Mifflin, 1998) and *Living Well Is the Best Revenge,* Calvin Tomkins (Viking, 1971; Modern Library, 1998). *Tender Is the Night* is one of my favorite F. Scott Fitzgerald novels. When I first read it, I knew it was loosely based on the dazzling American expatriates Gerald and Sara Murphy, but I had no clue how much of it was fiction, and I have remained fascinated by the Murphys.

With the publication of these two books, fact and fiction have been sorted out. Of the two, Calvin Tomkins, longtime art critic for the *New Yorker*, writes the smaller but not in any way lesser book. *Living Well* relates the Murphys' story concisely and engagingly, accompanied by black-and-white reproductions of Gerald's paintings and sixty-nine photographs from the Murphys' family album. Amanda Vaill's heftier *Everybody Was So Young* includes two inserts of black-and-white photos and some more recent material than the older Tomkins title, which focuses on the years before they returned to America in 1933. The Murphys were more legendary on the Côte d'Azur, where they lived in the Villa America on the Cap d'Antibes, but they held court in Paris just as eloquently.

The Italics Are Mine, Nina Berberova (Harcourt, Brace, 1969; Knopf, 1992, revised translation). Memoir of Russian writer and exile to Paris and the United States. Berberova, who passed away in 1993, is also the subject of "Going On," an essay in Kennedy Fraser's wonderful book *Ornament and Silence: Essays on Women's Lives from Edith Wharton to Germaine Greer* (Knopf, 1996).

The Letters of Vincent van Gogh, edited by Mark Roskill (Atheneum, 1963).

Madame de Sévigné: A Life and Letters, Frances Mossiker (Knopf, 1983).

Madame de Staël: The First Modern Woman, Francine du Plessix Gray (Atlas, 2008).

Édouard Manet: Rebel in a Frock Coat, Beth Archer Brombert (Little, Brown, 1996).

M. F. K. Fisher and Me: A Memoir of Food and Friendship, Jeannette Ferrary (St. Martin's, 1991; Thomas Dunne, 1998).

Matisse

Matisse and Picasso, Yve-Alain Bois (Flammarion, 1999).

Matisse and Picasso: A Friendship in Art, Françoise Gilot (Doubleday, 1990).

Matisse, Picasso, Miró: As I Knew Them, Rosamond Bernier (Knopf, 1991).

The Unknown Matisse: A Life of Henri Matisse: The Early Years, 1869–1908 (1998) and *Matisse the Master: A Life of Henri Matisse: The Conquest of Color, 1909–1954* (2005), both by Hilary Spurling and published by Knopf.

M. F. K. Fisher, Julia Child, and Alice Waters: Celebrating the Pleasures of the Table, Joan Reardon (Harmony, 1994). Fisher, Child, and Waters were the pioneers in the American food world: due to Child's PBS television series, the Food Network thrives today; due to Fisher's passionate writing on gastronomy, cookbooks and food magazines grew to flourish; and Waters's insistence upon fresh, seasonal food has prompted the growth of farmers' markets and the local food movement.

Henry Miller: The Paris Years (Arcade, 1995), by the Hungarian photographer Brassaï, whose given name was Gyula Halász.

Misia: The Life of Misia Sert, Arthur Gold and Robert Fizdale (Knopf, 1980). *Misia* tells the wildly entertaining but true tale of the vivacious socialite Misia (*née* Marie Sophie Olga Zenaide Godebska), whose third husband, the Spanish painter José-Maria Sert, decorated such spaces as Rockefeller Center and the grand ballroom of the Waldorf-Astoria Hotel in New York.

Napoléon

The Horizon Book of the Age of Napoléon (American Heritage, 1963).

How Far from Austerlitz?: Napoléon 1805–1815, Alistair Horne (St. Martin's, 1997). The years 1996 and 1997 marked the two hundredth anniversary of Napoléon Bonaparte's first successes in the Italian Campaign against Austria, causing historian Horne to reflect upon his earlier book *Napoléon, Master of Europe, 1805–1807* and ask, "Did he deserve it? How did his reputation look, nearly two centuries later?" and "What paths led him to his final, wretched exile?" Austerlitz has been referred to as "the first great battle of modern history," Horne notes, and was Napoléon's greatest victory; it was also the beginning of Napoléon's downfall. Though *How Far from Austerlitz?* isn't a biography of Napoléon, it provides a great starting point from which to view his life. (The title of this excellent book, by the way, is taken from Rudyard Kipling's "A St. Helena Lullaby," which stuck in my head long after I'd finished reading. Each line of the poem begins with "How far is St. Helena . . . ," referring to the island where Napoléon served out his exile. One stanza is: "How far is St. Helena from the field of Austerlitz? / You couldn't hear me if I told—so loud the cannons roar.")

Napoléon, Vincent Cronin (Collins, 1971).

Napoléon Bonaparte: A Life, Alan Schom (HarperCollins, 1997).

And though it's historical fiction, a trilogy about the life of Joséphine Bonaparte is a unique take on the life of Napoléon's wife: *The Many Lives and Secret Sorrows of Joséphine B.* (1999), *Tales of Passion, Tales of Woe* (1999), and *The Last Great Dance on Earth* (2000), all by Sandra Gulland and published by Scribner.

Picasso

A Life of Picasso: The Prodigy, 1881–1906; The Cubist Rebel: 1907–1916; and *The Triumphant Years: 1917–1932,* all by John Richardson and published by Knopf (2007).

Life with Picasso, Françoise Gilot and Carlton Lake (McGraw Hill, 1964). Gilot and Picasso never married but had two children together, Paloma and Claude; Gilot later married Jonas Salk in 1970. If you admire Gilot as much as I do, you may know she's an accomplished artist in her own right: see *Stone Echoes: Original Prints by Françoise Gilot,* edited by Mel Yoakum (Philip and Muriel Berman Museum of Art at Ursinus College, 1995) for her printmaking oeuvre and *Françoise Gilot: Monograph 1940–2000,* Mel Yoakum and Dina Vierny (Acatos, 2001) for her oil paintings and works on paper.

Picasso: A Biography, Patrick O'Brian (Collins, 1976).

The Success and Failure of Picasso, John Berger (Penguin, 1965; Pantheon, 1989).

Renoir, My Father, Jean Renoir (Little, Brown, 1962; New York Review Books Classics, 2001).

Rodin: A Biography, Frederic Grunfeld (Henry Holt, 1987).

Rodin: The Shape of Genius, Ruth Butler (Yale University Press, 1993).

Saint-Exupéry: A Biography, Stacy Schiff (Knopf, 1994).

Speak, Memory: An Autobiography Revisited, Vladimir Nabokov (Harper & Bros., 1951; Vintage, 1989, revised edition).

Toulouse-Lautrec: A Life, Julia Frey (Viking, 1994).

Zola: A Life, Frederick Brown (Farrar, Straus and Giroux, 1995).

The history of Paris lies in her buildings and monuments. That of the Parisians in a host of little details.

—*Cahier de Paris*

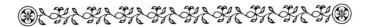

THE ÎLE-DE-FRANCE
AND BEYOND:
EXCURSIONS FROM PARIS

To understand French landscape one must visit the Île-de-France, that region northwest of Paris where small villages nestle in gently rolling hills covered with fruit trees and flowers. The human scale of the land, the humbleness of the steeple of every village church evoke another age.

—ALEXANDER LIBERMAN,
The Artist in His Studio

PARIS IS INEXHAUSTIBLE, but visitors wishing to explore outside of the city—and I do encourage exploring the environs—will find there is practically unlimited choice in what to see and where to go. (Some journeys will even have you back in Paris in time for dinner.) Within easy striking distance from the city, in the Île-de-France (of which Paris is a part), the options are many: the Château de Versailles; the forêt de Fontainebleau; the village of Barbizon with its showcase of pre-Impressionist landscape artists; the beautiful gardens at Marly-le-Roi; the châteaux at Saint-Germain-en-Laye and Chantilly; the village of Auvers-sur-Oise, where Van Gogh spent his final years and also frequented by another nineteenth-century painter, Charles-François Daubigny; the fabulous Musée National de la Renaissance in the Château d'Ecouen; the exquisite château of Vaux-le-Vicomte, built in the seventeenth century by Nicolas Fouquet, Louis XIV's finance minister (French history buffs may recall that the château was so stunning, and the housewarming ball Fouquet hosted so over-the-top, that the jealous Sun King imprisoned Fouquet and hired the very same team of architect Louis Le Vau, garden designer André Le Nôtre, and dec-

orator Charles Le Brun to redesign Versailles). In nearby Normandy, there are the D-Day landing beaches and museums, and Claude Monet's house and studio, where he painted his famous water lilies, in Giverny. The châteaux of the Loire Valley could easily occupy a full week's time, the pretty coastline of Brittany beckons, and the distinctly northern city of Lille, in the Nord-Pas-de-Calais region, is a mere one-hour train ride from Paris. . . . As you can see, it's difficult to decide!

INTERVIEW

David Downie and Alison Harris

For many visitors the decision for an excursion is easy: Burgundy—with its outstanding, world-famous wines, renowned culinary specialties, rivers, Romanesque architecture, and towns like Dijon, Beaune, and Vézelay— is tops on the side-trip list. As if additional reasons were needed, I like to refer to a special issue of Saveur *(Issue 30), devoted to Burgundy. There the editors encourage a visit because "it hasn't yet been discovered by the Eurochic or the mavens of the Mediterranean. Because its food is hearty, honest, and linked to the earth and its wines are delicate and elusive. Because it remains true, even today, to its ancient reputation for good living. Because it's not Provence."*

By happy coincidence, the Little Bookroom published another volume in its Terroir *series as I was completing this book.* Food Wine: Burgundy *by David Downie and Alison Harris (see page 369) is an absolutely essential companion to this region—don't even think about going to La Bourgogne without it. The book covers all the towns and villages of the region and includes superb recommendations—for places to eat, wineries to visit, charming places to stay, interesting shops and food artisans— as well as brief notes on a number of museums and historic sites and a very* good overview of Burgundy wines. Downie also provides a list of market days in Burgundy, a food and wine glossary, and a few pages of practical information. Here's one nugget worth repeating: "Nine in ten businesses are closed Sunday afternoons and a half day or full day once a week, usually Monday, sometimes Wednesday"; wineries are also often closed in July and/or August. As for restaurants, Downie focuses on those places whose chefs still work from scratch, "using fresh, locally sourced, high-quality ingredients, serving traditional or updated regional fare and cuisine bourgeoise *that captures the spirit—if not always the letter—of* terroir." *The word* terroir, *referring literally to the land, describes the proud sense of place expressed in locally grown and produced food, found in abundance in this region.*

I have had the great pleasure of meeting Downie on several occasions, along with his kind and talented wife, the photographer Alison Harris. Most recently, I met them both for lunch at one of my Parisian favorites, Ma Bourgogne, on the Place des Vosges, just steps from their apartment.

Q: What are some general words of advice you would give to travelers going to Burgundy?

A: First of all, give yourself enough time—enough time to slow down and really enjoy discovering and exploring the small roads of Burgundy. At least ten days is great, which is enough time to get lost and find yourself again, and our book will take you to many different places, and certainly many off the beaten track. One of the things we enjoy doing most in Burgundy is hiking. There are a great number of marked trails, and when you hike, you see much more than from a car window: you're actually *in* it—*in* the landscape, we mean.

Q: When did you first start exploring Burgundy?

A: We started going to Burgundy about twenty years ago thanks to some good friends we knew in Paris—they're English and American—who were at that time going back and forth to Italy, and they found that this was becoming too time-consuming. They then bought a little place in southern Burgundy—from which their forays to Italy took less time—and when we visited them we discovered this uncluttered, won-  derful, beautiful place in France . . . and we've continued to go back over the years. Though we're referring specifically to southern Burgundy, make no mistake: *all* of Burgundy is great. There are parts of the region that are very well known, of course—everyone roars up and down the wine route, everybody wants to go to Beaune. These are wonderful, and you should see them, but hardly anyone gets off that wine road and goes out into the hinterland of southern Burgundy. The wines of southern Burgundy, by the way, are not as well known, and for a long time everyone thought they were all lousy wines owned by a big cooperative. Actually there are many, many really good wines that are being made here, at prices that aren't crazy. So we got to know this part of Burgundy well and we began exploring the rest of the region.

Q: For visitors who are looking for pursuits other than wine, what else does Burgundy offer?

A: Vineyards cover about 2 percent of the land area in Burgundy, and there are about four thousand wineries in the region, which is about the size of Delaware, so it's easy to see how everyone thinks Burgundy is nothing but wine country. But Burgundy is much more: it has one of the largest forests in France (and in fact forests occupy 34 percent of the land area); it's the heartland of ancient Gaul; it's home to dozens of

Michelin-starred restaurants and hundreds of simple *auberges* devoted to *terroir* cuisine; and there are dozens and dozens of undiscovered rural areas with one-lane roads and about a thousand Romanesque churches, which were spun off from Cluny, which was the largest and most powerful medieval monastic complex outside Rome. Even people who don't really care much for architecture and art love to see these Romanesque gems on the horizon. Burgundy is almost entirely rural—60 percent of the land area is devoted to farmland—so for this reason alone it is worth visiting and is the perfect side trip from Paris. All you have to do is get off that main road and go up into the hills and you'll find all this wonderful stuff.

Q: Do visitors need appointments in advance to visit wineries?
A: Yes, usually in France—wherever you are—it's better to make an appointment if you can.

Q: What specifically about your Burgundy *Terroir* guide do you feel is especially useful for visitors?
A: I've worked on so many guidebooks over the years and I know their flaws. Sometimes the writer doesn't have time, or he or she really isn't suited to the assignment, or the editor wants the writer to create the perfect guide but is prevented from giving the writer the proper resources. So as I started working on this Burgundy guide I decided I was going to make the perfect guidebook for my friends. This is the book I would want them to have because they would get to a town and they would have a little sense of its history, they would have a sense of what its unique foods and wines are, they would know of some worthwhile sites to see. Yes, the Burgundy guide is obviously about discovering famous wineries, famous chefs, and famous sites, but it's also about all these hidden places and wonderful little pockets of charm and beauty. All the *Terroir* guides are insider's guides, for curious,

intelligent people, but we don't want that to sound snobby. We can't stand the tone of some guidebooks that assume because the reader is American and perhaps not well traveled, the text is dumbed down. We assume that even though readers may not yet be well traveled, they picked up our book because they're interested to learn, and we respect that. The *Terroir* guides are not about the mindless pursuit of hedonism. They're about making it possible for someone who loves culture, great food, and great wine to go out and find the authentic food artisans and winemakers. And they're about preserving traditions that should be preserved. The guides are also not just for tourists—they're also for people who already know the area. We noticed with our Rome guide that a lot of copies were purchased by people who live there.

Q: Can you share just a few of your favorite aspects of Burgundy?

A: An afternoon visit to Cluny, which once housed ten thousand monks, and seeing where the abbey once stood. All you see now is the transept and a reconstruction, but it's well worth it. An autumnal walk in the woods, or perhaps a springtime walk, when you look out over a countryside which is made up of hedgerows and flowering fruit trees and wildflowers and a Romanesque steeple in the distance. A visit to Bibracte, the lost city of the ancient Gauls. There's a museum there, not a very great one but still with some interesting stuff. Walk up to the top of

the hill where Caesar dictated the conquest of Gaul and read Julius Caesar's classic *The Conquest of Gaul,* which, believe it or not, is a real page-turner. It describes the only military campaign of the ancient world for which we have a record. Truly, it's incredible to read this when you're *in* ancient Gaul, in the heart of Burgundy.

And after you've looked at all the Charolais cattle everywhere—cattle actually outnumber humans in Burgundy—go and eat a really good dry-aged Charolais steak in a traditional restaurant. You'll find many listed in our book.

TWO PERFECT DAYS IN BURGUNDY

Billing itself as the "world's premier active travel company," Butterfield & Robinson (butterfield.com) has had a long-standing relationship with Burgundy. B&R offers trips to sixty destinations worldwide, with four different journeys that include Burgundy: biking, self-guided biking, walking, and a wine "grand journey" that also includes Bordeaux and the Piemonte region of Italy. Though its most popular walking trip in 2010 was along the Amalfi Coast, its most popular biking trip was to Burgundy. (Additionally, B&R has at least nine other trip options in other parts of France.)

Founded in 1966, Butterfield & Robinson refers to George Butterfield, his high school roommate Sidney Robinson, and Sidney's sister Martha Robinson, who together coordinated a trip to Europe for forty-three students. (Martha later married George, thus becoming the only *true* Butterfield & Robinson.) Early B&R trips were only for students, who biked from youth hostel to youth hostel. But at some point along the way the trips were crafted to be more distinctive and more comfortable, and B&R is now known to have pioneered the concept of luxury biking tours in Europe. The three founders, who use the motto "Slow Down to See the World," also have a reputation for providing once-in-a-lifetime experiences and unique access to events, people, and places that are very difficult or impossible for travelers to arrange on their own. All three are still involved with the operation of the company, and in 2009 they welcomed Erik Blachford, former CEO of Expedia and onetime B&R guide, as a new partner.

In an interview with the *Globe and Mail*, George was asked to give some advice specific to running a high-end business. "It's pretty simple," he said. "Just get it right. People don't want to be treated like they're just one of thousands and thousands. You want everything to be special. And an awful lot of group travel is pretty routine, pretty predictable." His remarks really appealed to me, so I sent him a query asking if he would share some of his favorite things about Burgundy. Assuming he wouldn't have time to share more than a few sentences, I was thrilled to receive his reply, "Two Perfect Days in Beaune," reprinted here.

In 1986 we moved the B&R office from Paris to Beaune. Centrally located, with arguably the world's best wine and biking, our offices in Beaune are B&R's European headquarters and home to twelve hundred bicycles.

Start your first day with a buttery croissant from Pâtisserie Bouché before a morning visit to the Hospices Civils de Beaune. Head over to the patio at Le Conty for a light lunch. After lunch, drive to Gevrey-Chambertin along the Route des Grands Crus, passing through some of the most famous *grands crus* of the Côte-de-Nuits. Or bike up into the Côte-de-Beaune via Aloxe-Corton and Pernand-Vergelesses. Dinner tonight could be on the terrace of the lovely Le Jardin des Remparts, or for a more casual option, Les Caves Madeleine, a charming wine store and restaurant. For an evening nightcap try Le Bout du Monde.

If you are in Beaune on a Saturday, head over early to Le Grand Café on Place Carnot and watch the farmers set up for the spectacular morning market. Pick up some local Epoisses, a baguette, and a bottle of wine for later. Stroll around the cobblestone streets and the rampart walls of Beaune. In the afternoon you can head south by car or by bike to Meursault through the villages of Chassagne-Montrachet and Puligny-Montrachet. If you haven't had lunch already, you could stop at a great local restaurant, Le Montrachet, in Puligny-Montrachet, or if it is later in the day, just enjoy a glass of wine at the wine bar. Tonight a great bistro meal is right downstairs at the hotel restaurant, Le Bistro de l'Hôtel.

Dining Notes and Contact Information

Pâtisserie Bouché (1 place Monge / +33 03 80 22 10 35). This is the best shop in town for cakes, pastries, and chocolate. Madame Bouché—the very impressive-looking woman behind the counter—makes fabulous-quality goods and prices them as generously as the portions of butter on her croissants. (The top-notch Hôtel Le Cep gets its breakfast croissants from her, and they really are the best!) Some of her chocolate recipes are patented, and she ships them to shops in Paris as well as doing a hopping business here in Beaune. You'll find her at the opposite end of the pedestrian zone, in Place Monge.

Le Conty (5 rue Ziem / +33 03 80 22 63 94 / leconty.fr). A nice little restaurant with good food and friendly, quality service. In case of fair weather, the terrace is one of the best in town. Their menus are always a good choice and changed seasonally. Laurent Parra, a young chef from a local gourmet family, cooks some excellent local goodies! Closed Sundays and Mondays.

Le Jardin des Remparts (10 rue de l'Hôtel-Dieu / +33 03 80 24 79 41 / le-jardin-des-remparts.com). This restaurant has a fantastic terrace, some great innovative food, and a charming atmosphere. The service is not a speedy American-style affair; this is meant to be a longer meal that you linger over with great company. Closed on Sundays and Mondays.

Les Caves Madeleine (8 rue du Faubourg-Madeleine / +33 03 80 22 93 30). Friendly, intimate, and casual atmosphere. Featuring long tables with shared seating, this is a great spot for regional specialties and has both good, inexpensive set menus and a wide choice of à la carte options. It also boasts an excellent selection of wines sold in cooperation with the winemakers, and as such are not marked up like in other restaurants—some excellent deals are to be had here! Closed Sundays, Thursdays, and Friday lunch.

Le Bout du Monde (7 rue du Faubourg-Madeleine / +33 03 80 24 04 52 / leboutdumonde.net). The team welcomes you into the warm lounge bar for a simple beer or a more exotic drink. Nice, quiet terrace in spring and summer. Right across from Les Caves Madeleine.

Le Grand Café (36 place Carnot / +33 03 80 22 23 00). If you head here at the end of the day for a pastis, kir, or cold beer, you may very likely be sharing the terrace with some of our B&R Beaune staff who've just finished their day at the office! This is the grand classic of French cafés, and not only do they have one of the best people-watching terraces in town, but the service is impeccable as well. You can also eat lightly here; they have a small menu of sandwiches and salads.

Le Bistro de l'Hôtel (5 rue Samuel Legay / +33 03 80 25 94 14 / lhoteldebeaune.com). Le Bistro concentrates on serving simple food, using only the freshest high-quality produce from local suppliers, including fish, seafood, beef, *poulet de Bresse,* and Charolais veal. Truffles and wild mushrooms are featured *cuisine du marché*! This is simply one of the best tables in Beaune, with an amazing wine list. Open every day for lunch and dinner except for Sunday lunch.

Other Options and Accommodations

Bistrot Bourguignon (8 rue Monge / +33 03 80 22 23 24 / restaurant-lebistrotbourguignon.com). A relaxed bistro atmosphere, great for those who need a quick, simple meal. Wonderful wines by the glass with a few tables out front. On the weekends, they often have live jazz music playing—you can even just go by for a glass of wine to take in the music! Closed Mondays.

Le Gourmandin (8 place Carnot / +33 03 80 24 07 88 / hotelle gourmandin.com). This is an excellent bistro that has a real Parisian atmosphere. Excellent *boeuf bourguignon* as well as creative and light dishes and lots of unknown little wines available by the glass. They do have some weird things on the wine list that seem overpriced, but there are also some good finds. The maître d' can always suggest something delicious and not too pricey to drink, but the service can be at French speed. Open every day.

La Part des Anges (24 rue d'Alsace / +33 03 80 22 07 68). This wine bar offers a cozy ambience and great food. Run by young guys, La Part has a large selection of local dishes and some amazing wines on their wine list that can be enjoyed by the glass. Closed Sundays and Mondays.

L'Hôtel de Beaune (5 rue Samuel Legay / +33 03 80 25 94 14 / lhoteldebeaune.com). This mansion is the gem of Beaune. With only seven rooms, it oozes grace and charm, and is now considered the top property in the town. The spacious rooms are furnished with fine linens, mahogany furniture, and interesting artwork. Since the hotel is located right in the center of Beaune, the town awaits just outside your doorstep.

Bastion Ste. Anne (bastionsteanne.com). For a longer stay, you may want to rent our home in Beaune, Bastion Ste. Anne. Forming part of the centuries-old walls of the town of Beaune, this combination of secret garden and lovely cottage is a totally unique experience.

Other Burgundy Resources

"In Burgundy, Picking Up the Pace," Alexander Lobrano (*Gourmet,* September 2006). Inspired by Samuel Chamberlain's "Burgundy at a Snail's Pace," which appeared in the first issue of *Gourmet,* January 1941.

"Burgundy I: Parsleyed Ham, Two Burgundian Cheeses, and Spice Bread," Edward Behr (*Art of Eating,* Number 59, 2001).

"Burgundy II: Chablis," Edward Behr (*Art of Eating,* Number 81, 2009).

"Beaujolais: The Goal of a Gulpable Wine," Edward Behr (*Art of Eating,* Number 67, 2004).

Puligny-Montrachet: Journal of a Village in Burgundy, Simon Loftus (Knopf, 1993). This fascinating book is *de rigueur* reading for anyone with an interest in wine, Burgundy wine in particular. Perhaps the most interesting detail about it is the front endpapers, a color reproduction of *Le Terrier de la Seigneurie de Puligny*

et Mypon, preserved in the *mairie* (town hall) in Puligny "for the delight of anyone with an inquisitive nose." This remarkable land register, compiled between 1741 and 1747 in three enormous leather-bound volumes, is "one of the earliest, most detailed and most complete surveys of any of the classic vineyard regions of France." It indicates the name of every landholder, every tree, and every house in the village, the boundaries of each field and the subdivisions of every vineyard. What the wine enthusiast discovers, with Loftus's curiosity and expertise, is that a mere seven and a half acres of *terre* became the "most precious agricultural land on earth, producing the grandest of all white wines: Puligny-Montrachet." Three appendices—appellations, vintages, and tastings—complete this eye-opening and memorable work.

An Hour from Paris

Several years ago, writer Annabel Simms found herself in the middle of the woods, as completely lost as if she were in Africa instead of nineteen kilometers from Paris. There were three paths in front of her with no indication of where any of them led, so on impulse she chose the one on the left. She soon came upon some houses and knocked on the door of the nearest one. After following the owner's directions, five minutes later she was in front of a magnificent sixteenth-century château. It turned out to be the Musée National de la Renaissance in Ecouen, twenty-three minutes from Paris by train (and it happens to be one of my favorite museums in northern France). It was this experience that alerted Simms to how accessible the countryside around Paris really is, and how few foreigners—and the French themselves—are aware of this. (Those paths, by the way, are now signposted.)

More excursions (with much note taking) into the old *pays*

de France—the fertile plain surrounded by rivers to the north of Paris—led Simms to conclude that the Île-de-France has escaped the effects of mass tourism and is one of the least visited parts of France. She also realized she had the makings of a unique book geared entirely to foreign visitors arriving by train. These visitors, she envisioned, would be "curious about everything, rather than with a specialist interest in walking, architecture, gastronomy, or whatever," and they would be equally as interested in the present as in the past. Her readers would appreciate cafés and humble restaurants, and above all would be those "who avoided crowds and prepackaged experience wherever possible and were happiest when exploring off the beaten track." And thus *An Hour from Paris* (Pallas Athene, 2008, revised edition) was born.

Simms has really done her homework, and not for nothing has her book been referred to as a "groundbreaking work" (*Sunday Times*) and "a kind of Île-de-France *profonde*" (*Independent*). I urge anyone with even the vaguest thoughts of setting out for the Île-de-France to go with this book in hand—it's a slender paperback. Simms has thoughtfully provided updates on her Web site (anhourfromparis.com).

AUVERS-SUR-OISE

Only twenty-two miles north of Paris and easily reached by train from the Gare Saint-Lazare, Auvers-sur-Oise is a small village known not only as where Vincent van Gogh spent the last weeks of his life (having arrived by train, in 1890), but also as the home, from 1862 to 1878, of Charles-François Daubigny, a painter considered a forerunner of Impressionism. Other Impressionists and landscape artists were drawn to Auvers as well, including Paul Cézanne, Camille Pissarro, and Jean-Baptiste-Camille Corot.

At the village's Auberge Ravoux, Van Gogh rented room number 5, with full board, for three and a half francs per day. Van Gogh painted more than seventy masterpieces in Auvers in fewer than eight weeks, but his room there was his last: he shot himself in a nearby field and died at the auberge shortly thereafter. According to Alexandra Leaf and Fred Leeman, authors of *Van Gogh's Table at the Auberge Ravoux* (Artisan, 2001)—a book you must read if you go to Auvers—Van Gogh lived in at least thirty-eight places in four countries, all in his life of thirty-seven years. Due to French superstitions about suicide, it's unlikely that the room was ever rented again after his death. Both Van Gogh's room and the Auberge Ravoux were declared historical landmarks.

In 1926 the auberge was officially renamed Maison de Van Gogh, and in 1952 Roger and Micheline Tagliana bought it and lovingly revitalized it. Four years later, when Vincente Minnelli was filming *Lust for Life* with Kirk Douglas as Van Gogh, he shot on location at the auberge, finally correcting the misconception that Van Gogh had died in Provence. In 1985, Belgian businessman Dominique-Charles Janssens was hit by a drunk driver a few yards from the former Auberge Ravoux. While he was convalescing, he read Van Gogh's letters and became quite passionate about the artist's work and life. He also learned at this time that the auberge was for sale, and he decided to buy it. He writes in his foreword to *Van Gogh's Table* that he wanted to create a spiritual refuge where people could connect with Van Gogh's art and feelings, a place where they could really step back in time: "There, they would find Van Gogh's room, a small intimate space, empty except for memories. Visitors could furnish it with their own feelings or experiences. No mass tourism would trample through the tranquility of the place. It would be preserved as a refuge of silence from the frenzy of the external world." The Maison de Van Gogh (maisondevangogh.fr) also has a worthy restaurant; note that neither the restaurant nor the museum is open year-round.

Other attractions in Auvers-sur-Oise include the home of Dr.

Gachet, the cemetery where Van Gogh and his brother Theo are buried, the Romanesque Gothic church immortalized in Van Gogh's *Church at Auvers-sur-Oise,* the Château d'Auvers-sur-Oise (also known as Château de Léry), and the Musée Daubigny.

In addition to works by Charles-François Daubigny, the Musée Daubigny (musee-daubigny.com) features the works of other nineteenth- and twentieth-century artists, including some of Daubigny's own students (among them Hippolyte-Camille Delpy and Alexandre-René Véron), plus Jean-François Millet, Dr. Gachet, and Cézanne. I've been a fan of Daubigny's works since I first discovered them as a student in Paris. Daubigny had a boat he often used as a kind of floating studio, from which he painted landscapes outdoors, without reworking them later. (Among his works in the Musée d'Orsay is *Sunset Over the Oise.*) A few other works I particularly like in the Musée Daubigny are *Le Port de Rotterdam* by Norbert Goeneutte, *Bateaux au coucher du soleil* by Maxime Maufra, and *Le Travail champêtre* by Émile Boulard, all terrific Impressionist works by painters with whom I had been unfamiliar.

A good article to read before heading to Auvers is "Impressionist Visions near Paris" by Dana Micucci (*New York Times,* July 7, 2002). Micucci writes "I left Auvers-sur-Oise feeling that I had discovered the quintessential French village, overflowing with authentic rural charm and richly layered with culture and history."

CHARTRES

A visit to the town and cathedral of Chartres is an easy half- or full-day trip from Paris. "There is nothing comparable to the brilliance of Chartres' windows—not even the mosaics of Byzantium," notes Joseph Barry in *The People of Paris.* "Even without knowing the difference between Gothic architecture and the more earth-bound Romanesque from which it sprang, one can still sense the spiritual life of its vaults." Barry, "an architectural traveler with a pair of powerful field glasses rather than a pilgrim with a prayer book," recommends that travelers visit at twilight, when "all is calm and timeless. The gray of the sky merges with the warm gray of the stones. . . . Softly, dramatically, the night-lighting of the great cathedral commences."

I've been to Chartres only once, and unfortunately it wasn't at twilight; rather, it was on a gray, overcast day, but what was remarkable to me was that the famous blue in the stained-glass windows was still *really* blue, a shade completely unlike any other, as if light were shining through it. Robert Payne, in *The Splendor of France,* comments that throughout French history there has been an intense devotion to light, which for the French was "the purest joy, and they celebrated their joy in stained-glass windows, in brilliantly colored books and dresses, in Impressionist painting, in a continuing debate on the nature of light, in endless speculations on its strange and exhilarating behavior, as though it were a living thing. Because the light was feminine, and desired to please and to be seen, they opened up the walls of their cathedrals to let it in, and because the light was self-conscious and determined to be shown in its utmost splendor, they filled the windows with those thousands of pieces of colored glass, as thin as wafers, which are the great glory of medieval France."

Chartres definitely *vaut le détour,* and three worthy resources are:

"Seeing the Light in Chartres," Joan Gould (*New York Times,* December 18, 1988).

Chartres Cathedral, Malcolm Miller with color photographs by Sonia Halliday and Laura Lushington (Riverside, 1997). Miller has been leading tours to the cathedral for many decades almost every day without exception. Inquire at the *office de tourisme* (Place de la Cathédrale) or contact him directly (millerchartres@aol.com / +33 02 37 28 15 58).

Universe of Stone, Philip Ball (Harper, 2008). In this thorough book, Ball admits that it's somewhat foolhardy to talk about "why" Chartres Cathedral was built, but that is what he attempts to do. Only by confronting that question, he believes, can we fully experience all this cathedral has to offer. "There seems to be little point," he notes, "in knowing that you are standing in the south transept or looking at St. Lubin in the stained glass or gazing at a vault boss a hundred feet above your head unless you have some conception of what was in the minds of the people who created all of this." (And a "boss," by the way, is an architectural term that refers to a generally round, carved element located at the central crossing point of the ribs in Gothic vaults.)

Fontainebleau Postcard

My friend Ruth Homberg recently moved to Fontainebleau with her husband, Peter, so I asked her for some suggestions for a memorable Fontainebleau journey. Her detailed notes follow:

Located forty minutes outside of Paris by train, the ville *of Fontainebleau is nestled in the midst of a forest three times the size of Manhattan. The two main draws of the small French city are the campus of INSEAD, one of the world's leading business schools, and the Château de Fontainebleau, which has housed countless notables, including Napoléon and Marie Antoinette. The château sprawls across several acres of land and is adjoined by a park with carefully landscaped ponds and canals, which are also home to massive carp. On sunny days you can feed the ducks alongside French children and families enjoying* pique-niques.

The best days of the week to make the journey to Fontainebleau are Tuesdays, Fridays, and Sundays, when the heart of the town is converted into a lively farmers' market. Be on the lookout for souvenirs, including hand-woven baskets, jewelry, quilts, and clothing, as well as country-fresh produce and fruit, cheeses, and charcuterie. Sundays promise the most vibrant market, but be warned: after noon the entire town shuts down until Tuesday. (One of our favorite days here has been a Sunday morning at the market gathering food for a picnic in the park behind the château).

For an authentic and moderately priced French lunch or dinner, try Bistrot 9 (9 rue Montebello / +33 01 64 22 87 84 / lebistrot9.com) for a salad with chèvre chaud, *or the delicious* sole meunière. *For another bistro option, also try Bouchon de Bleau (32 rue de France / +33 01 64 22 30 99). (Note that both are often fully booked.) My other favorite in-town restaurant is Ty-Koz, a* crêperie *on a cobbled side street (18 rue de la Cloche / +33 01 64 22 00 55). With a glass of French wine or a pitcher of traditional cider from Bretagne, any dish tastes delicious.*

If you're traveling by car, don't fail to make your way to the neighboring towns of Barbizon and Moret-sur-Loing. Both are sleepy, picturesque villages that boast long histories. The old city of Moret-sur-Loing is bookended by two arches that lead to a bridge over the river Loing. Between these arches lies the medieval town, parts of which are in their original state. It's fun to grab an ice cream cone on a cobbled side street and stroll through the ancient streets or down to the beautiful river. On a hot day, you may see campers kayaking over the small locks or children wading in the shallow parts of the river.

Barbizon once housed many painters and writers. As it borders the paths of the Fontainebleau forest, it's easy to see what brought them here. With only one main street lined with a few shops and hotels, it has a history steeped in the arts. Beginning in the mid-1800s, it became a popular vacation spot for Parisians. In addition to tourists, the town attracted quite a few painters, who would later be dubbed the Barbizon School. Among others, this group included Théodore Rousseau, Jean-François Millet, Narcisse-Virgile Diaz, and Charles-François Daubigny, and much of their work is on display at Musée de l'École de Barbizon at the Auberge Ganne. Later, the town also lured the younger Impressionist painters like Monet and Renoir. Writers were drawn to the area as well, and well-known French poets, like Paul Verlaine, Baudelaire, and Guillaume Apollinaire all made the trek to the town and spent time writing there. At the end of the main strip in Barbizon are trails that run throughout the Forêt de Fontainebleau, which is full of hiking paths and huge boulders that many use for rock climbing. Be sure to get a map, and beware of the wild boars that are in abundance!

P.S. Peter and I recently checked out the town of Troyes, which is about an hour from Fontainebleau. It's also really cool. Have you been?

> Note: I haven't yet been to Troyes, but an interesting arti-
> cle to read about its culinary specialty, andouillette sausage, is
> "The Andouillete of Troyes" by Edward Behr (*Art of Eating,*
> Number 78, 2008).

LOIRE VALLEY

In addition to your guidebook of choice (my own favorites in-
clude *Knopf Guides: The Loire Valley* and *Michelin: Châteaux of the
Loire*), and perhaps an illustrated book, such as *The Châteaux of the
Loire* by Pierre Miquel and with photographs by Jean-Baptiste
Leroux (Penguin Studio, 1999), the very best, hands-down-
number-one resource you need is *A Wine and Food Guide to the
Loire* by Jacqueline Friedrich (Henry Holt, 1996). Honored with
Julia Child and James Beard awards, as well as being named
Veuve-Clicquot Wine Book of the Year, you need this encyclo-
pedic book if you're going anywhere at all in the Loire Valley.
American journalist and former lawyer Friedrich moved to
France in 1989 and stayed, and she now divides her time between
Paris and a small village in the Loire near Chinon. She spent two
years researching this book, a practical, interesting, and mouthwatering guide, and she's working on the second edition (to be
published by University of California Press). But don't think this
first edition won't be helpful: I can attest to its usefulness even
now, more than a decade later. The first part of the book is about
the river, wine history, climate, soil, and grapes, followed by a section focusing on food and a wine route that takes travelers
through the Nantais, Anjou and Saumur, Touraine, Sancerrois,
and Auvergne. At the end of the book are four useful appendices:
listings of *bonnes adresses* and recommended itineraries, a glossary,
wine-serving tips, and conversion charts.

I'm a huge fan of Friedrich's writing—I have all of the

"Choice Tables" articles she's contributed to the travel section of the *New York Times,* and her *Wines of France* book is also indispensable. And I'm not alone in praising her: noted wine authority Jancis Robinson endorsed Friedrich's Loire book by saying, "I've waited twenty years for this book. I am truly impressed by it and so grateful for its existence. I didn't know who would find the energy to write it, but for decades we will be grateful that it was someone of Jacqueline Friedrich's talent and passion." I also love that Friedrich's favorite word is "delicious." Readers may keep up with her at Jacquelinefriedrich.com.

COMPIÈGNE

I have long been fascinated by the signing of the armistice that ended World War I, which took place at a spot in the Forest of Compiègne, about seventy-five kilometers from Paris in the Picardy region. At five thirty a.m. on November 11, 1918, a German delegation signed the truce with the Allies. The two sides met in a clearing in the forest on railroad tracks: in one railcar was the German delegation, including imperial secretary of state Matthias

Erzberger, and in the other were Allied commander in chief General Ferdinand Foch and First Sea Lord Admiral Sir Rosslyn Wemyss, the leading British delegate on the Allied side. The armistice terms had already been prepared by the British and French governments and were not open to further discussion. The thirty-four clauses were read aloud to the Germans, and "hearing these conditions, one of the Germans wept openly," notes the Australian Department of Veterans' Affairs World War I memorial Web site (ww1westernfront.gov.au). All the Germans reportedly had tears in their eyes, and according to *A Stillness Heard Round the World: The End of the Great War,* Erzberger, whose son had recently died in a military hospital, said, "The German people, which held off a world of enemies for fifty months, will preserve their liberty and their unity despite every kind of violence. A nation of 70 millions of peoples suffers, but it does not die." Foch, whose son had been killed in action in 1914, ended the event by saying, "*Eh bien, messieurs, c'est fini, allez*" (Very well, gentlemen, it's over, go), and he ordered a cease-fire for eleven a.m. that morning. The German delegates signed the armistice after it was referred to Berlin, and Kaiser Wilhelm II abdicated the throne and went into exile in Holland.

The Glade of the Armistice (Clairière de l'Armistice) was established shortly after, and it "remains a shrine to those who perished in World War I," as Catharine Reynolds puts it in her *Gourmet* article "A Weekend Interlude: Imperial Pleasures North of Paris" (November 1996). A stone plaque there bears the inscription, loosely translated into English, "Here, on 11 November 1918, the criminal pride of the German Empire was brought low, vanquished by the free peoples it sought to enslave." The Paris newspaper *Le Matin* raised funds to erect a memorial to the liberators of Alsace and Lorraine, and the Glade was officially dedicated on Armistice Day 1922. Ferdinard Foch's railroad car—Wagon-Lits car #2419D—was once again a dining car after the war, and it was brought back to the Glade on Armistice Day

1927. A statue of Foch was also installed in the Glade in 1937, after his death.

On June 21, 1940, six weeks after Germany began its renewed attack on France, the Germans moved Foch's railroad car back onto the track where it had stood in 1918. Hitler had chosen this place for France's de facto surrender "to efface once and for all by an act of reparative justice a memory which was resented by the German people as the greatest shame of all time," according to William Shirer in *The Collapse of the Third Republic*. After the agreement was signed, the stone plaque was broken up and sent back to Germany, as well as the Alsace-Lorraine memorial. Foch's railroad car was sent to Berlin, where it was placed on display until 1943. Curiously, the statue of Foch was not taken down or defaced. It's not likely that this was an act of soldierly courtesy, but rather, as the World War I memorial Web site explains, "another bit of petty revenge on the part of the Führer; the victor of 1918 left in solitude to contemplate the annihilation of his work."

Compiègne was liberated in 1944, and German POWs restored the Glade on September 1. After the aerial bombardment of Berlin in 1943, the Nazis had moved Foch's railroad car to the Thuringia Forest for safekeeping. But in April 1945, with the Allies moving in, the Nazis set fire to the car. After the war was over, the pieces of the stone plaque and the Alsace-Lorraine monument were found in Berlin and returned to the Glade. Another railroad car, #2439D, crafted in 1913 like the original, was brought to the Glade; because the original furnishings and documents from Foch's car had been saved before war broke out, the full restoration of the Glade's pre-1940 appearance was possible.

In addition to the Glade and the Musée de l'Armistice, Compiègne offers other diversions for visitors, including the forest itself with hiking trails and bike paths. The Château de Compiègne, designed for Louis XV but more noted for the reign of Napoléon III and Empress Eugénie, is also worth a trip; in addition to the historic apartments there, the château also houses the Museum of the Second Empire and the Museum of the Automobile and Tourism. (Reservations are required; see the Web site, musee-chateau-compiegne.fr, for more information. The American Friends of the Château de Compiègne, at afcdc.org, is also dedicated to increasing awareness of the château's history). Also check out the sixteenth-century High Gothic–style *hôtel de ville,* which has one of the oldest city clocks in France, featuring a *bancloque* in the belfry with three *Picantins*—wooden figures in sixteenth-century attire representing the three enemies of France at that time: Flandrin the Fleming, Langlois the Englishman, and Lansquenet the German—that strike bells with their mallets every quarter hour. The regional cuisine is noted for its chocolate and *gâteau de Compiègne,* also known as Napoléon's dessert, made with cherries. The Compiègne town Web site (mairie-compiegne.fr) is in French only but still useful.

CHAMPAGNE

A great book to read that is not only about the bubbly drink but also about the Champagne region is *The Widow Clicquot: The Story of a Champagne Empire and the Woman Who Ruled It* by Tilar Mazzeo (Harper Perennial, 2008). I had no idea how fascinating the world of Champagne was until I read this book. Though I

adore Champagne—if I were asked that desert island question, *bien sûr* Champagne would be the one drink I would request—and I really like Veuve Clicquot, I had no idea what a remarkable woman *la veuve* (the widow) Barbe-Nicole Clicquot Ponsardin was. Mazzeo does an excellent job of piecing together Barbe-Nicole's life, even with relatively few resources available (the Veuve Clicquot archives hold many detailed account books but no personal documents). Interestingly, as Mazzeo points out, in the nineteenth century, when the story of Champagne begins, the history books rarely included the lives of entrepreneurs or commercial innovators, especially if they happened to be female. It's not difficult to find letters and diaries of royalty or notable statesmen, "but few librarians thought to collect personal records of businesspeople, even businesspeople who did exceptional things." This is still true today, but it was particularly true in the nineteenth century for a woman, unless she was either royalty or the sister, wife, or mother of a notable man. Nicole-Barbe wasn't any of these, but she was formidable, independent, and determined. As Mazzeo writes, "Her success was not in bucking the system, but neither did she slavishly follow convention. . . . She had a talent for seeing the opportunities that existed in moments of cultural and economic instability." Her triumphs and failures make for interesting reading, and a few myths are busted along the way: Dom Pérignon did not discover sparkling wine, for instance, and some wine historians now claim that a Champagne-like beverage was first invented in Great Britain, where there had been a small market for sparkling wine by the 1660s.

I like that Mazzeo gives us good descriptions of the city at the center of the Champagne region, Reims (pronounced as "*Rans,*" she tells us) both at the time of the *ancien régime* and today. She also reminds us that, like the other great widow of her day, Great Britain's Queen Victoria, the widow Clicquot helped to define a century. "For decade after decade, her name was heard on the lips of soldiers, princes, and poets as far away as Russia. Before long, tourists came looking for a glimpse of the woman whom the writer Prosper Mérimée once called the uncrowned queen of Reims." She was known locally simply as *la grande dame*—the great lady—and rare Veuve Clicquot vintages are still named La Grande Dame today. Nicole-Barbe is revealed in these pages as a woman of contradictions: a generous philanthropist but also a hard-hearted business owner, "a small, gruff, and decidedly plain woman with a sharp tongue who sold the world an exquisitely beautiful wine and an ethereal fantasy."

Mireille on Champagne

"With the recent addition of a Paris–Reims TGV, one can easily visit the Champagne region for a day, but ideally an overnight or even two to three days make a winning difference. Especially if staying at Les Crayères (64 boulevard Henry-Vasnier / lescrayeres.com), a top hotel and restaurant located in a huge park in Reims with three restaurants, from *haute* gastronomy to more casual to a super brasserie. Visiting the city and region in May or June or early fall is ideal. The weather and vineyards are superb. Driving across the quaint, grape-growing hillside villages with their manicured vineyards, and stopping for dinner at my favorite country restaurant, Le Grand Cerf in Montchenot (50 Route Nationale 51 / le-grand-cerf.fr), is my idea of a weekend in the country. Experiencing a few Champagne houses is, of course, a must to discover the complexities around each bubbly: my favorite cellars belong to Ruinart (small), Taittinger or Pommery (medium), and Veuve Clicquot (larger but discreet). One should not neglect the center of Reims for its famous cathedral, whether you go for the *rosace* (rose window), the stained-glass windows by Chagall, the viticultural panels, or the *grisailles* (monochrome paintings in shades of gray typically painted on the outside panels of altarpieces). And don't leave Reims without stocking up on the famous *biscuits de Reims*—pink cookies that are a little crunchy on the outside and soft inside that were originally meant for dipping in

Champagne—available in *pâtisseries* near the cathedral, notably at Maison Fossier (fossier.fr), founded in 1756."

—Mireille Guiliano,
author of *French Women Don't Get Fat*
and former president and CEO of
Veuve Clicquot, a subsidiary of
LVMH

BRETAGNE (BRITTANY)

Visitors to Paris can easily visit the region of Brittany for a more extended excursion. Trains leave from the Gare Montparnasse; most require changing at Rennes or Vannes, the biggest cities in the region. Those cities are 250–300 miles from Paris, so even with high-speed train service, plan for a couple of days at least. Brittany is quite different from the other regions near Paris because its history is predominantly Celtic, and its unique architecture, culture, geography, and Breton language are distinct from any other region of France. Within Brittany, my husband and I have thoroughly enjoyed visiting lovely Pont-Aven, with its water mills and the Musée des Beaux-Arts, which features works by Paul Gauguin, Paul Sérusier, Meyer de Haan, Émile Schuffenecker, Maurice Denis, and other members of the Pont-Aven School. Though Gauguin was a central figure of the Pont-Aven School, his works do not dominate the museum's collection, which is rather refreshing, as it allows visitors to discover lesser-known but wonderful artists; for example, it was at Pont-Aven that Sérusier, under the guidance of Gauguin, painted his famed *The Talisman* (now in the Musée d'Orsay), launching the group known as the Nabis (Hebrew for "prophets"). Not far from Pont-Aven is Quimper, the very same town that the charming ceramics come from, where fans can buy not only brand-new pieces but also *deuxième choix* ("seconds") at good prices. At Carnac, check out the mysterious *alignements,* megalithic stone monuments which date back to the Neolithic period, and throughout the region enjoy eating (too many) of the delicious butter-filled specialties—my favorites are the delicate *galettes de Pont-Aven* and the thicker *traou mad* ("good things" in Breton).

When I learned of a new book entitled *I'll Never Be French (No Matter What I Do): Living in a Small Village in Brittany* by Mark Greenside (Free Press, 2008), I wasn't sure I would like it because the title seemed a little too cute; plus, some reviewers said it was "laugh-out-loud funny," an accolade about which I am always suspicious. But the praise was enough that I broke down and read it, and I'm so glad I did. Greenside has written a positively wonderful book that now joins the pantheon of similar books treating other parts of France.

Not only is the book great, but Greenside is, too. I met him for a *café* in New York when he was en route to France, at the beginning of the summer. After only a few minutes, it was clear that, despite the cutesy book title, he is genuinely respectful of his Breton friends and neighbors. Greenside currently spends summers and some holidays in Brittany, though he ponders a possible permanent move to France. In his book he notes that after living in the hills of Oakland, California, for nearly twenty years he didn't know any of his neighbors, but in Brittany, in less than a month, he already knew two families—one that didn't even speak English—and his social life was fuller than in the States. After more time spent in Brittany, he's concluded, "This is what I love about France, the small things are large: a *bonjour, ça va,* a flower, a glass of water. It's a good way to live."

When his book was published in French in June 2010, Greenside was a little worried about how it would be received in his village. He decided he really needed to tell everyone, since he couldn't be sure how people would respond to what he'd written about them. The first person he went to was the insurance guy—when you read the book you will understand why Greenside told me, "He was the one I was most worried about, because of all the characters he was the most exaggerated. I walked in without an appointment, I gave him a book, and I walked him through the chapters that he appears in. At first, I don't tell him it's coming out in French, and I explain that obviously I'm giving him this book because I don't mean anyone any harm, and that I've only had good intentions. As I'm leaving his office, he says, 'You know, my wife reads and speaks perfect English.' And I thought to myself, Well, I've now lived my last day." (Postscript: At Christmastime he received a letter from the insurance guy's wife—she loved the book!)

I asked Greenside to share some of what he loves most about Brittany, and what follows is his short list:

• The light. The light is just extraordinary here. It's that famous, northern, shimmering, glittering light, and even when it's overcast it's illuminating. It's truly why all the Impressionist

painters, every single one of them, came to Brittany. Along the whole coast the light is just magnificent. In the summertime, you have a long dusk because it doesn't get fully dark until midnight. Brittany is known for its horrible weather, which is one reason why there aren't a lot of tourists. But the weather changes dramatically all the time.

- The coastline, which is fantastic and is a lot like the coast of Mendocino, California. Some of the largest tides in the world are right here, and every year you hear about people drowning at Mont-Saint-Michel. The difference betweeen high tide and low tide is 1,500 meters. At low tide the beaches are endless.

- A *crêpe.* My first *crêpe* was the simplest of all *crêpes,* with just butter and sugar, and every time I think of it my mouth waters.

- Oysters. The Belon *huîtres* (oysters) are among the best in the world and I can get them an hour and a half south from my house. They're best in the winter. One afternoon I got sixty oysters and went over to a friend's house and we just shucked and ate them. The price is very affordable. There is oyster farming all around southern Brittany and there's a fresh catch every day.

- *Cochon grillé* (grilled pig). Every village has its own summer *fête*—it can be a religious day or a civil day and there is dancing, food, and music. As Brittany was home to several Celtic tribes by the time Caesar came to Gaul, you'll see more Irish flags than you will French flags. And there will always be a huge meal. In my village the *fête* is known for salmon, but in other villages it's *cochon grillé.* It's delicious. I always look forward to my first *cochon grillé* of the season.

- The strawberries of Plougastel. These are the sweetest, juiciest strawberries I've ever tasted. They are unbelievable and this village has adopted the strawberry as its mascot. There's even a strawberry museum! At the Fête des Fraises (Strawberry Festival) everyone wears costumes and all these kids run around dressed as strawberries.

- Three generations of entire families, often hand in hand. I'm constantly amazed at seeing families together and enjoying one another. Even the teenagers are enjoying themselves, and not just on *fête* days. Sunday family dinner is still a tradition, and the basic social unit is still the family. It's just amazing.

- Time, and everyone's relationship to time. In the States, I'm very much of a control freak, type double-A: I control my life and I control my environment, I get from point A to point B, if I need help I know where to get it, and I know how to accomplish things. In France I am 100 percent dependent—there I am used to standing in line and used to understanding that this is the way you do it, this is how it works. My American friends don't even recognize me when they come and visit and see how I am in France. In America I want everything quick, fast, direct, and to the point, and I want to do everything I can for myself. In my village, it's okay if you spend a few minutes chatting with the proprietor of the *boulangerie* when there's ten people behind you.

- War monuments. Brittany was occupied during both world wars, so every village has its World War I memorial—it's staggering—and you'll also find De Gaulle monuments for World War II. Plaques with De Gaulle's famous speech imprinted on them are mounted on many of the Breton ports, and from what I understand, more people from Brittany joined up with the Free French and the Resistance than anyone else in France. There's a war presence in every town, especially because the German fortifications are still there along the entire coast. Every bay you go to you see the triangular formation of the machine guns—they can't get rid of them.

- The churches. In Brittany, it's very Catholic, as the Bretons supported the Church over the monarchy. But the churches are Gothic scare-the-hell-out-of-you churches, with pictorials explaining to illiterate people the stories of the Bible. Bretons are Gaelic and they're very fatalistic. Stuff happens; what are you going to do about it? They're not a depressing people despite all of this. They're extremely curious about everything. It's not like the States where when someone asks you how you're doing they don't really want to know. Bretons really want to know. They want to know about my geraniums, my car, and my wife, who is Japanese.

- The granite stone for the houses and the bridges. It's all schist, and the colors just have a solidity to them; this is where they belong. You might think that with all this stone everything would be harsh, but it's very soft and welcoming, and it looks really nice with my door—I painted my door a bright blue color and I love it. It's typically Breton style and I just like looking at it. With all the stone around, everything feels like it has a solidity to it, a permanence to it, a history to it that is very, very real and tangible. Nothing about Brittany feels ephemeral—and that's also part of what I love about it.

It seemed to me that Parisians had taken care to ensure that even the smallest details of life were beautiful.

—BARBARA WILDE,
OWNER, L'ATELIER VERT

A PARIS MISCELLANY

I envision this A to Z section of my books as an informative and interesting sourcebook, one that could almost be published as a separate volume. Compiling it is both fun and overwhelming—fun because I love enthusing about these engaging subjects and overwhelming because I could have submitted hundreds more under almost every letter of the alphabet. For me, this section is a compilation of good things and favorite places—and of course a list of anyone's Parisian favorites is almost impossible to compile because it would be too long. I am always adding things to the list each time I visit, so it keeps changing, some entries replacing others. So in the spirit of sharing and comparing, what follows are worthy entries for all sorts of sites, lodgings, shops, museums, views, words and phrases, culinary treats, souvenirs, and noteworthy bits of trivia. I've tried not to repeat favorites of mine featured elsewhere in the book, but forgive me if I enthuse again about a few. And, as always, please browse my blog, Thecollectedtraveler.blogspot.com, for many more recommendations and updates.

A

Accommodations

Architecture critic Paul Goldberger has written that "a good hotel is a place, a town, a city, a world unto itself, and the aura it exudes has almost nothing to do with its rooms and almost everything to do with everything else—the lobby, the bar, the restaurants, the façade, the signs, even the corridors and the elevators." Hotels like the ones Goldberger describes exist in all price categories, and they are, to my mind, the kind of places most of us seek. Paris has an abundance of selections in all categories and in all price ranges, and if anything it will be difficult to choose from the many appealing places! In fact, for a stay of more than a few days, I recommend making reservations at more than one place. In this way visitors may experience different types of lodgings as well as neighborhoods, perhaps choosing a combination of a modest inn and one very special place for a splurge. I do not buy into the idea that accommodations are only places to sleep—where you stay can be one of the most memorable parts of your trip, and the staff at your chosen accommodation can be enormously helpful in making your trip special. Deciding where to stay should not be taken lightly and deserves your best research efforts.

It is not my intent to visit dozens of hotels in Paris and report on them—that is the purview of guidebooks, Web sites, and accommodation guides. But as someone who pays close attention to the tiniest details, has stayed in accommodations ranging from campgrounds to five-star hotels, is practically allergic to must and dust, has an exacting idea of the words "customer service," and has been known to rearrange the furniture in a few hotel rooms, I do think I have something valuable to share with readers. And besides, because many people ask me for recommendations, I move around a lot when I travel, changing hotels and arranging visits to those that are fully booked or that I otherwise might not see. I make sure to see lodgings both moderately priced and expensive, so that readers have personal recommendations for both. Most often, I am drawn to the moderate places that also represent a good value, as I've found that these sometimes receive the least attention. It's never hard to find out about the budget or luxury places to stay, but the places in between—which I believe suit the pocketbooks of the majority of travelers—are often overlooked or given cursory consideration.

I myself do not generally prefer chain hotels, especially American ones, but those who do will find a number of them in Paris. I prefer to consult specialty hotel groups (assuming there is one for the destination I'm visiting), and among my favorites for France are Châteaux & Hôtels Collection (chateauxhotels.com), Gîtes de France (gites-de-france.com), Relais & Châteaux (relais chateaux.com), and Relais du Silence (relaisdusilence.com). Additionally, I like Small Luxury Hotels of the World (slh.com) and Leading Hotels of the World (lhw.com).

Regarding books about accommodations in Paris: there is no shortage. Here are the books I consult when I'm contemplating where to stay (and, yes, I really do peruse *all* of these—there is hardly any overlap and I like to know I've turned over every stone in considering my options before heading out):

Alastair Sawday's Special Places to Stay series, with editons on Paris, French châteaux and hotels, and bed and breakfasts, and *Go Slow France and French Vineyards* (Alastair Sawday Publishing). Over the years I've used a great number of Sawday's books for locations throughout the world, with great success. There's also useful information on the Sawday's Web site (sawdays.co.uk).

Boutique and Chic Hotels in Paris by Lionel Paillès (Little Bookroom, 2008) is a chunky little book with fifty-two great recommendations for places that Paillès refers to as "pocket palaces, boutique hotels, or neo-Oriental nests . . . atmosphere is their stock in trade, so it takes very little time to feel at home." There are a number of hotels in this book with rates under one hundred and twenty euros per night—among them the Hôtel Eldorado (eldoradohotel.fr) and Villa Toscane (hotelvillatoscane.fr), both of which are far more appealing than many places I've seen for the same price. However, the listings vary widely, with some places over three hundred euros per night. The photos are satisfactory for giving you a sense of where you'll be staying; there are also brief suggestions for things to do in each hotel's neighborhood at the back of the book.

Karen Brown's France Bed & Breakfasts and *France Hotels* (Karen Brown Guides, updated for 2010). Award-winning Karen Brown Guides have been great resources for accommodations for over thirty years, and are admired for their meticulous research. The guides differ from the Alastair Sawday series in that they typically focus more on exceptional high-end (rather than moderately priced) places to stay. Also find tips on her Web site (karenbrown.com).

Parisian Hideaways: Exquisite Rooms in Enchanting Hotels by Casey O'Brien Blondes and with photographs by Béatrice Amagat (Rizzoli, 2009) is my newest hotel resource and I just love it. Blondes's vision of an idyllic Parisian location is a quiet street as opposed to a wide avenue, and she prefers places that are intimate with lots of personal contact, leaving out the palace hotels, franchises, and chains. Especially helpful are her own categories of hotels, such as Brocante Chic, Design Classics, Timeless Elegance, and Historic Flavor. She invited each hotel's owner or manager to share their *coups de coeur* (favorites) for their respective neighborhoods, because, as Blondes wisely notes, "the most valuable resource a Parisian hideaway has to offer is the knowledge and rich culture of its owner and management. They know their neighborhood and relish sharing its secrets with guests. . . . There is a good chance your stay will engender an ongoing friendship, as these hotels, like the city they encapsulate, foster fidelity. It's hard to find someone who has visited Paris and doesn't dream of returning."

Paris: Hotels and More by Angelika Taschen with photos by Vincent Knapp (Taschen, 2006). I admit I was initially drawn to the beautiful *feel* of this book (I even like the smell of the paper!), but it's as useful as it is pretty. Taschen has chosen hotels that capture the character and atmosphere of Paris, and includes her favorite shops and sites in each neighborhood; she's left room for readers to record their own favorite finds as well.

I highly respect the writers of the hotel guides above and don't pretend to share their level of expertise, but I do stand by the lodgings that I particularly like. I believe any one of the places listed below will make your stay in Paris special:

Four Seasons George V (31 avenue George-V, 8ème / +33 01 49 52 70 00 / fourseasons.com/paris). I have long been a big fan of the Four Seasons brand, and the company's Paris outpost is a splendid success. Four Seasons acquired the George V from Trust House Forte in 1997 and basically gutted the building before re-opening in 1999; before the association with Four Seasons, the original George V hotel, opened in 1928, had an illustrious his-

tory: in 1944 the hotel was General Eisenhower's headquarters during the liberation of Paris. The recent $125 million renovation included interior design by Pierre-Yves Rochon, a reconfiguration of the guest rooms—there are now fewer rooms (245) but they are larger—and a restoration of the building's Art Deco façade.

It's easy to enthuse for pages and pages about the George V. There's so much to recommend it: its service; restaurant Le Cinq, with two Michelin stars under the direction of chef Éric Briffard; a wine cellar with more than fifty thousand bottles and twenty new labels added each week; recreations manager Claudia Caringi, responsible for the hotel's younger guests (numbering up to eighty children a month during peak times), who makes it easy to see why the George V was named a family favorite by *Travel + Leisure* in 2009; the house Rolls-Royce Phantom (Hermès-inspired, hand-built, and available for airport pickups, day trips, or business in Paris); its concierge desk and specifically Adrian Moore (referred to as "a food-savvy culture maven who knows Paris inside and out" by *Bon Appétit,* and whose blog, Adrian

moore.blogspot.com, is a great resource); its truly beautiful spa, inspired by Marie Antoinette's beauty secrets and a summer walk in the gardens of Versailles; the list goes on. But to my mind the best feature of the George V is the flower arrangements by artistic director Jeff Leatham. Even if the hotel is too costly for a stay, drop by the hotel's lobby, the Marble Courtyard, and the lounge La Galerie so you can see Leatham's breathtaking creations. Approximately nine thousand blooms are purchased every week from the Netherlands, and Leatham and his seven assistants design new themes for the hotel, refreshing the flower sculptures on a daily—sometimes hourly—basis. Leatham, who had no formal training in flowers but did have a landscape artist for a father, has observed that "flowers bring out the passion in people, they exude energy, color, and light, and they can lift us above the brouhaha of every-

day life." His arrangements have set the standard for all Four Seasons hotels. (Leatham provided arrangements for Chelsea Clinton's wedding and has his own show on TLC, *Flowers Uncut*, plus he has a studio in New York; see Jeffleatham.com.) Rates at the George V range from approximately 825 to 13,000 euros.

Paris Splurges

In addition to the Four Seasons George V, there are a number of palace hotels and other very grand places to consider for a splurge, for just one night or several, including Le Bristol (112 rue du Faubourg-Saint-Honoré, 8ème / +33 01 53 43 43 00 / lebristolparis.com), Hôtel de Crillon (10 place de la Concorde, 8ème / +33 01 44 71 15 00 / crillon.com), Le Meurice (228 rue de Rivoli, 1er / +33 01 44 58 10 10 / lemeurice.com), Plaza Athénée (25 avenue Montaigne, 8ème / +33 01 53 67 66 65 / plaza-athenee-paris.com), and the Ritz (15 place Vendôme, 1er / +33 01 43 16 30 30 / ritzparis.com). Of this last, *Travel + Leisure* special correspondent Christopher Petkanas has said, "For sense of arrival nothing can touch it." I am partial to Le Meurice because of its history and its location on the rue de Rivoli (I love the arcades), and the view from the rooms on the Tuileries side— overlooking the Eiffel Tower and the Louvre—takes my breath away.

Pavillon de la Reine (28 place des Vosges, 3ème / t33 01 40 29 19 19 / pavillon-de-la-reine.com). This lovely inn, among the most romantic in Paris, takes its name from Anne of Austria, who slept here just before her wedding to King Louis XIII (after which she became *la reine,* the queen).

It's wonderful enough to stay in the vicinity of the Place des Vosges, but even more special to stay in a building that is actually a part of it. Pavillon is the only hotel on the *place* and its entrance is tucked away, so unless staying here tourists don't usually wander by, adding to the hotel's exclusivity. Pavillon was recently completely renovated; the interior décor, which blends soft and bold colors with velvets and arabesque-patterned fabric in the hallways, was the vision of Didier Benderli, formerly with Jacques Garcia and designer of David Bouley's namesake restaurant in New York. A member of Small Luxury Hotels of the World, the hotel remains privately owned by the Chevalier family and is managed by director Tim Goddard, who oversaw the multi-

million-euro renovation and has been at the hotel for nearly twenty years.

Each of the forty-two guest rooms and twelve suites is unique, but they all are elegant and evoke a sense of calm and intimacy. Indeed, from the minute you step into the Pavillon's lobby you feel you've entered a different world, peaceful and far removed from the bustle on nearby rue des Francs-Bourgeois. There are lots of antiques and exposed wood beams throughout the hotel, but in addition to this Old World quality there are plenty of contemporary touches in both the public and the guest rooms, notably with the flat-screen TVs atop carved wooden chests and Molton Brown toiletries in the modern bathrooms. The duplex rooms on the first floor were decorated by interior designer Nathalie Prost—whose other hotel credits include the Lancaster, Sofitel Bora-Bora, and Club Med Kos—and they are warm, cozy, and fantastic. The Suite de la Reine, with an enlarged, handwritten parchment page from Rimbaud's *Une Saison en enfer* above the bed, is one of the most unique and comfortable hotel rooms I've ever seen. A small Carita spa (two treatment rooms, fitness room,

Jacuzzi, and steam room) was added during the renovation, and offers an anti–jet lag massage; there is no restaurant, and the breakfast room is open only to guests.

The hotel still attracts an artistic clientele; Jean-Paul Gaultier once lived in the hotel, and a look at the guest book reveals the names of John Malkovich, Jane Fonda, Christian Lacroix, and Jeremy Irons, who wrote, "What? Write in a book / Where gentlemen look / And ladies spy / Not I, not I!" Rates range from

375 to 835 euros. Note: A sister hotel, Le Pavillon des Lettres (12 rue des Saussaies, 8ème / +33 01 49 24 26 26) opened in the fall of 2010. I haven't seen the hotel yet, but it's also designed by Didier Benderli, and it pays tribute to letters written by such authors as Baudelaire, Hugo, Ibsen, Kafka, Nerval, Shakespeare, Tolstoy, Yeats, and Zola. Particular passages from their letters are printed on the walls of guest rooms. Rates range from approximately 300 to 460 euros.

Hôtel Verneuil (8 rue de Verneuil, 7ème / +33 01 42 60 82 14 / hotelverneuil.com), **Hôtel Thérèse** (5–7 rue Thérèse, 1er / +33 01 42 96 10 01 / hoteltherese.com), and **Hôtel Récamier** (3 bis place Saint-Sulpice, 6ème / +33 01 43 26 04 89 / hotel recamier.com). Sylvie de Lattre, a stylish and savvy entrepreneur, now owns a trio of hotels that are my current favorites in Paris. The oldest in the group is the Hôtel Verneuil, a cozy twenty-six-room inn just off the rue des Saint-Pères in Saint-Germain that de Lattre acquired in 1997. For De Lattre, it was her first step into the hotel world. She had studied political science, worked in property management, and had lived in England, Hong Kong, and Singapore with her husband, but then realized she wanted to start her own business in hospitality management. She took over the Verneuil, which had changed hands a few times over a thirty-year span, and had it redecorated completely—and, she told me, she'll likely change it all again in the next few years. The renovation and redecoration were done by Michelle Halard, a well-known designer and decorator also responsible for the interiors of restaurant Pierre Gagnaire and, in Provence, the Hôtel L'Oustau de Baumanière (as well as some dinnerware pieces for the French earthenware company Gien).

Each guest room in the seventeenth-century building is decorated differently and the overall feel is that of a *maison particulière,* or private home. Most of the guest rooms are small and space is tight—though imaginatively used, as in the narrow closet space on either side of the bed—and some rooms have doors so close

together that occupants can't open them simultaneously. This is a common feature, however, in very old buildings in Europe, as are other quirks, such as uneven steps, which you will also see at the Verneuil, and elevator service begins on the second floor, so your bags must be carried up a flight of steps first. I have no quibble with these features, as they contribute to the overall charm of this lovely hotel, and at any rate the staff here is so accommodating, and so genuinely concerned that you have *un bon séjour* (good stay), that it more than compensates for any architectural limitations.

Guest rooms combine (mostly) bold colors with printed fabrics; my room was a warm shade of red while a friend's was a light mint green. The lobby and adjoining *salon,* with a black-and-white tiled floor, pretty wood paneling, bookshelves, and fireplace, are great public spaces where guests may gather and enjoy glasses of wine or Champagne. Breakfast is served in a subterranean room of bright whitewashed stone arches, another example of a creative use of space. It didn't take me long to notice that every time I stepped through the Verneuil's front door I was greeted by a really lovely scent, which was from a customized candle created for the hotel by the skilled perfumist Gilles Dewavrin (gillesdewavrin.net). Happily for me, guests may purchase these candles, and now every time I light one in my home I immediately think of my stay at the Verneuil (I also beg anyone who's going to Paris to bring me back another one). The Verneuil's location is superb: ten minutes' walk from the Musée d'Orsay, ten minutes to Saint-Germain-des-Prés, fifteen minutes to Saint-Sulpice, and two blocks from the Seine, with the Louvre just on the other side of the Pont du Carrousel. Guest testimonials in the *livre d'or* attest to the hotel's popularity, so advance booking is advised. Room rates range from approximately 148 to 240 euros.

Hôtel Thérèse is the only inn of the three on the Right Bank, located between the Louvre, the Opéra, rue Saint-Honoré, and

the Palais Royal. It's popular with business travelers (there is a seminar room for meetings) but its uncluttered comfort and airy feel appeal to leisure visitors as well. The talented Jean-Philippe Nuel supervised the décor of the forty guest rooms and three junior suites; rooms are larger than those at the Verneuil and are more contemporary, yet in a classic way. The street-level lounge has a very clubby feel and is a great place to read the paper, meet friends, and relax. Overall, the clientele at the Thérèse represents a more balanced international range; fewer Americans stay here than at the Verneuil or Récamier. Room rates range from approximately 155 to 320 euros.

Hôtel Récamier, opened in 2009, is the jewel of the group. Recently featured in the pages of *Elle Décor* and *Maison Côté Paris,* the Récamier is chic and classic at once. The hotel has a very similar feel to the J.K. Place hotels in Florence and Capri—in fact, when I met Sylvie de Lattre, she told me that although she'd not yet seen those noteworthy hotels, the designer she hired for the

Récamier, Jean-Louis Deniot, had, and it's apparent that there is some J.K. Place influence in the rooms of the Récamier. I happen to love J.K. Place, and so I also love the Récamier's original touches. The Récamier was the first hotel project for Deniot, and the only direction she gave him was to create a cross between a traditional hotel and an elegant private town house, something that was special and that nobody had seen in Paris before. Deniot created twenty-four unique rooms using 150 fabrics and 50 wallpapers, and he put elements together that might at first seem not to blend. Each room mixes texture and pattern and each bed features patterned coverlets and a canopy, but every room is different and no two pieces of furniture are alike.

Every floor of the hotel has its own color scheme or theme—black and white, ethnic chic, gold and black, coral red and Asian,

blue-gray—and on every level of the central spiral staircase is a bust of Madame Récamier, each a newfangled interpretation of Jacques-Louis David's famous painting of the same name in the Louvre, in the styles of such artists as Niki de Saint Phalle, Christo, and Yves Klein. A nice feature is that, on every floor, the two rooms overlooking Place Saint-Sulpice can be opened up and made into a suite. The Récamier has a small outside patio where breakfast is served in nice weather; otherwise it is offered in the *petit salon* where complimentary tea, coffee, and refreshments are served to guests for *l'heure de goûter* (snack time) from four to six p.m. The hotel's location in the sixth right by Saint-Sulpice is just fantastic. Room rates range from approximately 250 to 420 euros.

Recommended Budget Choices

Hôtel Chopin (46 passage Jouffroy, 9ème / +33 01 47 70 58 10) and its sister property, the Hôtel de la Bretonnerie (22 rue Sainte-Croix de la Bretonnerie, 4ème / +33 01 48 87 77 63); both reachable at hotelbretonnerie.com.

Hôtel des Grandes Écoles (75 rue du Cardinal-Lemoine, 5ème / +33 01 43 26 79 23 / hotel-grandes-ecoles.com).

Hôtel des Grands Hommes (17 place du Panthéon, 5ème / +33 01 46 34 19 60 / paris-hotel-grandshommes.com).

Hôtel Mayet (3 rue Mayet, 6ème / +33 01 47 83 21 35 / mayet.com).

Hôtel Saint Thomas d'Aquin (3 rue du Pré-aux-Clercs, 7ème / +33 01 42 61 01 22 / hotel-st-thomas-daquin.com).

Mama Shelter (109 rue de Bagnolet, 20ème / +33 01 43 48 48 48 / mamashelter.com).

Port-Royal Hotel (8 boulevard de Port-Royal, 5ème / +33 01 43 31 70 06 / hotelportroyal.fr).

Recommended Hôtels de Charme

Hôtels de charme are in abundance in France and are perhaps a little hard to describe because there are so few in North America. An *hôtel de charme* is usually a place that is small, charming, not expensive or luxurious, and a good value. The phrase also denotes quality and character, and may be run by family members. *Hôtels de charme* may be found in rural areas as well as urban, and there are a number in Paris. Generally, an *hôtel de charme* is not the equivalent of a boutique hotel, which typically costs more and features more modern conveniences.

Hôtel d'Angleterre (44 rue Jacob, 6ème / +33 01 42 60 16 93 / hotel-dangleterre.com).

Hôtel Duc de Saint-Simon (14 rue de Saint-Simon, 7ème / +33 01 45 48 68 25 / hotelducdesaintsimon.com).

Hôtel du Jeu de Paume (54 rue Saint-Louis-en-l'Île, 4ème / +33 01 43 26 14 18 / jeudepaumehotel.com).

Recommended Rental Agencies

À La Carte Paris (alacarteparis.com).

I Love Paris Apartments (iloveparisapartments.com).

Paris Appartements Services (paris-apts.com).

Paris Home Shares (parishomeshares.net).

Vacation in Paris (vacationinparis.com).

Antiques and Auction Houses

Paris has long been a great destination for antiques, and visitors who love antiques shopping will not be disappointed in one area in particular: in the streets of the sixth and seventh arrondissements. Big news in the auction house world came in 2000, when a monopoly restricting auction sales to French nationals was declared void. (Previously foreigners had to arrange for a French person to bid for them.) The monopoly had been established by a royal edict of Henri II in 1556, and in the four centuries since, London and the United States had outpaced Paris in sales, as well as in market savvy and diversification. Christie's and Sotheby's (both British firms) now have a presence in Paris, but the Hôtel Drouot (drouot.com) is Paris's historic auction house, founded in 1852 and located on the corner of rue Drouot and rue Rossini in the ninth arrondissement; there are also salesrooms at 15 avenue Montaigne in the eighth, as well as at Drouot Nord and Drouot Véhicules (outside of the city). The house is actually an umbrella group now owned by a subsidiary of the bank BNP Paribas, with sixteen different halls and seventy independent auction firms, which can be intimidating indeed to would-be auction participants.

Antiques professionals, interior decorators, architects, casual collectors, or simply those interested in attending an auction or a flea market should contact Emily Marshall at Grotto Antiques *tout de suite*. Marshall is the only American to have earned a diploma from the famed École Boulle, a prestigious applied-arts school for the decorative arts in Paris. Named after Louis XIV's cabinetmaker André-Charles Boulle, students of the school must have a thorough knowledge of the history of French furnishings and demonstrate proficiency in drafting and hand sewing to earn the *Certificat d'Aptitude Professionnelle,* or CAP, degree. Marshall prepared for the CAP by training for two years with Madame Catherine Bientz, a drapery-maker for the shah of Iran. École Boulle is highly selective; in 1995, the year she began at the

school, only eighteen students were selected out of several hundred to attend. Since graduating, Marshall has created draperies for distinctive apartments in Paris and has continued to apprentice and train, acquiring professional techniques few, if any, other Americans know. In addition to operating Grotto Antiques (1399 East Tutt Road, Trenton, Kentucky / 615 430 5491 / grottoantiques .com) and specializing in *haute couture* for the home, Marshall and her husband offer an international antiques courier service in France. They also organize antiques shopping tours to the flea markets and auction houses, always negotiating for the best price.

Through a serendipitous saving of Marshall's business card, nearly ten years after first meeting her I tracked her down, and we reconnected by telephone and e-mail.

Q: When did you first visit Paris, and what was it that inspired you to go?

A: I'd majored in anthropology and Brazilian Portuguese in college and had lived and worked in Brazil. When I was job hunting, I discovered the Austin Company, a tobacco agency based in Greeneville, Tennessee, that bought tobacco for domestic and foreign manufacturers and it had plants in Brazil, so I decided to explore job opportunities with them. I was hired as Austin's first woman in the leaf department, which I was mainly responsible for buying at auction.

I'd work half the year and travel for the rest. I went to London and Paris, where Austin's second-largest customer, SEITA, the French tobacco monopoly, was based. So it seemed natural to inhale Gauloises and Gitanes *sur place.* Through family connections I was able to arrange a stay in a bohemian garret in the fifteenth, and Paris cast its spell. Once I returned to work, I began to scheme: how could I go back and stay longer? Austin gave me a year off to work on an MBA degree. I met a Parisian and fell in love—ironically his godfather headed up Philip Morris in Switzerland, one of Austin's clients—and I said *adieu* to the tobacco business. I stayed in Paris until 2006, returning to the States only then to start Grotto Antiques with my second husband, Mehdi Zohouri.

Q: Were you always interested in antiques and textiles?

A: Looking back now as an older woman, I realize one should never underestimate the ability of a child's eye to be educated

and cultivated to appreciate beautiful and worldly things. I grew up on a rolling cattle and tobacco farm in the middle of Tennessee, but foreign influences blew regularly in and out. My father was a sea captain, and his annual visit home would have him loaded down with silk from India and Egypt, ebony from Africa, and lacquerware from the Orient. My favorite uncle,

Jim Beaumont Marshall, was a career State Department employee and traveled the world. His keen eye and own fascination with textiles initiated me to the world of Indonesian ikat, Suzani embroidery, and Indian silks. I'm sure the textile bug comes from him. Also, a woman named Dorothy Ann Ross Russo was a great influence—she'd spent her junior year abroad studying at the Sorbonne, and her home had mysterious escargots and freshly baked French-style bread. She read us *Babar* in French. I'd sip coffee with her artist husband, Remo, in their kitchen nook and quiz her on those buildings taped to the wall: Chinon, Chenonceau, and Blois. I see those black-and-white prints even now; I was seven at the time.

I started sewing at six. Both my grandmothers did beautiful work and my mother made her own Vogue Paris Originals during the early sixties. By twelve, I could make most anything, and in my teens, I could make coats interlined and lined. When I was nineteen I had a job in Washington, D.C., working for a gift shop, where I learned of Cristal d'Arc, Limoges china, and Quimper ware. The back area had French fabric, and on my breaks I would drool over the material. So my eye developed in America, but it was École Boulle's Histoire de l'Ameublement Français (History of French Furniture) course that ignited the passion for French antiques, textiles, and decoration.

Q: You are the only American to ever attend Paris's prestigious École Boulle. What transpired that made you want to apply for admission?

A: A terrible French divorce! Did you see the film *Le Divorce,* based on Diane Johnson's book? Leslie Caron is nothing compared to my ex-*belle-mère*. Sewing calms my nerves and was a channel to relieve a whole lot of stress. But more officially, I was thumbing through a catalog of adult courses offered by the Mairie de Paris (mayor's office) and I stumbled upon the heading *Tapisserie d'ameublement,* and it got me thinking that I wanted to learn soft furnishing techniques. Later, when I sent in the application to the École Boulle, I was selected out of hundreds of candidates.

Courses at École Boulle include French, physics, industrial and hand sewing, technology, drawing, cutting patterns and draping, and the history of French furniture and architecture. Each subject has a coefficient. Meaning if you're not so hot in French (coefficient 2), you'll make up points with the sewing project (coefficient 10). Just don't make a zero in a subject: no diploma will be awarded. I became passionate for French antiques in the History of French Furniture class. Working chronologically, we worked our way up through the styles, starting with the Romanesque. It wasn't just furniture but the architecture and fabric associated with each period. I made up flash cards scrambling all the periods together, and I received a perfect score on the final exam. I loved it, and I'd discovered what I wanted to do with my life. I drove my husband crazy—he'd see me coming down the hall and duck out of the way, not wanting me to quiz him on some *fauteuil canné à la reine, époque Louis XV* or *duchesse brisée.*

Q: Where did you meet your second husband, and did he, too, have a passion for the antiques market in Paris?

A: At the *marché aux puces,* the Paris flea market, *bien sûr!* One Friday morning, I came around a corner in the Marché Dauphine and there was this gorgeous man with an equally gorgeous stand. *Voilà!* He'd grown up in Tehran's bazaar with his father, and when the shah's regime collapsed, he lost his scholarship and had to eat, so he sold antique photographs at the *puces* to survive. He's been there thirty years now.

Q: When did you establish Grotto Antiques, and what do you specialize in?

A: January 2007. The antiques side of the company deals in a refined eighteenth-century look. Unfortunately, a dealer has to
buy what the market wants, and now, modern rules. Magazines dictate the current look and most people don't have the
courage or taste to buck the trend. I like to think we hold
people's hands to help them be individualistic and noncon-
forming when it comes to creating a home. The other part of
our business is the École Boulle atelier. We just landed a prestigious project with one of America's top architectural and
interior design firms. Our specialty? Roman shades made in
the same fashion as the Élysée Palace.

Q: When did you start attending auctions at the Hôtel de Vente
Drouot?

A: Right after I got the CAP in 1996. The official visit at
Drouot is all day long the day before the auction. (Check *La
Gazette de l'Hôtel de Vente Drouot* for specific information on
hours and merchandise to be presented—for example, silver,
coins, books, wine, furniture, modern paintings, etc.) Still,
professionals huddle around the steel grates just before eleven
a.m., chatting and smoking, waiting for the one-hour visit,
eleven to noon. The steel grate opens and they're off! A mad
frenzy of hundreds of dealers, pushing and elbowing, up and
down escalators, all on a mission: to find things that'll make
money. There's an hour to scout through thousands of articles: sixty minutes to note the *salle,* estimate price, leave an
order, corner the *commissaire,* befriend the auctioneer, and spy
the competition. Promptly at noon the doors slam shut.

Auctions begin at around two, though longer ones can
start at one-thirty or sometimes even in the morning. You
stand—all day long—in the back or running between the
salles. You have to stand so you can see your competition or
whether the auctioneer has a pigeon (fake bid) in the corner.
Dealers crush you, on purpose. You're on tiptoes trying to

see. And the smell can be overwhelming—there is often a *clochard* (bum) in his filthy clothes, trying to warm up in winter weather. The auctioneer announces the numbered article and opens with a bid: *Monsieur, est-ce que j'ai cinq cents?* (Do I have five hundred?) Five hundred in an eloquent, slow chant. *Six cents?* (Six hundred?) *Six cents! Et sept cents?* (Seven hundred?) *Est-ce que j'ai preneur à sept cents? Sept cents! Sept cents! Adjugé, sept cents euros!* The *commissaire* flies to the person that's bought the lot, gets his check or cash, and hurries back with his name to the recording secretary, who makes out the bill. In the meantime, the *crieur* has already started taking bids on the next auctioned article. Back and forth and back and forth, all day long, every minute, a lot is sold.

Q: The Drouot auction house can be intimidating to visitors, which is where your courier service can prove to be invaluable. What exactly does your service provide, and what are some notable pieces that you've found for your clients over the years?

A: Drouot is a closed world where if you're unknown, you can't bid. The auctioneers don't know you—won't take your bid—and the dealers won't let you have anything anyway. Are you fluent in French? Can you follow the auction? Do you have a K-bis (professional license) and a business checking account? Foreign check? Forget it. Letter of credit from a foreign bank? Too expensive and too long to arrive. Credit card? Probably not. Most auction houses don't take them anyway. We make it possible to get over these hurdles, and it's worth it. Daily, Drouot has treasures for those who wait and happen to be at the right place at the right time.

We provide two services: buying at auction, and our courier service at the main Paris flea market (Puces de Clignancourt) and professional trade shows (*déballages*). We take customers under our wing at the flea market and protect them from dishonest dealers and unsavory characters who tend to congregate near the market. (We know a Manhattan dealer who got his cell stolen right out of his hand and an old woman whose teeth were knocked out at an ATM. Tip? Never put cash in your purse; thieves will rip it right off your shoulder.)

Tackling this sometimes seedy world, though, has its fruits: beautiful antiques found at great prices. We really do it all from A to Z, honestly and with a genuine pride in seeing to our customer's satisfaction.

Q: What are Les Grands Ateliers de France?

A: Simply put, they're the best artisans in France—*la crème de la crème* in their field, of upholstery, gilt bronze, embroidery, furniture restoration, etc. Maison Brazet is one; Rémy

Brazet's fine upholstery atelier may be visited in an inner courtyard on a shopping street in the sixteenth. Many locals don't even know it's there. Last time I went, he was placing feathers on Catherine the Great's bed that the Getty Museum had bought from Bernard Steinitz. Brazet also works for the Metropolitan Museum of Art and once had a New York customer who flew on the Concorde to discuss trim with him. His work is so perfect that one museum thought he'd cheated by using foam instead of horsehair. He sliced open the chair to prove them wrong.

Q: I know you have literally hundreds of Paris addresses, other than Maison Brazet and some known only to the trade, in your attaché case. Can you share some of your favorite and most distinctive with *Collected Traveler* readers?

A: Dealers never give out their sources. That's how we make our living. But here are a few I can share with my brief notes:

Fried Frères (13 rue du Caire, 2ème / +33 01 42 33 51 55 / friedfreres.fr). Supplies crystal beads, sequins, and pearls to *haute couture* houses. Sold prestrung for crochet embroidery. Stockroom stuffed to the ceiling! Minimum order. Worth a visit to feel the energy of the Sentier, the garment district.

Lesage (13 rue de la Grange-Batelière, 9ème / +33 01 44 79 00 88 / www.lesage-paris.com). François Lesage, the father. Right beside Drouot. The master of French hook (crochet) embroidery and has a school open to the general public. Courses, beginning level I, expensive. His *haute couture* atelier for designers like Chanel, Jean Paul Gaultier, and YSL is never open to the public.

Jean-François Lesage (207 rue Saint-Honoré, 1er / +33 01 44 50 01 01 / jeanfrancoislesage.com). François's son. Luxurious home embroidery produced in India; mostly gold and silver thread. Don't even bother calling unless you're professional or seriously interested in ordering. Works only with high-end customers: Saudi Arabian princes, aristocrats, and foreign governments.

Boisson (181 rue Saint-Denis, 2ème / +33 01 45 08 02 61). Rue Saint-Denis can be disturbing, as prostitutes of all sizes and ages hang out in doorways. A single woman, especially a pretty one, might be bothered if walking alone. Don't let that stop you from visiting this boutique stuffed with thread and yarn of all descriptions for weaving and embroidery. Cotton warp thread for tapestry and rug making. Owner welcoming and knowledgeable.

Au Ver à Soie (102 rue Réaumur, 2ème / +33 01 42 33 52 92 / auverasoie.com). The best store in the world for silk thread! Located in the heart of the garment district. Silk thread and ribbon in all forms, shapes, and sizes, even chenille. Color palette incredible. Minimum order. Can find retail at Ultramod (3–4 rue de Choiseul, 2ème).

Léobert (75 ter rue de Charonne, 11ème / +33 01 43 71 70 05). Wholesale-only upholstery supplies. École Boulle's source.

Brigitte Duros (27 rue Froidevaux, 14ème / +33 01 43 22 44 77 / tapisserie-paris.com). Judge for Meilleur Ouvrier de France embroidery competition. Restores tapestry, embroidery, and antique fabrics. Can duplicate most any textile. Dyes her own yarn, fixing the tint in *bouse de vache* (sounds better in French— fermented cow manure!) to restore antique *tapisseries*. Located on charming courtyard behind the Montparnasse cemetery.

La Galerie des Cadres (131 rue des Rosiers, Saint-Ouen / +33 06 80 65 22 33 / galeriedescadres.studio-batignolles.com).

Michel Idée owns this great source for frames at the Paris flea market. All periods and styles. If he doesn't have it, he'll find it!

Maison Degroote-Mussy (12 passage des Taillandiers, 11ème / +33 01 48 05 17 16). Last time we popped in, they had a back order of six months, fabricating furniture for Alberto Pinto. One of the few furniture makers still in the Faubourg Saint-Antoine.

Gauthier et Cie (68 avenue Ledru-Rollin, 12ème / +33 01 47 00 60 44 / gauthier-cie.com). Monsieur Tournay's boutique used to be hidden inside a courtyard on rue de Charonne. He's upscale now, with a beautiful shop. Why not, for the most beautiful curtain rods in the world? Massive gilt bronze Louis XV consoles. Hand-sculpted wooden rods tinted to the client's specification. Sells primarily to Russian and Middle Eastern markets. A downer? No new catalog nor price list. To-the-trade only.

Georges Le Manach (31 rue du Quatre-Septembre, 2ème / +33 01 47 42 52 94 / lemanach.fr). Upstairs, delicious silks produced by a *meilleur ouvrier de France* using Adidas-clad foot power. Jean Paul Getty's fabric source. Factory in Tours to visit by appointment only. Worth it to see men—tattoos and earrings—hand weaving silk. Sale on slightly irregular fabrics.

Passementerie Île-de-France (11 rue Trousseau, 11ème / +33 01 48 05 44 33 / pidf.fr). *Passementerie* (trims, cording, and tassels) for royal families and castles. Antique collection to view.

Q: And speaking of addresses, what are some of your favorite culinary haunts in the vicinity of Drouot?

A: A lot of dealers just cross the street to one of the cafés; having a *sandwich jambon-beurre* at the bar helps to pass the time before the doors open again. Order a *demi* and you'll hear the latest scandal or coup in the trade. It's more pleasant here since smoking was banned. For a real meal, Chartier (rue du Faubourg-Montmartre, 9ème / +33 01 47 70 86 29 / restaurant-chartier.com) provides bistro fare in an incredible Belle Époque atmosphere. I love it from the minute I walk in. The waiters dash about in their long white aprons, *torchon* swung over their arm, serving up steaming French cuisine. Try the *tartare de boeuf* just to witness the waiter's flair in whisking together raw hamburger, mustard, and egg. Orthodox and *pied noir* Jews (formerly of colonial Algeria) trade in diamonds and textiles in this part of the ninth arrondissement, so good kosher restaurants and bakeries exist down most any street east of Drouot. La Boule Rouge (1 rue de la Boule Rouge), owned by the famous *pied noir* singer Enrico Macias, offers typical Algerian dishes, including couscous. Watch out for the *harissa,* the hot chili and garlic condiment.

With fine weather, walk a block to the shopping street, rue Cadet, or continue on up the hill along rue des Martyrs, for a food lover's paradise of shops filled with foie gras, cheese, pastries, sausages, and bread. Order takeout (*à emporter*) and eat in the Square d'Anvers, at avenue Trudaine, with a glorious view of Montmartre. Afterward, hoof it down the hill to 3 rue de Rochechouart and stop for Aurore Capucine's lavender cookie. I'll travel five thousand miles just to gorge on one. Zazou (20 rue du Faubourg-Montmartre) specializes in North African pastries. Get a tray and load it up with *makroud* (date-stuffed cakes), semolina and honey cake, or homemade *loukoumia.* Eat standing up. Mint tea is wonderful on a cold day.

La Mère de Famille (35 rue du Faubourg-Montmartre/ lameredefamille.com) is Paris's oldest candy shop (*confiserie*) in its original location. The boutique's windows change with the seasons: giant chocolate bells at Easter, candied *muguet* (lily) for the first of May, mushroom-shaped *pâte d'amande* in the fall. All beautiful and delicious! Pricey, though. The same commercial cookies can be found at the local Franprix. Only locals go to Restaurant Petrelle (34 rue Petrelle, 9ème / +33 01 42 82 11 02/petrelle.fr). Food is bought daily at market according to the chef/owner's whim. It's totally magic at night and haunted mostly by actors filming in nearby studios. But there are only a few tables; you must reserve!

Q: Lastly, what do you find most rewarding about your work?

A: Welcoming the dealers from around the world, clinching the deal, *la chine* (the hunt, the pursuit), getting up at four a.m. to land a treasure out a truck's back end, and just being with our family, the thousands of people that make up the *puces.* Also, being surrounded daily by a world of beauty—a magic one where objects from the past bring joy.

L'Atelier Brancusi

Sculptor Constantin Brancusi was originally from Bucharest, but the majority of his works were created in his Paris studio. He bequeathed his studio and all its contents to the French government on one condition: that the Centre Georges Pompidou reconstruct the studio as it had been in its original Montparnasse location. The museum brought in architect Renzo Piano, who also designed the Pompidou, *et voilà:* the world's largest Brancusi collection—consisting of sculptures, drawings, tools, and more than fifteen hundred photographs—in a great, light-filled space on Piazza Beaubourg in front of the museum. It is firmly on my short list of favorites. (www.centrepompidou.fr)

Au Nom de le Rose

This mini chain of shops dedicated to roses—a favorite of mine for over a dozen years—carries bouquets and loose-cut roses in a great variety of colors as well as lots of other things having to do with the flower: candles, *extrait de parfum* to refresh potpourri, culinary items, soap, and rose petals—which I've scattered on a white tablecloth set for dinner, to great effect. There are several Paris locations (aunomdelarose.fr); it's a great place for picking up a small bouquet for your hotel room at a good price.

B

Le Bateau-Lavoir

Poet Max Jacob gave the name Le Bateau-Lavoir to a group of artists' studios in Montmartre, at the top of the steps leading to 13 rue Ravignan. By all accounts, the studios themselves were dark, dreary, and dirty; as to the origin of the name, accounts differ. Some have it that on stormy days the wooden planks of the studios swayed in the wind and creaked dangerously, resembling the laundresses' boats that used to float on the Seine—this seems reasonably plausible to me. The original building, which was destroyed by fire in the 1970s, is also reported to have been either an old piano factory or a manufacturing facility of some kind. Whatever it once was, in the late 1800s and early 1900s it was home and gathering place for a veritable hit parade of artists and writers, including Maxime Maufra, Juan Gris, Modigliani, Kees van Dongen, Apollinaire, Georges Braque, Henri Matisse, André Derain, Marie Laurencin, Maurice Utrillo, Jacques Lipchitz, Cocteau, Gertrude Stein, Ambroise Vollard, Daniel-Henry Kahnweiler, and Picasso. Picasso painted one of his most legendary works here, *Les Demoiselles d'Avignon* (Avignon refers not to the Provençal town of Avignon, as many people assume, but to a street in Barcelona, where he lived for some years when he was younger; whether or not the women in the painting may be prostitutes I will leave to art historians.) Picasso left the Bateau-Lavoir in 1911, and by the time World War I ended, everyone had left, migrating mostly to Montparnasse. Today there is a reconstructed display of the Bateau-Lavoir in Place Émile-Goudeau; for art history buffs it's worth stopping by while you're in Montmartre.

BHV

Short for Bazaar de l'Hôtel de Ville, the BHV (52 rue de Rivoli, 4ème / bhv.fr) is one of Paris's legendary department stores—see a very detailed and informative entry on *les grands magasins* on my blog. I reference it here not for its wares (though the basement hardware department, believe it or not, has incredibly cool stuff that you just can't find in North America) but for its rooftop terrace, which I rarely hear anyone talk about. I found it by accident and couldn't believe my good fortune to be sitting up there with a grand view all around and only two other people. It's a great outdoor space to know about—it's free, relatively quiet, and a good spot to take a break if you've been shopping or sightseeing in the fourth arrondissement.

Le Bonbon au Palais

I love La Mère de Famille, the most famous address in Paris for old-fashioned candies and confections, but I also love newcomer Le Bonbon au Palais (19 rue Monge, 5ème / bonbonsaupalais.fr). The shop is decorated to make you feel like you've stepped into a 1950s classroom, with a note to all written in chalk on the blackboard. On my last visit there, I learned: *La vie est bien plus belle avec des bonbons* . . . (Candy makes life better.) The owner has gathered the best sweets from all around France and displays them in large glass jars with lids. It is indeed a palace, filled with forgotten treasures and childhood favorites (for the French, anyway), and though it seems an obvious destination for kids, it's hard for anyone of any age not to appreciate the whimsical and exuberant atmosphere of this unique shop.

Bon Chic, Bon Genre

This phrase translates as "good style, good class," and is roughly equivalent to the North American word "preppy." It's commonly used when referring to restaurants, stores, and anywhere "*les BCBGs*" hang out (that's pronounced *bay-say-bay-zhay*). BCBG is also the name of Max Azria's line of clothing.

Bonjour Paris

Bonjour Paris is a terrific Web site (bonjourparis.com). It's an outstanding resource for visitors to Paris as well as anyone who is a devoted Francophile. American expat Karen Fawcett, who's lived in Paris since 1988, has been maintaining the site since 1995, and with each passing year it becomes more and more indispensable. May 1, 2010, marked Fawcett's twenty-second anniversary in Paris, and as she noted in a posting that day, "After all these years, more of me is French than American. . . . Paris has captured my heart and part of my soul."

Fawcett and I share not only a passion for Paris but also for the *Eloise* books, and for the idea that the more people are able to travel, the greater global understanding will become among people and nations. I caught up with her by telephone recently:

Q: Before moving to Paris, what had your relationship with the city been?

A: I fell in love with the Eiffel Tower when I was thirteen and in Paris on a teen tour. Years later, when my (now deceased) husband was transferred to the City of Light, at first I didn't want to leave the States, even though his gig was only for one year, but once there I was in love all over again. Though it bears repeating that living there is an entirely different experience than visiting. But I had one hell of a time! Eighty-seven consecutive nights of house guests, not knowing three words of French, and a husband who worked sixty-five hours a week.

Q: What are some features about Bonjour Paris that you think make it different or more worthwhile than other Internet sites devoted to the city?

A: Mainly, we're not for readers who just want to know where the Eiffel Tower is located. Bonjour Paris devotees have been there and done that. The site is known for featuring in-depth stories by good writers on Paris and other places in France, as well as for tons and tons of practical information and tips.

Q: You have been very honest in your postings about life in Paris—that it isn't all roses and foie gras. Now that you have the benefit of years there behind you, what are some of the most important words of advice you might share with anyone thinking of moving to Paris or France?

A: I would say that both for anyone thinking of moving here *and* for first-time visitors, come with the idea that things will be *different*. Look at the buildings, try to learn even the most rudimentary history, say "*Bonjour*" and "*Merci,*" and know that not everyone speaks English. We're guests here!

Q: What are some reasons why you feel living in Paris is rewarding?

A: I have such a feeling of safety, for one. I like being able to walk anywhere in my neighborhood and stop for a drink. And I am constantly amazed by the wonderful people I meet. I love feeling as if I am living in a global society.

Q: In a typical week or month, how do you spend your time in your *quartier,* and what places do you frequent?

A: No two days in Paris are the same, but I spend a lot of my life behind the computer working on Bonjour Paris. It's my passion as well as an addiction, having spent the past fifteen years typing away and sharing my love of, and more than occasional frustration with, France. At least once a week, I try to make a pilgrimage to a neighborhood with which I'm not familiar, but a lot of my free time is limited by the weather. As much as I try to go to the Luxembourg Gardens each day, if it's freezing cold or raining I don't make it.

I'm desperately trying to stay away from daily pilgrimages to Kayser, the wonderful bakery that's less than a block away from my apartment (even though I may have only one croissant on a visit, the calories gravitate to my thighs). My money is better spent at Monceau Fleurs, where you can buy moderately priced flowers, which, although ephemeral, give me pleasure. Rather than going to the gym, my exercise consists of walking and walking some more. When taking the Métro, there are invariably stairs involved, and even though I know better, I jog from one platform to another when changing trains, as if I'd have to wait an hour if I missed the next train pulling into the station. I do take taxis occasionally, when I'm very dressed up, but that's pretty rare since Paris has become a substantially less formal city (unless it's a three-star restaurant, men often don't wear ties anymore).

People who live in France usually have a favorite café, and it's more than a place to drink coffee: it's a front-row seat to observing others and living theater. My cafés tend to change according to where there's the most sun. And as much as some visitors assume all Parisians eat out all the time, those days aren't frequent unless you're made of big bucks. When I first arrived in Paris, I was horrified by the few kitchens I was allowed to see [typically, guests would not be welcome to visit the kitchen], because they looked like dungeons. The French are now into chic kitchen design—all you need to do is walk down boulevard Saint-Germain near rue du Bac in the seventh and you have your choice of one über-expensive kitchen store after another.

My main shopping venue is Ed, located at the end of my block on rue Notre-Dames-des-Champs. Initially, the store was kind of a dump where the neighborhood's residents would pretend they didn't see each other. The grocery store stocks its own inexpensive Dia brand and many generics that cost less than comparable items at Paris's mainstream groceries. This doesn't mean I don't go to La Grande Épicerie at Bon Marché if I want special goodies to serve to my guests. And I've become a *dévotée* of Picard, a chain that sells the best frozen foods anywhere. You can order via the Internet and a delivery truck will arrive the next day. One of the joys of living in France is the availability of first-rate cheese, one of my greatest weaknesses—it's hard to say no to a Vacherin Mont d'Or at its runniest perfection.

I've come to the realization that it's okay to let a place annoy you on occasion and still know it's an integral part of your heart and soul. At a party I went to recently I was greeted by a sea of unfamiliar faces, and people were from a great number of other countries. Everyone spoke French and English, and many people said they came to Paris on a year's assignment and were now still here ten, twenty, even thirty years later, and had no intention of ever leaving. Sometime after midnight, I walked home, and by the time I reached my front door I realized I'd been seduced by Paris again. I will always travel, and revel in it, but I wonder whether I will ever leave—except feet first.

Bookstores

If you like visiting local bookstores when you travel as much as I do, I feel certain you'll love these favorites of mine:

Librairie Florence Loewy (9 rue de Thorigny, 3ème / florence loewy.com). A truly unique store/gallery with books by artists.

Galignani (224 rue de Rivoli, 1er/galignani.com). The first English-language bookstore on the Continent.

La Hune (170 boulevard Saint-Germain, 6ème). For an impressive selection of art, design, film, poetry, literature, and philosophy titles.

La Librairie des Gourmets (98 rue Monge, 5ème). Wonderful store for cookbooks and culinary books of all types, as well as a great selection of posters, cards, and culinary maps of France. The shop was chosen to run the Paris chapter of Slow Food.

Librairie Gourmande (92 rue Montmartre, 2ème/librairiegourmande.fr). Also a wonderful, two-story culinary bookstore near the site of the original Les Halles food market, appropriately.

Paris et Son Patrimoine (25 rue Saint-Louis-en-l'Île, 4ème). Books (nearly all in French) about Paris neighborhoods, streets, monuments, architecture, music, and theater.

Taschen (2 rue de Buci, 6ème). Hardcover illustrated books on art, fashion, travel, design, film, etc.

Village Voice (6 rue Princesse, 6ème / villagevoicebookshop.com). An all-around terrific selection of books in English and a stellar lineup of author appearances and special events (plus a very thorough list of recommended books about Paris on its Web site).

Les Bouquinistes

I think the first time I came across the word *bouquiniste* was when reading Hemingway, and ever since then I've had a soft spot in my heart for these secondhand booksellers (sellers of *bouquins*) who set up shop along the banks of the Seine. Rhonda Carrier relates in *In Love in France* that the *bouquinistes* originated in the sixteenth century, a time when some of Paris's bridges had shops and stalls along their lengths. The booksellers sold their wares from wheelbarrows until someone came up with the idea to attach trays to the sides of the bridges with leather straps. This continued until the late nineteenth century, when the *bouquinistes* were permitted to fasten their boxes to the quaysides on a permanent basis. Apparently there is an eight-year wait for a *bouquiniste* spot! Over the years I've bought quite a few items from *bouquinistes*—old stamps, postcards, paperback books, prints—though admittedly the value lay in actually purchasing them from a *bouquiniste* rather than owning them. I do very much love the two colored etchings I bought and had framed, and they are joined by other etchings I've collected on one wall in my living room.

C

Canal Saint-Martin

The Canal Saint-Martin, in the tenth arrondissement, is one of my favorite places in Paris, especially on Sunday, when many shops are closed and museums can be crowded. The canal's construction was ordered by Napoléon in 1802 to supply Paris with a source of drinking water, to help eradicate diseases like cholera and dysentery, and to provide a shorter river traffic route *through* Paris rather than *around* it. Gaspard de Chabrol, then prefect of Paris, proposed a canal that would be four and a half kilometers long and would connect the river Ourcq to the Seine, and the project was funded by a new tax on wine. The Canal Saint-Martin was completed in 1825; in Paris it is bordered by the Quai de Valmy on one side and the Quai de Jemmapes on the other. The Hôtel du Nord—the very same from Marcel Carné's 1938 film—is at 102 Quai de Jemmapes and is now a bar and restaurant (with a cool Web site, hoteldunord.org). Readers may remember that in the movie the character Arletty utters a classic line implying that "atmosphere" is overrated; appropriately, there is a nearby bistro, L'Atmosphère (49 rue Lucien-Sampaix), serving inexpensive *plats du jour*. On the Quai de Valmy, at no. 95, I'm especially fond of Antoine & Lili, the most colorful shop (think pink and fuchsia!) I've ever been in, which specializes in women's and kids' clothing and lots of cool decorative stuff (antoineetlili.com). But the best way to experience the scenic Canal Saint-Martin is to take a barge ride on it: the cruise is two and a half hours and passes through nine locks. Canauxrama (canauxrama.com) and Paris Canal (pariscanal.com) both offer cruises.

Chairs

I love the wrought-iron chairs that are set up around the fountain in the Tuileries Gardens. People move them around to their liking, usually based on where the sun is shining (or not), and I have taken dozens of photos of them. There is something incredibly attractive about their shape and decorative scrollwork, and I remain fascinated by the fact that the chairs aren't permanently affixed to the ground (so that no one steals them) or covered with graffiti (the way they might be in many other cities). I was disappointed to learn a few years ago that the original Tuileries chairs had been replaced with far less attractive models. I have no idea why, so the photos on the facing page are for those of you who may have never known the beautiful originals.

Chèque-cadeau

A *chèque-cadeau* is a gift certificate, which I learned when I wanted to buy my friend Luc one as a birthday present to use at La Librairie des Gourmets. A staff member kindly taught me this phrase, and I thought an occasion might arise when you, too, would be happy to know how to ask for one.

D

E. Dehillerin

Dehillerin (pronounced *DAY-luh-rhain*), a family business founded in 1820, is the mother lode of stores selling *materiel de cuisine* (18–20 rue Coquillière, 1er / e-dehillerin.fr). If you have a passion for cooking, you have likely already read about Dehillerin and my voice will just be one more added to the chorus of those who love this store. I haven't yet bought a copper pot or bowl from Dehillerin—its copper cookware is usually the first thing enthusiasts note—but the help I received when I was looking for a *kugelhopf* mold was kind and helpful (many people say the service is frosty at best). My only other purchase here was a set of pewter skewers for grilling, with decorative shells, fish, and crustaceans at their ends, but even if I never buy anything else again, I will not miss out on walking around this (rather dusty and) rambling shop. The Web site is fine for seeing the vast assortment of items available here, but nothing beats a real visit.

The only store I'm familiar with in North America that is remotely similar to Dehillerin is Bridge Kitchenware, which is also a family business, founded in 1946 by Fred Bridge. Bridge was located in Manhattan until 2008, when Steven and Kathy Bridge moved the store to New Jersey (563 Eagle Rock Avenue, Roseland / 973 287 6163 / bridgekitchenware.com) so they could be closer to their family. The store, like Dehillerin, has been a favorite for home cooks and noted chefs; there is a customer story shared on the Web site about a young woman whose grandmother "grabbed her by her arm and said buy whatever Mr. Bridge recommends, he knows his stuff and *never* argue with him, just nod and be quiet and hand him your money." I think the Dehillerin family would recognize the story as being similar to many of their own.

E

Edible Idioms

A feature I love in *A Food Lover's Guide to Paris* by Patricia Wells is the sprinkling of French words and phrases throughout the book that are culinary inspired but used in everyday speech. *Beurré* (buttered) is a colorful way to say someone's had too much to drink, and *le temps des cerises* (literally "the time of cherries," equivalent to our phrase "salad days") is one of my favorites as well. Clotilde Dusoulier, on her blog, Chocolateandzucchini .com, calls these "edible idioms," and she regularly adds such phrases to her site. A few she's highlighted are *tourner au vinaigre* (literally "turning to vinegar," but implying a situation or conversation that's taking a bad turn; things going sour); *etre serrés comme des sardines* (being packed together like sardines, used when people are squeezed into a very small space); and *ne pas manger de ce pain-là,* or "not eating that kind of bread," meaning refusing to act in a way that goes against one's values. For each phrase, Dusoulier also gives an example in a complete sentence in French and provides a link for an audio sample; for the example for *ne pas manger de ce pain-là,* we have this translation: "I'd have to kowtow to the principal to get a spot for my daughter, but I don't eat that kind of bread." This idiom highlights two kinds of people, she notes: those who would do anything for a piece of bread and those who would rather do without than "eat bread that was acquired in a way that doesn't sit right with their sense of ethics or morals"—and we know how the French feel about their bread. The phrase was the title of a 1936 book of poems by Benjamin Péret, a French Surrealist whose tombstone in the Batignolles cemetery bears the phrase as its epitaph. His book in its English translation is titled *I Won't Stoop to That.* I just love how much you can learn from a simple phrase.

Eiffel Tower

No matter that it is one of the world's most touristy symbols: I love *la tour Eiffel.* Writing in the *New York Times* in 1989, the year the tower turned one hundred, architecture critic Paul Goldberger aptly noted that, compared with nearly all other famous architectural icons, the Eiffel Tower is *bigger* than you expect: "That is the first thing that differentiates it from almost every other well-known structure in the world: no matter how many times you have stood before the Eiffel Tower, it is always at least a little bit bigger than you expect it to be." Writing for *Gourmet* in 1977, Joseph Wechsberg admitted that ever since arriving in Paris some fifty years earlier he had never been up inside the Eiffel Tower until recently. Once he did go, it was an "astonishing experience—and not only for the view," and I completely agree.

Gustave Eiffel's other works are noteworthy as well, including the Tan An Bridge in Vietnam, the Oporto Bridge in Portugal, the Garabit Viaduct in the Massif Central, the frame of the Bon Marché department store, and the framework for Bartholdi's Statue of Liberty—but it is of course the Tower for which he is best known. If you admire it as much as I do, I encourage you to read the chapter entitled "The Ogre of Modernity: Eiffel's Tower" in Frederick Brown's excellent book *For the Soul of France* (Knopf, 2010). The building of the tower took twenty-six months, Brown informs us, and "eighteen thousand numbered pieces" were delivered to the Champ de Mars with military precision. Yet its construction was mired in controversy. Guy de Maupassant, along with other writers and artists, signed an open letter of protest—known as the Protest of the 300—addressed to Alphonse Alphand, minister of public works, referring to the tower as "useless" and "monstrous" and declaring themselves devoted to stone. In Paris, they wrote, "stand the most noble monuments to which human genius has ever given birth. The soul of France, the creator of masterpieces, shines from this august proliferation of stone." They criticized the tower as being "American," and "an odious column of bolted metal."

The details surrounding this structure are endlessly fascinating. For example, the Eiffel Tower is classified within a *catégorie spéciale* indicating that it is not designated as a historical monument. If you want to learn more, another good account is *Eiffel's Tower: And the World's Fair Where Buffalo Bill Beguiled Paris, the Artists Quarreled, and Thomas Edison Became a Count* by Jill Jonnes (Viking, 2009), a truly fascinating peek into the Paris Exposition of 1889 and the history of the tower, defined by Eiffel as "not Greek, not Gothic, not Renaissance, because it will be built of iron. . . . The one certain thing is that it will be a work of great drama."

F

Faire le Pont

The French word *pont* (bridge) is also used as the equivalent of "long weekend" in English. As Bryce Corbett humorously notes in *A Town Like Paris,* "Through a clever melding of the Christian and Socialist calendars, the entire month of May is one long public holiday in France." He exaggerates, though not by much. When a holiday falls on a Thursday or a Tuesday, for example, the French like to *faire un pont* ("make a bridge") by also taking off on the surrounding days. This is useful to keep in mind if there is a scheduled holiday during your trip (especially in May)—if so, do not expect things to operate as usual.

Fermeture Annuelle

This phrase, meaning "annual closing," is one you'll see often during the month of August, when nearly every resident of Paris (or so it seems) is on holiday, either for a few weeks or the entire month. It is an important one to remember because, similar to on *ponts* (above), some restaurants may be closed, sites may keep different hours, some shops may be closed, and the plumber will be unavailable to fix the problem you're having at the apartment you've rented. All this changes at the time of *la Rentrée*—the "return," and it is often spelled with a capital *R*—signifying that everyone is back from vacation, school is starting, and the busy fall season has just begun.

Films

One of my favorite forms of travel immersion is to invite friends and family over for an evening of a themed dinner and a movie. It's a great way to familiarize yourself with some of the foods you may be eating on your upcoming trip, and the movie is just icing on the cake. Potluck is especially fun for guests who enjoy the challenge of making something new or bringing an appropriate favorite, and guests who aren't cooks can supply the wine. There is no shortage of films featuring Paris to watch after dinner. Some I particularly like include: *Amélie* (2001), *An American in Paris* (1951), *Avenue Montaigne* (2006), *Le Ballon rouge* (*The Red Balloon,* 1956), *À Bout de souffle* (*Breathless,* 1960), *Le Dernier Métro* (*The Last Metro,* 1980), *Funny Face* (1957), *Gigi* (1958), *Hôtel du Nord* (1938), *The Last Time I Saw Paris* (1954), *Les Enfants du paradis* (*Children of Paradise,* 1945), *Paris, je t'aime* (2006, and my absolute favorite!), *Paris When It Sizzles* (1964), and *Paris la belle* (*Beautiful Paris,* 1960). This last is an unusual documentary directed by Pierre Prévert featuring black-and-white images of Paris from 1928 with the same shots—in color—from 1959, with his brother, poet Jacques Prévert, doing the narration and song lyrics.

Fin de Série

This is a good retail phrase to know, as it's used to refer to items that have been discounted because there are only a few left or will no longer be available (i.e., the line is being discontinued).

Flamant

Flamant Home Interiors (flamant.com), founded by brothers Alex, Geo, and Jacques, is a great store to browse in for anyone who loves the arts of the home. Its stated mission is "the revival of handicraft furniture and old objects adapted to the needs of today," and the selection includes dinnerware, tabletop items, paints, and decorative pieces. (I am partial to its Manosque line of white dinnerware.) The Paris store is at 8 rue de Furstenberg/8 rue de l'Abbaye, in the sixth.

Flâneur

Eric Maisel, in *A Writer's Paris,* defines a *flâneur* as "an observer who wanders the streets of a great city on a mission to notice with childlike enjoyment the smallest events and the obscurest sights he encounters." I like that definition, but I like Bryce Corbett's, in *A Town Like Paris,* even better: "The term *flâneur* exists only in French, describing a person who spends entire days wandering aimlessly with the express purpose of doing little more than taking in whatever he sees. A French man is never in danger of running too quickly past the roses to ever stop and smell them." The word *is* uniquely French, and though I keep the word in mind here at home, it is positively Parisian.

Fluctuat Nec Mergitur

Paris's coat of arms is a boat motif borrowed from the seal of the Watermen's Guild, appointed by Louis IX in 1260 to administer the city. In the sixteenth century, the Latin motto *Fluctuat nec mergitur*—"Buffeted by the waves, we shall not sink"—was added, and it remains today. You'll see this coat of arms around the city, carved into buildings and imprinted upon documents. To view some on the façades of buildings, log on to the creative Web site Ruavista.com and browse its selection of photographs.

France Magazine

There are very few pieces of mail that arrive in my mailbox that I am genuinely excited about, but *France Magazine* is one of them.

This wonderful, fully illustrated quarterly—filled with a heady mix of articles covering culture, travel, timely topics, and cuisine—began publication more than twenty years ago. Under the direction of editor Karen Taylor, the magazine is published by the French-American Cultural Foundation (FACF) in Washington, D.C., whose mission is to foster cultural and educational ties between France and North America. Previously available only by subscription, *France* is now for sale at select Barnes & Noble, Borders, and smaller bookstores nationwide, and I highly recommend becoming a regular reader (202 944 6069 / francemagazine.org).

Le Furet-Tanrade

I first learned of this shop from Patricia Wells in her first edition of *The Food Lover's Guide to Paris,* and I've been a loyal customer of Le Furet-Tanrade ever since (63 rue de Chabrol, 10ème / lefuret -tanrade.com). Initially, I went to the store in search of *confiture de poire passée,* a smooth, delicious pear concoction Wells recommended for mixing with plain yogurt. I did as she prescribed, and

I was rendered speechless by how delicious it was. Later, I discovered *pêche de vigne* jam, and all I have to say is if you think you've had better peach jam anywhere in the world than this one, you are dead wrong. Still later, I discovered the shop's orange-flower water made from the blossoms at the *orangerie* at Versailles, and the chocolates, which are of quite good quality. Tanrade has, according to Naomi Barry in *Paris Personal,* "enjoyed the reputation of being the first house in Paris for fine jams, jellies, and fruit syrups" for nearly 250 years. At the time Barry penned her book (1963), she considered Tanrade's *marrons glacés* the finest in Paris. I can't vouch for that, but I can for every single item that I've purchased here. Tanrade is positively *vaut le détour.*

H

Les Halles

In recent years, I've become incredibly fascinated by Les Halles, Paris's central food marketplace until 1969. Though there was a market on the site since 1183, it is Victor Baltard's iron and glass pavilions, constructed between 1854 and 1866, that captivate my imagination (ten original market halls were erected in the 1800s, with two reproductions added in 1936). *Les Halles* is pronounced *lay-AHL,* one of the few examples in French where *liaison*—the practice of pronouncing the final *s* in a word when the next word begins with a vowel—does not apply. (Other examples include *les hors d'oeuvres, les haricots, les homards,* and *les hot-dogs.*)

Les Halles, as Naomi Barry wrote in her 1963 *Paris Personal,* was "a kind of butter-and-egg Casbah, packed with history, glamour, traffic, trading, and vice. . . . To stroll through this brilliant, aromatic bazaar is to spin your senses until they reel with the colors and the smells of everything that grows on earth and comes up out of the sea." There was a profusion of two-wheeled carts at the market known as *diables,* belonging to neighborhood grocery owners who needed fresh produce for their shops. There were also porters, known as *les forts des Halles,* who had had their own guild since 1140. *Les forts* also served as pallbearers to the kings, who, upon their deaths, were carried to the Basilica of Saint-Denis, just outside of Paris, where French monarchs have traditionally been buried. In 1461 *les forts* went on one of the most successful strikes in French history: halfway to Saint-Denis, they set down the casket of Charles VII and refused to go any farther until they were promised more money. Lastly, Barry tells us that the word *clochards* (bums) may derive from Les Halles: a bell (*cloche*) would be rung after the day's trading was finished, and the *clochards* were the (hungry) recipients of anything left over. (Another theory about the name, Barry relates, is that *clochard* comes from *clocher,* a verb meaning "to limp" or "to bump along," as *clochards* are often observed walking in a rather uneven fashion.) The streets in the vicinity of the market that still exist today were aptly named: the rue des Lombards was so named for the merchants from Genoa, Venice, and Florence who set up shop as bankers and money changers. Rue de la Ferronnerie was named for ironmongers (iron is *fer*), and the boulevard Poissonnière was the street used for fish (*poisson*) transported to the market.

In the Middle Ages, the entire Les Halles *quartier* was prominent as *the* place for starting riots, hatching plots against the government, and seeking approval of the crowd, and royal ordinances and peace treaties were first read here to the market people. Émile Zola's 1873 novel *Le Ventre de Paris* (*The Belly of Paris*) is set in the Les Halles neighborhood, and his vivid descriptions are one of the best records we have of this extraordinary market. A more recent reminiscence is found in *Saveur Cooks Authentic French,* from Claude Cornut, second-generation proprietor of a market bistro, Chez Clovis: "Les Halles was a village unto itself in the very heart of Paris. We were so content and self-sufficient that we would forget that there was a world outside. Imagine the ambience of a place that is alive at least twenty hours of the day!"

But by mid-twentieth century the market's location, which took up about forty acres, became problematic: the nighttime truck traffic was unbearable, and much of the arriving foodstuffs had to be repacked and sent out again to other parts of France and beyond. In 1969, the decision was made to move the market to

Rungis, south of Paris (see Rungis entry, page 683). Only one of Baltard's pavilions survived the demolition, and it is now located in the suburb of Nogent-sur-Marne, to the east of Paris (reachable by the RER). According to Thirza Valois in the first volume of *Around and About Paris,* there were many people who lamented the end of the world Les Halles had created. A sculptor observed, "It was a place of bliss . . . the last vision of natural life in the city. It is now paradise lost," and a social observer and poet opined, "The death of Les Halles has tolled the knell of Paris." Fortunately, this last didn't come to pass, though what followed the demolition was justified cause for alarm: a giant hole in the ground remained for ten years, and then in 1979 the Forum des Halles opened.

The Forum does incorporate nice pedestrian and garden areas that I am fond of, but any mention of the Forum usually refers to its underground shopping mall, which quickly became seedy (and at times unsafe) when the Châtelet–Les Halles Métro station was expanded to become the largest station in the system—the suburban lines connect with the city lines here, and it's easy to get lost in the labyrinth of passages. Currently, plans are under way for a new glass canopy to cover the existing shopping complex, and a music conservatory, a museum, restaurants, and additional shops will be added. There will be additional garden space added as well, and the whole thing is slated to be completed in 2016.

If I rarely see any North Americans around Les Halles, I have seen even fewer at Saint-Eustache, bordering Les Halles to the north, the second-largest church in Paris after Notre-Dame and among my favorites. Built in the sixteenth century, Saint-Eustache is where Cardinal Richelieu and the Marquise de Pompadour were baptized, where Louis XIII made his first communion, where Jean-Baptiste Lully was married in 1662, and where funeral services for Molière and fable writer Jean de la Fontaine were held. In *The Belly of Paris,* Monsieur Claude (who is likely based at least a little on the painter Cézanne) tells Florent that he doesn't believe it was coincidence that brought Saint-Eustache's rosette windows in alignment with Les Halles. This is modern art confronting old art, he says: "Since the beginning of the century only one original building has been erected, only one that is not a copy from somewhere else but has sprung naturally out of the soil of our times, and that is Les Halles. Do you see it, Florent? A brilliant work that is a shy foretaste of the twentieth century. That is why it frames Saint-Eustache. There stands the church with its rosette window, empty of the faithful, while Les Halles spreads out around it, buzzing with life." Saint-Eustache is also known for its strong musical tradition due to its outstanding acoustics, and the church has one of the most prestigious organs in Paris. According to Thirza Valois, the organ's case was designed by Victor Baltard, and as it is "equipped with both a mechanical and an electronic transmission system, [it] is the biggest double transmission organ in the world."

Besides the *Ecoute* sculpture by Henri de Miller in front of Saint-Eustache, my favorite feature of this wonderful church is the haut-relief in resin and acrylic gouache entitled *The Departure of the Fruits and Vegetables from the Heart of Paris, February 28, 1969,* by Raymond Mason. It is entirely fitting that this artist's tribute to Les Halles is here, in the church that, despite its association with elite names of the past, served the working-class merchants of the market.

Baron Haussmann

Georges-Eugène Haussmann could trace his lineage back to Cologne, Germany, and Alsace, but history has made his name nearly synonymous with Paris. In fact, as David Jordan notes in his excellent *Transforming Paris: The Life and Labors of Baron Haussmann,* "No name is so attached to a city as is Haussmann's to Paris. The great founders of cities in antiquity, both mythological and actual, even Alexander the Great or the Emperor Constantine, who gave their names to their creations, have not left so indelible an urban imprint." The French (as is their wont) even created an adjective from his name, *haussmannisé*.

Baron Haussmann was named prefect of the Seine under Napoléon III, and the city of Paris as we know it today is the direct result of Haussmann's plans, which included the creation of the city's *grands boulevards,* the continuation of the rue de Rivoli, the redesign of the Bois de Boulogne and Les Halles, the addition of more parks, the blue and white plaques bearing street names, and apartment buildings that even today are coveted for their solid walls, good structural foundations, high ceilings, and well-lit rooms. Haussmann oversaw nothing less than the most extensive urban renewal project ever attempted. The elegance and even the sense of grandeur that Haussmann brought to Paris are undeniable, but in the mid-1800s his ideas were met with virulent criticism. In creating the boulevards, huge numbers of impoverished people were swept aside, unable to afford the new rents, and nothing was done to help them relocate elsewhere or to alleviate their conditions in the neighborhoods they were forced into, such as Belleville and Vaugirard.

In his preface to *Transforming Paris,* Jordan writes that initially even he had no affinity for Haussmann. "Hadn't he destroyed Paris so the army could deploy rapidly and shoot down demonstrators? My sympathies were on the other side of the barricades that Haussmann—so the cliché ran—had made obsolete." It's true that Napoléon III wanted a capital city that would never again allow protesters to so successfully fight against his troops as they had during the creation of his Second Empire, which was born out of a street battle that left four thousand Parisians dead. Haussmann proposed a modern and clean city, as opposed to the medieval city Paris was, with squalid living conditions, a lack of clean water, few trees, no plumbing, and narrow, dark streets. He especially admired the Marquis de Tourny, who under Louis XV had transformed Bordeaux, where Haussmann had lived for more than twelve years (if you've visited Bordeaux you may fondly recall the wide and beautiful Allées de Tourny). Tourny's Bordeaux also had some striking similarities to Haussmann's Paris, including an opera house in the center of the city, a major river, grand public buildings inherited from the past, and an old medieval core that had been successfully integrated into the new city. But, as Jordan notes, Bordeaux was not Paris: "There was no city like Paris. The concentration of money, energy, people, and institutions, the dominance of Paris over France, was unparalleled."

You don't have to walk far in Paris to experience a bit of the baron, and *Transforming Paris* (Free Press, 1995) is a wonderful companion. It's really a book about Paris that features Haussmann more than a biography of Haussmann. Included are many maps and photographs that excellently convey the changes Haussmann made, plus a moving epilogue about Jordan's visit to his grave in Père-Lachaise. Haussmann's grave is not featured on the Père-Lachaise map you can buy for a few euros at the entrance, but it's in the avenue Principale in the fourth section. "He is prominently placed for eternity," Jordan notes, "amid the graves of distinguished contemporaries, many now as forgotten as he. Visited, without deep emotion, by very few, he is best remembered by what he did. Take a moment to look down on Paris from the cemetery. It is the best memorial."

Heilbrunn Timeline of Art History

Launched in 2000, the Metropolitan Museum of Art's Heilbrunn Timeline (metmuseum.org/toah) is "a chronological, geographical, and thematic exploration of the history of art from around the world, as illustrated by the Metropolitan Museum of Art's collection." It is nothing less than an extraordinary achievement: "an invaluable reference and research tool for students, educators, scholars, and anyone interested in the study of art history and related subjects." A vast number of French works appear in the timeline, from the year 500 to the present (the timeline goes much further back), and I encourage readers to dip into it and get lost in it. The timeline—which is researched and written by the Met's curators, conservators, and educators—allows visitors to compare and contrast six thousand works of art from around the globe at any time in human history.

Hollins Abroad Paris

I'm very fortunate to be a graduate of Hollins University (formerly Hollins College), a private women's college in Virginia founded in 1842. Hollins has a fine liberal arts curriculum (*Forbes* recently included Hollins in the top one hundred of its America's Best Colleges list) and renowned undergrad and graduate English and creative writing programs. Graduates of other alma maters may feel equally fortunate, but Hollins has one other attribute that most colleges and universities don't: its study abroad program in Paris. Hollins Abroad Paris, founded in 1955, is one of the longest-established American programs in Paris. Its distinctive program was for many years located in the sixteenth arrondissement (rue Lauriston), then in the seventh (rue de l'Odéon), and is now a member of the Reid Hall campus, which it shares with nine other American schools, including Columbia University, Smith College, and Dartmouth College. I attended in 1979, and lived on the rue de Grenelle in the seventh arrondissement with a family of five that didn't speak a word of English. *Absolument*, HAP is greatly responsible for who I am today as well as for the creation of *The Collected Traveler.*

"Letter from Paris," a booklet written by the Hollins Abroad pioneers of 1955, perfectly conveys, in words I wish I'd written myself, the experience:

> If you are a girl with a call for adventure, with curiosity, a widening scale of values, and a bit of courage, then you are the one who should go abroad. You may cry when you leave, count

the days till you come home, and be a homesick pup, but you'll never—we promise you, never—regret it or forget it. When you're a sophomore in college and having the time of your life, we know it's no easy thing to consider throwing it all aside for a year of who knows what; but we, the ones who went in '55, are asking you to follow. Our year's adventure has been invaluable; we have seen and lived an existence preciously given to very few; we have stumbled on obstacles only to turn them into stepping stones; we have fought and then praised, living, we think, the most profitable year of our lives. So join us; leave the boyfriend, family, and half the wardrobe home; take a big step and live a year that's worth a lifetime.

One Hollins Abroader, Susan Gilbert Harvey, was inspired to pen a book weaving her own experience with that of her great-aunt, who lived in Paris in 1898. *Tea With Sister Anna: A Paris Journal* (Golden Apple, 2005) reveals the life Anna McNulty Lester led in Paris as an art student, which Harvey, also an artist, pieced together from letters she'd discovered in her great-aunt's steamer trunk. In her preface, Harvey says she admired her great-aunt's talent and tenacity, and enjoyed walking her streets in Paris, but she was surprised to find such passion in her great-aunt's solitary life. It was a simple typed quotation she'd come across in one letter that encouraged her to investigate Aunt Anna's sojourn and to examine her own life as an artist: "Let us hang our life on the line, as painters say, and look at it honestly." On the final page of the book, Harvey writes, "When I first read these words, I pictured a clothesline art display. Now I know that 'on the line' means hung at eye level, the most prestigious position for a painting in the Salon."

When I attended the fifty-year reunion of HAP, I met some other women who also lived in New York, and we had such a great time together that we now meet several times a year for a French-themed *fête*. As a group we are of varying ages and, with two exceptions, we all attended HAP in different years. But what doesn't vary is our conviction that our time in Paris irrevocably changed our lives. For this edition I asked *mes amies de New York* to share some of their memories and favorite things about Paris, and they were, *naturellement,* only too happy to comply:

> There is nothing like Paris at twilight. Enough daylight remains to allow the city's architecture to be admired in all its glory, but the exteriors now share center stage with glowing interiors. There's a fabulous juxtaposition of centuries-old structures and illuminated contemporary life. This contrast excites the eye—and makes the heart beat a bit faster.
>
> —Amanda Miller, Hollins Abroad Paris, 1984;
> vice president and publisher, John Wiley & Sons

MY SHORT LIST OF FAVORITE THINGS
TO DO IN PARIS

- Spend several hours at the Musée d'Orsay (my favorite museum in all the world).
- Have dinner at Le Grand Véfour in the Palais Royal.
- Marvel at the stained-glass windows of La Sainte-Chapelle with the sun shining in.
- Sip a *café crème* and people-watch at Les Deux Magots, the famous expat hangout on the Left Bank; or take afternoon tea at the century-old Angelina tearoom on rue de Rivoli.
- Stroll the Tuileries Gardens west of the Louvre.
- Have pre- or after-dinner drinks in the Hemingway Bar at the Ritz.
- Have your portrait sketched by street artists in Montmartre (and explore the neighborhood of *Amélie* while you're up there).
- Wander around the Île Saint-Louis and have an ice cream at Berthillon.
- For two splendid views, climb up to the top of the Arc de Triomphe and ride the escalator to the rooftop café of the Centre Pompidou.
- Have drinks at Harry's New York Bar (5 rue Daunou, 2ème) near the Opéra.
- Both the Musée Rodin and the Musée Marmotton are very special.
- For visitors with a sweet tooth, you can't leave Paris without going to Ladurée (16 rue Royale, 8ème) and sampling the pastel-hued *macarons*—they were invented here over a century ago. My favorites are pistachio, cherry-amaretto, lily of the valley, and grenadine. With its Jules Chéret décor, this branch of Ladurée is strictly an Old World experience.
- Have a meal at the Le Jules Verne restaurant on the second *étage* of the Eiffel Tower—it's open for lunch and dinner, is under the direction of Alain Ducasse, and has earned one Michelin star.

- Take in the after-dinner *spectacle* at the Crazy Horse cabaret on avenue George-V.

—Missy Van Buren, Hollins Abroad Paris, 1975;
former client relationship manager, IPC Systems

From a kaleidoscope of memories of a college student's year abroad comes this one: less pleasant or inspiring or soul-searching than some, but important in its lesson about living in harmony with *la vie quotidienne*—everyday life—in Paris.

My roommate Amanda and I had been in Paris already for several months when we happened to bump into our elderly French hostess on the street close to where we lived with her. We were stepping into a bakery to buy a baguette, and Madame followed us into the shop while we made our purchase.

Back on the street, she turned to us in fury. "Are you always so rude to the baker?" she demanded in French. Amanda and I looked at her, and at each other, in stunned silence. We had said please and thank you. We could not imagine that we had been anywhere close to rude.

Turns out, in Paris, it is *de rigueur* to catch the eye of the shopkeeper upon entering an establishment and to greet them with a heartfelt *Bonjour, madame/monsieur!* After making your polite request and payment, it is also important to conclude the visit with *Merci* and *Au revoir, madame/monsieur!*

While this might seem like a formality to Americans, it is a small ritual that echoes throughout *boulangeries,* newsstands, *pâtisseries,* and boutiques all over the city, day after day, woven into the culture of which the French are so proud and so protective.

I've shared this story with countless Americans who have asked about the (supposed) rudeness of the French, and I think it helps them to appreciate a timeless exchange essential to the fabric of everyday life in Paris.

—Nicole Osborn Ash, Hollins Abroad Paris, 1984; personal coach
and former vice president of marketing, American Express

In the back of the stage at the Paris Opéra is a beautiful room where cocktail parties are held after some perform-ances. While you are sipping Champagne and munching on wonderful treats the curtain is raised and you have this spec-tacular view of the orchestra. Each time it gives me goose bumps!

—Frances Hershkowitz, Hollins Abroad Paris, 1962;
former executive with McKinsey & Company
and Ballet de Paris enthusiast

A FRENCH REMEMBRANCE

Paris was the first real city in which I ever lived and is like a sec-ond home to me, even though I have only returned to visit a handful of times in the past twenty-five years (including my honeymoon!). In 1982, my roommate and I lived with a family at 115 boulevard Saint-Germain, just steps from the Odéon Métro station and a quick jog to the Palais de Luxembourg with its beautiful *jardins*. While our room-and-board contract did not include lunch, our family was generous, especially on the weekends, and often included us in their Sunday dinners if we were around. Because the Vietnamese maid had Sundays off, the fare was usually something simple, such as *choucroute* (sauer-kraut) with sausages, a spinach dish with hard-boiled eggs, or a roast chicken. One Sunday during lunch I offered to make the family a meal that was *typiquement Américain* the following week. I couldn't think of anything more American than meat loaf and baked potatoes. My roommate, not being much of a cook, decided she would contribute dessert—banana splits.

The following Saturday we went to the open-air market and purchased the ingredients, which was an adventure all on its own and a rather expensive endeavor for our meager student budgets. The family's kitchen was not exactly up to date, with a gas oven and stove that required using a lighting device to get started, a very small refrigerator, and quite cramped quarters. After almost setting the apartment on fire trying to light the stove, everything took twice as long as it would have in a normal American kitchen, especially the baked potatoes (no microwave to fall back on).

When everything was finally ready the family had been waiting for a very long time and they were *hungry*. I will never forget the father stabbing his baked potato with his fork, holding it upright with his left hand, and peeling the skin off with his right. So much for sour cream and chives! When dessert was served, the chocolate sauce was hard as a rock and the ice cream like soup. Needless to say, they never asked us to cook for them again!

—Judy Morrill, Hollins Abroad Paris, 1982;
managing director, Highmount Capital

The Hollins Reid Hall program (hollins.edu) welcomes students from all colleges and universities, so if you know someone who might be interested, encourage him or her to explore further!

Hôtel

The word *hôtel* in French not only refers to a lodging but also is a general word used for many other buildings or complexes. Some common *hôtels* are: a private, aristocratic mansion (*hôtel particulier,* like the Hôtel de Sully in the Marais); a city hall (*hôtel de ville,* which every French town of any size has); a hospital (sometimes called a *hôtel-Dieu*); a general post office (*hôtel de poste*); an auction house (*hôtel des ventes*); and, in Paris, a home for wounded war veterans (the Hôtel des Invalides, founded by Louis XIV, now also a military museum).

I

Interdit

The French word for "forbidden" or "prohibited," *interdit* can be an annoying word, especially when it is displayed on signs on the grass of many Paris parks and gardens, justifiably among the world's most beautiful. I used to bristle at the signs, but then I decided that a feature I really like about Paris parks is that they are part of people's daily lives, not a place for recreation only. Parisians walk through parks and gardens every day, to and from work, to take a break, to rendezvous with friends or family. We have very few urban parks and gardens in North America that are quite the same—New York's Central Park and Boston's Public Garden are two that are—as we tend to think of parks as places to go just to play sports or lay down a blanket for a picnic. In Paris, you can't separate the parks from the boulevards or avenues, and I think being prohibited from walking on the grass is a small price to pay to stroll or sit in such picturesque surroundings (and the grass is often the most perfect you've ever seen).

J

Jeu de Paume

Today reserved for temporary exhibitions with an emphasis on contemporary photography and video, the Jeu de Paume museum once housed the Impressionists. For many years after living in Paris as a student (when I was typically at the museum twice a week), I was able to still remember the exact placement of each painting in every room. Alas, my memory fails me a bit now, though I do remember whether a work was on the first floor or the second, on the rue de Rivoli side or the Tuileries side. It may seem pointless to mention something one can't really experience anymore—after all, we can still see the Impressionist paintings in the Musée d'Orsay (thankfully)—but there is something very special and worth emphasizing about viewing art in a small museum.

Thinking about how compact the Jeu de Paume is reminds me of a passage from the chapter "Hunger Was Good Discipline" in Hemingway's *A Moveable Feast,* in which he speaks of the small museum of *his* day:

> There you could always go to the Luxembourg Museum and all the paintings were sharpened and clearer and more beautiful if you were belly-empty, hollow-hungry. I learned to understand Cézanne much better and to see truly how he made landscapes when I was hungry. I used to wonder if he were hungry too when he painted; but I thought possibly it was only that he had forgotten to eat. It was one of those unsound but illuminating thoughts you have when you have been sleepless or hungry. Later I thought Cézanne was probably hungry in a different way.

I was hungry often in Paris, too, but I will never forget how standing and looking in the Jeu de Paume made me feel about art, about my life, about the extraordinary place that is Paris. I mention all this to encourage visitors not to overlook Paris's wealth of small museums—in any one of them, you may very well have your own illuminating thoughts.

Jewish History in Paris

France is home to the fourth-largest Jewish community in the world and the largest in Europe; after Catholicism, however, Islam is the second-largest religion in France. Though Jewish communities in France date back hundreds of years, France's reputation as a *terre d'asile* (land of refuge) for political or economic exiles emerged during the Napoleonic Wars, when the "liberating" army attracted immigrants from Germany and Italy. France was also the first of all Western European countries to emancipate the Jews, in 1791, and many Russians who enriched Paris in the late 1800s and early 1900s were Jewish, as Nancy Green recounts in *The Pletzl of Paris* (Holmes & Meir, 1986); *pletzl* is Yiddish for "little place." Green writes that "the mystique of France's appeal was embedded in both the embodiment of 'civilization' and the enduring aura of the French Revolution. . . . For the Russified Jewish intelligentsia, 'Russification' also included a certain amount of French language and literature. French civilization, from its poets and philosophers to its culture and cuisine, had even penetrated the Pale [of Settlement]." (The Pale was an area of western provinces in Russia where Jews were confined to live, as decreed first by Catherine the Great and then definitively established under Nicholas I in 1835. The population within the Pale rose from 1 million at the beginning of the nineteenth century to approximately 5.5 million by the end.) Not even the Dreyfus Affair was seen as an obstacle: *l'affaire* was in fact outside the realm of under-

standing of Hasidic and Orthodox Jews since, in Russia, no Jew (except a few doctors) could attain such a rank as army captain. There was also a proverb that Yiddish oral tradition adopted as its own: *lebn vi got in Frankraykh*—to live like God in France—which dates to 1693, when King Maximilian reportedly said, "If it were possible that I were God and I had two sons, the first would succeed me as God and the second would be king of France."

The *pletzl* in Green's book refers to the Marais quarter, which has a Jewish history dating back to the thirteenth century, though not continuously. At that time, present-day rue Ferdinand-Duval was rue des Juifs (Street of the Jews); nearby rue des Écouffes (pawnbrokers) and rue des Rosiers (perhaps, Green notes, from *ros,* the teeth on a loom) were already known as centers of Ashkenazic Jewry in Paris. Wealthier Jews, mostly of Sephardic origin, lived in the fifth arrondissement. Today the Marais is home to the Musée d'Art et d'Histoire du Judaïsme (71 rue du Temple, 3ème / mahj.org), a really great museum housed in the beautiful Hôtel de Saint-Aignon, dating from the 1600s.

According to Lucien Lazare in *Rescue as Resistance* (Columbia University Press, 1996), three out of four Jews present in France in 1940 survived World War II. However, not a single deported child survived. It is particularly sad to note, as Pierre Birnbaum explains in his chapter "Grégoire, Dreyfus, Drancy, and the Rue Copernic: Jews at the Heart of French History" in *Realms of Memory* (volume I), that in the 1980s "various administrative and political authorities refused one after another to provide sites for statues of Captain Dreyfus, Léon Blum, and Pierre Mendès France." At the site where once stood Paris's Vélodrome d'Hiver, built as a bicycle racetrack but now mostly known as the site where Parisian Jews were taken before they were deported, there is now only a small plaque that is somewhat hard to find (which I can attest to, though I did manage to find it and take a photo). "This place of remembrance *par excellence*," notes Birnbaum, "has simply vanished. Even worse, there is apparently no surviving photograph of the July 1942 roundup to preserve a visual record of the event."

It's true that, as Birnbaum maintains, "physical sites of Jewish memory in France are quite rare"; still, Paris, and many other cities and towns in France, has a number of noteworthy sites of Jewish interest. In Paris there is also the Memorial to the Deported behind Notre-Dame on Île de la Cité, as well as the Mémorial de la Shoah (17 rue Geoffroy-l'Asnier, 4ème / memorialdelashoah.org). Two books to consult are *The Complete Jewish Guide to France* by Toni Kamins (St. Martin's, 2001) and *A Travel Guide to Jewish Europe* by Ben Frank (Pelican, 2001, third edition). Both books devote large sections to Paris, and the authors note that visitors who keep kosher need not worry about where to take their next meal: there may be more kosher places to eat in Paris than in New York, Chicago, and Los Angeles combined! Additionally, the French Government Tourist Office publishes "FranceGuide for the Jewish Traveler," which can be accessed at Franceguide.com.

Just Campagne

This partially English-named shop (*campagne* means "country-side") is actually very French, founded in the South of France in 1990 by Azzedine Berkouk, who designs women's handbags. Berkouk's line of what I refer to as "regular" leather bags are perfectly fine and nicely crafted, but it's the open-weave leather bags with interchangeable linings that are truly distinctive. The leather is available in only two shades, but the linings, in cotton, linen, and wool, come in a variety of colors, and the price is dependent upon which lining you choose, wool being the most expensive. All Just Campagne bags are hand finished in Toulouse and each has its own serial number. Stores in Paris are at 159 boulevard Saint-Germain, 6ème, and 14 rue des Pyramides, 1er (just campagne.com).

L

Language

Everyone will tell you that it is essential to attempt to speak some French when in Paris. This is true—the French warm to anyone attempting to speak their beautiful language—yet it is also true that the natives of *any* country love it when visitors try to speak their language. What you might not realize is that French is still in many ways a universal language. It has been my experience that *someone* always speaks French, even in such seemingly unlikely countries as Egypt, Portugal, Turkey, Greece, and Croatia. Spanish may be the second language in the United States, but it won't serve you very well outside of Latin America, Spain, and the Philippines.

With this in mind, I wasn't surprised to learn, in Jean-Benoît Nadeau and Julie Barlow's excellent and fascinating *The Story of French* (St. Martin's, 2006), that though in terms of numbers of speakers French ranks only ninth in the world, French is flourishing. Of the six thousand languages now spoken on earth, French is one of only fifteen spoken by more than a hundred million people; it is one of eleven other languages that are the official language in more than one country, and among these, only four— English, French, Spanish, and Arabic—have official status in more than twenty countries (French, with thirty-three countries, ranks second to English, with forty-five). Two G8 countries, France and Canada, are French-speaking, as are four European Union members: France, Belgium, Luxembourg, and Switzerland. And French, along with English, is one of the two primary languages of the UN. Nadeau and Barlow also inform us that French "is the number two second-language choice of students across the planet, attracting learners as far away as Lesotho and Azerbaijan." And finally: "There have never been as many French speakers in the world as there are today: The number has tripled since the Second World War."

Nadeau and Barlow share their surprise at discovering, on a trip to Tel Aviv, that the first language they heard when they stepped out of their hotel was French. They were surprised because most Israelis speak Hebrew and English, and they figured it would be difficult for a third language to emerge among them. But what they learned was that 10 percent of Israelis speak French, including the large Moroccan population there, and that there are French-speaking communities in many more places than Tel Aviv. This solidified an impression that grew as they worked on their book: "that French is more resilient than people generally believe" and that "it has an enduring hold on the world, a level of influence that in many ways surpasses—and is even independent of—France's."

M

Macarons

The French *macaron* is distinct from other similarly named sweets, notably the American macaroon, coconut blobs sometimes dipped in chocolate. I once *loved* American macaroons, but some years ago I decided they were too sweet and, after trying French *macarons,* too limiting in flavor. French *macarons* are made with a large quantity of egg whites and are therefore very light, and they are a sandwich cookie—unlike a giant blob—with a flavored filling. Many people rave about the *macarons* at Ladurée, the *pâtisserie* credited with having invented them, but I think the *macarons* are substantially better at La Maison du Chocolat, Pierre Hermé, and Gérard Mulot—and, of late, at my own home.

Before I was in possession of *I Love Macarons* by Hisako Ogita (Chronicle, 2009), the recipe I used was from an old issue of *Gourmet* attributed to Mireille Guiliano, author of *French Women*

Don't Get Fat. The recipe is a good one, but required the assistance of my daughter to hold down the parchment paper on the pan so I could pipe the batter out of my pastry bag. Ogita explains so much more about the making of *macarons*—what can go wrong with the batter, how to make them with Italian meringue, how to add flavor to the batter, etc.—that I can't imagine I'll ever look back. It really helps that there are photographs, and I was happy to learn I can use my Silpat baking mat instead of rolled parchment paper! Plus Ogita is thoughtful enough to provide six recipes at the end of the book to use up all the egg yolks you'll have left over from making the *macarons.*

Maille

Boutique Maille, at 6 place de la Madeleine in the eighth arrondissement (maille.com), is the Burgundy mustard company's official representative in Paris, and it's a good culinary stop to add to your itinerary. Founded in 1747, Maille is now owned by the

LA MAISON
ivre

Poterie artisanale
Terre vernissée
Céramique d'Art

ouvert du Lundi au Samedi de 10h30 à 19h00
38, rue Jacob - 75006 PARIS
Tél : 01 42 60 01 85
métro saint-germain des prés
www.maison-ivre.com
info@maison-ivre.com

mega-conglomerate Unilever, a far cry from the day in 1769 when Antoine Maille was named official *vinaigrier-distillateur* for the royal court of France. The reason to come here is not for the ordinary jars of mustard and condiments, which can reliably be found throughout North America, but for the freshly pumped mustards on the central counter, which come in attractive stoneware containers in three sizes. Three different mustards are offered daily, all of which are more potent than the Maille mustards imported in the States. The staff pumps your mustard choices into the jars and seals them with lids made of coated paper and cork. (Don't worry: these will make it through your flight home just fine if placed upright in your carry-on luggage.) You can also purchase small wooden mustard spoons and some nice gift arrangements with mustards in painted faïence jars.

La Maison Ivre

Fans of Rimbaud will recognize the pun on his poem "Le Bateau Ivre" (The Drunken Boat) embedded in the name of this charming and hugely appealing shop, La Maison Ivre, founded by Sylvine Nobécourt in 1991 (38 rue Jacob, 6ème/maison-ivre.com). As Sylvine, who has a great sense of humor, tells it, she studied French literature at university and loved it, but didn't know exactly what she wanted to do with it upon graduation. She's not even sure she can pinpoint the day she came up with the idea for a store, but she does know that since the "great adventure began, I became entirely devoted to the store. In fact it is La Maison Ivre that has chosen me." She likes the association between literature and her shop, devoted to "a symphony of colors to brighten your home," and indeed the shop is filled with irresistible items. Here you'll find *torchons* (tea towels) in more than fifty patterns, aprons, coasters and trivets (including some with the store's logo), *poterie artisanale*—the store is a veritable showcase for handcrafted ceramics from several regions of France—and one-of-a-kind items like lavender wands.

Sylvine's wands are made by a woman in Provence who is one of the few people making them at all these days, and they are prettier and larger than others I've seen. I've loved these wands since I bought my first one thirteen years ago in the Provençal town of Vaison-la-Romaine—I remember it well because I was pregnant with my daughter at the time—and I intend to continue depleting Sylvine's stock. Sylvine's English is very good, and she loves nothing better than telling the stories behind all the items in her shop.

Metal Pointu's Bijoux

Founded in the 1990s in Paris, Metal Pointu's ("edgy metal") is a jewelry line created by designer and artist Bernard Bouhnik. I first learned of it when my good friend Lorraine gave me a Metal Pointu's bracelet for my birthday, and I absolutely flipped over it. With a number of boutiques in Paris (all the locations are on the Web site, metal-pointus.com), it's easy enough to stop into one and see if the *bijoux* line is your thing. Bouhnik works in tin, silver, and bronze, and some pieces also include colored beads and crystals; his works are bold and decidedly not overly feminine. Bouhnik's sister and partner, Sylvie Buchler, has described the collection—which includes neck pieces, earrings, bracelets, cuffs, and rings—as "definitely for a woman who is not shy," and she explains Bouhnik is inspired by "architecture, urbanism, and engineering." Some of Bouhnik's pieces are in museum collections, including the jewelry collection at Boston's Museum of Fine Arts. I am also drawn to the packaging: each piece comes in its own fabric *sac* with the Metal Pointu's logo stitched onto it, which is slipped into a black deckle-edged box tied at the top with a white ribbon.

I wore the bracelet Lorraine gave me almost every day for three years, until the day the elastic finally gave out. I was crushed, but I figured I would bring it with me on my next trip to Paris and see if it could be repaired. I was so happy to discover soon after that Metal Pointu's has opened a boutique in New York! I made a beeline to the shop (252 Elizabeth Street/646 454 1539), and Sylvie, who is overseeing the Soho outpost, had the bracelet restrung. I'm wearing it almost every day again.

Le Métropolitain

"Because it is so easy to understand," Franz Kafka wrote, "the Métro is a frail and hopeful stranger's best chance to think that he has quickly and correctly, at the first attempt, penetrated the essence of Paris." Mastering the Métro, which turned one hundred years old in 2000, does give one a sense of truly belonging to Paris. While it may be over a century old, Paris's system is elegant and (strike days aside) very efficient, and it is in a state of constant renewal. In addition to new tramways ringing the city, the newest line, 14, is one example: the Météor (MÉTro Est-Ouest Rapide), which debuted in 1998, runs from the Gare Saint-Lazare in the eighth to Olympiades in the thirteenth and is completely computer operated. It makes the trip *rapidement* and *tranquillement,* and there are no doors between cars, so you can see from car to car, end to end. There are a number of Métro ticket options available to visitors, so be sure to consider them all before you purchase one.

If, like me, you are fond of the original cast-iron Art Nouveau Métropolitain entrances—when I am feeling homesick for Paris, I'm so glad I can walk just a few blocks to MoMA in New York to see the Hector Guimard entrance in the museum's sculpture garden—and want to learn a little more about this famous subway system, you'll love these two books: *Paris Underground: The Maps, Stations, and Design of the Métro* by Mark Ovenden (Penguin, 2009) and *Métro Stop Paris: An Underground History of the City of*

Light by Gregor Dallas (Walker, 2008). *Paris Underground* is like a love letter to the Métro, with positively everything you'd want to know about the Métro's graphic history at your fingertips: black-and-white photographs of the original stations, maps, illustrations, reproductions of posters, the creation of the RER lines and the Météor, signage and logos, and a directory of designers. This is the kind of book you can dip into and out of at random, each time discovering some interesting bit of Métro trivia.

Métro Stop Paris is one of my absolute favorite books about Paris, a history of the city via the Métro. Dallas informs us that the underground train service came to Paris in 1900, after London (in the 1860s) and New York (whose elevated rapid transit service dates from 1870). But the *idea* of a railway system linking the city's *quartiers* dates back to 1845, when it was proposed to link the Gare de Lyon to the Gare du Nord. The Universal Exposition of 1900 was the event that propelled the creation of underground trains driven by "electric traction." Though today there are some fifteen subway lines and almost three hundred stations in Paris's Métro system (not counting the RER commuter rail), Dallas focuses on just five lines and twelve stations to take readers to certain key spots "where we will observe a building, a street, a statue, a tombstone or some other landmark that will spark off a story that tells us a lot about the character of the city." Dallas advises, "As you emerge from each Métro stop, look up those alleys, stare into those old shops, pass your hands over the stones in front of you" so that "you will discover what Parisians call . . . the 'genius' of their civilization."

Métro, Boulot, Dodo

This phrase translates as "Métro, work, sleep" and refers to the daily routine—*le train-train*—of urban dwellers in France. In recent years it has morphed into *Vélo, boulot, dodo,* the *vélo* referring to a bike, especially with the addition of Paris's public bicycle share program, Vélib.

Musée Carnavalet

The Musée Carnavalet (23 rue de Sévigné, 3ème) is the museum I recommend to visitors above all others, and I also suggest that it be the first museum you visit, as it is the museum of the history of Paris. The museum today consists of two homes, the Hôtel Carnavalet and the Hôtel Le Peletier de Saint-Fargeau, which were joined in 1989. The Carnavalet is one of the most beautiful houses in the Marais and is a rare example of a Renaissance mansion still standing in Paris. It was originally built for Jacques des Ligneris, a president of the Paris parliament in the 1500s, but is better known as the home of Marie de Rabutin-Chantal, Marquise de Sévigné, who lived there from 1677 to her death in 1696. The Peletier de Saint-Fargeau mansion was built in 1688 for Michel Le Peletier de Saint-Fargeau, state counselor and financial administrator.

Among the many remarkable items in the museum's permanent collection are medieval shop signs; a model of Paris showing the bridges over the Seine, which in medieval times had houses and buildings on them; furniture from the family of Jacqueline Bouvier; paintings, drawings, and ephemera relating to the French Revolution and the July Monarchy; photographs by Eugène Atget and Henri Cartier-Bresson; the ballroom of the Hôtel de Wendel, painted by José-Maria Sert and dating from 1924; the room, with original furniture, where Marcel Proust wrote *In Search of Lost Time;* and paintings by Paul Signac, Albert Marquet, and Maurice Utrillo. The garden of the

Hôtel Carnavalet is also beautiful. I recommend buying a general guide to the museum in the bookstore before you begin your visit, as interpretive text in English is limited.

Musée Marmottan

The Musée Marmottan (2 rue Louis Boilly, 16ème / marmottan .com) has long been among my favorite Paris museums. The building itself was once a hunting lodge for Christophe Edmond Kellerman, the duke of Valmy, who sold it a few years later to Jules Marmottan, a nineteenth-century industrialist. Upon Marmottan's death, he bequeathed the home to his son Paul, who initially devoted himself to collecting artworks of the Napoleonic era. When Paul died, he bequeathed the home to the Académie des Beaux-Arts, and the museum opened its doors in 1934. In addition to a superb collection of illuminations donated by Daniel Wildenstein (son of noted gallery owner Georges), and another exceptional donation of Berthe Morisot works by Denis and Annie Rouart (Denis was the grandson of Berthe Morisot and Eugène Manet), the Marmottan owns the largest collection of Claude Monet's work in the world. Among its many Monets is *Impression, Sunrise,* first exhibited in Paris in 1874 and considered the work that gave the name to Impressionism—a critic referred to the painting as "impressionistic" and soon after works by Degas, Pissarro, and Renoir were similarly described. This along with eight other Impressionist paintings were stolen from the Marmottan in 1987—a theft then valued at nearly twenty million dollars—but in December 1990 they were recovered in Corsica and returned. In addition to Monet canvases, the Marmottan also has one of Monet's palettes.

Since I first began visiting as a student, the museum has been enlarged and now also hosts temporary exhibits. Though it is receiving visitors in greater numbers, I still don't often see many North Americans here, and I urge readers to make time for this museum gem.

N

Nota Bene

Some readers may already subscribe to *Nota Bene,* a quarterly publication founded in 2001 dedicated to independently, impartially, and exactingly reviewing the world's finest destinations. It's aptly named, as the reviews are brutally, ruthlessly honest, and founder and chairman Anthony Lassman is keenly aware that many hotels, for example, command extremely high sums for service that seldom matches the price. Nota Bene offers three services: the *Review* (ten guides published per year, focusing on hotels, food, nightlife, and travel tips), *Pulse* (devoted to shopping, fashion, lifestyle, and well-being), and Bespoke (tailored travel management service for members). Plus it offers a full-service Web site (notabenetravel.com). When the Nota Bene folks rave about something, you can be assured it will not disappoint. But their expertise comes at a price: upward of several hundreds of British pounds per year. Register for white, black, or platinum membership online.

O

Oberkampf

The rue Oberkampf, in the eleventh arrondissement, has been hip for about a dozen years or so, and I very much enjoy walking along it and the streets nearby, stopping for some inexpensive international cuisine and poking into refreshingly different shops. I suspect many people don't know, however, that the street is named after Christophe-Philippe Oberkampf, a German-born textile entrepreneur honored as a royal manufacturer by Louis XVI. Oberkampf created the fabric known as *toile de Jouy,* cotton or linen decorated with scenic French patterns and printed in one color on a light ground. His designs were originally printed from woodblocks, though by 1770 copperplates were used; and he set up shop in Jouy-en-Josas, near Versailles on the river Bièvre. Fans of *toile de Jouy* may want to visit the museum there (54 rue Charles de Gaulle, Jouy-en-Josas / musee delatoiledejouy.fr).

Olivier Pitou

There are a number of notable flower shops in Paris, but Olivier Pitou (14 rue des Saints-Pères, 7ème) is my new favorite. Fleuriste Pitou is a narrow shop absolutely jammed with magnificent flowers, potted plants, garden specialty items, and statuary—it's more like a mini jungle than a shop. Pitou also has a terrific *épicerie* directly across the street, at no. 23, with prepared foods, olive oils and vinegars, wines, cheese, pâté, and bread; if you've forgotten a *tire-bouchon* (corkscrew), they'll kindly open the bottles for you.

P

Papier Plus

I'm a nut for fine papers and journals, and my favorite paper haunt in Paris is Papier Plus (9 rue du Pont-Louis-Philippe, 4ème / papierplus.com), which has been around since 1976. It stocks notebooks, binders, stationery, photo albums, boxes, and portfolios by French craftsmen. The notebooks come in a range of sizes and formats, and every year they're offered in a range of new colors. I especially like the photo albums, which feature a cut out circular window on the cover, perfect for your best photo of the City of Light.

Pariscope

I just love *Pariscope* (pariscope.fr), the weekly publication detailing everything happening in the city and appearing every Wednesday. Its small size—about five by seven inches—is compact enough that you can carry it around in just about any size handbag or satchel. Even though it's in French, you can easily read the listings, and it's great for double-checking current opening and closing times of museums, sites, and shows you want to see. (I usually try and pick one up at the airport before I even arrive in the city.) *Pariscope's* competitor is *L'Officiel des spectacles* (offi.fr), which is also useful, but it's not as *branché* (trendy) as *Pariscope*.

Père-Lachaise

The reason for my first visit to the Père-Lachaise cemetery was no different from that of many other American college students: to see Jim Morrison's grave. I owned only one album by the Doors (*The Soft Parade*), so I didn't even consider myself a proper fan, but it seemed like the thing to do—and anyway, the wine that was offered to me by a group gathered there was better than the plonk I bought at Félix Potin. Only later did I learn that so many other famous people were interred here, and that, taken together, they represented a broad cross section of French personalities. But Père-Lachaise, one of the world's largest cemeteries, is even more than that, as Alistair Horne notes in *Seven Ages of Paris:* "It contains probably more of France's past than any other forty-four hectares of her soil. . . . In it resides a whole history of Paris, indeed of France herself, in marble and stone." Catharine Reynolds, writing in *Gourmet,* observed that the cemetery "evokes *civilisation française*— for citizen and foreigner alike." Whenever I recommend Père-Lachaise to visitors, they always thank me, reporting that it was the surprise of their trip, and some say it was their favorite site in all of Paris.

In addition to the many famous names of the deceased—you'll find them all (except for Baron Haussmann; see page 650) on the map you can buy at the entrance—within Père-Lachaise are a few other spots of note. The Mur des Fédérés is a wall in the eastern corner where 147 Communards were lined up and shot during La Commune. The monuments honoring the victims of Nazi persecution are the most moving memorials I've ever seen, anywhere (my friend Sarah and I came across one that was simply footprints leading into a large, dark stone structure, and we were reduced to tears). There's also the tombstone of Victor Noir. I first saw a photo of Noir's unusual grave in John Berger's *Keeping a Rendezvous,* and I was so intrigued I had to go and take a look at it myself. The story goes that in 1879 Prince Pierre Bonaparte, cousin to Napoléon III, wrote an article in a reactionary Corsican journal that criticized *La Revanche,* a radical Paris newspaper. The editor of *La Revanche* sent Noir and another journalist to Corsica to seek an apology, but Prince Bonaparte shot Noir instead. The grave portrays Noir, just twenty-two, dead on the ground moments after he was shot. (As an aside, the groin area of the bronze work is a little enlarged, and has received an abundance of indecent rubbing by female visitors.)

In recommending Père-Lachaise (boulevard de Ménilmontant and avenue Gambetta, 20ème / pere-lachaise.com) so highly, I do not mean to slight Paris's two other famous cemeteries, Montmartre (avenue Rachel, 18ème) and Montparnasse (boulevard Edgar-Quinet, 14ème), each worthy of a detour as well. Among those buried at Montmartre are Degas, Jacques Offenbach, Vaslav Nijinsky, François Truffaut, and Stendhal, and within the grounds of Montparnasse are Brancusi, Baudelaire, Brassaï, Jean Seberg, Sartre, and Simone de Beauvoir. Readers who want to discover more will be happy to have a copy of *Permanent Parisians: An Illustrated, Biographical Guide to the Cemeteries of Paris* by Judi Culbertson and Tom Randall (Walker, 1996). This is a fascinating read, even if you don't have any desire to walk among tombstones; in addition to the three big cemeteries it also includes Les Invalides, the Panthéon, Saint-Denis, and others.

Point Zéro

The *point zéro* milestone set in the *parvis* of Notre-Dame is the point from which all distances in France are measured. Legend has it that if you stand on the *point zéro* plaque, your return to Paris is assured. I've never wanted to take any chances about *that,* so I try to make sure at least one of my feet touches the plaque on every visit.

R

Rez-de-chaussée

Remember that in France the *rez-de-chaussée* refers to the floor at street level, while the first floor—*premier étage*—is the equivalent of our second floor.

Romance

Paris is likely the most romantic city in the world. And you don't have to be in love, have a partner, or feel a certain way about a certain someone to know this indisputable fact. A walk along the Seine at night, when all of Paris's bridges and monuments are lit, a stroll across the Pont des Arts, a respite on a bench in the Tuileries, dinner at the Jules Verne, or merely a glance at Robert Doisneau's famous photograph *Le Baiser de l'Hôtel de Ville* is proof enough that Paris is synonymous with *l'amour.*

If you'd like to plan an especially romantic trip to Paris, with or without a companion, a book you must have is *Romantic Paris* by Thirza Vallois (Interlink, 2003). Vallois, also the author of the indispensable *Around and About Paris* series (see page 104), here outlines a love history of Paris in addition to providing great tips for a three-day romantic itinerary, restaurants and salons de thé, stores for the heart and senses, cozy museums, sentimental walks, and recommended nightspots. Most importantly, Vallois reminds us that "we come to Paris as to a stage on which to enact an episode of our love life, but before we know it we are caught under the spell and find out, to our astonishment, that it is Paris herself that has gotten under our skin, the one love that has no rival and that even time will never erode. It was when I realized that Paris was my one source of inspiration, the object, in turn, of both my celebration and desecration, that I understood that Paris herself is a tale of passion, full of turmoil and fury and dazzling charm, the very essence of romance."

One very wonderful romantic site not featured in Vallois's book is the Mur des Je T'aime (Wall of I Love Yous). The wall was created by Frédéric Baron, who first collected the phrase "I love you" a thousand times in more than three hundred languages in three large notebooks. Baron and Claire Kito, an artist who practices Oriental calligraphy, collaborated on the idea of a wall, and another artist, Daniel Boulogne, specializing in murals, helped to bring it to completion. The wall, ten meters wide, is composed of 612 tiles of enameled lava whose shapes are meant to symbolize the sheets of paper in Baron's notebooks. The splashes of color on the wall are "the pieces of a broken heart, those of a humanity which is too often torn apart and which the wall attempts to reunite." The *mur* is really very cool and very touching, and it's free. Just take the Métro to Abbesses, and the wall is right there in the Square Jehan-Rictus on Place des Abbesses (if that sounds confusing, it's not—you can't miss it).

For the record, some other spots I think are particularly romantic in Paris include the Place de Furstenberg, the little recessed seats on the Pont Neuf, the wall in the little park at the tip of Île Saint-Louis, and the Square du Vert-Galant.

In Love in France

It's hard for me to believe that *anyone,* a romantic or not, would not fall head over heels for *In Love in France: A Traveler's Guide to the Most Romantic Destinations in the Land of Amour* by Rhonda Carrier (Universe, 2010). I love this book, which is, *naturellement,* mostly devoted to Paris—"Paris loves lovers," as Cole Porter knew and Carrier quotes on the opening page. Carrier knows France intimately, as she has lived in and traveled around the country since she was a teenager. Other chapters cover the Loire Valley, Champagne, Normandy and Brittany, and southern France; there are also chapters on "Love and Food" ("Food, like love, can change your life," she says) and on getting married in France. I consider this book essential, as it is jammed with *coups de coeur*—her passions, places she fell instantly in love with—even as Carrier wisely notes, "Paris is also oversubscribed, and thus I've tried to point you in the direction of some of its lesser-known treasures."

La Ruche

The word *ruche* means "beehive" in French, and in Paris the word refers to the famous honeycomb-shaped structure housing studios for such artists as Fernand Léger, Jacques Lipchitz, Ossip Zadkine, Alexander Archipenko, Marc Chagall, Moïse Kisling, Chaïm Soutine, and Amedeo Modigliani. Academic sculptor Alfred Boucher created La Ruche just after the 1900 World's Fair. He bought a plot of land in the fifteenth arrondissement from the owner of a bistro, Le Dantzig, that was then sandwiched between the Vaugirard slaughterhouse and an area of slums called *la zone*. Boucher had a vision, however; he planted trees and flowers and bought Gustave Eiffel's octagonal wine pavilion that was left over from the World's Fair. (This was, according to Thirza Vallois, common practice at the time; other artist quarters in Paris are still made up of such pavilions.) Boucher planned to rent each octagonal side of the pavilion as a studio—yet he was also a philanthropist, known to overlook the unpaid rents of his extremely poor tenants. La Ruche provided a roof over the heads of struggling artists, but it was only marginally better than the hovels in Montparnasse, where the "better off" artists lived.

La Ruche almost met its end in the late sixties, when the heirs of Boucher intended to sell it to the French housing authority. President Pompidou stepped in to save it from destruction, with a chorus of supporters including André Malraux and even parties in the United States. Today there are only twenty-three honeycombs in the pavilion, as opposed to the original eighty, and while visitors are permitted only in the surrounding garden (unless you happen to know one of the painters or sculptors who live inside), it is nevertheless a site worth visiting, to spend a few moments reflecting upon the artistic fervor and spontaneity that existed within. Vallois's *Around and About Paris* (volume III) provides the best summary of La Ruche.

Rue Louise-Weiss

This street, and neighboring rue du Chevaleret and rue Duchefdelaville, in the thirteenth arrondissement, form a new art gallery center in Paris. Every month or so, the galleries here host an open house, which is a great and fun way to see what's happening in the contemporary avant-garde art scene. All the galleries are located at numbers five to eleven and twenty to thirty-four on rue Louise-Weiss, and are open Tuesday to Saturday from eleven to seven (Métro: Chevaleret).

Rungis

Rungis, located seven kilometers outside of Paris near the Orly airport, succeeded Les Halles as Paris's wholesale food market starting in 1969. Rungis (the final *s* is pronounced, by the way) is the world's largest wholesale food market, an ultramodern, extremely hygienic facility, about as opposite from Les Halles as possible, and it is extremely interesting to visit. Visite Rungis (visiterungis.com) organizes visits, mostly for groups, but individuals may visit during a specified day each month. A better alternative, I feel, is to arrange a private visit with Canadian expat Stephanie Curtis (stecurtis@free .fr), who gives tours for two to twenty people, 120 euros per person, including breakfast, round-trip transportation, and visits to about seven pavilions. I arranged a visit with Stephanie for a group of my friends and we all agreed it was a really special experience. Curtis arranges to pick you up from your hotel between four and five in the morning so that you arrive at Rungis when the most activity is occurring. After a stop at a café, you set out for the pavilions—we saw those devoted to seafood, poultry, meat, cheese, and produce. (Tip: Some of the pavilions are necessarily kept quite cold, so even if it's hot outside, bring a sweater or jacket.) Approximately five or six hours later most of the vendors are finished for the day. Though you're technically not permitted to purchase anything at Rungis, Curtis will take you to one store on the premises where you can buy some items; the selection is limited to packaged provisions, but I bought *fleur de sel,* chocolate, and dried mushrooms at prices far below what I would have paid in the States.

The Russian Connection

The Alexandre III bridge over the Seine isn't the only symbol of a very old friendship between Russia and France, but it's the most visible. The bridge was named after Czar Alexander III and was built in time for the Universal Exposition in 1900, and for many years it was my favorite Seine bridge. French was the second language spoken by the nobility in Russia, and in the late 1800s and early 1900s Paris was filled with Russian émigrés. Nina Berberova's *The Tattered Cloak and Other Novels* (Knopf, 1991) is a work of six short novels all set in Paris and peopled with Russian émigrés. Berberova, who passed away in 1993, wrote these stories of a "wistful, shabby-genteel society that a generation of Russians created in Parisian exile" which were first published in Europe in the 1930s. I think *The Tattered Cloak* deserves to be better known, and it includes one of the most memorable passages I've ever read about the city: "Paris, Paris. There is something silken and elegant about that word, something carefree, something made for a dance, something brilliant and festive like Champagne. Everything there is beautiful, gay, and a little drunk, and festooned with lace. A petticoat rustles at every step; there's a ringing in your ears and a flashing in your eyes at the mention of that name. I'm going to Paris. We've come to Paris."

S

Saint-Julien-le-Pauvre

When I lived in Paris as a student, I decided that my favorite park in the city was the one next to Église Saint-Julien-le-Pauvre, in the Latin Quarter. This was not because the park was particularly pretty—it isn't—or because the oldest tree in Paris, a false acacia, has reportedly grown there since 1601 (it was planted by Jean Robin, thus the name of the tree is *le robinier*). Rather, I chose this little park—more properly known as Square René-Viviani—because I was sure it was the one Joni Mitchell sang about in her song "California" on the album *Blue* ("Sittin' in a park in Paris, France . . ."). The reason I was so sure was because I went to every *jardin* and park in Paris and I sat in each one until I determined she could not possibly have been referring to any other park. (I really did this, by carefully perusing my *plan de Paris,* and I can honestly report that I dutifully visited nearly every park in the city. I have not been referred to as compulsive for nothing!) I have no verification that this little park is the one Mitchell sings about, but I'm still certain of it, and though I've since come to prefer other parks in Paris, I'll always be fond of this one. The Église Saint-Julien-le-Pauvre, which was built on the foundations of a sixth-century church, is among the oldest in Paris and serves the Melchite (Arab and Near Eastern) sect of the Greek Orthodox Church. Don't miss visiting the interior, which is dimly lit, very atmospheric, and features gorgeous icons (and it smells really old).

Scent

The French—like the Italians, Greeks, and Spaniards, among others—are very attuned to scent, as am I. Each scent I encounter—of a room, a food, a person, a locale—becomes a memory-smell and forever associated with a place. Sometimes the scent is obvious, like the time I drove through Boise, Idaho, at approximately four in the morning in the summer with all the car windows open and I got a huge whiff of potatoes (what else?). Other times, the scent is surprising, like the time I was fortunate enough to have lunch at the former Bouley restaurant in New

York. Upon entering, diners were greeted by a small wheel-barrow filled with apples—and though the meal itself was amazing, it is the smell of those fall apples ripening in the foyer that has stayed with me all these years. Every time I open one of my kitchen cabinets and smell the whole cardamom pods I have in a container, my memory-smell is of the Indian sweet shops I frequented in Mombasa and on the island of Lamu in Kenya; when I come across herbs growing wild, my first thought is of Corsica—one of my favorite places on earth—and its *maquis,* a unique combination of numerous herbs including juniper, myrtle, lavender, and mint (it's so distinctive that Napoléon allegedly said he would recognize it if he were out at sea with his eyes blindfolded).

Marcel Proust and the *madeleine* aside, the French make a commendable effort to ensure that their homes, shops, and workplaces smell pleasing. Scent is one of the easiest ways to bring an element of "Frenchness" into your home and, simultaneously, create a sense of well-being. Barbara Milo Ohrbach, in her wonderful and bestselling book *The Scented Room,* notes that she has made it a habit to buy flowers from a market or corner kiosk when she travels so she can make her hotel room feel and smell more like home (a habit I endorse!). Pico Iyer writes in *Condé Nast Traveler* ("Scents of Place," May 2010) that when he opens the cabinet above his bathroom sink, "all the perfumes of Araby—and Bangkok and Addis Ababa and Paris—come flooding out. . . . Ever since I began staying in the kind of hotel that offers high-end toiletries more than a quarter of a century ago, I've been unable to contain myself." Gretchen Rubin, in her wonderful book *The Happiness Project* (HarperCollins, 2009), noticed one day that "though I sometimes mocked the scented-candle-pushing brand of happiness, I discovered that there is something nice about working in an office with a candle burning." I, too, can testify to the effect something as simple as a candle can have on my mood, my happiness, and my level of motivation. Additionally, potpourri, lavender sachets, bowls of quince, dried rose petals, room fragrance sprays and diffusers, and ceramic lamp rings are all great mood pickups. (For particularly alluring room fragrances, check out Florence, Italy–based Antica Farmacista, anticafarmacista.com.)

Some of these can be made at home, and two good resources include *The Scented Home: Natural Recipes in the French Tradition* by Laura Fronty (Universe, 2002) and *The Scented Room* by Barbara Milo Ohrbach (Clarkson Potter, 1990). Some scents, of course, simply can't be replicated back home, like that of Gauloises or Gitanes cigarettes, the smell of very old churches like Saint-Germain-des-Prés, and some Métro stations, which is good: some scents don't travel, so attached are they to a certain *place.*

I became even more fascinated by the way things smell after I read *The Emperor of Scent: A True Story of Perfume and Obsession* by Chandler Burr (Random House, 2002). I felt like a whole new world had opened up for me, one that isn't always sweet: the competition between the world's largest scent companies is fierce and cutthroat. Burr informs us that "virtually all the smells in all scented products in the world are manufactured by [five] huge companies that operate in carefully guarded anonymity." These big boys—with power now even more concentrated, after several mergers since the publication of Burr's book—are International Flavors & Fragrances (United States), Givaudan Roure (Switzerland), Firmenich (Switzerland), Symrise (Germany), and Takasago (Japan). The story-within-a-story in this book is that of Luca Turin, a renowned biophysicist who wrote *Parfums: Le Guide,* a bestseller in France, and *The Secret of Scent: Adventures in Perfume and the Science of Smell* (Ecco, 2006). Turin is something of a scientific maverick, having proposed a new theory of smell to unravel the mystery of scent. Turin told Burr that he got into the scent world because it was part of his upbringing and heritage: "Because I'm French, at least by upbringing. Frenchmen will do things Anglo men won't, and France is a country of smells." Some of the scientific equations and explanations here are admittedly over my head, but I still love this inside look at a world where science, marketing, art, and nature come together.

Le Labo

One of the more creative olfactory items I've ever seen is the Santal 26 perfumed notepad produced by Le Labo, a really cool company that I only recently discovered. Founded in 2006 by Édouard Roschi (Swiss) and Fabrice Penot (French), Le Labo—short for *laboratoire* (laboratory)—aims to "enable people to access the art of perfume in a setting inspired by a perfumer's lab." Both Roschi and Penot worked previously on the fragrance team of Armani (licensed by L'Oréal) and their scents are developed in Grasse, on the Côte d'Azur. (Home, by the way, to the excellent International Perfume Museum, museesdegrasse.com, as well as another under the auspices of Fragonard, fragonard.com.) Roschi and Penot's mission is to "create ten exceptional fragrances, with no eye on costs and one goal: to create a sensory 'shock' as soon as you open the bottle." I think they have done this brilliantly.

There are Le Labo boutiques and counters around the world (lelabofragrances.com), but only two in North AmericA: New York City (233 Elizabeth Street / 212 219 2230) and Los Angeles (8385 West Third Street / 323 782 0411). Not only are their scents exceptional, but the Santal 26 notepad—with its leather cover and brown kraft paper—is, too. The notebook is referred to as a *carnet de boucher,* or "butcher's notebook," which must refer to the brown kraft paper sometimes used to wrap purchases at a butcher shop. Other than the name, there is nothing remotely butcherlike about this wonderful creation! It's handcrafted in France by the also terrific La Compagnie du Kraft (lacompagnie dukraft.fr) and is scented with Le Labo's cult interior scent, Santal 26, characterized by a smoky, leathery essence. It comes with an elastic band, and it is just one of my absolute favorite *objets* on the planet. "Use it and abuse it," note the founders, "as it's made to outlast you. And it probably will."

When I visited the New York boutique, I decided to sample a few scents to see if I could find one more perfume to add to my (very small) stable of scents—they're not easy for me to find, as perfume tends to be very fleeting on my skin. I tried four and loved them all, but six hours later the scent of only one still remained: Rose 31. So, yes, Rose 31 is now next to the other two bottles of perfume I own, and I'm extremely happy this scent is a part of my life. Each Labo scent is freshly bottled at the time of purchase and the label is personalized with the customer's name. Each boutique has a unique city-exclusive scent: for Paris it's Vanille 44, for New York it's Tubéreuse 40, and for Los Angeles it's Musc 25. Each perfume has an accompanying body lotion, and Le Labo's line of candles and home fragrances are composed of completely different scents.

Sennelier

In Paris since 1887, Sennelier (magasinsennelier.com) is a renowned art supply shop founded by chemist Gustave Sennelier. He opened Maison (now Magasin) Sennelier on the Quai Voltaire, just across the Seine from the Louvre and not far from the École des Beaux-Arts, and happily Sennelier is still a family affair.

According to the company, Sennelier's work "was so meticulous and his eye for color so accurate that the artists soon began to consider his palette as the ultimate standard of quality." Sennelier began packaging some paints in metal tubes, which enabled the painters of the day—notably the Impressionists—to paint outdoors; Cézanne, Pissarro, Bonnard, and Picasso are said to have been frequent clients.

Today the shop—known also as Couleurs du Quai—doesn't look much different, inside or out, from its original appearance. The small glass door and creaking wooden floor seem perfect for an art supply shop, and there are papers, large rounds of colorful pastels, pencils, paints, watercolors, brushes, and drawing pads stuffed everywhere—this is not a pristine space, but rather a gold mine for anyone who is artistically inclined. Even for nonartistic types like myself there are quite a few things of interest: I found some great pads of paper in varying sizes and textures that I use for note-taking and journals, as well as a beautiful refillable leather case that snaps closed and holds a pad of paper inside. There are very handy Couleurs du Quai journals, in several sizes and with an elastic band, with standard brown kraft paper and covers featuring a photograph of the store dating from the early twentieth century.

But the best find here are the 24-carat gold-plated *accroches-tableau de décoration* (picture hooks). These old-fashioned hooks with decorative symbols on the top—such as the Eiffel Tower, the Arc de Triomphe, Napoléon, an artist's palette, and so on—hold the picture up at the top (not from wire strung from the middle of the backing) with the decorative symbol showing above the frame. I just love these, and at a reasonable price of about thirty euros they're a unique and lightweight souvenir. The original shop is at 3 quai Voltaire in the seventh arrondissement, and there are two other locations: Magasin Sennelier Frères (4 bis rue de la Grande-Chaumière, 6ème) and L'Atelier des Couleurs du Quai (6 rue Hallé, 14ème).

Serge Gainsbourg Wall

The rue de Verneuil, in the seventh, is home to the Serge Gainsbourg wall, at no. 5 bis. Born Lucien Ginsburg in 1928, singer-songwriter Gainsbourg was a French legend who recorded a great number of albums from the 1950s through the 1980s (a good place to start if you're unfamiliar with his music is the 2006 compilation *The Originals*). He was also a sensation who made headlines often due to his relationships with Brigitte Bardot and Jane Birken and his sometimes public displays of drunkenness. The "Serge Gainsbourg Wall," which is covered with graffiti and has been visited since his death in 1991, is the exterior of his former home, now owned by his daughter Charlotte. In an interview with *Vanity Fair* in 2007, Charlotte revealed that one day about seven years prior she'd discovered that all the graffiti had been

covered up with "disgusting yellow" paint. She presumed it had
been done by the police, but learned that the neighbors thought
the wall was offensive and had organized a paint cover-up one
night—"But the great thing was a week later, it was all covered
with graffiti again." Now she is hoping to turn the house into a
museum with the help of architect Jean Nouvel. True Gainsbourg
fans may also want to visit the newly dedicated Jardin Serge-
Gainsbourg, on the northeast edge of the city at Porte des Lilas—
where, unlike in the Tuileries, the chairs are permanently affixed

to the cement! If the location seems odd, keep in mind that an early hit of Gainsbourg's was "Le Poinçonneur des Lilas" (The Ticket Puncher at Lilas Station)—the Porte des Lilas Métro station is very nearby.

Les Souvenirs / Shopping

It is next to impossible to find anyone who knows more about shopping—for souvenirs or, well, *anything*—than Suzy Gershman, author of the bestselling and terrific *Born to Shop* series (Frommer's) and the memoir *C'est la Vie*. Gershman's shopping guides—which I read cover to cover—are packed with store suggestions for every type of shopper and pocketbook, and include tips that can save you bundles of money. After a number of years in France, with an apartment in Paris and a house in Provence, Gershman moved back to the States, and now lives in Southern California, where she is near her kids. I reached her by phone a few days after she moved back.

Q: When was the first *Born to Shop* guide published, and how did the idea for the series come about?

A: It all began with a lunch in 1984, just before the start of the Olympic Games in Los Angeles. A lot of people felt then that the Games would be a nightmare for L.A.—huge amounts of traffic, etc.,—and at this lunch I learned that all these women had rented their houses out and were leaving town until the Olympics were over. They were going to Venice, Treviso, the South of France, and so on, and everyone was excitedly sharing all their shopping tips for these various destinations. Not highfalutin tips, but everything from cut rate to couture, Monoprix, factory stores—real people shopping as opposed to designer shopping—and the idea was born to put all these tips together in one book. My husband came up with the title and the original concept was for a really big book, but

Stephen Birnbaum's guides were really popular then and statistics showed that travelers would buy a more specialized book rather than one large one. Bantam, my original publisher, decided to break up the big book we created and spin it off into smaller editions. Four different editions came out in 1986—London, France, Italy, and Hong Kong—and it grew from there. It was destination-based and very timely, and it was the tight revision schedule that made the books last. (And as it turned out, the L.A. Olympics were hugely successful and there was hardly any traffic, but we couldn't have predicted that.)

Q: When did you first show an interest in retail shopping?

A: It all started when I was eleven years old. My father was a chairman of the World Health Organization, and in those days he worked for a division called the Pan American Health Organization. We lived in Caracas, Venezuela, for a year. We went to the markets a lot, and my dad often gave me the equivalent of fifty cents and said, "Here, Sue. See what you can buy with this." I loved the theater and excitement of shopping.

Q: What are some organization tips you employ when researching a *Born to Shop* guide?

A: I was a correspondent for *Time* and *People,* and have basically been a reporter for most of my life. I've learned that the more organized you are, the more you get done that you wanted to in the first place. I have basic charts I create for each destination—these show the streets of my neighborhood's hotels and transportation. I have developed a theory that tourists want to see specific sites and they want to know about shopping that is nearby those sites. I'm not a nighttime person, so I order room service and I turn on CNN and I sit

in bed with my maps and my notes and I work the charts. I will send you to an out-of-the-way place only if I think it's worth it. I really believe that people use guidebooks to *eliminate* things as opposed to following everything, and that's really valuable information. I'm like an Indian scout who's riding up at the head of the wagon train to tell you what's ahead.

Also, I stay in the same few hotels every time because I know my way around most quickly—if I stayed in different hotels, I'd have to learn new neighborhoods constantly. I usually have three to five in each city. I need to know where my grocery store is, where I can get a rotisserie chicken, etc. I really lead a far less glamorous life than people might think. I choose hotels by nearby transportation, extra amenities, and whether there is a club floor or a lounge with food I can call dinner. I just don't really use concierges. The first thing I do when I arrive in town is go to a kiosk and buy every local magazine on the stand, and then I spend that down time in bed, turn on local television, and start turning the pages. I don't need to be able to read everything comprehensively, but this gets me in tune with the community.

Q: What are some hotels you particularly like in Paris?

A: The hotel I really like to recommend is the three-star Hôtel de L'Élysée (12 rue des Saussaies, 8ème / +33 01 42 65 29 25), across the street from the Élysée Palace. The location—half a block off the rue du Faubourg-Saint-Honoré, midway between the Champs-Élysées and rue Royale—is superb, and it's a bit over a hundred euros per night. Some of the rooms are better than others—you have to be able to say, "I don't like this room; I want this one instead." Recently I stayed in a hotel that knocked my socks off: the InterContinental Avenue Marceau near the Arc de Triomphe (64 avenue Marceau, 8ème / +33 01 44 43 36 36 / ic-marceau.com), with twenty-eight rooms designed by Philippe Starck protégé Bruno Borrione. I have never been a contemporary-art person, having long preferred an old *grande dame* hotel, but this was so *intime* (intimate) and interesting, the décor a mix of Kenzo and wild and wacky and very creative without being offensive. Also you could get Wi-Fi access everywhere—often the old hotels don't have the IT that you expect.

Q: What are some Paris souvenirs you recommend?

A: Well, it's important to define what a souvenir is, because for each person it's different. To me a souvenir works if it fits into your real life back home—it's not necessarily a blinking Eiffel Tower. To me, something real life is the best souvenir: a kitchen towel, baby bibs with writing in French . . . I'm not so big on traditional touristy souvenirs.

Monoprix is probably my favorite store, and visitors should know that not all Monoprix supermarkets are created equal—you may have to go to more than one to find what you want. (Some have wonderful grocery stores—I have bought salt, sugar, lavender sugar, and and great gifts there.) I usually tell people to avoid the big department stores because I find them overwhelming, but I was just in Galeries Lafayette and it was terrific! Upscale grocery stores are great, including Lafayette Gourmet and the Grande Épicerie at Bon Marché, which is just *so* great. The arcades of the Palais Royal are a great place to find more unique things. I've also just found two new stores that are fab: Uniqlo (17 rue Scribe, 9ème / uniqlo.com), a Japanese version of Gap; and Igloo (111 avenue Victor-Hugo, 16ème), which at first glance seems kind of a tourist trap, a little like Pier 1 with weird stuff, but it is very cool, like a little department store—they have everything.

Q: Why did you decide to leave France?
A: It was hard to think about leaving France at first, especially Vaison-la-Romaine, where I was part of a little community, but everybody had left except for me and Patricia and Walter Wells. It just suddenly felt right. At my age I should be downsizing. My kids are in Paso Robles, which is just this amazing community. It's truly in the middle of nowhere and exists because it's halfway between L.A. and San Francisco. It was once the heart of the salad bowl but is now grapevines—about 80 percent are only five years old. There are a few people who've been there for thirty years making wine, but not many, and tastings are free or around five bucks. Some bottles of wine are fifty dollars, but the average is ten to twenty dollars. It's thriving here! The French will tell you that one of the most important things in life is sitting down and sharing a meal and talking, and this happening in Paso.

Q: Is there any place you've not yet been that you're dying to visit?
A: There are a *million* places that I'm dying to visit. *Born to Shop* books are chosen by numbers of visitors to various

destinations, so I've never been to Cape Town, for example. There are a couple cities in Vietnam I'd like to go to, and I'd like to get back to Bangkok. I *always* want to go someplace else.

In addition to Gershman's *Born to Shop* books, I also like to consult a few others that I've found very helpful over the years:

Chic Shopping Paris, Rebecca Perry Magniant with photographs by Alison Harris (Little Bookroom, 2008). Magniant founded the Chic Shopping Paris company (chicshoppingparis.com), a service offering personal tours of Paris's *bonnes adresses* by bilingual guides. I have yet to work my way through *every* boutique in this book, but I'm almost there, and I can report that each shop I've visited is unique and interesting, even those I left empty-handed (which didn't happen very often). Most of the shops Magniant recommends offer goods and services available only in Paris, and she regularly updates these listings and posts her new finds on her Web site.

The Flea Markets of France, Sandy Price with photographs by Emily Laxer (Little Bookroom, 2009). Though this terrific book covers a number of regions in France, one chapter is devoted to Paris and includes the *marchés aux puces* at Porte de Clignancourt, Porte de Montreuil, Porte de Vanves, and Place d'Aligre. As Price notes, the objects for sale at these markets "provide a glimpse of everyday life in decades past, and also suggest how that heritage continues to resonate today." She includes much practical information for the flea market experience (when to go, how to get there, how to communicate, how to bargain, market schedules), as well as good suggestions for other things to do and other markets close by. I think this is indispensable for flea market aficionados.

Markets of Paris, Dixon Long and Ruthanne Long with photographs by Alison Harris (Little Bookroom, 2006). The authors, who also wrote *Markets of Provence* (William Morrow, 1996), "have a love affair with markets," and so might you after flipping through this book. As the Longs note, the attraction of markets is that, "above all, it's the opportunity to observe a social experience that is quintessentially French and independent of class." They include markets with food, antiques, artisanal crafts, and books, many of which I'm eager to explore—plus restaurant recommendations. The two-page primer "When in Paris, Do as the Parisians" is very helpful, as are the suggested daily itineraries.

Paris Chic & Trendy: Designers' Studios, Hip Boutiques, Vintage Shops, Adrienne Ribes-Tiphaine with photographs by Sandrine Alouf (Little Bookroom, 2006). As the title suggests, this guide focuses exclusively on fashion, and includes jewelry, lingerie, shoes, and handbags. The fifty-four recommended shops "together make Paris what it has never ceased to be: the all-time moving and shaking capital of fashion."

Paris: Made by Hand, Pia Jane Bijkerk (Little Bookroom, 2009). Stylist Bijkerk adores all things *fait main* (handmade), and she presents an enticing selection of papermakers, shoemakers, jewelry designers, milliners, umbrella makers, dressmakers, ceramicists, and more. She also explains the interesting concept of *fait main:* it's not only about creating something by hand, but also includes the act of restyling, restoring, or reinterpreting a found object. "In French," Bijkerk notes, "the act of finding vintage objects has its own verb: *chiner.* And *chineurs* are the talented individuals who *chinent.* Many of the *chineurs* I have included in this book have the ability to see a found object in a whole new light, and they can't wait to get back to the studio and get their hands dirty." Packed with memorable ateliers and boutiques, the book also includes a list of her dozen favorite *fait main* stops.

The Paris Shopping Companion: A Personal Guide to Shopping in Paris for Every Pocketbook, Susan Swire Winkler with Caroline Lesieur (Cumberland House, 2006, fourth edition). Winkler has "pursued the enigma that is French style" for some time: she imports French linens for her own shop in Portland, Oregon, she lived in Paris as a graduate student in French literature, and she was a Paris-based fashion journalist for *Women's Wear Daily.* Coauthor Lesieur is a native Parisian and a personal VIP guide, so between the two of these specialists, readers are in good hands. They inform us that the first tourist guidebooks to include information on French luxury goods and boutiques appeared in the seventeenth century. "Even then, during the time of Louis XIV, the shops were put together as nowhere else, positively seducing their customers. Little has changed and the world still flocks to Paris to be seduced by the charm, elegance, and glamour of its offerings."

Winkler's shopping favorites represent a very personal selection, and in fact she covers a limited range of neighborhoods, but what she does cover is thorough. I particularly like that she not only chooses her favorites and points out good values, but also has "made a special effort to highlight wise purchases in even the most expensive shops. These often make the most distinctive gifts because they come so beautifully wrapped and packaged." Practical information—sizing charts, tax refunds, shipping, customs, a "shop talk" glossary—is included, as are some places to stay and a chapter called "Paris on a Budget." They leave us with this parting thought: "In a culture where style of life is a source of national pride and pleasure, shopping as the French do is an invaluable approach to understanding French culture."

The Riches of Paris: A Shopping and Touring Guide, Maribeth
Clemente (St. Martin's, 2007). Amid other similar titles, Clemente's book stands out and is very much worth perusing. For
seven years Clemente operated the Chic Promenade shopping
service in Paris, and she lived there for a total of eleven years; she
is also the author of *The Riches of France: A Shopping and Touring
Guide to the French Provinces* (St. Martin's, 1997). In this book,
Clemente reminds readers of Paris's long history of commerce,
with its first trading outposts set up along its bridges, "where
people could bargain for their essential goods as they plodded
along the route from northern Europe to the Mediterranean.
The actual shops during the mid-seventeenth century were
merely storerooms for the goods lined up outdoors; store windows didn't begin to appear until the end of the seventeenth
century. . . . But somehow I imagine that the Parisians found
their own alluring way of displaying their wares . . ." (I completely agree.) Clemente admits, "In Paris I relish the idea of entering a boutique that is quaint, enticingly decorated, and, most
of all, has a soul all its own." But don't let this preference lead
you to think this book will lend you to the passé or the dé-
modé—there are plenty of contemporary, appealing, dynamic
establishments here. As Clemente says, having a soul of its own
is the most important quality of a retail shop. Organized by specialty rather than neighborhood, Clemente also includes dozens
of "Riches of Paris Tips" and great sidebars with topics such as
"Ten Ways to Find the French Look for You."

Shopping Tips

Here are some good retail vocabulary words to know, especially if you're in Paris during the national sales in January or
August: *soldes* (sales); *dégriffés* (clothing where the labels have
been cut out; more generally, "marked down"); *moitié prix*

(half price); *coin des affaires* (the bargain section of a large store); *deuxième choix* (seconds); and *tout doit disparaître* (everything must go!). *Je regarde* (I'm just looking) is a useful response when someone asks you, *"Vous désirez?"* (May I help you?).

You might want to adopt my motto of "When in doubt, buy it now." I learned years ago that the likelihood of being able to retrace my steps to a particular merchant *when it was open* was slim. A number of individual shops are closed on both Sunday and Monday, or open only on Monday afternoon, and many are still closed for two hours at lunchtime.

In short, remember that stores in Paris are not open twenty-four/seven, so if you spy a baguette in the window of a *boulangerie* or an article of clothing that has your name all over it, *allez* (go) and get it, for Pierre's sake. One has regrets only for the roads not taken—or in this case the *objet* not purchased!

Spas

Spas and salons have become wildly popular, even *de rigueur,* in many hotels and inns, and in a city like Paris, where well-being and beauty are taken seriously, spas are plentiful. Some are quite lavish, as you might expect, but even those that are not are still something special. Only recently have I begun to appreciate how wonderful and truly beneficial spas are, especially during travels, and though it is easy enough to obtain the names and addresses of spas and salons in Paris, it isn't so easy to compare them or know what to expect when you show up. Thank god there is now *Pampered in Paris: A Guide to the Best Spas, Salons and Beauty Boutiques* by Kim Horton Levesque and with photos by Kristyn Moore

(Little Bookroom, 2010). If you are even remotely interested in spending some time at a spa or salon while in Paris, you positively need this book.

I had the great pleasure of meeting Levesque in New York when the Spa Vinothérapie Caudalie, in the Plaza Hotel, hosted a *fête* to celebrate her new guide (the Paris Caudalie spa is one Levesque recommends). We are very much kindred spirits; she told me, "I think I'm like you in that I am obsessive about pre-trip research. I always have several guidebooks and a folder of photocopies with me when I travel." Levesque first visited France as a high school exchange student, and she returned to France every summer throughout college and worked variously as an au pair, farmhand, and cook at an auberge in Normandy ("I was cooking mainly for British travelers who wanted to get off the beaten path and experience authentic France—they didn't know there was an American in the kitchen!"). She attended the Sorbonne as an undergraduate and taught French in an International Baccalaureate high school program in Phoenix. Her husband's family is originally French-Canadian, "so it was a pleasant surprise," she said, "that my father-in-law's first language was French and that I was able to communicate with my husband's entire extended family in their native tongue." In addition to her French background, she'd been doing writing and translating for companies in the beauty industry; plus some of her favorite skin-care products are French, and she's long had an interest in well-being. All of this made her a natural for authoring a spa book. Levesque thought many of the books about beauty in France created caricatures of French women, and she set about to improve upon that: "I wanted to offer more of a holistic and practical guide to Parisian beauty." She was fortunate, while researching her book, to rent an apartment next to the Luxembourg Gardens, as she had her two daughters with her and was pregnant with her third. It was exhausting, she said, "but my parents came along to help with the girls and they spent part of almost every single day in the Luxembourg. I think it is one of the most beautiful gifts I can give them, the experience of travel."

There are useful chapters in *Pampered in Paris* on basics such as French words and phrases and etiquette, which is essential, as Levesque can tell you: "I had a spa experience a few years ago that would have been much more relaxing if someone had told me what to expect. I was not anticipating a male masseur or a chest massage on my first Parisian spa day, but that's what I got!" Levesque introduces readers to more than fifty spas in the first through ninth arrondissements, plus the twelfth and sixteenth, as well as four in the suburbs. They are quite varied—some offer traditional French treatments while others specialize in Thai, Chinese, or Indian therapies—and range in price from budget to very expensive. (Also included is the rare Nickel Spa for Men, which opened the first men's salon in a department store in Paris at the Printemps on boulevard Haussmann and operates another outpost in the rue des Francs-Bourgeois in the third.) Levesque discusses *thermalisme* (thermal cures), hammams (Turkish baths), and thalas-

sotherapy (treatments from the sea). She recommends manicure and pedicure salons as well as makeup boutiques, chains, and perfumeries. She explains that the French regard weekly salon visits for manicures and pedicures as "peculiarly American"; only a few salons are dedicated to nail care, but almost every spa offers a full menu of nail treatments.

My favorite chapter, "Beauty Secrets Revealed," extolls the virtues of French *pharmacies,* which I adore. Pharmacies are identified by a light green neon sign; every neighborhood has a handful, so you are never very far from one (they also take turns staying open on weekends and holidays). Not only can you fill prescriptions here, but you can also find some items available over the counter that in the United States are available only by prescription. Levesque shares a list of must-have *pharmacie* items, including Avène and Nuxe products, which "have a mass popular and critical following." Perhaps best of all is her recommendation of Be Relax, a kind of mini spa at both Charles de Gaulle and Orly airports. Walk-ins are expected, and a number of services are offered, including deep massage, massage designed to help travelers relax before a long flight, and foot massage. Though I understand why these services are popular *before* a flight, I actually think they would be better *after* a flight—how much better I would feel if I arrived at my hotel after a thirty-minute foot massage!

Levesque, who has dry and very sensitive skin, chooses Nuxe Crème Fraîche de Beauté Suractivée as her favorite moisturizer. "Also, as my French friends told me and I confirmed with research, Bioderma Créaline H20 Sans Parfum is many a French woman's well-kept secret—it's a gentle cleanser, and Bioderma Atoderm is a wonderful body lotion that doesn't irritate my or my girls' skin." When I asked her which Paris spas or salons she would choose if she were forced to name only a few of her absolute favorites, she replied, "Well, I change my mind on any given day of the week, but this week my favorites are Wassana and Anne Fontaine for massage; Anne Sémonin Spa at the Bristol

Hotel for facial, and the Détaille and Artisan Nature boutiques for perfume."

Statues of Liberty

I like walking through the Luxembourg Gardens and coming upon the Statue of Liberty there. The first time I saw it, it came as a complete surprise. Likewise, when I saw the other one, on the Île des Cygnes, a man-made island in the Seine at the Pont de Grenelle, I couldn't believe it (and I think I got a little teary eyed). I was reading Gertrude Stein's *Paris France* and I completely latched onto her remark that "America is my country and Paris is my hometown." It's a beautiful and almost startling moment to see a Statue of Liberty in Paris.

Le Système D

The *D* stands for *débrouillard*—resourceful—or for the verb form, *débrouiller*—to untangle. Think of *le système D* as "winging it" or "getting by," but it can also mean "beating the system." Ross Steele, in his book *When in France, Do as the French Do,* explains that it is a French "national pastime to find a way around a government regulation or administrative decision," and he notes that the expression says a lot about the French temperament. From the French point of view, "the chaos of a French line is a logical consequence of a mass of individuals untangling the knotty problem of getting to the head of the line." Anyone who has witnessed the French inability to stand neatly in line knows that this is true. *Le système D* is present in nearly all aspects of French life, and one of the highest compliments in France is *Il/Elle sait se débrouiller* (He/She knows how to get things done). As Steele notes, this is "always sincere and expresses admiration for a person's resourcefulness."

T

Le Thé des Écrivains

The name of this original shop in the Marais, Le Thé des Écrivains (16 rue des Minimes, 3ème / thedesecrivains.com), translates loosely as Tea of Writers. Founder Georges-Emmanuel Morali has created an incredibly appealing concept that weds tea with writers and readers. There are, for example, canisters of teas blended to evoke Russian, Japanese, American, French, and English writers, alongside a terrific assortment of handmade journals, photo albums, and notebooks. I have a great memory of the first time I stepped into this shop: it was an uncharacteristically overcast, chilly day in late September, and I was offered a complimentary cup of tea brewing in a samovar at the back of the store. I soon discovered one of my favorite souvenirs on earth: a *carnet de voyage* composed of three notebooks and one accordion folder housed in a handmade paper case held together with an elastic band and a brown bead. I've bought about a dozen *carnets* since then, filling up three and giving the others as gifts. The handmade notebooks come in a great range of bright, cheerful colors, and the store's Collection Vacances features luggage and gift tags. If you love reading, writing, tea, or all three, you will not want to leave this shop.

Travel Journals

I've never been the kind of person to record daily personal entries in a journal, but I've known many people who find that "Dear Diary" approach meaningful and positively addictive. When I'm traveling, however, I want to record as many details as possible— where and what I ate, what the weather was like, how much money I spent, how a site, monument, or event made me feel.

Recently, I've also borrowed a habit from my good friend Arlene, who likes to record a quote of the day in her journals. This can simply be a funny or memorable remark, uttered by a traveling companion or, really, anyone encountered on a trip. Sometimes more than one quote is worthy of inclusion on a given day, and these are great fun to read after a trip is over.

My journal is indispensable to me not only while I'm traveling but before I depart—I typically fill up at least half a journal with notes and clippings that I glue onto the pages. The journal then becomes my main resource on a trip, eliminating the need for lots of other books—otherwise I bring only one or two guidebooks, plus a novel or two and a work of nonfiction. By the time my trip has ended, my journal is a complete record—a true souvenir— of everything I experienced, bulging with even more handwritten notes, paper ephemera, pressed flowers, wine labels, postcards, you name it. Yet it's also much *more* than a souvenir: compiling the journal before I depart and while I'm away is among the most treasured experiences of my life.

Over the years I've purchased a great number of journals, a few of which have had features I've liked and many of which have not. So a few years ago, I created one of my own: *En Route: A Journal and Touring Companion for Inspired Travelers* (Potter Style, 2007), which includes general travel tips and recommendations, wonderful travel quotations, lined pages for your own notes, sketching pages, address and emergency information pages, and a clear sleeve at the back that zips closed. Additionally, I asked several noted travelers to share the titles of books that inspired them to hit the road, and the replies—from Colman Andrews, Melissa Biggs Bradley, Dana Cowin, Ina Garten, Frances Mayes, Peter Mayle, Barbara Ohrbach, Fred Plotkin, and Ruth Reichl—are sprinkled throughout.

Kids like journals, too, and without doubt the best one I've seen is *The Children's Travel Journal* by Ann Banks and with illustrations by Adrienne Hartman (Little Bookroom, 2004), which is spiral-bound and has lined and blank pages and a pocket in the back. There are sections for the destination, first impressions, food and restaurants, landmarks and monuments, museums and galleries, people, best and worst days, and "I'll never forget . . ." This is just so creative and so much fun, a real opportunity for younger globe-trotters to create a masterpiece of memories. My daughter already has two of these, each stuffed to the gills with her drawings, notes, photos, dozens of entry tickets, postcards, maps, stamps, and even some restaurant menus (it's remarkable how waiters will let you keep one when a child is asking).

U

Un Jour Un Sac

Translated loosely as "one day, one bag" (*sac* refers to a handbag), the concept of the store Un Jour Un Sac by François Rénier is one that I love: it's mixing and matching handbags with different handles that clip on and off—or "it's all the bags you can imagine," to borrow from the Web site. The possibilities are practically endless, and it's like having a bag custom made just for you. There are six stores in Paris (unjourunsac.com) and each bag is made entirely in northern France.

V

La Vaissellerie

La Vaissellerie (lavaissellerie.fr) is a chain of five stores—"*les petites boutiques chic de Paris*"—with inexpensive tabletop wares and

kitchen items you didn't know you needed. I have bought a number of useful and attractive items here over the years, and it's a
good shop to know about for gifts. My favorite find is a cylindri-
cal plastic container meant to store Camembert cheese in: there's
an upright piece of plastic on the bottom half that acts as a knife,
so when you put a round of unwrapped cheese inside, the "knife"
actually cuts it, and each time you lift up the round and move it,
the cheese is sliced in a new place. You can find sets of white
porcelain platters and plates at great prices, plus linen towels, silverware, ceramics, place mats, glassware, utensils, and more. When
you make a purchase, you automatically receive a *carte de fidélité*
that entitles you to future discounts.

W

WC

Le WC (*vay-say,* or *double vay-say*), is how you refer to a restroom
in a public place in France (as opposed to a bathroom in a private
home, which is often composed of two rooms, the *toilettes* and the
salle de bain). Some visitors may be surprised to find that many
bathrooms in older bars, cafés, and restaurants are chronically
short of toilet paper (it's never a bad idea to start out each day
with some tissues in your pocket), and many are still even *à la
turque,* meaning squat toilets. I have read (and I believe) that these
are actually physiologically healthier than our fashion of sitting on
a toilet seat; however, anyone who has trouble squatting and
standing up again—to say nothing of those who find the prospect
repellent—may not enjoy navigating one of these. It can also be
confusing to figure out how to flush the toilet. Typically, there is
a chain or a lever marked *tirez* (pull), and when you do water can
produce quite a wave, sometimes coming up over the basin and
your feet—so you should prepare to flush as you simultaneously

open the door of the stall and step out. If these seem like unnecessary details, I share a comment from author Bill Gillham in *Parisians' Paris:* "All I can say is that a bad experience in a Parisian lavatory can spoil your day; or at least put you off your meal." Gillham also reminds visitors that, "if you are not to experience a minor trauma," if you find yourself in complete darkness when you close the door to some bathroom stalls, don't panic: the light will come on when you slide the bar to lock the door.

Wine Shops

Lovers of the fruit of the vine will find wine sold mostly everywhere: in supermarkets like Monoprix and small neighborhood grocers, at the wine retailer Nicolas—the oldest wine chain in France, founded in 1822, with more than four hundred stores in France and some other European countries—and at renowned and beautiful shops. Here are some of my favorites:

Lavinia (3 boulevard de la Madeleine, 1er / lavinia.fr). This three-floor shop, Paris's largest wine store, carries many very affordable wines in stock as well as rare bottles.

Legrand Filles et Fils (1 rue de la Banque, 2ème / caves-legrand .com). In the beautiful Galerie Vivienne, Legrand is one of the oldest grocers and wine merchants in France. On one side of the *galerie* is a shop selling glasses, books, and other wine paraphernalia, while on the other side is the actual wine store, with more than four thousand wines and a great *espace-dégustation* for tastings.

Les Caves Augé (116 boulevard Haussmann, 8ème / cavesauge .com). Founded in 1850, Augé has a reputation for carrying the very best wines, but there are lots of bottles for twenty euros and under.

Clos Montmartre (9 bis rue Norvins, 18ème / commanderie -montmartre.com). Paris's own vineyard, fifteen hundred square meters planted with Gamay and Pinot Noir grapes. The land was set to be exploited by property investors for a housing development but was saved by artist François Poulbot in 1929. The first vines were planted in 1933, and every October since then a five-day Fête des Vendanges has been held, with proceeds from all the wine sold going to children's charities. Clos Montmartre's location seems appropriate, as Romans built a temple here on this hill dedicated to Bacchus.

Z

Zouaves

The stone Zouave soldier on the Pont de l'Alma, built in 1856 to commemorate Napoléon III's victory in the Crimea, is one of my favorite symbols of Paris. The Zouaoua were a fiercely independent tribe living in the hills of Algeria and Morocco; in the summer of 1830 some Zouaoua lent their services to the French colonial army, and later that year were organized into two battalions of auxiliaries. Over the next decade the Zouaves, as the French called them, proved their valor in dozens of bloody desert encounters. Even as Zouave units began to be increasingly composed of native Frenchmen, their distinctive uniform remained a derivation of traditional North African dress: a short collarless jacket, a sleeveless vest, flowing trousers, a long woolen sash, white canvas leggings, and a tasseled fez and turban. By 1852, the Zouave units were made up entirely of native Frenchmen, and Louis Napoléon restructured them into three regiments of the regular French army. Algerians and Moroccans alike were assigned to units of the Tirailleurs Algériens, or Turcos, and wore their own distinctive light blue version of the Zouave uniform. According to the Web site Zouave.org, U.S. Army captain George B. McClellan, observing the Zouaves in 1855, praised them as "the finest light infantry that Europe can produce," and soon after American militia units began to adopt the baggy trousers, braid-trimmed jacket, and tasseled fez of the Zouaves.

The Crimean War of 1854–55 confirmed the reputation of the Zouaves, and after the battle of Alma, Marshal de Saint-Arnaud noted, "*Les Zouaves sont les premiers soldats du monde*"—The Zouaves are the best soldiers in the world. It was at the battle of Sebastopol, however, that the Zouaves won immortal renown. They went on to play major parts in the battles of Magenta, Solferino, and Mexico, and in the Franco-Prussian War and World War I. But the Great War saw some Zouave battalions lose as many as eight hundred men in a single charge, and as camouflage, not color, became standard dress, their uniform passed into the pages of history by 1915.

Vincent van Gogh painted five works of Zouaves; with the exception of one in a private collection, all are on view in public museums, including the Metropolitan Museum of Art and the Guggenheim in New York and the Van Gogh Museum in Amsterdam. The Pont de l'Alma originally had four statues of Zouaves built into its span, but now this one soldier stands alone, and he is Paris's official flood gauge. During the worst overflowing of the Seine, in 1910, the river waters reached his beard.

Paris, to be Paris, must be the place where the great moral dilemmas of mankind are identified and where the experiments in the life of thought—if not of action—take place at the highest register. Paris should be infuriating, as it must have been to millions when, for example, Édouard Manet painted a naked woman lunching on the grass. . . . Above all, for Paris to be Paris, it has to be free. The question thus is not: Are there too many Arabs in Belleville, too many Chinese in the thirteenth arrondissement, too many neighborhoods that have lost their character? The question is: Will the fear that there are no longer any Parisians lead the inhabitants of the great village on the Seine no longer to fashion a place that matters to all humanity?

—Richard Bernstein, *Fragile Glory*

ACKNOWLEDGMENTS

A book of any type requires the efforts of a staggering number of people, but an anthology requires the involvement of even more people as well as a staggering number of details. The likelihood is great, therefore, that I have neglected to name some people who helped create this finished book or who kindly inquired about it, and I can only hope that they will understand and forgive me. Once again, I extend an enormous *merci* to Vintage publisher Anne Messitte, Vintage Editor-in-Chief LuAnn Walther, and my editor Diana Secker Tesdell, who likely never anticipated that an anthology series could prove to be so *compliqué*. Other patient and talented colleagues in the extended Vintage family who diligently helped this book along include Cathryn Aison, David Archer, Bette Graber, Kathy Hourigan, Jo Anne Metsch, Roz Parr, Nicole Pedersen, Russell Perreault, Anke Steinecke, and Allison Zimmer. *Merci bien* also to Steven Barclay, Sebastian Beckwith, Carol Bonow, Ceil Bouchet, Joan DeMayo, Lindsey Elias, Barbara Fairchild, Ina Garten, Suzy Gershman, Mark Greenside, Mireille Guiliano, Linda Hollick, Ruth Homberg, Judith Jones, Sylvie de Lattre, Kim Levesque, Alec Lobrano, Kermit Lynch, Emily Marshall, Caroline Mennetrier, Jennifer Paull, Emanuelle Sasso, Clark Terry, Patricia Wells, and Molly Wizenberg. Sincere thanks to each of the individual writers, agents, and permissions representatives for various publishers and periodicals without whose cooperation and generosity there would be nothing to publish, and I would not have the opportunity to share the work of many good writers with my readers. Extra special thanks to traveling companions and friends Amy Myer and Lorraine Paillard, and to Arlene Lasagna, who bravely stepped in as amateur camerawoman in the absence of my official photographer, Peggy Harrison (www.peggyharrison.com). I am appreciative of the kind and courteous assistance from the staff at the Mount Pleasant Public Library in Pleasantville, New York, and I remain deeply grateful to my brilliant and kind boss and mentor, Chip Gibson, who has long supported *The Collected Traveler*. Finally, thanks to my husband, Jeff, and our daughter, Alyssa, whose favorite Parisian experience (so far) is riding the carousel near the foot of the Eiffel Tower.

PERMISSIONS ACKNOWLEDGMENTS